AF251531

THE METAHUMAN SYSTEMOLOGY HANDBOOK

COMPLETE GRADE-IV MASTER WIZARD EDITION

THE METAHUMAN SYSTEMOLOGY HANDBOOK

Piloting the Course to Higher Universes
& Spiritual Ascension in This Lifetime

COLLECTED WORKS BY JOSHUA FREE

ISBN : 978-0-578-29872-6

This book is not a basic course text or beginner's guide.
To be effective, this material requires a Seeker be
familiar with knowledge and methodology
presented in "Tablets of Destiny" and "Crystal Clear"
(and "Systemology: Original Thesis" and "Power of Zu")
which are all also contained in the former Grade-III
master edition textbook "The Systemology Handbook."

Complete Mardukite Systemology Grade-IV Research Library
Prepared for publication by the Joshua Free Publishing Imprint
representing Mardukite Truth Seeker Press, Mardukite Zuism
and Mardukite Academy of Systemology.

FIRST PRINTING—MAY 2022

mardukite.com

THE METAHUMAN SYSTEMOLOGY HANDBOOK

An advanced-level operator's manual to the Human Condition and unlocking the true power of the Spirit for a metahuman evolution and ascension in this lifetime!

In *Grade-IV* Mardukite *'Metahuman'* Systemology, wisdom of the *'Arcane Tablets'* is combined with two years of additional experimental research, workshops and lectures carried out after the 2019 completion of Grade-III objectives, goals and publications. For the first time ever, the complete fundamentals of systematic processing may be understood and applied directly toward freeing considerations for a 'new human' ideal... conditions for a 'metahuman' evolution on planet Earth!

Advancing even further on the developments and premises first established in "Systemology: The Original Thesis," "The Tablets of Destiny" and especially "Crystal Clear," the director of the Mardukite Academy and Systemology Society, Joshua Free, provides a complete handbook illustrating the principle steps of correcting – or "defragmenting" – the basic points that have entrapped viewpoints and determinism of the Spirit to the programming and encoding inherent in the standard-issue Human Condition.

All essentials from the "Professional Piloting Courses" delivered by Joshua Free in 2020 and 2021 are collected together for the first time in a single oversized Master Wizard Edition hardcover volume. This includes all materials from the former anthology, *"Metahuman Destinations"* (*Liber-2C*, *Liber-2D* and *Liber-3C*), in addition to the latest developments of spiritual technology found in *"Imaginomicon"* (*Liber-3D*) and the transitional title by Joshua Free (leading to *Grade-V*) called *"The Way of the Wizard"* (*Liber-3E*).

Together the most actualized members of society can help "Pilot" the course of Human Evolution toward ideals that will free the Human Condition and return the ultimate command and control of *Life* back to the *Spirit.* Here, we have discovered the *"Way Out"* – hidden for 6,000 years. Here, we have a *Key* that is accessible and practical. Here, we finally have *answers* and *solutions!*

Essentially, *"The Metahuman Systemology Handbook"* is a revolutionary futurist "grimoire" that allows Seekers to summon and invoke, command and control, the most powerful spirit to ever exist... *Your Self.* Here you may access the truth beyond physical existence. Fly freely across the *Gateways* and return to where it began and reclaim that *Personal Universe* which the *Spirit* once called *"Home."*

It's time to break free from "The Matrix" – this "Prison Plane" of existence! Learn and practice the command of a Mind and control of a Body from outside the artificial systems of this Universe, using a methodology never before experienced by Humanity – because you were *never* "Human." Fully realize what it actually means to be a Spiritual Being – then rise up through the Gateways to Higher Universes and *BE!*

We all strongly benefit from the fact that at its basic state, the *Alpha Spirit* – the true *Self* or *'I-Am'* – is actually righteous and good (if not otherwise *amoral* down here on Earth when serving a higher Ethic) simply working to get along and maintain the continuation of its own existence. Were this not the case, we would have no chance at rehabilitating *Presence* and *Awareness* of the actual *Self* that is behind the helm and restoring to it the full control of how we experience the *beta-existence* that we each participate in maintaining as reality.

The world manifested "out there" is an agreement of participation by what is going on "in here" and there really is no distinction between the two when we get right down to it.

Accumulated involvement in dangerous situations, states of confusion, unjust destruction and being at the effect end of faulty – or blatantly false – information, all lend to fragmented purposes that may well be painted to appear "for our own good." Instead they are actually non-survival (or counter-survival) oriented, leading us away from routes to achieve "greater heights" – higher more ideal states of Knowing and Beingness – including the former "Magic Universe" preceding this one.

Here then is the collected works by Joshua Free presenting the next great frontier of the *Pathway* used by the Mardukite Systemology Org and which was crossed by participants and Systemologists at the Mardukite Academy during 2020 and the *"Freedom From"* workshops led by Joshua Free at the Systemology Society in 2021 (and part of 2022).

Here are the Secrets of the Human Condition, Life, Reality and the Universe known only to the most secret underground cabals throughout history and the highest echelons of elite – and even the Illuminati – still alive and operating today!

THE METAHUMAN SYSTEMOLOGY HANDBOOK
< TABLET OF CONTENTS >

.: INTRODUCTION :.
EXCERPTS FROM "A BASIC COURSE IN SYSTEMOLOGY"

.: UNIT 1—LIBER 2C :.

.: UNIT-2—LIBER 2D :.

.: UNIT-3—LIBER 3C :.

.: UNIT-4—LIBER 3D :.

.: UNIT-5—LIBER 3E :.

.: APPENDIX :.

∞

EDITOR'S NOTE

"The Self does not actualize Awareness
past a point not understood."
—*Tablets of Destiny*

While preparing this book for publication, the editors have made
every effort to preserve the integrity of the original material as
presented in a straightforward manner by the author—using clear,
easy to read and understand language.

Wherever appropriate, ambiguous and archaic terms are defined
in the glossary and appear in **bold** when first introduced in the text.

A clear understanding of this material is critical for effective
comprehension and personal benefit from *Mardukite Zuism* applied
philosophies and *Metahuman Systemology* spiritual technology.

These transcripts are prepared for research and posterity as
used by the *Mardukite Academy of Systemology (Systemology Society)*
and spiritual piloting or counseling services of *Mardukite Zuism*.

The *Seeker* should be especially certain not to simply "read through"
this book without attaining proper comprehension as "knowledge."
Even when the information continues to be "interesting"—
if at any point you find yourself feeling lost or confused while
reading, trace your steps back. Return to the point of
misunderstanding and go through it again.

Additional assistance and research support may be obtained from
other *Mardukite Systemology* volumes from the *Mardukite Academy* as
sponsored and published by the *Systemological Society*.

And *now* responsibility for this power and its
actualization is passed on to you, the *Seeker*.

Take nothing within this book on faith.
Apply the work directly to your life.

Decide for yourself.

∞

—INTRODUCTION—
EXCERPTS FROM THE BASIC COURSE
FOR METAHUMAN SYSTEMOLOGY
—GRADE-IV—

:: General Introduction to Mardukite Systemology ::
THIS IS SYSTEMOLOGY—A HISTORY & OVERVIEW
[Summation Presented by David Zibert]
REVISED GRADE-III INTRODUCTION

Since the inception of the Mardukite NexGen Systemology Society a decade ago, many things have been brewing quietly and unseen in the underground; but, fear not, as slowly but surely, everything will be brought to light... as a "New Babylon" *is rising*—and the Grade-III work is now complete.

Original literary presentations of NexGen Systemology occurred underground in 2011 and continued through 2013. Essential materials from this period were reissued as *"Systemology: The Original Thesis."* These materials first began to appear in 2011 as a series of booklets by Joshua Free, which at first glance were actually quite different from anything he had really presented before. The booklets were the first to present "Systemology"—or else, the work of the "Systemological Society"—as an offshoot of the Mardukite Research Organization and extension of the Mardukite Chamberlains group, which previously participated in development of our former Grade-II "Mardukite Core" research library, now collected in its entirety within an anthology titled: *"Necronomicon: The Complete Anunnaki Legacy."*

> Of course, "Systemology" stands for "system logics"—or else, "the logics behind the systems," which is also to say, in more esoteric terms: "the magic behind the magic."

In 2011, several booklets were released in the original Systemology "thesis" series; the first titled *"Human, More Than Human: Awakening to the Next Evolution."* It was really a down to earth approach; a simple user-friendly booklet about how, quite literally, "Humans are more than Human"—that we are more than our physical body and that there are actual "worlds" out there that most individuals are unaware of in their daily lives. It was really just taking the reader by the hands and saying in a rather basic and gentle way how *"we are more than human."*

The original underground release and presentation of Systemology was quite peculiar at the time. Even I wasn't sure what the goal was behind all this. But in the end, it made sense—and there was a brief follow-up published soon after: *"Systemology Defragmentation: Self-Honesty for the Next Evolution."* This title delved into the core of the matter and explained the basic theory behind "defragmentation" processes; which is the same as *ascent* up the "*Ladder of Light*" as we know it from our *Grade-II* presentation of the Babylonian "*Spiritual Star-Gate*" paradigm.

Systemology presented a new approach to the core *Pathway*; the same *Pathway* represented by the previous "Mardukite Core" and our explorations into the Babylonian paradigm proper—but these new booklets presented main tenets of this core without the more esoteric, magical or religious semantic trappings that we commonly find with other literal interpretations of the *Arcane Tablets*.

Then, a third booklet continued this original thesis series, arriving in 2012 as "*Transhuman Generations: The Next Evolution of a Species.*" It relates how worldviews are programmed in the generational cycles that repeat over an over—and, of course, when most individuals are unaware of that taking place, such as we see today in the world that we live in, a cyclic history is bound to simply repeat itself. Although the material is quite basic, it is an important consideration for Self-Actualization.

Another installment appeared in 2013, titled "*Systemology For Life: Patterns and Cycles.*" This one continued in the spirit of "*Transhuman Generations,*" but emphasized personal cycles—and about cycles repeating themselves—yes, through the generations, but more specifically, cycles repeating themselves as we experience them as individuals: how to notice them, and go beyond them, of course, toward the goal of *Self-Honesty* which is, again, achieved via "defragmentation."

In addition to these, a few other small underground releases were not as widely circulated. One of these being "*The Games: Portals of Self-Transformation & The Underground Occult Initiation.*" It was a very controversial booklet when it was first published; relating some of Joshua Free's adventures in the West Coast Occult Underground. Excepts continue to be reprinted in various volumes. These booklets are combined for an anthology reissued officially as "*Systemology: The Original Thesis.*" They also appear in the complete Grade-III anthology: "*The Systemology Handbook.*"

It became apparent in 2013 that many individuals, even those among the Mardukite network still studying the *Grade-II* "Mardukite Core," were not ready for Joshua Free's new "Systemology" developments at face value. Very few outside our elite close-knit membership of the original "NexGen Systemological Society" really took notice of what we were working toward from 2011 to 2013—and we continued to work even more quietly and unnoticed thereafter. Of course, this was all about to change with the public reboot that is presently going on now as we enter the 2020's.

There is also an interesting aspect of "Mardukite Systemology" uniquely experienced by an individual that follows the work of Joshua Free chronologically from its beginning—and seeing how "Systemology" *was* the goal; seeing how it was always the *unspoken goal* standing in the center of everything since the very beginning of Mardukite Ministries and the Mardukite Research Organization in 2008. An individual sequentially studying the materials for our complete "Master Course Grades" may still experience this development personally for themselves. Anyone who has read certain introductory material from "*Necronomicon: The Anunnaki Bible*" or "*The Complete Anunnaki Bible*" by Joshua Free—even those individuals that read "*The Great Magickal Arcanum*"—will notice that the "logic of systems" *and* an aim toward applied spiritual technology of "Systemology" is what has been there all along, underlying the journey, driving the work forward.

△ △ △ △ △ △ △

In October 2019, the Systemology Society experienced a new public debut with an arrival of the first true core textbook for Grade-III, catalogued as *Mardukite Systemology "Liber-One,"* released globally as "*The Tablets of Destiny: Using Ancient Wisdom to Unlock Human Potential*" and published from the new *Joshua Free Imprint*. It concisely presents the entire fundamental foundation for "Mardukite Systemology" itself—and upon which a series of further Systemology publications are now based upon.

Great care has been taken with "*Tablets of Destiny*" (*Liber-One*) so that everything in the book is as clear a message as possible—particularly for a novice of this paradigm—including concise definitions of each word that could be problematic or misunderstood during solitary studies. Care is also taken in clearly defining vocabulary newly introduced for our Systemology. Furthermore, *Liber-One* includes a summary of each lesson, given at the end of a chapter for optimal clarity. I also found that these summaries are great for just a quick second reading and review.

"*The Tablets of Destiny*" (*Liber-One*) is actually *not* a rehash of what was done before (with "*Systemology: The Original Thesis*")—it is a completely new presentation. It presents, for example, the logics behind the systems, and of what "Mardukite Chamberlains" had discovered concerning Babylon. We had once been like: "Okay, we found *that*. Now, *what* do we *do* with it?—And how does everyone get *benefit* from it?" But now, *this* is where we are. This is what we *do*. And *this* is Grade-III "*Mardukite Systemology*."

At its most basic core: Mardukite Systemology is an applied spiritual technology of the 21st century AD, based on the spiritual wisdom from the 21st century BC; which were compiled in their rawest tablet forms and presented for the *Grade-II* Mardukite Core—*"The Complete Anunnaki Bible,"* *"Sumerian Religion,"* and so on. *Grade-III* launches with *Liber-One*, introducing what we have termed the "Standard Model" (of Systemology), otherwise known as the *"ZU-Line"* (in Mardukite Zuism). This, in itself, is a workable, non-

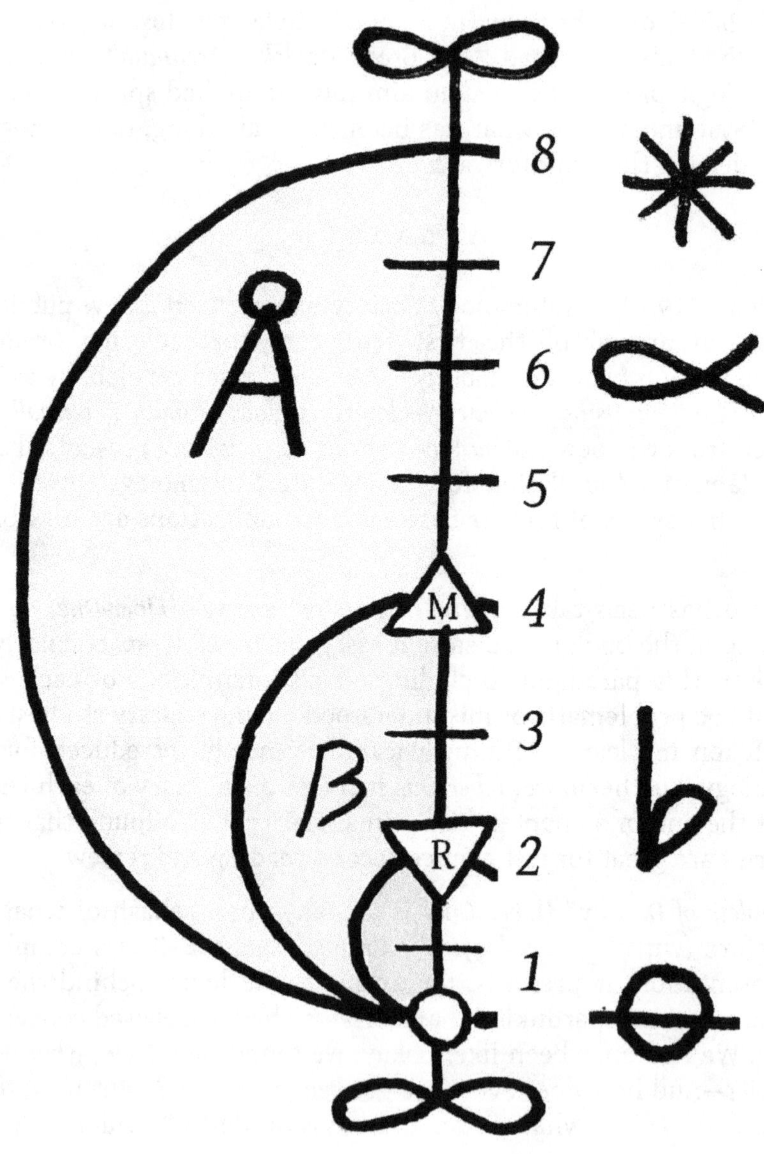

dogmatic, applied spiritual technology of the same *Babili* "Ladder of Lights"—the StarGates of this Universe—of which a *Seeker* is already familiar with by first working through *Grade-II*.

So, how does the "Standard Model" or "ZU-Line" work? Well, first of all, these are an abstract construct, graphically defining parameters for a Systemology of the Human Condition. It is divided as *seven*—or *eight*—steps for practical purposes, but theoretically extends to Infinity, above and below its scale; just like the Ladder of Lights paradigm of *Gates*, or any such similar Kabbalistic Model.

"The Tablets of Destiny" (*Liber-One*) focuses on the lower levels of the scale —from *0-to-4*. This work emphasizes building a strong personal foundation of emotional health and mental strength before an individual is introduced to more advanced practices—such as those included in its follow up manual, *"Crystal Clear"* (*Liber-2B*) and the other upper-level Grades. But, most importantly, we found out that a sane "Mind-Body Connection" is a prerequisite to experiencing a *Self-Honest*, clear and unfragmented realization of Self as "I-AM" ("Alpha-Spirit") in this lifetime.

This new approach is actually quite different from previous attempts and other traditions; even the most pious *Gnostic* paradigms still continue to *reject* material existence—what we refer to as *"beta-existence"*—as an "illusion." We are not rejecting the Physical Universe in Mardukite Systemology; no, rather we acknowledge that its existence is based on artificial agreements regarding an otherwise very real universe, in which a Human being—operating as a *"genetic vehicle"*—is the tool used to experience such a reality. Lower gradients of the *ZU-line* (*Standard Model*) run as follows—but, be aware that these descriptions are something of an over simplification; there is more to it, though this should suffice for our present introductory review:

0 — Inert Matter (theoretical zero, since everything in existence is basically a motion), or else Body Death (for the "genetic vehicle");

1 — Physical Body (basic physiological functions/cellular "fight/flight") receiving communications from...

2 — Reactive Control Center (or "RCC") which includes survival programming ("reactive response mechanism") inherent to the development and experience of all physical life.

Between "0.1" and "2" lies the standard emotional range of the Human Condition, which can be, and is, programmed and encoded with *imprints* preventing the Self from access to its own experience of higher levels of *Awareness* in *Self-Honesty*. Then we have:

3 — Thought (associative knowledge) and activity communicated from...

4 — Master Control Center (or "MCC") which is the point of contact from the True Self, or Higher Self in some paradigms, and is the highest gradient relating to the genetic vehicle or physical body for the Human Condition in the Physical Universe.

Self-Honesty is to be sought at each of these gradients as one moves upward on the "Pathway." This means that, for example, if you are not at a point of Self-Honesty regarding gradient "1" and "2," then you won't be certain to have a Self-Honest command of the thoughts and programming beyond that, which is preventing you from experiencing the *knowingness* and *beingness* of your "Higher" or "Truest" expression of Self; which we refer to as the "Alpha Spirit"—the "I-AM"—a spiritual being which merely maintains *considerations* of experiencing a beta-existence.

In effect what is sought on this "Pathway" is a clear *communication* with the continuity of All Life—and that starts with your own—and when you have a Self-Honest experience of your own life, you practice the same for ALL Life at each Sphere of Existence, or else it isn't truly Self-Honesty. This systematic process—as we present it in our "Systemology"—begins with removal of emotional imprinting; all of which is coming from the *Reactive Control Center* (*RCC*) and so cannot be seen rationally and analytically by the *Master Control Center* (*MCC*). This means that most people live their life in a reactionary fashion, often under the control of their emotions without even knowing it.

Here, it is important to mention, that what is implied by references to "emotions" really concerns the negative states of the Human Condition —which are all reactionary in nature—such as hopelessness, fear, anger, lust, jealousy, and so forth. For example: usually when you are angry, you are operating as a reaction to something—and the encoded mechanisms are commanded by the *Reactive Control Center* or *RCC* (plotted at "2.0" on the Standard Model or ZU-line). This is quite different from experiences of more positive states, such as being "in love" or personal enthusiasm about *willingness* to act on something, &tc., which puts the individual at *cause*, rather than as an *effect*, and which are commanded by the *Master Control Center* or *MCC* ("4.0").

Much of our Mardukite ("NexGen") Systemology paradigm could be summed up as returning the Self to the state of being Cause rather than the Effect. An individual should always be able to use the *Master Control System* to control their thoughts, noticing if the *Reactive Control Center*

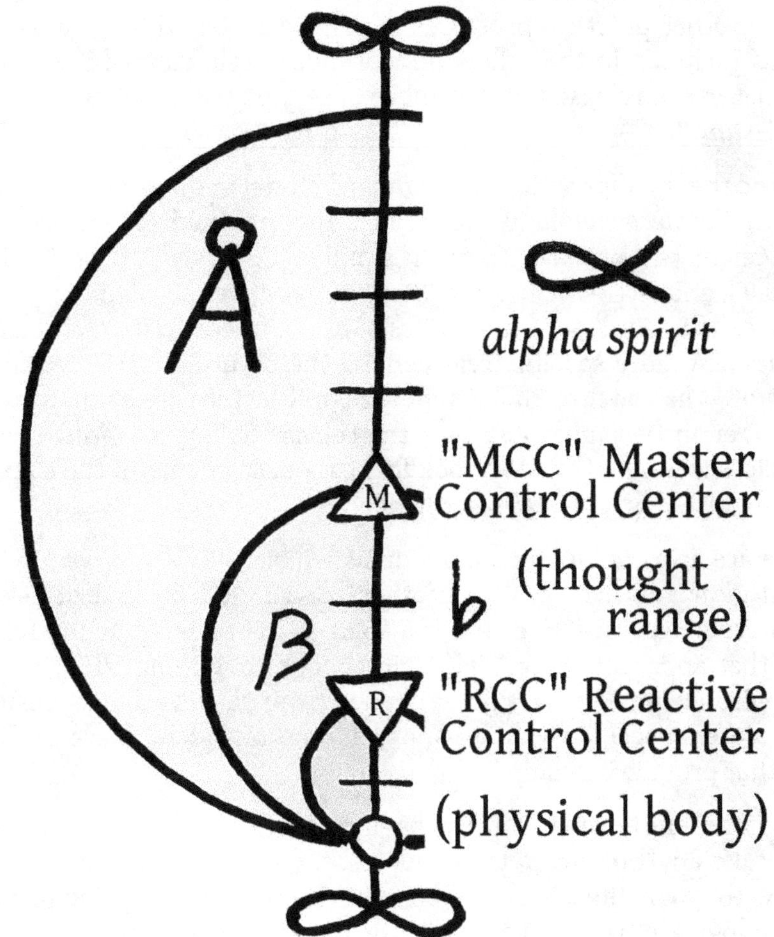

takes over with its emotion control, and even correct this condition with methods of "*Self-Processing*."[*] Pre-programmed automated reactivity may eventually be dissolved altogether—and that's *Self-Honesty*; *that is* our "Systemology" in a nutshell. Of course, there is much more to this and our methodology of application; but the important part to understand about the "levels" is that *Self-Honesty* is still to be sought at each *gradient* —and a *Seeker* will quickly discover that these tiers of *true realization* act as *Gateways* to accessing increasingly higher points of "*Actualized Awareness.*"

The first of our basic practical method to systematically process "emotional imprinting" effectively is described and outlined fully in "*Tablets*

---

[*] Details for "Self-Processing" are introduced in "*Crystal Clear*" (*Liber-2B*), also contained in the complete Grade-III anthology, "*Systemology Handbook.*"

of Destiny" (*Liber-One*), referred to as "Route-1" in later Grades. And there are many other practical processes to assist a *Seeker* within *Grade-III* material as included in the follow up workbook style companion, "*Crystal Clear*" (*Liber-2B*), released in December 2019, just two months after "*Tablets of Destiny*."

The basic theory supporting the Standard Model and *ZU-line* is represented by a simple cosmology rooted in lore contained on *Arcane Tablets* from ancient *Mesopotamia*. To put it simply: you have "AN" which is the "*Spiritual*"; and "KI" which is the "*Physical*"—between which exists a *continuum* called "ZU," which manifests as "*Life*" or else "*Spiritual Life Awareness.*" A more specific treatment og the nature of "ZU" became the subject of "*The Power of Zu*," a supplemental lecture series delivered by Joshua Free in December 2019, for the release of "*Crystal Clear.*" Lecture transcripts were published in book form and also appear in the complete Grade-III anthology, "*Systemology Handbook.*"

Yes, we are aware that some individuals will see "*Tablets of Destiny*" and "*Crystal Clear*" as merely just another "Self-Help" book series—which from a certain perspective this *is* a "Self-Help" series—but my take on this is that apparent these "Self-Help" books containing "deep esoteric occult wisdom" makes for a great change from all those books posing as "deep esoteric occult wisdom" and yet turn out to be mere Self-Help books that provide "no help."

But, as is generally written at the beginning of each volume of material: "Don't take anything from these books on faith. Apply these principles directly to your life..."—then confirm whether these principles and methodology are true for you, from the perspective of Self; and thus not only discover, *but live*, the *Life* you were meant to *live*, Self-Honestly as a Free Spirit.

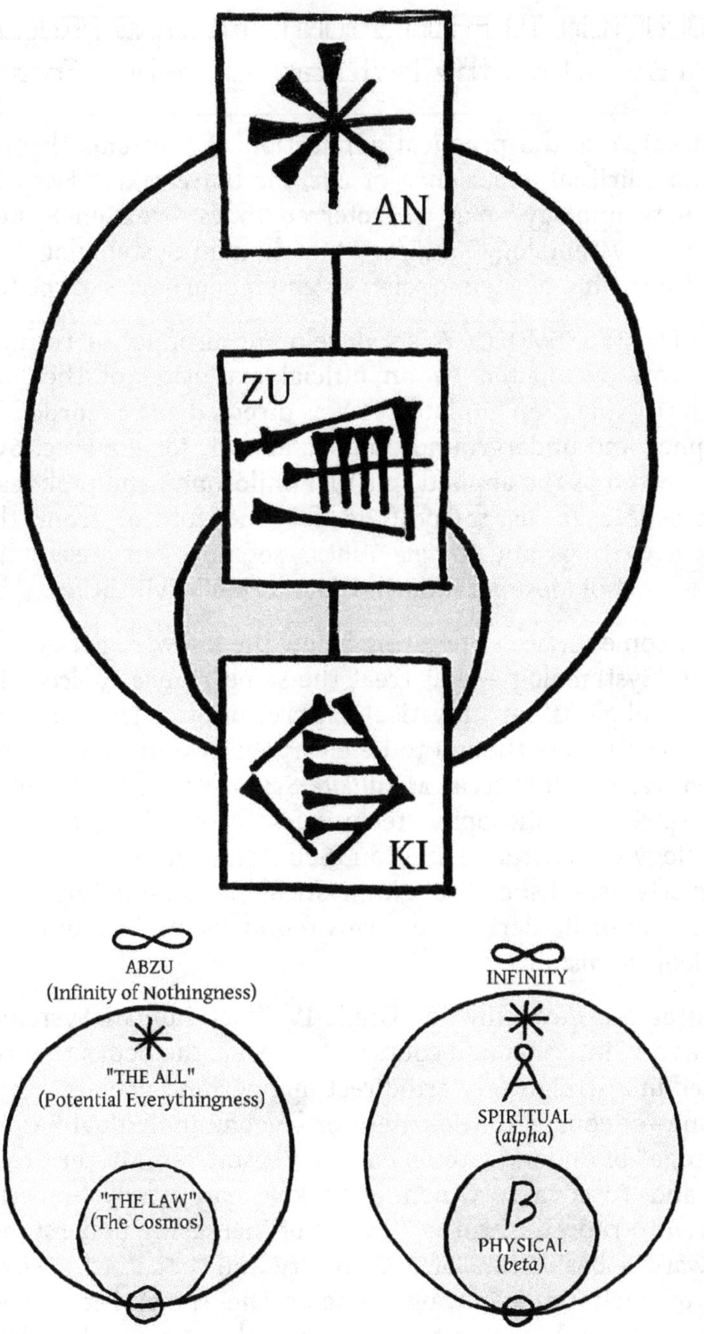
AN
ZU
KI
ABZU
(Infinity of Nothingness)
"THE ALL"
(Potential Everythingness)
"THE LAW"
(The Cosmos)
INFINITY
SPIRITUAL
(alpha)
PHYSICAL
(beta)

:: THIS IS GRADE-IV MARDUKITE SYSTEMOLOGY ::

INTRODUCTION TO PROFESSIONAL PILOTING PROCEDURES
[Based on the lectures by Joshua Free]

SYSTEMOLOGY is the practical application of "systems theory" to the study and spiritual experience of *Life, the Universe and Everything*. This "spiritual technology" may be referred to as "NexGen Systemology," "Mardukite Systemology" and/or "Metahuman Systemology" to distinguish it from other academic sciences and modern uses of the term.

MARDUKITE SYSTEMOLOGY is a developing product or result from intensive work conducted by an official extension of the "Mardukite Research Organization" in late 2010, as directed and recorded by mystic philosopher and underground esoteric author, Joshua Free. *Systemology* work is treated as the applied spiritual philosophy and practical technology accessible to us today (and for the future) from the oldest cuneiform writings and *Arcane Tablets* set down in ancient Babylon—from the heart of Mesopotamia and "Sumerian" civilization.

There are some *Seekers*—operating below the knowledge tier of Grade-III Mardukite Systemology—that treat the same *Arcane Tablets* with an exclusively religious or mystical appreciation. This is known as MARDUKITE ZUISM—though to be clear, the two movements are mutually *inclusive*. We now treat *Mardukite Systemology* as the "upper level" applied spiritual philosophy, techniques for spiritual counseling and methodology of spiritual evolution (Self-Actualization) methodology *for* the formerly established "religio-mystical" understanding of *Mardukite Zuism*, in any of its derivative forms found today, including "Mesopotamian Neopaganism."

Training at our Academy for Grade-IV "Metahuman Systemology" is treated as an "intermediate course." However, the books themselves are presented in a straightforward direct manner and may be "understood" by anyone—of course, to the extent or level an individual has actualized their "ledge" of understanding. For this reason, our Master Grades of Research and Discovery, which a Seeker may study separately, are structured to represent three "levels" of increasing understanding that lead toward a basic state of *Self-Honesty* and *Actualized Awareness*. The subject of each Grade always remains the same: *Life, Universes and Everything*. The only factor that differs is the "level" of understanding used to treat study and practice of the information.

"*Systemological Self-Processing*," introduced in Grade-III ("*Crystal Clear*"), developed after a decade of additional experimental esoteric research privately conducted by remote members of an underground "Systemological Society." This ongoing exploration into "applied spiritual philosophy" is established in light of all collected wisdom from various mystical and spiritual pursuits during the last 6,000 years of record history—most of which is found to be either erroneous and/or unworkable in effectively producing consistent stable results for higher states of *Actualized Awareness*.

Whether performed alone using a workbook (like "*Crystal Clear*"), with assistance of a friend, counseling from a Minister of Mardukite Zuism or by a Professional "Pilot" of Systemology, the functional purpose of "*Systemology Processing*"—or "*systematic processing*"—is for a *Seeker* to effectively *actualize* true *realizations* that produce positive movement upward on the "Pathway to Self-Honesty."

During a twenty-five year engagement with the underground esoteric and "New Age" community, Joshua Free discovered that the majority of practitioners following the "Route of Magick and Mysticism"[*] or "Route of Druidism and Dragon Legacy"[‡]—and other esoteric traditions amalgamated from diverse well known "organizations," "orders" and "fellowships"—were not independently arriving at the intended *realizations* from these philosophies, much less an *actualization* of the same, that might lead an individual steadily *outside* of the "Human Condition." This is just one of the stumbling blocks Joshua Free discovered concerning most contemporary approaches to "enlightenment" and various metaphysical "Self-Help" regimens.

A primary goal of our Systemology—which should be evident by the techniques and training for *Grade III*—is raising an individual's state of *Actualized Awareness*. This requires, by definition, bringing what is hidden into the light, or else carrying those aspects of "consciousness" existing below a level of analytical surface thought up to such where they may be treated "consciously" or "knowingly" by *Self*—from the perspective of the true and actual *Spiritual Self*—which we call the "Alpha Spirit."

Raising a *Seeker's* "level" of *Awareness*—*Actualized Awareness*—means very simply bringing more of an individual's "actual present space-time" **(beta)-*Awareness*** in "phase" or "synch" with the "Alpha Spirit"—the True "I-AM"-*Self*. This brings power and attention of *Awareness* more under control of the *Seeker*, which is to say a "clear communication" of *actual* potential.

---

* Grade-I, Route-A; see "*The Great Magickal Arcanum*" by Joshua Free.
‡ Grade-I, Route-D; see "*Merlyn's Complete Book of Druidism.*"

> "It is my goal for NexGen Systemology that we can elevate the *Actualized Awareness* of all *Seekers*—all able *Humans*—on Earth and to provide a true vehicle for their spiritual evolution in Self-Honesty. It is an objective for all Systemology Pilots and Mardukite Ministers to bring conscious *Awareness* of *Humanity* up and out from the heavy sticky murky mud they are subjected to. By cumulatively shedding skin and layers of everything that is not the true I-AM Self, achieving greater realization in Self-Honesty and increased *Actualized Awareness*, a *Seeker* ascends through a sequence of Gates to Higher Understanding—and ultimately to experiencing the Higher Universes that we have merely forgotten about."

A *Seeker* is introduced to *Grade-IV* with the third professional volume in our series, *"Metahuman Destinations: Piloting the Course to Homo Novus"*—and therein discovers that they are at an intermediate stepping stone between two great planes of realization:

   a.) what has come before—treated as the "Master" levels, including basic *Grades I-II,* and the *Grade-III* "Pathway to Self-Honesty" distinguishing "Mardukite Systemology"; and

   b.) what we are leading into now—using *Grade-IV* as a stable reaching point toward our higher "Wizard" levels, distinguishing remaining Grades of "Actualized Technology" (*A.T.*) still forthcoming.

"Professional Piloting Procedure" is introduced in the *Grade-IV* volume, *"Metahuman Destinations"*; meaning we now can provide both the Pilot *and* Seeker with skill development, education and strengthening personal certainty of the "Alpha Spirit" as an "Actualized Technician" (*A.T.*) of this spiritual technology.

Joshua Free first announced an integration of "Systematic Self-Processing" and "Professional Piloting" into Mardukite Systemology during a lecture given on August 9, 2019.[*]

> "There are many solitary methods of heightening Awareness and increasing mental skills necessary for *'processes,'* but I bring up this example... because when engaged in [professional] processing, there are two people involved: one of them is going through the *'processing'* toward Self-Honesty and one of them is assisting from a point of Self-Honesty. We identify the one receiving the service, or going through the *'processing,'* as the Seeker. In order to differentiate a very specific role that the assistant has in

---

[*]   Transcripts appear as an extended course reprinted in the complete *Grade-III* Master Edition anthology, *"Systemology Handbook."*

this process, the individual administering the *'processes'* is referred to as the Pilot. And let me make this point clear from the get go: the Pilot is specifically and exclusively responsible for Self-Honestly assisting the Seeker in reaching their chosen *destination—*nothing more or less. The Pilot is not a tour guide; not an interpreter; not a doctor; certainly not a therapist in the traditional sense—they are offering no actual advice toward or against anything that is uncovered as a result of systematic processing. Any and all realizations are meant for the Seeker to discover, determine and actualize on their own. The Seeker merely has the confidence now of knowing there is a safety net of travel by someone who has already been where they want to go!"

Based on this description, your first thoughts may be that *Grade-IV* course material must pertain exclusively to rigorous "procedures" and esoteric philosophies useful only to upper-level students of our unique underground brand and style of knowledge dissemination. But, this could not be any further from the truth. *Anyone* can benefit from the instruction and applied spiritual philosophies explained and demonstrated in every Mardukite Systemology publication.

Many believe that all respectable spiritual, mystical or philosophical "routes" regarding *Life, the Universe and Everything,* are headed in the "same direction" or considered in equal regard. If humanity's historical timeline and workable effectiveness of their methods are any indication, we can be certain the resulting "destination" for this plethora of "routes to knowledge" brewed within the intellectual labyrinths of the "human condition" are anything but equal to one another. In fact, what—if anything—could be truly identified as "equal" to anything else in this "physical universe" (which we refer to as "*beta existence*"). In fact, "associative knowledge" and the inability to properly *distinguish* "things" from other "things" in *beta-existence,* is one of the primary sources of "personal fragmentation"—resolution of which is a main priority of our Systemology.

The purpose of systemology and systematic piloting is to support responsibility of the Prime Directive in *beta-existence* of all *Life, Universes and Everything*—which is *to exist* and to act toward a continuation of *existence*—and for this purpose: to actualize the highest reach as "cause" on the Spheres of Existence. This is to say "defragmenting"—or clearing energetic channels—all the way up to to the highest states of knowing and being, or *Actualized Awareness*. At this higher truer point of *Self-Awareness* as an Alpha-Spirit—beyond compulsive and unknowing participation in the "Human Condition"—the original Alpha Prime Directive finally returns: *to create.*

Being high-level "cause" means *Self-directing* communication and control of energy and power consistently toward continuation of a higher and truer personal viewpoint from this "Alpha" state. This includes *Self-directing* effects that will promote the highest ideals of "ethical utility" as the individual reaches across the "Spheres of Existence."

△ △ △ △ △ △ △

In the first professional *Grade-IV* installment published as *"Metahuman Destinations,"* a Systemologist learns the fastest route toward actualizing the highest extent of reach as "cause" is to act toward assisting all existence insofar as it mutually helps to maintain the Prime Directive at all levels; "help" being one of the highest forms of communication, which allows an individual to *be* at a position of *cause* and also increase energy frequencies on the Zu-line. The ability to extend our reach as "cause" is accelerated by the "help" and "assistance" of whatever we may take responsibility for, even if its only responsibility of being in communication with a Universe.

When we consider the role of "Pilots" in Systemology—they are helping and assisting a Seeker, which in turn is helping and assisting the Pilot's reach. A *Seeker* must be willing *to be* helped and assisted—and be willing to help and assist the Pilot—by providing a full "attention" (presence) for participation in the session and processing communications. The Pilot or Minister must also be willing and able to help and assist a *Seeker*.

The first part of *Grade IV* emphasizes defragmentation of *communication*—all personal communication systems—and proper command of the same. "Communication, Command and Control" is a particularly important stable orientation point for fully accessing further work. For experimental and training purposes, this part was originally released for the Academy as *"Liber-2C"* and *"Liber-2D"* in Spring 2020; later revised as "Unit-1" and "Unit-2" for the *"Metahuman Destinations"* volume released in October 2020—and contained in the Grade-IV Master Wizard Edition of "Metahuman Systemology Handbook."

The remainder of *Grade IV* introduces the systematic design of Bodies, Minds and Universes. Emphasis turns toward a new methodology of techniques to put personal power of consideration, creative ability and command of imagination back under full *Self-determination.* An extension of earlier work as it applied to newer goals composed an Academy draft of "*Liber-3C*" in Summer 2020, but reissued as "Unit-3" in "*Metahuman Destinations.*" This development allowed a cross-over for Grade-IV—and the completion of its objectives and goals—as "Systemology Wizard Level-0" with publication of "*Imaginomicon*" (*Liber-3D*) a year later in Summer 2021.

"And when one truly realizes the full considerations that a combination of communication and imagination truly has upon the individual, an entirely new or previously unreachable universe of possibilities suddenly becomes real again; becomes a potential Reality again within the reach of Self as Alpha Spirit. Each an every one of us is a participant in the creation of universes and realities and we have the responsibility to our Self to permit the highest freedom of the Alpha Spirit to once again unfold as the present Awareness as Self. This is a state that is completely within reach of all individuals on planet Earth today; all we have to do is free ourselves to create a better world. So, let's get together and help one another create a better world."

:: AN INTRODUCTION TO METAHUMAN SYSTEMOLOGY ::
OBJECTIVES AND GOALS OF MARDUKITE GRADE-IV
[Based on a lecture by Joshua Free]

Completion of the "Core" for *Grade-III Mardukite Systemology* allowed our work to move up to a new level of understanding and practicality; and now we are able to speak from an even greater, higher, more widely encompassing perspective with *Grade-IV Professional Piloting Procedure*—as presented in the "*Metahuman Destinations*" (*Liber-Two*) compilation; and also the Grade-IV Master Wizard anthology "*The Metahuman Systemology Handbook.*" We are still moving upward on the *Pathway* and not simply restricting this knowledge exclusively to *Piloted* processing. We are dealing with new vistas for our understanding and are achieving significant advancements toward our true end goals at an accelerated rate. But it is important that we do not miss any steps along the way—important for all *Seekers*, whether *Pilots* or otherwise. It is apparent to many working through this material that we have tapped into something that shifts us up and beyond what we find at the *Master Grades*, but it was always dependent on what realizations were in reach up to this point.

Grade-IV builds upon former instruction given as the *Grade-III* "Master" level of Mardukite work that precedes our present "Wizard" *Grades*. To make certain no stone has remained unturned, a Seeker is prompted systematically through the *Grade-III* work as an integral part of *Grade-IV*, and combined, the "whole package" is intended to yield very specific attainable goals. Before we move a *Seeker* beyond *Grade-IV* there are certain things we expect from the processing taking place and realizations held. There is no question that an adequate education of true knowledge can accelerate this journey—but this is only on an assumption that a *Seeker* is ready to receive and interpret the information. Otherwise, its just more data added to a heap.

We have all made decisions—however much they may seem influenced by external or other-determined sources—about what we are *willing* to be, *willing* to do, *willing* to have a communication with—and *Self* does not like to be wrong. So, here we are systematically unwrapping this mess of convoluted beliefs and confusing agreements we made as Self along the way. You would think it should be an easy task, but the Human Condition is very much tied to the "physical" way of things—and the more greatly an Alpha Spirit identifies *Self* or "*I*" with this "physical" way of things, it becomes that much harder to change considerations about anything; and I mean *real* "change." If an individual really could freely change their considerations about existence as freely as they might like to think they can, then states of strong fragmentation would not exist and persist. And yet they do.

The purpose of "systematic processing"—within the tradition of ministry in Mardukite Zuism and applied spiritual philosophy in Metahuman Systemology—is to increase free range of consideration available to an individual; regain command and control of their Human Condition *knowingly* as an Alpha Spirit. We have traveled down a long pathway to the present state of affairs in this Universe—and this journey has indeed left us in a state of severe fragmentation; has left us fragmented about the identity of *Self.* With absence of true knowingness, the true creative ability of the Spirit diminishes if fixedly stuck in *considering* that these conditions of the Physical Universe are the absolute. I am here to tell you that this entire Physical Universe—this *beta-existence*—that the Human Condition is presently anchored to, is but a speck of dust in the widest encompassing considerations of the ALL.

There is no reason for me to be unnecessarily esoteric here: each and every one of you carries a certain knowing that you have descended or "fallen" from some higher consideration of space-time energy and form —and just about every spiritual, philosophical and scientific methodology of the contemporary age seems to hint around a bit about this; but few of us are now content in waiting around to see what any further *agreement* with knowledge about the design of this physical beta universe is going to offer. Some of us have already peeked behind the screens and know what it is going to offer: a way of further dividing what is already here into another sub-level universe that the consideration of *I-as-Self* can get entrapped in.

The subject of *willingness* appears very frequently in our Systemology— and if we are going to think about things in terms of "magic" or "will" or "intention" and everything else along those lines, then this is the common meeting ground and a place to start; and it is why we consider this upper-route of Mardukite Metahuman Systemology as "Wizard" work; this position to be that some in our *Piloting* courses have referred to as "Actualized Technicians" and "Alpha Tech" and so on. Many have realized this is getting us where we want to be—and there is no question about this.

The questions, at least for me, have always returned to organization and delivery, the means of structuring research and way in which its discoveries are analyzed—all of which has occupied nearly a decade now of my current lifetime, just in regards to the Systemology that I have been involved in developing behind-the-scenes of the more publicly visible Mardukite *Grade-II* work and the "Routes" explored in *Grade-I.* But all of this contributed to our "Complete Mardukite Master Course"—these other "Routes" are excellent entrance points onto the *Pathway* so long as they are treated as such and not as the ends in themselves. That is too often the alluring trap, and why such methods are allowed to be so freely explored in contemporary society: they are just betting you will get trapped in them.

By its very definition, "fragmentation" implies separation and disconnection; or what some define as dissonance, disharmony and discontinuity... a lot of "dis" words in there. It is for this reason that we emphasize "communication" at the very start of *Grade-IV*, in "*Metahuman Destinations*"—because a *Seeker* is not going to get any further with their Master Grade material without some remedy of being very blatantly "out of communication" with *Life,* the *Universe* and whatever the individual is *unwilling* to "know," *unwilling* to "be" or "face" or "confront" and so on. A *Seeker* has narrowed their decisions of what is acceptable or conceivable to "know" or "be" within preexisting programming and thus has become an "effect" of the same—thereby giving up responsibility for Self-determinism of the Alpha state.

This isn't a "fire and brimstone" sermon; I'm not here saying all this to judge or condemn; you have actually already accomplished that part on your own for your Self—and there is more value in my working to remedy *that* condition than there is in my reinforcing it as others have done in their methods of using knowledge, religion and spirituality to further trap humanity in the lower systems. We are all here now because we suddenly found ourselves *unwilling*—or believe ourselves *unworthy*—to consider any *Higher Universe* to occupy—and that, in a nutshell, defines the actual present state of affairs we are treating in our Systemology.

Δ Δ Δ Δ Δ Δ Δ

The journey down a *Pathway of Fragmentation* that led us to this point did not happen all at once—nor is it important that we grasp a complete understanding of our full Cosmic History at this juncture of work in order to deliver or receive effective processing. We are most concerned with what a *Seeker* is able to relate to concerning *this* lifetime, before we begin to compound matters any further. We already demonstrate the significance of these principles with application to *this* lifetime using systematic methods of *Analytical Recall* ("Route-2") as introduced in our text, "*Cryst-*

al Clear"; and newer methods linking circumstances and experiences to energetic flows referred to as "circuits" for of *Communication Processing* ("Route-3") in "Metahuman Destinations."

When a *Seeker* is brought to consider moments they have gone out of communication in their life experiences, the realizations that may occur can be startling—but they are what we are targeting to overcome. Of course, if we emphasize only the negative states and conditions, we would only be effective in validating the negatives—which is only one type of flow. So, we may, for example, have the *Seeker* recall a time when they were in "good" communication in alternation with those times when they had broken ties or "cut" communication lines with others and yes, even "things"—really any "form" with "mass" that we assign a label to and which can hold, carry or incite some kind of energetic charge; and this is referred to as a "terminal."

Another excellent example to demonstrate to *Seekers* is what *willingness* has been diminished in connection—or rather "disconnection"—to certain *facets* that are emotionally charged or otherwise imprinted to restrict considerations. Each and every one of us has certain "charged" *places*, or *people* or *ideas* that trigger something—some kind of "ping"— just by their being flashed into our view. Sometimes we do not even need a physical representation of this to be present in our physical environment. Merely the thought or *concept* of it—being formed in our Personal Universe, or as some consider, the "Mind's Eye"—puts us in a position to be "for" or "against" some mode of consideration. We are not even talking about "intuition" here, although it is sometimes mistaken as such when these channels aren't clear.

For example, an individual experiences some type of traumatic event or *Imprinting Incident* at such and such place and around such and such type of facets and suddenly the *willingness* for any later *duplication* of these is diminished. The individual doesn't even want to be around that physical area location any more and will even go to great lengths to avoid this "other-determined" restimulation that exposure incites. We've covered this stuff in *Grade-III* pretty well, especially in regards to the emotional encoding discussed in "*The Tablets of Destiny*" text. The point that was not necessarily driven home within that volume is that this successive validation of being "out of communication" with existence led *Self* down a dark spiral of intentional forgetfulness; and this is a state that we are only now discovering any real remedies for, after having swirled about within this murky mess for countless aeons.

When we talk about "communication," we often mean *willingness* to reach for *knowingness.* There is also the method of processing that we consider "objective," and this targets the *willingness* to reach for action and the command and control of *doing* things as cause. Yes, we want to understand Cosmic Law or Causal Law; but it is not hard and certainly not as convoluted as physical sciences make it out to be. The average *Grade-II Mardukite* or Hermetic philosopher "understands" Cosmic Law pretty well—they have a handle on some of the basic principles by which beta-existence has been Ordered. But we are not trying to get entrapped any further into this Physical Universe and therefore do not need to make our sole occupation a discovery of more intricacies to agree with. It is, for the most part, a closed system with the illusion of recursive infinity so that it may become the sole occupation of its inhabitants; infinitely divisible by "discovered knowledge"—which has to be created and forgotten just get a sense of being discovered again.

A 6,000 year legacy of secret and esoteric knowledge to mastering the worldly universe is what is "mastered" at the "Master" levels of our work, or rather the "*Master Grades.*" Most individuals who have come and gone never even reach the apex of *this* much during their lifetimes, then alone move past it. It is a quite enamoring study—and it has been concisely condensed within our series of Master Edition hardcover volumes including: *The Great Magickal Arcanum, Merlyn's Complete Book of Druidism, Necronomicon: The Complete Anunnaki Legacy* and especially our *Grade-III* compendium, *The Systemology Handbook.* Corresponding Mardukite Academy lectures and supplements are collected in an additional companion volume: *The Complete Mardukite Master Course.*

The *Pathway* that led us to this point is treacherous and tortuous. As much as we are set out to desensitize or discharge more commonly known implanted terminals of the Human Condition, it should be observed that there are just as many—if not more—potential trappings when one crosses that first *Gate* and has stepped beyond exclusive considerations of mundane existence. This is when a lot of dissonance starts to occur and a ritual magician of the present age does not realize they are sitting in their circles talking to themselves, changing themselves or their considerations if effective; but more often than not, they are waiting for the *Books* and *Candles* to start talking *to them*, and well... we have already seen the personality effects that result from hanging suspended too long within that first sphere.

None of the lower Graded Routes are inherently wrong or bad in the moral or ethical sense. What they are—and what we have presented them as—are tiers on a very well-known "*Ladder*" of ascent that lead us through the same barriers of consideration that we contributed in setting up for ourselves on the way here. When this responsibility is dismissed, we have no actual authority or control over the matter. It is true we have given it up; have decided at one time or another that it would be better not to have it—but, now we know our mistake. The only issue, until fairly recently, is that there have been no successful demonstrations of a map to remedy this mistake. We've just sort of "lived with" it and agreed to it as a reality. They've just kept telling us to "suck it up" and "this is how it is" and we have agreed to be this effect via the very participation with this Game.

Handling of systematic processing—at Grade-IV—is codified by a schedule called: *Systemology Operating Procedure 2-C*, since it was introduced in *Liber-2C*, it is our second official outline of procedure, and is also a step toward basic restoration of the Alpha Spirit's ability "to see." *SOP-2C* is fully outlined in the text, "*Metahuman Destinations*." Its structure continues and incorporates what we already set out in *Grade-III*. For example, Resurfacing from "*Tablets of Destiny*" and Analytical Recall from "*Crystal Clear*" are still both retained and valid in *Grade-IV*.

Willingness to "recall" and "resurface" and "remember"—the consideration that it is acceptable to *do so* without reservation—is where the *Seeker* arrives directly in *Grade-III*. At least, this is where we should expect them to arrive. If they aren't getting there on their own—and we're not going to leave them behind as a result—we simply incorporate *Grade-III* work as a preliminary to approaching the full extent of *Grade-IV*, and development of *SOP-2C* allows for this. There is no reason that a *Seeker* cannot "self-process" themselves through the full extent of *Grade-III* work, either. The thing of it is: there is no short-cutting these processes and side-stepping realizations.

Without a free and total *willingness* for analytical recall on any aspect on an internal level, there can be no clear communication and certainly no demonstration of *Piloted* processing that will prove effective. We can process a *Seeker* to increase willingness for analytical recall and thereby improve their reach as communication, but until this whole matter is satisfactorily been resolved, there is no reason to even consider work of "higher" *Grades* and *Routes*. They will not prove to be as effective as they otherwise would be in the right hands or applications.

At *Grade-IV* we apply processing that directly targets energetic flow of communication and the *Seeker's* willingness to engage or reach as a *Self-directed* action—which again requires working through a whole host of energetic masses that have accumulated from heavily charged experiences; those that lay as a mass or resistance on an otherwise freely dispers-ing wire or energy current. If that seems too esoteric, let us just say that we must clear the obstacles that exist in the pathway of true *Self-honest* vision for the Alpha Spirit.

Fragmentation at this level of processing—particularly as it applies to the most readily available memory that we can resurface from this life-time—is, at its core, entirely *analytical* or *mental* in nature. And by this, I mean that it is linked to the realm of "Thought." The fundamental inhib-itions and excuses, the inabilities and hindrances we attach to our personality, the blocks and long lists of things we don't want to know or acknowledge—all of this accumulates over time, persisting to affect our range of present-time considerations and thoughts, based on fixed solid-ity of former considerations and thoughts; including those we have chosen to forget about and no longer take responsibility for.

All of this contributed to where we have considered *Self* to be; and all of this, once recognized and realized and accepted, becomes a map *out* of the mess we got ourselves into. All that is waiting, is for us to take the responsibility and resume command. That's it! That's all we have to do. But since we have so carefully and systematically arrived at this state we are at now, it seems it takes a bit more than a single moment of passive "positive thinking" to pull us completely out of its gravity. It shouldn't have to; though for the amount of fragmentation that most individuals are carrying around, it seems to take a little more work. But, I am pleased to say that: systematically, we *have* found a way, and that *is* the essence of our work now today.

:: A Mardukite Academy Lecture by Joshua Free ::
SYSTEMOLOGY—THE ORIGINAL THESIS
[Master Course Lecture #39]

Grade-III "Mardukite Systemology" as it is presented now—and its continuing evolution—is a consequence subsequent to application of my *original thesis* on Systemology, itself a composition of multiple essays and various papers I presented to the underground *"Systemological Society"* nearly a decade ago.

During the past ten years, "Mardukite Chamberlains" Alumni and members of *Moroii ad Vitam* continued to assist and support the original *"NexGen Systemological Society"* even though very little had been published on the subject officially between 2013 and 2019. A combination of *those* individuals *and* incessant application of my *"Systemology: Original Thesis"* theory *to* Grade-II work resulted in, *finally, "The Tablets of Destiny"* nearly a year ago, which is *"Liber-One"*—really the public inception—of what took nearly a decade of underground work to establish officially as "Mardukite Systemology."

Although, it's not—it's something that's used for "posterity." We don't really require, for example, an individual to have read *"Systemology: The Original Thesis"* in order to understand *"The Tablets of Destiny"* or to apply the material in *"Crystal Clear"* to their life. However, for purposes of having a "Master" understanding of how this all developed and what this all entails, it *is* all included in the Grade-III Master Edition textbook, *"The Systemology Handbook."* It is also available as a stand-alone title.

"Systemology: The Original Thesis" applied a *philosophy* to a general universalist understanding of the Human Condition. It was definitely of a "Mardukite" flavor, because, of course, it incorporated the idea of the ancient Anunnaki, the establishment of civilization and its progression—as we've cover it Grade-II and *"The Complete Mardukite Master Course."* But, it was mainly a *philosophy*.

It wasn't until we *crossed* this philosophy numerous times with ancient cuneiform texts—which we refer to numerous times as the *Arcane Tablets* —that we were able to get any kind of *workable* effective systematic methodology out of this information. And this, of course, spawned "Mardukite Systemology," which has actually been able to develop at an exponential rate—as a result of finally breaking through with these *Keys*.

It's ironic, because what we are talking about in Grade-III is the "Ishtar

Gate," and so, the level of—well, I've made jokes in the past about "getting beyond the Ishtar Gate"; that it was something that just didn't seem to have happened anywhere, as far as recorded traditions in history, and in the literary preservation of these systems—in regards to how "actualized" the various "initiates" and "followers" of these other "routes" really were.

The objective *goal* of Grade-III to complete the Master Grades, has always been about *breaking through* the Ishtar Gate; actually being able to surpass the point of initial "beta-fragmentation" as it concerns, for example, emotional reactivity and all of the "pre-patterned" forms of behavior that seem to override and take over our sensibilities, or an individual's ability to command experience as *Self*, and actually be *Self-Directed* and *Self-Determined* in totality. So, it was at *that* point—in delivering material to that point—that we finally capped off the "*The Complete Mardukite Master Course*" with three Master Grades; because, what else is it but, you know, a gradient of Self-Mastery. And so, that's where we're at.

In the original presentation of the thesis, the first booklet is referred to as "*Human, More Than Human.*" The catch phrase for this—and the pamphlet for it—and the way we've even reintroduced "*The Tablets of Destiny*" when we were promoting it a year ago was that:

> "The Universe exists within a Sea of Infinity, an ocean of pure potentiality. Do you know your place? Sealed within the Human Condition is a unique life program special to you. Unlock the power of your true identity and live the life you were meant to, Self-honestly as a Free Spirit within NexGen Systemology."

> "And what we discovered—or rediscovered—is not a *new* methodology, but the *first* one: the archetypal System of Systems known to the ancients. We used it. We applied the acid test of reality—and only the truth remained. We saw it first hand; beneath the veils and levels and layers of the systems... only the truth remained."

And therein, I began a series of booklets to compose "*Systemology: The Original Thesis*"—trying to drive in the direction of "metahuman" or *homo novus*, this next level of Awareness and Realization and Beingness, that seemed to be only scraped upon or alluded to in all these former spiritual systems and mystical traditions; but of which has never seemed to be obtained or never seemed to be able to be delivered—at least, never to *my* satisfaction.

There was always this allusion that "well, there might be something in the afterlife; or if you do good now, well good things will eventually happen to you" or something of this respect. But, other than this "morals and dogma" mentality, there didn't seem to be a delivery to any point; no one even seemed to be any *happier* or *better off* in the long run for the fact that they were actually working through whatever it is they were working through—they were always still lost in their own fragmentation and operating on various imprinting and so forth.

So, what I was really working to establish in *"Human, More Than Human"* is the idea that humans are *more than* human; I mean, it's kinda given in the title. And this has been kind of joked about in the past, by those that have commented on it, about how blatantly forthright some of this really was. Then again, it could still be taken kind of "tongue in cheek"—with a "Well, we've kind of all known *that*, but then we've been told we *have a soul* and there's spiritual forces at war over us and then we go to Heaven or we go to Hell" and so forth.

Well—[*sniffs*]—I really didn't find any of that to be the case within our Systemology. *But*, I did find that an individual *was* themselves this thing they had separated as "soul." The individual *was* "spirit," *was* "I-AM," *was* the "Alpha" of this other existence, and that any of this other stuff that had been attached to it *was* basically *that*: energies and masses and fragments, memories, different emotional encoding, implants, that had been *attached* to the individual by their own considerations and identification of "I-AM" *to* anything.

It was *those things* that were weighing down the quality of the Spirit, the quality of what they were considering "soul." *But*, it isn't like an individual "had" one; like, they were carrying it around in their pocket or something like that—but that it *is* what the individual actually *is*; and that is what we consider the "Alpha Spirit" in Systemology.

Another concept introduced at the very beginning of the thesis is this very idea of "fractioning" of reality—that there's separations—and that these separations are what an individual has a sense of. As separation of individuality and true knowingness takes greater hold—as more and more fragmentation is basically standing in the way of a clear view and a clear channel between Self and its own experience—that's when an individual begins to feel more *solemn*, they feel more *hollow*, there is a certain *sadness* that takes over; they become more *introverted*.

Now, when I say *introverted*, I don't mean someone that has the ability to, you know, "self-analyze" or "look within" or be able to observe their own behavior or correct patterns of the Mind and so forth—but an "introverted person" that's basically just *withdrawn* from their interaction and communication with energies, their interaction with flows and energies, the social environment and so forth. This is one of the things that seems to *dim* along with the decline of *Actualized Awareness*.

The other thing pointed out in *"Human, More Than Human"* regards the "standard issue" state of a Human being—and how they basically go about their everyday lives *believing* they're "Self-directed" and *believing* they're "Self-determined" and that they are actually experiencing life and everything with clarity, but that there is actually so much artificial programming and fragmentation and "conditioning" taking place—and control over the mental imagery, the associations of knowledge, all of the emotional responses that are attached to experience and former encounters with different facets of life—that really get in the way of that.

The purpose of *"Crystal Clear"*—because we knew it was going to take a while to establish any kind of "Piloting Program" or get a solid "Ministry" and elements of "clergy" and "Zuism" on the road—is that *"Crystal Clear"* is really meant to be a *"self-processing"* guide, although it can be used quite effectively along with Piloting. But it was really meant to be a self-processing guide that an individual could use on their own. Back when I was writing material for *"Systemology: The Original Thesis,"* we *didn't* even have a workable concept of "self-processing" available; we didn't have any kind of practical effective aspect to apply our philosophy until we really spent many more years with it.

When you start to look at what we've done with *"Tablets of Destiny"* and *"Crystal Clear,"* a lot of the stuff from *"The Thesis"* seems very *elementary* and basic; but when we're talking about a *"Complete Mardukite Master Course"* or the intellectual-academic level *of* treating Mardukite Systemology as Grade-III within the Academy or schooling or in your own "apprenticeship programs," the material from *"Systemology: The Original Thesis" is* a fairly accessible introduction to our work, if not using *"The Tablets of Destiny"* directly. Another, more recently released, publication of ours excerpts introductory material from all Grade-III sources—*"The Way Into The Future: A Handbook For Humanity"*—with selections from my writings edited by James Thomas, one of our Publication Staff Officers.

An individual that doesn't really have a background in Mesopotamia, that hasn't worked through Grade-II materials, might actually be able to *reach* a few of the realizations on their own, just by working through the material of *"The Thesis"* prior to treating, for example, *"The Tablets of Destiny"* directly. It's for that reason that I bring this up, because although we treat Grade-III in a certain way now, my aspirations toward it may be even found in *"The Great Magickal Arcanum."* In fact, since the 1990's, I had always intended on this gradient of work being an upper-level of, for example, the *"Hermetic Order of the Crystal Dawn"* that I was operating underground in the "Merlyn Stone" days.

The whole purpose—or the actual reasoning behind the name "Crystal Dawn" had to do with this same "crystal clarity," the same "metaphors" that we apply all the way up to present day, you know, *twenty years* later with *"Crystal Clear."* That was essentially the functional purpose of the establishment of the "Crystal Dawn" *project* back in the late 1990's. At the time, before *"Arcanum"* and the Mardukites, we didn't have a "Master Grade" system to actually bridge this kind of understanding.

I was primarily dealing with Grade-I type involvement in the 1990's and the first few years of the 21st century—and the individuals around me, the ones I was encountering, for example, in the "New Age" marketplaces and bookstores and so forth, were still primarily stuck still considering things only at that level. The rest of them, those that were considered "Lightworkers" or dealing in "Eastern Spirituality" and "chakras" and whatnot, they seemed to be pretty much, you know, attached to their own paradigms with that—but were still not *quite* breaking through to find effective means of *really releasing* from the Human Condition.

It's really that element—the idea of the Human Condition being something *separate* from *Self,* separate from I-AM, that is actually one of the pinnacles of Grade-III realizations. This is something that former levels of understanding (or former Grades) are not necessarily impressing fully. They kind of make it seem like, "Well, you're this being or an Awareness and when you die you just float around as this ghostly being and so forth" or "your shackled to one of these or another afterlives" or "you go off to happy hunting grounds." These are artificial spiritual beliefs; they're attached only to certain "religions" and so forth; they don't necessarily have any other basis in fact.

In the language of Grade-III, when we're talking about *"encoding,"* we're talking about the *emotional* level of *"imprinting."* And this is what, in the past, or in psychology or in other philosophies, we might refer to as "conditioning." And then, when we're talking about *"thought,"* when we're talking about beliefs—when we're talking about the associative knowledge that an individual has with the actual understanding that they're maintaining with the world around them—we're talking about basic mental programing; we're talking about the Mind-System at that point.

Our Standard Model is not just spiritual puffery. It also demonstrates that in *beta-existence,* a "Mind" and a "Body" *communicate* through stimulation of biochemicals. So, again, what we find is that there are certain "push-button" mechanisms attached to the Human Condition, where it can be "conditioned" or "fragmented" or "controlled" or "manipulated" or given false knowledge based on sensory stimulation and *encoding* of essentially either *"pleasure"* or *"pain."*

We see a lot of imprinting and fragmentation attached to points of, for example, *pain,* or in other elements, *loss*—any sense of suffering on the individual; because, you're talking about *that* individual's experience from *within* that Body, and the more that happens, the individual begins to *feel,* the individual begins to start *thinking as* identified with a Body.

The programming for parameters of *beta-existence* all come from within, *interior* to Mind-Systems and the Human Condition. The more an individual, for example, feels pain, and isn't really able to confront or face the nature of that—or maintain control over that experience and their *Mental Imagery* and *imprinting* of that experience—they begin to become more and more the *effect* of, for example, their experience of and as the Human Condition. They begin to associate and then identify more and more of what they believe Self or I-AM *is* with the Human Condition.

In the past, this has been treated only loosely in some "regressive" techniques and certain forms of "creative psychology" and so forth; but, it's never really been brought into the level of "mysticism" or being treated at, for example: just last week at the Academy we were talking about "ritual magic," we were talking about "Anunnaki"—potentially "alien gods" and things, you know, for the last few days—and now we're talking about ways of basically relieving the suffering of the Human Condition enough to get an individual to *free* their considerations outside, the fact that they're not their body.

Now, when we talk about things like the "Matrix-System"—today, this is an example where we have certain pieces of *inspired* science-fiction media and so forth, which kind of demonstrate a certain understanding or at least give tangible *examples* for concepts—that many years ago would be harder to explain, and harder for individuals to understand. For example, now everyone has at least some kind of idea of a "Reality Matrix-System" now. But really, we consider a "matrix" like a "grid." The "grid" implies action in multiple directions, so we're talking about a *duality*— we're talking about systems that basically operate with energy flows due to considerations of polarity. This is even touched on in *"Liber-R,"* the final installment of Grade-II, *"Novem Portis"* or *"Necronomicon Revelations,"* which was written and released simultaneously with the first portion of "*The Thesis.*"

But, we're talking about the "Matrix"—we're talking about a visible series of lights, the "array," the "light-matrix"—the System—that basically is what you can see; what is around, what is given substance. And an individual participates in this regularly. That is one of the functions of the Alpha Spirit: that they can *create*—if nothing else, they *create* the imagery experienced within their own Universe. This is what is basically being "snap-shot" around us—we, you know, there is a certain sense of newness or "novelty" when we discover something or see something for the first time; and there is a certain *imprint* that takes place, which kind of dulls our Awareness thereafter, when we basically lead off the *imprint* we carry as what is real.

So, let's say you've got a certain encounter taking place. It's basically just energy and mass moving through space and giving a concept of time or duration. Then experience takes over—the parameters of what the senses can experience; the Human Condition can take over; and then all of this is given a classification and other associations for identification. And so the next time an individual encounters the "same" thing, there is a certain energy signature—key waves and frequencies that are picked up by sensory faculties of the body, since the Spirit is no longer interested in handling it directly—and rather than give it full attention, like as if it were new, we get basically just a replay—we get basically just an experience of the former snap-shots that have been taken, and thrown up at us. That's basically all of what we are experiencing in *beta-existence*; because the *Self* still has to *create* the *image* of the form that is being treated, based on the energy signatures received. A lot of times, this is what causes the "world around us" to kind of "cave in"—because we aren't really (consciously) participating in its creation anymore; we've just basically passed on that responsibility. Although we are still creating it, we're creating it just on basic pictures and imprints and snap-shots from the past that we are compulsively still creating.

The second text that was developed—the second booklet that was released for "*Systemology: The Original Thesis*"—was called: "*Defragmentation.*" Again, a very self-explanatory title. After establishing the nature of the Alpha Spirit in "*Human, More Than Human,*" the "*Defragmentation*" booklet was about, basically, getting back to that point. This is where Self as an Awareness Point or Total Consciousness is treated as the I-AM or the "*Alpha Free Spirit*" (as it was originally referred) and that a Self-Honest experience of the I-of-Self *is* the only *True Identity* of the *Individu-*

al and the only *True Point-of-View* of the Observer; the most basic, prime—*Alpha*—state of Self.

Programming—and what some have called "conditioning"—or encoding, is what dictates fragmentation of the. And, of course, you have a material existence, since it is consciousness-created, it is fragmented and developed by these creative Alpha Spirits; and we are *all* participating in doing this. The stuff of Universes has been created, compacted, recycled, turned to dust, compacted again and made a bit more solid for the next condensed level of material Universes. Basically, these systems are composed of fragmented parts; and then, of course, they work and are interrelated to each other—and that's where we start to deal with this idea that what we're dealing with is called "Systemology." Because even when we're talking about traditions and different paradigms and all of the ways in which this ancient wisdom has been extended to us, you still have modern systems that are essentially fragments of an ancient wisdom.

Here we start to treat the nature of systems, systems operating within each other, larger systems operating upon smaller ones—kind of "*cogwheel*" aspects and dynamics; and that's what it is—it is "*dynamic systems*" we are treating. But, this isn't—it's not the mechanistic "clockwork" universe as a lot of physics would have you believe; it's *dynamic systems*, where each one is—it's not just "billiard balls" hitting against "billiard balls." There's other considerations that work upon that. Other "unseen" forces that perturb what is apparent; all of which mainly relate to the individual.

I mean, the individual is the one that is basically able to tip the scale on that. Yeah, we would have a very "clockwork" mechanistic universe *were it not* for the fact that there is *Life* in this Universe—and *Life* has the ability to *change* things, to *create* things, to *destroy* things; and all of these are not parameters that are necessarily totally fixed.

The individual—the Awareness—that is making these choices is not a part of this Physical Universe. There's no mechanistic "cog" definition that applies to the individual; with the one exception that comes close, only because it acknowledges it at all, and that's "game theory." But this is what has separated, for example, *our* Systemology and what has kept "religion" and "science" at various odds: most material sciences can only really be concerned with a material *objective* universe as it applies *almost* free of the Observer; which is not actually the Universe we cohabit as a POV with other POV. So, material science is unable to do that since even it's *Point-of-View* is always impinging upon it its own expectations, its own observations and, of course, the limits that sensory organs or the perceptions or what have you are able to *view* and *define* its "observed" *causal effects.*

Because, that's what we're dealing with: *cause* and *effect*, pretty much at all points here; we're dealing with an individual trying to be as much at *cause* as possible over their experience of reality, over their creation and direction of energies and so forth—as opposed to becoming the *effect* and slowly *succumbing* to all of these forces of this material universe, which will definitely, if allowed to—you know, it's a *hungry* universe—it will definitely take over, if allowed.

When we talk about "programmed-identity-personas" or "*phases*," we're talking about these "*personalities*" that act as "filters" in which to view the world—more POVs. We're talking about, from the perspective of the "Mind-System," filters for the Human Condition that are embedded with *emotional* energies. They have their own harmonic *resonance*; they have their own *inclinations* as to what is considered attractive and what is considered repulsive for that "personality package."

And by putting one of them "on"—by having these filters "on"—you filter more of the experience and that actually *validates* function of the filters and basically makes things more solid. So, experience becomes reality and reality becomes experience; and then *emotional encoding* and the *memory imprinting* and all of that determine what the definitions or parameters of that reality experience are—as they are perceived and associated and assigned meaning.

This is basically what constitutes the experience of *Life*, the *Universe* and *Everything*; and at a "philosophical" level, this stuff all seems, you know, real *easy...* it all seems to make sense. But *still*, it took ten years to bring it to anything practical; primarily the best example of that for Grade-III being the material presented in "*Crystal Clear.*" Even in that sense, we talk about distortions or fragmentation of an individual right *in* the text of "*Defragmentation*" in "*Systemology: The Original Thesis*" as "crystalline distortions"—distortions in the perception lens; basically, referring to preprogrammed *compulsions, obsessions, tendencies,* and what is ignorantly generalized as "disorders" and "phobias."

Unfortunately, most of psychology is no longer dealing with anything about "consciousness"—if it ever even did before. It's only concerned with "behaviors." And I have an academic background in that, but I don't find it helpful. If you ever take a look at the "*DSM-IV*"—it's this huge diagnostic manual used for psychology concerning mental health and mental behavior—really, it's just a bunch of classifications; it's just a bunch of definitions. Every little quirk that an individual has, or could potentially have, is somehow in there and classifiable as a "disorder" and so forth. But, they have no methodology behind actually *correcting* any of this—that's never been established; nor has there ever been, within that paradigm of "mental health," an establishment of what "*sanity*" actually is—or when an individual is finally "*done,*" for example, with their "therapy." Beingness never seems to get returned to the patient.

That's why we take this up in the sense of "spirituality" and even the "religion" of Mardukite Zuism *and* a pursuit of a *higher* level of "metaphysics" and so forth, because honestly, there's no reason for me to endeavor into the fields of "medicine" and "psychology" and interfere with the realms of "doctors" because, we're not even playing in the same realm. We're treating a *Spirit*, which they've no longer acknowledged even *exists*—as far as their practices are concerned. We're dealing with the *Mind*, which because it's not fixed strictly to the "brain" as an "organ" as far its actual existence—yeah, sure it uses the "brain organ"—but, because they were never able to find the "I-AM" or Alpha Spirit, because they were never able to find "consciousness" and put it under the microscope, because they've never been able to define the "Mind" and actually be able to determine what it is, for example, independent of the brain as a physical organ, *none* of that stuff exists in the realm of physical sciences and psychology. Our domain and their domain do not seem to overlap in any way shape or form, except for the fact that, well, you can kind of classify the knowledge in the same vicinity many times.

These "crystalline distortions" can become *crystal clear*, when this crystalline catalyst, for example, the "function machine" that I was referring to in an *earlier* lecture [of "*The Complete Mardukite Master Course*"]—whatever is being used by the Mind-System to process the energetic transmission of information; if this is crystal clear of fragmentation, then the experience can be.

You can see the *effects* in everyday life of just what external fragmentation programming actually—and the encoding—leads to, in terms of the Human Condition. You see a lot of people with irrational or erratic or completely chaotic thought; the inability to concentrate or focus—the kind of fatigue and irritability that seems to plague the Human Condition more and more everyday; and of course, this increased attention on ailments and diseases of the body. This all affects what we're treating or looking towards in Mardukite Systemology as a "Self-Honest" experience.

That's what we're trying to correct even within Grade-III and our application of the work and the milestones that we consider capped off with Grade-III, because as much as one uses the *nomenclature* or the concept of "Wizards" and what not, no real "Wizard" work can be done until we get a person back up to *zero*; back up to at least a point of—you know, even though they are occupying the Human Condition, they are not completely trapped by all of the "push–pull" mechanism that are attached to that.

And there are *mechanisms* that have been created along the way, affecting what they've been treating as an experience; and both the mechanisms and the experience they feel a real need to hold onto, because without holding onto that experience, they feel like they don't *have* something. And so, this concept of *loss*, the programmed conditioning about *loss*, it's really what keeps many people from letting things go —old ideas, old energetic masses, the inability to forgive, the inability to look at something new.

Like in *"objective processing,"* we might have an object on the table—we get an individual to look at it as if practically for the first time with full awareness, over and over again, to be able to duplicate that action perfecting and without mental strain. We treat this kind of stuff at higher levels of "Systematic Processing" and it yields results, because we're looking at the highest-level application of all those old *rites* and *lores* and *rituals* and *pathways*—and all this stuff that's come before—we looked at the highest-level of what we could apply from that and what it might do, and therein we found Mardukite Systemology.

:: First Steps to Grade-IV Wizard Materials ::
THOUGHT PROCESSES, THOUGHTFORMS AND FRAGMENTATION OF MENTAL SYSTEMS
[A Summation by David Zibert]

Although not exactly encouraged in our society—or formally trained in any way—it is not only interesting, but also rather important, for you to inquire about the Mind; its various fragmentation and thought processes as a system. What I'm referring to here as "The Mind," is the human faculty of "reason," or else "Awareness"—which, in part, differentiates humanity—and systems of the Human Condition—from other basic organic lifeforms.

Surely, all life has its own capacity for reasoning—within the limitation of its own species or genetic vehicle; its own "Mind-System" you could say—be it animal, insects, plants, even minerals are alive in their own ways and grow based on a crystalline pattern.[‡] But there is definitely something that sets operating as the "Human Condition" apart from all of these other forms of life—and that's what I am referring to here as the "Mind-System." It is our grand peculiarity as a species...

That being said: we sure have a lot in common with other life forms —"All-as-One" interconnected by "Spheres of Existence" in the Physical Universe—but if this "Mind" we are talking about is what sets us apart: *what* is unique to *our* current experience of life on Earth? Maybe that's worth exploring a bit; worth spending some time understanding—as human beings—what we have in common with, for example, dogs. What have we completely overlooked or dismissed in this existence. Might we appreciate dogs more when living life as—or extending our point-of-view to experience life as—a dog, don't you think?

> Command of the "Mind-System" is the key to a superior experience of life and reality, not just in this beta-existence, but as a key to unlocking potential to experience life and reality of *Higher Universes.*

When you're "thinking up" something, functions of the "Mind-System" appear to be quite straightforward. You just "do it"—and either ideas and/or memories seem to simply pop up in your "head"; often even in

---

‡   See Joshua Free's edition of John Toland's "*Pantheisticon*"—also reprinted in the Grade-I "Route of Druidism & Dragon Legacy" Master Edition anthology, "*Merlyn's Complete Book of Druidism*" by Joshua Free.

words for more abstract concepts—but also perceived as images, sounds, even smells or tastes. This is especially true when it comes to memory recall, since all information from the senses is associated and imprinted as ideas and mental images too.

What you might be unaware of, is that there is a systematic process going on in within and as the "Mind"—and, of course, at another level of activity, biochemically taking place throughout the brain as you "think up" stuff. This is all part of what I refer to as the "Thought Process." The brain is a biological machine used to process activities of the "Mind-System" (mental machinery) for a genetic vehicle in this Physical Universe. So, let us certainly not confuse ourselves here: the "Mind" is not the "brain"—the brain is an organic meat machine; the Mind is machinery composed of only energy.

∆ ∆ ∆ ∆ ∆ ∆ ∆

When you think up something, where does it come from? Basically, from nowhere—or what can be described as the "unmanifest reality," or else "infinite potentiality." In effect, *thinking* is simply a means to communicate with reality—solidifying it. Just thinking a thought instantly manifests it within the reality of your mental universe, engaging the "Mind-System," which is always comparing and evaluating thoughts and data with previous experience and former thoughts in order to have it "make sense."

Your Mind-System is always "on" and always computing right, correctly within itself; essentially incapable of a wrong computation. All of the errors come from erroneous data supplied and collected through experiences; the analytical functions of the Mind as an operating system simply calculate what it is given. *Self* assigned the value. But there are also labels, patterns of association and attribution of Identity. Every thought gets stored in some folder within the Mind-System, creating a memory-chain or track, associated together to create artificial structures and patterns. Each subsequent thought is compared to each file—and "processed" through each circuit—for each associated folder. This further validates classification and evaluation of these patterns as "memory."

Thought Processes operate like circuits and channels of a communication system, communicating the *reality* of a Universe; your own *Personal Universe* and the *Personal Universes* of others. The same thoughts and memories might be filed differently by different individuals and given quite a different consideration as reality. That's why, for example, different individuals might "recall" different *facets* from the same event, or associate the same *facets* in a unique way.

Paradigms and semantic systems are all approximations of reality. Each contributes to the creation of biased "thought-forms" ultimately leading the individual to a biased experience of reality—and thereafter, a reality and understanding limited by the experience. The same erroneous data is stored for future evaluations of perception. These biased or "rigidly fixed" paradigms—operating in exclusion to Self-Honesty—*are* the artificial illusion that philosophers chase after, first consciously and knowingly created and then maintained as compulsively created automatic mechanisms.

The true origin of all personal thought is Self, the Awareness that is monitoring the Mind-System. Energy is created at command of Self, in Alpha States, not from lower-level machinery restricted to material senses. When one is considers a "mental" *point-of-view* "interior" to the reactionary level of a physical body, the "brain" may independently operate as an organic machine that relays orders to other control centers related to the "body" functions and motions as a genetic vehicle, but these are all easily manipulated reactive stimulus-response mechanisms.

Δ Δ Δ Δ Δ Δ Δ

One might notice how some individuals have a tendency to invoke accepted authorities in order to validate their own agreements and data association—such as in academia. Generally in the contemporary academia of any age, promoting original ideas is not only frowned upon, but mostly forbidden, whether by the "*laws*" of specially funded sciences or "forces" of organized religions. Both have their coffers to fill. The irony here being that these alleged "accepted" authorities go through the same thought process and are subject to the same fragmentation described by Joshua Free in the professional series of Systemology books: "*Metahuman Destinations,*" "*Crystal Clear*" and even "*Tablets of Destiny.*" Consensual reality is indeed both malleable and corruptible—and whomever controls the most agreed upon paradigm controls that reality.

If you are seeking an actual Self-Honest reality experience, the way is to free yourself and be able to think beyond the paradigms and semantic systems you have been formerly programmed with. Some esoteric mystics have called this "Crossing to the Abyss," or else "Antinomian Thinking." But whatever name given—the core material inspiring our Systemology and routes toward Self-Honesty is not a *new* discovery; for it has been long whispered of in select underground circles. It was, for example, acknowledged by early Christian Gnostics—and is reflected stronger in even older historical texts such as the *"Chaldean Oracles"* or the Babylonian *"Epic of Creation."**

The QBL or *"Kabbalah"* (*"Cabala,"* etc.) is perhaps one of the more widely known mystical paradigms employed in Western esoterica and contemporary mysticism. It developed through Rabbinical Jewish lore based on knowledge first concealed as the "Gate" (or "Star-Gate") system of Babylon. I use the Semitic Kabbalah here only as an example, since it is not directly a part of Mardukite Zuism or Mardukite Systemology; but it is a way some *Seekers* will already be familiar with the more "esoteric" concepts explored in our Systemology.

In the example of QBL: When you "think up" something, it comes from AIN, the sea of infinite potentialities, then it manifests in the reality of Kether, the "Crown," and then *swoosh!* The whole "Tree of Life" manifests rather instantly in response, and the thought is computed to fit somewhere on this systematized model—largely based on associative semantic data within the paradigm—to make the content and evaluations of the thought compute with reality, preventing the individual's universe from collapsing on itself. And, of course, several different semantics and interpretations for the same Qabbalistic model exist to even fit *that* knowing into some predisposed category of knowing.

You, therefore, unknowingly—or even knowingly—place each and every thought and memory upon one or another "Sphere of Existence"—called *Sephiroth* in the QBL—and these get fixed and stored in your memory bank. And when thinking or recalling something else, the Mind-System takes into account everything that is already stored in this memory bank as a comparison in order to file the thought or memory once again into a "Sphere of Existence" and fix it upon a timeline, confirming it and having it make sense, thus once more preventing the mind from collapsing. We could just as well apply this to any version of the "Tree of

---

* The Babylonian *"Epic of Creation"* or *Enuma Eliš* is a primary emphasis of Mardukite Zuism and Grade-II materials contained within *"The Complete Anunnaki Bible"* edited by Joshua Free, reissued in the complete Mardukite *Grade-II* Master Edition 2020 hardcover anthology, *"Necronomicon: The Complete Anunnaki Legacy."* As it applies to the Standard Model and cosmology of Systemology, refer to *"Tablets of Destiny."*

Life" or "World Tree" or "Chakra Centers" or "Gate-System." They are all semantic paradigms for relaying some level of understanding concerning the circuits and channels of Thought Processes taking place in the Mind-System.

In this sense, thoughts confirm and feed other thoughts endlessly; keeping you busy in a "mental maze," never letting you see the actual thought or clear memory as it truly is in a defragmented state, outside of a paradigm system or other erroneous associations. This mental fragmentation is what defines how you experience the reality of your own Personal Universe, falsely measure against and superimposed by reality of other Universes.

Now, in regards to an individual trying to get out of this process: you can, of course, attempt to shift paradigms all you want; and this is pretty much what most of the mystical occult scene—and even the "New Thought" movement—is presently concerned with; with endless presentations of personal "gnosis," offering only a different paradigm for a different experience of reality semantics. But these, while interesting, have a tendency to only fragment and obscure one's understanding of reality and their personal universe even further. Hence these other paths are really akin to simply getting out of a cage just to enter a more alluring one. Do you see that?

What we have developed over the course of a decade for Mardukite Zuism and Systemology far surpasses attempts made by these former paradigms—each one reaching further and further away from its original source, never returning the Mind and its control back to the original state that it once maintained before its fragmentation into the various human systems. And perhaps for the first time, in a long time, there is a recognizable way out; solutions revealed to us now in the 21st century A.D. of what has only been touched upon in obscurity since the original cuneiform tablet renderings of the 21st century B.C.

We are ready to face these challenges now... *Are you?*

—UNIT ONE—

COMMUNICATION & CONTROL

—LIBER-2C—

:: 1 ::
THE SYSTEMOLOGY OF COMMUNICATION

There is a chapter in *The Tablets of Destiny* titled *"Communication of Thought, Will and Action on 'The Tablets of Destiny."* It describes activities and properties of *"ZU"* or *"Spiritual Life Energy"*—which is communicated through an entire series of **channels** and flowlines—but the actual systemology of "communication" may not be equally apparent to all *Seekers* from these descriptions. The *Systemology Society* realized that communication was the fundamental unifying key underlying all other action, motion and *Living* in systems.

In former presentations of *NexGen Systemology* composed a decade ago—such as the old *Reality Engineering*[*] lecture series—the concept of "communication" *was* defined in our earliest manuals as:

> "successful transmission of information, data or energy (&tc.) along a message line with a reception of feedback."

Of course this is a stable definition for some applications, but it deserves expansion for our "Pilot" course regarding the "control" of energy and power as it applies to higher-level understanding within Systemology. Therefore, we now also define "communication" as:

> "an energetic flow of intention to cause an effect (or duplication) at a distance; the personal energy moved or acted upon by will or else 'selective directed attention'; the 'messenger action' used to transmit and receive energy across a medium."

An individual consistently "interacts" with all manner of energies, information and forms in everyday life—including those found at more rigidly solid levels of the physical universe (or *beta existence*), but not limited to them. An understanding of communication of *Awareness, Actualized Awareness* or *ZU-energy* is what allows *Self* to properly direct the relay of energy between "control centers" such as what is often very generally referred to as the "Mind" and "Body," which are systems controlled and commanded from a higher state of *spiritual beingness.*

When it comes to the individual—the *Alpha Spirit* as *Awareness or ZU*—communication involves all spiritual, psychological, emotional and physiological 'messenger actions' taking place along the "personal identity continuum" or Zu-line. This activity is essentially what many refer

---

[*] See also *The Systemology Handbook* anthology by Joshua Free or *Grade-III Mardukite Master Course.*

to as **"*consciousness*"** and it is a "communication of Awareness" relayed to and from various "control centers" **extant** on that *Spiritual Life Energy* **continuum**.

The "Standard Model of Systemology" (and Zu-line) demonstrates systematic communication of *Awareness* at any point between the continuity of physical solidarity in *beta-existence* and essentially *Infinity*. This workable "Standard Model" is explored quite extensively in the *Grade-III Mardukite Systemology* material.[*]

Humans are prone to viewing communication exclusively in external or objective forms and mediums—such as speech or writing—but this is only one type of communication. However, in whatever manner we decide to view communication, it is an energetic **"flow"** of energy changing in space and this creates a cycle that in essence defines what we experience as "time." There is *no* treatment of time as an illusion within our systemology, because the observable cycles of energy, by their very nature, define **"time."**

When an individual is experiencing "internal" (subjective) activity, this is a form of communication (energetic exchange, &tc.) that we can call "processing." An individual receives an incoming communication from the environment—or generates one internally—and then processes the energy as "information." This then "in-forms" or "forms-in" some kind of analytical significance for an individual; that is to say—it is given "consideration" or "meaning."

Knowledge concerning "influx" and "outflow" of communicable energy from the physical (beta) environment and the manner it is "processed" subjectively is now fully systematized for purposes of: study as *Self*, effective application to *Life*, and the establishment of "Professional Piloting Procedure." The beauty of "systemology" is that training on this subject remains consistent regardless of applications thereafter, because the basic data applies to all systems. When we consider specific qualities used to describe vibrant, radiant and charismatic individuals on Earth's **timeline** demonstrating an ability to *cause an effect* onto objective reality and the world-at-large, the common point to them all is the *ability to communicate*.

—Communication is the primary means by which "personal fragmentation" takes place.

---

[*] See specifically *The Tablets of Destiny* (*Liber-One*) and *Crystal Clear* (*Liber-2B*)— materials which also appear within the collected works Master Edition *Grade-III* anthology: *The Systemology Handbook*.

—Systematic use of communication as "processing" is a primary means to "defragment" an individual.

Communication is potentially the most effective workable tool an individual may employ. Its proper handling means successful manifestation of will and intention to the highest level of cause; but improper control leads to becoming an effect, trapped by one's own **thought-forms**, **thought-habits** and reactive-responses automated by systems of the biochemical genetic organism an individual Alpha Spirit tends to identify as in space-time of *this* "beta existence."

There are many forms of communication that originate at higher levels of understanding or command of action, generated from a point of *Self* that is "exterior" to "beta-existence" as cause. This is also communicated through a series of personal (relay) channels (along the Zu-line) before an expression is manifested at another "level" of existence.

In most cases—where the origination or source-point of energy communication is Self-directed from the Alpha Spirit—the transmission of any current or flow of energy that carries an intention (or form) is treated as a **"thought-wave"** or "thought-vibration" in systemology.

Self has an incredible ability to use the **Mind-Systems** to generate and direct specific currents of energy which directly influence the experience of Reality in the Physical Universe. We know that thoughts *can* have a "reality" to them—and that the extent of this "reality" is equivalent to the strength of the original intention and clarity of the channel by which it is transmitted on.

Thoughts which manifest solidly enough for others to take a position, or "point-of-view" on, earn some quality of "reality" in the physical universe to the extent they may be communicated. This takes place even when an individual's point-of-view is *"against"* something; for there is now a "mass" or "solid" on that channel or flowline *to be* "against."

In *NexGen Systemology* it is just as important to understand how these "thought-waves" and "thought-forms" are communicated to create an effect on others as it is to realize the powerful effects our cycles of thought, belief, behavior and reaction have on us, working together to develop a particular "artificial beta **personality**" that we present to the world and which is the product of accumulated personal fragmentation and erroneous programming.

Success in the Game of Life is particularly dependent on the ability to communicate clearly not only with those other individuals and *Lifeforms*

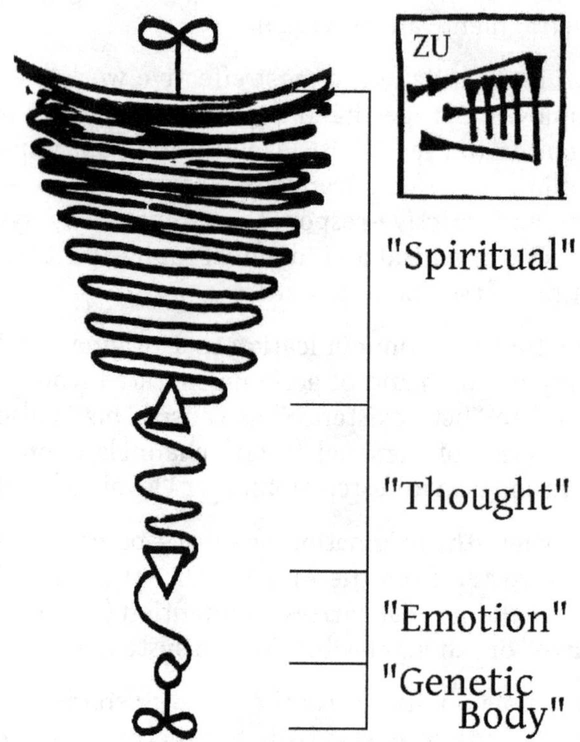

we interact with, but also with our Self, which is a state often referred to in *Mardukite Systemology* as *"Self-Honesty."* Our systematic method of achieving this as a basic beta-state is called *"The Pathway to Self-Honesty."*

The functions of Communication exist in all facets and aspects experienced of *Life, the Universe and Everything.* When we consider the spiritual, religious and mystical applications of communication throughout history, there is no shortage of examples wherein the human population has made attempts—however successful—at reaching toward the Infinite, which is otherwise considered some kind or another type of "communication with God."

We find practical applications of communication in any effort or intent to "make something known" or "bring to light" what is otherwise unknown or not treated as presently existing. We find interchange of "thought energy" taking place wherever **knowledge is imparted**" or a medium is used to share in or partake in the transmission of energy or "information."

There are two basic components that correspond with <u>communication</u>: <u>intention</u> and <u>attention</u>. These are comparable to the Three Principle Systems of "Cosmic Manifestation" as described on the *"Arcane Tablets"*—*

COMMUNICATION—"Motion/action"
INTENTION—"Substance/form"
ATTENTION—"Awareness/consciousness"

Those continuing their studies from *Grade-III* would be most familiar with the concept of *Intention* as an application or active property of the WILL at (5.0) on the Standard Model.

<u>intention</u> : to intend, have "in Mind" or signify (give significance to) for or toward a particular purpose; in *Systemology* (from the *Standard Model*)—the spiritual activity at WILL (5.0) directed by an *Alpha Spirit* (7.0); the application of WILL as "Cause" from a higher order of Alpha Thought and consideration (6.0), which then may continue to relay communications as an "effect" in the universe.

When we consider the act of *attending* with our *presence*, the direction of focus for *Awareness* could very well be toward a specific aspect or thing. There are, however, a few more components to this activity.

<u>attention</u> : active use of *Awareness* toward a specific aspect or thing; the act of "attending" with the presence of *Self*; a direction of focus or concentration of *Awareness* along a particular channel or conduit or toward a particular terminal node or communication termination point; the Self-directed concentration of personal energy as a combination of observation, thought-waves and **consideration**.

Communication is a systematic process by which an intention is given attention; the intention is projected by a sender or source-point and given some quality of attention by a receiver or receipt-point where it is treated as an effect. The cyclic action actually creates and defines space and time as it is occurring.

Whether treated as an interpersonal exchange among human bodies or between universes, the nature of a communication defines the range or boundaries (**parameters**) of the relationship between any two "things"—or "system terminals." On a purely systematic level, communication is a flow of energy between two terminals (terminations or end points): one projecting and one receiving. When communication is "two-way," when

---

*   Explored more directly in *"The Tablets of Destiny"* (*Liber-One*) by Joshua Free.

it is flowing in both directions, a **"circuit"** or "cycle of actions" has formed.

$$\text{INTENTION} \rightarrow \text{ATTENTION}$$

(Directing Attention) → (Accepting Intention)

Where communication appears in any system on any level, it is treated as a pathway, bridge, conduit, gateway or channel between two "points." Quality of any two-way circuit of communication is defined by clarity of transmission and its ability to relay clearly across a proximity (distance of space) or between terminals. The "Standard Model of Systemology" demonstrates how all existence—*Life, the Universe and Everything*—is a composite system of intricate "two-way" pathways all acting together "systematically" as one whole, but composed of parts (or "sub-systems").

NexGen Systemology is the result of thousands of years of research and experimentation concerning the highest ideal state of Knowing and Being —the most effective efforts toward Self-Actualization and freeing the innate power and identity of the Spirit. It should come as no surprise for us to then treat the nature of existence as a "communication of energies" or "energy flows" taking place between all points and "terminals" in existence as an intricate "web-like matrix."

Communication terminals (or "nodes") within a functional system—even a "living" one—are not restricted only to other *Lifeforms.* Anything that has been put forth as an "intention" into existence is given a sense of "being" and "form" when it is permitted *to be.* And this *beingness* is the result of "attention" on the "intention" enough to validate "it exists."

Fragmentation of any kind is a distortion that inhibits free flow of energy (or clear communication) and the understanding (comprehension) or duplication of the energy received as an effect. An individual also maintains a chronic level of *Self-Honesty* and *Actualized Awareness* (experienced as the "freedom of the Spirit") equivalent to the degree that their "lines" of communication for experience with various terminals are "free and clear."

The goals of "systemology education," "systematic processing" and "piloted procedures" are all to assist the *Seeker* to free the restrictions and barriers erroneously agreed to on communication lines and thereby "defragment" the flow of energy. An individual is principally as **"capable"** as they are freely able to clearly communicate *Self-expression.* Effective "systematic processing" is heavily dependent on successfully managing these flows.

:: 2 ::
THE CONTROL OF COMMUNICATION SYSTEMS

Thoughts, just like other forms of energy and matter, are "waves" or "wave-forms" that carry the cosmic property of communication: *motion.* A "wave" is a messenger action (or *'motion'*), carrying a "point" of some type or degree to another "point" across a distance, and therefore changing "space." Rate of transmission across space defines "time." We often express a "wave-action" with considerations of "time" as "vibration" and "frequency." This is a "measured observation" of "time" between "points" in "space"—which is to say "communication of Reality."

"Clear communication" or "clear channels" of energy transmission, mean a "duplication with certainty" of a message or energy flow. Without such "understanding," what many pass off as "communication" is really only "distortion" and noise—erroneous fragmentation promoting "turbulence" of an energy flow.

> <u>turbulence</u> : a quality or state of distortion or disturbance that creates irregularity of a flow or pattern; the quality or state of aberration on a line (such as ragged edges) or the emotional "turbulent feelings" attached to a particular flow or terminal node; a violent, haphazard or disharmonious commotion (such as in the ebb of gusts and lulls of wind action).

The common expression in *Systemology* for clear relay of communication, between *Self* and the universe, is "*A-for-A.*" This means a relay or projection of energy, information or thought—as "A"—is directly and perfectly duplicated with the same "intention and meaning" at its receipt-point— as "A."

When an individual's attention is directed or focused on some specific bit of incoming energy (therefore becoming a receipt-point of energy/information), the information comes in on an attention line and given significance and meaning based on either a *Self-Honest* experience of the energy or based on associative data collected from the past.

"Associative knowledge" is often times quite solid as a "thoughtform" or "mental image" which manifests and solidifies along energetic channels of experience quite literally as "beliefs" about Reality. Rigid solid beliefs, particularly at lower levels of realization, automate the "significance" assigned to any reception of energy and its related experience. *Self* (as Observer) is not able to "see" past these artificial solids, filters and screens, which creates turbulence on the pathway of what should otherwise be a clear communication of Will and Intention between *Alpha* and *Beta* states—between the Alpha-Thought of the Alpha Spirit and the control maintained over the beta-form that it operates and monitors.

In *Grade-III*, the "*Pathway to Self-Honesty*" is described as a journey of clearing spiritual energy channels of debris and erroneous associations imprinted by the environment—those entwined and solidified energies inhibiting total experience as an actualized *Self*. The "*practicum*" of *Grade-IV* employs "*Professional Piloting Procedure*" to engage two-way communication flows between a *Pilot* and *Seeker* in order to manage turbulence on lines directed toward terminals or terminations (objects, ideas, events, memories) which otherwise do not "talk" or "respond" and which result in no systematic repair on their own.

Once fixed in place, an individual is likely to keep hitting such fragmentation as a "barrier" to communication of true *Self-Honest* reality experience unless properly managed. The significance cannot be overemphasized: experience of *Life* is a communication between *Self* and a *Universe.*

The greater a *Seeker's* true understanding about *Life, the Universe and Everything,* the more certain and willing they are to project communications; which in turn is an increased ability to manage the "personal environment." We can be certain that in all of its creative expressions, the responsibility and capability attached to the true nature of the Alpha Spirit as a "being" is to *create, experience, know*—all of which is based in the personal control of communication.[*]

A specific channel by which an individual manages control of the communication line as Self, is described and demonstrated in *Grade-III* materials as the "*Zu-line.*" Clear communication and control is only possible by a "clear pathway" between relay points on the "*Zu-line*"—a "straight line" of energetic communication on the Standard Model, between the Alpha Spirit at (7.0) and continuity of the "physical universe" as *beta existence.* There are other relay points on this channel while an Alpha Spirit controls a genetic body—meaning many points at which *fragmentation* may occur and an intention is later diverted by some other crooked or jagged wave-form that provides distortion in the follow through of a communication to be accurately duplicated A-for-A. Fragmentation is what inhibits the clear passage of communication and therefore its control.

---

[*]   Or from the Welsh Druid Triad: *to see, to study and to experience all things.*

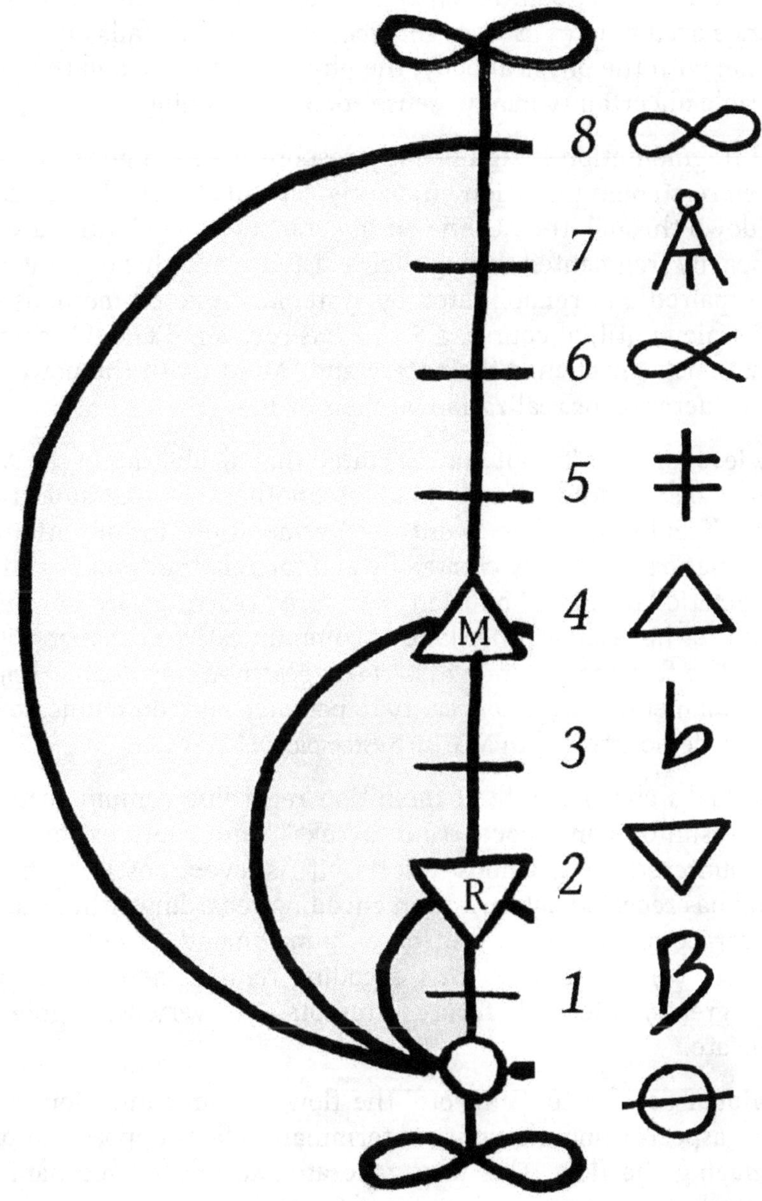

Many communication circuits exist on the "Zu-line" (Standard Model). Any of these may store erroneous or misguided personal "**charge**" as fragmentation. When not resolved, this state of fragmentation generally increases over time and even through many lifetimes. To begin: we can productively concern ourselves with inhibition to communicate and improper management of control experienced in *this* lifetime. As more emotional turbulence, painful experience and intellectual programmed **dissonance** accumulates as *fragmentation*, an individual falls out of communication with the physical body, the physical universe and then finds considerable uncertainty in any "sense" of *Self* remaining.

Personal fragmentation is significantly responsible for a general inhibition to express communication efficiently "at WILL"—which is to say at (5.0) on down through the ZU-line on the Standard Model. An individual is very heavily fragmented during their existence and this is a state that may be repaired and rehabilitated by systematic piloted methods on a gradient scale—until, of course, a *Seeker* has recovered enough personal certainty to *actually* change their state and "Mind" with the power of a single consideration or realization on their own.

At every level or definition it may be stated that all abilities of the Alpha Spirit may be reduced to one kind of another of communication— between *Self* and some other "point" or "termination" for our attention. Even if its nature is entirely created by and for *Self*, the "point" still acts as a systematic "terminal" one can therefore "reach toward" or "move away from" or have some other kind of communicative exchange with as a "form." The fact that an individual *takes perceived stimuli* and *then creates their own* mental images of reality to perceive and communicate with is generally demonstrated in *NexGen Systemology*.

An individual's chronic state of inhibition regarding communication is often the result of many reoccurring "breaks" "interruptions" or "barriers" encountered in previous efforts. It is even possible that an individual has received authoritarian encoding regarding either the "demands" for communication, and/or a "punishment" is enforced as a consequence when one does. This encoding remains as fragmentation and may greatly affect all future attempts—the very willingness—to communicate.

An individual decides to "shut off" the flow of communication with a particular aspect, thing, thought, or terminal-node as opposed to properly managing the flow. This may generate "automated mechanisms" that similarly treat more and more of these flows outside of Self-determinism. These are the first considerations that create defining "walls" that limit personal willingness and clear view of existence.

When we consider strong lingering *fragmenting* effects of communication and our relationship with the environment: it is often *what we did not say* or *the answers we did not receive* that cause us to still energetically "hang on" to these lines or anchor points with part of our attention thereafter.

This attention—and generation of any reality on its channel—will be fragmented. This type of fragmentation is reinforced by "internal communications" with an individual's own personal "interior" systems. Very often these flows of attention are directed toward mental walls and screens used as a substitute terminal-node in place of the actual objects, life-forms, &tc. When a stimulus presents, the individual projects images treated as reality "within the mind" and then proceeds to interact with them, playing out and reacting with all manners of fragmented considerations.

You may have witnessed—or even yourself experienced—how internal circuitry with such fragmentation can "work a person up" or "down" or get them "spun" on some particular aspect. Humans can cause themselves sickness and ranges of anxiety with no other outside influence but their own internal considerations of fragmented communication. The Standard Model suggests that Cosmic Spiritual Life Energy ("*Zu*") comes into and flows through the Alpha Spirit from Infinity as a continuous and essentially unlimited "inflow." This being the case, the only matters that have detrimental affects on the Spirit's experience of *Life, the Universe and Everything*, would be those places, points, circuits and flows where energy is restricted, fragmented or otherwise blocked.

If energy is flowing in at a constant, then any energetic barriers, imprints, considerations of limited belief, emotional response-reactive charges on "mental images"—or any other blockage—*will* build up pressure and concentrate free energy as more solid masses. All systems are composed of interchanges and interactions, flow-lines and actions—and they are **dynamic** in that each level is affected by and/or affects other levels...systematically. All personal systems and universal systems operate on energetic principles—no matter what terminology is used to define them. For this reason, all of the most paramount lessons of the magician, mystic, spiritualist or systemologist concern ENERGY.

Many factors lead to a *Seeker's* sense of communication fragmentation—some easier to process or more quickly recalled in analytical sessions than others. Most involve encounters with perceived barriers or improper external control (and authoritarian enforcement), but all of them affect willingness of an individual to generate or communicate a creation, even as simple as a single thought.

The human condition—and even considerations of the Alpha Spirit—essentially evolve out of a sequence of observations that lead to what an individual is or isn't willing to communicate freely with, and therefore be a part of as a responsible creator or *Self-determined* being. Each time an individual is blocked from extending their reach, they are less willing to "speak up" or "engage" thereafter. This does not generally happen all at once; unless there is a very serious heavily charged incident far back on the spiritual timeline.

Beta existence is among the lowest levels of cosmic communication—ideals and intentions readily as solid as billiard balls banging against one another and reconfirming the heavy solidity of a condensed universe. That is the truth of *this* universe; there is no illusion about that. The only *holograph* is the one projected in the mind—turning the energies and waves we place attention on into definable solids and forms with meaning and significance when we duplicate its imagery in our mind as "Reality." We are always interacting with reality and the universe in proportion to the clarity that we duplicate in the mind (A-for-A) the clear or true nature of the "inflow." Response-reaction mechanisms and associative identifications evolve based on how "images" in the mind are treated and communicated with in the past and not as the product of a present environment.

Being "out of communication" or "out of touch" is a result of too limited of consideration, responsibility and willingness to be *Self-directed*. It is constrictive and limiting insofar as it defines or dictates the free range of *Self*. The more places we are unwilling to go; the more people we are unwilling to talk to; these begin to define stringent limitations when an individual identifies *Self* with a physical form that may be so easily entrapped through automated mechanisms. That which we dislike or want to avoid; what we disagree with or attempt to reduce the reality of; the entire idea of what we are willing to keep close to us in proximity—these are all matters of consideration that are either given a free span of accessibility or else are limited to associative fragmentation, which at the lowest forms of human experience seem very much attached to "reactive emotional charges" on the images we conjure to mind every day.

A *Seeker* or *systemologist* that has completed *Grade-III* materials (that are the literal foundation for the present work) and is familiar with the Standard Model, should come to the realization that: communication is an exercise or expression of *Self* as Will and Intention—which may be directed fully from *Self* at cause from an *Alpha* point "exterior" to the physical universe (*beta*); however, its expression is managed by the "*Master Control Center*" (MCC or "Mind Systems")—and potentially the "*Reactive Control Center*" (RCC or "Emotional Response")—when the genetic vehicle or physical form is used as the catalyst to communicate this Will and Intention with the universe.

:: 3 ::
COMMUNICATION AND PILOTING
AS A COOPERATIVE GAME

As an intellectual pursuit and field of applied spiritual philosophy, *Nex-Gen Systemology* is notoriously connected to two basic preexisting studies that developed strongly during the past century: "systems theory" and **"games theory"**—of which are treated only with the highest-level mathematical jargon in all approaches outside of *NexGen Systemology*.

> "If we consider the Physical Universe we are experiencing as a 'game-board' on a table, then the table, the chairs, the manner of the room in which they sit...none of this is 'in play' or in any way existing within the parameters of the <u>game</u> itself. Other than, of course, at a higher level, someone choosing to manufacture the <u>game</u> and the Alpha-players choosing to play it, there is no existential correlation between 'Dimensions.' From *within* the <u>game</u> we cannot ascertain anything about some other all-encompassing environment directly, although we are certain that whatever the 'I' is, it must occupy this other space with its spiritual existence and then project its Awareness and Will into this <u>Game</u> as Life."
>
> —The Tablets of Destiny (Liber-One)

> "The higher states that we achieve result in higher complexities of the System we are in. It just works out that way. We tend to equate it best to '<u>game theory</u>' at this juncture because we are talking about systematic variables that, yes, are governed by Law, but we cannot apply this Law directly to the true force that is doing the determining of action—and that is the Self. The Self is making choices."
> —The Tablets of Destiny (Liber-One)

> "The paramount signature <u>Game</u> of the actualized Alpha Spirit is an ability to create and un-create at Will. At every turn in Systemology we find increasing realization of abilities and education regarding applications of <u>Games</u> and Systems to the management of our beta-existence and our environment—and every step of the way we are working **successively** toward the Actualization of the Alpha Spirit as 'I' of Self. All of these aspects, conditions—and even the very Processes themselves—point toward one key theme:
> CONTROL."
> —Crystal Clear (2B)

An individual is probably already familiar with the idea of "games"—especially in the sense of "competitive sports." At basic: a "game" is "any strategic situation where the power of choice is employed or affected." We then refer to individuals in the game as "players" if they are "an individual that is making decisions in a game and/or is affected by decisions others are making in the game, especially if those other-determined decisions now affect the possible choices."

In establishing the "game" and "players" we discover what some call "common knowledge," which is to say the facts that all "players" know, and they know that all other "players" also know. One might assume that the very structure of the "game" shared between players is a "common knowledge"—though this does not appear to be shared equally as true *Awareness* among all players of the Game of Life. This immediately creates another condition for players to consider, which is also treated by Game Theory: "Rationality."

"Rationality" is the extent to which a player seeks to play the game—make decisions, &tc.—in order to maximize gains (or else survival conditions) achievable within the parameters of any given game. In *NexGen Systemology*, we extend this definition to describe "the ability and willingness of an individual to reach toward conditions that promote the highest level of survival and existence and thereby make the best choices and moves to see the desired goal manifest."

When Game Theory is applied to Life, it demonstrates very clearly that "power of choice" is only as free as an individual is able to consider all choices. At high levels, the Game of Life, Universes and Everything is demonstrable with precision logic and affected directly by Alpha Thought; so then why aren't these same realizations accessible to the average person today? Well, they are. However, most individuals no longer carry a free range of consideration with them as a spiritual truth and instead have begun to think purely in terms of mechanistic qualities inherent in the low-energy condensed **continuity** of the physical universe.

Understanding the "power of choice" has been a constant staple of the social sciences and is even of significant interest to a *Seeker* as they work their way on the *Pathway to Self-Honesty* and beyond. Modern esoteric interest in these matters is even as antiquated as the academic pursuits—to which we find significant increase of attention being given to "systems theory" and "games theory" as society moved through the 1900's. Nearly all contributors to these fields during the 20th century were highly educated mathematicians.

Systemologists look for many ways to demonstrate objective truths. In fact, processes are developed so that a *Seeker* may experience principles of truth demonstrated with as much significance of "reality" as their former fragmentation has been instilled. After an individual has already accepted or "agreed" to a particular statement or barrier of reality, they put up another fact or statement or solid **postulate** against it; and confusion often ensues.

We refer to "Piloting" and "Processing" in *NexGen Systemology* as a form of "two-person cooperative game"—which is a concept formally developed by John Nash in 1950. "Piloting" would be a "game"; it involves "two persons" and is "cooperatively" engaged specifically for overall improvement (gain). A "Piloted Session," by definition, is a formal interactive situation that follows a model; and much like other games, it involves more than one player. Otherwise, a game with only one player is usually called a "decision problem"—and we can be assured that *Seekers* already have much practice playing at that one, with all of the fragmentary free-association and loop-patterns that tends to result from operating states outside Self-Honesty.

John Nash (a famous mathematician) explained that "a game is 'non-cooperative' if it is impossible for the players to communicate or collaborate in any way" and that players in a two-person cooperative game are "not 100% opposed; but not 100% coincident." They are not necessarily a "team" in the truest game-sense of the word; but they are both invested in or have their interests in the mutually beneficial results that ensue. Since we are not earning our "gains" through conflict, the "two-person game" of "processing" is, however, 100% cooperative.

As a cooperative game between two people, the most powerful strategies toward sharing a reality and presence, discussing and agreeing on a plan of action for sessions, and then actually conduct processing sessions to any notable gain...all utilizes "two-way communication."

The "Game of Processing" is carried out between two "players"—a "Pilot" and a "Seeker." It is the "Pilot" that is responsible for managing and handling the *flight*—which is to say, the "session." The "Professional Pilot" is trained and experienced to manage the environment and processing of a session as a means of assisting the *Seeker* in reaching a destination; which in most instances is a general increase in the *Seeker's* chronic state of *Being* and *Knowing.*

A "session" is all aspects/facets concerning a "session." The environmental setting; the focus or presence (set) of the *Seeker*; the methods or techniques used in practice by the Pilot—these are all considered a part of the "session" as a 'game-field'. This is to say: the agreed upon reality between players for a space and time in which to play a game. This is no dissimilar to the concept of a mystical microcosmic playing field, 'sacred space' or 'ritual area' as desired.

A Pilot may be said to employ both "two-way communications" and **"processing command lines"** (or PCLs)—yet even the "command lines" are transformed back into a "two-way" flow with proper use of **"acknowledgment"** and "communication processing." For a *Seeker* to communicate freely in session they must feel safe and uninhibited to do so, which a Pilot must assist. The purpose is not to have a *Seeker* merely talk endlessly over the course of a session—because such would render no gain at all—but the *Seeker* must be fully present in session and willing to participate in the game.

Systemology presents a Game of Self-Actualization. If a *Seeker* wishes to play a different game, or wishes to be in some way intentionally difficult or unwilling as some other misguided personal exercise, it is only their own loss. We will assume (in this manual) that a *Seeker* is a systemologist that at least understands something of what is expected of them—in terms of compliance and cooperation—in order to participate in an effective session that produces real spiritual gains. The entire purpose of the session is to increase the *Seeker's* certainty of ability and sense of knowing and being—in spite of any greater higher-view interests the Pilot may have for "serving the betterment of society" or the esteem of "certifying an A.T. Actualized Technician" &tc. Any success the Pilot has toward "greater" goals is dependent wholly on actual gains achieved by the *Seeker* they are in "communication and control" with.

Discipline of the Pilot is a primary concern at this juncture of "*Flight School.*"* Just as a *Seeker* must be encouraged and ensured that they are in a safe environment (and among safe company) to produce necessary communications (and arrive at any "self-realization" on one's own), a Pilot requires practice maintaining a non-reactive state in the presence of a *Seeker*. That is to say: the Pilot is able to meet (confront/face) any encounter or communication with the *Seeker* in session without exhibiting or displaying an emotional response-reaction. This is practiced with precision as part of "Pilot Training." It is also important for Pilots to practice methods of "two-way communication" demonstrated within this manual.

---

* *Grade-IV ISS* material is sponsored by "Systemology Air Command"—the official underground Guild Union of Professional Systemology Pilots and Mardukite Zuist Ministers.

This handbook is prepared as a result of carefully researched experiments and trials conducted in person—either by the present author directly, or via long-standing elite systemologists. In any case, instruction and research were inseparable to culminating any objective presentation as a book—especially one that might allow for understanding and use of this technology outside or independent of direct supervision and input from the present author.

There are many reasons a Pilot should seek to control their own reactive-response mechanisms, but when it comes to piloting a "*systematic session,*" then high-level Self-control must be demonstrated to a *Seeker* at all times. For example: while running a process during a session, the *Seeker* may begin to produce any number of personal realizations. These are "acknowledged" in live communication and recorded in a "Flight-log"* without necessarily having to "certify the truth" of the received communication, neither dismissing or adding data to validate anything further on the "comm line." In other words, this is not the time for a Pilot to start bringing up personal anecdotes about some time or instance when they thought about such and such or that such and such happened to them. That's what classrooms are for.

A Pilot must be uninhibited in their willingness and ability to *listen* in spite of the actualized level of a *Seeker*. Likewise, the *Seeker* will naturally gain greater confidence with the Pilot and with the application of practices as more time is spent in session together. This "familiarity" seems to have a positive impact with producing greater levels of communication and thereby increasing the potential gains for higher-level processing.

Most methods developed for *Grade-IV Systemology "Professional Piloting Procedure"* are based on years of "energy-work" and "esoteric experiments" regarding "communication with the physical universe." Until full certainty of Will and Intention is returned to the Alpha Spirit—whereby a *Seeker's* consideration of one thing or another can actually be changed with Alpha Thought and free of emotional reactivity—the caliber of work alluded to throughout this manual is particularly more challenging to manage directly as "self-processing" (speaking to those who are previously familiar with the "Crystal Clear" text).

In some cases, elementary self-processing was found to promote additional circuitry in some individuals that are likely to "hold on tightly" to their heavily charged "mental images" and set up terminals for addition-

---

* Also available—*"Systemology Truth Seeker's Adventure Journal."*

al "internal communication" or "self-talk" long after the session has ended; long after any function or purpose of a mental image had expired. When a *Seeker* does not (or cannot sanely) differentiate between the level of reality (or state of agreements) of the internal subjective from the external objective communications with the physical universe, all manners of fragmentation likely will ensue. Systemology processing simply assists an individual put "phases" and "identities" of various universes in line with one another.

Whether a Pilot or *Seeker*, the effective purpose behind the *Grade-IV* course on "control and communication" is to establish a state of uninhibited willingness to communicate on clear channels. This is one primary aspect to rehabilitating or regaining the higher faculties of the "Mind and Spirit." This often involves analyzing deeply laden postulates or barriers that restrict what and with whom we communicate for fear of invalidation, error, loss or pain.

:: 4 ::
FUNDAMENTALS OF COMMUNICATION
FOR NEXGEN SYSTEMOLOGY

Clear understanding of the subject of communication is a benefit to all individuals—yet it is of particular interest to systemologists, *Seekers* and Pilots. In *"The Tablets of Destiny"* textbook, "Levels of Understanding" are defined based on the general "grade" that a knowledge base is collected and how data is organized and evaluated. There are many levels of consideration or significance; and each relatively defines similarities and differences.

"Understanding" is: a clear 'A-for-A' duplication of a communication as 'knowledge', which may be comprehended and retained with its significance assigned in relation to other 'knowledge'. This means that personal experience of an event, static piece of writing or the information relayed in speech (*&tc.*) is rarely given the same 'significances' by all Observers— nor is the presentation of true knowledge of *Life, the Universe and Everything* treated with the same degree of understanding by all individuals maintaining a relationship with the human condition.

It is for this reason that true understanding—which is to say *actual realization*—cannot be enforced, instructed or even demonstrated with simple language to those who are not yet in a position (or willing to put themselves in a position) to be a receipt-point for a true A-for-A understanding. This very fundamental prompted such esoteric axioms as: "the lips of wisdom are sealed except to ears of understanding" or "when the student is ready, the teacher appears."

We then may describe the exact relay and duplication of a communication or knowledge as:

A-for-A
A = A ; B = B ...
A → A

In technical terms, we could even treat communication as a teleportation between points. But—what about fragmented knowledge manifestations? Imprints? Etc.?

B=A; C=A; D=A ... (differences are generalized as similar; all *facets* equal "A")

A=B; A=C; A=D ... (similarity is erroneously distinguished as something different)

Elsewhere this is defined as **"dissonance."**

In *NexGen Systemology*, the nature of communication and nature of energy flows are essentially synonymous studies. We are treating a systematic relay of energy as a communication; whether we are engaging our attention across a room for a piloted session or across the veils of cosmic existence: the fixing in place of a thought, will or intention as cause or as a source-point and transmitting it clearly across energetic channels *is* the very action of all *Life, the Universe and Everything* in communication with all *Life, the Universe and Everything.*

Even when we are not engaged in formal "two-way communication" (by which we may directly receive positive feedback and acknowledgment about reception and comprehension of a message), the purpose of any origination, creation, message or communication *is* for it *to be* received. "One-way" flows are simply communications for which no answer has been sent back as an acknowledgment or response, which can also manifest as a *compulsion* to communicate.

A Pilot may be surprised to discover just how many individuals have energy held up in their life still waiting for a "response" on some line. And far too often, an individual following standard issue human programming fails to differentiate the inert continuity of the physical universe from the "living beings" also identified with some kind of energy-matter system or "physical body."

Beta-Existence is not a "living form"—and it tends to only communicate on the lowest-levels and these are among the most solid that we know of. When we *push*; it *pushes* back. We have already, at this level, come to think of it as a some thing to push against and therefore validate its solidity. It is composed therefore entirely of solids far more condensed and compacted then any of the upper levels from which this debris has clearly settled from.

Communications of thought, intention—any energy, &tc.—are all transmitted or projected from a source-point and they create a certain space-time around them that carries potentially observed qualities. There must be some "thing" to be sent and received. It must occupy a unique space and by passage through any medium, may be defined in terms of time. This means that at upper levels: space-time energy-matter may all be *created* with Alpha Thought.

The channel of communication may be direct, but it also has many relay points, even within the most basic form of expression. The Cause-Point

(Sender) intends "A"; the Comm Line travels across space (Messenger Action) as "A"; received by a Receipt-Point (Node or Terminal) as "A"; and finally results, or is comprehended, at the Effect-Point as "A."

"Fragmentation" and "distortion" are words describing "absence of clarity" in a message or communication. Whatever has been fed in on the "line" is not being processed in the same way across all distances. Of course, a greater likelihood for a distorted communication exists the greater the distances, the greater the number of relay points (or points of "duplication"), the greater the perceived barriers to divert, and thus the greater the communication lag or "time" between relay points.

Fragmentation is generally a consequence of "associations" and "significances" assigned as a meaning to any facet, concept—whatever "A" actually *is*. And therein lies the issue for many individuals in differentiating "A" not as an "A"—or what has been instructed or emotionally encoded to mean "A"—but as an actual *is*. If something *is*, then we consider it *real*, but only then. Therefore, we can only communicate "reality" or "what *is* real" to the extent that it is able to be exchanged— both sent and received—across a distance between two points as an *is*. The degree of understanding as shared communicable reality with any "terminal **node**" (anything that may be distinguished as an *is*, and therefore as a 'termination point' of a system) is said to be the degree to which one is "in" or "out" *of communication* with said 'point'.

Proper relay of clear communication is very important for the optimum continuation of all life, but is also particularly important on a formal technical level in *Professional Piloting Procedure* and even upper-level work. As it is the key to remedy and realize all other stations along the *Pathway to Self-Honesty*, the repair of "personal communication" is where most assistance begins, because without it there can be no higher-level work; this is to say that the higher-level work in no way substitutes what is intended to be earned at subsequent *Grades*.

There is an illusion by many not properly initiated into the folds of the Ancient Mystery School, that somehow, the "higher Grades" are "higher" in their superiority or power to the "lesser" ones—and yet as one works through a properly graded scale, one does not actually notice much greater of an incline or increase in the next tier than the former. There is an illusion that if one could simply gaze upon the words of some higher order of knowledge, with the symbols arranged in just such and such an order, than an explosion of effect will instantaneously occur and the *Seeker* will immediately sprout wings and catapult them entirely out of any consideration of the material cosmos and back into a state of Alpha cause.

However, the likelihood or "quantum probability" that such phenomenon is to occur is low. It is not impossible. In fact, if anything, it is a semblance or memory of a former time of spiritual actualization when the Self was very much in control of its own directed energies and in the clearest and strongest modes of Self-determinism, even while monitoring a "body."

This type of phenomenon is, of course, not what we are claiming to reproduce with a pursuit of the *Pathway to Self-Honesty* via methods given as *"NexGen Systemology"*—since ours is a methodology systematically **graded** to provide no sharp peaks or drop offs for those that wish to follow the map. Of course, the more we wish to push away, the more space is created and thus we have the illusion of a perpetually 'expanding' physical universe solely due to the solidity of the considerations taking place at these lower-level concentrations.

It is the consideration of "distance" that we will treat next, because for some this is only thought of in terms of literal spatial distance—and this is fine, so long as one adds to their consideration of "distance" the association of the willingness to have something "close" or "far" in proximity. This means that on a communication level, the distance is equivalent to our literal proximity but also our willingness to allow some 'thing' to come "close" to us.

We use these terms very specifically because obviously a person could be standing right in front of you but still be refusing to listen or be a receipt-point because they don't *like* you—or they have some other associative fragmentation connected with the kind of "terminal" you represent—they could be said to be "at a distance" or "out of communication." And when this behavior is enacted intentionally, or is noticed between individuals, or is stated in conversations related to the same, humans generally are aware that in spite of physical locales attributed to space, an individual is in fact "distancing" themselves—at least energetically.

It is also noticed that this "distance" can be reduced with "interest" and "agreement"—and then suddenly individuals are in energetic proximity to be in communication. The state of agreement and interest leads to a shared reality from which additional attention may be applied on the communication line. It is only after this "distance" is bridged that any productive "two-way communication" can ensue.

An individual will keep that which they *like* (or feels *familiarity* or fond *emotional ties*) in closer communication than what they do not *like* or *agree* with. Hence they have no real understanding of whatever is "not liked" and therefore continue to exercise no real *Self-directed* control toward it on those energetic comm-lines. These may become metaphoric "walls" and "imprints" that add to the "distancing" factor of clear communications.

One of the issues for the Alpha Spirit that is a creative force outside beta-existence is that it is identifying with control centers (for a form) that are very much anchored in the physical universe. Of course, this is not the only potential existence for a Spirit—but it does come to believe so as it starts to associate more and more with the solidity of the physical body and both the considerations and restrictions associated with the physical universe.

A *Seeker* must actualize a realization—through processing—that objects and walls found in the physical universe are a solidification, result or effect from concentrations of thought-energy or attention applied to give these things there solid forms. They aren't living terminals and they do not communicate. They have only the significance of being a solid; an inert part of physical continuity that are an *is* only because someone has assigned an existence to it.

At this (0.0) level of solidity of largely gathered particle masses, billiard balls and concrete walls, it requires something of equal solidity to even communicate with it—and for this the human condition is given a standard-issue array of sensory inputs in which to receive data from the environment as assigned to a "physical body."

Our level of communication projected as a willingness to reach from a room might be limited to feeling the solidity of the surrounding barrier-walls by touch—and so we know that they are there for the body, and we are even in control of the body as we direct its motions to do this. But we are also aware that there is a higher truer and more eternal part of us— the actual "I" that was never *in* the body in the first place, and need not be restricted to walls.

Communication in the physical universe can involve any perceptual channel that the genetic vehicle (organic organism) has the faculties for. There is already a wide range of energies and motions taking place around us—but we must have an appropriate type of "terminal" or "receiver" that operates along a level to communicate with it; even if it is only to receive the impressions of a communication at the effect-point.

The basic energies are already in existence, but when we "tap those wires" and put any attention in the directions of their flows, we are "aware" that something is taking place. We selectively use the word "awareness" in instances of actualized knowingness and beingness because it denotes that there is a range or field of "unawareness" just by the consideration. Therefore, what we are "unaware" of is no less true or extant or an *is* on an objective level than it otherwise would be—the difference is what is brought within the realm of control or the proximity of reach in order to share responsibility in it. Control without responsibility is simply *enforcement*; and it is generally to this lesser level of awareness that most systems are brought in the absence of responsible control.

When an individual opens up channels of communication—any type of communication—they are essentially directing attention along a "flow-line." This "flow-line" could be systematically demonstrated in various states with various wave-form graphics, but what is most important or critical to us for practical purposes is simply whether the line is heavily charged with fragmentation *or* not.

In systemology, we treat all projections (or radiations) from a point, or point-of-view, as a communication; whether regarding energy or its condensation as matter—a particle or bit that must ebb and flow and therefore creates a wave-flow motion to exist. The distance between the source-point and any other receipt-point defines "space"; and the interval of transmission, "time."

An Alpha Spirit may originate a communication for expression along the Zu-line into existence, but there is already a significant amount of past communications, erroneously imprinted associations and incomplete cycles of action still running on personal circuits. This type of fragmentation actually inhibits clear communication because there is existing interference on the line. Even when it is coherent enough to be relayed among them, most human communication is **aberrative**.

At the upper (*Alpha*) levels of the Standard Model:

The Alpha Spirit (7.0) is a communication or wave-crest ridge on a Sea of Infinity (8);

Alpha Thought (6.0) is a communication or wave-form projected from the Alpha Spirit (7.0) into the ALL of "Spiritual Existence" where the Self may postulate, theorize, create and form any images for consideration;

Will-Intention (5.0) is a communication between the *Alpha* states and control systems for beta or material existence—or else, where the Spirit commands the Master Control Center (or MCC) for managing experience of beta-existence.

Goals for basic systemology include increasing defragmented channels for considerations—meaning free and uninhibited consideration and a willingness to communicate any willed intention based on true judgment and not based on the fragmentary images and emotional associations that may be heavily attached to these channels.

Full capability along any/all channels to any terminal would be simply the:

Willingness to send/transmit any communication;

Willingness to receive/accept any communication; and

Understand/Duplicate the communication free of turbulence/emotional charge.

In systematic processing of the "Willingness to Communicate" a Pilot is assisting the *Seeker* in overcoming inhibitions, reducing fragmentation, dispersing emotional charges and other erroneously imprinted beliefs and associations regarding the "Willingness to Communicate." Systematic processing may be applied to any facet of the human experience and beyond even that—but it seems relevant and appropriate to provide this one as a practical example here.

All basic processing presented in systemology is toward the increase of ability by increasing an individual's willingness *to be able*—and in essence, *be* responsible *for*. We treat the subject of responsibility as a separate class of processing, but that is not to say that a *Seeker* will not come to the appropriate realization that all "power" comes from the responsibility to be Self-directed as a creative force in existence. A *Seeker* may even come to the greater realization that all of their fragmentation is self-fed and unnecessarily reproduced in the mind.

:: 5 ::
THE SYSTEMOLOGY OF TWO-WAY COMMUNICATION

Communication puts a potential pathway into existence between two points—of which we may refer to as "view-points" (POV). Every point in space is a potential POV—which is an upper-level *realization* that results from processing. Our knowledge is a "systemology" because we may use it to apply a philosophy that is effective for all relative systems, not just specific instances. For example: the same "source-point to receipt-point" (or sender-receiver) circuit between a Pilot and *Seeker* in a session describes a cycle-of-action called the "communication circuit" which also demonstrates truths of communication between Alpha and Beta control points (or **anchor** points) of an Identity-Continuum.

Direction and flow of two-way communication in the piloted session is a responsibility of the Pilot. The Pilot must be in control of this flow in order to ensure proper processing. But, it should be understood that as an applied spiritual philosophy, Systemology is not some newfangled psychoanalysis mental health science concerned with talk therapies and associative free thought. Undirected communication cycles are a waste of time for both the Pilot and *Seeker.*

Systematic processing is a "selective direction of attention" and when engaged properly, the methodology does produce *actualized realizations* for a *Seeker.* But, the Pilot and *Seeker* must be both *fully present* and participating in the session to yield any benefits. This requires a very specific and controlled handling of communications. Communication and control are the keys to all effective systematic processing sessions.

Piloted Two-Way Communication is not a "conversation" in the traditional sense; certainly not as such that the *Seeker* might receive from their average friend or family member—or anywhere in the typical social environment of the standard-issue human condition.

Systematic Processing is not designed to directly treat conditions of a "body" or "genetic vehicle" with the exception of increasing personal "control *of*" a body *as* a vehicle. This conception is envisioned by some as "control of" a marionette doll—but under no circumstances should a Pilot validate entrapment of a Seeker *being* stuck "in" a "physical body."

The proper use of systematic processing and command lines should always direct a *Seeker's* attention to the control and monitoring of the body, rather than any identification of *Self* being forced "into" a body. Whenever a body is treated, the statements are always in relation to controlling the centers of "a" body or "that" body, but never enforcing a *Seeker's* considerations that *they are their physical body*. The sooner a *Seeker* can begin to treat the control and imagery of the body as though it is out "in front" of them, the better.

In the "systemology of universal physics" explored in *Grade-III*,[*] a *Seeker* discovers that the cosmos and entire Identity-continuum related to I-AM-*Self* is entirely composed of energetic interactions and communications taking place between the two cosmic principles: substance and motion. And of course when we add personal *Awareness* to the equation, we arrive at the various 'circuit-flows' able to be experienced as an *is*. As a 'motion', Zu is the energetic activity in the cosmos, exchange of information and interactive communications that vibrate within and also radiate flows from out all forms, which carry them through space as points measured in time.

> "Zu is not literally and exclusively the 'Mind'—which is a 'system' of manifestations that processes and otherwise <u>communicates</u> the Zu apparent as 'personal awareness'... A *Seeker's* own understanding—and the ability to share such 'Reality' with others—will always rely on the <u>communication</u> of information and energy, both among one's own personal systems and in any interactions with other systems."
>
> —The Power of Zu (Liber-S1Z)

Whenever a Pilot determines a *Seeker* has a source of turbulence on a particular channel or with a particular terminal, the most basic solution is to regain control of the communication with that aspect or terminal. Imprinting creates barriers to a full range of consideration and willingness, creating conditions that enforce specific programming or reactive-responses in place of true Self-determined thought activity. A Pilot must eventually be able to distinguish between true Alpha Thought and mechanistic automation ('automatic circuits') often substituting such.

Beta-existence is very much 'physical' and very much 'mechanistic'—having reached such a state of solidarity in particles and flows that at its most continuous level it can be seen to be arranged or 'cosmically ordered' as a series of 'clockwork' systems. The slippery slope or downward spiral begins with accepting consideration that all systems must be rigidly material and 'clockwork', thereby keeping the 'free range of thought' of the individual fixed into certain-or-specific modes along certain-and-specific channels with certain-and-specific terminals, &tc.

---

[*] Specifically found in the materials for *The Tablets of Destiny* (*Liber-One*) and *The Power of Zu* (*Liber-S1Z*)

Two-way communication—as it relates to a piloted session—assists in determining if a *Seeker* is "in **phase**" and "present" (which addresses the "presence" factor of the session). Part of this step in the process includes establishing what, if any, current "problems and concerns" might be keeping attention on matters outside the session.

The purpose here is not to literally solve an individual's perceived problems one by one, but simply to make certain that they are acknowledged and then treated as not being present in the session. Whatever the specific nature of these, it is doubtful that any one of them is the actual source of fragmentation to be treated with systematic processing. It is much more likely that the chronic state of uncertainty an individual maintains is simply a contributor to their "handling" or "management" of problem-solving capabilities.

Using basic relays of communication at the beginning of the session will assist in directing the *Seeker's* attention to the session itself. For example: asking a *Seeker* if there is anything you should know about, or if there is anything going on in their life right now that might put focus out of session. An interest in the *Seeker* and their management of living conditions outside of the sessions also assists in establishing greater trust in the Pilot by the *Seeker*. It should also be evident, though not necessarily stated directly, that assistance is available and the Pilot is there to help them.

Communication is Will-Intention *in action*. It is the intent to cause an effect; even if that effect is simply duplication of some message or energy. We have established that the effective quality of the communication is proportional or equivalent to the duplication (perception, understanding and interpretation) "A-for-A." The "sender" of a communication acts as the primary 'cause' for that cycle, and the "receiver" must be willing to accept the communication flow as an 'effect' in order for there to be duplication or reproduction of the intention as effect.

Previously, "communication lag" is described as distortions in circuitry that fragment a "communication line." This fragmentation is noticeable during systematic processing or when an individual is communicating their considerations. Rather than acting from an *Alpha* point of Will (&tc.), the individual's *Actualized Awareness* is heavily charged and engulfed in a lot of "sticky-like" beliefs, postulates, personal creations and agreements with others that filter a communication with the environment where Awareness is fixed. As we know, the greater the distance, even on something as abstract as the "Zu-line" on the Standard Model, the greater the probability of fragmentation and distortion; and the longer its communication lag.

The immediacy and "presence" found in being centered in the "Now" (or the "kNow" as we used to write it a decade ago in the original systemology thesis papers) is of such importance, that without this prerequisite state, no actual "session" has begun. Once a session has begun, a Pilot must make certain that each cycle of communication in the session is completed before originating another.

The basic wave-arc or cycle-of-action for two-way communication is:

a) origination at source-point
→ b) reception at receipt-point and response
→ c) response is acknowledged by the original source-point
→ d) receipt-point knows that the cycle has been completed

All systematic processing requires completing the cycle of action for each command line.

The command line is an "input" into a system. The communication line is a "flow of information" and a "circuit" is formed when there are "two-way comm-lines" established between two "terminals." All masses and "resistances" create fragmentation, ridges and jagged flows. This all sounds rather technical; though in practice, the demonstrations show that the technicality of our vocabulary is simply best for the widest range of systematic application.

We discovered that one of the reasons "Self-Processing"[∞] has limitations, is that even just the continuous use of autosuggestion or auto-commands concerning recall or other directions has a tendency to set up new "circuits" in the mind to relay this type of third-person communication to *Self.*[*]

The creation of any point or consideration or thought or energy stream requires an equal creation of appropriated space for it to exist—which is to say a "field" by which the encoding and decoding of a message can take place between two terminals. This "field" or "zone" is also known as the area of potential interference, because it exists in a space between the sender and receiver. The space will carry the message clearly in the absence of interference.

Another source of interference is the "personal circuit"—which is to say the processing (of Zu) taking place interior to the Personal Identity Con-

---

[∞] A self-processing regimen is presented in the Grade-III textbook *Crystal Clear (Liber-2B)* by Joshua Free.

[*] Solo-Piloting (or Solo-Flying) is only instructed and practiced at higher *Grades,* operating quite differently than the types of systematic processing demonstrated in *Grade-IV Professional Piloting Procedure.*

tinuum of an individual. Yes, the individual is a terminal, but they are more than just a solid wall (we would hope anyways; it's possible that they *are* that apathetic) and therefore have an entire systematic process taking place within the domain of their own personal beta (internal) or alpha (exterior spiritual) experience.

A "personal circuit" can also become fragmented when an individual sets up additional internalized communication circuits with terminals that have been imagined into beingness and used as a substitute to discharge communication flows against. If an individual does not feel or perceive any response from a communication line, a sort of self-made mechanism of automatic response will be generated to maintain a continuous energy action on that terminal—even outside the conscious awareness and Will of the individual that first set it up!

The more an energy flow is generated toward mental images on an automatic loop and seemingly without *Self-direction*, the more that these imprinted "facsimiles" or "copies" of reality will seem more and more solid; treated more and more like the "real thing" when the control of these automatic response mechanisms is no longer treated as the responsibility of the *Self*.

A response by the *Seeker* to the 'processing command line' is not the end of a communication cycle. Doing so would keep the attention flow on the *Seeker* as an effect only—which is simply one step toward poorly handled interrogation. The *Seeker* remains an effect-point until they (their answer/response) is acknowledged. Acknowledgment is acknowledgment; the *Seeker's* response only needs to be acknowledged as extant in order to complete the current cycle. For example: the delivery of the same command line a second (or third...&tc.) time is not a repeat of the same communication; each is its own cycle—its own space and time. Proper management of communication of energy is what control of true power *is*!

A fragmented Alpha Spirit left to its own devices has already traversed uppermost **echelons** of spiritual existences and various universes as reality—but the true underlying nature of existence can become quite empty and forbidding when the Spirit projects its Awareness to points in this newly perceived space and then finds nothing in the environment answering communications. This is the nature of Alpha fragmentation: a Spirit waits longer and longer for a response and becomes more and more fixated on the spaces and "things" as a result. Differentiating energies (material solids from living forms) is resolved during "communication processing."

The Pilot and *Seeker* are both treated (rightfully) as "live terminals" during the "session." They are not the only "terminals" extant; but for purposes of *Professional Piloting Procedure*, they are the only "live terminals" with a "presence" in the "session."

Objective processing also produces great results on the *Pathway to Self-Honesty* prior to pushing a *Seeker* through a series of intensive mental exercises. It is suggested to alternate subjective and objective processing during a session. Pilots use objective processing to assist getting the *Seeker's* focus and command of the body under their own Self-control. This provides an ability to grant "presence"

as *Self* within the session. Entangled energy may even be discharged on solid forms (physical terminals) in the physical universe, which do not otherwise act as living terminals—such as inert matter, objects and walls. Hence, the incorporation of 'objective processing' which can assist in both grounding or centering the *Seeker* in good communication with the physical universe and also helping to consciously knowingly maintain their own perspective or "viewpoint" (POV) on reality "in phase" with the "*present.*"

Pilots assist a *Seeker* in establishing communication lines (or flows) with the appropriate terminals so that a seeker may discharge their own fragmented stores of energy on another terminal (other than the Pilot) and 'ground out' the energetic charge. The Pilot is of course educated to understand and maintain full knowledge of the types of phenomenon or manifestations that may potentially present themselves while processing a *Seeker*, including intensive emotional discharges and/or other "loop patterns" expressed.

Piloted sessions are effective when a *Seeker* is successfully directed to access their own programming and emotional encoding, imprinting and fragmentation, when facets that would otherwise be unknowingly restimulative are not actively present in the environment. This gives a *Seeker* the chance *to see* a facet, bit of data or mental image for what it *is* in Self-Honesty—and **"process out"** stores of reactive-response charges along the way.

Basic establishment of a "session" and the communication cycle-of-action that follows as "processing" is easily summarized in four fundamental steps:

A.) The Pilot (*sender*) sees that the Seeker (*receiver*) is in session, prepared to be a receipt-point for communication;

B.) The Pilot (*sender*) selects a communication channel or line and directs a query or transmission to the Seeker (*receiver*);

C.) The Pilot (*sender*) sees that the transmission is received by the Seeker (*receiver*); and

—a secondary cycle-of-action ensues while the Seeker performs a personal communication on their own circuits after processing it; and

—the resulting response to the query or processing line is communicated from the Seeker (now a *sender*) back to the Pilot (now a *receiver*).

D.) The Pilot then acknowledges receipt and comprehension of the communications to complete the cycle.

Any breakdown in this flow (cycle-of-action just described) must be addressed immediately during the session in order to maintain an effective session and before attempting to resolve or complete additional cycles (commands, processing, &tc). Remember that it is the Pilot's responsibility to ensure this flow takes place as described; so, we will examine each of the parts a little closer before moving on.

A.) The Pilot (*sender*) sees that the Seeker (*receiver*) is in session, prepared to be a receipt-point for communication;

Before any actual systematic processing begins, the "presence" of both the Pilot and the Seeker must be established; and subsequently prior to the transmission of each cycle of communication. Of course, once a session is running well, it may take but a moment to be sure that the Seeker is ready for the next command line. Although technically some kind of "processing" begins as soon as the Seeker has walked in through the door to the session environment, an actual "session" has not really begun until "presence" has been established.

There are many ways in which "presence" may not be able to be present, therefore preventing a proper session from actually starting. These may include any personal issues that the Seeker is experiencing regarding the location of the session, the individual acting as the Pilot or any other pressing concerns affecting the mind from outside the environment.

Once these preliminaries have been addressed, the next major concern of the Pilot is making sure that the Seeker is able to "duplicate communications"—that a willing Alpha Spirit is able to maintain enough control over functions of the physical body in order to actual be receipt-point, receive transmissions properly, comprehend them and process them internally—all of which is implied when we define these qualities at once as a "duplication."

These are many gradient levels of response to systematic processing; including the entire band of potential "experience"—from the lowest range of near-body-death up to the moment when a being now actualized with the full state of *Awareness* as the I-AM-Self would be able to generate an entirely new universe for itself whilst standing at its own Alpha state of existence as a wave ridge or peak amidst a sea of Infinity. Unnecessary stresses on the Seeker (and a Pilot straining to be successful) are avoided by not making the Seeker confront a larger gradient or higher tier of actualization than they have achieved a realization for. An individual is only capable of being *Aware* and willing and determined to the extent that they have established for themselves. This must be increased at a pace that is effectively appropriate.

   B.) The Pilot (*sender*) selects a communication channel or line and directs a query or transmission to the Seeker (*receiver*);

The Pilot is trained to direct the Seeker's attentions with communication; therefore if these skills have not been reached, there is more likelihood for a breakdown in the cycle. Processing is dependent on the ability of the Pilot to maintain and hold the Seeker's attention for the duration of the session. "Interest" levels lie within the band of "thought" and not "emotion"—meaning that interest is not manged by the RCC (reactive-response) system, but requires that this system not be engaged or restimulated so that a Seeker may be *Self-directed* in their focus of attention. If the Pilot pushes the Seeker into too steep of a gradient in processing, the Seeker will find themselves confused and "stalling out" in interest (which may trigger reactive-responses). Maintaining control of the communication and command lines is the Pilot's responsibility.

   C.) The Seeker receives the communication, duplicates the data and processes it. Communication of the result is returned to (sent back to) the Pilot. The return communication is a performance of the process (such as an answer), or an indication (announcement) that a creative command line has been run.

Pilots encourage continuous flow of communication during the session, including to notice when a Seeker is getting hung up. Keep in mind that we are dealing with an active flow between living terminals of a system, so a Seeker should be encouraged with gentle prompts to continue any flow they are processing; but also making sure that the Seeker is not lost in their own circuitry. We can assume that Seekers have already spent too much of their lifetime (or several lifetimes) internalizing with various circuits or running around the physical universe trying to communicate with dead terminals. Systematic processing is meant to remedy this condition.

    D.) The Pilot then acknowledges receipt and comprehension of the communications to complete the cycle.

In order to complete (close) one cycle of the communication circuit, the Pilot is required to acknowledge the communication flow of the Seeker. Failure to do so is one of the most invalidating aspects of the communication process; and this truth is not exclusively limited to applications of *Professional Piloting Procedure*, but in all aspects of Life and the Universe.

An acknowledgment within the session assists the *Seeker* in their certainty to realize greater flows of attention (*Awareness*) are placed onto the circuits processed in the session than would otherwise be the case if the *Seeker* were left alone to their own resolve—either to Self-Process or to be allowed to bump against all of the perceived blockages encountered in their environment as a radiated explosion of unfocused uncontrolled volatile chaotic energy.

Remember not to introduce a new communication/command cycle until the existing circuit has been either completed or repaired. It is better if no need to repair is present; hence we establish the most ideal practices for a Systemology Pilot (Air Command Pilots and Ministers of Mardukite Zuism, &tc.) that may be applied to any and all systematic processing session regardless of their level.

The Pilot therefore accepts any and all answers with an acknowledgment before proceeding to another, even if the earlier command line is to be used again. Even if the message is being repeated, it is for a new "prompt of an answer" and a new communication cycle.

Often the methods of systematic processing require the use of the same "command line" numerous times in order to breakthrough to the level of answers that will provide true realizations. This is not really the same command repeated many times, but each is its own command, with its own space-time.

A Pilot should never ask a Seeker to repeat their answer as if it were wrong—or to press the Seeker in any way as to whether or not *that* is actually their answer or if they actually performed the creative (subjective or mental image) command, &tc.

The answer *is* the answer; it is at least the Seeker's answer for that moment or instance of space-time. It is the answer for that moment of consideration toward the definition or implication of what a command means. But, as systematic processing undoubtedly demonstrates, the significances and meanings ascribed to things are purely circumstantial and entirely self-created. An individual has an ability to change these considerations at will—and as a result, has the ability to change how they are going to interact with any flow-line with any terminal in existence.

:: 6 ::
UNIVERSAL COMMUNICATION AS
A SYSTEMATIC CONTROL ACTION

Communication is a primary requirement for existence. There is a communication of *Spiritual Life Energy* ("ZU") present directly at each of the principles of manifestation: substance, motion and *Awareness*. Circulatory communication of Zu is present within and as each/all level/aspect of existence and manifestation. Everything alive is a communication. This activity within a Mind-System is the communication with the ZU/Awareness of a specific 'Personal Identity Continuum' that extends between an Alpha Spirit and a beta form.

Mardukite Systemology is derived from only one single assumption or primary postulate for which we have an understanding of Life, the Universe and Everything simply by further logical deduction and practical experiential experimentation directly in said universe by said Life to determine anything and about everything. (This is otherwise called "*epistemology.*")

The original premise is this: that the true *Self* or actual identity of the individual is an Alpha Spirit. This spirit is capable of the highest creativeness and is itself set in a high state of beingness, which later became the effect of its own creations: considerations, beliefs, imprinted associative knowledge, fragmented experience and over-identification with fixed states of beingness other than the *Self* as Alpha Spirit—which means, usually, an over-identification with the genetic vehicle (physical body) as the *Self*, and a belief that there is some way able to permanently hinder or harm the *Self* beyond or exterior to this beta existence. It is a primary purpose of systematic processing to return a Seeker the certainty of this state.

For all of its technical speech, *NexGen Systemology* is not a superficial presentation of *Life, the Universe and Everything*, such as we actually tend to find more within the lesser-level domains of physical knowledge and even conventional metaphysics. Our entire field is based on only one grand assumption—one main tenet that cannot necessarily be directly proven within the confines of *beta-existence*, and that is:

> YOU, the actual *I-AM-Self*, is an Alpha Spirit.

This is all that an individual is required to "take on faith" until it may be known—and since we are dealing with the "spiritual" in these matters, there are many who simply find the validity of *Mardukite Systemology* as an extension of one of the oldest religious and mystical orders to develop from the Ancient Mystery School, called *Mardukite Zuism* for our purposes. There are many schools of thought that are based on opposite assumptions, and these tend to be more in line with what an individual is typically indoctrinated to believe. There are many esotericists, elitists, philosophers and other intellectual authorities, which believe (or enforce the belief) that "common man, the animal" (the standard-issue human condition) is not capable of actualizing any greater state of beingness—or that only a select demographic of the population is somehow capable. We have not actually found any workable truth to these statements.

A more effective truth, which may be demonstrated with systematic processing, is that while not entering the "Great Work" on the same level, *all humans* have the innate ability to reclaim and reawaken the knowing embedded deep within as the power of the Spirit. Just as an individual's *Awareness* (sense of Self) can be fixed to lower-points of beingness by selective direction of attention, so can it be "unfixed." In doing so, and being free to consider its more natural Alpha States, it finds that far more than an "identifying" with a particular body or set of life-memory and emotional mechanisms, the Alpha state is a beingness equivalent to the other alpha states it gives consideration to—which means the actual true I-AM-Self *is* Spirit, *is* Alpha Thought, and *is* Will. This is just as comparable to the beta-experience of a "Mind-Body" that carries thoughts and emotions and applies effort, though these are treated at a lower-order of existence, being confined entirely to the "beta"/physical universe.

Levels of *Awareness* correspond to communications exchanged by an individual—which is of course more significantly noticeable in family units and social organizations. Fragmentation becomes most obvious within generalization. We also see the chronic beta-state of *Awareness* manifest in the very types of communication that an individual is *willing* to pass along; or how they filter or alter a message to meet their level of understanding and emotional condition.

You can look at any point on the *Beta-Awareness Scales* (and the simplified *Emotimeter* scale) and identify individuals in your life (or perhaps in your past) that only seem to communicate after engaging one of those lower-level reactive-response mechanisms for the processing: an individual, for example, that only communicates bad news; or another that only communicates antagonistic gossip; or another that insistently invalidates others with only counter-points, and so forth.

As memory gathers mass, other people attach certain "personality" stereotypes to individuals carrying chronic states. These observations become basis for additional judgments and considerations that further enter the equation. This is simply another example of why all interpersonal communication outside of a state of Self-Honesty is highly *aberrative* and leads to personal fragmentation.

In our modern "electronic-age"-meets-"space-age" society, we are most likely to best understand the concepts of "terminals" in relation to how we tend to socially use the "term" today: as a mass that is able to communicate data, process commands—essentially any of the input–output functions that we should expect—such as in the case of a "computer terminal" which may also "interface" or communicate with *other* "terminals." When we chart out "network systematics," these terminals are also treated as "nodes."

> terminal (node) : a point, end or mass on a line; a point or connection for closing an electric circuit, such as a post on a battery terminating at each end of its own systematic function; any end point or 'termination' on a line; a point of connectivity with other points; in systems, any point which may be treated as a contact point of interaction; anything that may be distinguished as an 'is' and is therefore a 'termination point' of a system or along a flowline which may interact with other related systems it shares a line with; a point of interaction with other points.

To provide another application, let us take up the example of "Systemology" as a "terminal." It is an *is*—meaning it *is* some *thing* which may be ascribed data, associations and significances. You can read a book about it. You can talk about it with friends. You can form an opinion about it if your experience with it suddenly becomes imprinted by some or another emotional charge, and so on.

As an *abstract* concept, "Systemology" would not be considered a "living terminal"; it is not a specific individuated lifeforce-entity which will communicate with you. But that does not mean it is not a *real* terminal—it is simply not a *concrete* one. That later quality is something which individuals actual cause by concentrating more and more mass on the terminal. But so long as it may be brought to an individual's level of *reality* in some way, it will be *real* to the extent that a person can hold a circuit of reality on it.

For example, if you take up communicating about Systemology to another individual, most will usually respond positively unless it is somehow already associated with some imprint that has a heavy emotional charge that the individual takes as negative. An example of this is would be someone that associates the individual, unique, specific idea of Systemology with something else—for example, an "alien cult." A person reads the word "Anunnaki" on a title of a book by Joshua Free, watches a television program by a completely different author, then sees something about "processing fragmentation of the human condition" and finally reads a website about a sci-fi alien cult in California that committed suicide. They then start to group these different terminals along the same line and suddenly decide that this method of Self-Help is actually an alien cult... *False logic.*

We cannot dismiss the very fact that this is how the human condition learns and associates its knowledge. The Mind-System is an incredible tool for interaction with the physical universe, but its certainty of calculation is always 100% no matter how valid the inputs really are. When an individual does not have any "reality" on some terminal, they do not share communication with it; they aren't going to "like" it—thereby will not want it "close" to them in proximity. They are not going to be "interested" in it—and are likely to dismiss it with a response of "boredom." All of this is due to numerous past failures to understand something new, which after accumulating, will inhibit an individual's willingness to "reach" toward a terminal to understand it or bring it "closer." How an individual might treat an object (terminal) in space is no different than their handling of mental images treated as "things."

We notice certain tendencies with those that have self-made or agreed-upon deficiencies in learning new things—mostly stemming from emotional encoding on the circuits connected to education, studying, learning, schoolwork, new databanks (books), and other such inputs. Some individuals have had "such a bad go" at these terminals in the past that they now have become entirely convinced there is something wrong with them. This can happen with any "terminal" in existence; we are simply using "learning" as an example. New materials (books) or new information are intended to lead to new considerations. First among these are the **semantics** (or syntax) connected to the vocabulary and terminology used to define the paradigm. This is important for understanding the rest.

Once the arrangement of semantics has been grouped and organized as a preliminary level of understanding, later incorporation of new data within that paradigm or field of study is then "learned" based on definitions of the vocabulary in relation to demonstrations made that are then compared as similar or dissimilar to what an individual already knows (has established as fact cumulatively up to that point). As an increased understanding is maintained, more focused attention may be given to the subject—and the increased familiarity will result in an increased liking, acceptance or agreement concerning that subject/terminal, and therefore a greater willingness to "reach" toward and bring into closer proximity and thus responsibility of communication.

Something that is found effective toward positive results is likely to be of interest; and the increase of true understanding in Self-Honesty is most certainly a very positive result and a reassurance for effectiveness. A person is likely to repeat or follow or keep close that which *works* and is *effective* in *producing positive results.* For what other basis do we have for anything?

Control and communication operate systematically to create considerations of space-time:

COMMUNICATION—the idea, thought, concept, wave-action, bit or
    particle that is in motion creating the space about it.

CONTROL—the direction/directed intent that drives focus or
    attention of the idea, thought, concept, wave-action, bit or
    particle as a communication.

SPACE—the energy/mass created as a result of communication
    and control.

The *Grade-III* Textbooks/Self-Help Manuals—*Tablets of Destiny* and *Crystal Clear*—are combined to help resolve some of the most basic issues facing operators of the human condition, which correspond with increasing personal management beyond the common level of standard-issue programming and fragmentation-producing social involvement. Using the material given in the previous Grade, it is expected that a *Seeker* or *Pilot-in-Training* has:

a) accrued a basic education in the terminology and basic theory of Systemology;

b) ability to effective apply the basic tech to personal life and yield results;

c) attained a certainty that their personal situation will not get any worse;

d) increased determination to self-process and receive professional processing toward greater improvement of Self-Actualization;

e) ability to achieve higher actualized Awareness and knowing to manage most affairs of physical existence with certainty and as cause, over-coming worries and false hopes;

f) the actualized ability to "self-help" (literally) and the realization that we must use our abilities to help others—*all* Life in Existence...

...which naturally brings us to *Grade-IV* and the basic tools inherently necessary for such ventures—being the emphasis, of course, of the current textbook of Piloting Procedure.

Communication is a direction of control, which is of course most applicable to the personal identity continuum and its control of a body in the physical universe. The communication that makes this systematically possible actually originates from outside of, or exterior to, the *beta-existence* (physical universe) itself. It is quite simply a sheer act of Will, and therefore the highest facet of beta-control that *Self* has at its disposal. Everything that the *Self* is *doing* is a communication out into universes—at least two: a personal spiritual universe (*Alpha*) and a physical universe (*beta*). Alpha Communication is a creative expression of the Alpha Spirit as I-AM-Self. Self generates an Alpha Thought as manifestation—and this creation is controlled by Will-intention at the upper-levels of Alpha or Spiritual existence, exterior to a physical body and even the Mind-Systems that connects the Alpha Spirit as an identity along the *continuum* of energetic control centers that make *beta-existence* with a *genetic vehicle* even possible.

The nature of Intention and the activities of the Will are the closest points from the Alpha spectrum to the Beta spectrum (of the Zu-line on the Standard Model). On the beta side, the uppermost reach is the "Mind-System" itself. The Mind-System is an intermediary between what is taking place as Will-Intention (Alpha) and what information is directed toward the control of a physical body. But these flows are not one-way. They also send information back to Self, which constitutes any further considerations or analysis or estimations.

When the channels are not cleared, but are instead filled with debris and fragmentation, the information and energy that is communicate along the lines in each direction will be filtered or altered by some other type of imprinted or encoded influence—and thus we say that the information, the experience of the information and any further considerations of significance assigned to the information is all "fragmented."

As a Seeker resurfaces their associations on any given channel (circuit with a terminal), data may be brought to a scrutiny at analytical levels based on a specific "point-of-view" (POV). Each consideration has the ability to change the way in which the channel is treated until the Seeker is actualizing a realization that they have the ability to change this POV at Will.

Each terminal node is a potential point of contact and it is that "contact of a terminal" that the Pilot is most concerned with in directed the focused attention of a Seeker. An individual has the ability to "contact" points of energy and matter in space and across time (as recorded on their personal timeline)—and this includes the points on the timeline when we have fixed those considerations, imprints and beliefs in place, even if we have since forgotten that they are there. The point is to remember that they are there, so they may be brought to a scrutiny analytically as a consideration the individual is free to create anew—but how would this be possible if the individual did not realize they had put the first point out there as a "solid" in the first place? Otherwise the original creation would go on continuing perpetually to exist outside of the responsibility and control of its creator.

Accumulation of "experience" seems to create more barriers to communication and willingness than it resolves; yet humans tend to very much value "experience" above the achievement of an ideal state of Knowing and Being, even when such begins to define or restrict the individual to smaller more rigid parameters of what is real or possible.

A Pilot uses systematic processing to assist the Seeker in widening the consideration of their "viewpoints" (POV)—which in turn allows for a natural increase in actualized personal realizations without educational indoctrination toward a specific result or concept. It is simply a matter of allowing the Seeker the freedom of ability to manage the mental images and their associations that have all been collected, quite simply, by what a Seeker has been exposed to.

Inflows and outflows of energy are exchanged in a circuit. A completed circuit allows a flow of energy. An imbalance in flow direction alone is enough to cause turbulence on that channel and increases likelihood of imprinted fragmentation. You can easily notice in a conversation how an individual that is projecting a communication will become frustrated when they are not receiving back any kind of answer or response. And those which are in the habit of only accepting inflows of communication equally become frustrated when they are not given a chance to originate their own communications. One of the most important steps for good communication, managing personal life, managing abilities of the spirit and conducting the most effective optimum piloting is capability and willingness to *confront*.

<u>confront</u> : to come around in front of; to be in the presence of; to stand in front of, or in the face of; to meet "face-to-face" or "face-up-to."

Many individuals may have a fragmented understanding of the concept of "confronting" due to its improper handling and associative "experiential knowledge." There are some that have come to "opinion" that all *confrontation* is "bad." Apparently they have the concept of confronting confused with semantics of *conflict*, or opposition to "good communication." And then there are those which seem to have mastered no other levels of communication but to be in conflict with everything in their environment and seek to impose or enforce any and all manner of arbitraries onto it in lacking for true control.

An ability to hold attention and control of the session; the ability to deliver communications as though they are your own even when read from a book or list; the ability to ensure complete communication cycles during processing; these are responsibilities of the Pilot—and additionally to be able to conduct this activity without becoming fragmented by the Seeker or the operations of the session. All of this may be resolved with proper practice of communication skills, the ability to confront/interface properly with a Seeker (or any individual that you maintain a presence with), the ability to deliver communications, then acknowledge receipt of a response to those communications and expertly bridge them to the next cycle of communications.

Individuals who are able to direct their attention with fixed focus and concentration easily are able to also manage their own internalized communications and handle their own reactive "Self-talk" and "out of phase" assumptions taken on from others with greater ease—if these types of reactive-response mechanisms are still functioning at all. The ability to be at ease and comfortable "in the face" of other individuals and terminals is one of the indicators of Self-Honesty—and what we mean by the ability to confront.

Those who are more *Self-directed* and operate more clearly from the Alpha states of Will and Intention are also able to better focus their own energies and direct their own attention as needed without becoming either unnecessarily fixed or distracted, but under the full control of Self. The greater certainty an individual maintains that they are able to handle a situation or terminal, the more willing they are to face it. Often this must be practiced or worked up to on a gradient scale, but it is possible to achieve states whereby an individual is willing to confront and manage anything that "life" can throw... and still walk away smiling.

"We should not be surprised that behaviors and realities—activities and motions—manifested in the Physical Universe from individuals 'blocked' or 'fragmented' by many imposed artificial solids are also blocking others in their energy flow. These are often the same individuals that seek incessant validation of their own 'fragmentation' by forcefully trying to 'make us as they are.' It is only when we return to our true sense of Self that we are stronger as individuals—with a higher frequency of operation—in our ability to <u>confront</u> energy and transform obstacles to our survival in the Physical Universe as daily life, and free our Self to experience its highest spiritual evolution and Awareness as 'I AM.'"

—The Tablets of Destiny (Liber-One)

"Aside from those memories assumed through direct 'bodily injury,' disruptive Imprints are mainly a result of authoritarian enforcement of beliefs, 'emotional baggage' and other programmed responses that strongly influence our thought fragmentation from beneath an emotional surface—and which is prone to resurface unbidden and undirected by the Self. These types of Imprints must be systematically 'resurfaced' and '<u>confronted</u>' on the *Pathway to Self-Honesty* before effectively defragmenting 'higher energy' thought-bases of manifestation: substance, motion and Awareness—of which these Imprints will undoubtedly distort in the Mind. Remember that we cannot move forward past the point we do not understand—and this very much includes ourselves and our relationship ties to the past." — Tablets of Destiny (Liber-One)

"When we are able to Self-Honestly resurface and <u>confront</u> the ridiculousness of our past—'look back and laugh'—we are immediately released from the emotional hold that it has on us. We have brought it all up to the surface for the Mind-Systems to deal with appropriately by Self-direction and we reduce the automated programming that is attached to it."

—The Tablets of Destiny (Liber-One)

"Too often, this idea of 'positive thinking' or 'creative visualization' or a few minutes spent in front of the mirror chanting 'axioms' and 'affirmations' is not enough to override lifetimes of bombardment—or even the interference prevalent in a single lifetime in the 'modern' world. The Human Condition requires a bit more assistance now to grant the certainty necessary to rise up and <u>confront</u> the sources of turbulence—thereby preventing further and additional fragmentation." —The Power of Zu (Liber-S1Z)

As a Pilot: the ability to confront or face the Seeker is the first step to having any flow of communication for a session. This means the ability to *be* and share a *presence* with the Seeker. Just as it is important to get a Seeker to be focused and attentive to the session with their presence, so too must the Pilot be fully present for the session—and fully able to face the Seeker with actualized Awareness.

A Pilot practices facing turbulence with ease; or at least the demonstration to all concerned that it is being handled with ease. Even when the "plane is going down," the Pilot must be expert at maintaining their own composure to ensure that they can control the communication of energy taking place in their environment and thereby provide greater certainty or stability to the composure of the passengers. It may be assumed that a Pilot will encounter an entire array of potential phenomenon and manifestations from Seekers as they handle the processing sessions—and it is the responsibility of the Pilot to simply maintain the integrity of the session in every instance.

A Pilot practices using communications and processes alone, using basic objective processing[*] or even a "stuffed animal." It is better if they are able to be coached by someone that can observe them; particularly in exercises that are meant as training for "living communication" between beings. The purpose is to practice "not reacting" to whatever the other person is doing or saying. Before even introducing other steps, such as delivering a communication or acknowledgment, a Pilot should begin by practicing simply *being* in the *presence* of another without flinching or apologizing or performing any unnecessary (and often unintentional) body movement, coughing, fidgeting &tc.

A person might start by just getting used to being in the spatial vicinity of some terminal, and therefore not even look; just sitting a few feet across from another person even when you are not looking at them will still require you to *be* in their *presence*. You can try practicing with eyes closed and then when that is comfortable, with eyes open; simply being in the presence of another for several minutes and able to do so comfortably. This may be practiced rigorously as needed. It is a valuable skill. It does not denote any type of agreement or status with what is being confronted, but simply the ability to face it and not quiver away from it or evade it or react to it out of discomfort with small smirks and giggles, noticeably widening eyes or even verbal responses and interjections that are not specifically part of the process.

---

[*] See *Crystal Clear (Liber-2B)* for details regarding practicing systematic objective processes alone.

The most important thing to understand about the ability to confront, if nothing else, is that it is a state of *beingness;* it is not something you are doing. True ability to confront as Self does not require any other automatic mechanisms or social conventions, such as those that we might inherently begin to assume for ourselves after repeated experiences with the company of others. There are certain tendencies that often get set up based on these experiences and then used toward the handling of future experiences, nearly automatically. In other words, many have lost the ability to *confront and be* without *doing* something, particularly with regard to the body. This is one more consideration that an individual has made and agreed to at some point, which actually keeps them snapped harder *into* a body with beliefs that they are not to be able to confront anything of any universe without the body.

Technically, communication *is* the *Self-direction* of *intention.* An individual is *intending* something when they originate a communication or creation of any kind. This includes a written command line or some other piece of communication from another source. It must be owned and understood to be communicated. Due to the nature of individualism, creativity and the actualization of Will-Intention needed to engage a true communication, it is no wonder that so many individuals have dropped off their pathway with this step; whether approaching it as we currently describe, or even in the manner of which these very same type of preliminaries are found in many esoteric schools and philosopho-mystical traditions. For example, the purpose of any "ritual" is to *Self-direct* intention, and yet most practitioners will tend to get caught up in intricacies of the "ritual." As soon as considerations of ability become fixed to only having such and such power and ability during such and such times and by the authority of such and such of the umteenth legion of the second order of angelic hordes...well, then they have missed the whole point of "magic."

As with many other very critical preliminaries of both our "applied systemology" of the future and "applied magic and mysticism" of yesteryear, the significance, for example, of properly directing Will and Intention is so overlooked and yet is essentially the definition of what the individual has set out to do in the first place. If your current tradition, practices and techniques are not moving you along the Pathway in the direction of an increased certainty and willingness to direct intention, then you may want to rethink your approach. The purpose of practicing a controlled delivery of intended communication is so that the Pilot has the certainty and command to direct very clear intention as a message or direction of attention and *know* that this intention is being received and effects (duplicated) properly.

:: 7 ::
UNIVERSAL COMMUNICATION, WILL
AND THE POWER OF INTENTION

Intention generates energy behind communication—not the words. Of course there are many associations with words, starting with definitions we ascribe to them—and yet in true communication, intention is superior to words. The stronger the intention, the more likely it is to push through filters and fragmentation, but that does not mean that the intention itself is any clearer. Clarity is also subject to the debris, imprinting and filters on the communication line or channel—and any meaning assigned to symbols, words, &tc.

> The Communication is the Intention (Alpha) on a line;
> the Words are a Medium or Catalyst of the flow.

In fact, sometimes if your intention is strong and clear enough, it will be received even if the words are not ideal. But it is directed and focused toward a receipt-point or spot in space; whether or not we have identified that spot as occupied by an individual. In objective processing, this may be practiced as simply as saying "hello" to an "object," but more than simply using the words, actually practicing the intention that the message is to be carried to the receipt-point.

Another version of this exercise would have you practice projecting the same intention previously used out loud, but communicating it silently and projecting it into the center of the object. You could extend this exercise by changing a consideration that some other (nonsensical) word actually *means* "hello"—and then applying that word with the same intention, first as a spoken method and then silent. The real point is to practice the direction of Will as communication. This is not a general **elocution** course we are presenting here.

When we speak of intention, we literally mean Will-Intention (5.0) on the Standard Model and it is an alpha quality of existence; you will not actually find it directly within the Physical Universe, nor in the Mind-System that is connected to body. The act of intending comes from *Self* and is practically a creative opposite condition to being reactive.

> intention : the directed application of Will; to intend (have "in Mind") or signify (give "significance" to) for or toward a particular purpose; in *NexGen Systemology* (from the *Standard Model*)—the spiritual activity at WILL (5.0) directed by an *Alpha Spirit* (7.0); the applic-

ation of WILL as "Cause" from a higher order of Alpha Thought and consideration (6.0), which then may continue to relay communications as an "effect" in the universe.

As harmonics of the Standard Model suggest, the alpha quality of Will-Intention at (5.0) is the higher-dimensional equivalent along the personal identity continuum as we would find "Effort" (1.0) in the Physical Universe. At (5.0), the Alpha spirit is impressing the most condensed part of spiritual beingness into its environment—strong enough to impinge or influence the physical universe, using the Mind-System at (4.0). At (1.0) the physical body or genetic vehicle is engaging its most condensed part of physical beingness as a physical effort into the environment—strong enough to produce an effect at that level that it will be inertly balanced by the continuity of energy and matter in the Physical Universe (0.0).

"Of the many ways in which beta-existence may diminish willingness (and capability) to Self-direct with certainty, the most critical fragmentation consistently received from others—and social environment—may be reduced to two main categories:

a.) **Invalidation**; and b.) **Enforcement**.

Both methods involve strong emotionally charged communication of <u>intention</u>, effort and belief—and both '**wave-forms**' of energy operate outside of Self-Honesty as a '**fallacy**' purely for the fact that they come from (allegedly) 'authoritarian' sources. Any 'appeal to authority' in logic is a 'fallacy' and therefore fragmentation by definition." —Crystal Clear (Liber-2B)

"'Imagination' and 'Individuality' are properties of the Alpha Spirit that exceed the boundaries of the Physical Universe. They may certainly be realized in the Physical Universe, but the 'ideas' begin or have a cause that is exterior to the Physical Universe—the parts used to express a unique individual creation are not just duplicating an existing archetype. We aren't talking about conceiving a 'better table' or something. We all know what a 'table' is. But that idea was first formed exterior to the Physical Universe and then realized into beta-existence by an <u>intention</u> of Will. They aren't just growing ready-built tables on trees or mining them out of the ground." —Crystal Clear (Liber-2B)

"Each and every one of us has the ability to both **incite** or dissolve 'creation' with our Attention—our focused application of Self-directed Awareness. We may do this many times a day: we form an

<u>intention</u> in our mind, create an entire 'mental image' and then erase it. This is the innate ability of Self to 'imagine.'"
—Crystal Clear (Liber-2B)

"Emotional energy can be created by WILL (<u>Intention</u>) without succumbing to the actual low-level emotional fragmentation in-and-of itself. As cause, WILL intends effect. It does not require exciting a personal display of emotion to accomplish this either—it may be accomplished solely due to <u>Alpha-Intention</u>. This is precisely how the 'I AM' as Alpha Spirit directs all cause and consciousness activity form the 'ACC' (7.0). Everything above (4.0) on the Standard Model and ZU-line (and any Systemology model, chart or scale) is considered 'causal' in terms of beta-existence. Using the power of Intention, the Seeker can simply 'Will' a desired effect to take place 'lower' down along the ZU-line."
—Crystal Clear (Liber-2B)

Suppressed communication—the inability or unwillingness to extend the reach of communication—tends to result from the assumption of more timid personality characteristics once an individual believes that they will not be understood or that the receipt of their message would be invalidated through laughter, belittling or punishment. Therefore an unwillingness to communicate or extend a creative reach from Self begins to become automatic; and any function of the personal identity system that is running on automatic is running on other-determined control as opposed to Self-determined (assuming of course that the automatic mechanistic relay was not intentionally set up knowingly and intentionally as Self; because then it could be changed, altered or stopped on command).

The reason we introduce the subject of "confront" before "directed application of intention" is because the individual (Pilot or otherwise) must be able to face or direct the intention as a communication *to* some spot in space. True communication is not addressing an empty room or wall—and it is not even addressing an audience. In the case of groups, the directed application of intention is directed between the sender and each individual as a multiplicity.

Often times lack of actualized Self-certainty and fragmentation causes individuals to fail to properly direct their intention; in which case we tend to attack those that speak too softly to hear, address opposite directions from where the receiver is, or are even noticeably hesitant in their delivery of speech to the point where a person must strain to keep their attention. All of these are forms of inadequately directed intention.

Of course, we can just as easily find the other extreme cases where an individual is incessantly loud and unreserved in all manner of channels of speech, even trains of thought that are not relevant to the present situation or a direct response to the communications directed at them. These chaotic flows of energy are not focused and are therefore not under control.

A person who cannot start talking, stop talking or change the flow of direction to be sender or receiver fully at will is not in control of communication or themselves. Much like the operation of a car, ship or other vehicle—the only true applications of Will by the Alpha Spirit as an operator, are to start, stop or alter the direction of motion. These are literally the only fundamental components of control in a system.

Another facet of personal control in both the delivery and receipt of messages involves the added physical expression or efforts attached, which may be distracting or make the flow less clear. These include hand gestures, facial changes, lifting eyebrows, rolling eyes, &tc. An individual in Pilot Training can be observed and reminded that these things are happening, therefore allowing the individual the opportunity to practice specific types of self-control. These automatic mechanisms exist in place of delivering true controlled communication.

A Pilot maintains the integrity of the session using specific methods of controlled communication and specifically designed processing command lines. Failure to maintain control of communication renders the session ineffective for the goals of processing as it degrades into a basic Q-and-A conversation maintained under the control of the Seeker, or at the very least one of their automated mechanistic circuits of communication. Such types of "casual talk" prevent any real processing from occurring.

This type of zigzag shifts the focus of attention on the line among many points or terminals without any direct line back to the actual processing that should be taking place in session. The resulting effect of the communication is always an ongoing feed into the next cycle without actually reaching an understanding or bringing a circuit to a scrutiny.

The following is an example of Q-and-A and poor confronting abilities (the Pilot reacts and changes the session); this is NOT an example of a good flow of communication for a systematic session.

PILOT : Imagine the living form of a cat there in front of the body.
SEEKER : I don't like cats.

PILOT : Oh! (*alarm, raised eyebrows, then frown*) What don't you like about cats?

SEEKER : Well, see, they remind me of when I was a child.

PILOT : Did you have a lot of negative experiences as a child?

SEEKER : Its hard to remember my childhood. I don't like to think about it.

PILOT : Would you like to process out some events from childhood?

SEEKER : I was thinking maybe we could just take it easy today.

PILOT : Is there something else you would like to run?

SEEKER : Run? Oh, you know...the last time I was running, you know, jogging down the street, I kept getting this image in my head that I was running a marathon.

PILOT : Have you ever run in a marathon? ...

As the reader can probably see, this above conversation is not going any-where and is far and removed from any kind of effective systematic processing. The Seeker is anxious about something that they are treating as an existing problem—enough to be an interference to the session—than it should be assumed that the problem, at the very least, exists *for* the Seeker. It is a part of their "reality." It is an occurrence or an 'actual thing' taking place in the world.

Whatever the Seeker's present concerns are, and although they may carry some type of fragmentation with them, they are simply treated as a work-a-day issue common to simply being present in society, which may be subject to the considerations of the individual, but are not the actual subject of the session ensuing thereafter. Careers, money, love-life, legal issues... these may all be picking away at the Seeker's attention and bringing their presence away from the session if they are not simply acknowledged at the start. They are simply acknowledged—and that is all. They may not even be tangible problems to be solved; they are whatever the Seeker is carrying with them "off the street." This raises the next subject of discussion for Pilot communication in session, which is the acknowledgment.

Acknowledgment is part of the feedback loop portion of the communica-tion cycle. It is an arc of energy on the comm-line that confirms or validates the very fact that after the original communication point was sent and received, that a response generated has also been received. The Seeker's answer is the validation or acknowledgment of their own re-ceipt of the original communication; otherwise what would they be responding to? However, it is very important that the Seeker receive an acknowledgment of their response in order to close or complete the original circuit. Otherwise the communication cycle is not completed and anything further added to the line will only be adding confusion.

Acknowledgment is a necessary part of true communication if an individual wants to know with certainty that their communication actually arrived at a receipt-point. If you were to throw a ball over a hill in front of you—and therefore to a point out of your actual view—you might hear the ball "hit" something, and lacking a line of sight, that sound would be the acknowledgment that the "point" (ball) traveled a distance and reached its terminal.

Incomplete communication cycles—an answer not given or an acknowledgment not received—are a basis for fragmentation, confusion and an unwillingness thereafter to reach (communicate), at least along certain channels, assuming the individual has not yet generalized all terminals as unworthy of communication. When left to their own devices, this is sometimes the only approach that an individual will take in regards to communication in view of the fact that they have seen poor results of their efforts time and time again. The message that the reactive-response systems send out is "don't bother, nothing's happening."

Systematic Communication Processing assists a Seeker in "tying up" energetic loose ends that have accumulated on various lines. The more incomplete communication cycles extant on a particular line, the more distortion and fragmentation will occur on that line. This "debris" inhibits clear communication between two terminals. One of the techniques employed is to imagine a terminal responding to the Seeker with an acknowledgment, such as "okay." This may even be treated as an additional step toward objective processing.

Acknowledgment is a key component to maintaining control of the communication line; for the Pilot to maintain control of "command lines"; and for a Seeker to stay in session without accumulating more incomplete energetic circuits. Because an acknowledgment is not a prompt to "continue" talking along a circuit, we consider that it is controlling the line by stopping and completing the communication cycle of actions. By acknowledging receipt, we are informing the sender or originator that the intention has been received and they need not keep putting attention on that point. A new cycle may now begin. Even if the utterance is the same, such as in many types of systematic processing, it is still its own cycle of communication and is meant to produce an original response in a separate unit of space-time than the former answer.

The key demonstrated here—and required for the session—is that a person will stop their flow of communication once the acknowledgment has been received. This is important, otherwise the Pilot would lose control of the session and the communication. By letting another person know that their communication has been received you are taking control of the line, because they have completed their action.

If no acknowledgment is made, their actions are inclined to go on being applied until an effect has been observed.

Controlled communication is not generally a practiced discipline; seldom even given much significance by the standards of most humans. Most individuals are communicating on automatic circuits that they have set up at one time or another in order to handle inflows from the environment. The Pilot cannot allow automated mechanisms to run rampant throughout the session; and it must be assumed that these are not yet under the Seeker's control or they would be not taking place.

Crudely stated: anything that we may stop or start or even change or alter in some way, we have a certain degree of control over. And this control and the nature of the thing being stopped or started (*&tc.*) is only a consideration or point-of-view. It is the responsibility of taking control of the lines as a source-point and exercising that Will-Intention on the flow. Now it is true that this is always the case; except however outside of *Self-Honesty*, because if an individual is not in full conscious control of their flows—or the mechanisms they have set up to automate the control —then the *Self* is not in control. So what are we really doing with systematic processing? We are dealing with communication and control of energy and power. No effort has been made to disguise this fact. The Pilot is demonstrating the control and responsibility of the line until the Seeker truly can as *Self*.

One of the first steps is to get a Seeker to realize they are the one *doing* whatever they are doing. This means the Pilot is observant in recognizing the ability level of the individual at the start, and simply selectively directing the Seeker's attention to that action—whatever it is that they are or can do. If they are simply sitting in the chair, make certain that *they are certain* that *Self* is making that body sit in the chair.

A compulsion is a failure to be responsible for the dynamics of control— starting, stopping or altering—on a particular channel of communication and/or regarding a particular terminal in existence. The flow has an appearance of being stuck however it is already or by the control of some automatic mechanism. As a practice you would start a person intentionally doing what they already do and then show them that the willingness to alter or change directions is their choice by simply demonstrating the opposite dynamic.

For example: an individual who is a compulsive talker may be systematically processed to realize acknowledgments or lack thereof in the physical universe; that would be one technique. Another technique would be a blatant demonstration of control on that channel. So a Pilot says to the Seeker: "When I say the word 'start', you will begin talking and you will continue to talk until I say the word 'stop' and then you will stop speaking, do you understand?"

Of course, we are not suggesting that a few cycles of this will clear a person of all their difficulties, but this is an effective technique that has been found useful. Although the Pilot is appearing to be the director of effect, controlling the line of "start" and "stop," this is not some covert attempt at "making a person do something" or "becoming a robot." A Seeker is awake, they are aware of their presence in the session and they are willingly participating in some demonstration that is found to produce an effective result toward some realization in many instances of its application; if not always, when applied correctly and run completely.

Another aspect that a Pilot will encounter is that most systematic processing involves "duplicating" a command line many times over and over again in succession. This very idea, in traditional society, is the very nature of automation. However, if the Pilot is not able to apply the same actualized intention and Will to the thirtieth time a particular query was used as the first time, then the Pilot too has become nothing more than a machine.

A complete circuit of communication fails blatantly when it is simply not responded to at all. The acknowledgment is part of a receipt of an answer. But if we have not even received an answer to the original question, we do not have a flow of communication. We cannot be certain that the original message was understood or even received. This is very important to know about because it *is* something that will happen in a Piloted session and if it is not handled appropriately, the channels by which the entire session operates on, will begin to become fragmented right there.

When control of communication is not managed in the absence of proper responses and acknowledgments—and yet is still allowed to continue to run noise on the channel—the resulting "conversation" will have no "point" or "direction" and no interested parties will be likely left "interested" in it by then end. No one will have known what anyone else is even talking about. This is what we consider "noise" or interference—or blatantly a "distraction."

A Pilot extends a communication out on the line even when we are using objective processes at the start of a session to orient the Seeker's presence. These are commands or selective directions of attention toward something that the Pilot can actually *observe.* We ask a Seeker to perform a series of basic actions and notice the lag in receiving the command and the ability to transmit the command to a body, and make it do something on command.

An individual following standard-issue human conditioning has become so accustomed to operating on "autopilot" that even these basic steps toward actualization are found to have observable results in increasing an individual's control of their own actions. No matter how basic this all may seem, the full actualized application of Will on the direction of Self worked up on a gradient scale of reach is the only aspect that has ever made other "rituals" and "therapies" even remotely effective.

When a Pilot is operating any of the subjective processes or upper-level techniques, we are dealing with instances when a command line is directed to the Seeker for them to do something within their own personal universe—which is to say imagination and creative imagery using the "Mind's Eye" and eventually total 100% "Spirit Vision" as Alpha/Self. However, it would be impossible to assist a person in performing tasks the Pilot is not able to "see" directly if we cannot even be certain the Seeker can perform the basic tasks that we *can* "see."

Consider the individual that, when asked to perform a task, gives no response, does not perform the task or performs a different task. Consider the confusion that may take place on a line of communication if after asking a question (A), the person is responding to some question (B) from a previous incomplete communication cycle. Even the simple accumulation of unanswered questions and incomplete tasks is enough to cause fragmentation on a line.

Fragmentation is composed of misappropriated *Awareness* (or *Attention*) that is fixed and no longer under the free control of *Self.* This, in a nutshell, is what *all* fragmentation is, whether imprinted as imagery or encoded emotionally or programmed through associative knowledge. It is something left incomplete or misunderstood and so "a part of us" as energy-matter is still left with that anchor point suspended in space-time. You even hear observant people refer to someone like this as being "hung up on something." Whatever it is a person is "hung up" *on*—that individual is "still waiting to receive an answer."

It is extremely important that a Pilot completes every communication cycle before initiating another. As much as this seems evidently practical, it can also be applied to the energetic interactions between ourselves and the entire universe. Repetitive processing methodology is a subject of confusion in Pilot Training because in actuality, we are never repeating or duplicating a previous communication. It does not matter that the same words are used in one command as the former command; the idea that it is actually a "duplicate question" is a false consideration. Communication is only duplicated when a specific point moves across a channel from the source to a receipt point on that channel. A second point with the same characteristics sent along that channel is *not* the "same" point as the first one. That being said, to have the same characteristics it would also have to be carrying the same quality of Will-Intention—without variation—as the first time; which we do observe in proper systematic processing. One consequence of experiencing the standard-issue Human Condition is inability or unwillingness to put any interest into repeated actions... Well, that is one bit of encoding which may be resolved with these skills.

According to the Standard Model, the Physical Universe is commanded and controlled by Will-Intention (5.0) and it is not a point present in *this* physical universe (beta-existence). This means an Alpha Spirit (Self) must direct its intention at a body and then the body will play out the actions attributed to its own physical location. It can be identifiable in space-time as a body and can communicate with other bodies it shares proximity and understanding with in space. If all bodies were potential terminations of a phone line, they would still not be the Self that is holding the receiver at the end and directing the communication.

In modern society, we have put an emphasis on the possession of a body with that of a phone because without these channels we are essentially cut off from the direct experience of communications of reality in the physical universe. But the *Self* is no more a body than it is a phone. It is given value because it is used by *Self* to experience a world of bodies and phones.

When a Pilot is processing a Seeker, they are *not* giving the "same command" over and over again. In fact, each command is its own unit or point of existence carried cross its own arc or curve of space—its own flow on a circuit. It is only when that particular message or command is not received, that an individual will simply begin to put more and more charge on the same flow as the previous time and build up a greater and greater store of personal fragmentation and general confusion.

Most "natural" upper-level successful individuals in society have already gotten a sense of how to manage this. They have learned how to get their questions answered and see their intentions carried out by those they are entrusted to. An individual that is successful in facing terminals in the universe, willing to maintain their own emotional resolve, willing to effectively communicate their intention and acknowledge when attention of others is applied to a flowline to receive it—this is a person that is successful in public life.

:: 8 ::
CONTROL AND RESPONSIBILITY FOR
SELECTIVELY DIRECTED ATTENTION

Ability to command attention is probably one of the more commonly ascribed traits or characteristics to those who are considered successful or charismatic or confident... or dare we say it, "powerful." To what else are we basing our considerations for comparison of such traits if not for the "ability to command attention"? Here then we discover another important key to the success of controlled communication and the systematic processing session.

It is a lot to ask, given the current state of the human condition, for a Pilot to say, "we will now begin the session" and suddenly everything outside the session goes out of view and the Seeker is "present right there with full attention" (which we call "presence"). Of course, a proper command of the communication line with clear intention would make this possible—and in some respects is a goal—and yet we are not restricting the potential of our methodology to only cases that have already assumed the state of *Homo Novus*. Doing so renders the entire concept of what we are doing for the present state humanity null and void.

An exceptionally low-level of interpersonal communication that may be used by a Pilot—or anyone wishing to establish a communication line with someone at the lower ends of the Beta Awareness Scale—and that is the ability to "Mime" or "Mimic" (and by this, we do not mean mimicry in the antagonistic sense). It may be used as an entry-level step to the selective direction of attention, but only when absolutely necessary.

"Low-Level Systematic Methodology" is more of interest to a Pilot processing a random individual off the street, or even a physician interested in mental science, but not necessarily a Seeker that is actively interested in studying Systemology and carries enough actualized Awareness already to want to "see themselves through" to higher points of beingness. The entire idea of "pushing" the "secret realizations" (intended behind the transmission of these exercises) or even "forcing" processing on someone that does not want to provide their presence to the session is too counter-productive for our intentions. There are plenty of willing Seekers that can benefit from this work. This isn't a cult.

But to at least provide an example: an individual who cannot at first follow the command to pick up a "bell, book or candle," might be able to mimic an action. You say, "watch what my hand does, okay?" and they should respond in some way—even a facial twinge—to show they got some sense of recognition a message is received. So, you pick up a [bell] and then you ask them, "did you see that?" and if you had their attention before—if you had enough intention on the line for them to look—they will indicate a response.

You can experiment with—and perhaps actualize a few realizations on your own—by trying the most socially recognized example of mimicry out in the world laboratory: "waving your hand" with the intention of "hello." And there you have it. Communication *is* powerful.

Many humans do not maintain control over their attentions; as a result, beta capabilities of the Alpha-Spirit (Will-Intention) get fixed to automatic mechanisms no longer under determination of Self. These functions are resolved as a gradient effort, slowly increasing reach of a Seeker with each new certainty of (or capacity for) ability, hence: "capability." This includes the ability to process "directions."

Keep in mind, we are not asking a Seeker to do anything dangerous; it would seem more dangerous to leave someone in such conditions of fragmentation where they might actually be a danger to self and others by being that "out of touch" with the universe. Unfortunately, this is exactly the state of standard issue human participants. Therefore, control of communication is demonstrated for the Seeker on the body and their attention; then the determination, responsibility and control is gradually returned to the Seeker progressively during the course of processing.

Once a session is begun and a Seeker's presence is established, the two next steps of control involve objective processing and motions/actions of the body. This is as basic as the Pilot directing the attention of the Seeker to "look" at a specific object that is present in space-time. This could graduate into having the Seeker direct themselves to find an object to look at on their own determinism.

Improper management of "control" has led a Seeker to misappropriate responsibility—and therefore control—of the body, the mind, the creative imagery of the mind, and reactivity of the same. Control of these communication lines is passed to some "automated circuit," and this is, at first, willed into action and permanent existence. It remains permanent so long as the responsibility and control of it the mechanism is passed off to some unknown cause or other-determinism.

Greater fragmentation on a line, especially along any specific circuit or toward a specific terminal, is a result of energetic "masses" accumulated

rigid imprinting and fixed programming. This will produce greater communication lag from the Seeker while various considerations or barriers are processed through. Often times, the method of using a "repetitive command" is to actually "run out" of all the considerations of a circuit at one level and then have a "breakthrough" in finding a new consideration or definition or perspective on that flow, which then produces a new set of answers.

A Pilot should not rush the Seeker to answer or respond; but the Pilot needs to keep track of the energetic flow and make sure not to add confusion to the line by acting impatient or any other misappropriation of communication. We expect a change in communication lag concerning any particular circuit or terminal as the processing toward defragmentation takes place.

Answers to many questions themselves are not nearly as important as the personal processing used to arrive at them and range of total free consideration available to the Seeker. Answers given may quicken after a lull of reshaping a consideration or altering a definition—but this is left to the Seeker to resolve, because the question or command line proposed is not altered with each cycle in that process. Answers may become scarce if the Seeker is reaching to the "bottom of the bank" concerning something finite.

When a Seeker declares at any time that there are no more answers "coming to Mind" acknowledge ("okay") and continue the session. If the channel still requires defragmentation (but nothing else may be "recalled"), a Pilot's additional route available is having the Seeker "imagine" various scenarios and the practice of **"thought experiments"** on a channel, which may also lead to the optimum actualized realization.

It is every human's responsibility to learn to handle communication, control and commands because of how much they have a tendency to fragment daily life with their common use. It is in our benefit that we may systematically use these same channels to "undo" the fragmentation that exists on the lines. Our proper handling of communication during sessions and in everyday life is the key to resolving the problems of the human condition. Here we point out that "commands" are impressed onto the systems of the personal identity continuum at a relay point—which are indicated specifically on the Standard Model as the:

"ACC" – Alpha Control Center; (7.0) on the Standard Model
"MCC" – Master Control Center; (4.0) on the Standard Model
"RCC" – Reactive Control Center; (2.0) on the Standard Model

These are abstract in relation to our experience of solids in the physical universe when compared to (1.0) at the biochemical level and (0.0) as the inert material continuity of condensed energies in the physical universe. However, these are not any less "real." The RCC has, in the original presentations of systemology a decade ago, been equated to a Mind-of-the-Body, running on reactive-response mechanisms that control automated functions of the body. This semantic is simply in contrast to the MCC, which was formerly considered as the Mind-of-the-Spirit.

The MCC *is actually not* the Mind-of-the-Alpha-Spirit, but it is the uppermost level of "Mind" that is still connected to the human condition. The Mind is actually a bridge between the influence of the Will (from a higher order of Alpha existence) and what is treated as the control centers and functions of the physical body, which are governed by the RCC. It is the interaction of the Alpha Spirit with the systems of the genetic vehicle or organic entity that creates a field of relay between them, that we consider the Mind.

For example, we may demonstrate the entire design and makeup of a genetic entity as controlled by reactive-response mechanism at (2.0). In theory, this means that independent of the Will from an Alpha-Spirit, a living organism would function at its most basic level of survival needs solely by the RCC.[*]

There are some systemologists that have often referred to this reactive control center as the "animal mind" or "primitive mind" because some presumed it to be the limit of intelligence of "conscious life" short of being imbued by some additional element of "divine consciousness." This is not entirely the case; it is simply the way in which the relay control centers seem to be wired in appearance when compared to standard-issue knowledge about "life." Animals demonstrate a greater capacity than the RCC alone—and so, the RCC is simply the extent of the genetic cellular stimulus-response inherited in a physical form. It is also established that a spiritual entity controlling a body can "step out of that POV" and still leave the body as a living and breathing organism running on its own most basic functions. Some believe this is what happens when we sleep.

Causally, communication is always a means of producing effect—but the fact that it may be "wired" directly to points of fragmentation is a concern. Because then, all someone would need to do is know our "buttons"

---

[*]   A fundamental analysis of these relay systems and the Standard Model may be found in core volumes of Grade-III, *The Tablets of Destiny* and *Crystal Clear*, which are also compiled in *The Systemology Handbook*.

to be able to control us; thereby usurping the Will of the Alpha-Spirit by engaging a direct line on the RCC. The Alpha-Spirit would be helpless but to watch the games of the body play out without their control. This is actually what happens for the human condition when the Self no longer maintains responsibility and control of communication lines with the physical universe. If not *you*, then *who*?

Many individuals fragmented from improper handling of control have a difficult time demonstrating "self-control"—failing even this, they go on to find ways to enforce control on others. Keep in mind, this is the same individual that is not demonstrating the ability to have their own best spiritual, mental and physical interests in line. This all provides a finite number of conditions of control an individual could be in:

   a) maintaining actualized control as Self on the personal identity continuum and knowing it;

   b) maintaining no actualized control as Self and having functions of the RCC or Mind-Systems operated by some other-determined cause; and

   c) maintaining an actualized conscious agreement for the function of the RCC or Mind-Systems to be operated by a Pilot for purposes of systematic processing.

This breaks down roughly to: being aware one is in control; not being aware one is not in control; and being aware that one is not in control. In *Grade-III*, we stated similar conditions about *Awareness*: being aware that one is aware, not being aware... and so on. On a systematic level, we find just a few of these basic states of control and system dynamics at work. It is the combination of just a few dynamics at work that creates a functioning system.

There are several conditions that may be fragmented in an individual, which when brought to light in this education, will be found to strongly affect the Pilot-in-Training, and also the quality of processing an individual would bring to a session. These matters are all part of an Alpha-Spirit's considerations; they have no other true moral implication other than what is associated to them as an imprint and then as erroneous programming. Consider then:

> the willingness to control others;
> an inability to control others; and
> the compulsion to control others.

An individual agreeing to processing in session is therefore providing a presence of willingness to "play the game" of "systematic processing."

Of course, Willingness is a quality of the intention supplied into the physical control centers of the Mind-Systems. These share a systematic and dynamic relationship with the RCC and reactive-response mechanisms of the body. This is important to understand because of phenomenon that may take place during processing, when a Seeker is suddenly "unwilling" or has hit a "blockage."

Let us assume for a moment that when uninhibited, not in a state of fragmented stimulation, and free to decide on the course of actions, has decided to pursue a study of Systemology, proceeds to read through the *Systemology Handbook* and various course manuals and decides that this is actually something they are interested in doing. Where then should we place cause when the same Seeker is suddenly resisting and opposing their progress in a session?

We might be left to wonder very quickly if we have made an error as Pilots. This is assuming we have not considered that the difficulties a Seeker is having in controlling the body is not restricted to a few isolated incidences, but is actually deeply ingrained in their fragmentation, imprints, programming and self-created mechanisms (automated machinery).

Past imprinting concerning control, communication and responsibility are just as likely to hangup a Pilot that has not achieved an actualized beta state of Self-Honesty and is not in a position of Self-control themselves. For these reasons, as an applied spiritual technology and demonstration of the name of "NexGen Systemology," it will be noticed that Pilots are put through an even more intensive course of instruction within our official work as the "Systemology Society" than what at average student is impressed with, for example, via the "International School of Systemology" and "Mardukite Academy" at lower "Grades."

Quite frankly: ministers, instructors and Pilots are "drilled" on skills much harder and more rigorously than the average Seeker or student experiences, approaching this field of study, philosophy and spirituality from the other side. One of the reasons is because the Pilot is also a Seeker, or starts off as a Seeker, and here we are delivering manuals that essentially have answer keys within them that bring to light some of the most coveted esoteric realizations from over 6,000 years of recorded history...but they are still being *read*, not *realized*.

A Pilot that has not started their own journey as a Seeker being processed from a point of naivete, has not had the opportunity to reach these same realizations on their own through processing. This means that we have to substitute the attainment of realizations from the systematic processes themselves as a form of demonstration. The Pilot is given the unique opportunity to see the fundamental systemology of all *Life, the Universe and Everything* play out right before themselves in every application of processing—and even during training, with the intellectual consideration and "thought-experiments" possible, simply by working through the manuals—and previous *Grade-III* materials. A certainty of things *will* develop.

Education and training in Mardukite Zuism and Systemology Technology is an application of a precision spiritual philosophy to all *Life, the Universe and Everything*. It is not exclusively a field of training for "Pilots" conducting *Professional Piloting Procedure*; such is only one avenue of direct application, and yes, an official one within the capacity of our work as a "group organization" that delivers materials, educational training and spiritual services.

The individual that has achieved a beta state of Self-Honesty is an individual with the ability to confront—face up to—and thus communicate on all channels of *Life, the Universe and Everything*. Whether trained with recognition and a fancy-lettered certificate or trained within the confines of one's own residence, the principle tools and skills administered under the banner of Mardukite Zuism and NexGen Systemology may be applied "out of session" in the world-at-large with considerable benefit. To restrict an application of this knowledge in any other way is to limit it to the very boundaries that it has proposed to resolve.

:: 9 ::
CONTROL AND RESPONSIBILITY FOR
MIND-BODY COMMUNICATIONS

Fragmentation is reinforced by validation of the RCC (reactive control center) as the command center of the body. Unfortunately, this is one issue with overuse of *cathartic processing* (Route-1 methods) as the sole means of resolving personal turbulence: it repeatedly validates the mechanistic functions of the RCC. Yet, all upper-level knowledge is still true at a *Grade-IV* level of understanding: the Alpha-Spirit, having become more and more engrossed by the data and masses identifying Self with beta-existence then discovers itself (or never discovers this point) that they have become entrapped within—or are suddenly barred by—only the mechanistic considerations of *Life, the Universe and Everything*, following only a nature of the "machines" it has witnessed as "reality" at this lower-level of fragmentary and condensed physical existence.

The truer nature of reality and existence is far more fluid. The ability to change and alter flows of energy; to start and stop the motion of any system; to create and dissolve universes; all of this lies at the upper reaches of spiritual existence that lies outside the domain or realm of this physical existence. According to the Arcane Tablets, these two basic distinctions of existence are separated and defined by the LAW, which sealed physical existence away from spiritual existence.

To the extent to which we may determine anything with certainty, we can be sure that an Alpha Spirit begins to associate the identity (and nature) of Self with a physical body and the senses of the physical body. In this instance it is not treated as a "genetic vehicle" but as a consideration of the totality of Self, right there in-and-as the body. This is the only consideration that can even logically promote the existence of a "finite afterlife" which is contrary knowledge to what we know to be true. If you are to go to a "heaven" for all eternity after a lifetime, how would you live again? And how did you live before? These are contradictory considerations and are a perfect example of the cognitive dissonance that emerges from fragmentation. Only by the Alpha-Spirit considering that they are the body can they be affected by the body. Otherwise there is no other real access point for fragmentation to the "true" Self.

Until the Alpha-Spirit makes the consideration (and reality-agreement) that what happens to the body will in some way affect the I-AM, there is no real concern about the events that one is experiencing. The ability to confront and face-up to all terminals in the universe is simply an ability to share communication and let everything pass through as a wave without putting up blocks and other points of strain on the line.

We are very active creative beings, but until we can handle and manage the reactivity of the experience of our creations, we are not in a command position of control and responsibility. This is what defines the states of actualization—and to the extent by which a spirit is both willing and able to reach. If we can consider the ALL without the limits of the mechanistic LAW, then we have *really* stepped outside the box into Alpha Thought. Even a fragmented individual not yet beta-actualized can be brought to a realization that these points of fragmentation—when examined on the Standard Model—do not actually affect the nature of Self at (7.0); they impinge upon the personal identity continuum that one is attending to (has attention on).

It may be assumed (though not treated at these beta levels of knowing) that since the Infinity of Nothingness (8.0) is likely to produce an equal infinity of all wave crests of I-AM peaks—at (7.0)—that the Alpha-Spirit at this state may very well be connected on a line to more than one personal identity continuum operating in beta-existence; and this may very well account for multiple lives, or perhaps even all possible lifetimes, each still operating independently on their own existential timeline. We are, of course, most concerned with the one presently knowingly using sensory faculties of a body to read this book, or the one sitting in front of us as a Seeker. We are here now because apparently this is what has significance; this is where it *is* at.

We have been led to believe that the human condition is very "mysterious" and that there is nothing that we can truly know about it; because of course, it's all theory, and mostly all self-serving information anyways—used by one authority to prove a point, then changed and altered to prove a completely different point. This is what we have discovered as "progress" among the conventional scientific community ever since it was able to resume its work after the Dark Ages of Roman Christianity. It has never returned to an apex of its former Golden Age of intellectual and spiritual balance.

The challenge in applying *Professional Piloting Procedure* to a session—or even the manner of handling communications in the everyday world—concerns selecting the appropriate channel and applying the right intensity. A Pilot should master a full understanding of the *Beta Awareness Scale* and corresponding *Emotimeter* of the human condition in order to assess the status of a Seeker during processing, or anyone that you in tend to communicate with.[*]

Keep in mind that an individual is meant to run through an entire course of reactivity in a circuit with a terminal, and the intensity will be felt to the degree that a circuit is fragmented. Once the line is defragmented, a Seeker has no difficulty maintaining responsibility and control of the communication of energy on that line—and that is what we call "true power." A reader that is not yet as familiar with the Standard Model, the *Zu-line*, *Beta-Awareness Scale* or *Emotimeter* can simply treat the material of this book on a gradient of fragmentation. Energy comes into the system at (4.0) and this is considered full *beta-Awareness*. To the extent that the energy is allowed to have a clear pathway to travel toward the continuity of the physical universe (0.0), there is no fragmentation on the line and there is an "honest" POV (point-of-view or viewpoint) accessible from Self.

Between (4.0) and (0.0) we find the entire system of the human condition. An ideal state is to operate this human condition from a point of actualized *Awareness* that is "exterior" to the system, where the Self actually relies in its Alpha condition; however, the more an individual has decided to operate from lower POVs on the line, the more fixed and rigid those points become and there is no room for higher considerations. Reality has been fixed to the experiences on the line from a certain point down to (0.0) and it is within this new range or band of considerations that we would say a Seeker is stuck.

If a Pilot were able to determine the point at which an individual has fixed or stuck their beliefs along a certain channel, this would be of benefit. Well, this is actually the entire purpose behind the *Beta-Awareness Scale* (and even the administration of the *Beta-Awareness Test*)[*]—to determine a chronic state. A Pilot should be familiar with the *Grade-III* materials concerning *Awareness* because they are likely to encounter an entire array of expression from a Seeker during a process that has a lot of imprinted energy-stores on it—of which we would say that the line is heavily "charged"—or it is a "hot button" as some of the younger systemologists assisting research at the offices often refer to it as.

   (4.0)   "Vibrancy" – feelings of accomplishment and great success of triumph over life's challenges; a new realization or achievement of knowing and beingness; full operation of Mind-Systems; local presence and control of the physical body.

---

[*]   *Beta-Awareness Scale* and *Emotimeter* are fully described in *Crystal Clear.*
[*]   "*Beta-Awareness Test*" (*BAT*) is described in *Crystal Clear.*

(3.5) "Outgoing" – pointed speech and focused attention; very directed with intention; confident and positive in outlook of future application of ability; the minimum expectation (condition) for defragmentation of an energy current, session, &tc.

(3.0) "Content" – friendly disposition and engages in casual conversation with attention and interest on the comm line, session or processing; best results for progressive or effective communication, especially in processing, are conducted at least at this level of interest and control, even if not their chronic state (or BAT score); at (3.0) a Seeker has already reached a point of only 50% present-time beta-Awareness.

Lower levels of actualized session presence (*Awareness*) below 3.0 actually require a greater emphasis on "control processing" to elevate a Seeker to higher "Session Awareness" (SA). Session Awareness is treated separately from a BAT score or an interpretation of an individual's chronic state.

Personal actualized *Awareness*—and control over the Mind–Body system communications—drops to lower points on our abstract scales and models as more barriers and solids are imposed on an individual during their lifetime, and particularly as they are imposed or added onto the channel or circuit to any terminal as fragmentation.

Desire to improve ability is present at lower-levels of beta-thought but too often overshadowed by indoctrination, encoding and repeated enforcement along some channel. So much invalidating communication has been received from others in these circuits that it becomes too difficult—or out of the willingness to reach—to maintain high levels of personal determinism.

(2.5) "Tolerant of Existence" – ranging from such states as dismissive of a subject to being completely bored; present in body, but otherwise marginally occupied with an interest in exercising personal Will-Intention on the environment.

If a Pilot is successful in delivering such an individual to higher levels of communication and actual get their attention focused in the session as a presence, then the individual is increasing the handling of *Awareness* and more "content" with their environment (3.0). However, if the Seeker has a significant amount of distortion on a line and it begins to trigger "sensations" or "somatic discomfort" then less *Awareness* is being applied to the management of personal reality and the they will go into a point of "invalidation"—which we register as (2.0) on the scale simultaneous with the RCC.

> (2.0) "Invalidating" – uncomfortable with the environment, mental images and facets incited by the environment; an individual that is experiencing turbulence along one of their lines/channels of communicative energy and exhibiting suspicion of the session, the intentions of the Pilot and a general pessimism about the processing.

"Session Awareness" (SA) begins with the Pilot's encounter with the Seeker "at the door" and not necessarily the "start" of session. We are, of course, gauging the communication level and presence of the Seeker in session, though after this, the SA will adjust during the session based on whatever fragmentation is being processed (imprints, programming, &tc) or whatever line, channel or circuit on the RCC is being run.

If we consider "boredom" on the spectrum of potential reactivity to a terminal circuit, it is actually up in the range of mental beta-thought, albeit low-energy levels of thought. Yet, when we compare even this to the alternatives engaged by the RCC, the state of boredom would be an amazing achievement *forward* in responding to a terminal than any of the lower emotional states of pain, anger, sadness and apathy. In this instance, processing a line of experience that formerly incited personal feelings of rage and sadness to a point of "boredom" would be, in itself, the most therapeutic phenomenon some people might ever have the opportunity to experience in their lifetime—and we are certainly not limiting the potential effects of systematic processing to be a state of "boredom."

When presence drops below a state of boredom, the direct line of *Awareness* to Self is withdrawing its actualized Will and as a result we see a general increasing "withdrawal" of the "spirit" from the "body," as it descends into lower and lower levels of emotional solidity.[*]

Once a Seeker is accustomed to systematic processing procedures and is readily able to "be" in session with their presence, then it becomes easier to start working directly with terminals that are likely to be in stimulation immediately after the session has ended. That being the case, it is better to improve a Seeker's own basic state of certainty conce-

---

[*] The nature of emotion, withdrawal of Awareness from the body, and other materials describing activities of the personal identity continuum at the emotional levels of experience, are described more completely in the *Grade-III* text: *The Tablets of Destiny: Using Ancient Wisdom to Unlock Human Potential.*

rning Self-determinism before having hours of processing effort immediately nullified by subjecting them to the same circumstances that they are still developing the willingness and reach to manage. For this reason, in special instances, a Seeker may wish to at least temporarily relocate away from certain terminals in life while developing the certainty to face them. It does not work out well for a Seeker that is receiving a daily dose of invalidation while working toward a greater state of knowing and beingness.

All control of the Mind-Systems (MCC) and genetic vehicle/entity (RCC) are a matter of Alpha Thought (6.0)—pure consideration that is directed into *beta-experience* of the human condition (via Will). Relay across the other control systems follows but it is now beyond the proximity of Will-Intention (5.0). It is important then to return control of the automated machinery and the reactive-response mechanisms to the Seeker. For some who are not very actualized, the very idea of the ability to "change your mind" seems too superficial to be important. Those with a lot of "gum in the works" are not experiencing clear communication as the Alpha-Spirit with its own spectrum/continuum as an identity.

One important necessary part of "two-way communication" is quite simply: getting your question answered. As such, we are using systematic processing methods that use repetitive questions, though each is issued in its own cycle as its own unit or point or bit of data being transmitted independently of any other. It is not a "repeat" of a command formerly just given or a build upon a previous answer. It is the same words used to issue a new processing command line,

which is brought to a finality. The communication lag is not simply an interval of time in getting any response, but literally the period of time that passes before the actual answer to the original question manifests.

Original Q	PILOT : What's your name?
(lag)	SEEKER : I can't believe the traffic today and how long it took to get here.
	PILOT : I understand. Now, what is your name?
(lag)	SEEKER : That's a funny word—"name."
	PILOT : Okay. Now, what is your name?
Answer	SEEKER : Oh, it's John.
Question 2	PILOT : Thank you. What's your name?
(lag)	SEEKER : (*pause, blockage, processing*)

(lag)	SEEKER : (*confused, shaking head*)
Repeat Q2	PILOT : Okay. I will repeat the command line. What's your name?
Answer	SEEKER : It's John.
Question 3	PILOT : Thank you. Now, just to be sure—What's your name?
Answer	SEEKER : John.
	PILOT : Thank you.

Whether piloting an airplane, a spaceship, Self or a Seeker, all of the control and communication requires the certainty and determination to manage space and time—and for purposes of specifically piloting: the environment of the session, the status/location of Pilot and the status/location of the Seeker.

Actualized control via Self-honest management with certainty means the ability to accelerate, decelerate or change direction—all of which are descriptions of the actions, motions and flows of any system. It does however apply very well to the analogy of piloting a ship or the control of a vehicle or the handling of processing or handling of energetic flows —the beauty of working from the systemological paradigm is that the same principles apply across the boards of all systems.

In applied systemology where "Piloted processing" is extant, the focus on control pertains to the direction of attention. The ability to determine or control a "body"/"ship" toward a destination where a Seeker finds themselves rehabilitated in their control of self-determinism, is a matter of controlling attentions. The control of personal attention is the key to applying the power of personal Awareness and the Observer-Effect onto existence in the universe. This is how an individual is made to "agree" to something or is imprinted about the meaning of what things are. There is always someone along to come tell us what and how things *are*.

As communication lags get shorter and control over the body and the responses become more direct, the entry-level processes do not have to be run on an individual as long. This means that while some basic Mind-Body control processing might be introduced at the beginning of every session, these techniques would not necessarily need to be run very long before the Seeker would achieve the same result that a previous session may have spent a greater amount of time on.

For example, if the first few sessions of a Seeker's official piloted journey on the Pathway to Self-Honesty each involve 30-60 minutes of basic objective processing and Mind–Body circuit control, it is very possible that after clearing these circuits, such an exercise would require less and less time at the beginning of later sessions to produce the same results, which then puts the Seeker in a better position to spend session time on successively higher levels of processing. All of which is conducted on a gradual scale of operation.

In other mystical and esoteric applications of personal development, the same type of cumulative gains might be equated to the ability to work on some type of preliminary ritual or meditation prerequisite whereby the first time an hour is spent properly visualizing some symbol as solid in the air; the next time the symbol and a circle around the area where one is sitting; then the next time the individual would be able to add more steps to the same period of time because the ability to conjure a symbol and a circle would only require a smaller portion of the time to concentrate attentions on and make real in the Mind's Eye with a consideration.

This is the type of gradient you would find in some "magical" development program whereby an initiate must be able to visualize more and more solid symbols in a shorter period of time while also conducting various actions and gestures. The effectiveness of any of this is the initiate having spent time mastering the ability to consider and create the parts—each individually—and then be able to summon a reality on them collectively much quicker and stronger than before.

Attention is a powerful tool for Self—and others seem to instinctively know this. It is the direct conduit to our flow of energy, which follows our attention. When an individual applies attention and interest along any line, channel or circuit, they are validating both the nature of the circuit and the terminal it is connected to. This is how things are given their reality.

Simply by directing our attention to what others are presenting something as an *is*, we are offering our own agreements to that "thing" as an *is*. Whatever it *is*, whatever it is determined to be, the energetic line simply follows. If there is fragmentation on the line, then the experience of the *is*, will be considered valid with a moderate amount of intellectual interest.

As we analyze and consider what something *is*, it becomes more and more our own. In fact, this is what many people refer to as an "idea." If an individual loses the ability to direct their own attention and the ability to control emotional reactions connected to the circuit on that line of attention, then it will be found that the line itself—or whoever is managing the other end of the line or access to the "button"—is given all the causal control and responsibility and the individual will consistently assume a victim-phase when encountering it.

The dialogue given previously is illustrative only. There are many points of it that are bad practice. The main fault with actual application of the script in real life is that the Pilot did not handle the present concerns of the Seeker before putting them into a directed line of communication. The Seeker is still brushing off the emotional residue of navigating through traffic to get there on time and the Pilot is only partially acknowledging this fact.

Another major concern is that a Pilot must be certain if what a Seeker says is actually the Seeker saying it or if there is a "language imprint" somewhere on the line that is in stimulation. When individuals reach certain emotional levels and/or they reach out and touch the wires on a certain circuit to a terminal, they may go into a reactive-response manifestation on language channels. They simply start playing a "recording" containing programmed thoughts and various self-talk "commands" encoded on that line.

One goal of systematic processing is for the Seeker to be able to differentiate their knowing and assignment of significance. There is a wide sweeping difference between Self-determination and the "buttons" linking automated response mechanisms to erroneous programming and a fixation on what is no longer in control or held with responsibility. Increasing the Seekers ability and certainty to be Self-determined resolves many of the automatic functions that inhibit actualized *Awareness* as an Alpha (spiritual) being.

The standard-issue human condition is fragmented. The ability to *be* and direct personal experience is too often controlled and dictated by another authority—until an individual's agreements finally resolve in setting up automated machinery, because systematically it is the most effective way to resolve delivering the same conditioned responses without having to place any higher-level personal intention into it. Even the genetic vehicle is wired this way at a cellular level.

The ability to *know* or *think* is also subject to considerable authoritarian control for the average Human. The irony is that whatever is considered or postulated as fact from within the standard-issue condition of humanity is likely not to be an individual *thinking* for themselves any time that one of their "buttons" is activated. As a result we cannot say that the *actions* exhibited in the Physical Universe are solely efforts triggered by Alpha Will-Intention if the individual is heavily fragmented. Energetic blockages on the line literally inhibit the transmission of clear communication between Self and the control of the body.

In *NexGen Systemology*, "mental blockages" are treated as communication lines that have been imprinted or encoded or heavily charged with emotion and condensed as a kind of mass. In earlier *Grade-III* materials, we refer to this as "belief," and it has been written by modern philosophers that "Belief Imparts Reality"[*]—which means it is up to an individual to decide what something *is* and what meaning and significance it should have. Even in mythologies, an ability to "name" physical existence and "classify" experience was the first "sentient" quality that allowed humanity to commandeer Spaceship Earth.

---

[*] "Belief imparts reality, and beliefs will continue to be real so long as people pour energy into them by faith." —Douglas Monroe, author of *21 Lessons of Merlyn, Lost Books of Merlyn* and *Deepteachings of Merlyn*.

:: 10 ::
THE ENERGY AND TRUE POWER OF
SELECTIVELY DIRECTED ATTENTION

There is little reason in putting a lot of intellectual emphasis on fancy words and definitions to describe *attention*. As far as we can tell, it is an inherent knowingness that we are aware of as *consciousness*. This is one aspect that does not require being taught about (although we seem to benefit from a reminder as we go further on in our 'years') since it is the very thing that all living beings have an innate sense of. They have an attention they are directing as a focus, or which is being demanded by some authority or distraction, and there is an inherent *knowing* attached to the experience that we are directing our personal energy wherever our attention lands.

As a child discovers this, they also realize there is a benefit to having those attentions; they can inherently feel the energy that accompanies it because they are still that sensitive—have not projected a bunch of screens and filters through which to view life yet—and they learn ways of managing it. When it is not received through one or more productive efforts than an effect will be earned some other way, and the naïve child begins to "act out" because they want their beingness as an identity validated with "attentions."

If we examine all *Life, the Universe and Everything*—we discover our "attention" *is* valuable. In fact, it is so valuable that it has been likened to our very spiritual life-force energies by many mystics and sages of the past. And as soon as we find ourselves locked into a world of sensory fragmentation, the demands on attention become great—more and more of the system seeks validation; everyone wants the certainty to know that they exist.

There is certainly no shortage of energies running rampant, flowing all throughout the world in every which direction. Those who constantly speak in references of being "depleted in energy" or "cannot focus" or "always tired" or "can't seem to get things done"—all of this stems from the inability to properly recognize and manage the energetic continuity that is taking place all around us at all times.

Some time spent directing personal attention around a room or at various objects at Will is not simply an exercise used by a Pilot to manage controlled communication—there is actual energetic value in many types of objective processing that increases the flow (and personal certainty of managing the flow at will) of clear communications between Self and any and all terminal-circuits of attention maintained with the physical universe or another living being.

All focused selectively directed attention—whether Self-determined, demanded/enforced, distracted by a "button" &tc.—carries our personal ZU-energy—or Actualized Awareness—into the cycles and systems of manifestation described throughout "NexGen Systemology." These systems—as demonstrated on our Standard Models and Charts—

> carry "Alpha Thoughts" (6.0) as "Will-Intention" (5.0)
>
> from "Spiritual Beingness" (*spiritual consciousness*)
>
> into "Mental Knowingness" (*mental consciousness*)
>
> where it is carried into—and realized for—
>
> the Physical Universe by the "beta-Thought" (4.0)
>
> of a "beta-Lifeform" connected on the ZU-line ("*Identity*").[*]

From this degree of Self-direction on downward, it is the MCC (Mind-System) that is responsible for gauging "Effort" necessary to enact the desired change/manifestation in the Physical Universe—and it is generally "correct" to the degree that it is defragmented and actualized.

It is not difficult to understand at this juncture, perhaps, the meaning behind the statement that: "best intentions are not enough to gain desired results." Validation of "Alpha Thought" (6.0) and Self-direction of "Will-Intention" (5.0) are very significant demonstrations of our higher levels of beingness and knowingness. Yet, at the same time, we can easily see how, as this communication signal travels "down" the conduit of the personal identity continuum and solidifies (lowers) its frequency, other relay centers are required to properly cycle and "channel" energies to the extent that these "channels" are free and clear of fragmentation.

The mystery of life is therefore maintained by not being able to apply our attentions appropriately at Will. Other erroneously associated data and programming can also encode a fixed imprint on the line of a specific channel. We can, in essence, allow ourselves to see no further past the point we don't understand—and those facets and terminals with significances we don't understand are simply those which we do not have a controlled communication with or the ability to fix and unfix our attention upon by Will. What else is the Alpha-Spirit even "directing" in *beta-existence* when acting "Self-directed"?—if not the application of their own energies by controlling the flow via selective attention.

---

[*] Excerpting the *Grade-III* volume: *Crystal Clear (Liber-2B)*; also available in *The Systemology Handbook.*

The cliché statements about being "afraid of what we don't understand" and "only fearing fear itself" have not brought humanity to any higher realization on the handling of personal attention and the right communication necessary to "understand" anything. In many cases an individual is energetically treating any aspect that they are not willing to face or handle as the "darkness," the "distortion," the "distraction" and the "unknown" simply by a basic unwillingness to confront, communicate and understand. Once these images and their facets are turned into unknowns, they are attended to with fear and dislike mechanisms.

That the original channel and true data remains extant underneath the nature of all "personal mystery" is a strange phenomenon. Just because a person has thrown up a filter on a channel, or attended the dark screens and mysterious "blacknesses" with fear, does not mean that there is not actual information still in play for this game of which we are simply not seeing.

Mishandling of energy and communication; the formation of blockages, barriers, filters and mechanisms; attending things we don't understand with our energy and *Awareness*; all of these actions actually contribute to making what is already misaligned even more solid and rigidly fixed in place as a consideration—even when the moment when that consideration was agreed to and fixed in place is forgotten.

When we consider the "magician" conducting a ritual, every single aspect of the ceremonial demonstration is meant simply to selectively direct attention. The illusion and trapping of the lower Grades of "magic" lies in the consideration that some otherwise inaccessible power is concealed through the utterance of a secret word at the appropriate time when such and such planet is visible in the sky and the initiate is standing on one foot hopping about the circle nine times backwards trying not to trip on a series of magical tools laid out in the four directions as they swing a wand in their right hand and making certain to keep the incense censor fed with the left hand, lest they be able to catch a breath of real fresh oxygen and begin to wonder what they are doing this whole time.

This is not meant to invalidate personal realizations and gains of self-determined certainty that are equally possible at the *Grade-I* and *Grade-II* designations of magic instruction, mysticism, religion and hermetic philosophies.[*] However, when the magician displaces the "source and

---

[*] For Grade-I Route of Magic & Mysticism, see *Arcanum, Sorcerer's Handbook*, and *Vampyre's Handbook*; the Grade-I Route of Druidism & the Dragon Legacy is collected in the omnibus anthology, *Merlyn's Complete Book of Druidism: A Master*

cause" of Will to other-determined responsibilities, an "out of the box" paradigm serves only to entrap an initiate in another, different or larger "box."

Fixing a line of attention is very similar to fixing attention on a line of communication, and when this is controlled properly, amazing things can happen. Ability to selectively direct and fix attention (and really really fix it well) is what we attribute to the "power to create." And there is no higher faculty that we have discovered for Self other than the ability to freely consider and be willing to create—which is only actualized to the degree that one is willing to take responsibility for creations as cause. When they are attributed to some other-determined cause, the power and energy attached to the creation is surrendered—and yet the individual still remains very much connected to the solidity of the creation.

Fixation on an issue or problem limits the scope of Attention that an individual is willing to apply—and thus limits the amount of actualized *Awareness* that is given to control of the personal identity continuum and functions of the Mind-System: to be able to change, at Will, the ideas, thoughts, considerations, postulates and mental image creations.

As a Seeker works through *Grade-III* and *Grade-IV* type systematic processing and systemological education, the realizations demonstrate that we are increasing the "apparent ability" of the individual by increasing the span of potential uninhibited thought activity—thereby freeing it from its erroneous associations and reactive-response mechanisms. Much of this is handled directly with "systematic subjective processing," which is then alternated with the more "objective processes" that allow an individual to reclaim and recycle the stores of mental energy that have been managed during a "subjective" exercise.

It may be stated that the focus of subjective processing is aimed specifically at a Seeker's thought activity, conceptions, considerations and significances attached thereto. They are exercises, usually elevated to an analytical level, that address the *knowingness* maintained by the Self, or at least the present awareness as Self. This is also comparable to where attention is fixed. In contrast, objective processing focuses on an increased awareness toward control of what the Self is *doing*, which is also to say: energy that is directed onto the attention line. This basic systemology of function is where we discover the compartments of Self-

---

Course in Druidry for Modern Druids; and the entire Grade-II Mesopotamian Mysteries curriculum is found in *Necronomicon: The Complete Anunnaki Legacy (2020 Ed)*.

identity; a spirit that is *being*; a mind that is *knowing* and a body that is *doing*; however these are relayed.

An individual may very well have been strongly conditioned, deeply emotionally encoded along some channel to simply no longer want to recognize it or look at it—its power and energy has become so fixedly designated as inhibiting and destructive and the individual no longer wants anything to do with it. This leads to later considerations that "this is bad" and "that is pain" and "I don't want to know" and of course ultimately, "I don't want to be responsible for control and energy and power because it is bad and painful and I want nothing to do with it as cause so I will be the effect because I cannot change it then and I don't have to be responsible for damage and pain which now someone else has caused to me..." This is not an Alpha-Spirit talking, thinking, or acting in a Self-determined fashion at all.

One technique—that many spiritual philosophies have each developed their own versions of—concerns the ability to "imagine problems" or literally "create problem scenarios" in the mind that Self knows that they are creating and of which they can apply some attention to. If it is closely similar to the original channel or terminal-circuit, then all the better. If a Pilot can get the Seeker to consider similar problems to the one that they are overwhelmed with, new realizations can result and a greater certainty for solving problems in general.

Problems are not inherently bad—much like everything else—and an individual is likely to respond or handle them as they would any terminal-circuit to the extent that such channel is clear of fragmentation. Even delivery of a communication requires solving problems; and an individual will always be found solving a problem about something—whether or not they are fixed, obsessed and operating on automation is the other matter altogether.

Presence is "personal orientation of Self or POV located in space-time and handling the energy-matter present in the environment"—so that is a condition we want to make sure is present before the actual start of a session. Keep in mind that the preliminary steps of Piloting are drawn from the same methodology that others use improperly to cause fragmentation; for example, as "social programming" and what some refer to as conditioning—this is accomplished with four basic steps (which we then actually handle more responsibly in *Professional Piloted Procedure* than we are to expect that a Seeker has had the opportunity to experience in the normative standard-issue world-at-large).

1. get into communication on a channel
2. maintain control of the communication line
3. demonstration (of communication and control)
4. widening (or fixing) of considerations (beliefs)

Information within Systemology—materials contained within esoteric Grades and the applied practical philosophies of *Grade-III* and *Grade-IV*—is only "dangerous" if it remains suppressed below common knowledge. It is only "dangerous" when it remains exclusively in the hands of upper-level echelons of society—and too often such individuals use the knowledge only to impose more barriers on the public, producing more and more personal fragmentation by way of erroneous enforcement.

Knowledge that is researched, discovered, experimented with and demonstrated throughout *NexGen Systemology* is only "new" to those individuals being permitted access to the secret wisdom for the first time. The truth is that Systemology and systematic processing is not based on "new" information that suddenly developed out of nowhere, but it does take a more practical approach to esoteric knowledge contained on the Arcane Tablets—even more practical and direct than many of the quasi-mystical magical orders and "secret societies." Such organizations have already been in possession of some reflection of this knowledge for thousands and thousands of years since the **Ancient Mystery School**.

An individual applies their "attention" to such subjects, objects and environments that are equivalent to their level of interest. Obviously a person will give more attention to the things they are interested in—including the terminals of "magic" or "religion" or "spirituality." A person is likely only to give such things attention if they are demonstrated to have some level of relevancy for daily life. Other individuals may not even be aware that their interests in such things as "wizard-dragon fantasy" and "science-fiction space-opera" are most likely resonant energies connected to flows on channels to past lives and past life memory.[*]

The power of attention may be summed up to be: "the consideration of Self to selectively direct its own *Awareness* as a focal point on any line,

---

[*] Such subjects are treated only at higher *Grades* of Systemology and upper-levels of systematic processing in order to prevent a Seeker from mishandling the information prior to having increased certainty and ability to confront, which can cause further fragmentation. A Pilot should emphasize the management of Self-determinism and application of *Awareness* for *this* life and the automatic mechanisms that Seeker's already find themselves held in suspension to by the repeated direction of their attentions in *this* lifetime.

which is to say a point in space." The actual consciousness of an individual that is so often fixed and tied only to the considerations and *Awareness* as a physical body, is able to be transferred at Will by Self to any other point that it can consider in space—and if there isn't a point in space, the Alpha-Spirit creates it simply by the consideration that it is there, and fixes attention on it.

Understanding the physical universe has been a great strain on the standard-issue human condition, because as a form wired solely to sensory information about the tangibles and solids of existence, the entire background reality to *Life, the Universe and Everything* has completely eluded the semantic-set and vocabulary of most conventional sciences; they are in the position of only seeing effects.

Even the points attributed to cause in the physical universe are only treated so in relation to the visible effects and relationships that are observed at the level of continuity making up the physical universe. Just as the "RCC" *Reactive-response Control Center* may be said to be a cause on the physiologic functions and biochemistry of a genetic-body, we can be certain that it is not the definitive cause for all of its activity—but rather a relay station that operates much more closely to the level of manifestation than we deem physical and observable at that level of existence.

Therefore, the "RCC" is approximately the extent to which conventional physical sciences have had any understanding or reality on the human condition. "Stimulus-Response" is about as far as they ever reached in understanding what the being *is*, and yet not one of us who has at least taken a peek behind the curtain a time or two would actually believe that *Self* is nothing more than physical chemical elements charged with a bit of electricity. This is the basic "humans are animals" mentality that has kept the state of the human condition forever trapped amidst the lowest level meanderings.

Keep in mind that the identification of *Self* with the physical is what has gotten the Seeker into their mess in the first place. In fact, we can actually gauge just how "solid" an individual has become simply by taking a look at the *Beta-Awareness Scale*. The lower their attentions are fixed on the scale, the more solid they become. And when the *Self* has identified with a body that is experienced deep levels of depression, apathy and hopelessness... they are quite solid in their existence and they are much more subject to the "impact" of condensed "solid" energies. They are only a few units of *Awareness* away from being at the level of the inert material existence as a genetic being—and as a spiritual being, we have discovered that the Alpha-Spirit can sink into much deeper trappings of consideration than even "body-death."

Barriers imposed in the "Mind" and those extant in the physical universe are all "solid," which is to say, all "things." And as such, "things" and "solids" begin to be treated synonymously with no distinction—and yet we know that there are many levels of manifestation and solidity. As an individual begins to consider only the mechanistic and material basis of their *beta-existence*, the "things" and "solids" are treated by Self as a higher significance or range of evaluation than they actually are. It is the *Awareness* that has been lowered or fixed upon the line, but the "things" are not any more solid at the higher-levels where Self actually *is*.

This issue causes fragmentation, which is simply treating things other than what they actually are. But then we say, well, everyone deserves an opinion and has the ability to makeup the reality and universe that they wish to see things as. And this is, to a great extent, very true. However, we have already placed upon ourselves a condition—or been put in agreements with a condition—that we still are identifying with the lower-level range of experience exhibited by a physical body.

An individual must operate outside the confines and boundaries put in place in order to ensure an actual higher-level cause to a beta-effect. Otherwise we are still operating from within confines of a small cubicle of potential considerations and believing we swim in free expression. It is only free to the extent that barriers have been enforced or designed or agreed to—and while we can be certain that the physical universe and its level of existence is bound by the LAW, the majority of an individual's barriers and imprints and fragmentation are not necessarily due to the LAW imposing some arbitrary punishments. Instead these result from a person not operating in conjunction with the basic energy-matter LAW, and therefore creating and considering more barriers to be in place than there actually are. The barriers are made real, at least to the individual, by acting or reacting on them as terminals—and fragmentation ensues on the line.

Philosophies behind "objective processing" are many—but if nothing else, the methods represent a powerful toolkit to help remedy attentions and increase certainty of an individual in focusing on what they *can* do and the ability of control they *do* have. But there is another reason this is important, because it serves a purpose to resolve another an issue that has been found to come up in most intensive experiments of effective processing; and that is the subject of "loss."

An individual can get a sense that they "lose" something important by giving up a hold on some reactive-response mechanism or mental image or another facet of automatic programming that they have become accustomed to as perhaps even a small basis of fact as reality. Even the dissolution of solids on a communication line or energetic circuit with a terminal can actual generate a great "feeling" of loss; sometimes the individual even feels as though they have just been witness to an explosion. This is one reason why we alternate internalized or subjective work of any kind with "objective processing" as a standard. This should limit the intensity of these occurrences naturally, rather than waiting until after a Seeker has blown off so many charges that they are too confused to bring their attentions back to objects and spaces in their immediate environment.

This information is based on research conducted and discoveries resulting from experimental methods used at the *NexGen Systemology Society* of the *Mardukite Research Organization*. It is provided in hopes that an individual working to be a *Professional Pilot of Systemology* is working toward the betterment of the planet and the elevation of their fellow humans to a higher state of existence known as *Homo Novus*. The work is not perfect, but it represents the best of what we have developed to date—and obviously, given this is *Grade-IV*, the full extent of potential work is not yet completed; yet the journey ahead is well founded—it has been traveled by a select few of now and a few that have gone on before us.

Those who do not adhere to these practices and suggestions will simply find that their own experience of this work is not really "systematic" and open to a lot of set-backs. Those that try to simply plunge through to the uppermost routes of potential work or run nothing but intensive mental exercises to attempt to expedite overt "mental abilities" (while believing that objective processing is a waste of time) &tc.—these individuals will not find balanced stable progression on the *Pathway* and will be likely to be the same individuals that later denounce it.

It is a Pilot's responsibility to make certain that our Systemology continues to effectively grow, be represented appropriately, and through this, always working toward the ideal goals for the spiritual evolution of the human condition—and its highest state of potential knowing and being as the Alpha-Spirit.

—UNIT TWO—

SYSTEMOLOGY OPERATING PROCEDURE #2-C

(SOP-2C)

—LIBER-2D—

:: 1 ::
INTRODUCING PILOTED SYSTEMOLOGY
OPERATING PROCEDURE 2-C

The idea of "Piloted Procedure" was introduced in "*The Tablets of Destiny*" (*Liber-One*) with "RR-SP-1" (Resurface-and-Reduce-Systemology-Process-1).[‡] This is the first route where systematic processing was explored and it remains "Route 1" hereafter; introduced as seven basic steps, each identified by a unique cuneiform sign. A Pilot should study the basic outline of the original procedure and summation of research on the subject of **Cathartic** *Processing* at that time.

Although processing has been expanded upon with alternate routes, the same ancient "seven-step" format of a "processing session" remains true. We have updated the context for its application in *Grade-IV*, but this does not in any way invalidate former presentations of any procedure. As a Seeker, Pilot or Systemologist increases their ledges of knowing (knowledge) with each step along the *Pathway*, there is a higher-level or wider-angle view in which to look upon, examine and analyze that which we have already crossed and new horizons to reach. Our considerations are more encompassing of what *is*.[*]

Research and discovery work for the present manual and Grade began alongside work for "*Crystal Clear: The Self-Actualization Manual & Guide to Total Awareness*" (*Liber-2B*). Within that volume, several methods of processing are described and demonstrated, but most specifically the methods of *analytical processing* or *analytical recall*, designated therein as "AR-SP-2." This method of processing appears in *Grade-IV* exactly as it is given in "*Crystal Clear*" and is considered "Route-2" of *Standard Operating Procedure 2-C*.

It is strongly suggested that a Seeker, Pilot or Systemologist reading this manual is familiar with the previous material and knowledge lectures available in "*The Tablets of Destiny*" (*Liber-One*) and "*Crystal Clear*" (*Liber-2B*) or in the "*Systemology Handbook*" anthology, before putting *Professional Piloting Procedure* into practice on a living being.

The two previous (*Grade-III*) textbooks are each a treatment of a specific "Route" on the *Pathway to Self-Honesty* whereby individuals better come to "Know Thyself." A Seeker is not restricted to any one route to achieve

---

[‡]   This method was reexamined and reissued in 2022 as "R-1-R" or Route-1-Revised.

[*]   When following *Grade-IV* (SOP-2C) applications of *cathartic processing*, the procedure is referred to as "RR-SP-2."

progress, but obviously a person can only be taking one at a time. Even if multiple routes are applied during the course of a single session, each "process" and each communication within that process is treated in its own unit of time in space.

A perceptive Pilot will also be certain that after a particular route has been taken for any length of time to produce a result, a form of "objective processing" will assist in maintaining attentions on the session before suddenly diverting to another route of processing. An individual who has just worked their way through all of the emotional stores on a particular line for fifteen or thirty minutes or more will have difficulty in maintaining what they have just accomplished if they are suddenly plunged into some analytical thought process.

"Route-1" is directly concerned with flows of emotional energy and emotionally encoded imprinting, which is the main subject of the "practicum" within *Liber-One*. It is quite apparent that *Crystal Clear* (*Liber-2B*) presents a more intellectual application of systemology to functions of Mind-Systems and programming within the "thought" range of activity; that is what "Route-2" is concerned with.

The primary difference is easy to consider when one understands the actual nature of fragmentation and the means in which an individual may be encoded or programmed. If a reader has familiarized themselves with the principles of systemology, than it is easy to recognize that a person may be taught "A is A, and A is for 'Apples'." This *is* technically a form of programming, but it takes place at intellectual/thought level of processing. It is, essentially, a learned or socially conditioned means of understanding, relating and communicating with the universe via associative language and semantics.

But what if someone were to beat you over the head repeatedly with a bag of apples—and thereafter even the idea or mental image of apples were to suddenly make one sick or uneasy... this is what we consider emotional encoding and it is nearly always completely erroneous because it removes Self from the equation (at the RCC) to determine the significance. If this were not enough, it is found that various other *facets* present during the encoding can also be associated; such as, for example, the location it happened, the people involved, different sights, smells, sounds, &tc. all are encoded as imprinted *facets*.

In an extreme situation, we would consider someone in this condition "psychotic" because they are still heavily "hung up" on an event that has since passed on the timeline. It is the event or choice or sensation that we do not understand—or are not willing to understand—that may become a source of fragmentation. These isolated instances in themselves do not always appear to be serious, but if you compound a lifetime (or several) of such fragmentation, you would find that considerations have become finite between many barriers.

First experiments for *Systemology Operating Procedure 2-C* first began with the intention to refine the basic RR-SP-1 seven-step process to coincide with the introduction of AR-SP-2 in *Crystal Clear*. In the end, rather than combining the processes prematurely, a Seeker using *Grade-III* material is simply presented two different "routes."

> "Routes of defragmentation all involve some measure of 'emptying out' whatever is not 'Self.' When we are running Cathartic or Kenostic techniques we are always 'emptying out' the emotional charges stored within imprints or the thought-formed 'beliefs' we feed our energy into. In order to reclaim the energy, the ZU, the Knowingness, and the freedom of the Spirit that takes up this Human Condition, it is obviously required that we 'purge' everything that is not the Alpha Self. These are all methods to ultimately return the Awareness of the Seeker back toward the 'spiritual.' The only reason there is any sense of 'wonder' and 'discovery' attached to this is because we have apparently forgotten that we have trod upon this very same Pathway at least once before, on our descent into the Human Condition for at least this present lifetime—and however many other countless times our Spirit has crossed with the planet Earth." —Crystal Clear (Liber-2B)

SOP-2C is a refinement of the seven-step process given in *Liber-One*. Rather than treat a completely separate sequence of operations for each Route, we have simply amended Step-3 and Step-4 to include any applicable route, including either "Route-1" (RR-SP) or "Route-2" (AR-SP). SOP-2C is written to make Step-3 and Step-4 specific to each Route, but the general session-style of all systematic processing may operate as a standard procedure for all of *Grade-IV*.

A Seeker should be encouraged to provide answers and responses freely. They are working to change their mind about considerations and agreements they have made about the way things are; and this is an *ability*, which therefore means it should not be enforced and it should not be invalidated. The end result is a Seeker that is better able to apply Will-Intention using Self-determination.The purpose is to increase a general certainty toward ability and not an emphasis on only how something applies to specific situations or events. The reasoning and analytical discovery concerning such events and memories are up to the Seeker to work out; the Pilot is only offering the safety net and tools by which this "experience" may be properly processed.

Systematic processing is effective when it can operate beyond mere "conversation." The Seeker does not need more fragmentary conversation in their life; the real conversation is already taking place in the circuitry of their own mind—and it is this very activity that we must get under the Seeker's control again. All communication present during the session will have an effect on the Seeker's presence in the session, their certainty to contact the physical universe and their willingness to communicate with any terminals. Actualization increases as the realizations begin to occur and in the process, a Seeker discovers their own inherent ability to control and manage as Self.

Step-1 for any *Professional Piloting Procedure* is the establishment of *presence*, which is to say that a "flight session" is in existence and that at least an initial level of communication has been achieved. We make certain that we have a person there in contact with us, that we are communicating with a living terminal and they are at least present enough in space-time to be in session. The next step is logically to make sure they are in session and hold their attention with an increased level of communication and control—and specifically communication and control over the physical body. It is important to get the Seeker's attention focused on the command lines that target operation of the body and their orientation in present space-time before you applying additional Routes.

In more metaphoric terms of our application: the early control of the session (and the first steps of operating procedure) is similar to the basic "take off" practices of a flight. At Step-1 we have a basic "check-in" process involving greeting, identification and then "welcomes" and other niceties to establish communication and contact (boarding). Then, in Step-2 we *know* we have a Seeker on board and can proceed to "take off" with the session. Communication and presence are required, then established more strongly as the control and responsibility of the session is assumed fully by the Pilot.

Technically, Step-3 is Processing/Maneuvers and it is coupled with Step-4. In essence, Step-3 and Step-4 are all that is defined by each individual Route. These are then performed back and forth in succession until whatever channel being treated is cleared (Step-5) and the new realizations are discovered (Step-6) at which time the Pilot can "land"/end the session (Step-7) or bring the Seeker through additional Routes.

The Pilot makes their own assessment notes regarding the session and condition of the Seeker. It is very important that assessments are not ever articulated as an "evaluation" to the Seeker. The Pilot is not to *enforce* what the Seeker needs to know from the processes; the Pilot is only to professionally provide the processes. A Pilot is educated and earns more certainty about Systemology. They receive knowledge—advanced foreknowledge—regarding targeted realizations that processing is meant to provide within our systemology as taught within our literature and at our workshops and conferences. In essence, the Pilot is already given the answer key—whether or not they have actually been processed to achieve the information as a genuine "realization"—but it is otherwise cheating the Seeker from the benefit of actually arriving at the proper realizations from the processing directly, if the Pilot keeps cutting into the flow with what everything actually *is*.

At different stages of actualization the same type of processing will actually yield different results and so each point must be treated as its own unit of space-time because the Seeker's condition will be in a constant state of movement—if processed correctly—and the considerations on something at one moment are likely to change. We would also expect a Seeker to change in some ways between sessions as a result of any outside/environmental encounters they will have with the world-at-large.

As *Awareness* increases, the reality on things increases; the ability to confront or recall various things or communicate on various channels also increases. In fact, the more a Seeker is processed, the more there is to process; and hence we find upper-level techniques necessary at higher Grades in order to satisfy the newer levels of realization that are achieved. We are, of course, working our way to Infinity—though we we settle for an Actualized Alpha-Spirit. Along the way, the Seeker is finding new terminals, circuits and facets for consideration; aspects that were not in the reach of reality for them only just previously.

A phenomenon may take place whereby something may seem unreachable, hidden or a complete mystery at the lower levels of processing, but then suddenly after breaking through a former barrier, a new ledge is reached and things are within accessibility that formerly were not. The Seeker is able to face up, confront and take responsibility for more and more.

There is another side to this phenomenon whereby some "thing" or aspect will at first be treated as though it is very significant and heavily charged at one level of consideration, but then as an individual is able to increase their willingness and ability, these matters seem less important than before. It is evident in these situations that the Seeker has "risen above" the fixed considerations of a former belief or the former associations attached to any line. In brief: at different levels of processing, different facets are confronted and faced and other facets and circuits are no longer a part of the reactive-response mechanisms.

The highest understanding and application of communication in *NexGen Systemology* is, quite literally, how it relates to the Standard Model—meaning the systematic interactions of all *Life, the Universe and Everything* all the way up to Infinity. We are using techniques that demonstrate the communication of energies between all systems—including all personal systems, such as the "Mind" and its interactions with the physiology controlling the genetic vehicle and other interactions with the physical universe. This all contributes to what we call "experience"—what we are able to experience and how we are going to treat the experience of an *is*. Personal *Awareness* increases with understanding what we *are* willing to experience, know or do. Ultimately this leads to the realization that these considerations will define, more importantly, what we are willing to *be*.

Systematic processing reveals how fixed beliefs are generally not facts about the world but simply an agreement to associative knowledge that is programmed—leading naturally to the set up of programmed tendencies and emotional responses that are encoded. A person will often speak about "thinking for themselves" or "having their own opinion" or "getting their way" or some other screaming call for subjectivity—yet too often these tendencies have also been strongly impressed, and the individual is just reacting to times of stress or confusion. They are no more in control of having their opinion when they believe they have their own opinion than when they are conditioned to lash out demanding to have their own opinion. All of these are programmed tendencies.

Everything that the individual or Seeker is actually seeking in their existence and in the games that are played out as Life is simply a means of getting back to the original state that has been detoured from before. For example, the willingness to succeed, be certain of Self, to act pointedly and be "self-driven"; these are all tendencies we admire in those particular individuals that simply do not appear to be as "run down" as the rest of society. Systematic processing is intended to repair reduction in *Awareness* that a Seeker has incurred over the course of their life (or lives) and thereby improve their own proper handling of control and communication with others.

Systematic processing brings out the "tendencies" and "characteristics" that are attached to the artificial identities that Self has accepted as "personality." Unfortunately, these personalities, so acutely developed and nurtured, suddenly become vehicles of our own entrapment, all of which reinforce a restriction to freedom of consideration and willingness that must be made to fit into some or another prescribed "character package." Over the course of a lifetime an individual appears to identify Self more and more solidly with the physical body—and when improperly managed, this too becomes a source of fragmentation.

A Pilot will find that too often in everyday life an individual is unwilling to throw out the stability that they have used for so long to hold up their perception of reality. When a Seeker is processed and comes to a new realization or has discharged a heavily laden imprint from a line of communication, there is a sense that they have still lost something that has been familiar to them. Former generations still alive among us have gotten along for so much of their lives operating at a certain state or condition that to think of things being in any other way than how they have seemed for so long would, in their own mind and according to their own considerations, be more devastating in itself than the attainment of any truer realization of life. In short: they are satisfied with the lies they have grown comfortable with. They prefer the more familiar state of misery that they have agreed to rather than face the fact that they did not have to suffer for an entire lifetime and could have actually reached these new vistas of knowing and being at any point along the way—had they simply set their attentions on it.

:: 2 ::
UNDERSTANDING PILOTED SYSTEMOLOGY
OPERATING PROCEDURE 2-C

Preliminary steps for a piloted systematic processing session are described throughout the present manual.

(*SOP-2C*) (*RR-SP-1 Version*)

Step-1 : "Presence" 1 : "to lead off; accompany; to
  \ first point of contact impose a process or path"
  \ basic communication

Step-2 : "Communication & Control" 2 : "to begin; start; fasten/
  \ increased communication hold level"
  \ beingness in session as Self

These steps being met, the next two steps would represent whatever actual "processing" technique or "Route" is being used, but we may generalize it as a "STEM" formula:

Step-3 : "Systematic Processing" (Maneuvers Part-A)
  \ orientation point in space-time (ST)
  \ attention on the line

Step-4 : "Systematic Processing" (Maneuvers Part-B)
  \ management of energy and matter (EM)
  \ intention on the line

These two steps apply to each effective Route of systematic processing. The basic pattern is the same: 3) getting attention on the line; 4) putting intention on the line. Each of the Routes follows this formula, and each is emphasized in one of the manuals. The first two routes are established in former texts as follows:

	Route-1 "RR" (*Liber-One*)	Route-2 "AR" (*Liber-2B*)
Step-3 :	\ Resurface	\ Recall
Step-4 :	\ Reduce Charge	\ Analyze

In each of the Routes, there is a direction of attention by the Pilot, which is a query to bring something about or cause the effect of getting the Seeker in touch with a particular current. Once a "subject" is the focus of attention—or a point/spot/object in space has been identified—then the action or Will-intention may be put on that line of attention and the communication or energetic flow ensues.

A Pilot assists the Seeker in personal processing by using a systematic use of communication. The Pilot puts out a query on the line (even if it is in the form of a command) and the Seeker generates an answer and responds (even if it is only the physical act of completing a basic command). A Pilot is not supposed to be "answering questions" for the Seeker. This is not a game of "tell me what's wrong with me." A Pilot simply directs the Seeker's attention and then puts intention on the line in lieu of the Seeker directing the command. In either case the command is put forth and a process ensues. It is still up to the Seeker to identify the content of their own "Mind" and respond to the questions/commands.

The flow necessary to generate the realizations for effective systemological work is as follows:

    a) the Pilot selectively directs attention with a "what is it __"-type flow; and

    b) the Seeker processes to generate the "it is a __"-type resulting answer.

If at any time the direction of flow on this basic fundamental is reversed, the entire benefit of systematic processing is easily nullified. The opposite flow of directed attention is called "education"—and it is not one of the techniques used in a systematic processing session; save it for the classroom. Even when an individual is confused about some vocabulary or semantics, they should be directed to discover the answer in one of our books, or a dictionary that is kept available in the room and retrieve the information from a glossary.

For example, a Seeker says they don't understand a particular word (and we are referring to specifically the meaning of a "word" and not necessarily "the point of a process"), then the Pilot can say, "okay, let's look that up and find out together." And then they are directed to the book— or if they have difficulty with this, the Pilot can find the page in a book or a dictionary where the definition is stated; but make sure the Seeker is reading it for themselves if they are able. The point here being to always work with whatever the Seeker *is* able to do, making sure not to invalidate their potential gains by pushing them past the threshold or reinforcing what they are unable to do or unwilling to reach for in their current state.

Another important feature of systematic processing is the "demonstration," which is done to assist a true understanding of some concept. A "demonstration kit" (similar to an objective processing kit, such as the

"*Bell, Book & Candle*") contains various small items, trinkets, paperclips, marker stones, game tokens, bits of string, &tc. which may be used to demonstrate or model a particular concept or systematic function. This is exceptionally useful when you can actually get a Seeker to demonstrate their own understanding of something. Whatever level of understanding a Seeker is at, a Pilot must simply acknowledge and not "push" anything.

Once willingness and determinism has been returned to a Seeker through processing, the ability to "change the mind" and its considerations at will increases and incorporation of new information or education is actually of some benefit, because the Seeker is in a position to actually *do* something with the information. To do otherwise or follow a different course of actions is to place something that is already misunderstood even further out of reach; and it is has been discovered that many traditions and paths in the past have done just that.

Introducing heavy education onto someone lowers their levels of *Awareness* when improperly handled. When someone is constantly telling you "it is __; this is __; that is __" a lot of your attention is being directed or determined outside of your Will-Intention. And the significances of the *is* always belongs to someone else; on their word or authority. However, when someone asks you "what is __," suddenly you are able to engage personal processes to generate answers and you are able to self-determine the creation of a reality.

Of course, in the world-at-large we find a lot of give-and-take concerning these types of flows; though it will be noticed that certain individuals are predominantly projecting an outflow and certain individuals are predominantly receiving inflows; and the key to balancing this acrobatic act is to return control of attention and intention back to the Seeker—allowing them to determine where to place their attention and what intention to put on the line. The Seeker is determining the significances of things for themselves; and that is the essence of a **consideration**. Systematic processing at *Grade-IV* concerns questions that have "open answers" or wide ranges of consideration as opposed to simply prompting for "yes/no." There is a time and purpose for such "yes"/"no" types of assessment, but *Systemology Operating Procedure 2-C* does not incorporate these methods directly.

Before introducing any additional Routes that apply to *SOP-2C*, the remaining steps are listed below regarding a completed session (regardless of the Routes taken). This revises a seven-step basic format of a former Systemological Procedure presented in "*The Tablets of Destiny*" manual.

Step-5 : "Clearing the Channel"
  \ purify; cleanse; clear away
  \ handling the energy flow or circuit

Step-6 : "Realizations"
  \ beingness; to become; to arrive at; to ascend
  \ spiritual rehabilitation; increase in Self-determinism

Step-7 : "Landing Procedures"
  \ attainment of destination; actualization of more ideal state
  \ End of Session

Where "Route-1" is generally referred to as "emotional processing" or "imprint processing" and "Route-2" is often considered "thought processing" or "deprogramming," it is actually quite difficult to limit the function of any route to only one or another type of defragmentation results. The irony continues when we view "Route-3" as "communication processing" or "control processing" when such attributes must always be present in a session for any Route to function. It should thus be considered that these are merely the "emphasis" of a Route.

Internal communication between Self and Self, and those between Self and the "Mind-Systems" linking Self to *beta-existence* and control of a genetic vehicle, is an actualization of the first "sphere of existence"[*] and the reach of the Alpha-Spirit to communicate as Self. Self is always the spiritual energy source for whatever is communicated and experienced as its universe or reality. The Mind assigns considerations to particles and waves as forms and these are thereafter treated with some significance and meaning for experience as beta existence.

Communication with others in our immediate proximity constitutes the solidity of the second "sphere of existence" and the first circle of reach or influence that expands from a consideration of Self as an epicenter of potential reach. This expands through various spheres, levels, veils or thresholds, all the way back to the *Gateways of Infinity*. The second systematic "sphere of existence" that we communicate an energetic exchange with is primarily our "home" and domestic life; perhaps also our immediate family and friends—essentially whatever an individual keeps closest in "reach" or "around the house" to maintain the sense of Self as a physical being incarnate and connected.

Survival as Self and the assurance of preserving a Home in a society requires extending reach beyond Self and beyond Home and immediate

---

[*] Materials regarding "Spheres of Existence" are included in *Crystal Clear* (*Liber-2B*); also collected within *The Systemology Handbook* omnibus anthology.

family and close friends and actually engage a reach toward the greater world-at-large, but most specifically in Groups. And by this, we do not mean exclusively one group or identity-title versus another. A Seeker is considered part of many groups or demographics in society; so in essence we could either refer to the third "sphere of existence" as Groups or as Societies. The organization and function of Systemology or Mardukite Zuism operates on the third "sphere of existence" as an intermediary between Home/Family (2) and All Humanity (4).

Therefore, when we refer to "Route-3" as "communication processing," we mean very specifically processing the imprinting and fragmentation encoded or programmed as "communication"—and this is not, of course, restricted only to communications which have been spoken or written, but any activity or motion or event or exchange that may be observed. In theory, the same events or channels could be treated by any one or another of the Routes; however, each has a particular emphasis which may be applied for more effective results than another. All are equally effective when operated for their ideal level of use.

	Route-3 "2C" (*Liber-2C*)[*]	Route-0 "AT" (*Liber-3D*)[‡]
Step-3 :	\ Contact	\ Imagine
Step-4 :	\ Communicate	\ Create It

There are then a total of four possible "Routes" composing an infinite number of potential techniques that may be applied within the structure of *Systemology Operating Procedure 2-C*. Since *Analytical Recall* (*Kenostic Processing*) and *R&R* techniques are discussed in previous texts, our present emphasis for *SOP-2C* is "Route-3"—which is to say, "communication processing" or "operative processing."

Some terminals and circuits that seem inaccessible at one level of processing or actualization are suddenly within reach from a higher level of realization. For this reason many of the processes are used regularly as "standard" procedure; they effectively apply to whatever level a Seeker is at in their progress. It is not the processes themselves that are elevating an individual to specific levels. They work systematically to provide the most effective general increase in actualization and when a process is applied again on a new terminal from a new POV and range of considerations, it will not be just the same process being run again.

Once control and communication are established in a session with preli-

---

[*]   Included in this present anthology manual.

[‡]   The designation for "The Imaginomicon" (also contained in this anthology).

minary processes, it is customary to use basic recall commands to refocus and concentrate the Seeker's attention onto the session and onto the communication line with Pilot. This is done at the beginning of each session as a basic standard practice before any additional more intensive Routes or exercises are employed. It requires the ability to "recall" imagery in the mind—at least what the Seeker is willing to reach on for their level of development. This also requires the ability to contact the "terminals" as they are carried with us as experience—which has been described previously in this text. Then, finally, it requires the ability to "confront" or "face-up to" the mental images of these individuals that are attached to the other ends of the circuits of experience running in our Mind.

With "communication processing" a Seeker is given the opportunity to confront and face up to the interactions with individuals and the environment without being in direct emotional restimulation and without making programmed effects on the Seeker (from contact with the line) more solid. The Seeker gradually regains ability to face these terminals without inhibition and without experiencing distortion/turbulence on the line.

As a preliminary to higher grades and Route-0 handling of mental imagery described in a forthcoming manual. It may be said that whatever a person is not willing to handle or reach for; whatever they are not willing to know or what has not been answered or responded to; whatever blackness and distortions appear in what is seen or treated in the mind—all of this could be said to be facets of "the primary thing we cannot see beyond." Whatever that "thing" is, it has become a mystery and it has been enshrouded by layers and layers of other erroneous fragmentation.

To run "Route-3" processes, a Seeker must be willing and able to face the terminal at the end of the channel; see it clearly and recall activities that took place—the energy flows concerning that terminal at that instance. Another version of these processes involves "imagining" events and interactions that have not actually taken place between terminals, but of which by running through them as a mental exercise, provides greater considerations on events that *have* actually taken place.

We generally consider the blackness of a mystery or the backside of an individual as the opposite of knowing something or getting a response (or a question answered). When attention is directed onto the mystery, the unknown, the unanswered question and the beingness that is not acknowledged, we are often looking at blackness, emptiness and in the case of live terminals, we tend to "look away from" or divert our attention to another terminal or else create one in our Mind in lieu of actually facing or treating them in the physical universe. In one practical exercise, the backside of someone is imagined a mystery and the front side is an answer.

The original purpose of "Route-1" was to handle various "physiological pings" or "somatic responses" that emerge automatically if wired as a reactive mechanism in a circuit. These naturally affect thought-flow and generate into thought-forms that go beyond control of the creator (the Seeker). A Pilot must become accustomed to emotion if they are going to handle processing that has the ability to incite it. Even more likely is an encounter with "pings" that trigger a Seeker's discomfort—and therefore affect their willingness to continue working on a certain line or stay in session altogether.

A Pilot can generally determine a Seeker's charges on a line or their level of communication and control with any terminal based on their willingness or ability to literally be responsible for the reactive-response "pings" that kick up when "facing that direction." How can an individual be "free" when their considerations and willingness to reach are so thoroughly tied to how this, that and the other is "*making* them feel"? Or if they are to only agree with what they "like"—how easily could this be controlled.

An individual is then as well off mentally and spiritually as they are able to properly manage and handle the energy and matter of present space-time by knowingly maintaining true relationships or communication with these "things" in present space-time. Most fragmented individuals are "hung up on the past"—treating the energy and matter in present space-time as though it is still happening at some other point on the timeline. This is a direct contradiction to the state of Self-Honesty.

Whenever the Self reaches—whether in the natural state of the Alpha-Spirit extending its consciousness as arms in front of it to feel around in the emptiness, or whether putting out a line of attention to contact another individual just to know they exist—the individual is putting out a query or request for answers, and awaits the response. The human condition may be said to be the result of a ceaseless "quest for answers" that has resulted in the experience of the most lowest-level condensation of consideration for potentiality of existence. It is quite clear that the Mind-Systems are occupied with resolving the inflowing information with the considerations otherwise programmed and encoded. And when approached with an experience or the confrontation of some object or mental image, communication ensues.

When an individual puts out their attention—extends their reach—information is returned on a circuit as a communication flow. To make sense of this, an individual:

1.) searches their own databanks of experience for an answer/response;

   (*and failing to receive this...*)

2.) inquires or requests answer/response (communication) from another;

   (*and failing to receive this...*)

3.) observes others and/or the environment for other cues/information; or

   (*the first method used by an Actualized Technician...*)

0.) experiences direct "**gnosis**" or other actualized realizations internally.

Of course, true gnosis would require having cleared the channels (used to receive such data) of fragmentary debris or erroneously programmed limitations on consideration or any other reactive 'pings' that would otherwise inhibit the reception of total understanding. This is the component—the practice of defragmentation—that is too often missed by other forms of "enlightenment," which can in themselves become just another type of trapping for the more intellectual or mystically inclined when operated outside of Self-Honesty. We have found that those who are formerly so ingrained into these methods and doctrines as an endpoint have actually had difficulty in extending their reach to any higher *Grades* in our Systemology.

While there is *no* reason for us *not* to encourage the study of ancient esoterica and the work developed over the past 6,000 years—which is revealed quite adamantly in *Grade-I* and *Grade-II* material—it should be noted in Self-Honesty that magicians and priestesses, however much enlightened they may be within their own paradigms, run the risk of being entrapped in their systems by actively imposing higher-level barriers on themselves than the average human would even understand. In this respect, lower *Grades* always seem more dangerous than the upper-level work, due to the likelihood of misuse of such material—whereas most upper-level work is so refined and esoteric that it protects itself by being essentially "not useful" to those unprepared to understand it; it's functional meaning is not properly communicated to an individual that has no reality on a particular channel.

"Circuit-0" is an energy flow treated as *Alpha Defragmentation*, which is to say the condition of Self as "Actualized Technician" (A.T.) or "Wizard" consciously operating from "exterior" to *beta-existence*. This does not mean that the individual is "out of touch" with the Physical Universe— on the contrary, they are operating the human condition from a point that is outside the consideration that they are stuck *inside* "being" human.

We limit added discussion and commentary in a processing session because of how "fragmenting" and aberrative most human communication is. This is the very type of fragmentation **processed out** in Route-3. All of the "got to" "ought to" "should" "shouldn't" "must" "must not" statements compound into a certain pattern of thoughts, associative 'pings' and empty communications with a Mystery. All of these communications that have been stored up as "experience" over the course of our lives are imprinted and will become challenges against our ability to experience free range of consideration, conception, thought and creation.

:: 3 ::
INTRODUCING "ROUTE-3"
COMMUNICATION PROCESSING FOR SOP-2C

Can you recall a time when you told someone something? Can you recall a time when someone told you something? How about when someone else was talking to another or a group? Can you recall a time when you told yourself something with intention?

In each of these instances—What was said? How did the communication make you feel? What did you see around you at the time? How does that communication cause you to see the world differently? How do you feel about that communication now?

All forms of contact with the world outside is a form of communication; and systematically these communications are linked to the energy and circuits taking place "within us"—*interior* to the Mind-System. All external sensory data must be received and processed as Self to have any kind of registry as real—and how clear are these channels dictating the relay and reality of this "experience"?

The same rules of communication taking place in session between the Pilot and Seeker (as terminals) are the same fundamentals of "communication processing" when a Seeker has set up lines of communication (or been enforced to put attention on a line) in their life and been subject to an inflow or outflow that they are now responsible for "carrying around as experience."

The function of systematic processing is not actual erasure or elimination of a Seeker's memory. In fact, it has been demonstrated that the type of exercises we employ may actually contribute to improved abilities of recall and analytical memory. This actually happens because an individual's willingness to reach even within themselves (and the circuits already existent) increases; they find themselves with more free range access to their own "Mind-System" than they did before.

We can assume that the development of an RCC or *Reactive Control Center* (inherently part of the ZU-line communicated between Self and a genetic body) is likely the product of survival experiences early on the cellular line and of which collected its own energies and information centers to communicate between various nerves and systems that later developed as an organism extended its reach further and further from one cell.

An organism develops response-reaction mechanistic systems during encounters with various barriers and other material interactions of the Physical Universe. These mechanisms begin to define the very **parameters** of what the organism is willing to *be, know* or *do.* Some mechanisms of the genetic vehicle are not only the result of *this* lifetime, but of which have been inherited along the "genetic line" on which the physical body evolved from an organic being. This is, of course, separate from "past lives" that Self would associate with its own personal identity, since it is not likely to have controlled a body in the past that is on the exact same genetic line as the current one; but we have encountered some cases where, for example, a woman's daughter born in this lifetime was actually her own mother in a former lifetime—in that they shared an opposite role to one another in a former period on the timeline.*

The machinery set up along the evolutionary line—which we refer to as the RCC at (2.0) on the Standard Model/Zu-Line—is still very active in the human condition. The issue is not that it exists; but that Awareness as Self is too often reduced to the consideration that the Self is operating as a "body" and not even as a "Mind" and especially not in realization of being a "Spirit" commanding the other two systems. Information is stored below the surface of the RCC and given heavy emotional charges to keep it there, therefore barring an individual with free access to the energy it contains. It is not the energy within the imprint or mass that an individual is seeking to reclaim, because inflow from source is unlimited; it is actually the "blockage" that needs to be freed so new incoming energy is in full circulation—and a lifeform can actually reach toward its own continuation.

Objective processing is also "communication," providing increase of *Awareness* and presence by establishing a realization that in the physical universe—concerning matter and "need to know about" compulsions—the answer *is* simply the answer, or rather that the question *is* the answer, but its sometimes treated as the "other side of" because it must be "hidden." Yet, things are not hidden; individuals hide—they hide themselves from the truth and reinforce everything they "don't want to know about" as opposed to that which they are willing to reach toward—and quite literally, "know about."

Humans—by programming or agreement—are convinced that continued existence from one day to the next is something to *do,* meaning: a "problem" to be solved—because life has to serve a purpose and to serve as purpose is to solve a problem. So, we have resolved ourselves to the fact

---

* The systemology of "past lives" is handled at higher *Grades* of work with our structured paradigm.

that in order for Self to have its own purpose and be its own reason, it must have "problems" to solve. But there are many orders or levels of problems that could be solved. The only issue is when the Alpha-Spirit is so enamored with the Physical Universe and fixed on the association of a physical body that the primary "problem of life" remains at a lower order of reasoning. Since every day is a new problem to solve, new reasoning and new answers are constantly being sought to erroneous questions and the repeated quest for a truth that has all been beaten over their head time and time again and yet still they feel it is something that they must "go looking" for. There is a small semantic irony in referring to a systemologist as a "Seeker" until they reassign enough of their consideration to be an Actualized Technician (A.T. /"Wizard").

The lower an individual is considered on the emotional range of the *Beta-Awareness Scale*, the more literal or solid we would expect them to take words. Below (1.0) on the Standard Model, words have the ability to inflow on someone as solidly as throwing a ball at them. Yet, they are only words—and here we mean specifically "words" and "language" and "images" and any basic form of communication regardless of the intention behind it. At (1.0) on the Standard Model, "association" includes "all things as all things" as all "things" reach closer a state of inert continuity (0.0)—and where everything is as equally solid and as equally significant as everything else, which is exactly the way in which the RCC processes data.

One of the primary qualities of personal fragmentation is the misappropriation of associated identification; and while this seems like some fancy word play, we are talking about *facets* of *imprints*, where dissimilar aspects of existence are suddenly encoded together. At one level, this happens with painful and traumatic experiences with others and the environment—and again, potentially even with ourselves. At another level, this happens when we feel experiences of loss or strong invalidation— the sense that others have taken something from us, or that the cycles-of-action taking place in the environment are somehow "unfair." This all leads to greater and greater misunderstanding—and if we have no solid *ledge* to stand on to *know*, where does that leave us?

Symbols are often used in the place of actual "things" during communication—the exception being "objective processing" but that is when we realized something else: those "things" are also symbols. Everything that we can treat as a "thing" is a symbol at its own level or gradient. This creates an entire scale, then, concerning what a symbol can actually be— since it appears that it is the symbol that is being communicated as an energy pattern and not actual "things." These symbols are simply treated as "real things."

Everything that is transmitted on the Zu-line or a line or flow is a "symbol"—the pattern form by which we recognize it for what it is. How else can we determine the nature of one type of wave flow or, dare we say "sensation," from another? We must be inherently able to identify differences in the energy flows and then assign significance and meaning to it by our consideration. The end result is "our concept" or "reality" *on* whatever line we are treating. But the meaning of symbols may be altered or programmed. And in the absence of true *knowing*, a "symbol" is a poor substitute.

Various processes repair a Seeker's communication with the Physical Universe, but these are meant to focus attention on the answers simply being the answer or specifically that "the thing *is* the thing" and has no other significance or emotionally encoded reactivity, &tc. This seems basic and yet if a Seeker is unable to do this in their handling of the Physical Universe (in objective processing) the same practices will be implemented when handling control and power of their own personal identity continuum. Another purpose behind objective processing is resolution of any considerations that past memories should have any hold over the Seeker, that the present is too unsafe to confront and manage, and that the future is some unknown Mystery that is inherently dangerous. It may or may not be surprising to some individuals just how many of their programmed and encoded considerations of *Life, the Universe and Everything* have essentially led them to be trapped within these very conclusions.

Creative ability is an *Alpha* quality. The willingness to create is to make something real and solid as an absence of nothingness—including points in space. The willingness to create also means the ability to freely create again and again. When a Seeker realizes that they are not "losing" anything by giving up the hold on heavily charged images and fragments— because they can recreate anything at Will—than they will feel more certain in maintaining control and responsibility of the mental images.[*]

An individual is responsible for the creation of and reaction to all activity taking place on the Zu-line (personal identity continuum). Emotional charge present on the line of any circuit is in many ways reinforced by a resistance to loss; the idea that another consideration would somehow dissolve our existing "beliefs" is treated as a loss. This only comes from a

---

[*] See the section: "*The Imaginomicon: Liber-3D.*"

consideration that *Self* is somehow unable to duplicate creation of any such things again. Willingness for an individual to create and communicate (and even control a piloted session) is dependent on the responsibility, *Awareness* and ability to carry a source particle, bit or thought to its receipt-effect point.

The Alpha-Spirit learns very early in its existence that to be a source of creation or communication is to be the generator of an energetic effect. Then we learn, in the presence of others, that our creations and communications have an effect on others and the solidity of these things somehow increases. These are exactly the type of flows of energy that we treat as "circuits" for "Route-3" techniques.

The Nothingness does not appear to communicate (any more than than the walls and solids of inert physical existence communicate) and so the Alpha-Spirit develops its reach, willingness and communications in the direction of "somethingness." Of course as more and more of these "somethings" develop and as more beings begin to create "somethings" to show off to others, the energy becomes more and more compressed and solid and the remnants of these creations filter down into the lower-energy environments and existences of shared agreement. These considerations all become more and more solid as they are concentrated at these lower-levels of existence. They begin to act as walls to considerations at those lower-levels and if the sense of *Self* is placed within them as a POV, those considerations actually do become as solid as walls are experienced at the continuity level of the Physical Universe.

Each of these "levels" of existence have been treated as dimensions, layers, veils, gateways and so on, in previous Grades of instruction based on the cultural or mystical context where they appeared. The same "seven-plus-one" levels that we find plotted on the Standard Model and the Zu-line do, in many respects, align with lore of the Babylonian StarGate system that is described in *Grade-II*.[*] Even the mystics, priests, priestesses and magicians of the Ancient Mystery School treated these zones as some type of barrier or gateway—apparently fixed in place by some original group of Alpha-Spirits that participated in cosmic ordering of the Physical Universe. Later, mystical traditions created religions and alchemical beliefs regarding sevenfold lore of planets, colors, notes of music and chakras, &tc.

The *Graded* system within our paradigm also follows the conception giv-

---

[*]   See the *Grade-II* materials, the entire collection of which is available in a hardcover Master Edition omnibus anthology titled: "*Necronomicon: The Complete Anunnaki Legacy*" by Joshua Free (2020 Edition).

en of seven-plus-one levels toward total *Actualized Awareness* as *Self* realized as *Alpha-Spirit* and hence the uppermost reach of an "Actualized Technician" during this lifetime, when they are freed from all the trappings that result from being entangled to fixed lower POV—when the Seeker was less and less in phase with Self as Alpha-Spirit.

The final steps of *SOP-2C*, regardless of the Route taken, regard clearing the channel (or line-circuit of communication) and allowing the Seeker an opportunity to arrive at new levels of realization.

Whatever you wish to call them: realizations, awakenings, cognitions, true gnosis, deep insights, or increased actualization—these are all indicators of a fully completed process or that a communication line-circuit is defragmented. It is important for the Pilot to acknowledge the forward progress a Seeker makes on the *Pathway* without invalidating what they have not yet realized and without conditioning the Seeker to become dependent on validation from others to determine their successes or achievement of a new realization. The realization is for them to make—and whatever is true for them at that moment *is* what is true for them at that moment, and any other impression or enforcement of another POV is going to be received as an invalidation.

We assume that the Seeker has spent a lot of their time experiencing existence outside of their own true viewpoint as an Alpha-Spirit. And, of course, it is the ability of the Alpha-Spirit to project or reach to any point at Will, but if they are suddenly stuck at some lower-level of consideration believing they are trapped in the barriers that have been imposed at those levels, then they are no longer freely operating as *Self-determined*.

There are two main categories of intention that exist on the flow of a circuit with a terminal:

> a) the insistence of; a reach toward; and

> b) the protest against; a withdrawal from.

It is these two categories that tend to form into functions of an automated mechanism, especially if not acknowledged. Response-reactions can be automated because a system works in the direction of greatest efficiency. Of course, as soon as these functions become automatic, and the individual has forgotten this agreement, responsibility and control are misplaced.

Basic processing commands that apply to a **dichotomy** on these circuits, differentiating considerations of what a Seeker would reject/protest or accept. For example, the Seeker has experienced communications where they were "enforced" or "had to have *x*" or were "prevented from having *x*" or has "had *x* imposed" on them or an "outright denial of *x*" &tc. &tc. This will come out of considerations concerning:

a) With what might you protest? *-or-* With what might you reject?

b) With what might you agree? *-or-* With what might you find acceptable? *-or-* What would you accept?

In practice of actual processing, these specific commands would be used alternately from (a) to (b) to see if there is a heavily charged emotional reaction with any terminal, or if the analytical treatment of this will essentially free up the ideas that they are holding on strongly to, and if necessary—once a terminal has been identified—worked on via multiple routes to make certain that the emotional charge on the line (sadness, anger, frustration, pains, pings, &tc.) have been properly desensitized (literally "discharged").

Rejecting, blocking or persisting—anything other than a free-flow of energy—on channel is the first steps toward making something undesirable more "real" or "solid" on that line unknowingly. The masses that build up continue to receive a steady flow of energy, but since it is not passing through, it creates turbulence on that channel and creates a disturbance in the Self-Honest experience of existence for the Alpha-Spirit. When barriers and restrictions are encountered—including no response—you can actually see an individual's "mood" or *beta-Awareness* level decline as they enter increasingly lower states of consideration as Self. We would expect a person to be very hung up on any circuit that it has had this kind of relationship with for a long period of time.

Primary considerations for any turbulent circuit—or which a communication has not been properly acknowledged or answered:

What were you intending to create/effect/communicate?

Who were you intending the communication for as a receipt-point?

What mechanisms are you now operating in order to continue this communication so compulsively?

A Pilot may not be able to ask a Seeker the third question directly. Therefore, the last part is simply a consideration of what the resulting realization should be once relevant information or facets of specific events are accounted for and run through in "recall" a few times. Some additional ways in which we may pose considerations in language:

What are you rejecting/protesting against/insisting on?

How did you communicate that in the past?

How are you still communicating that now?

Who/what are you waiting on acknowledgment/response from?

"Route-3" is named so for two reasons: it is the third Route established (chronologically speaking) for *Professional Piloting Procedure*, and it involves identification of terminals and processing of three circuits of energy-flow related to that terminal. The purpose of this is to process *all* three energy flows that are related to a terminal, concept, event, idea, emotion, &tc.

Processing all three circuits to a terminal is far more effective than emphasizing, for example, *only* "what has happened *to* the Seeker." The other side of this is "what has the Seeker done?" But even that is only two circuits of energy; so, we balance this with another circuit—and that is "what the Seeker has observed another doing to others"; therein we have the third. Example:

Step-3 : Contact Terminal
\ example terminal : "*communication*"

Step-4 : Communications Monitored on Circuits to Terminal
\ Circuit-1 : "what could you *communicate* with?"
\ Circuit-2 : "what could *communicate* with you?"
\ Circuit-3 : "what could others *communicate* with?"

Although our example is a perfectly legitimate model, and one that it *is* actually effectively workable, this is a slightly confusing way to learn "Route-3"—here, "Communication Processing" is used for "*communication*" as a terminal. If this seems esoteric, the same example might be restated for example as: "what would be acceptable to communicate with?" or "what would you be willing to communicate with?" In this sense, "willingness" is essentially synonymous with what would be "considered acceptable"—meaning no heavy emotional charges or response-reactivity on that line. It does not necessarily mean that a Seeker must then "agree" with any other significance or sentiment attached to it.

"Willingness"—the word is used quite frequently to describe the range of consideration and personal ability that an individual has achieved—and we mean literally the willingness to confront or face some terminal, subject, live-form, &tc.; increasing the willingness to hold a reality—and even create reality—without becoming the effect of it, or subject to some mechanistic reactivity or associative conditions that restrict any other consideration.

Accumulated "experiences" and "agreements" along some channel are a cause of many lingering automatic "problems" and "pings" that may be restimulated into action by various facets and conditions. These begin to define and restrict a very specific range of what an individual will find acceptable to confront in their lives. How many times has an individual said that they "don't want to know" or "don't want to deal with" &tc. &tc. And over time they begin to give up their determinism and control of knowing and dealing or managing the energy flows on various channels of information and experience.

As an individual finds difficulty with maintaining control on certain parts of the body as they become more and more "out of communication" with them—meaning that they are rejecting or blocking a flow between the Self and that part of the body. It is easy to understand, systematically, how such improper handling of personal energy (attention and intention) can actually result in having energetic blockages on the channels with the body.

Communications of Self with Self is also a circuit, but do we not treat it as part of the "three" and therefore refer to it as Circuit-0. This information is treated specifically in later work regarding "Actualized Technician" (Wizard Grades) for which *Grade-IV* is a "bridge" to. In the case of "Route-3" practice, Circuit-0 would be "what has Self communicated to Self?" This is not absolutely necessary for *Grade-IV* processing work and should only be introduced if it will always be applied thereafter. Essentially, once a Pilot is using "Route-3" to treat systematic processes, than "Route-1" and "Route-2" would also require incorporating all three circuits in order to get the same effective results.

The following outlines standard practices of using "Route-3" (also logged as "SP-2C") for *Systemology Operating Procedure 2-C.*

 Step-3 : Contact Terminal
   \ terminal, live-form, belief/attitude, emotions/sensations

 Step-4 : Communications Monitored on Circuits to Terminal
   \ Circuit-1 : Self *to* others/terminal (*out-flow*)
   \ Circuit-2 : others/terminal *to* Self (*in-flow*)
   \ Circuit-3 : others/terminal *to* others/terminal (*cross-flow*)
 (*Opt.* AT)   \ Circuit-0 : Self *to* Self (*Alpha-flow* or "postulate")

It is a common mistake to focus only on events rather than the consideration, emotion or feelings attached to that channel. Isolated event should be run with "Route-3" only if it has just recently taken place, as a means to manage it better. Otherwise, trying to use SOP-2C to process "every time a tree branch hit you in the face" is not very productive; however, processing out energetic flows regarding times you experienced stinging pains in the face, times you caused others to experience stinging pains in the face and then also times when others caused another to experience stinging pains in the face... suddenly the idea of being at cause again over the sensations felt in the face becomes stronger. This applies to those incidents which later continue to carry heavy emotional charges that *make* us "*feel*" a certain way when a terminal or channel is active. These matters treated "outside of our control" are what require systematic processing to bring back under controlled communication by and as Self.

:: 4 ::
UNDERSTANDING "ROUTE-3"
COMMUNICATION PROCESSING AND SOP-2C

An individual can resume true authority of Self by undoing all considerations and agreements that inhibit this original and true actualized state of knowing and being. The ability to *be* as *Self*—actualized as an *Alpha Spirit* independent of sensations that continuously snap our *Awareness* into a physical vessel—is barred by inclinations that are not properly *Self-directed*, but are instead *other-determined* causes to whatever we are thinking and feeling at a given moment. With so many of these channels tied to some kind or another of an *encoded event* or *encoding event*, it is any wonder that so many individuals are convinced that they remain responsible and in control of the *genetic body*, *Mind-Systems* and *Alpha-Thought* of the *Spirit*.

One of the most effective efforts a Pilot or Seeker can do to assist another seeker (whether or not they are Piloted in their development) is to introduce them to the text of *Crystal Clear*. By allowing a Seeker to work through material within *Crystal Clear* <u>with</u> assistance of a *Professional Pilot*, the most efficient results can be accomplished *within* the sessions.

Certainly the ideas behind our method of progressive Self-Actualization, rehabilitation of Will-Intention, spiritual evolution toward Ascension as an independent Alpha-Spirit able to direct the course of its own knowing and being during this lifetime and thereafter... all of this is very familiar to a Seeker that has poured over stacks of dusty volumes on esoteric philosophy, participated in various mystical lodges of the supposedly enlightened, or otherwise have found themselves conducting various rituals, techniques, meditations, guided visualizations and prayer sessions... but we all know the extent to which the results are yielded. As stated in our materials leading the Seeker up to this point: "there is a magic behind the magic" and it is only in uncovering the true nature of *this*, that the Seeker will have any chance in actualizing Awareness as its Source.

Effects from systematic processing actually exceed results found in conventional forms of "New Thought" and mysticism that will leave Seekers either trapped within the confines of a rigidly structured system (too many barriers) or left to their own reverie and considerations of various "axioms" and "motivational statements" that clash with preexisting programming and encoded emotional reactivity that is far too ingrained to be washed away with a few moments of "light positive thinking."

Various practices and demonstrations of "Will" found throughout the esoteric underground, New Thought schools of thought and other theosophical, Rosicrucian, magical and hermetic revivals in modern times have all become noticeably only a "shadow" of their former positions in the development of *Homo Novus*—and while we certainly are not going to invalidate what they have had to offer for the preservation of human history (as explored in *Grade-I* and *Grade-II* material), we cannot rely—or otherwise place expectations—on what they offer, which exceeds the very understanding demonstrated to the most common denominator of its membership, and the caliber of teaching fed to an "outer circle."

An organization may develop around the words and works of a brilliant individual that *has* actually accomplished its ultimate goals—yet this may not be properly communicated objectively; and even if it is, we cannot be certain that a transmission of this information and its context is carried out properly thereafter, particularly by those charged as its scions, those with little, if no true, reality on the material they handle. Access to information or original source material is often controlled—and this too is demonstrated by those that use the information (first developed in order to "free the human condition") to effectively manifest the completely opposite result of further controlling and entrapping individuals.

Rituals and ceremonies were once conducted very powerfully—and still may be today—when they were practiced by priests, priestesses and magicians operating in a state of true Self-Honesty and a more perfect communication with the universe. In fact, there was once a time when you, as a more actualized Alpha Spirit, identified with an existence that was not nearly as concrete as this form of *beta-existence*, and which had not yet resorted to putting all of the control and communication of energy and matter on an "electrical wire," and so it was thus much more common for a person's considerations to direct this flow; they had not yet relied on an other-determined source to provide this control. This is just one example of higher-level considerations that result from defragmenting the channels.

As in any ritual, the environment of systematic processing sessions is deliberately created on several levels; not only limited to the physical preparations. There is a physical universe in which space of the session location is fixed—and this is just as representative as a microcosm of the greater physical universe extending in all directions as any magic circle. This becomes more evident when there is a flow of communication bridging the personal universes of both a Pilot and a Seeker, which then generates a shared universe between them, also set in phase with present space and time of the physical universe.

A beta-actualized Seeker should be able to recognize that the various terminals and solids in space are simply each a POV of the universe and have no other specific significances. If all is actually *one* at both the continuity of *zero*—or (0.0) on the Standard Model—and at Infinity, than we would expect that the true nature of everything is equal to everything else. Of course, these two points seem incredibly "hypothetical" as a point of knowing and being—so, everything in between is "charged" with some kind of intention or another. Systematic processing reduces this charge to something within reach of handling by consideration, even if it does not completely eliminate the charge. An individual is Piloted only to increase their own Self-determinism and willingness to reach for *Self-Honesty* and the certainty of knowing that there is *somewhere* still to *go* thereafter. Several Seekers that were able to reach significant plateaus of *Grade-IV* rather quickly, all seemed to share the same sentiment thereafter that the state of *beta-fragmentation* was actually still just one further rung on a longer ladder.

A Seeker should be brought to a point of realization that the *beta-existence* that they have had encounters with *is* a *beta-existence* and not the *only* POV-location for *Self*. We are not even, at this time, stating that a Seeker must emphasize "leaving"—stepping "out of"—the physical universe; however, the standard model marks the boundary of the physical universe as *beta-existence* at (4.0), which also coincides with the relay of the Mind-System (between Spirit and "Body") and the *fourth* "Sphere of Existence" (which is the "human condition" collectively as a "species"). This is mathematically established on all our models because this is the "existential limits" of the Mind-Systems specifically attached to current considerations of the "human genetic vehicle" as a condition or system of personal identity.

Appropriate realizations from "communication processing" include the very simple fact that being in good communication with the physical universe means recognizing it as the effect and not the cause. We can intuit how solids of the physical universe are some type of concentration or condensation of something taking place at another "level" but we should not assume that it carries any live communication or purposeful intention from some other source. If the energy-matter composing a solid that we identify as "baseball" is suddenly thrown at our face and causes us pain—why should we have any reason to assign that bit of solid as anything more or less than any other? Why should we suddenly accept receiving 'pings' whenever a baseball is present—even when used among others that we are merely observing?

These matters may seem trite at the time, and even when restimulated, because we justify it by telling ourselves we can live without baseball. But this does not negate validating the effect that circuits with that terminal still have over an individual. When we consider just how many of these types of 'pings' begin to compound about what we are or aren't willing to do (regardless if we would want to or actually will go and do them) then suddenly life seems more and more of a trap, out of our control and even sensations of the body start to operate in a "button-like" mechanistic nature. An individual's personal timeline is composed of a sequence of events and communications stored as mental images with emotional charge—information that could just as easily be filed away for retrieval at will (and the intentional creation of images at will); without them occurring as a reactive-response 'ping.'

> ping : a short, high pitched ring, chime or noise that alerts to the presence of something; in computer systems, a query sent on a network or line to another terminal in order to determine if there is a connection to it; in *NexGen Systemology*, the sudden somatic twinge or pain or discomfort that is felt as a sensation in the body when a particular terminal (lifeform, object, concept) is 'brought to Mind' or is contacted on a personal communication channel-circuit; the accompanying sensations and mental images that are experienced as an automatic-response to the presence of some channel or terminal.

Good communication realizations include: that the physical universe is an effect and not a cause; it is a medium for the experience of communication—but it does not communicate; it does not answer or respond and will provide no live communication to an actualized individual that has not first put the intention in place or decides to get the idea that it has responded. The effects are always their own answer. The universe *is*. To consider any more significance to it—outside of the properties of Cosmic Law—is to be thrown into chasms of a Mystery; one that will never be solved to satisfaction. Such thinking—and attachments to encoded or associative knowledge—is simply not the pathway that an actualized individual chooses in order to extend their reach back to the point where they have been all along. Position of the Alpha-Spirit never changes—only consideration that it has changed its location as an *Awareness-POV* is in flux.

When we refer to communication with universes, we mean Alpha-Spirit as Cause; the consideration of an Alpha-Spirit as a wave-crest or peak at (7.0) on the Standard Model, which is extending its reach out into the potentiality of ALL in generate and project its Alpha Thoughts as creations. Of course, once *Awareness* is fixed down in the *beta-existence* planes of the physical universe—*all* existence becomes an effect, but we are still in communication with all of it. The actualized individual all two-way communication with the physical universe as matter and energy; all of it is Self-generated—both the query and response. So, the answer to the physical universe *is* the answer, because it is an effect. All of the Mystery is a result of failure to properly realize and acknowledge this.

For example: the individual that had a pretty bad experience with the "baseball," the communication flow is still being assigned improperly, that the "baseball" is cause. This means the "hang-up" of encoded imprinting, is very literally a case of a person *waiting* for the "baseball" to now respond!—waiting for inert matter of the physical universe to suddenly make things right again as if it were a living terminal. This may sound incredibly "crazy"—but it is exactly what is taking place.

There are thought-exercises within the field of "New Thought" and application of *NexGen Systemology*, where a Seeker is prompted to establish a communication line with some terminal—living or non—and actually get the sense that a proper flow of two-way communication is taking place and that is a response comes from the other end. When practiced consciously and intentionally, there is no actual fear of fragmentation or distortion as a delusion. The Seeker *knows* that they are causing themselves to get the sense that they are receiving a response. They are not actually waiting for baseballs and uncomfortable arms and legs to *actually* speak—because we all know on our sanest days that such things simply do not happen. And yet, somehow, the use of creative abilities of imagination actually repair the lines of communication and the response-reaction mechanisms that have been "imagined" into place by the same functions.

"Route-3" targets emotionally encoded imprinting; those moments that carry a significant charge that later affects our experience of life. This is treated differently than learned or "programmed" knowledge that is based on other associative knowledge and stores of information maintained an analytical level. At such frequencies within the thought-range, the computation is perfect but only to the degree of the knowledge maintained as analytical memory. Information that carries an emotional charge is not treated analytically and is instead connected to circuitry of the reactive-response mechanisms developed from a deep laden emotionally encoding experience: the original experience which actually formed the imprint. Later experiences only deepen it by a reinforcement or validation that the reactive machinery is still operating automatically.

From the standpoint of continuity of the physical universe and observation of matter around us, the entire existence of the Zu-line, personal identity continuum and any control center relays along the way seem incredibly abstract. The entire array of matter in the physical universe is cemented abstraction—all of which must first be given significance as "form" in the Mind. At the level of experience observable as *beta-existence* and from the confines of an *Awareness* POV that is fixed to lowest-level energetic mechanistic understanding of the universe, much of what is relayed in *Grade-III* and *Grade-IV* material seems very abstract or metaphysical. But is it any more the case now than with the *Grade-I* and *Grade-II* materials, when one first takes up those? Our emphasis and vocabulary have shifted, but we are still dealing with the same universes —and the same Self.

Mechanisms and circuits are always in play as Self extends its reach to more and more variables. A conduit of energy, communication and receptacle for storing experiences as memory, may be found with each and every terminal contacted in the universe—whether in this lifetime or even this universe. These are formed by attention. These are never automatically "unformed" but they may be reconsidered and do not have to be wired like a bell on a string, set to send us a 'ping' or twinge of pain each time they are in stimulation by the environment. It is not the environment that is at cause, ever. It is our agreements to this chain reaction that allows it to seem so. The environment presents a bit of information, "A," and suddenly we process the data as "b-c-d-e-f" and then constitute that as the basis of reality and our agreements to it. All of this is within the responsibility and control of Self to dictate—once it is *realized*.

Imprints are generated by a significant event that is then impressed very strongly onto an individual's personal timeline with a heavy energetic charge. There are really only a handful of situations that can severely imprint onto a spiritual being during their association with a physical incarnation—but we can assume, in the long journey that the Alpha-Spirit has taken to arrive "here" that essentially all of these imprint-type events have taken place and been reinforced through restimulation countless times since. The amazing truth behind this applied spiritual philosophy of Systemology is that its use has been found in various traditions and scientific techniques even over a century ago and practiced by several individuals in several different fields during the course of the 20th century. Their legacy and writings have all been left there for us to find;[*] a direct trail from the revival of theosophy and the Western Magical Tradition into the rise of the American "New Thought" movement and other practices of early creative psychology prior to WWII and the psycho-politics that ensued thereafter.

The only reason the present author can find for these various schools of thought to have abandoned their experiments and therapies—or at the very least discontinue any public admission to their existence—is because in virtually all cases where it has been intensively applied, the practice of "regression techniques" ultimately places ones *Awareness* into "past lives." Given modern standard-issue religious indoctrination on this very subject in the **Western** world, you might understand how it was not "acceptable." Of course we tend to hold off emphasis of such subjects until we can be certain a Seeker has a proper handle of their presence in *this* lifetime and ability to handle the communication without simply stimulating it, reinforcing it and then leaving it even more solid than before. Any heavy charge found activated on an imprint must be processed-out or it will simply strengthen the integrity of the machinery.

During any session or any light *analytical processing* or even considerations of communication on any channel, if the Seeker is experiencing a 'ping' or indicating that some other turbulence of energetic flow is existent on the line, a Pilot should recognize this and handle systemological processing to locate the "imprinting event" on the Seeker's timeline and **"process-out"** the "charge."

---

[*]   The subject of which would require an entirely separate volume to catalog properly.

:: 5 ::
APPLICATION OF "ROUTE-3"
COMMUNICATION PROCESSING AND SOP-2C

A Seeker is willing to reach for higher levels of communication and accept greater responsibility and control of higher faculties of knowing and being by first demonstrating controlled communication with energy and matter, thoughts and efforts that are present *in* the present. Demonstrations of effective Will and intention applied to the physical universe (*beta-existence*) will increase certainty that there are higher levels of basic communication channels existent at higher "POV" just as real and just as able to cause effects as anything we see or experience as solid in the physical universe.

As a Seeker increases their sense of certainty on control and the Self-determined control of their own experiences and reactions to those experiences, a greater sense of Self-Actualization naturally results. We are treating the level of willingness and acceptance an individual manages as a communication line with all masses—and even the absence of matter, as points in space. Any mass, which is an object in space—and any space that contains a POV, but which has no mass—may be observed and given significance. These significances are the consequence of very fixed considerations about what some thing *is.* And the reason an individual starts to get trapped in their *Awareness* at these low levels of the physical universe is quite simply a consideration that they cannot reach any higher than the barrier imposed or agreed to by the lack of proper communication.

By releasing emotionally entangled charges of energy on imprinted information, an increased certainty of control and Self-determinism is reached whereby an individual is better able to manage mental imagery and responses to the environment inherent in experience of existence. These stores of energy that we refer to as a "charge" are essentially the same as "emotional encoding."

> emotional encoding : the substance of *imprints*; associations of sensory experience with an *imprint*; perceptions of our environment that receive an *emotional charge*, which form or reinforce facets of an *imprint*; perceptions recorded and stored as an *imprint* within the "emotional range" of energetic manifestation; the formation of an energetic store or charge on a channel that fixes emotional responses as a mechanistic automation, which is carried on in an individual's spiritual timeline or personal continuum of existence.

Emotional encoding is the "substance" of the *Imprints*; it is what an *imprint* actually *is* composed of or *is doing*. This is explored more extensively within *The Tablets of Desinty (Liber-One)* manual. But, this knowledge alone does not suffice in providing a Pilot with adequate tools to actually "discharge" the energy and return information contained within imprinting to a level of analytical thought and its memory banks. At that time, an individual is free to take it out and create (or re-create) imagery at Will by intention as a Self-determined action *if* they choose to. But the imagery and its stores of energy are not forced upon an actualized individual by their own mechanisms.

> <u>imprint</u> : to strongly impress, stamp, mark (or outline) onto a softer 'impressible' substance; to mark with pressure onto a surface; in *NexGen Systemology*, the term is used to indicate permanent Reality impressions marked by frequencies, energies or interactions experienced during periods of emotional distress, pain, unconsciousness, loss, enforcement, or something antagonistic to physical (personal) survival, all of which are are stored with other reactive response-mechanisms at lower-levels of *Awareness* as opposed to the active memory database and proactive processing center of the Mind; an experiential "memory-set" that may later resurface—be triggered or stimulated artificially—as Reality, of which similar responses will be engaged automatically.

An *Imprint* may be restimulated by later "activating event" that in some way resembles conditions or *facets* of the original "Imprinting Incident"—which is the first or original event instance communicated and *emotionally encoded* onto an individual's "timeline implants" (events over the course of all lifetimes). This forms a permanent impression that is later used to mechanistically treat future contact on that channel.

The imprinting incident may be chronologically the "first" event of a certain type even if it is not necessarily the first "image" or "memory" that comes to mind when an activating event triggers this chain into present *Awareness*. In fact, an imprint carrying a heavy energetic charge may be restimulated thousands of times over the course of one or several lifetimes and simply add to the validity that it does exist. Each time an activating event triggers the energy of reactive-mechanisms outside a session, validation occurs; it solidifies and strengthens the encoding as valid.

Two reasons why amateur use of "Route-1" has not always eliminated the hold that an imprint maintains on the individual is because the operator of the procedure:

a) does not have a good controlled communication with the individual; or

b) is processing symptoms from an activating event and not the imprinting incident.

This second reason is precisely why "Route-1" is not demonstrated in *Crystal Clear* (*Liber-2B*) as a suitable method of "self-processing." With the exception of potential upper-level work, the only real avenue for a Seeker to operate on their own solitarily *is* "Route-2" or *Analytical Recall* (AR-SP-2) as demonstrated in the exercises found within *Crystal Clear*. The greatest gains earned from *Grade-III* work is found from a combination of study in combination with its exercises as *Piloted Sessions*. Of course, this method is not always functionally available, but it is quite ideal.

Primary energetic stores of an *Imprint* are fixed by the original event—the *imprinting incident*. Some relief may be earned from working out emotional stores on later *activating events*, but the true impression that holds an imprint in place is always connected to the original *imprinting incident* and cannot be completely defragmented unless processed-out directly. Application of any "Route" to an event other than the *imprinting incident* is really only to either bring information up to analytical ranges for consideration on an intellectual level or else as a direct avenue toward uncovering whatever the *imprinting incident* actually is, which again, may not be a part of the surface memory that an individual carries until that channel is willingly contacted with attention and traced back to its source.

An *imprinting incident* will be a time when *Self-determinism* was removed from the equation of actions—when an individual greatly considers themselves as the *effect* of some channel of communication. *Imprinting incidents* include moments when Self was held fixed at a location of space against its own will, and yes, even when it spread out its own reach and discovered to have caused *imprinting incidents* on another; moments when Self can no longer leave on its own accord or can no longer approach some terminal, lest they be punished. In *Grade-IV*, we might consider that an individual "falls out of" proper communication with their environment, universe, channels and terminals as a result of these incidents—and later *activating events* only reinforce this further, building greater and greater stores of entwined entangled energy creating turbulence on the line.

When attention of *Self* is so strongly thrown onto reactive-response circuits and they engage without being *Self-directed*, the imprinting gets stronger—the emotional encoding deepens. This is not the case when a Seeker deliberately knowingly applies attention on a channel during systematic processing and therefore may defragment and discharge the stores of energy when applying attention intentionally. During a session, attention has not been forced or triggered by some activating event and so power and control remains under responsibility and certainty of the Seeker to handle and manage, running through the sequence of events and images until emotional ties are desensitized. It is actually not a very complicated ordeal, and certainly not supernatural, but the average individual carrying the human condition is not educated or given the experience that contribute to regaining certainty and ability to be a Self-directed Alpha Spirit in command of a body.

The sequence of intervals between *imprinting incidents* and additional *activating events* create a type of "chain" that carries the quality of time for an individual. It may be said that these *incidents* and *events* are what compose the heaviest weights attached to an individual's spiritual timeline, which is their own personal energetic record that reaches across all lifetimes since their origins as an Alpha-Spirit. It may also be said that an individual's freedom and vitality as an Alpha-Spirit is only thwarted or dimmed in relation to the amount of personal energy entwined on a timeline. In essence, the spirit is only as free and eternal as it remains to consider itself so. It can also feed attention continually into considerations that support entrapment and allow the spirit to "feel" diminished.

The more an Alpha-Spirit considers memories and images of a past to be important and carry emotional significance, the less likely they are to take over ability to create and dissolve images and memories at Will, treating them only for the information they actually contain and assigning no deeper significances otherwise. This is now a skill that apparently requires systematic practice by an individual that has formerly been given no instruction or encouragement on maintaining metahuman control of the "body" and "Mind."

Although specific language is used for "processing command lines" in a session, no amount of memorization of particular scripts can substitute actual understanding of our systemology. Unfortunately, this is exactly what an esoteric or mystical practitioner is after: a set formula of movements and incantations that will instantly take over their Will as operator and do the work for them. No such luck here.

Self is always *Self* regardless of where *Awareness* is fixed as a POV. The personal identity continuum (Zu-line) is carried with an individual during their lifetimes and is still a part of the considerations of Self in whatever form it controls. It is perhaps the closest thing to a "soul" that we have discovered (without confusing our systemology with any extraneous religious sentiment than it already has in the light of "Mardukite Zuism").

If a Seeker were truly determined enough to "fly up" and grab hold of the Truth from the heights right from the start, the remaining work would seem unnecessary. But, it has been recognized that those working within considerations of the standard-issue human condition are not able to do this—and when they try and fail, the willingness to even extend the reach again will dim. The action will have been registered as pointless, or even worse, painful or punished. Best to just "keep our feet" on the ground, is what they tell us. And so the ancients realized that some gradient would be necessary if an individual were to actually seek the heights and yet still maintain solidity and certainty necessary for achieving the original ideal Alpha state of knowing and being from *this* beta side of existence. We find evidence for these tiers, levels, gateways and thresholds in virtually all extensions of the applied spiritual technologies that resulted from a dispersion of teachings from the Ancient Mystery School and the ziggurat-towers of Babylon.

Grade IV is a very critical tier, mid-way between where things have come from and to where they are going—and beyond that, to Infinity, we could hardly comprehend from this vantage point; and still we are here, moving forward. We know this *is* the way, not only because it is effectively workable, but because we can find evidence for its use in ancient times, when there were still actualized avatars among us that seemed very "god-like" in their command of *beta-existence*. What has since been lost can be reclaimed—as can our actualized *Awareness* returned to and as Self, the Alpha-Spirit.

What we are essentially describing from the greatest heights of mystical, spiritual, magical and/or religious terminology is nothing short than true ASCENSION; yes, **Ascension** after our incarnation in this lifetime, with the same certainty and direction of Will that we execute in this lifetime —so that is something worth developing greater control of; and systematic processing does just that, returning the control of Will to the Seeker far more efficiently than the performance of arbitrary ceremonies and the utterance of unique poetry. Real "magic" is Will and Intention; the control and communication of both. That *is* magic.

The progressive sequence of mystical *Grades* and various "initiations" are representative of achieving higher states of actualization and release that lower-level attachments have on considerations of Self. Of course, this is not what is actually found to be the case in the ranks and orders and lodges that propose various *Grades* and levels of knowledge exploration and corresponding titles for various degrees, each elaborated upon with ceremonial rites. Rituals and esoteric lore has become only a symbol, a shadow of mystery in contrast to former states of illumination that these paths once led to. They now lead no further than what they were understood to be in their relatively recent reconstruction during the wake of Dark Ages and in the presence of rapid industrialization and mechanization of the world.

We are then working toward a greater, higher, upper-echelon goal that is quite esoteric, spiritual and mystical by many folk's definition of such things, and we are working toward an increased freedom of the Self as the Alpha-Spirit by progressively releasing the hold that ties and attachments to mundane things and emotional solids have had in restraining any further considerations of Self. This is, by definition, the pathway to true *Ascension.*

There have been many models of this *Pathway* in the past—many traditions composed of cultural semantics and **allegory** attempting the same goals we do today. Each proposed their own *Kabbalahs* and *Standard Models* representing veils of existence, the separation and fragmentation of Self from its own spiritual identity and all manners of classifying various Gates and thresholds, which have been so carefully cataloged for the living in "Books of the Dead." It is true that we find many clues about the direction we should be headed in—but the easy answer to this is that the only way out is always the way through. The mystic, magician, priest or priestess stands apart from others because they *do* know this is the way through. And they have been given many maps and points of orientation from every angle. The secret lies in finding the direct path between them all or else the Seeker will become trapped and enamored by the myriad potential of ways and paths they *could* travel.

The subject of "Ascension" and the intentional design and control of "etheric bodies" after this current lifetime, is actually treated esoterically in a former multi-*Grade-bridge* volume titled *"The Vampyre's Handbook."** This "Liber-V" material was specially researched and developed for a faction of Mardukite Chamberlains Alumni called "Moroii ad Vitam Paramus," which treats the mystical side of systemology within the cont-

---

* *"Vampyre's Handbook: Secret Rites of Modern Vampyres"* (2020 Edition) by Joshua Free includes complete *Liber-V* materials from two former publications: *"Vampyre's Bible: The Moroi Book of V"* and *"Cybernomicon."*

ext of "vampyre energy work"—in the spirit of a long-standing tradition of such that actually emerged from the original Ancient Mystery School (as is explained in greater detail within that volume).

However, one unique elements of "Liber-V" is an emphasis on the connection between the Egyptian Mystery Tradition alongside more familiar applications of the "Route of Mesopotamian Mysteries" (*Grade-II*). In fact, "Liber-V" actually bridges incorporated knowledge from all three initial *Grades* under the context of a 6,000 year historically valid Vampyre Mystery Tradition; and of the subjects treated by "Moroii ad Vitam Paramus" for their research and discovery: *The Egyptian Book of the Dead*.

We know that the Spirit *does* go on from here; but how can we be sure that we will have any greater control then, or any greater sense of *Actualized* ability than we have been able to demonstrate in *this* lifetime. Basing our beliefs simply on potential of what is possible with no regard for how one would employ any of these higher faculties is to again put the Self in the position of being an effect and assuming that we will just *know* and automatically be able to *do* in some greater capacity (after this life) than we have been able to demonstrate with direction of Will and intention at the very level we are operate at now.

Seven-fold gate symbolism of the Mesopotamian "ziggurat star-gate" tradition is accessible for study within the full context of *Grade-II* material.‡ And when we consider some of the colorful presentations for similar lore provided in the *Egyptian Book of the Dead*—better translated as *Coming Forth into Light*—it becomes quite clear: the way "out" is the pathway of "defragmentation."

An individual is always led through a series of seven veils or thresholds that each require shedding garments, artificial layers of Self, or whatever it is that ties and holds a Seeker to that particular level of existence. It is therefore a sequence of "releases" and "lightening the load" that the Alpha-Spirit has taken on as a burden, and which otherwise keeps it from the experience of its own true nature. This is, in essence, what fixes the human condition trapped in low-energy loops of thought and behind artificial self-imposed barriers.

In the classic presentation within the Egyptian paradigm, a spirit is marched through several gateways, confronting various gatekeepers and demonstrating various faculties along a way that is so pointedly fixed

---

‡ Available in its entirety as the *Grade-II* omnibus mega-anthology of collected works by Joshua Free titled: *"Necronomicon: The Complete Anunnaki Legacy"* (2020 Master Edition Hardcover).

within the paradigm that its details, names of each gate, passwords and the nature of the gatekeepers, &tc.,[*] are all found within the leaves of the most ancient books—along with explicit instructions for traversing through and about these planes on an ascent to a greater point. But!—at one juncture, the Egyptians describe the "weighing of the heart," which is to very specifically say the weight of masses of emotional encoding and stores of heavy energy accumulated in this lifetime.

If the *Awareness* of a spiritual identity (being) has become so heavy in opposition to its natural state—compared to "weighing against a feather"—then the Spirit does not Ascend, does not Actualize itself as the Alpha Spirit, and is sent back down to resolve this matter further. Of course, afterward, they are given no further tools or keys to actually resolve this for themselves—and here we find the cycle of death and rebirth at low-level potentials of the spectrum that the standard-issue is suspended by. Even outside of a body the Spirit finds itself trapped because it has no sense of its true existence aside from its former body. The literal description of weights and scales may be entirely symbolic and only for the benefit of our material understanding—but the intended message rings clear.

"Route-3" is the preferred method for defragmenting emotional encoding and other stores of energy that we consider an *Imprint*. Much like the former "Route-1" (that this method is built upon), it is most effective for managing emotional encoding and *Imprints*, whereas a further development upon it—in conjunction with "Route-2"—may better serve the nature of "thought considerations" and conceptions formed as "mental images."

If a Pilot has studied this present manual and all of the materials contained in *Grade-III*, such as is collected in *The Systemology Handbook*, then the amount of difficulty in bringing a Seeker closer to their goal of beta-defragmentation—or the *Pathway to Self-Honesty*—is actually quite minimal. Difficulties will arise if a Pilot does not stick to the criteria and instruction we have presented in *Grade-III* and *Grade-IV* material and decides to "get inventive" on a Seeker and begin experimenting with various theories or mixed practices from other traditions. Even including materials from *Grade-I* and *Grade-II* in systematic processing is a mistake and will cause a Seeker to "go out of communication" and a Pilot

---

[*] See also information given in *Grade-II*, available in *"The Complete Anunnaki Bible"* or the complete *Grade-II* anthology, *"Necronomicon: The Complete Anunnaki Legacy"* (2020 Edition), where literal Egyptian versions of similar Mesopotamian lore are given as an appendix to the *Tablet-B* and *Tablet-C* series.

to lose credibility with the Seeker.

We are not, here, invalidating any of the work from former *Grades*. Even the premise of *Mardukite Systemology* or *NexGen Systemology* is actually an extension of "Mardukite Zuism," which is reflected in the *Grade-II* core materials far better than ever in history since ancient Babylon. But!— Systemology is a futurist extension of this, drawn from over 6,000 years of esoteric wisdom passed down from the Ancient Mystery School and it has been developed and cultivated in present time as an entirely unique, but all-encompassing, paradigm that is not directly reflected one-to-one or A-for-A with any preexisting tradition.

Once we start conducting systematic processes using *Grade-III* work and above, we are introducing a higher level of understanding to what foundations we have stood on before, and we are releasing the hold on whatever need not come along with us. We are not trying to take the *Grades* up with us and try to now fit *them* into a higher order of reasoning. That is a backwards way of flow and one that automatically produces fragmentation in programming. It is better likened to a removal of all that is unnecessary from a former reasoning and a development of only that which is true for the higher order of reasoning and there developed as a foundation. From that higher vantage point, if you still wish to peer over the edge and see what is what about the lower *Grades*, well, then you will have a much wider-angle view to understand it from. But if you literally try to take it all with you on your ascent, you will be disappointed.

Difficulties that could arise using *Systemology Operating Procedure 2-C* can be avoided by using best practices of *Professional Piloting Procedure* and by not pushing a Seeker to confront a terminal they are not prepared to handle. If the channel cannot be avoided, then work on it as a gradient scale. An individual that becomes angry at the Pilot or is otherwise skeptical of the entire practice of applied systemology will require a greater handling of control and communication; emphasizing exercises appropriated as Step-2. Rudimentary exercises and basic processing are more effective if, the individual is operating at lower-degrees of actualized *Awareness.* No "higher-route" method will remedy this; it must be resolved first.

Step-3 : Contact Terminal
　　\ terminal, live-forms, belief/attitude, emotions/sensations

Step-4 : Communications Monitored on Circuits to Terminal
　　\ Circuit-1 : Self *to* others/terminal (*out-flow*)
　　\ Circuit-2 : others/terminal *to* Self (*in-flow*)

\ Circuit-3 : others/terminal *to* others/terminal (*cross-flow*)
(*Opt.* AT)   \ Circuit-0 : Self *to* Self (*Alpha-flow* or "postulate")

In "Route-1," the assumption is that the easiest fragmentation to contact, are those *imprinting incidents* where something happened *to* the Seeker, when the Seeker was at *Effect* and on the receipt-point of a direct line of communication with intention. This is true—and when a terminal is imprinted by such an energy flow, then it is run as such. But "Route-3" advises that at least two additional circuits are processed on that same terminal. And per the standards of *Grade-III* (SP-2B)[‡] if *activating events* on these other circuits are not found accessible as "recall," then they should be "imagined."[*]

"Route-3" does not only emphasize "in-flow." To only focus on the "in-flows" is to consistently validate the position of the Seeker as *effect*, which will force a greater deal of introspection on the body and reinforce the lower-level experiences *imprinted* on that "form." Although "in-flows" do serve as motivations for a Seeker to "act" as they *do*, it is only one part of the circuitry that is established as an imprint with any terminal. All three circuits contribute to "personality" programming.

Step-3 seems fairly straightforward, because you are simply selecting a terminal or concept to run systematic processing on. Of course, this could be performed on anything. The real trick is assessing terminals that both: a) have a heavy charge emotionally encoded that will make a real difference if released; and b) are within willingness and certainty of the Seeker to reach and confront at their current point of development. As a general rule, any automatic reactive-response exhibited or chain-sequence that leads to a 'ping' would be considered to qualify these two conditions. However, severe lags in real progress may develop from either: a) contacting the wrong terminals; b) not discharging enough from a channel; or c) not locating the *imprinting incident* and only processing *activating events*.

There is only one basic method that we have found effective for *Grade-IV* in order to be certain that the energetic stores on automatic-response circuits is lessening or simply charging up more, and it relates specifically to the manner in which the mental imagery of the event is experienced and controlled. When a fragmenting event is run through, the Seeker experiences it in all of its stimulation and color and accounts for what they are reactively seeing and any other sensations that are att-

---

[‡]   See *"Crystal Clear"* (*Liber-2B*) or the *Grade-III* anthology, *"The Systemology Handbook."*

[*]   Imagination, imagery and creativity is treated in *"The Imaginomicon"* section.

ached to it. The Pilot does not necessarily prompt for individual pieces of information, but instead encourages the Seeker to relay whatever is happening with a simple acknowledgment of, "okay, continue."

After a Seeker has run through a sequence of what has happened, they are then returned to the beginning of that event again—just as demonstrated in the instructions for "Route-1"—and run through it at least a second full time. At this point, the Seeker may be asked if the mental images are "getting stronger or dimmer" or "erasing or getting more solid." This is as good of an indicator as we currently have at *Grade-IV* (without electronic assistance) to determine the energy discharge on a channel.

If it is erasing and the sensations attached are lessening, then a Pilot simply continues on this same line of processing until the Seeker demonstrates a higher actualized *Awareness* in the presence of the same terminal. If the effects are getting stronger, there is only two reasons for this (all other aspects of systematic processing being satisfied) and that is: the actual *imprinting incident* has started earlier than the moment the Seeker is treating as the "beginning," or only an *activating event* has been contacted, and the Seeker should be asked if there is an earlier incident of *x*—being the same terminal. If there is a new starting point of the same incident, then simply direct the Seeker to start at the "new beginning" of the incident and scan through it. Don't get upset and start demanding why we weren't starting at the "real" beginning in the first place.

Often times, it is the deliberate contact with what is otherwise only an automatic circuit that will bring more to the surface than was originally known or remembered—hence why the "Route-1" method is referred to as "resurfacing." An additional point of fact for a Pilot is that "Route-3" may also be used to "repair" any *Grade-III* sessions that have only used one circuit of contact to defragment a channel. This is why records are kept; we have a specially designed "Journal" for noting any terminals and facets contacted. Those run on only one circuit previously in *Grade-III* should be later run on additional circuits as a "repair."

We have treated use of "Route-3" almost exclusively for emotional encoding and *imprinting*, although it is not the only potential application. In fact, the basic practice of all three circuits as methods of Self-Processing considerations is treated in *Crystal Clear (Liber-2B)*. Many of the exercises for "analytical recall" are actually structured on what is now a "Route-3" method. For example, processing in the section titled "Defragmenting Self-Consciousness" runs as follows:

—RECALL an incident when you were invalidated by someone else. (*Circuit-2*)

—RECALL an incident when you invalidated someone else. (*Circuit-1*)

—RECALL an incident when someone invalidated someone else. (*Circuit-3*)[*]

Here, of course, the reader will see from this excerpt that the chronology or sequence of the original *AR-SP-2* ("Route-2") outlines all followed a different ordering of the circuits. (And of course they were not distinguished as "circuits" in that text; yet the practices themselves were still found effective.) Here is another example from *Liber-2B* that treats "interruption" as the terminal:

—RECALL a moment when you were suddenly interrupted by someone. (*Circuit-2*)

—RECALL a moment when you interrupted someone else. (*Circuit-1*)

—RECALL a moment when someone interrupted someone else. (*Circuit-3*)

And here, this example treats enforcement of belief:

—RECALL an incident when a belief was enforced on you. (*Circuit-2*)

—RECALL an incident when you enforced a belief on others. (*Circuit-1*)

—RECALL an incident when someone else enforced a belief on others. (*Circuit-3*)

Many lighter analytical processes of *Grade-III* have a capability of "hitting on" a "hot button." This *must* be handled "in session" if it occurs. This means *Grade-III* work is used as a preliminary assessment of where a Seeker is actually at in their life and their certainty and responsibility of control (&tc.) before applying (or learning) upper-routes and higher-level work. Since this is all effectively demonstrated and experimented with before publishing, one should assume there is good reason behind our methods of delivering the work as such.

---

[*] An additional circuit could be monitored here for advanced A.T. (*Actualized Technician*) work whereby in "Circuit-0" we would recall the times when "Self invalidated Self." This is an applicable but higher order of processing work not directly instructed within the present manual (*Liber-2C*).

—in "Circuit-1" we have *Self* as the primary source-point, and it is extending its reach or sending its "point" to a distant "receipt-point," as if we are starting a flow of communication; which in essence, we are, because *Self* is *doing* something;

—in "Circuit-2" we have a second definitive live-terminal as the source-point and *Self* as the receipt-effect-point of a communication, when something is *happening to Self*; and finally,

—in "Circuit-3" we are a part of the third sphere of existence where "others" and "groups" are exchanging energy and we are still receiving the communications in connection to some terminal.

The assurance that systematic processing and fundamentals of *NexGen Systemology* are an avenue to the ideal state of the Spirit is a responsibility that each and every systemologist and Pilot is representing whenever employing the methods and name of Systemology and *Mardukite Zuism*. We are dealing with the nature of all *Life, the Universe and Everything* and we are bringing Seekers to the forefront of accessing the very fabric of space-time as the creative spiritual individuals that they are. This *is* a "Game"; but it is also very *Real.* Treat it so.

:: 6 ::
OBJECTIVE-BASED SYSTEMATIC PROCESSING
⟨ INTRODUCING "BELL, BOOK AND CANDLE" ⟩

"BELL, BOOK & CANDLE" : three dissimilar objects that are kept accessible during a processing session; a term meant to indicate a **Pilot's** portable "objective processing kit" or objects generally present in the session room (accessible on a shelf, table or pedestal stands); in *NexGen Systemology,* the name of an **objective** processing philosophy pertaining to command of personal reality; historically, a formal ritual used by the Roman Catholic church to ceremonially declare an **individual** "guilty of the most heinous sins" as "excommunicated (to hold no further communications with) by **anathema**"—a *bell* is rung, a *holy book* is closed and all *candles* are snuffed out—thus we therapeutically use the same symbolism historically representing religious fragmentation for modern systematic defragmentation purposes.

—from the version 4.1 NexGen Systemology Glossary

"Objective Processing" within the tradition of *Mardukite Zuism & Systemology* is based on several years of experimentation using esoteric, mystical and mental exercises—those that orient a **Seeker** with the reality of an "objective universe"; which, for current purposes, is the "Physical Universe."∞ Although we can be sure that each individual—each "**Alpha Spirit**" or "I-Am-Self"—maintains their own individuated "subjective universe," there is also an "objective universe" that we all agree to. And a Seeker is not very well off if they are unable to approach objective qualities of the "Physical Universe" or treat it as anything other than what it actually is.

Many spiritual philosophies and mystic schools operate on principles based on a rejection of the Physical Universe—the pretense that there is no "objective" reality taking place at the physically material" **level** of **beta-existence.** This is actually a surefire way of being trapped; within the very confines of a level or **condition** of **existence** not appropriately faced.

Delusion results from holding on too strongly to misinformation—and this may even be found within most material passed through the "New Age" movement. Beyond this, the sciences—social, physical and technological—are also **fragmented.** Even most ancient methods evoked by

---

∞ Referred to as "KI" on the Arcane Tablets of Mardukite Systemology (*Grade-III*).

modern practitioners are only successful in sealing initiates deeper and deeper into crevices and confines of rigid systems, or else drop out from the bottom (of our **existential** concept of the **Zu-line** or **Standard Model**) back into high levels of fragmentation and spiritual entrapment.

Many "esoteric, mystical, occult, spiritual" individuals do not rise above the first *Grade* or *Level* or *Gate*. Regardless of what information or experience is later accumulated, it will only be treated at that *first* potential level of **understanding** outside of the mundane, but then treated as "everything" (or **encompassing** everything). Initiates in the past have often run the risk of treating each new **gradient** as a *final arrival point*. Such is not the case within our Systemology, where **successive** gradients are treated exactly as they are: a sequence of *Gateways to Infinity*.

"Objective Processing"—as a *NexGen Systematic Processing* method—is first introduced in our "systemological" text, *Crystal Clear*.[*] Technically speaking, *any* systematic processing pertaining to the "objective universe" is considered an "objective process." This is not only restricted to use of *actual* "objects" as identifiable forms. *Any* points and spots in **"space"** that are part of the objective-physical-material universe are considered as such "objective."

Our present focus concerns demonstrations with physical objects—their identities, associations and control—this same methodology is also applied to higher "Actualized Technician" (Wizard) levels operated exclusively in **Zu-Vision** as Self, clear and free of any limited **considerations** of a physical body or astral form in order to spiritually exist. For now, we shall focus our treatment to the "objective" universe.

Personal **defragmentation** involves erasure of "automatic tendencies" and reactive-response mechanisms that apparently can usurp personal command over the *genetic vehicle* when operating under the "RCC" (**Reactive Control Center**). This "control center" developed for the operation of the *genetic vehicle* independent of the Alpha Spirit that commands it. As a systematic **dynamic** of our experience in *beta-existence* using a physical body, command of the "RCC" is an integral part of maintaining Self-Honest **Self-Determined** control of the Mind–Body connection.

Although an Alpha Spirit may command a "body" to do one thing, fragmentation and other automatic mechanism can distort this line of **communication**. Given that the Alpha Spirit *is not* the *genetic vehicle* it commands, it should be able to fully direct the body to perform tasks in much the same manner as we might witness a puppeteer operate strings

---

[*]   See 'Unit-4' in "*Crystal Clear*" (*Liber-2B*) or in "*The Systemology Handbook*."

of a marionette doll.

Naturally, "to be" a powerful and creative Alpha Spirit with energy to consider and **manifest** all nature of universes—as do other Alpha Spirits —there must be a willingness for things to happen (including what has happened before). This requires taking **responsibility** to exercise control of effects. What else is communication but "directing an energetic flow of intention to cause an effect (or duplication) at a distance."[‡] An individual carries many **imprinted** "associations" from former "experience" that **inhibit** full Self-Honest willingness to Self-direct as cause in the present. Such "tendencies" operate on automatic circuits communicated by the RCC.

Obvious examples regarding development of automation in response-actions of a *genetic vehicle* all involve **enforcement**, **invalidation** and/or *counter-efforts* by others. These are the most easily recognized because they result from **"imprinting incidents"** involving other **terminals** in the objective universe (*beta-existence*) that are more easily recalled from memory stores or **resurfaced** from **emotional encoding**.

The most heavily encoded personal fragmentation—in regards to experience of *beta-existence*—pertains to "RCC" circuitry shown on the *Expanded Grade-IV* demonstration of the Standard Model (of the Zu-line) as Spheres of Existence (in Universes) that include **sub-zone** values for the *Pathway of Fragmentation*—the first two spheres of existence relating specifically to:

("2.0") — Self as *Aware* of "Physical/Material Havingness"

("1.0") — Self as *Aware* of *Life-existence* as a "Physical Body"

("0.0") — Genetic Vehicle/Body ("Physical Universe Continuity")

("–1") — Pain and **Unconsciousness** of the Physical Body

("–2") — Loss (or threat of) and Emotional imprinting on the "RCC"

Fragmentation and personal automation result from an accumulation of mental imagery that is heavily **charged** with emotional energy. Even a single charged incident can create an "imprint." Above we have listed the most basic categories for this range, being: "physical pain," "physical **trauma**," as well as any perceived "loss" and "emotional encoding." Of course, these are only **POV** (viewpoints) **assumed**; none of these levels are the actual Self—or Alpha Spirit. In fact, nothing at this level can actually affect the Alpha Spirit at all, *except* that there is a consideration that it can—and by this **agreement**, entrapment ensues.

---

‡ Quoting *"Version 4.1 Systemology & Mardukite Zuism Glossary"* (see Appendix).

An individual fixes their *Awareness* as being "in" a "body" and thus considers their Self exclusively "as" that body and, of course, able to be the *effect* of it. But, we know—from basic systemological knowledge—that this is a backwards way of operating, or rather not operating (and being reactive), and the only way which Self as the Alpha Spirit can become fragmented: to be the *effect* of its own *cause.* Inevitably the Self becomes ensnared by the same traps and mechanisms set up for others.

Doing something and *knowing* that you are doing it is a basic **premise** of commanding the presence of Self in the objective universe. However, there are numerous ways in which the natural state of willingness *to be cause* has been "*dis-courage-ed*"—increasingly more interactions with the physical universe and other individuals are responded to on automatic fragmented circuitry. An individual finds themselves (or rather doesn't) considering increasingly limited and more finite courses of action in lieu of "other-determined" automatic-responses, tendencies and reactive mechanisms—none of which have any place in the **ascending** condition of **Homo Novus**.

∧ ∧ ∧ ∧ ∧ ∧

When we consider "**apparent** reality"—the way in which things *seem* to be. All associations and significances are assigned values; they are easily fixed in place as they condense, but more appropriately maintained fluid to the true Will-Intention of Self that is able to shift its POV with any consideration that is within reach.

Use of our "*Bell, Book & Candle*" methodology as a **repetitive** technique is likely to run a Seeker through the emotional **band** outside of their Self-determined intention while they keep applying a directed unit of *Awareness* on each part of the activity. The same as before, the same as next time, but each treated as its own unique application of energy without expectancy: not as a "build up" from any former occurrence or cycle-of-action and certainly not in the anticipation of what they next cycle of action (or command line) will be—because after more than 20 minutes it is already "assumed" that the next line will be "such and such" and then we are back to an "automatic" state that is outside full presence and application of Will to the NOW.

Appropriation of the name "<u>Bell</u>, <u>Book</u> and <u>Candle</u>" erupted from a desire to systematically defragment individuals that were formerly heavily imprinted on *Grade-I* and *Grade-II* type work—often resulting from many years of their own studies and practices before discovering or receiving instruction from Mardukite Systemology on these subjects (*Grades*); meaning those who held significant emotional encoding and intensive mental programming with a fixed belief-set concerning subjects (terminal circuitry) of, for example: symbols, education, magic, politics, religion, spirituality and God. Many of these are subject to artificial implants on the **identity** of Self. The "charge" holds them in place as a "solid" (in the sense of a fixed **pattern** of energy flow).

Systematic personal processing toward higher routes and states of consideration encourages ability to free one's Self from any fixed or rigid pattern of thinking—even those automatic-response mechanisms that tend to develop without the Self *being Aware* that they continue in their operation. This takes place in repetitive tasks; yet we are aware of how important repetition is in spiritual practices and mental processing. For some Seekers, it is too difficult to effective work a simple task in repetition and duplicate results toward an end. A person **transmits** message "A" and another person hears "B" understands it as "C" and somehow communicates it to others as "D."As soon as someone gets it in their head that this objective universe is simply an illusion and not "real"—particularly after having already "agreed" to a "physical body"—well, where does that leave them grounded at all? Where is Self as a point of Source in the experience? To suggest an "un-reality" is to give up all control and responsibility for the experience and creation of *Life, the Universe and Everything.*

Due to improper handling of communication and control over the course of an individual's lifetime (or several), they are likely to find the "span" of their attentions quite limited. Even when Will *is* applied by *Self* in its greater moments of "clarity," the Alpha Spirit often discovers that a "body" is not "cooperating"—that it has fallen out of direct communication with it and therefore lacks a direct command of its functions as actualized *Awareness*. This may actually manifest in systematic processing during even earlier basic sessions that are intended to orient the Seeker in space as a "presence" in objective reality to the extent of their actualized *beta-Awareness*. If this occurs, a Pilot should be very careful about running any further types of more advanced creative and imaginative processes (which occur subjectively) until the Seeker has resolved the ability to properly manage and direct their "intentions" on the objective universe (in a way that the Pilot can see and observe).

The "duplication factor" is apparently behind some of the great "mysteries" we have carried with us in memory to this lower level Physical Universe: teleportation and levitation and other facets of a magical universe that we inherently can recall from a former lifetime. These are considered anomalies today when fixed to rigid mechanized considerations of "material **continuity**" in the physical universe as being all there is, was or will be. But the rules of the **Game** here, governed by **Cosmic Law**, only applies to the Physical Universe and the Human Condition (at "4.0" on the Standard Model). As such, basic rules *do* apply within *beta existence* under Cosmic Law that no two points can be the same in space and that all objects must be separate from other objects to *be*, and so on and so forth.

An ability to actually perform or intend an action over and over again with full *Awareness* and command of Will is not a skill equally developed and practiced across the boards—and it is certainly not found present in the standard-issue Human Condition. The standard-issue Human Condition is riddled with massive amounts of implanted hypnotic programming and emotional encoding that actually prevents total command of these abilities by the average individual; at least the fullest extent by which they may be demonstrated.

"Command processing" promotes the opposite effects of hypnosis and improperly enforced control—a defragmentation of former mishandling of these alleged conditions. If anything can be said about the standard-issue state of the Human Condition, it is that it has long been asleep; hypnotized by a vast array of systematic programming since the **inception** of civilization on Earth—and even before then.

Defragmenting the ability to duplicate repetitive actions is as important for the Pilot as it is for the Seeker; it is important for the delivery of *Professional Piloting Procedures*; it is important for all individuals on the Pathway—it is a critical step. Since it is referred to as the "Magic of Will and Intention," several members of the *NexGen Systemology Society* encouraged treatment of this upper level of work as the "Wizard" *Grades.*

We treat the subject of what "communication processing" requires as a "process" and the skills to deliver it as a Pilot within the same context simultaneously. This unique approach contributed to our original designation of *Grade-IV* as "*Professional Piloting Procedure.*" We have expressed the necessity to equally deliver repetitive commands each within their own unit of time and existence and each with the same degree of Will-Intention as any other—as if each is the only in existence, not building upon a former cycle-of-action or leading up to anything other than that present moment in space-time.

Λ Λ Λ Λ Λ Λ

Each command line and response response must be treated with full "presence" in that cycle of communications and/or actions involving the Pilot and/or Seeker, no matter how many repetitive sequences are applied. This is a basic prerequisite of systematic processing—for the Pilot and the Seeker—and thus it is treated most rigorously at *Grade-IV* in order to permit the work of any further upper-routes and *Grades* to be actually effective.

Regarding *Systemology Operating Procedure 2-C*, the methodology of "*Bell, Book & Candle*" is applied as an extension to Step-2b "*Presence in Space-Time*" as shown below.

Step-2 : "Communication & Control"
\ increased communication and control
\ beingness in session as Self (in phase)
\ Step 2a : "*Basic AR*"
\ Step 2b : "*Presence in Space-Time*"
\ "*Bell, Book & Candle*"

Following this formula:

—"*Basic AR*"[‡] puts the Seeker in contact with their "subjective universe" and its communication to the Pilot (Seeker's personal experience/memory : "personal/subjective universe");

—"*Presence in Space-Time*" puts a Seeker in communication with the "physical/objective universe" while maintaining internal communications with their "subjective universe" (Seeker's personal contact with "physical/objective universe"); and finally

—"*Bell, Book & Candle*" bridges a Seeker's contact with the "physical/objective universe" as a communication with the Pilot, a live-form representing other "subjective life" occupying an objective reality along with the Seeker (Seeker's communications with an "physical/objective universe").

---

‡   Analytical Recall (*Route-2 "AR"*); see also *Liber-2B*, "*Crystal Clear.*"

:: 7 ::

UNDERSTANDING COMMAND PROCESSING
WITH THE "BELL, BOOK AND CANDLE"

Systematic processes associated with the *"Bell, Book and Candle"* range from the most basic demonstration examples of "objective processing" given in *Crystal Clear,*[*] to some of the most "testing" or "trying" methods, which are, of course, intended to "process out" many forms of fragment-ation, including tendencies or **compulsions** regarding automation (rather than command), the command of one's "attention span" and the resistance to automatic-response mechanisms that tend to develop as a result of repetitive tasks. It may be assumed that most individuals carry some encoding attached to their implants regarding performance of re-petitive tasks as an action, or any duplication of another "thing" or "communication" in existence.

Realizations and skills established in *Grade-IV* are the foundation for all "practical" use of our applied spiritual philosophy as developed for up-per-routes. They build upon one another and are unforgiving of any de-ficiencies of effective **actualization** required from a former route in order to be effective. This "progression" becomes most evident and paramount for success at *Grade-III*, from which the present *Grade* is based.

"Step-2" of SOP-2C includes varied methods derived from the most eso-teric mystical methods to the most critical findings born of "psycholo-gical" and "philosophical" fields in the past century. However, the focus of "Step-2"—and emphasis of this manual—is always "communication, control and command" of the Mind–Body connection. Basic "command processing" is an extension of "communication processing." We are still dealing with energy flows relayed as "source-to-receipt" and "cause-to-effect." Systematic processing is *not* a "magical action" by the Pilot to "command the actions" of the Seeker; it is a relay of communication.

"Communication processing" and "command processing" are a precurs-or to "creative ability processing." Each leads into the other. To have a true *Self-Honest* "command" of anything—including control of the *Genetic Vehicle*—the facets and functions of "communication" are treated. In or-der to **enact** true *Self-Honest* "creative ability" as a source-point, an individual must execute total "command" as Self, which includes rehab-ilitation of the selective directed attentions as treated in this expanded methodology of "Step-2."

---

*   *Liber-2B.*

Proper handing of repetition, attention and reproduction puts command back under control of Self. Improper management of repetition, attention and reproduction puts command under some type of automatic control of a response-mechanism. When an individual has systematically created one of these types of automatic-devices for themselves, and they *know* that they have created it, then the responsibility and control is easy to recognize. However, a Seeker is likely to set up automatic communication relays and then forget about them—or worse, they will not realize that they are being created by a patterned system function of the lower control centers (such as the "RCC") and then will be operating with that response-mechanism running on automatic and beneath the surface of analytical control. This is exactly the type of systematic fragmentation that we are applying our spiritual philosophy toward in order to achieve systematic defragmentation.

The purpose of "command processing"—such as *Bell, Book & Candle*—is not to establish new patterns of automatic function, but to return greater certainty of control back to the Seeker. Any concepts held as imprinting, programming or Alpha fragmentation ("implants") that suggest "reproduction is bad," "repetition is pain," "duplication is unoriginal," "actions are not to be repeated," "what exists cannot be undone," &tc. all contribute to restrictions in willingness, reach, controlled command of personal action, that all lead to automated responses and reactive mechanisms inhibiting Self-determination. And at its Alpha state, the Self requires no greater determination; therefore Self-Determination, as a synonym for Self-Honesty, is not an end-state, but a point of *beta-defragmentation*, upon which all other upper-route work is treated in further *Grades*.

In Step-2, "*Presence in Time-Space*" orients a Seeker with the environment (physical/objective universe) by deliberate contact with it. It is a form of "objective processing" because it directs the attention of a Seeker onto the "objective universe." This allows an individual to locate themselves in objective space-time as an actualized *Awareness POV*, irrelevant if it involves maintaining a "physical" form or not. Variations on this may be found in traditions of mystical, spiritual, or otherwise religious use of "sacred space," "nemetons," "holy mandalas," "ritual areas," &tc. Establishment of "*Presence in Space-Time*" is a critical component to successful systematic processing sessions.

Our present chapter-lesson, however, concerns the next step in *SOP-2C*—the association and **differentiation** of "objects in space." It is no secret that entry-level *Grade* material applies this type of methodology adamantly. The "magician" wears a separate attire, which then is given a significance of putting them in **"phase"** with... well, we would hopefully assume to be *Self-Honest* **faculties** of Self, free of heavy mundane burdens and other emotional attachments that fix themselves to what they consider their identity. Other objects and tools are taken up, each in turn, and given a significance that is meant to endure for the remainder of a ritual, &tc. Such demonstrations are given in *Grade-I* materials and are mentioned here only as an illustrative comparison to one of the numerous ways in which "objects" have been used as focal points for developing Will-Intention, or rather the *command* of the same.

Λ Λ Λ Λ Λ Λ Λ

It is only when one is unwilling to be "cause" of their *beta-experience*, or believes that the conditions or patterns put forth are unable to be controlled, that they suddenly find themselves trapped by their own emotionally encoded mental images that they use in place of an actual Self-Honest experience of the objective universe.

The Alpha Spirit exists as a point of *Awareness* that extended its reach and therefore developed a construct—an "astral" or "mental" form—in which to do this from as a POV. It is part of communication and experience of *beta-conditions* in the Physical Universe, but bodies are to be commanded by Self and not allowed to establish their own systematic automation based on programming and implants. This is precisely what the "RCC" is for the *genetic vehicle*: a relay point to yet another "constructed" form that is tied to "sensation." To treat any of these various points on the Zu-line as "unreal"—or to allow automatic mechanistic relays to determine their reality—is to lose command of their function. At lower levels, the *Reactive-Control-Center* (*RCC*) governs most activities experienced from the POV *of* a "physical body."

In the past, the levels demonstrated on the Zu-line between Infinity-Source (8.0) and physical continuity (0.0) have often been expressed as separate *Gateways* or **thresholds** that resemble veils or layers of clothing (or other "shells") that one might assume as an attachment or extension of personal Identity. It is hardly worthwhile to simply say these points are not real and be done with it; or to say well, I guess that is how things are and take no further responsibility and control for the phenomenon. If one considers the condensation of energy along the Zu-line and the descent of the Spirit through successive "universes" and varied degrees of *Awareness* that are carried with them, we can consider that the Alpha Spirit has very much "imagined into being" the various

POV viewpoints that are accessible in experience—but! then has also very much lost Self-directed command of its own creations, as an individual further **succumbs** to being the *effect* of the same.

The Alpha-Spirit emerges as wave peak of nothingness—a mere consideration of thought as an individuated *Awareness*, being the "I" or "I-AM"—and to which we frequently refer to as Self or "Alpha Spirit." They are the same; the Seeker, the Pilot, the individuals that are behind these *vehicles, is* the Alpha Spirit or I-AM-Self. Any associations of identity to any other forms, be it *physical* or *astral*, are merely considerations—points of view that are assumed by Self in order to experience a particular universe (reality). Of course, when communication of these considerations is improperly handled, we find a Seeker that is unable to "change" their POV at "Will"—or maintain any degree of strong Self-determined control over true creative ability of the Alpha Spirit. This is when fixations and compulsions and tendencies tend to become a part of the Seeker's personality programming, no longer under Self-directed command.

Just as a channel of water cuts out the terrain to make for an easier, more efficient, pathway of flow—so too, do we find, with the automatic reactive-response mechanism established within the personal systems of the Zu-line. We are still treating "systems" and "energy" as always; only the "type" changes from case to case, or example to example.

When command of the first few "run offs" out of the original circuit or channel are not attended to, we find an immediate tendency toward automation. The trickle of water becomes a stream and then a river—and the origination or source of this manifestation is so long gone and forgotten, along with its responsibility and control. This is where we have found the standard-issue Human Condition at this present time; and this state is what we are resolving with the same systematic "objective activity" that mirrors the original means an individual became fragmented in the first place.

Responsibility ultimately does equal commanding power to create and control creations. It very much defines the degree to which a person is willing to reach in order to make something happen—meaning, to create an effect. In most cases, satisfaction of this need to create effect is only treated at the lowest orders of manifestation. In fact, as an individual fails to direct communication at a particular channel or circuit along the Zu-line, the result is for energy and *Awareness* to shift further and further down the *Beta-Awareness Scale.*

—Fragmentation by "Loss" (–2) is only possible after an Alpha Spirit is implanted to believe (and then agrees) they cannot "create" or "have" *again.*

—Fragmentation by "Pain" (–1) is only possible after an Alpha Spirit is implanted and convinced to believe (and then agrees) that the Spiritual Self can actually be hurt, affected or punished when a body is hurt or punished.

In setting up mechanisms to "avoid all effects," the Seeker is no longer willingly a receipt-point for communication. Many restrictions are imposed by limiting actions to a systematic response. Unwillingness and avoidance actually strengthen the programming. By putting up blocks or counter-flows, a "solid" is formed in which to impact. By allowing such energies to "pass through without reaction" an individual is not fragmented by an experience.

By our agreements, the power these automated mechanisms have is great when left "other-determined." By giving up responsibility and control an individual is forced into an effect "unwillingly." Increased Self-Determinism is a necessary factor for the next evolution of the Human Condition—which we simply refer to as *Homo Novus*, a **metahuman** state that archaic German philosopher Friedrich Nietzsche vaguely defined as the *Ubermensch* in his discourse *Thus Spoke Zarathustra*. This is a state of actualized ability in *Self-Honesty* that represents the next "issue" of the Human Condition on planet Earth and in the physical universe: elevated to a point of *Awareness* that reflects the former glory of past kingdoms and universes that we all once inhabited prior to the one here now.

The Alpha-Spirit is *always* the Alpha Spirit, varied by its own degree of actualization; and the Human Condition is *always* the Human Condition, but the manner in which it is treated and defined is altered based on consideration. We are simultaneously improving the state of the Human Condition as a *being* in *beta-existence* while rehabilitating commanding power of the Alpha-Spirit, which *does not* "dwell within" (except by considerations currently enforced) but instead communicates and controls its reality experience of *beta-existence* from a **static** point of the true spiritual *Awareness* as *Self* that we treat as (7.0) on the Standard Model.

Λ Λ Λ Λ Λ Λ Λ

Reproduction or duplication pertains to several aspects in *NexGen Systemology*. On the one hand, we find an occurrence of repetitive cycles-of-action, communication and/or creation (and unwillingness to command the same). There is the other more literal or tangible idea of making "copies" of some "thing"—such as an image or a message—so as to make the cumulative (created) presence and reality of a thing more solid. The same repetition is applied to "other-determined" flows in order to make them less solid. By repetitively altering consideration of ownership/responsibility of some energy between Self and others, the kinks generally get worked out. Finally, we can also direct our *Awareness* to reproduce or duplicate any "remote" POV.

Free unrestricted access to all viewpoints and considerations is within the realm of command for the Alpha Spirit; it is only when these alternative POV are assumed unknowingly or without ability to knowingly change them (and associations attached to them), that we say an individual is out of "phase" with Self and Reality. They are in "someone else's phase." We see this fluidity in creative abilities of children, where they are able to direct their *Awareness* into any POV as *Beingness* that they can imagine. Often, adults respond to this: they are "just going through a *phase.*" It is rather like that; except that a Seeker begins to assume "phases" as their *Beingness* or *Identity* unknowingly and without a command that permits their fluidity for change or alteration of direction.

We refer to personality traits as "tendencies," but they are often programmed and encoded by emotionally charged memory—and as a result, they have a "tendency" to displace, distort and fragment Alpha communications; thus also the command, by Self, of the Human Condition. We tend to "learn" by experience; yet much of this experience is erroneous and highly charged with energy and other forms of emotional encoding.

It is true that each of us, in our Alpha state, is an individualized entity—differentiated as separate from other individualized entities—even at that upper-most point of Spirit that we designate as the I-AM at (7.0) on the Standard Model. Certainly each "I-AM" is an individuated wave crest separate from other individual "*I-AMs.*" But that is not what most refer to as "personality." Beta personalities are an accumulation of material and mental mass on which personal experience of "time" is oriented on a "line."

We observe a correspondence between the health and vitality of an organism in **proportion** to the heavy "charges" and "masses" carried—all of which inhibit ability to freely create, reproduce and duplicate cycles-of-action that lead to a continuous creation. Even at a cellular level, we see that this programmed inhibition is what actually contributes to breakdown of **organic** bodies as it fails to properly command consistently duplicated cycles-of-action. Those who then simply push off the subject of "time" as "another illusion"—as with other facets of Causal Law—refuse responsibility and control of these systems.

"Repetitive" activity or "copying" the POV of someone else generally carries some emotional encoding. In the furthest reaches of our **genetic memory** we have the imprinting assigned by an Alpha Spirit that set this genetic-line into motion. We have also found reoccurring evidence throughout history supporting the idea that the original standard-issue Human Condition is primarily **engineered** for specialized "slavery"—and this is very deeply ingrained within pattern programming of the "RCC." The mechanisms cause a tendency to go on "automatic" for these activities.

An individual that begins to accumulate "experiences" that are painful or invalidating or otherwise producing an "other-determined" result (from the Alpha POV or state of Will-Intention), will then be less likely to follow those courses of action again; the willingness to allow any cycles to repeat diminishes. This especially becomes a factor over the course of one's ongoing accumulation of such heavily charged encoding and imprinting across many lifetimes. When too many things in the objective universe are considered and treated as barriers, and too many cycles-of-action are deemed disadvantageous, an increased inhibition in willingness to act, communicate, reach and create (as an **associative** generalization) will thwart achievement of the highest ideal state of knowing, being and *ability* that is accessible to the true Self as Alpha Spirit.

A great source of confusion occurs when an individual decides that something is not to happen again, for whatever reasons, and then they find themselves facing the thing happening again. This is a great source of confusion for an individual when it is not Self-determined. Yet, this confusion is only a matter of consideration—often based on what the individual *expects*. Here, we find this subject addressed directly in "Route-3, Communication Processing":[*]

\ What would you be willing to have happen again? (*Circuit-1 alt.*)

\ What would you allow to have happen again? (*Circuit-1 alt.*)

\ What would be acceptable to have happen again? (*Circuit-1 alt.*)

\ What wouldn't you mind allowing to happen again? (*Circuit-1 alt.*)

These alternate examples are provided for when a *present* or *attentive* Seeker informs a Pilot that they "don't understand" immediately follow-

---

[*] See appendix for "*Step-2a*" and "*Route-3 Processing Command Lines.*"

ing receipt of a **"processing command line"** (PCL). However, we can only be certain that the misunderstanding is a result of the "wording" and not the willingness of the Seeker to be in communication—or provide "presence" to the session. But, once a variation has been agreed to, the same "wording" should be used consistently. Otherwise new "comm-lag" will be introduced to the session based on new wording and terminology and not based on the actual PCL.

At first, we apply basic *Analytical Recall* to simply test the presence and *Awareness* of the Seeker during Step-2, before orienting them directly with their environment (time-space) using Step-2b. These are always practiced at the beginning of a session—as is some variation of *Bell, Book & Candle*—although the purpose and duration for which they are applied varies as a Seeker is able to get into higher-level communication more easily (sooner) with additional sessions.

The remaining circuits of our previous example would be treated as follows, using "have happen again" as the primary terminal:

What would ____ be willing to have happen again?
   (*Circuit-2, alt. POVs*)

     or \ What could ____ find acceptable to have happen again?

What could others be willing to have happen again? (*Circuit-3*)

     or \ What would (*sphere of existence*) find acceptable to have
       happen again?

Other applicable terminals for this processing include: Reproduce, Duplicate, Repeat and Copy.

:: 8 ::
APPLICATION OF "BELL, BOOK AND CANDLE" IN SYSTEMOLOGY OPERATING PROCEDURE #2-C

An individual that maintains many erroneous agreements that fix their "identity" or state of "being" *to a* "physical body" will often treat the concept of repetition, reproduction and duplication in only its most "materially literal" interpretation. Rather than subject a Seeker to a rigorous study and intensive period of instruction—from which the Seeker may or may not arrive at a proper understanding—these same progressively "higher" realizations are attainable using systematic processing.

When following the SOP-2C formula, a Pilot brings the Seeker into the room and establishes the start of a session after resolving any preliminary concerns. It is important to note and address any of these "world-at-large" issues that the Seeker may have—and which they have "brought in" with them, so to speak. They are considered "present" in the session because the Seeker's attention is fixed on these channels from the beginning even more than any processing that may be introduced thereafter. If it is established quickly and to satisfaction that these "problems" are not "present" in the room, then the session can immediately continue into Step-2.

It may be that when you (*as the Pilot*) are first introduced to a Seeker for processing, that the initial session is rather more like an "interview" than an "intensive" progressive experience. The same formula of SOP-2C is still applied. The methodology works along up to whatever level of actualization and defragmentation a Seeker is presently at. Each "part" of each "Step" is taken in turn as its own unit of processing and operated until the intended end result is successfully reached; no more and no less.

A Seeker is not "pushed along" or "held back from" their own progressive *Self-Actualization* when they have *Professional Piloting Procedure* applied to their condition. It is applied "intuitively" and with judgment and **discernment** on the part of the Pilot. If all of this were not the case, we could just as easily produce audio recordings of rigid guided meditations and so forth—but such methods have already been explored throughout the 20th century, in the New Age movement, New Thought philosophies and realm of social sciences, and they were not found to deliver the type of workability that we have set as a goal for our Systemology. Consequently, *Piloting* is dependent on, and effective only with, *real communication*.

It is quite possible that the first *Piloted* session that a Seeker experiences with our systemology will consist of Step-1 brought through to its completion. Personal introductions—at a casual level—should be kept brief and focused on the Seeker. Piloting is not a time for an individual to try to dazzle a Seeker with a lot of fancy words and book-learning. We are interested only in the Seeker and *their* background during these sessions. The Seeker's attentions should only be on the Pilot in order to remain in session and receive communications, but should not be taken up with any other gimmick or effort on the Pilot's part to "seem interesting" &tc. The Seeker is the focus.

An entry **assessment** of the Seeker can be taken using the *"Beta-Awareness Test"* (*BAT*)[*] so effective results of systematic processing (regarding repair/beta-fragmentation) can be charted and graphed as a confirmation. This "tool" provides a Seeker with an objective point of certainty regarding their own condition. The *BAT* material speaks for itself and does not require additional validation (or evaluation) by the Pilot.

The purpose of the *BAT* is to establish an individualized, yet objective, point of reference for the Seeker—and we have found that the most significant *BAT* improvements take place within the first three to six months of intensive systematic processing. In fact, many Seekers are able to demonstrate a noticeable improvement within the first few weeks. It is important that this successively gradual increase of certainty is maintained—especially at the beginning of their journey on the *Pathway to Self-Honesty*—or a Seeker may become discouraged and steer away from the *Pathway* in confusion and abandon it, falling again to the downward spiral of going out the bottom of the *Awareness* scale of existence.

It may very well be the case that an initial session—if scheduled for longer than one hour—would be able to complete a basic introduction and personal assessment, then move on to Step-2. If this is not the case, it may be assumed that the initial intros and assessments and resolution of "presence" would not require the same duration. Each step is treated until the conditions of completion are met. In this case, we mean "basic communication" and "presence" between the Pilot and Seeker as present in the room. Such essentially meets the requirements of Step-1, *and the Pilot says the words: "Start of session."*

Once a systematic processing session may officially start, a Seeker estab-

---

[*] First introduced in *Liber-2B,* "*Crystal Clear*" – a method of *psychometric evaluation* developed for *Mardukite Systemology* to determine a "basic" or "average" state of personal *beta-Awareness*. An additional "Spheres-Assessment" is introduced in "*Way of the Wizard*" (*Liber-3E*) within this present Master Edition anthology.

lishes greater subjective communication with themselves. The Pilot directs this initial handling of the "Mind-System" using "*Analytical Recall*" techniques—given as Step-2a—which is based on the applied spiritual philosophy and *tech* introduced in *Crystal Clear*.[∞] This is conducted at the start of each session until basic "recall" is operable and coherent, and the communication lag on basic channels is reduced to a consistency or nullified.

As with previous steps, the first time that Step-2a is introduced to a session, the Seeker may have to spend a significant duration—if not the entire session—developing basic "Analytical Recall" (AR) abilities required to satisfy the goals of this step. As with any other steps or systematic processes, it is usually found that the duration spent on each (to meet a basic state or end result) will shorten with each session. A Seeker that is not successfully processed through Step-2 will be less equipped to handle any of the additional "Routes" that are provided.[*]

In Step-2a, the Seeker is directed PCLs from the most basic and non-invasive (or non-restimulative) list possible, using "AR" (Route-2) tech. This should be very extensively applied when first introduced, making certain that a Seeker has a very fluid ability to recall moments and events recorded on their personal **timeline**. The other directive is to encourage the "sensory perception" possible through recall. This means directing attention to various *facets* of the record until accessible information is communicated successfully to the Pilot with ease—and without any associated emotional disturbance to memories recalled. Any imprinting discovered with a heavy emotional charge should, of course, be resolved before continuing with other goals. The "Route" taken to resolve this is on the Pilot's judgment.

Step-2a is not intended to be an intensive process; only an introductory one that opens up channels of energetic communication for further processing. This should not be confused with the idea that the step has no inherent value on its own. An individual that is actually present in Step-2a is developing their ability to manage the Mind-Systems from the start; earning the same benefit as any other "Route-2" application. But the purpose is not to simply enter Step-2a and treat all processing thereafter as a "Route-2" extension. Step-2a is, exactly as listed: only *one* part of Step-2.

Once the Seeker has some handle on themselves—has established that

---

∞   *Liber-2B*

*   The only true accelerator for *Grade-IV* is the material found in *Grade-III*, esp. "*Crystal Clear*," which Pilots distribute as part of their professional practice.

they are an actual presence in session; an Alpha-Spirit operating a Mind-System in command of a particular "body" being monitored—then we redirect attention and communication from this line, toward the space of the environment: the "objective" physical universe in Step-2b.

Simplified objective processing, if introduced on a gradient scale, is also an emergency session-remedy for a Seeker's entry-level difficulties, inability to recall, or an unwillingness to get an increased reality on "Basic-AR." Clearing the channels of "recall" are an important part of *beta-defragmentation*, and so Step-2a cannot be skipped, but it may be alternated with various forms of objective processing. The Pilot returns to AR procedures after each cycle with a "lighter task" to complete until the Seeker discovers that they are able to recall something "actual" from their mental stores; something that actually carries a mental image—and preferably at least a few *facets* of analytical information along with it.

After application of *Basic-AR*, Step-2b is dedicated to "objective processing"—fixing attentions on the external realm of the Physical Universe as the primary "terminal" to knowingly"get reality on"—essentially a *reality* on the nature of *beta-existence* as the space and environment that the corresponding *beta-anchored* "genetic vehicle" occupies. In this instance, we increase a Seeker's own reality on their *"Presence in Space-Time."*

"Presence in Space-Time" is a fundamental component of "communication, control and command" (described within this anthology). It is the primary part of the objective stage in Step-2; and it must be established for each session. Results from the systematic processes for accomplishing this are achieved "sooner" in each successive session, but Step-2 is never dismissed altogether in a formal *Professional Piloting* session. Data for every process used—its type, duration run and realizations attained by a Seeker—are recorded in a logbook/journal for each session.[√]

After an introduction and completion of *"Presence in Space-Time,"* and after successful completion of *"Bell, Book & Candle"* as its own process, additional "Routes" of Piloted processing can ensue.

Considerations for the Physical Universe (operating under Cosmic Law) concern only the "body" and its POV—not the actual identity of the Seeker as Self as Alpha-Spirit; not that which governs the *genetic vehicle*. In this respect, the only considerations that lead to personal fragmentat-

---

[√] The *International School of Systemology (ISS)* has prepared a special economical publication for this purpose titled: *Systemology: The Pathway to Self-Honesty: Truth Seeker's Adventure Journal*.

ion are the product of improper beliefs that the True Spiritual Self *is* the Mind-Systems, or worse, the "body." The "Zu-line" (illustrated on the Standard Model) represents a "personal identity **continuum**" but it is an extension or projection generated by the Alpha-Spirit from its upper-most POV; its POV and identification as *"Beingness"* is not fixed to any other point along that line except as considered so by various "agreements" and "mechanisms."

Over-identification with the lower-level material existence leads to a very literal belief that "I-AM" *equals* "body" or even the "Mind"—and in our moments of greatest clarity, we inherently know this. However, many contrary *reality agreements* about *beta-existence* and automation of reactive-response mechanisms—which are experienced as an effect from the perspective of Self—further fix rigid considerations of the *Identity* and *Being* of the Alpha-Spirit.

"Bell, Book & Candle" employs the type of "objective processing" that actually handles "objects" in space. This is obviously treated after a completion of the first parts of Step-2, since to hold a reality on the "objects" in space, one would first have a reality on "space" itself.

> A sense of agreement on reality must be maintained
> before any communications can occur with a reality.

And this sequence of operations follows a natural logic that is quite effective. However obscure and esoteric it may seem at times, *Mardukite Systemology* follows a basic logic sequence that allows us to treat states of *knowing* and *being* "systematically" in relation to all potential existence.[*]

Putting this all together we find a sequence of processes in Step-2 that raise a Seeker's actualized *Awareness* and "communication, control and command" for the remainder of the session. If the line of attention or willingness is thereafter broken, the Pilot uses their judgment to return the Seeker to a point in the processing where things "dropped out."

By the end of Step-2, a Seeker should be in a condition conducive to additional work. It does take a few sessions, depending on the Seeker's level of development, to really get through these processes individually —and *"Bell, Book & Candle"* is no exception. The first time it is introduced, it should be operated minimally for an hour to achieve desired results. After this, if the Seeker demonstrates good reality on the physical universe (and has successfully attained the goals of the process) and they do not have any significant "setbacks or upsets" during this course of their journey on the *Pathway* (which may require going back to a former regi-

---

[*] Most of this logic is demonstrable using the Standard Models of Systemology.

men to establish the foundation state again), the time spent on introductory objective processing as "Step-2" is reduced and consolidated.

After several sessions with a Seeker successfully processing well, the entire Step-2 chained sequence of operations (as described) may be completed in as little as 10 minutes. This, of course, would require an intuitive and efficient Pilot and a "cooperative"* Seeker that is maintaining their presence in session with proper "communication, control and command."

Objective processes pertain to the objective universe, which is the physical environment that a Seeker knowingly applies their *Awareness* to, and therefore their *presence as* an *Awareness* that can hold a reality on the "physical universe" even if not bound to it as an *Identity* or POV. Erroneous knowledge or belief associations concerning *beta-existence* are a consequence of, and continuous contributor to, personal fragmentation. Denial of Cosmic Law or beliefs that the Physical Universe is "not real" will only further entrap a Seeker as a low-level effect. We would not expect such an individual to get along very well experiencing a "physical life." Of course, we need not be in total agreement with what we are given in regards to the Physical Universe either, and it must be stressed that the observation of Cosmic Law is applicable to *this* universe only—and an Actualized Technician is one that has successfully broken agreements with identifying the POV of Self with beta-existence.

In spite of examples of "objective" techniques appearing within "magical primers" and other esoteric, philosophical and "Self-Help" sources, it is interesting to observe just how many magicians and wizards and mystics and spiritualist lose their *reality on* the Physical Universe as they enter through the "First Gate"—such as the Seeker finds accounted for in *Grade-I* materials (describing an entry point to higher realizations via the "Route of Magick & Mysticism.")‡ These lower Gates are not end-games, although they are often treated as such. And each "plane" distinguished by these gates is also subject to its own "microcosmic copy" of the Seven-plus-One structure within them. This is what constitutes the feeling

---

*   *Liber-2C* regards piloted systematic processing as a "cooperative two-person game."

‡   The Mardukite Esoteric Research Library for the Grade-I *"Route of Magick & Mysticism"* is contained within the new 2020 edition of *"The Great Magickal Arcanum: A Master Course in Magick for Modern Wizards."* A separate related, cycle of *Grade-I* material appears as the *"Route of Druidism & Dragon Legacy."* This *Liber-D* cycle of material Free is composed of *The Druid's Handbook, Elvenomicon* and *Draconomicon,* which were all compiled (along with additional supplements) for a single Master Edition anthology in 2020, titled: *Merlyn's Complete Book of Druidism: A Master Course in Druidry for Modern Druids.*

of "Arrival" after successfully accessing the systematic divisions of a single Gate. As a result, the world of mysticism and occultism and even religion has a tendency to trap those individuals that simultaneously lose their grasp on the truth of the material world.

Many individuals "lose themselves" by fixing *Identity* of *Beingness* to the first level beyond material continuity. Most "magical" lore still in existence (and still being contributed to by those confined to the *Grade-I* paradigms) is fragmentary and collected from very ancient memories that were themselves carried over or inherited from another space-time or universe that we all once occupied prior to the descent of our considerations to this present physical plane.

Even the "religious"—not only the "mystical"—associate erroneous significance to the physical universe with identification of solid objects as a "symbol" for some other *beingness.* We find this throughout *Grade-I* whenever an initiate is made to so carefully fix their attentions on something and then assign it the significance of something else. A twig becomes a wand; a tree becomes a world-axis between universes; &tc. Although realizations are found within that level of understanding, the initiate is more likely to **"collapse the wave"** fixing reality with treatment of *that* level as the "sum all of everything" just as much we find with more mundane mind-sets on physical "reality" at essentially *Gate/Grade-0.*

> —How can someone even hope to hold any "communication, control or command" on some thing treated as "unreal"?
>
> —And what type of fragmentation would ensue if these new **"postulates"** about reality were in opposition to agreements about the physical universe previously made and forgotten about?

Even the magician, mystic, priest or priestess that prides themselves on a "higher understanding" and treatment of reality has a tendency to become so enamored (as an effect point) by experiences demonstrating that something (anything) *more than* or *external to* the Physical Universe exists, that the fundamental communication, control and command maintained with *beta-existence* begins to falter. Such individuals are observed to be "out of touch" or "lose grasp" on "Reality," which as we treat it objectively amongst all Seekers, *is* the Physical Universe! We can accept that there are higher universes that we have descended from without rejecting the reality of the material one we have found our considerations entrapped in.

Methodology behind *"Bell, Book & Candle"* is simply rooted in the application of attention and contact with objects in *beta-existence* free of any other significances assigned. The actual "object" itself is irrelevant; it's just "mass." The concept of using a "bell" or "book" or "candle" is simply a way to **codify** the idea with some standardized title for our tech. The most basic point of this is to get a reality on objects in space after identifying the reality of space itself previously in Step-2. We do not wish to fix any additional significance to the "objects" themselves, beyond the basic fact of their physical composition of energy collected and condensed by agreements as "mass." This same principle is applied to "space" in "*Presence in Space-Time.*"

Throughout Step-2, a Seeker is directed to knowingly contact and communicate with the solidity of the physical universe and acknowledge the relationship maintained with *beta-existence*—which is usually taking place unknowingly. On one operative "level" of processing, basic objective techniques work to increase attention span, concentration skills and focus—much in the same manner that many other esoteric traditions observe. However, as a Piloted process, Step-2b and specifically "*Bell, Book and Candle*" assist in resolving sources of heavy fragmentation and imprinting, such as automation, fixed attention and intention on repetitive tasks, erroneous associations, or significances attached to "mass" in the physical universe.

At every level of *Beingness*, an entity seeks to "have" and "possess" *things*. And while there are no other logical reasons as to why we should stress an importance of *Living* in order to accumulate dense piles of mental and physical *stuff*, this is what takes place in the absence of attaining any greater satisfaction from the *effort* applied to *Living* while fixated as an effect of the Physical Universe and its "sensation-based encoding."

It is suggested on the *Arcane Tablets* that the state of Self-Honesty is directly related to an individual's freedom from physical and mental attachments, solids, *stuff* and *things*—whatever "energetic charges" and "fragmented waveforms" they are carrying around. And we find elements of this demonstrable in virtually every "mystical" or meta-spiritual methodology that churned up in the history of this planet.

"Systematic objective processes" provide a sense of Self-directed reality on *beta-existence* and "objects" in the physical universe as solid matter. Even creative uses, first demonstrated in *Crystal Clear** are not in any way a "delusion" when the Seeker is *Aware* that *they* are directing the intention and creating the idea that a particular object "feels" or "seems" a

---

*   See *Liber-2B, Unit-4 and Unit-5;* currently available as "*Crystal Clear*" or in the complete *Grade-III* omnibus anthology, "*The Systemology Handbook.*"

certain way. The purpose of this is to get a Seeker *realizing* that *they* are always the one that is assigning the significance or association to any *thing* found in the Physical Universe. By "thing" we, of course, mean some kind of solid matter or mass—and we know that at the level of the Mind-Systems such "masses" are called *beliefs* and *implants*, and at the emotional level these solids develop in the form of rigid distortions as automated reactions and responses.

Many mystical traditions and philosophies operate on a principle of "rejection" of the Physical Universe—but this has not been discovered to be widely effective for earning the results we are after in our Systemology. In fact, the absence of *Self-determinism* involved in such pursuits does not actually strengthen any upper-level qualities of the Alpha-Spirit beyond that which pertains specifically to *beta-existence*, the division of which is essentially (4.0) on the Standard Model. Esoteric initiates remain suspended within the effect-range of the Physical Universe, simply on an oppositional side of it.

When we give up the responsibility and control to manage effects of the physical universe, we become the effect, regardless of how far away we wish to remove ourselves from the equation. Sitting up on a mountaintop for half of a lifetime, encountering no one and not moving around for fear of unbalancing causation or karmic effects from hurting a blade of grass or stepping on a bug... this might be satisfactory for a select few today on the planet, but it does not play a role in our Systemology, because it is no way systematic—no matter how many insanely long **Eastern** hymns have been written and codified about it.

Many philosophies and teachings warn against attachments and over-identification with the material world—but that does not mean we should treat it as *evil* (as the *gnostic* does) or as a *glamour* or *maya* (as the *mystic* does) or as some incredible *mystery* (as the *academic* does) or as holding some kind of *magical significance* (as the *occultist* does)... when does a stick become a wand and by whose authority other than the consideration of *Self*? Only at the lowest order of causative creative expression and consideration could "objects" ever *become* "symbols." That the imaginative efforts of "New Age Wizardry" should have fallen so far into symbols from its once glorious heights is only one sign that it is no longer in-step or in "phase" with an actualized higher POV of existence. But this is about the extent to which an initiate will reach if following the lowest levels of the *Pathway* out as an end-game.

The true "Wizard" is one that has graduated *being* the *effect* of other-determined causality. Note that our purpose in *Grade-IV* (and beyond) is not to invalidate lower "Routes" and *Grades*. There is nothing inherently wrong with "magical" methodologies that lead an initiate toward greater certainty, willingness and ability on a gradient scale—but once an initiate begins to agree to the practical limitations of its paradigm and structure, then they have come up to yet another barrier—the *second* veil —that is considered the same type of boundary as what one had crossed from the mundane just to get through the *first* gate! A systemology of these "Gates" constitutes esoteric technology behind *Graded* material developed for the "Mardukite Esoteric Research Library"—which includes *Mardukite Zuism & Systemology*.

It will be eventually *realized* that whatever we encounter as a "solid" or "object" of the Physical Universe, it is <u>Self</u> that determines the qualities and experience that is registered. We can easily direct attention toward physical objects and note their solidity and the condensation of energy that they contain as a "form"—and this is a matter of consideration or "thought." But, most of the time it is not the actual *Self* that is in the determinant state of cause on these experiences when information being fed to the Alpha-Spirit is filtered and colored by all manners of fragmentation, particularly as commanded by the *Reactive-Control-Centers.*[*]

When we "look" at something, we are giving it our attention and receiving various information as a communication from it; and this information is processed as the "reality" we have on something. In order to have any reality on it at all, the nature of the "thing" is duplicated or reproduced in the mind as a copy—which is then viewed within the **Mind's Eye** as a mental image. The nature of how we are seeing and interpreting this information from the POV of a *genetic vehicle* is widely examined in **physics** and psychology, but it is not generally considered much further.

Most individuals are not able to actually experience a true "copy" of external stimulus inflowing from the Physical Universe due to various degrees of fragmentation developed along perceptive channels. This says nothing even of other biological conditions that might affect how information is received and communicated; for example, an individual who is "color blind" is usually not "blind" but processing visual information from their environment through physical filters acting as an anomaly to what is considered the standard-issue Human Condition.

An ability to reproduce information from one's environment is critical;

---

[*] The remainder of this chapter-lesson is based on a February 2020 *NexGen Systemology* workshop lecture given by Joshua Free that was not adequately recorded to be included in this manual as a full "extended course" transcript.

but not because of how important the *facets* of the Physical Universe actually are (since such is arbitrary), but on the contrary: of how easily we may simply duplicate "imagery" *at Will*. A realization here regarding "clinging to experience" with emotional charge (or a sense of "loss"): there is no need to cling so tightly to that which we could just as easily recreate for ourselves in the moment of a breath! And this is indeed one of the innermost teachings derived from the *Arcane Tablets*, which carry a truth that is otherwise lost in the **Western** world.

Λ Λ Λ Λ Λ Λ Λ

The version of "*Bell, Book & Candle*" employed at the Mardukite Offices is the most intensive systematic "objective processing" that we have standardized—but it *has* been applied for a minimum of one hour on all *Grade-IV* Pilots that contributed to research (for this manual). Our first experiments with a "standard version" only involved two objects—and they were not at first a *Book* and *Candle*, but that was what the present author settled on when being processed on this method for 90-minutes. It is only effective as a defragmentation intensive when used for a minimum of 30-minutes; and the first time it is introduced to *SOP-2C* directly, it should be conducted for at least 60-minutes (until the Seeker has appropriately *flattened* the waves it is meant to defragment).

The Pilot does not need to run the "standard version" of *Bell, Book & Candle* in all repeated sessions if the Seeker has already received its benefits. This step is not meant to provide some "miracle" or "remedy-for-all" by itself either; it is simply a step. Objects used may be anything of an appropriately manageable size; and a *Book* and *Candle* seemed to apply very well to this, carrying a particular esoteric flavor. Individuals in our Offices suggested the phrase of "*Bell, Book & Candle*" due to its other religious associations in excommunicating witches and heretics from the Roman Catholic Church. The name stuck. In fact, it even led us to additional considerations for processing that involved three objects as opposed to two (or one) and the concept of giving a Seeker the "ability" to choose the object(s) for various processes. "Power of choice" is returned to a Seeker after an objective process where they are being directed to give attention to specific objects or spots on command of the Pilot. The Pilot directs commands only to defragment the channels and then returns command ability to the Seeker as a more able—or more *actualized*—being, with an increased ability to direct their own command more directly (such as with "*Presence in Time-Space*" processes).

In the "standard version" a Seeker is presented with an environment that contains two distinct objects that are not similar in any particular way other than being easily handled and composed of "matter." These may be placed at some distance on a desk or table that is used between the Pilot and Seeker or they may put up on stands/pedestals across a room with some distance between. Another variation on this processing simply places an object in each hand of the Seeker, and they are directed to focus attention and give various responses about each alternately.

It is best if a Seeker is able to "move around" as much as possible for "objective processing"—but it becomes more a matter of physical stamina and exercise in the beginning, if one were to process a Seeker through an hour of "*Presence in Time-Space*" and then an hour of "*Bell, Book & Candle*." Without properly handling "*Presence in Time-Space*," a Seeker will not necessarily achieve the same benefit from a 60-minute intensive of "*Bell, Book and Candle*."

The basic process directs attention back and forth between the two objects. They could be simply "object-one" and "object-two." Each is treated in their own unit of space-time with *Awareness* and no other assignment of value until it is knowingly granted. This is not a "first object"-to-"second object" and back to "first object" type operation; but that is *exactly* what the RCC will try to engage during the process—and that is what we want to effectively defragment. A single run as an initial intensive is not some magical fix-all, but variations may be employed thereafter that raise a Seeker's *actual* objective *Awareness* high enough for additional processing during a session.

In our original runs of "*Bell, Book & Candle*" we asked a Seeker to look at the object by name after differentiating it as an object for processing; so we said, "Here we have a *Book* and we are going to put that right there; and here we have a *Candle,* which we place there." We want the Seeker to physically pick up an "object" up and observe it. They then pick up the other and compare differences and note similarities. As an "A.T." exercise, you can have the Seeker make a duplicate copy of the object that occupies the same space-time as the actual object. Eventually the Seeker can even be directed to send their *Awareness-POV* "in to" and "out of" the object; an exercise that will encourage future Spiritual "Zu-Vision" practices.

In a later refined version, we had the Seeker *Identify* objects themselves as part of the repetitive commands for the processing. In this case, we said, "Look at that object." *And we would acknowledge that they have done so.* "Identify the object." *And they do and we say, good—they are communicating with us too.* "Pick it up." *Another command for silent action that should still be acknowledged.* "What is it?" *Yep, it's the object we identified before it was in our hands.* "Okay, put it back exactly where it was." And then we move on to the other object the same way and just keep repeating this over and over again. This basic version demonstrates the effective basics of the operation very well.

The newest version of *Bell, Book and Candle* now requires the same details be asked with each cycle, such as "what is its color?" "what is its texture?" "what is its weight"—but whatever it is, the command-lines need to be exactly the same for both objects and every cycle throughout the process in order to be effective. Even this is just one variation discovered in an old philosophy book from the 1950's on thought-exercises —which suggested details could be noted including: "solidity," "temperature," "significance," "purpose," &tc.

∧ ∧ ∧ ∧ ∧ ∧ ∧

"Attention" as an application of Self-directed *Awareness.* Proper development of an "attention span" is not encouraged in today's society—and too often we find our attentions are demanded and scattered by others when they are not fully under command of the Alpha Spirit. Keep in mind that the Spirit is *using* Mind–Body systems during its experience of *beta-existence.* Therefore, systems themselves only operate under command of Self to the degree that they are able to be given clear attentions that are not distorted by other forms of fragmentation.

Various forms of fragmentation cause the system to form tendencies and patterns that are not always within the scope of "attention" when diverted elsewhere. It will be noticed that one of the strongest of these is "automation" and one of the only ways the standard issue Human Condition manages this is through "variety." There is a tendency that takes place in the human condition after about 10-15 minutes of repetitive processing intensives where the Mind–Body systems disconnect from actualized *Awareness* of Self, and treat the inflow on automatic. This is because the experience is being accumulated along a timeline and not as an individual unit of time—hence the phenomenon of anticipation. The Seeker's mechanisms begin to *anticipate* the next command-line based on a "build-up" of "experience" from the former series and then operate from the RCC and not *Alpha*—all the while, actions are still being carried out.

To ensure a Pilot is actually applying systematic processing to the "I-AM" Self as Alpha-Spirit and not simply treating the exercise of a physical organism, the automation should be sporadically tested approximately every ten minutes to ensure the Seeker is still *present* and running the process. This means, for example, after many repetitive cycles of working back and forth from "object-one" to "object-two" the Pilot should direct the Seeker's attention on the same object twice; for example, using "object-one" and having the Seeker take their attention off and then back on "object-one" again. If you get a hesitation, smirk or emotional reaction of any kind, you can be certain that at least part of the Seeker's actualized *Awareness* had momentarily been removed in lieu of an automated response, but then it "snapped" back in.

The Self obviously has the ability to direct and command systems and even create energetic mechanisms and automated functions of the systems it controls and monitors. There is nothing wrong with this *if* the Self is fully *Aware* that these creations exist; that they are Self-made and thus may be dissolved (taken off of "auto-pilot") with the same degree of intention via Alpha-Thought ("postulate") or consideration. Tendencies of Mind–Body Systems to *go on automatic* outside of our command are what we want to resolve; this is different from combating a fundamental truth that all systems *can be* automated.

Full intensive processing of *Bell, Book & Candle* is formally introduced to a Seeker as an exercise meant to raise *Awareness* and tolerance for confusion and repetitive action in the Physical Universe. A Pilot must explain basic directions of any procedure they intend to run and ask the Seeker if it is okay to run it. If you have established *Presence in Time-Space*, then this will not be nearly as difficult for them, although it is not unheard of for a Seeker to just simply go "out of session" after 20 or 30 minutes of this and just say they've "had enough." However, if they can be encouraged to push through, a demonstration becomes obvious that this procedure is very much possible to endure.

Many individuals do not believe it is possible to perform the same cycles of action repeatedly without "blanking out," and therefore find no resolution to the fact that our society and its material systems have a very hypnotic effect. This renders programming and imprinting easier and its calculated restimulation for external "other-determined" command of the Mind–Body. This effect is what systematic processing resolves when properly conducted. And once the Seeker is able to release the hold a former moment has on their considerations of a future moment, while maintaining full presence as Self in the present, then you know you have found some modicum of success implementing these methods. Make sure to get them securely grounded and centered when the process is completed before moving on to another process or ending the session. Have them *find* the "floor" or get a *sense* of the ground; or you can have them *contact* its solidity. Make certain you end the session with the statement: *End of session.*

Fragmentation, encoding, imprinting, programming, implanting—and dare we say it, the "hypnotic effect"—are all the result of a "pattern" that goes unchecked by Self. And this *is* important to keep in check because we are likely to interact with all manner of various "patterns" of "existence and form" all throughout *beta-existence* and beyond; so best get a handle on it now. By regaining the skill or natural ability to direct a constant flow of full actualized *Awareness* into each new moment that a "pattern" of any kind is contacted (or restimulated), a Seeker increases certainty of *Self-determinism.*

There is an illusion maintained by some of our systemologists, that these practices in Step-2—or any systematic process found in our methodology —is a treatment of the body, or even its Mind–Body mechanics directly; it is not. We are not treating a body or the mechanisms of the connection that Self maintains with a body; we are directing all of our communications to *Self*, to the *Alpha-Spirit*, bypassing all other circuitry and returning the power of command over these other facets of the human condition. These are *their* things to resolve—their own creations and devices—and no one else has the right to take them away. You will most certainly find this to be the case if you try. And it is perhaps for this reasons that systematic processing has been found effective where so many other methods have failed in successfully improving the spiritual metahuman certainty of an individual.

:: 9 ::
UNDERSTANDING METAHUMAN SYSTEMOLOGY*
[GRADE-IV PROCESSING]

A Mardukite Systemologist that is studying with us in *Grade-IV* will immediately note the absence of any emphasis placed on "Route-1" methodology as explored during the extended course delivered for *The Tablets of Destiny*. It is true that deeper emotional encoding may resurface during some of the processes we use now for other "Routes," however it is not the intention of *SOP-2C* to target this directly. Naturally, emotional turbulence is not avoided or invalidated either. However, what we have found, and rather quickly, is that these newer methods that focus on increase of personal ability and certainty and willingness to reach for greater responsibility and *Self-determinism* are actually more effective and workable on a practical basis—especially in regards to this "paid-by-the-hour" work-a-day world; and it is assumed that a *Pilot* would also need to make certain to cover their own expenses and those of their operations with their professional practice. So, this means delivering the highest quality *Piloting*.

Most fragmentation you will encounter using *Grade-III* and *Grade-IV* material is based on "associative knowledge," which is to say: regarding *facets* that carry associated meaning and significance. Of course, in *Grade-IV*, we refer to such encoded *facets* as a *charged terminal* because we are working with communication circuits. An individual's true understanding of the nature of things becomes quickly blurred as the Alpha Spirit or Self begins to take on more and more rigidly fixed considerations from their environment. The Alpha Spirit begins to assume that the mechanistic nature of the Physical Universe is attributable or associative with the actual existence of the Self as Alpha Spirit; and herein we find the greatest and deepest trap of associating Self with a Body and then associating the whole package exclusively with beta-existence.

We sometimes refer to "attentions" of the Alpha Spirit or Self as an "Awareness"; but the truth of the matter is that Self *is* the Awareness and it finds that it actually invests itself *within* viewpoints it takes on; and the range of these POV is only fixed or limited by considerations, which are often also fixed or limited. This is not an incredibly complex puzzle to solve once we remove all of the erroneous information attached to "truth" throughout the ages; but it does require some working

---

* Based on transcripts to a lecture given by Joshua Free on the evening of May 15, 2020; first published in "*Command of the Mind-Body Connection*" (*Liber-2D*).

out, and that is what we are here to do; in essence, what you keep coming back down here to do. Once you are no longer the effect of all of this, then you will be truly free. There is no substitute for seeing this all the way through.

There is an inherent knowing that at the base of all *Life,* the *universes* and *everything* that is, was or could be—we discover this concept called "energy." We instinctively know that there is such a thing as "personal energy" and it seems to be tied to "attention." This is actually learned very early on, even as children, and does not need to be taught. But it *should* be taught, because lack of *Self-determinism* over attentions is actually what allows fragmentation to even exist or have any kind of hold on an individual whatsoever. There is an old axiom that actually guided our earliest experimentation in Systemology that: "Energy flows where attention goes," and then later we found on *The Tablets of Destiny* that "Whatever the Mind creates or believes, the Spirit reinforces." Well, this stuff was found to be quite true in our processing experiments and not just fancy words.

The term "Actualized Awareness" is introduced in *Grade-III* to differentiate the amount of beta-Awareness actively and actually present in an individual. These energy units are the basis of the exchange whenever we are communicating. And these communications are not only restricted to other living beings as terminals, because it has been found that we have the ability to grant "living" Beingness to virtually any object or thought and treat it as a suitable terminal for communication. Humans do it all the time without realizing it. So, while the processing that pertains to analytical recall or communication circuits may seem "light," it is practically "everything" at once. "The entire bowl of soup is tasted in the first spoonful."[∞]

Personal energetic stores or charges of energy accumulated from experience are often given attention in lieu of objective reality that is in front of us—and this is one of the magician's former mistakes: in simply ignoring the fact that a physical universe is taking place. We often impose, or superimpose, some other mental image or picture over what things are when we experience them. Yes, we certainly do have the ability to "create and make our own reality" and so does the next guy and the next one—we all have a personal universe that we occupy in the Spirit, and since it is first, foremost and exponent of our existence, we call it Alpha. There are many ranges and universes and divisions that exist between our Alpha state and this present Physical Universe that we refer to as "beta,"

[∞] Paraphrasing Deepak Chopra in *"Way of the Wizard."*

but this vocabulary has made it far more successful to actually yield some results and not just present a colorful mythology, philosophy or *kabbalah.*

At *Grade-IV* we blatantly confront *facets* or *terminals* that make us "think" or "feel" a certain way. As soon as we assess that something *does* produce an effect on us, it must be processed out or noted. Advanced practitioners that have been involved in experimentation along the way have even learned how to use *Self-processing* for emergencies and even have mastered a delivery of "Route-1" practices for emergency applications on others; particularly in these times we are living in when we must also conceive of effective ways in assisting others that are not yet even aware that our Systemology is an option for them in this lifetime. But this all comes down to the handling of "energy" and it is here at this point that we find at least some common meeting ground for all that has been explored in the previous *Grades* since the beginning. Energy.

In 2015, a division of the *Mardukites* (known as the *Moroii*) began conducting energy experiments concerning "flows" and "depletion." The final discovery, not even disclosed within any editions of *The Vampyre Handbook,* actually revealed something unexpected to those involved. Matters of energy depletion and charges were discovered to be entirely based on personal consideration alone and nothing else. An individual was as spiritually unrestricted as they were abundant in energy and this was found to be fed in from an unlimited source. So, why, then was anyone ever feeling depleted or spun-in if they were also being fed unlimited energy? It occurred to me that most individuals were wasteful with their own resources; that an individual low in beta-Awareness would unwisely use their own unlimited energy in contrast to another individual that was simply more Aware; but there had to be another way of considering this issue.

Then it became abundantly clear to me that if you were to create some type of mass in the way of the flow—just like debris caught in a canal or aqueduct—then it would more likely pick up other mass as the flow continues across that point. Water continues to come in, feeding with it a host of other potential debris to be caught up in the mass until finally there is a blockage. This blockage creates more and more turbulence for the flow as it works its way past it and essentially changes the nature of the flow in general until it potentially stops the flow altogether. Here we would have material still fed into the system from its source but allowing nothing, or very little, to get through. There is every reason to believe that something very similar is taking place in the energetic conduits that channel the personal energy of our experience as *Life.*

When we refer to "communication" we mean any exchange of energy and the type of flow that is taking place. This is not just about "talking," although we do find that language programming—the literal "language" that one thinks in—can also be assigned associative and erroneous meaning. But, we are also concerned simply with energy at its most basic or universal common point of existence as a communication; which we know is tied to attention and intention. This is precisely the information and realization that we are working with at *Grade-IV.* And it is important that the *Pilot* remain in good communication with the *Seeker* during the processing to make sure that these realizations aren't missed as the *Seeker* hits them. So give the session some attention and keep the *Seeker* communicating about what is happening with their internal universe.

Realizations are more important than any answers given to processing lines. The exception is the type of processing meant to reduce encoding or energetic charge of an imprint or other fragmentation. This means that we really have two types of processing—in addition to what we have already differentiated as "subjective" and "objective." The other type includes processes meant to bring the *Seeker* toward a certain conclusive realization on a "cognitive" or analytical level of thought. For example, if we were to use a PCL or "Processing Command Line" that directed a *Seeker* to "look around" and "spot something" that would be "acceptable" to remain and then "identify" it, we would do this repeatedly until the *Seeker* realizes that they are the determinant factor of what they are willing to find acceptable, or in a variant of the same process, to "reach" for. Now, how would you know that they are realizing this unless you allow them to say something other than a response to the next line? Communication!

The original type of processing we encounter involves discharging emotional stores held on a line; and while this may be accomplished with "high level thought"—or what some simply call "postulates"—such are aided by the type of **abreaction** processing that is first introduced as "Route-1" in *The Tablets of Destiny.* The basic principles of this are the same in *Grade-IV;* only the script-pattern has been updated for *SOP-2C.* The same type of effect can be drawn out from a precision use of "Route-3" as well; which in many ways is a refined version of "Route-1"—but treating imprints and implants as a multifaceted energetic charge.

The primary difference between "Route-1" and "Route-3" methods in handling imprinting is that when a *Pilot* discovers an area of the *Seeker's* life that has a heavy imprinted charge on it, the specific event or trauma does not have to be targeted directly as in "Route-1"—although it could be. Instead, multiple circuits running on that line are treated in succession until the *Seeker* has a better handling of it; at which point, the matter may even be resolved analytically.

In some variations of "*Bell, Book & Candle*" work, we asked a *Seeker* "what would it be okay for this book to be?" And they come up with all kinds of answers for a while until they say, hey, you know, I think I'm basically just the one determining what this could be and then I guess it could be anything I want it to be, and I'm the one that's doing this...and so on and so forth; things like that. It seems strange to some of you that we would feel the need to make demonstrations, or rather, conduct processing, in such a manner—almost juvenile, right? But you might just surprise yourself on how effective all of this is.

Some basic processing from *Crystal Clear* can bring an individual to the realization that what they think affects how they feel, which affects what they think and what they do, which is in turn managed by the way in which their mode of thought has been set up, and so forth—this is the first time that some are actually realizing this in their lifetime. I mean we all seem to "know" and "talk about" various ideas and I've seen even the lowliest individual have their most philosophical glimpses of truth—and yet all of the other programming and encoding is so deeply ingrained that these few sparse moments are not enough to put the individual back on the right track in the right direction. Full systematic demonstration of these truths and the true power of personal realizations earned, simply do not have an adequate substitute in this existence.

If we ask a *Seeker* to recall moments of "non-communication" with a specific terminal or facet they are dealing with, it should be alternated with moments of "communication." Here, we want a *Seeker* to realize that the "cold-shoulder-avoidance-game" is not even a Game; its boring and unproductive, right? And you can run something like this as a process with all of the circuits using "Route-3." So, you say: "Recall when you were in communication with *such-and-such*." And then, "Recall a time when you were in non-communication with *such-and-such*." And then right down the line of circuits: "Recall a time when *such-and-such* communicated with you." And, "Recall...not communicating with you." And so on. I mean, what's our end goal here? Get your *Seeker* to realize that being "in communication" is the *only Game* in town. They have to realize these things. Sure, you could just tell them all this stuff; and they would nod and go "mm-hmm" and then go right back to their old programming. So, we employ "processing" and it proves more effective.

Once a Seeker makes it through the basic processes leading up to this point, there is every reason to begin employing a regimen of more advanced "Actualized Technician" prep-work—meaning our introductory "Wizard" processes—so long as they are within the *reach* and *willingness* of the Seeker. And we would expect that they should be if this has all been handled correctly.

Our Systemology is concerned with an applied knowledge of "causation" and "source" in regards to the energy behind all *Life*, the *universes* and *everything* we can conceive of, right? The nature of this "chain" is fundamentally illustrated within the Standard Models of Systemology and our graphic Zu-line demonstrations—however much these may or may not be considered esoteric, allegorical or figurative to you. A grasp on the greater reality behind what these models represent is realized personally and directly as a Seeker moves along the *Pathway*. There is no reason to force or instruct those that are not yet ready to have a reality on something. "Lips of wisdom are sealed except to the ears of understanding." All we can do is assist a Seeker along the Pathway toward their own realizations.

At this point of *Grade-IV*, our "A.T. Source Processing" is mainly restricted to "communication," since it is in this form that the Seeker has been introduced to the fundamentals of energy. We are dealing with four main aspects of consideration—or POV—that a Seeker may identify with and which are treated directly with systematic processing. This has always been the case; although it is only now that I have been satisfied with a simplified codification of these conditions. There are some philosophers and mystics that have referred to them separately as "universes" or "bodies" in regard to the *Self* or *Alpha Spirit* having lost the ability to differentiate between them as potential viewpoints only. If that is the case, then systematic processing most certainly assists in untangling this web. They are, quite basically:

External – Internal – Interior – Exterior.

    —By "<u>External</u>" we mean the objective <u>Physical Universe</u> existence, or *beta-existence*, that the Physical Body or *Genetic Vehicle* is essentially anchored to for its consideratons as a locational space-time dimension or POV;

    —By "<u>Internal</u>" we mean the personal physical existence viewpoint that is associated with a <u>Body</u>, the personal physical shell that we consider a Beta-Body or *Genetic Vehicle*, which is in the command of an Alpha Spirit with an anchored POV;

—By "<u>Interior</u>" we mean the POV of Self that is fixed to the "internal" Human Condition, including as the RCC (*Reactive Control Center*), but more often referring to the complete <u>Mind</u>-System connected to the Human Condition (everything between "zero and four" on our Standard Model) when we might say that someone is still "inside" their head, so to speak; even unhealthily avoiding contact with the body (then finally)

—By "<u>Exterior</u>" we mean the POV of Self that is "external" to the Human Condition, which we have also come to refer to as ZU-vision, but which is essentially just our way of differentiating the metahuman range of considerations directly as the <u>Alpha Spirit</u>, free of the physical and mental trappings of the Physical Universe.

> <u>External</u> = physical <u>Beta-Universe</u> (objective)
>
> <u>Internal</u> = physical <u>Body</u> (objective)
>
> <u>Interior</u> = subjective <u>Mind-System</u> (Mental Universe)
>
> <u>Exterior</u> = subjective Zu-Vision (or <u>Alpha Spirit</u>)

We assume that, regardless of what fanciful philosophies, spiritualities or popularized religions that a Seeker has run across in their multiplicity of lifetimes that, in the here and now, they do not have a good handle on these conditions: what they are and how they are distinct from one another. In fact, the great conspiracy behind the structure of this beta-existence is that somewhere along the line we have all agreed to collapse the others into this one Physical Universe and have refined any and all beliefs about *Self* as the I-AM and *Alpha Spirit* based on what we have learned and observed in the Physical Universe. We have patterned all of our knowledge for each of these facets of potential beingness all on the same mechanistic ordering of *this* Physical Universe. *This* is part of what we are progressively unraveling along the *Pathway* through the *Grades* of defragmentation.

What is likely to happen in processing, is you are going to hit on something with an energetic charge on it, and if that happens, then you have to resolve that. You will have to at one point or another anyway, but if you can get broader realizations to occur, then the Seeker is going to have one foot up already when they confront their next charged terminal, such as the type of "genetic vehicle"—which runs into roles and phases and identities—or the type of "physical universe" location specifics, which runs into a whole list of associations with potential imprinting on them. And if you are planning on taking a *Seeker* up the higher routes of the *Pathway to Infinity*, you had better listen to everything they say and make notes of these lists in your log-books for later, because these will become important for assessment along the way.

If you use our current *SOP-2C Tech* for "Route-1" type work, try the "Route-3" techniques using any related *facet* or *terminal* that carries an energetic or otherwise reactive charge on it. Just plug it into the processes and flatten those collapsed waves that way. You want a Seeker freely and willingly able to recall and communicate anything without inhibition. You have the tools now. Make it happen.

:: 10 ::

PRESENCE IN SPACE-TIME AND SOP-2C STEP-2B[*]

There is a considerable amount of information that could be attached to the subject of *Presence in Time-Space.* This matter is the basis for our actualized Wizardry; what we pursue on the *Pathway to Self-Honesty* and through successive *Gateways of Infinity* later on as we continue to extend our reach toward higher developments.

We know that the inherently true and highest nature of the Alpha Spirit is as a *creative force.* We will not assign to it an arbitrary belief of being the "Absolute Source" with a capital "S," but it *is* the Source of the I-AM or POV perspective of the Spirit. We know that we are creating and feeding energy into what we concentrate our focuses upon and that combined, these aspects are inhibited by conditioned implanting, encoding and other programming taken on and carried along the way and assigned and associated as, and to, the Identity of Self; I-AM; the Alpha Spirit.

At our own core—and as our own Source—we are Eternal beings, fed in with an unlimited supply of energies only restricted by the solidity or mass that we have decided to take on along the way; and of which we consistently continue to validate through our agreement with the Physical Universe. And there is nothing wrong with an agreement that this Physical Universe is in existence; we see it and we experience it and it is very much solid—but it is not *All* there is; is not *Everything*; is just *one Universe*—and there is much that is passed off as "knowledge" about our *beta-existence* that we do not have to agree with.

The Alpha Spirit has, through a succession of other implanted agreements and assignments of Identity, come to essentially agree with the structure of the Physical Universe as being *All* there is; at least in the sense of providing no room, opportunity or belief that would allow the POV of the Alpha Spirit to be anywhere else but entrapped in the considerations of the Physical Universe. It likewise has developed a sense that the *Self* is so firmly tied to this; that the Alpha POV is somehow now confined to this Physical Universe and has created many "postulates" and made or reinforced and validated many agreements about this condition that are not altogether true at all.

In *Mardukite Zuism* and *NexGen Systemology* we tend to treat the Physical

---

[*] Based on transcripts to a lecture given by Joshua Free on the evening of May 22, 2020; published in "*Command of the Mind-Body Connection*" (*Liber-2D*).

Universe as little more than a *Game*; thereby we do not delude ourselves with accepting that it is anything other than a *Game* and with the same qualities that we should expect from a *Game*, which is to say a "barrier" to the playing field: the "interior" of the Human Condition—between zero and four on our Standard Model.

The Alpha Spirit has been engaged in the *Game* of the Human Condition for a very long time; and probably has been playing at the *Game* of the Physical Universe for much longer. Most of you know our teachings on "experience" by now; it's "fragmenting" and "aberrative." All the individual does is start to develop further and further conditions for themselves and more and more excuses and reasons and motivators for why they are doing this or unwilling to do that or not be this or not know that. You start to put *this* many artificial conditions on something as powerful as the Alpha Spirit and eventually you are just going to practically snuff it out and force it into considering that it is, itself, even lesser than what it once was. There we see a pattern of decay as "time" that is registered as states of "having" or "not-having" alternating across our spiritual timeline.

An Alpha Spirit exists—as the actual "I" or *Self*—in a universe that far and exceeds the considerations of a *beta-existence*—and hence our definitions for such a distinction when we speak of *Alpha* and *beta* qualities. We speak a lot now of—or "point-of-view"—and reproduction or duplication because that is essentially what an individual is doing with their Reality at every moment. Things *are* real; and that *reality* is based on *agreements*. There are some agreements that we can say are valid about *beta-existence*; they were ordered as so—though I have purposely treated this subject with a minimum of colorful cultural mythology. We previously assigned the Anunnaki paradigm to this work at *Grade-II* and *Grade-III* because it is the oldest complete point of visible and historical reference we have between what is not physically recorded in the distant past and the point that we are sitting at now in the present.

When we talk about the nature of Reality—the nature of agreements—the basic quality of what a thing *is*, we are talking about duplication or copying of programmed information used to generate the Reality perceived. This is like an embedded code processed and producing particular displays on a screen. The average user interacts based on the interface on the screen and is not usually working at the code directly; for example when the individual is playing a "video-game" they are interacting based on the graphic imagery that they can see and not necessarily the coding embedded beneath—but its still under there, defining parameters of the *Game*; there is no illusion about that. Maybe the *Game* really *is* composed of smoke and mirrors and is the complete *B.S.* some individuals are likely to assume—but most *Games* are, right? But its still a *real Game*—and here you are, *really* "playing" it. Right?

So here you are, projecting or extending your reach as a POV onto the command of this Human Condition and you're *in* the *Games*. What are you gonna do? You gonna avoid it? You gonna sit and stomp and pout and cry about how you don't like this *Game?* Oh, come on now. So, that's where we sit—and at this point, the barriers of the *Game* have become as a prison for the Human Condition and the extent of its reach and willingness to do, know or be anything; all of which are based on the considerations or "postulates" that a Spirit has fixed in place about itself.

The Alpha Spirit—*I-AM Self*—does not actually change location. What happens is that it considers other POV in existence and thereby creates or generates necessary factors of that experience, which is not limited to our physical conception of space-time or even the manner in which energy and matter operates within the confines of *beta-existence* under the Law that governs this Physical Universe. However, somewhere along the line, the Alpha Spirit got fooled or led into thinking that the only potential POV for an existence was out of this one physical body and somehow in order to continue to be an Eternal I-AM, the body would have to persist; to exist and survive in this environment, lest we "die." Well, we know that's all wrong; at least we say so in passing. So, why then does the programming continue to affect our willingness and reach of thought and action? Do you see?

As a Seeker is processed they experience a greater sense of command over the Mind–Body connection as opposed to remaining entirely in the realm of its effect; less and less reactive and responding to the programming and encoding of the *genetic vehicle* as a source-point of considerations. And it is hardly an appropriate source-point for *Self*. At one point on the timeline, the Alpha Spirit was most likely involved with an entirely voluntary and potentially reversible experience of a *beta-existence* POV, but at some point, the experience of the Physical Universe became the sole occupation of focus and attention to the point where the *Self* found itself trapped within the context of the Human Condition. This has become a permanent condition only due to the reinforced and validated consideration that it is so.

Willingness to communicate and handle communications is a definitive milestone of *Grade-IV Systemology*—being the primary deficiency in prior attempts at getting the Spirit to release their fixated hold on the Physical Universe—and thereby keep the Physical Universe from maintaining a hold on the Spirit. It is the resistance between the two that creates the bindings we are to shed. The more you resist to that which you have agreed, the more of an effect you are to it. This got the old-school magician into trouble, because in failing to understanding being Source—in failing to understand and properly handle the Mind–Body connection and its ability to direct communication—the magician often becomes an effect of the cause that they themselves created the condition for, but to which they did not understand or did not take responsibility for as Source.

All individuals will tend to believe that they are at Cause at those instances when they are not operating properly as such—and they tend to believe and present themselves as the victim of Effect of another or some other condition or motivated by another person's actions, when they themselves are actually in the pilot's chair for the decision to know and be and act. The willingness and reach, for most fragmented individuals, will be considered inhibited and yet the individual themselves will believe themselves to contain the whole, that they have it all in the bag—but they are not considering all of the "intentional forgetting" or the "unwillingness."

A Pilot can use *SOP-2C* or "Route-2" processing to get a *Seeker* into realizing, eventually, that *they* are only willing to communicate in areas that *they* themselves are willing to communicate on. This seems fairly basic and yet many are unaware that it restricts their reach and ability to know. Really, you don't even have to actually "look" at something to have a "knowing" about it. But there is a slippery slope here to where an individual begins to put up a lot of resistance on various lines of communication not even to look; and more often than not, these are the same channels that may later serve as "hot buttons" that are influenced from external sources; those "other-determined" forces that we have simply allowed to be the cause of whatever we are *thinking* or *feeling* or *doing*—and which have ultimately impressed or imprinted some sort of picture—or mental image—as to the limits of what we can "*be*."

If you were to straight ask, as a PCL, the most obvious—"What would be okay for you to talk to me about?" and "What are you okay with me talking to you about?"—through the circuits—you might be surprised just how far you could bring someone to realizing, for themselves, the type of material presented in this manual. But, you would have to make sure you are communicating with them about their answers. And of course you have to know the material in order to recognize the realizations. But, get them to tell you more about "why" or "why not"; they'll figure it out. You can make notes about the subject or themes—or what we call "terminals"—of willingness for later assessments, but the point here is not about the having them talk about anything—or you talking about anything—its to reach a conclusion, or a *realization* as we call it. These *realizations* are not necessarily linked directly to the content of the subjects, but newer considerations can lead to them...systematically.

An individual will only allow someone else to talk to *them* about things that they will allow someone to talk to *them* about. Pure and simple. An individual, who sits at the cause-point, is the determinant about what they are willing to speak about—and yet the control over receiving and duplicating the communication is actually on the receipt-point. Do you see that? This is demonstrable, right? Just get thinking along these lines. That's what we want to see: an increased use of *crystal clear* demonstrations of truth in *piloting.*

The subject of repetitive objective processing is taken up in chapter-lessons on "*Bell, Book & Candle*"—and there is no reason to reiterate these basic fundamentals of applications for "*Presence in Space-Time,*" because principles are the same; except, rather than dealing with objects in the environment—which is actually the step taken after *Presence in Space-Time*—we want the Seeker to take command over the POV with the Physical Universe environment in general. The demonstrations have potential as amazing reminders that rehabilitate the Alpha Spirit. Objective processing may even eventually be conducted from the perspective of the Alpha Spirit in "Zu-Vision."

In "*Bell, Book & Candle*" the emphasis is on control of objects in the Physical Universe via the direct Self-determined command of a Mind–Body connection. But, prior to even this—"*Presence in Space-Time*"—we want to raise certainty of a Seeker's direct command over that very Mind–Body connection. This way, it may be operated and monitored very deliberately to perform all other steps and processing, including "*Bell, Book & Candle.*"

An individual has developed a significant resistance toward subjects of "control" and "command" simply as a result of agreeing to the conditions of their improper management stored in memory. All of those encoded mental images and "pings" come up and some restriction on the wide-angle potential experience. When an individual is greatly the effect of other-determined conditions, sensory based experiences are often the basis of fragmentation when they result in energy flows an individual is simply not willing to manage—thus they become the effect. A distaste for the very idea of "control" or "command" is only a further demonstration to just how easily controllable our conditions really are when reinforced with "sensation" and "emotion"; and if they can be encoded to give such a response, then they should just as easily be controlled by *Self*, which is the only one ultimately responsible for duplicating the basis for reality in the end; and by this we mean the significances and charges to which things carry subjectively.

Physical pain is actually a high level of internal communication in the Physical Universe as it relates to a physical body; and it is a great source of personal fragmentation. The individual then falls out of proper communication with the physical body or *genetic vehicle* that it so heavily identifies with. As soon as response-reactions fall out of responsibility and control of the Alpha Spirit, other mechanisms and automatic functions begin to develop in regards to being an effect of some or another kind of command. And while that command is still technically directed by Self, it has, by its own admission and agreements, attributed all cause and motivation for being, knowing and acting to another (other-determined) source. This is how the Alpha Spirit descended from a powerful godlike creative being to limiting its considerations to implanted programming of the Human Condition, entrapped within the interior of beta-existence.

The main issue of the Human Condition—why it can be even fragmented at all—is too great of association of Identity between Self and solidity of the *genetic vehicle* operating in the Physical Universe. And while parts of this are echoed in various creation myths and Kabbalahs, there is no real substitute for the true knowledge accessible from the Alpha point of beingness and POV. When willingness and reach goes down, then *beta-Awareness*—or *Actualized Awareness*—of the individual also diminishes. And the lower it goes and the longer it stays there, the more solid of an effect all considerations for *Self* become. When we have considered ourselves and our body the total effect of the Physical Universe, then we are basically done here; the Spirit withdraws more and more and decides not to apply as much creative energy into reality—duplicating the reality of the same body day after day—and thus it begins to decay from no further creation applied.

The Human Condition, or parameter of the Physical Universe, is held as between the range of "zero-and-four" on the *Standard Model* of the *Zu-line*. We can calculate, that as a Spirit—which has so tightly identified with this existence and a body—it actually can operate from even lower levels on this scale than "zero." These sub-zero levels come up into hopelessness and helplessness and apathetic sympathy and all this—anger and pain and up into the band of attentions and boredom and on up, right? Well, we can assume when we introduce a line of processing to the individual that they are going to be coming up from the bottom, and you will see this in their reactions to repetitive objecting processing more readily than anything else.

Reactivity, for example, in *"Bell, Book & Candle,"* is not a "falling out" from a high point when they hit those first stages of "this is pointless" and then "fine, let's do this" and then "I don't like this" and then to "this hurts" and "this is boring, I don't care"... You might think you aren't getting anywhere, but you take a look at this *Beta-Awareness Scale* that we have established and you will see that the Seeker *isn't* moving "downward" at all—they are actually coming upward in their handling! Imagine that! It's right there for you to see if you are paying attention—and that is information from *Grade-III* used in all future processing. So, you want to be familiar with those scales and models because it lets you know where things are at. The amount of foundation material collected for our *Grade-III* anthology, *"The Systemology Handbook,"* cannot be under-valued.

Here are the basic instructions provided in a section of *"Crystal Clear"* titled: The Self-Processing of Attention Patterns. [You will find this listed in the "appendix" as "Selective Attention: Objective Processing for Presence in Phase."] This is pretty close to what we are processing in "Step-2" of *SOP-2C.*

> —*Look* around you and *Spot* an object in space.
>
> —*Identify* its solidity and *Contact* its substance.

In *Grade-III,* we suggested repetitive use of this basic command of attention with various objects, walls and corners, until, as it states: "completely *in phase* and interested in your Path." That's as much as is stated on this subject in *Grade-III.*

In *"Bell, Book & Candle,"* lag or in a communication is not simply answers to subjective questions, but is visible in the responses to objective processing PCLs. We are not interested in cult practices or any kind of brainwashing; but we *are* demonstrating that an individual who is not willing to participate in a *Game* of control is not willing to exercise control over themselves. They don't want a *Pilot* to control them; they don't want to control *themselves*; and they start to just become what they consider to be the random effects of invisible causes. At the same time, they believe, have no actual influence or interest in the subject of control. Well, we get that worked out here, early on.

The automatic mechanisms and other issues that are dissolved during processing is not always noticed as blatantly as analytical or cognitive realizations. Certainly the Seeker gets a sense of "betterment" during the course of things. If the Seeker can get through this part, the rest will come as it comes; but if there are a lot of *SOP-2C Step-2* hang ups, then get them all flattened out before you start dropping anything more onto a Seeker to process. Keep in mind, if a Seeker comes to some realizations—actual or otherwise—acknowledge them appropriately.

Functionally, *"Presence in Space-Time"* and *"Bell, Book & Candle"* go together and operate similarly. I wanted to discuss this process with you in a lecture rather than simply write a narrative is because I am more likely to fluidly explain this type of work, candidly, then if I were to actually write it out as precision data. We want the Seeker to get a sense for something as much as I want you to get a sense for something. Communication. Now, the script that I have seen used for this in other traditions is the most basic line of directive attention you can imagine. [*To audience member*] Let's just have—*would it be okay if you came up to participate in a demonstration?*

Audience Member/Seeker: Yes.

Good! Okay! Thank you! ... An example of willingness to engage in a *Game.* ... Now, right here, we're just now gonna do this to show some stuff —to give a demonstration—here, so you can see this isn't going to kill anyone.

Audience. [Laughs.]

We're not going to run this out to any real extent—this isn't to actually process you. *We could do that later. . .* Okay. This is basic. Let's say we've already got them there—your Seeker—and here we are. Okay, you see that wall?

Seeker: Um... Yeah?

Okay. Well, do you see it? Don't just take my word. Is there a wall?

Seeker: Yes.

Okay. Good. Now, walk over to that wall. ... Okay. Thank you. Put your hand—right hand—on that wall. Thank you. Now, take it off and turn around. Good. Now, you see *that* wall?

Seeker: Yeah.

Go and walk over to that wall.

Audience. [Laughs.]

Seeker: Okay.

Good. Thank you. Now, touch the wall. Alright. Thank You. Now, take your hand off and turn around... You all see where this is going? So, you would want to do this for a while and I think I may have altered the wording, but you are going to want to keep a consistent repetitive use of PCL. And now, then you want to move through this in a certain progression. For example, you want them to start taking greater command over this. So, you say—*if you want to do this for us*—you say: okay, so you see that wall? Now, *you* start that body moving toward that wall. Okay. Now, *you* decide when to place your hand on that wall and then *you* do it. Thank you. Alright. Now, *you* decide to take your hand off the wall and then *you* do it. Great. Decide when to turn around and then *you* make that body turn around. Good. Thank you. Do you all see this now? *Okay, thank you for assisting with this.*

So, there you have it. There is a considerable amount of metaphysics behind "Step-2" that you don't necessarily need to know a lot about to make it effective. To be honest, you can understand most of these fundamentals—and even reach most of the realizations—starting from even the earliest *Grades*, as we have demonstrated even with the earliest practices of magic and mysticism, and its evolution into religious and other various worldly systems. But, as we have found: the practice of the lower Master Grades in exclusion to the remainder, more often than not, will just keep a person mulling about on those planes if left there too long. We can do better now. We can move further. We will continue to move further and reach. And I don't see us slowing down here any time soon. Thank you.

—UNIT THREE—

ADVANCED PROCEDURES

—LIBER-3C—

:: 1 ::
PROCESSING THE MIND-SYSTEM TO
DEFRAGMENT PROBLEM IMPLANTS

Our tradition of systematic processing is a highly specialized form of applied spiritual technology—a practical application of philosophy in such a way that seems to have alluded the reasoning and education of the human population. Fundamental instructions for "home study" and "Self-processing" are introduced in *"The Tablets of Destiny"* (*Liber-One*). *"Crystal Clear"* (*Liber-2B*) supports this foundation with practical exercises.[*] A Seeker may successfully employ *Grade-III* for *"Self-Processing"* and/or as a guideline for entry level *Piloted* procedure.

A "Master" of any former esoteric or "mystery school" is expected to have achieved what was once universally identified as the "third degree" or *Third "Gate"* of potential realizations—a state that would put the initiate at the boundaries between physical and spiritual existence, with an alleged footing in either universe, but never fully in either. Rather than reaching further toward Self-Honest clarity that lay hidden beyond just one more plateau of obscured thought, the path ended there. Oh, sure— the high-level initiates could take the continuity found at this higher vista and demonstrate to those that still worked below that there was a *"greater than"* (and even divide that realm into thirty-plus more "degrees"), but that was it.

Computations devoted to associated knowledge allowed for near-infinite combinations, correspondences and "things to know" within the "mental universe"—but the Masters had not yet *gotten out* of their "heads" and were still operating very much *interior* to the fragmentation of the Human Condition.

Those individuals and Seekers that occupy their attentions on lower *Grade* work for extend periods of time begin to develop their personal universe around semantics and parameters presented within each potential paradigm. Even the physical scientist and mechanic runs in to this danger when linger too long, too closely, to the mechanized nature of the Physical Universe. The mystic magician and esoteric priest and priestess does the same when focused too strongly on the nature of **"Cosmic Law"**—a Law which, if nothing else, only can be certain to dict-

---

[*] Materials from both *"Liber-One"* and *"Liber-2B"* are available within the complete *Grade-III* Master Edition hardcover anthology *"Systemology Handbook"* by Joshua Free.

ate the course of energy and matter across the **space** and time of *this* version of the Physical Universe. The purpose of esoteric instruction was originally to remind the Spirit what it chose to forget; what it first chose to no longer be in communication with and then eventually obscured from view with automatically created barriers.

> The truth being that we already came from a higher level of exist-ence and only later continued to limit our considerations and the acceptance of enforced agreements to succumb to *this* one. Those *other* Universes are no less real than an abandoned property or ghost town that simply no longer receives creative attentions.

As personal fragmentation and universal condensation became more re-fined—leading toward *this* Physical Universe—the *Self-determined* consid-erations and allocation of data regarding "conceptions" fell more and more in line with a particular "Law" or cosmic decree that is otherwise treated as some kind or another of "divine ordinance" or "Ordering" in religious explanations.

It is always presumed that this Order was "enforced" from the beginning —but there are spiritual indicators that this was a once equally created or agreed upon Order, which at the time seemed to "make sense" to all those involved; it seemed like a "good idea." But it was still a system— and as such, you will always find that certain individuals become anom-alies, kinks and trouble sources within the system; and along the timeline, it seemed to make good sense to the majority of those involved that there needed to be some kind of "penalty system" in place to keep this Order from going away, and if anything, make it more solid.

On the surface—"on paper" as it is said in this world—this graduation of Order into an "ethic" is a very logical progression of events, once multi-tudes of spirits started occupying "shared universes." The policing force of a higher universe would create a lower-level universe in which to "im-prison" those that went against the established Order of a particular "Realm" or "Kingdom" (as they were sometimes known, as opposed to "universes"). But, given the decay of enough time and stricter and stricter system of enforcement, eventually everyone ends up in "prison" and it seems like the "universe" in the prison is now suddenly "where it's all happening." At some inevitable point, even the guards and upper-class citizens and kings all decide "it's the place to be." —And the whole mess starts up all over again at increasingly lower and lower levels. And now... *here* we are.

In the very beginning, the Alpha Spirit was still more interested in their own personal universe and their own creations than the "game of universes." The real fragmentation of the individuated Self came later along with that, primarily as a result of interactions with other energies and creations from other Alpha Spirits and the ensuing "experiences" that came to define an otherwise "artificial personality" laid over the original one of simply "I" as *Self.*

As Alpha Spirits began to experience creations of others, certain inclinations and tendencies formed. This is what we call "Alpha Fragmentation" because it took place on the timeline of the "spiritual universe" that is *exterior* to any *beta-existence.* It most certainly contributed to later programming, but in the spiritual existence we did not yet take on form that had to be fed or protected; and such low-level implant programming is dealt with more concretely in systematic *beta-defragmentation* processing. But, we should be aware, as we begin to weed out the fragmentation and "separate the wheat from the chaff."[*]

The subject of "communication" is the common denominator of all personal fragmentation—and as a result, it is where a Seeker begins. A basic methodology of systematic processing is found previously, so what we are concerned with now is taking the next steps in untangling the communication channels and circuits *interior* to the Mind-System; those that lead directly to the most fundamental "implanted problems" of the "Human Condition" as they are experienced in *beta-existence.* We treat this work as "Wizard Level-0" because it represents the bare minimum actualization, as an upper *Grade* starting point, that we have found necessary for an individual to achieve effective success with "higher level" work. While all of this material may make for an interesting read, if a Seeker is actually serious about their progress on the *Pathway to Self-Honesty* and beyond through the *Gateways to Infinity*, it is critical that they actually do the work, whether *Self-guided* or with professional assistance of an accredited Systemology Pilot or qualified Mardukite Minister.

Δ Δ Δ Δ Δ Δ Δ

As the Alpha Spirit (*Self*) became aware that there were other individuated Alpha Spirits (entities) that separated as an "I" from the Infinity, it became readily obvious that *Self* was not creating in a vacuum. Other POV were there to experience a creation; and *Self* also maintained a personally determined POV to experience creations of others. Interest and desirability became a personal taste regarding what was deemed accept

---

[*]   We are speaking here of matters that have very deep roots stemming from very early (relatively speaking) in our spiritual existence (on the spiritual timeline).

able and what was rejected. *Self* discovered that it found things it did not like about the creations of others.

We do not find much fragmentation taking place with an individual and their own creations so long as they know they are creating it, can un-create it and re-create it at will. Such is the natural inherent creative ability of the Spirit.

Creative abilities of *Self*—or rather "considerations" of the same—only became fragmented as a result of other-determined acceptance and re-jection of our creations in addition to the enforced acceptance (or rejection) of other creations made by other entities. It is only here that we begin to see **turbulence** on personal energetic communication lines. It is only here that we begin to see the Alpha Spirit demonstrate any "protest" against handling communication and creation in a universe. What this did, at *Alpha* levels of existence, was start creations in the dir-ection of needing to be "more solid" in order to receive wider validation. "Protest" developed into an **"insistence"** or else repeated use of a communicated energy into a form that is simply more difficult to avoid **acknowledgment** of or be ignored.

Self is completely **capable** of *directing* any manner of communication and creation and accepting the same without fragmentation or spiritual turbulence. So, how does it happen? It happens whenever anything starts to get set on automatic and the *Self* is no longer the determinant cause. This can happen very easily whenever there is an "insistence" be-cause, in the lack of an acknowledgment, the *Self* will continue to direct energy in a way that demands attentions and validation from others that something exists, is solid, as should remain to be created. This patterned tendency may be found underneath "compulsions" to repeatedly per-form an **"intention"** or creative use of energy. In time, there is a lot of personal energy directed by these "masses" (mechanism) unbeknownst to Self. If there is anything that "ages" or contributes to the decay of time for an "eternal spirit" it is *this*; and embedded beneath each and every one of these imprints and compulsions is one more thread holding together a firmly agreed-to belief that *Self* and its source of energetic po-tential is in any way *finite*.

We approach the subject of "Human Problems" as an extension of the communication processing. "Protest"—as a communication barrier—is a contributor to fragmentation when it becomes a "compulsive" mechan-ism, because any decrease in Self-determined ability is a decrease in *Actualized Awareness*. Many early implants were installed prior to *Self* tak-

Systematic Functions of the MCC

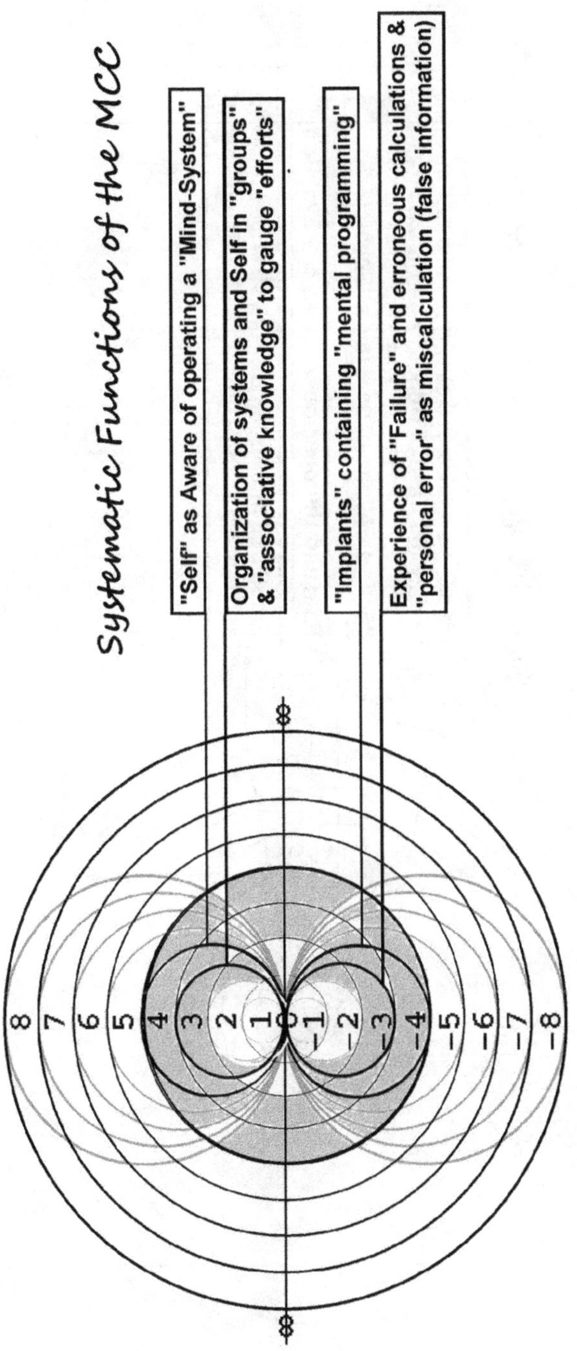

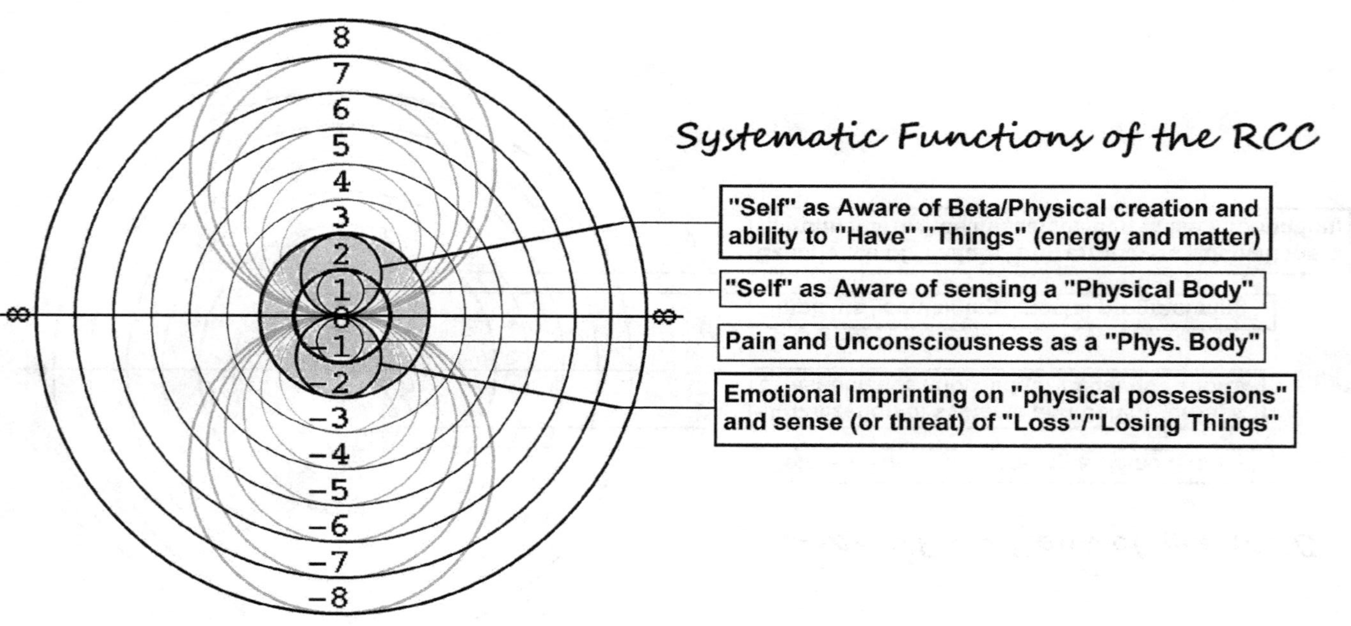

Systematic Functions of the RCC
"Self" as Aware of Beta/Physical creation and ability to "Have" "Things" (energy and matter)
"Self" as Aware of sensing a "Physical Body"
Pain and Unconsciousness as a "Phys. Body"
Emotional Imprinting on "physical possessions" and sense (or threat) of "Loss"/"Losing Things"
8
7
6
5
4
3
2
1
0
-1
-2
-3
-4
-5
-6
-7
-8

ing on a stringent Human Condition POV; they stem from deeply seeded imprinting that falls within the domain of "past lives."

We cannot dismiss the obvious apparent nature of "past lives" and yet at *Grade-IV*, we are not directing Seekers (or Pilots) to push this. There are many individuals not yet prepared to meet implications of "past lives" or their own spiritual timeline throughout "Cosmic History" and it is not suggested that this information should be in any way enforced until the Seeker is ready to confront it.

If we consider the POV from *Self*, the systematic processing to reduce the imprinted charge on channels that are presently engaged in "protest" and/or "rejection" (especially as an automatic tendency), would run repeatedly as follows until a Seeker can resume control over the nature of the "communication barrier."

Circuit-1:	What is it that you are protesting?
Circuit-2:	How have you communicated that protest?
Circuit-3:	Who should be acknowledging your communication?
A.T. (*opt.*):	(*Visualize the terminal accepting the communication.*)

A Seeker begins with most recent and easily accessible examples, then processes them out. It may very well be the case that an earlier similar "protest" or "rejection" appears from an earlier incident or event. This begins a personal journey of exploration into various degrees of higher and higher barriers that have been generated and agreed to over time. It did not happen all at once. Whatever state a Seeker is in today, they did not arrive there overnight. And the systematic imprinting and programming is laid in or keyed in differently for each individual. Encoding is embedded to a line of implanted systems programming that is generally found similar across the board of all individuals. This is fortunate for us, because it gave us something to work with: a basis for systematically understanding and therefore resolving the subject of "Human Problems."

After the Seeker has worked effectively through the most accessible events regarding their own "protest" and "rejection" of communications from *other* terminals and source-points, the same systematic techniques can be used to approach circuits on each direction of flow regarding, in this case, terminals representing "protest" and "rejection." For example, we can easily alter the above PCL format to apply to the POV of others: "What is (*terminal*) protesting/rejecting about you?" "How are they communicating?" "Who should acknowledge them?" &tc. This can even be applied to the third sphere of existence/influence regarding the mass communications of society as a whole, such as: "What are *others* protesting about *others*?" and so on. The time-tense of the PCL can be changed to "have" instead of "are" in order to better apply to past instances (once present ones have been reduced).

Self does not only goes out of communication with other "living" terminals or entities but also its own "things" and "creations." This is actually a very sad state of affairs for the Alpha Spirit, but it happens nonetheless and contributes to manifestation of greater pain and illness when identifying too closely with a physical body or genetic organism itself. For example, when an individual experiences "pain" tied to a specific part of the physical body or even a physical locale, the reactive-response tendency is to "avoid" such; which the RCC assumes its doing us a favor by manipulating our perception of reality to demonstrate the best chances of material survival. It simply registers everything that is connected to imprints of "pain" or "loss" as "to be avoided," rejected and protested *automatically*, and therein lies the fragmentation.

A Seeker or Pilot can apply this basic systematic processing formula to defragment channels all the way up through the *ZU-line*, applying the PCL to each of sphere of existence that we can reach to. "What have you protested about that physical body?" "What have you protested about your home? Family?" "What have you protested about your career?" "What have you protested about your organization? Church? Neighborhood? City?" "What have you protested about the Human Condition? Life on Earth?" ...and so on.

Once a Seeker is brought to understand the nature of "protest" and "rejection" we then bring them to understand—and take back the command —of their ability to "accept" and "acknowledge" and then begin to go through the entire process again with an emphasis on times when they have failed to accept or acknowledge other terminals; times when other terminals have failed to accept or acknowledge, &tc. This can all be reasoned out very simply and an A.T.—"Actualized Technician"—or "Wizard" can effectively cap this off with the appropriate use of "mental imagery." We are simply working our way back out through the circuitry that formed along one's personal spiritual identity continuum. It requires some directed attention but is not impossible to **process out**.

∆ ∆ ∆ ∆ ∆ ∆ ∆

Our *Grade-IV* systemology is referred to as "Wizard Level-0" because it is encroaching on the levels of work that have only been dreamed about by mystical magicians and philosopher priests for thousands of years. We are providing a new practical level of advancing through *Gateways to Infinity* that previously, from the standpoint of Master Grades, seemed fantastically out of reach and little more than spiritual pipe-dreams. It may be for this reason that so many other paths and traditions have fallen by the wayside before reaching this point; it may also be the case that after a few *had* reached this point, almost as if by accident, that they were not actualized enough to lead anyone else along—or else felt so possessive over the realizations inherent to the path that they disguised and distorted the knowledge so that those coming after would find only more fragmentation. The reasoning here is irrelevant now that the way ahead has been cleared.

Digging into the nature of "compulsive behavior" and "communication barriers" took several months of applying "*SOP-2C*." All the while, we kept throwing the procedure at every *facet* of every *terminal* of "Human Problems" we could think of until eventually a pattern emerged that correlated with our Standard Model. This led us to chart what we consider the *interior blueprints* for "implanting problems in the Human Condition for beta-existence." After several revisions, this current presentation of "Implanted Human Problems" registers quite effectively for processing all cases of the **standard-issue** Human Condition.

> 1.0 Physical Body (Genetic Vehicle)
> *To Exist* = Survive, Sustain, Eat, Sense
> –1.0 ... able to experience "pain" imprints
>
> 2.0 "Having" (Emotional Association)
> *To Exist* = Reproduce, Protect, Satisfy, Cope
> –2.0 ... able to experience "loss" encoding
>
> 3.0 Associated Knowledge (Calculations)
> *To Exist* = Organize, Reach, Cooperate, Compete
> –3.0 ... able to experience "failure" in evaluation
>
> 4.0 Mind-System (Human Condition)
> *To Exist* = Solidity, Control, Division, Invalidation
> –4.0 ... able to experience "enforced agreement"

When automatic mechanisms, obsessions and compulsions are appropriately identified in a Seeker's case, they should scan and process only the most immediate imprinting events that seem to reinforce these tendencies and patterns. Trying too excessively to get at the true underlying core of implants will, every time without fail, force the Seeker to confront "past-lives" that they may not be ready to confront. It is for this reason that such knowledge and memory is often concealed (again, as a result of "automatic mechanisms") until more readily available "solids" on that channel have been cleared away. Each time this occurs, the POV of the Seeker, as Actualized Awareness, is able to move further and further back in command of their own personal timeline, which is to say their personal identity continuum as reflected on the "ZU-line." The two are the same; one is merely a symbol of the other.

Wherever an implanted terminal node is in place within the *interior* of the Mind-System of the Human Condition, there is a channel of communication that should otherwise be under the command of *Self*. When these are allowed to go on automatic, then mechanisms form and energy is supplied to them from the Alpha Spirit but outside of conscious determination. There may have been a determined intent put in place at the start, but that has long since been overridden by allowing the automation to take over. This is one of the reasons that we impress *Bell, Book & Candle* techniques.

When there is a tendency, pattern or compulsion that manifests in this lifetime and which appears to be outside of the Seeker's control, our current practice is to begin with *Analytical Recall* ("Route-2") and see if we can determine what the mechanism is a response to. It may require some repetitive inquiries before the "Mind" gives up its veil on better answers; and it may very well be that these answers seem utterly ridiculous to the present lifetime or even *this* Physical Universe. Make note of them all; pay particular attention to any that lead toward the type of *realizations* we are after in *Grade-IV* regarding the source of automatic or reactive-responsive tendencies.

It may be too far of an entry level reach to simply ask a Seeker "What are you protesting with that behavior?" or "What were you protesting when you started doing such and such?"—but you may be able to approach the truth of things by applying the PCL: "What could you protest by doing X?" or something similar. Get the Seeker to come to some possible reasons why they would have set up that communication line in the first place. You may not be able to eliminate the original "Alpha" nature of the implant by processing events from *this* lifetime, but you *can* discharge some of the energy that keeps an individual from being able to ever reach back any further. Too much has been placed in the way—entire universes have been occulted from sight—and the progressive journey through the *Gates* cannot be bypassed in any way if it is to be true. No one can simply buy their way onward to the upper levels with goods wrought from *this* world. Such organizations exist only to further entrap *Self* into being an other-determined effect.

Tendencies toward "acceptance" or "rejection" are tied to closeness and proximity, or else willingness to keep something close; meaning it would be safe to keep close. When we are dealing with tendencies and reactive-response mechanisms, keep in mind that these are all originally built upon a premise of logic that was structured for survival. That which was deemed "safe" or would contribute to survival was deemed "acceptable." This is all fine and good until it begins to have its values assigned (or "determined") on an automatic or reactive basis that eliminates *Actualized Awareness* of *Self*. In the past we alternately have asked Seekers "What could you accept about *X*?" and "What could you reject about *X*?" until they realize that whatever they are rejecting, blocking, not wanting or avoiding is all based on past emotional imprinting. In other words, the "threat to survival" is not clear and present, but instead cast up into one's reality as a reactive-response with mental imagery intended to control thought and action in place of a Self-determined Alpha Spirit.

There is a "Route-3" PCL formula that may be used to weed out some of the fragmentation on these channels. After running the process on general events, the *term* "someone else" could be replaced with another appropriate "terminal" requiring specific attention. These PCLs are alternated within each circuit to prevent from getting "mentally spun" by running negative command lines. We extend the same principle from former "communication processing" and simply replace terminals and wording to apply to "presentation" of a creation as a more specific type of communication.

Circuit-1:   What wouldn't (someone else) want you to present to them?
What have you presented to (someone else)?

Circuit-2:   What wouldn't you want (someone else) to present to you?
What has (someone else) presented to you?

Circuit-3:   What wouldn't (someone else) want others to present to them?
What has (someone else) presented to others?

The same methods used to defragment channels of events during *this* lifetime may be further applied later to access deeper laden data of implants that are carried between lifetimes. In some experiments that involved past lives, or the spiritual continuum, the first two circuits are reversed to see if any further information can be gleaned concerning a motivator. But, essentially, it is these same methods that were applied (simply at higher levels) in order to discover and verify the way ahead.

:: 2 ::

PROCESSING HIGHER REALIZATIONS
IS ACCESSED WITH SELF-HONESTY

When we speak of willingness to communicate, reach, accept, help and so forth, we are not enforcing any moral ethic on what an individual *should do*. What we discovered is that unwillingness on any lines is a point of other-determined control. An individual does not necessarily need to *agree* with anything, but it can be accepted as a communication and given acknowledgment without actually **participating** in its creation. We have found that we tend to add more solidity to that which we are rejecting and protesting than that which we simply allow to pass us by. Ability to freely alter considerations and evaluations still allows *Self* an ability to determine these; but at least they *know* they are the ones doing it.

You don't have to agree with the way things are in the world, and you don't have to like so-and-so enough to want to be around them, and you don't have to necessarily become a "teacher" or "law enforcer" and you don't necessarily have to be a "vegetarian" or sit through long lessons about "math, science and history"... but shouldn't you be freely able to consider any of these things at will without some automated response-mechanism kicking in and taking command of your attention, focus, energy and behavior? You can practice this fluidity easily enough by **repetitively** using the following formula with whatever you may find that you are protesting with a lot of emotional energy. This can also be practiced as objective processing on arbitrary items.

> —*Contact* the channel of mental energy connected with the "terminal" or "condition" that you are protesting.
>
> —Get the *Sense* (or POV) that <u>you</u> are "protesting" X.
>
> —Get the *Sense* (or POV) that <u>you</u> are "admiring" X.
>
> —Get the *Sense* (or POV) that <u>you</u> are "creating" X.

If this is not found to be effective after several runs through the process, it may be that the content of the channel needs to be handled on a gradient scale; meaning that perhaps too "large" or "general" of a terminal is being processed. Keep in mind that a Seeker can only reduce emotional charge on *facets* and *imprints* related to events that they are prepared to "confront" as they actually are, not just as they seem to be from a fragmented state. This all has to be worked with. The Mind-System has a lot of checks and balances in place to make certain that this is the case.

"Protest" is not the only relevant example of communication blocks and rejection of objective universes; it does however seem particular applicable to the present state of the world. An examination of human history will demonstrate that this type of activity is cyclic in nature, but also part of even larger cycles; systems within systems. This is illustrated quite clearly in our "*original thesis*" of systemology.* There are many visible signs indicating present conditions on this "prison planet" are on the cusp of great change; and it is of utmost importance for an individual to achieve *Self-Honesty* and arrive at higher *Gates of Realization* to avoid succumbing to entrapment further down into an even lower level universe than where we have already fixed our POV.

When you are blocking, inhibiting, rejecting or protesting a line of communication, *you are doing* something. This is a projection of energy and active use of creative spiritual ability. This is far and beyond simple "dislike" or "disinterest" of some creation. This literally creates a spiritual "beam" of energy; a wave of personal emotional energy that is sent out *in response* to another **waveform** so as to keep it at a distance. This, of course, also creates an additional layer to the individualized concept of "distance" within one's personal universe, and therefore "space."

Beyond word play we can literally suggest that anything you want to actively keep out of your "personal space" or "personal universe" is being *protested against.* While this may have first started out as Self-determined and freely chosen, the patterned tendencies developed into their own automatic mechanisms using personal creative power. By taking over **responsibility** for creative ability to be at every point-of-view, which is to say every source-point and effect-point of creation, and yet not remain fixed or reactive to any, the freedom to selectively apply these energies is returned to *Self.*

When we approach energetic qualities of universes from an even *higher* level of reasoning for *A.T. Wizard Grades,*‡ it may very well be the case that our automatic "rejection" and "protest" of *this* version of the Physical Universe is what fixes our POV to these *beta-existence* "**anchor**" points and which holds the material existence around us in place and all the while actively making it more solid. This may seem incredibly "metaphysical" for a Seeker, but it is something to consider since whatever we are willing to take the full responsibility for creating no longer seems to

---

have an effect on us.

Δ Δ Δ Δ Δ Δ Δ

An individual declines on the scale of *Actualized Awareness* as their considerations become more solid to meet that of the Physical Universe. As perceived fixed solidity of the Physical Universe increases an individual finds that they are the *effect* of more and more low-level "problems." This fixation is what reduces *Awareness* to confront any greater level of problem solving. An ability to approach problems and consequences (or penalties) increases as a Seeker reaches higher vistas of understanding and the determinism to shift around considerations of "what is a problem." The Physical Universe therefore is able to maintain a hold on the POV of an individual to the same degree that the individual permits fixation on the "mystery" of solving implanted problems of the Physical Universe. As such, decision-making and actions employed by the Alpha Spirit is treated as *Game*, which is a concept quite **prevalent** within our systemology.

The *real* problems that face the Human Condition are those that "*must* be solved; but *cannot* be solved" and therefore get a person hung up on a "mystery" or "unknown"—which is to say a perpetual "maybe." So long as a "problem" is suspended in such a state, so too is the *Awareness* of the individual. A *true* problem involves "**conflict**"—whether of a conceptual thought or an intention to *do*. For example, an individual has thought put out on a line and it comes up against a counter-thought coming in from the other direction and there you end up with this cluster mess of energy that we call a problem. A source-point or individual is projecting a concept of "is" or "am" and they are coming up against the "isn't" or "not" along the same channel.

This same principle applies to the will to intend to *do* something, or direct an action or motion of energy, which we refer to as *intention*. This is much different in practice from simply deciding about how one is going to solve an equation. Imagine being told you needed to take a test and you agree to locate yourself in space-time to take this test, but you were not given instructions on the material being tested or even where the test was to be taken. This absence of information poses a serious problem, and yet the directive is now in place that you *must*. Or perhaps you have the intention of focusing on taking a test and the person next to you has an intention of distracting your attention. Anywhere we find two persisting flows of energy in direct conflict with one another, we have a "problem."

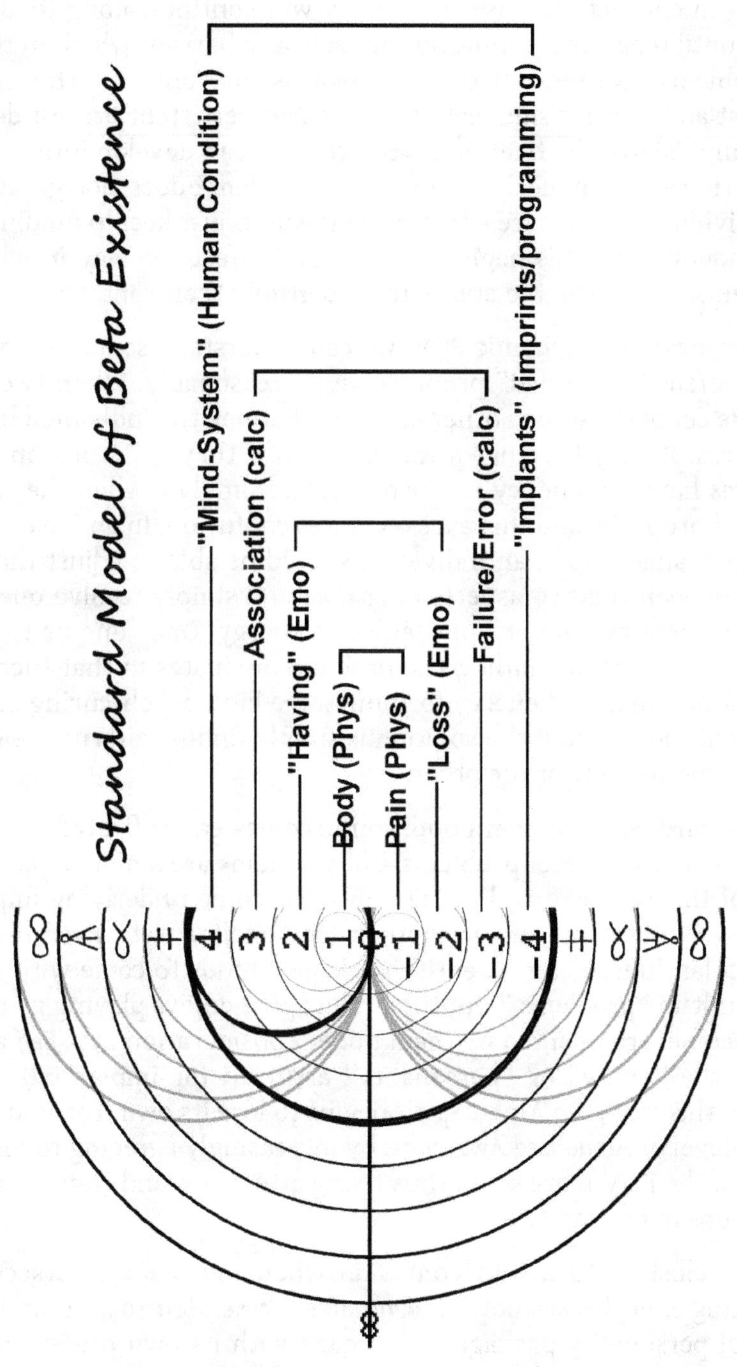
Standard Model of Beta Existence
"Mind-System" (Human Condition)
Association (calc)
"Having" (Emo)
Body (Phys)
Pain (Phys)
"Loss" (Emo)
Failure/Error (calc)
"Implants" (imprints/programming)
4
3
2
1
0
-1
-2
-3
-4

An Alpha Spirit seldom finds itself having *real* "problems" when there is nothing in conflict, because the energy will continue along its directed course until meeting a condition that acts as a barrier, which in the case of "problems" we tend to treat in regards to "conflict." This can also manifest and imprint similar to the way that persistent protest develops into compulsions; the fixation on the conflict can develop into obsessive automatic behavior mechanisms. The "problem" does not go away, so the individual sets up a reactive mechanism to just keep pounding away on it indefinitely. This begins to filter and affect the way in which all "problems" (and even the ability to responsibly "confront") are handled.

By incorporating a dynamic POV, we can understand semantics of "one-sided" versus "two-sided" problems quite reasonably. When two intentions are countering each other on same channel, the individual hits it as a problem. It only becomes a *real* problem if they get stuck on it. And problems have a tendency to cluster and accumulate when they are not managed properly; and this excess creates confusion. In an ideal well-adjusted actualized state, an individual should be able to adjust their POV freely between the two aspects of *conflict* and simply resolve one or the other by some avenue or application of energy. Once one or the other sides is no longer in conflict, the problem dissipates in that there is no longer a suspension of energy forming some kind of "obscuring mass" or "fragmentation." Often the solution is simply finding alternative considerations for one side or the other.

The standard issue Human Condition becomes easily fixated on "trying to solve" very low-level problems, but problems are simply a part of the *games* of this universe and in many ways become underlying implanted "purposes" that drive one or another "personality" sets. Even taking on a particular "phase" (or "identity package") tends to come with its own set of built-in "problems." But the Alpha Spirit enjoys playing games and only becomes fragmented by them under consideration that *Self* and the POV of the "phase" or "personality" assumed (or implanted) are the same. In this case, the Alpha Spirit begins to lose its own freedom of ability and level of *Actualized Awareness* by increasingly agreeing to make the reality of the POV more solid, thus fixing attentions and conceptual considerations to the same.

Problem clusters turn into confusion when too many intersecting or conflicting energies are not *Self-determined.* When left to automation, the artificial personality package will engage with its own preset means of treating a "problem" based on its *facets,* and this we know from observing behavior of the RCC, which imprints all *facets* of knowledge toward "pain" or "loss." The problems continue to exist because the individual is still providing active energy for it to exist; and for many, this is what provides a sense of "purpose" in life, because life in this universe is wired for solving problems. So, the implanted problems are simply agreed to and accepted as part of this game in order to have an activity here rather than invent and play a new better game.

When a two-sided problem (intention/counter-intention; purpose/counter-purpose, &tc.) is locked into a "cluster" of confusing energy, the individual is likely unwilling to confront (face up to) one side or another of the problem. The other side of these problems does not necessarily have to be initiated by another individual, but simply by another opposing terminal that is introduced as an arbitrary or variable, such as a "rule" of the game. One side of the problem may be an implant on the individual whereas what it is coming up against is a barrier placed in the game. Combined, the two are supposed to provide some sense of purpose in the game, matching freedoms and purposes against the rules and barriers. And so the world continues on.

For example, one common implant for beta-existence states that: "to exist is to be in a body which must be protected to endure." So we solve this with the concept of houses. Now the problem becomes that we "need a house to live in to survive, but houses also cost monies." An individual can have a lot of emotional imprinting and mental fragmentation regarding the concept of money. So, now the game for the Alpha Spirit has been reduced to resolving the "financials" to solve sheltering the body that it has been tricked into agreeing that is Self and must be protected in order for Self to survive. Is it any wonder that the god-like Alpha Spirit is waking up to the fact that it has slid into a very low-level of considerations just to keep playing a game with everyone. But here the Seeker should see the difference between the "imprinted directives" and the "barriers"—both of which are still subject to an incredible amount of fragmentation.

Now again, ideally, an actualized person should be able to manage their considerations of a problem without getting all bungled up, but past fragmentation (imprinted on the beta-personality of an individual) can play a strong part in affecting how the individual perceives and confronts external universes. For example, an individual should be able to decide on the appropriate type of home for their means and supply the appropriate means to it by operating in a Self-determined manner; but of course there are so many *facets* of a fragmented Human Condition that are likely to get in the way of success.

△ △ △ △ △ △

The *real* problem that a person cannot get beyond is the one that they cannot take responsibility for on either side. This means they are unwilling to appropriately *be* on either side, which means they are unable to properly confront it. We use the term "POV" or "point-of-view" to denote the sense of *beingness* that can be acknowledged in all things. This leads us to consider occupying more than simply the POV of the genetic vehicle and its artificial personality package—but also to recognize when we have adopted another person's POV unknowingly and are really operating from their programming, for whatever the reasons the RCC has deemed it more effective for material survival to do so (and keep in mind that the RCC does not operate on rationale and **reason**). The nature of Human Problems is generally cyclic and continuous when left to standard-issue conventions. As soon as a fragmented individual begins to think clearly on the matter

of shelter, the imprinting and encoding on the subject of money gets them all confounded. Then as soon as they start to apply some attention to the money half, that fragmentation stirs up so many emotions that now they can't think clearly about shelter needs. They have fallen into a trap that honestly very few in today's society successfully rise above without critical third-party assistance. Even then, that may only solve the immediate proximity of a problem that the individual is still no better equipped to manage properly in the future without systematic defragmentation of these channels.

One of the main issues, long observed on the Human Condition, and defying all reason and logic for the social sciences: when an individual has found themselves stuck in this loop with an unwillingness to confront it, personal energy goes into reinforcing the solidity of both sides of the problem—putting out energy, and putting out an extension of more energy against it. In essence, the *Self* is placing its POV between the opposing forces and holding both of them in place, hence maintaining the confusion by an unwillingness to *change.*

Self will only knowingly give up its hold or fixation on something if it knows it can create or communicate on this channel again at will. In systematic processing we demonstrate that any condition can be created again. This is as simple as getting a Seeker to invent problems, knowingly and willingly to return control over management of problems. A deeper truth will be revealed: that although barriers to the true creative ability of the Alpha Spirit have been blocked on the descent through a condensation of universes, in order to balance the Infinite of Nothingness with an infinite potentiality of form, the Self still wants something to *do*, and it will set up automatic mechanisms to create those conditions if necessary. If a Seeker can practice being at cause with the creation of problems (as an imaginative exercise) there is a less likely chance they will be compelled to do so compulsively on an automatic basis.

Another type of problem also operates within the Human Condition, called the "hidden implanted standard"—and there are several of these, most of which are formed during an Alpha fragmentation sequence, meaning even prior to Self ever even assuming a humanoid POV in this Physical Universe for the first time. There is also a "hidden implanted standard" for beta-existence, and this is the underlying "directive" that the artificial personality is composed around. It is the ultimate filter or piece of fragmentation by which everything that is experienced or directed in the Physical Universe must first pass through. It may even be found in the patterned responses to PCL by a perceptive Pilot—or it may be found that the Seeker compulsively applies this "implant" as a filter to carrying out the directive to any PCL they receive in session.

Records of confronting confusion—as held in memory as programming—usually are imprinted with "fear"; fear is the lowest denominator attached to implants that will keep an individual in the position of "effect." Fear is a "holder" on the Mind; it freezes the Mind in place with an inability to think analytically. This is so strong that many have had the experience of being able to *go outside themselves* during periods of intense fear/terror and watch just how unreasonable or irrational the response-mechanisms are during these periods. The *Self* is out of contact with the body because it no longer registers it as a safe POV to operate from.

When a problem is treated (emotionally) as a "Mystery" and then linked with "Fear" (being a "Mystery") it is easy to associate "fear" with the "unknown." By keeping personal *Awareness* in a low-level effect or POV, the true Self as Alpha Spirit is kept from achieving true realizations about existence. Where we have previously considered problems, overcoming of barriers or solving communication breaks, we may add to this concept the consideration that it is also overcoming a "mystery condition" or else an "unknown"—something that the Mind-System is wired to pursue naturally in order to occupy its own faculties. It sends its energies out to uncover the unknown mystery, but Self is inhibited from confronting it and again finds itself in the middle of a confusion.

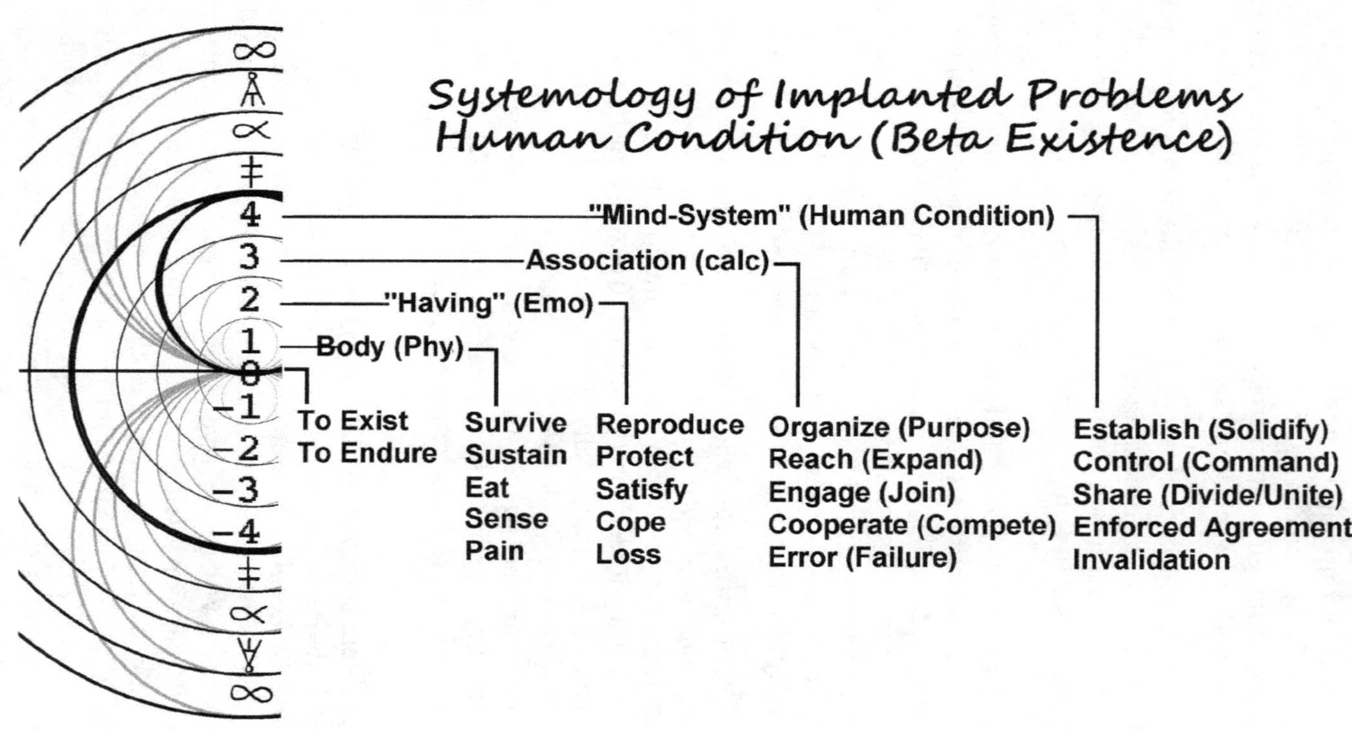
Systemology of Implanted Problems
Human Condition (Beta Existence)
"Mind-System" (Human Condition)
Association (calc)
"Having" (Emo)
Body (Phy)
To Exist
To Endure
Survive
Sustain
Eat
Sense
Pain
Reproduce
Protect
Satisfy
Cope
Loss
Organize (Purpose)
Reach (Expand)
Engage (Join)
Cooperate (Compete)
Error (Failure)
Establish (Solidify)
Control (Command)
Share (Divide/Unite)
Enforced Agreement
Invalidation

The "compulsive need and insatiable craving to *know* things" falls into this category; and so, things will be invented to be *known* about. The Mind-System is implanted to pursue data ceaselessly, which when operating compulsively, becomes an obsessive need or insatiable craving to simply "know"; and it doesn't matter what it *knows*, it just *has to know* "something" and there must be something more to be known because no solution is satisfactory to reducing the "unknown." Granted, this is a high level Alpha concern, but it is present throughout human activity in daily beta-existence at whatever point an individual is implanted to believe that "*To Know equals X.*" For many in the animal kingdom, "To Know —" might equal "To Eat" and so the better places to find better food might be the perpetual mystery to solve.

The implanted impulse "To Eat" is not itself a *real* problem; but it *is* a problem implant, which for purposes of the Physical Universe, produces an encoded effect on the individual that can be manipulated or imprinted on. This is to say that the "penalties" and "consequences" of the *game* of life in *beta-existence* is the "product of" the problem implants. These are merely **activated** when the one-sided problem is confronted, such as "how to acquire food" &tc.

The manner in which an individual can confront, take responsibility for and willingness to be *Self-directed* will all determine their successful management of "problems." The simple event that a car is on fire is not a problem; the one-sided problem becomes "how to put it out" and other factors (sides) only add to this confusion when the situation is not managed properly and are allowed to be oppositional to simply accomplishing a goal.

Our goal in *Mardukite Zuism & Systemology*—and the ministers and Pilots representing our paradigm—is not to simply "solve" all of a Seeker's problems for them. They don't want this anyway; the Alpha Spirit is a creative entity that likes to solve problems for "*purpose.*" Systemologists learn to solve their own problems better—managing and handling personal control of their Mind-System (and the Mind-Body connection) better—and in the end, simply *play a better game.*

:: 3 ::

THE GATES OF BETA-EXISTENCE AND BEYOND:
PROBLEMS TRANSFORMED INTO POSSIBILITIES

It would be an acute simplification to simply push off onto the Seeker the idea that "they" create all their own problems—or at least the perception that things can be problems or that *Self* can be so unwilling to confront the nature of problems as to wind up in the middle of *confusion*. Whether or not this true, the actualized realization of this—and the ability to confront it with total responsibility as *Self*—is a very advanced "metahuman" state, which we would consider among the greatest apexes of the *Pathway to Self-Honesty*. Such a *realization* cannot be firmly impressed with enforced knowledge; it simply lies in wait for when *Awareness* is high enough that the *Self* can handle it directly.

Systemology introduces systematic methods to bring an individual closer to full responsibility of their own Mind-System—since they have been far too long under an illusion that everything that they are seeing in their reality and its mental imagery and all that associated encoding and supposedly logical reasoning is all being dictated, or otherwise externally determined; and this is one of the greatest tricks that has ever been pulled on the Alpha Spirit to make certain their consideration of *beingness* is entrapped within the confines of *this* Physical Universe.

Inability to confront, approach and face the nature of present reality and existence, taking place in the Physical Universe and within one's own personal universe, is what triggers the automatic-responses and reactive mechanisms to be employed. The individual doesn't have the *Awareness* to be responsible for the present-time POV, so this is overshadowed with a lot of "suppositions" impressed as the "supposed to's" and "must haves" and other associative knowledge based on past circumstances. That which we have *lived* through is suddenly "safe" as a validity to our continued existence and survival—and this causes a tendency to form patterned reasoning. If left simply to the old **dead-memory** images held in the Mind, you can be rest assured that these dead images can be infused with life and treated as a present-time reality—and the Mind-System will find no shortage of ways of justifying all of these reactions and associates based on its stores of experience.

Back down the spiritual timeline of Alpha spiritual existence, the *Self* does not prefer to give attention (or "look") at things which it is not prepared to confront or be responsible for. There are old sayings regarding knowledge and learning that speak of the responsibility for what you "know"—and there is undoubtedly some truth to this, since we have discovered that "responsibility is power." But just as this responsibility deteriorated on a gradient scale, coinciding with the fragmentation of *Self* and the condensation of (and then entrapment in) *this* Physical Universe, so too can we systematically restore it by operating in a reverse order. It is *this* concept that is embedded behind mystical, spiritual and magical symbolism of various *"Gates," "Dimensions"* and *"Levels"* in former traditions and cosmologies, but very often the truth of things is much simpler than graphically presented in Mystery Traditions; because what is a "dimension" really, but just a "POV."

> The next step at this juncture of the *Pathway* is to "flatten the wave" of "collapsed" considerations regarding "handling of problems," and ability to manage the Mind-System.

Various techniques of instruction that we employ for our Systemology and spiritual presentation of Mardukite Zuism are, in essence, "game changers"—and any time such efforts have been demonstrated to any success in the past, they have usually been overrun by material-system corruption and the usurpation of less actualized individuals that use the same tech that could otherwise elevate the spiritual evolution of our planet but, because this *is* a "penalty-prison" fabrication of reality, these efforts resemble something more akin to a "jailbreak" than to a widespread rescue mission.

As we approach the *Gateways to Infinity* we require a wider scope of PCLs. These involve freeing up a Seeker's considerations beyond "what has happened to them" already or their accessible memory recall of the same. These newer processes involve differentiating between what we are *knowingly* creating and willing versus what is set to go on automatic.

In this first set of PCLs we are dealing with "concepts" and the intention or spiritual effort behind them on an Alpha level of interpreting Mind-System data, which is to say "sense." We are not asking for any specific concrete imagery to come to mind, nor are we directly prompting a reactive response from former programming and imprinting (but should this come up—and it undoubtedly will—each point of turbulence should be processed appropriately before moving on); we are simply asking a Seeker to *get a sense of a concept*, and then we can see where this leads the Mind-System. In other esoteric terms, we are asking to "conjure" or "evoke" to Mind, because in actuality it is always *Self* that produces the *sense of a concept*—so we want to practice this knowingly.

As for our "Route-2" research technique, the most basic session PCL uses: "Recall solving a problem" (or "Recall a time when you solved a problem") *alternated with* "Recall not solving a problem" (or "Recall an unresolved problem"). These were not found to yield very effective results, so they weren't included. This path is graded for a reason. The practice of "imagining" *Self* solving and not solving problems worked marginally better, but without *Grade-IV* training, even this proved difficult in getting a Seeker to the point of optimum *realizations.* Therefore, the methodology of this present manual relies on an understanding of all former "Routes" of systematic processing, because elements of them all were included in order for a Seeker to "make the grade" so to speak.

These PCLs are applied following instructions given for *SOP-2C* and "*Route-3*" and guidelines in *Crystal Clear (Liber-2B).* A Seeker/Pilot should work one "circuit" through (alternating the positive and negative flows) until it can be handled with ease before working with the next one. Then after working through all the circuits, a return to the first one again is usually beneficial because it may be treated at a "higher level" of understanding than formerly. (This is generally true of most systematic processing because as a Seeker's *realizations* increase, so does their scope on reality.)

Circuit-1:   Contact a sense of solving a problem.

                        Contact a sense of not solving a problem.

Another example of this PCL could be stated:

Circuit-1:   Get the concept of solving a problem.

                        Get the concept of not solving a problem.

The idea of "contacting a feeling" or "conjuring the idea" is also acceptable for beginners. Each individual is going to find a pattern of speech that "resonates" more effectively for systematic processing in early stages. But whatever pattern of PCL is selected, the same style should be used throughout each circuit. Other circuits of this processing cycle are as follows—

Circuit-2:   Get a sense of (*terminal*)° solving a problem.

                        Get a sense of (*terminal*) not solving a problem.

∞ "Terminals" can be *any* communication terminal or any conception that can carry an emotional imprint or mental programming. Terminals could simply be the term "others" or "another person" or it could be identified more closely to a specific terminal (if it is a problem area), such a certain individual or the "phase" they represent, such as "mothers" or "teachers"—any specific "*is*" that the Seeker carries energetic turbulence with. See also *Liber-2C.*

Circuit-3:	Get the sense of others solving a problem.
	Get the sense of others not solving a problem.

It may be, without supplemental book instruction, that a Seeker in session will need to work up to the idea of even treating the subject of problems, for which they can increase their considerations by running through each of the following in series.

Circuit-1:	What (is a) problem could you confront?

Or using another style of PCL—

Circuit-1:	What problem would be acceptable for you to confront?

Following the formula of *Route-3*, this PCL series continues—

Circuit-2:	What problem could (another/terminal) confront?
Circuit-3:	What problem could others confront?

Even small "problems" are quite challenging for some Seekers to approach, simply because they are still hung up on basic semantics associated and encoding to even the very word "problem." For some Seekers, being directed with a PCL that implies confronting the entire problem is too steep of a gradient. This is one of the reasons we prefer to arrange *Professional Piloting* for processing through these Wizard Grades, because a solitary Seeker can easily become hung up on a part of the processing with no other expert advice or support on how to move through it. So as an alternative, the Seeker can consider (or be directed by a *Pilot* to consider) some type of problem and then inquire as to "what part of the problem" a Seeker could confront. It may be that even small problems must be confronted in pieces until an individual develops the certainty to manage the whole packages.

Δ Δ Δ Δ Δ Δ Δ

Individuals approach the field of problems based on their level of *Actualized Awareness*. Any facet or directive could be developed into a problem, but that does not mean that they are in themselves the source of problems. Considerations again return to *Self* and ability to manage Self-determined decision-making in *Self-Honesty*. At the lower spheres of reach within beta-existence, we have already taken great lengths to codify the nature of human problems and subject of their implantation. This knowledge or learning alone—without supplemental systematic processing—does not necessarily accomplish the necessary "release from condition" that we are ultimately after, but it at least leads a Seeker in the right direction for processing.

The first sphere of existence represents the lowest operable domain of *beta-existence* as this Physical Universe, which implants the problems of survival. The individual is a survivor and little more. In the second sphere, which is also within the "Reactive-Response" range of a genetic vehicle, we see even more built up on the subject of accumulation and loss, competition and scarcity. We find the development of the artificial personality and the ability to be encoded by deeper imprints of fear or threat to survival. All of this keeps an individual tightly wound in a small package, reacting against all conditions encoded to fear, abandonment, guilt and victimization. The being is now fully aware or conditioned to be aware that they are pitted against the problems of a material universe in order to secure the longevity of their own material survival as the end sum of their true spiritual POV—and herein we have discovered the lowest-level trappings of material existence; to get the Mind-System operating on reactive-response mechanisms which can otherwise be occupied to direct an individual between very rigid parameters of potentiality.

> Since the true nature of the Alpha Spirit is a near-infinite Source-point of pure creative energy and activity, what passes for classification of a Mind-System—any part of the Mind-System, including MCC—must therefore be made up of some type of systematic "pattern" in order to operate as programming.

This means that even outside the domain of the RCC, we are still dealing with some kind of reactive-response mechanisms for an "analytical pattern" to form any kind of association in the upper-levels of the Mind-System. They may not be as crude as the reactive-response and fight-flight mechanisms of the RCC, but they are still patterned after some type of associated reasoning and thus full under the domain of a "mental universe" and not necessarily the true *Alpha* state of *Self.* As much as we would like to view the MCC as a kind of "higher Self" for the individual occupying a lower-level POV, it is certainly not the ultimate POV for *Self.* It is more commonly viewed as a **threshold** between interior *beta-existence* and the *exterior* spiritual or "Alpha" universes.

Following a similar formula as former levels of systematic processing, a Seeker can conduct "objective processing" techniques to supplement subjective PCLs. In this instance, we want to practice with an arbitrary object—such as a *bell, book* or *candle*—that a Seeker does not have significant emotional encoding with (meaning an preexisting problem already). Eventually the same formula could be applied to processing out other actual problems, but the point of this exercise is simply to increase the range of considerations regarding the conception of "problems" and "solutions." After the object has been properly *identified** (as a terminal) for processing, the following PCL are run similar to the first process in this chapter-lesson.

Circuit-1: How could (terminal) be a problem to you?
How could (terminal) be a solution to you?

Circuit-2: How could (terminal) be a problem to (other terminal)?
How could (terminal) be a solution to (other terminal)?

Circuit-3: How could others be a problem to (terminal)?
How could others be a solution to (terminal)?

Circuit-AT:∞ How could you be a problem to (terminal)?
How could you be a solution to (terminal)?

Some of the answers to these may seem hard to come up with at first, but when considerations expand, even more ridiculous answers can be accepted as an increased realization that it is *Self* determining these evaluations, now and always. Another form of "objective processing" that may be employed between "subjective processes" could include the same or similar item with the intent that a Seeker invents ways in which the object is the answer or solution. In fact, as the former, this process can be applied to problem terminals just as usefully as it can be applied to creative practice.

Circuit-1: What problem could you have with someone with which (terminal) is the solution?

Circuit-2: What problem could someone have with you with which (terminal) is the solution?

Circuit-3: What problem could others have with someone with which (terminal) is the solution?

Circuit-AT: What problem could you have with yourself with which (terminal) is the solution?

---

* See *Liber-2B, Liber-2C* and *Liber-2D* for more information.
∞ "Circuit-0" or "Circuit-A.T." is optional for the first pass through this present material (particularly for those still working through *Grade-III* instructions) and is included here for reference purposes only.

Δ Δ Δ Δ Δ Δ Δ

Our intention is to get a Seeker to increase their willingness and ability to solve problems by understanding that they can just as easily create conditions for the problem as the solution simply by reassigning evaluations. This is a tremendous ability; true to the state of the Alpha Spirit.

At these upper-levels of basic systematic processing, ability of *Self* is very noticeably tied to "responsibility" and so we tend to emphasize *that* much more in the journey to regain and resume the original conditions for the Alpha Spirit to operate from as a true POV independent of the Human Condition. Of course, this does not happen all at once, but it is found to occur as a result of increased responsibility for energetic management of creative faculties attached to being an Alpha Spirit.

"Responsibility" is a steep gradient for a *Pilot* to thrust on a Seeker with their first pass through the processing prior to arriving at an *Actualized Technician* or "Wizard" status. This state is "actualized" more permanently by making a second pass through standard processing while occupying an *A.T.* State. We are not limiting the application of the work in this manual only to *certain* Seekers—hence its inclusion—but it is only recommended that PCLs for "Total Responsibility of Problems" be applied to those Seekers actually ready to confront the reality that they are the one's in the *pilot's chair* for their existence. Once a problem (or turbulent channel/terminal) is contacted, the Seeker is prompted: "What part of that could you be responsible for?" And when that is no longer generating a response: "What part of that could you admit to causing?"

Since the nature of our "problem clusters" also seems to involve having two oppositional or separated POV, subjective processing can be supplemented with brief objective processes that include directing attention between two objects alternately, such as those methods connected to "*Bell, Book & Candle*." This is then applied to defragmenting previous unresolved problems by identifying the problem and then alternately spotting some point or facet from one side and then the other side—which is a further development on the suggestions given for *Route-1*.[*] This is particularly useful for reducing the energies holding together specific "problem cycles" that seem to reappear during the course of one's life.

---

[*] See "*The Tablets of Destiny*" (*Liber-One*).

:: 4 ::
COMMAND OF A MIND-SYSTEM
USING BETA-DEFRAGMENTATION

Prior to solidifying considerations and a POV for *this* Physical Universe, the "Mind-System" was constructed, created or formed—presumably by *us*—to engage with a "mental universe." The mental universe was constructed as a composite of personal spiritual universes collapsed together. They have ever remained personal to an Alpha Spirit at its truer state of beingness and existence, but from which the POV descended. More and more "communication barriers" were installed and more automatic mechanisms were established so that a "Mind-System" could actually exist and function.

> The "Mind-System" is no more *Self* than the "genetic vehicle" or a physical body is. But, much like a physical body, it is used to direct information that the *Self* should otherwise have a clear observation of. When it does not, we say that this personal identity continuum and Mind-System is "fragmented."

Although we have "compartmented" our understanding of the "Mind-System" by dividing it into the RCC and MCC as a classification of function, the two parts actually do work together as a system of the Human Condition is concerned. So, up to at least "7.0" on our Standard Model we have the Self as the Alpha Spirit in its original state, and down at "1.0" we find an organic body that has roughly about the same solidity as the Physical Universe that it occupies as a body. We don't occupy that universe, but our considerations apparently do, and as we have moved down through a series of condensing universes, so have parameters for the POV we agreed to (and so with the vehicles we command). In between the functions and relative existences of these two states, we find a relatively large portion of the Standard Model—all of what is classified a "beta-existence"—dedicated to the Mind-System. It is *this* system that directly links *Self* with *any* consideration of "form" as a beta-existence.

Somewhere along the spiritual timeline we received a distinct impression that we could be identified with a locatable form that could be harmed, that we could lose things, that we should protect our survival, &tc.—and while this may have originally taken place up in the *Alpha* regions of *exterior* beingness, it was *these* basic considerations on which the Mind-System was eventually formulated upon, which we refer to as "*implants.*"

Circuitry of the Mind-System was cemented through by repeated validation of its use as a medium or **catalyst** to evaluate experience and
observations for us. And it is certainly no mystery as to how this could
easily have compounded upon itself to set up a vast network array of
channels and circuits to literally "compartment" its own systematic operations. This means that while upper levels of the Mind-System may not
operate at the same material reflex level as "stimulus-response" and
"flight-versus-flight" mechanisms of the RCC, it should be presumed that
it at least must have *some degree of reactivity* to maintain any communicable preexisting programming or associative networking. Therein we
discover the nature of what these "implants," which underlie any all all
other mechanisms, metaphorically being the very gel and membrane **receptors** that make all other encoding, imprinting and programming
possible.

As *Self* decided that more and more "things" were "unsafe" (not contrib-
utory to a continuing existence) to "look at" (given attention to),
patterns of experiential memory developed; naturally leading to form
"preconceptions" about things. These assign values or evaluate a reaction or response to a *past* "imprint" of something, which is then stored
for future usage and treated then as "present-time" knowledge or experience. The only reason any being stores any information (or anything)
anywhere is because of a potential for future usage. This is actually
somewhat troublesome when we consider the amount of information
stored from each circuit on a channel. These network chains of information will all be aligned to seem reasonable and yet, result in a sequence
of cumulative "*must...*" and "*supposed to...*" directives.

After an individual has repeatedly validated lower ranges of POV as *Self*,
the implanted problem network of directives in the Mind is not always
clearly visible. It is, in essence, easier to demonstrate these principles
using the electrical signals that are sent to muscles, or even in the range
of emotion, where there is a great deal of solidity in sensation and its
evaluation; but when it comes to mental imagery and evaluations assigned to the same, it all looks so reasonable and logical from *down below*,
as if any of the preconceived notions carry any data at all worth *knowing*
about, and certainly not appropriate as a "filter-screen" by which we observe and interact with existence.

Elsewhere in esoteric lore, these "filter-screens" are treated as "*veils of
existence,*" although fragmented knowledge throughout the ages left
these traditions with no effective technology to effectively work through
them, with all importance and significances generally assigned to cor

responding "magical facets" and other "ritual specifics" with little regard for whether or not the mystic-magician or priest and priestess would actually arrive at the true *realizations* for *Self-Actualization* indicated for each of these "*Gates.*" This is what prompted our development of the Mardukite "Grades" and an advanced "Systemology" that could surpass all former "paradigms" and reach for ultimate goals of a *metahuman spiritual evolution*; thereby correcting the direction on the track that the standard-issue Human Condition has found itself (or in many cases, still not found itself).

> Since no preexisting system or paradigm of the past four millennium has demonstrated a motion in the direction toward correcting itself, we did not see it fitting to directly base our futurist evolution of Mardukite Zuism & Systemology on any one of them; with the exception, of course, being the consideration that we are an accelerated extension of the 20th century "New Thought" movement.

Systematic paradigms, traditions, religions and even material systems of the past have all kept attentions of the Alpha Spirit headed in the wrong direction—further entrapping *Self* into deeper and deeper material conditions of *this* Physical Universe—by promising (yet eluding evidence for) a greater evolutionary existence of the "spirit" by agreeing to more and more conditions of the Physical Universe and its systems.

While each of the paradigms may have been set up around a qualified source-point that *knew something,* the failure to adequately duplicate this original *knowing* across an organizational structure creates mechanistic systems that ultimately lead to their breakdown. More attention is given to the repair and support of the failing system as an organization or paradigm than to the actual resolution of what is causing it; assignment of *cause* and the *responsibility* of creation has long since been lost to an unknown mystery—and so the existence of the "problem" perpetuates.

Some of the more "gnostic"-minded philosophers and traditions developed paradigms on a fundamental that the Physical Universe is somehow not real at all; which unfortunately removes *all* sense of responsibility for it from the individual. When we say it isn't there—setting up "communication barriers" with a universe along the liway—we are leaving it up to something else for control of the communication of experience and reality for us.

One of the primary functions of the Mind-System that we know about quite readily from *Grade-III*, is the evaluation of personal knowledge to estimate the application of "effort"—which is sometimes interpreted as "force" in the Physical Universe.

The only true directive force that we know of in this universe *is* the Alpha Spirit, but its own essence is not *of* and *as* this beta-existence and thus is not able to be defined by any of its parameters of weights and wavelengths. Therefore, *Self* has set up channels of communication between relays and control centers that make this estimations of effort based on past experience. This "analytical pattern" in itself becomes something of a reactive response mechanism that can operate as a "push-button" system—and that is very detrimental to maintaining *Self-Honest* clarity of the Alpha Spirit as fully *Self-determined.*

An interesting correlation between *beta-Awareness* and the estimation of effort to create an effect is: as one moves down on the *ZU-line* (in *beta-Awareness*) they feel the need to exert more and more effort at the POV level they are occupying in order to earn the same effect at that level—as if pushing against more and more resistance.

You can demonstrate a registry of this in the "emotional state" an individual is suspended in at those levels where it is conceived that more and more effort will be required in order to create a change of state—even violently, if necessary—until an individual (upon failing to accomplish their ends at each point) finally succumbs into being the effect of oppositional forces, such as the basic material of the Physical Universe.

Of course, when this registers fully as being "total effect of external forces," the Alpha Spirit withdraws completely from the Mind-Body connection; we generally speak of such "genetic vehicles" as being dead and abandoned. The physical aging cycle could even be considered a reduction of high-level *Awareness* "POV" (as cause) being transformed into an effect. The individual eventually decided they could do no more to create an effect and be responsible for no more cause in this existence; so the Alpha Spirit just stops "looking" and the organism goes more and more on autopilot (accumulating more and more "experience").

A *Pilot* should note that a Seeker can also come to a realization of a problem simply being a "no-problem" or even a solution that seeks or creates problems. This comes up more frequently when imagining, inventing or creating problems as an energetic practice. Anything willingly and knowingly created within the personal universe can be controlled as "ownership" or "having" (which is again, to say, "responsibility")—and there is no need to worry about having to hold on too tightly because we can throw these away and easily create or duplicate any former creation again. Scarcity of this *Awareness* is part of what causes *Self* to "hold on" so tightly to traps in any material *beta-existence*. As a Seeker comes to an increased realization that a problem can be easily created at will, then there is less of a drive to remain suspended between existing ones.

The "Mind-System" is designed to essentially copy images of the universe in which the *Self* is extending its POV, which for our purposes now, has been restricted to the "games" of the Physical Universe (*beta-existence*). Since there is any number of creators putting forth their energies in this objective reality, it can be assumed that from the perspective of the "genetic vehicle" and Mind-System that *Self* is not directly responsible for "creation" of other-determined existences encountered in the Physical Universe. It does, however, begin to make copies of images that it encounters, which along with encoded programming and evaluations, is stored in the Mind-System as a representation of the external world. It is the contents of *this* Mind-System that an individual *is absolutely* responsible for—and it is *this* contents that contributes to experience of a personal universe that esoteric philosophers in the past have referred to as the "mental plane." We could go on to include the "astral plane" within this domain, because our mystical experiments revealed that even traditional "astral work" does not liberate *Self* from the "stuff" contained in the Mind-System. A "magician" is still very much operating from a POV within the *interior* of the Mind.

In most cases, *Grade-I* pursuits on the "Route of Magick & Mysticism" are not the most effective in achieving the highest *realizations* toward the ideal state of being for *Self;* even if their original underlying purpose was to get there, most simply don't. In most cases, the remedy for material problems (at low levels of operation) is a solution that in itself creates more problems. The root of problems and the Mind-System is never fully uncovered, only demonstrated—and repeated lifetimes of use, with a practitioner suspended at the *First Gate*—simply validates and reinforces more and more of the mechanisms present in the Mind-System.

> As the subject of "problems" becomes more interesting to lower-level understanding than pursuing *"Self-Honesty,"* an individual spends more and more of their directed attention on simply finding more creative ways to remain suspended in lower level considerations.

One reason our Systemology work is built upon foundations established as the *Grade-II* "Route of Mardukite Mesopotamia," is because the only effective elements from *Grade-I* that lent assistance to achieving access to the true *Second Gate* were all connected to the highest pursuits of mysticism in the direction of "Divine" and "Celestial" branches of magic and mysticism, including Druidism—which may have been repeated in their own fragmentary designs throughout history, but of which, in their purest form, can be traced back to the systematization of the ancient world in Babylon, by the Mardukite Babylonians.

Although many who have delved into esoteric and mystical pursuits are generally familiar with the more recent Judeo-Semitic interpretation of the "Kabbalah"—upon which the last two millennium of "ceremonial magic" is strongly based—even a casual amount of research into the much more antiquated *Grade-II* presentation of "Stargates" in Babylon (or *"Babili System"*) easily demonstrates that the more commonly known "Kabbalah" is an importation of older "stronger" Babylonian lore.[*]

If we follow the track laid down by *Mardukite Babylonians*, then:

The *First Gate*, being the lunar level, would correspond directly to pursuit of magic, mysticism and enchantment discovered in *Grade-I*, as an initiate moves up into the various "elemental" dimensions of the Earth Gate and beyond, tapping the first veil;

The *Second Gate*, is of course linked to Mercury and the hermetic spiritual quasi-religious styling of *Grade-II*; and in ancient Babylonian Mardukite tradition, this position was correlated to the Anunnaki demigod "Nabu," the systematizer of Babylon, developer of the stylus and refiner of cuneiform script in order to structure the first "priesthoods";

Which brought us to the forefront of the *Ishtar Gate* in *Grade-III*, the Venusian veil that most have never successfully crossed beyond from the Human Condition, because it requires attainment of *Self-Honesty* to the degree that reactive emotional ties to the lower realm are resolved;

As are the higher analytical systems of the Mind, which are confronted and disintegrated directly at the *Fourth level*; the Sun...[*]

---

[*] See especially the *Grade-II* volume, *"Practical Babylonian Magic"* by Joshua Free (also available in hardcover as *"Necronomicon: The Anunnaki Grimoire"* and within the complete Grade-II Master Edition hardcover *"Necronomicon: The Complete Anunnaki Legacy"* edited by Joshua Free.

[*] Which should prepare one for the *Wall of Fire* one must pass through to get beyond the *Fifth Gate* circumvented by "martian" and "martial" energy.

Such information is provided solely as reference to the esoterically inclined that may have missed this basic structure of ascent up the "*Ladder of Lights*" that is present in our interpretation of the *pathway* for Mardukite Systemology.

Δ Δ Δ Δ Δ Δ Δ

We have, at this stage, uncovered most low-level *beta-mechanisms* of the Mind-System that seem to "key-in" a "push-button" response association with reality, and its communication, which contributes greatly to an entrapment to the Physical Universe by consideration. There are many ways of working to undo these mechanisms—most of which continue to be explored throughout the forthcoming manuals covering these upper-level "Wizard Grades" of Mardukite Systemology. However, there is *more* instruction and practice that is critical here at *this* stage, before we leave an ambitious Seeker (or *Pilot*) off on their own to go treating "all the problems of the world."

We've come to realize that "problems" are simply a part of the "game" scenario; without them, you don't really have any conditions for which to operate a "game"—there doesn't seem to be any real purpose without something to "solve." This is confined to parameters of whatever "game" is in play—and the most unfortunate event for the Human Condition is when it stopped *knowing* that it was playing this "game." Did you ever play "cops and robbers" as a child? You would invent a set of rules and parameters; might even take turns—playing one side and then the other. It was a "game," you knew you were playing it, and so did your friends. But maybe after a while, maybe that wasn't interesting or challenging enough to occupy attention, or be considered "fun."

> So, what would happen if, in the middle of this game, you forgot it was a game and all you knew was the identity role persona that you had taken up to play it? What then? Well, this is a fair approximation of the current state of the Human Condition; and what's more—the *Self* is left to remember and rediscover all that it chose to forget to play *this* game. It's high time we found a final resolution to *this* one, so we can play a better one. If you haven't noticed yet, there is no way to "win" *in* the Physical Universe, but we can uncover the rules and break the chains to when we first agreed to occupy a Will *under* **Cosmic Law.**

The nature of lower universes, such as the one we occupy, is a penalty-prison system developed beneath a higher order POV (existence)—

and this sequential deterioration has continued to go on for some time. Many have an innate sense of the "Otherworld" or the magical lands of "Faerie" and other elements of fantasy, which seem as if they are a memory of a former time on *this* planet, but they are not. In fact, even when such periods of history *were* taking place prior to the industrial mechanization of society, they were themselves developed on and meant to stimulate memories of this *other* universe. Such made *this* version of Earth more resonant and familiar or similar to the immediately preceding "home" from which we came. After all, it is up to the inmates to create and maintain their own standards within the cells. So, naturally there is plenty to *do* in *beta-existence*, and countless ways to occupy attention during one's imprisonment—but to what ends?

For those that have risen above the lower-level of sensation—beyond living reactive lives based on immediate gratification of pleasure centers in the body—there are just as many, if not more, "intellectual traps" installed into the Human Condition once the POV of *Self* is fixed to the range of this Physical Universe. Most parts of the Mind-System are simply driven by discovery and craving for "new information" in an attempt to understand whatever previous layers of information have already been collected. It is ceaseless in this pursuit and stores information across many lifetimes, so it is unlikely to be **localized** in the "brain" although it appears to use that physical organ as a communication control center for the genetic vehicle as part of the organic RCC Mind-Body relay system.

Accumulation and storage of new information by the "analytical" database of the Mind-System is always appropriated an evaluation based on what has already been stored along appropriate "nodes" of that subject (as associative data held in the Mind). When this is left completely on automatic, outside control of the Alpha Spirit, the tendencies and patterns of circuitry becomes fixed—thereafter the individual is unable to consciously adjust their POV or considerations from a strongly impressed set of operations that they stopped being responsible for. The true stability of a Seeker—as it relates to *Grade-IV* guidelines—is measured observably by their ability to handle the problems and solutions of life, which is undoubtedly reflected in the communications during a systematic processing session. Up to this point, an individual's own point of stability is essentially the fundamental implants and premises that they will eventually group all of their other accumulated associated data around.

Freedom to create and un-create within the Mind-System is the focus of all systematic processing whereby a Seeker is directed to generate, imagine or create various concepts, ideas, scenarios, and flows of energy along any channel, all freely at will. As a related area of focus, we are also dealing with the concept of "change" because problem solving is innately about movement—or any growth or continuation along a line or track. Even if the "problem" to be solved is simply only stated as getting from "point-A" to "point-B" there is still *some game* to play; something to solve and *do*. Of course, in the Physical Universe we have misaligned our priorities of beingness and repeatedly substitute *doing* anything in place of *knowing* something real.

So now we have come to a point in the Mind-System where experience and familiarity lead to some quality of reactivity. An individual has "gone through" some experience or another and since they have obviously survived through it, there is some sense that there is something to *know* about it—and this of course creates a sense of familiarity with something, which we then can assign all kinds of associations and predisposed evaluations for. This could have started out very innocently and not as a means to entrap an individual, but ultimately that is what we see with its improper handling. It leads to associations that are limiting only for the fact that *Self* applies its own familiar experience from the past in order to experience the present—and where the "Mind-System" is concerned, this is done automatically by the very nature of its function when *Self* is not in "command," (which is also to say "responsible" for handling a present experience). The "Mind" (or in many standard-issue cases, the "Body") is allowed to do the "looking" and "analyzing" because the Alpha Spirit no longer deems it "safe" (*willing, able, &tc.*) to do so directly.

∆ ∆ ∆ ∆ ∆ ∆ ∆

We have expressed a requirement for a *Seeker* to actually *be* "present" *in* a "session" for any systematic processing to be effective. That means that the *Seeker*—which is *Self*, the individual, the "I" or "I-AM" as Alpha Spirit—must be "present" in the space-time *of the* "*present*" and able to experience it. How is this even possible for anyone to achieve when there are so many "filter-screen-veils" of imprinted reactions and logical reasoning standing in between *Self* and experience of "present-time" reality? It is *this* factor that led many philosophers into the field of "reason" and "knowledge" and the entire academic pursuit of "**epistemology**"—because the nature of using a "sensation-based body" as the observer or measuring device of reality is always found to have serious flaws. Rene Descartes wrote about how the senses could be demonstrate to the fool the *Self* and therefore could not be trusted; yet a conventional practice or spiritual technology to remedy this effectively was still in need.

If we could know for certain that the Mind-System was fully operational in *Self-Honesty*, then it might not be so bad to have some automated mechanisms doing some of the work for *Self*, but the information that it passes is always fragmented; mainly because it does not actually do any of the looking and experiencing and is instead dictating information back to *Self* based on imprinted programming already installed through experience. *Self* is no longer doing any of the experiencing and is simply receiving a series of images on a screen that have very little to do with the present space-time taking place.

:: 5 ::

COMMAND OF THE MIND-SYSTEM
FOR A METAHUMAN EVOLUTION

What we are approaching in *Grade-IV* is a heightened *beta-Awareness* that when compared to the standard-issue nature of the Human Condition, would seem quite *metahuman*, quite simply because the individual is not rigidly fixed on a POV within the biological or intellectual confines of this Physical Universe.

The common denominator of all advanced pursuits by an individual, whether physical mechanics or esoteric mysticism, is the handling of "energy." Energy, as we have found, is the fundamental unit of whatever is taking place in existence—any existence. The practice of personal control and determinism over the control of energy has been the subject of pursuit by every scientist, magician, priest or priestess, separated only by their semantic applications to observable levels of energetic interaction.[*]

As with many subjects within our Systemology, the ability to handle the energy we face everyday and its ideal use to increase our own spiritual abilities (those that extend to more than this lifetime or else beyond *beta-existence*) should be a commonplace education; and yet we find it nowhere expertly given in any universal applications, with the lowest possible understandings of it rendered as "science."

> There is nothing inherently wrong with a "science"; it seeks simply to *Know*, but it also must invent its own knowledge to *Know* about since it has eliminated from its equations the only lifeform that can actually do any *Looking* and *Knowing*, which is, of course, the Alpha Spirit in its true and defragmented POV.

Others have made attempts at getting to a point of "more than human" as well, but nearly all the current efforts are directed toward external **transhuman** technologies that really do not serve a purpose in achieving the actual state of beingness we refer to as "*Homo Novus*"—and therefore, to differentiate from these materialists, have attributed the main brand of our *Grade-IV* (*Wizard Level-0*) work as "Metahuman Systemology." This state appears to be primarily attained by *beta-defragmentation* of the "Mind-System."

---

[*] This matter of energy and semantics of "Zu" is best explored in the *Grade-III* lecture, "*Power of Zu*"—transcripts included in "*The Systemology Handbook.*"

The accumulation of energetic "mass" in the form of imprinting and programming through the course of many lifetimes has led a once god-like spiritual being into the position of carrying a lot of "baggage"—all of which has increasingly weighed the *Awareness* of the individual down into agreements of *this* Physical Universe due to an inability to unload these burdens along the way. It seems as though we felt we really needed to carry this weight with us in order to "have" something from the journey; not realizing we could have released ourselves from the hold and just created it all again later.

Mental images themselves do not seem to weigh us down—because they may be easily dispersed and created if Self-determined; only associations that are tied to them cause us the fragmentation—whether from emotional encoding or mental programming. It seems that at this point of the journey there are at least enough individuals now starting to take notice of this to make it a "thing" and the subject of a "New Thought" movement that is, in the words of this generation, working to liberate Alpha Spirits from the *Matrix*; freeing considerations to a higher POV that it has otherwise agreed to be shielded and blocked from in order to experience *this* "down here."

We have learned that electrical charges directed from *Self* as "ZU" (*Spiritual Life Awareness Energy*) operate quite differently in *beta-existence* than they do in the Alpha zones of a spiritual one. In fact, there are many instances where it seems that the Physical Universe is designed, being the expertly crafted prison that it is, to deliver the opposite results to what we are after, all of which is related to fragmented problem-implants.

For example: have you ever noticed in your experience with the Physical Universe that when you really really want and crave something—practically to the point of obsession—it always seems just a little bit out of reach? How about avoidance?—Did you ever notice that when you put up enough resistance to avoid something too strongly that you end up with it staring you right in the face? It's rather like getting a bit of dust or particle matter out of your cup of coffee: you reach at it with your finger and the wave-force distances it away from you; then when you withdraw it returns to where you had originally targeted.

Given how low *Awareness* levels tend to reach in *beta-existence*, it is found that an individual believes they need to apply an excessive amount of effort and force to create the change they want. This is, of course, after experiencing many diminishing universes that each became just a little bit more "solid" than the one before. Even the material universe of the "Otherworld" or "Magic Kingdom" that immediately *precedes* or *envel-*

opes this one (depending on your opinion of dimension) is not that much different in terms of solid forms, except that consideration for the power of the electron is not restricted to a "wire" which is therefore what makes "magic" possible there. And most of us have had some sense or memory of such a place, but it will not be found on this planet—although, there are times when those sharing this same memory have again made attempts to create a facsimile of it here.

Δ Δ Δ Δ Δ Δ Δ

Obviously we all have the ability to create, we have the ability to apply will as intention, and certainly not every effort or reach that we extend in this existence is **thwarted**; but somehow the important ones—at least the important ones to defragment your personal wiring—are placed in the category of "implanted problems" which are not otherwise *Self-determined* if following standard-issue programming. So, the individual that craves something to the point of obsession is wired to never receive it so long as they continue to apply those patterned efforts. For all of the hard-wiring that is attached to the response-mechanisms of the genetic vehicle, energy does not respond very well to a source-point of erratic desperation or force.

If you consider the projection and reception of energy as the force and suction demonstrated on the speck of dust in coffee cup, it is easy to see how we again return to the intention-counter-intention cluster of energy that we have formerly referred to as a *real* "problem." In the case of an implanted problem, these channels are encoded to exhibit polarities of "must have" and "can't have" on a particular terminal. Unlike a traditional "problem" cluster, these implants can actually create a vacuum of energy by directives that we "must" draw in and keep away various currents in order to satisfy programming.

Most materially successful individuals that achieved success via their own actualization have realized that the key to it all is "acceptance"; which someone maintaining a much more fragmented Mind-System would only be able to realize as "indifference"—and they are not the same. In fact, we have a place for "indifference" on our *beta-Awareness* scale, and it is not very high. Acceptance, however is a much higher state that revolves around a freed consideration of potentiality that they can "have things" without being obsessive or compulsive about the efforts to attain them. This relies heavily on one's own *determination*, but that again is not the same as repetitive application of an effort against opposition; it is instead a directing property of *Will* and *Intention*.

Exercises where an individual is maintaining their own control of their mental imagery may be used to assist the fluid willingness to "have" and "not have" without emotional reactivity. Even a casual disinterest is better than supplying more energy to rejections, blocks and barriers. When it comes to emotionally dramatic displays of behavior, it is simply best not to engage. Although direct handling of creative imagery handling in the Mind-System is relayed in greater detail later on in *Grade-IV,* for our present purposes, we have been using the PCL technique of "getting the sense of" something, which is especially useful for those Seekers not yet already managing their own mental imagery for systematic processing. This too is developed with further practice along the way.

We use the terms "acceptance" and "rejection"—and we can find this semantic present in our processing when a *Pilot* asks what a Seeker could "accept" about something, such as the situation they are having a problem with, or even something in the room (as practice), and then what could they "reject" about it, alternating with each PCL. For example, in an objective process for *"presence in space-time,"* we could prompt: "What about this room could you find acceptable" alternating with "What about this room could you reject." The point here is not to necessarily *have to* accept or reject anything about anything, but that the practiced *Self-determined* consideration for this fluidity remains unfixed.

Considerations of energy management *may* be contacted with "getting the sense" or "concept" of something—and, of course, if any automatic reactive-responses or mental images *are* triggered by working with a particular circuit, channel or terminal, this should all be noted within the session journal or Pilot's log.[*] Keep in mind that anything that *is* uncovered, should be handled on the spot since it is obviously a "problem" area that the Seeker is prepared to face.

Any "thing" or "concept" that a Seeker is compelled toward and uncovers as a source-implant or directive toward something they aren't achieving can simply reverse the charge at will, by "wasting" or "throwing away" mental images and other imprinted symbols that key this cycle in. It is apparent that the Mind-System has treated it as a scarcity and therefore has encouraged hanging on to it just a little too tightly. This can also be practiced further in a session by "imagining" or "getting the sense of" the free circulation of these energies, which would run along the lines of:

---

[*] There are specially prepared *Systemology Adventure Journals* or *Flight-Logs* now available specifically for recording the various facets, conditions and tech applied during the course of systematic processing sessions.

Circuit-1:   Imagine (get the sense of) giving X away to another.

Circuit-2:   Imagine (get the sense of) another giving X away
to you.

Circuit-3:   Imagine (get the sense of) another giving X away
to others.

Another alternating PCL technique to assist in freeing up the considerations surrounding *"having to X"* as the only solution or answer is—"What could X be a substitute for?" and "What could be a substitute for X?" Also returning to our previous **alternation** of consideration—"What X could you accept?" and "What X could you reject?" Or, if more applicable for lower levels: what *about* X, &tc. You can practice this in regard to aesthetics or survival any terminal that can be alternated with "desirable" (wanted) and "undesirable" (unwanted).

In addition to what we have presented, the "must have"/"can't have" problem implants are equally found in the "must avoid"/"must keep" programming. In the same way that the "having" is most strongly linked to circuitry pertaining to *loss*, the "must avoid"/"must keep" implants are often related to registries of *pain*. This is logical, because "pain imprinting" is the most solid reactive-response encoding, so its memory is intended to remind an individual of what they "must avoid" by giving them heavy pain imprinting they "can't get rid of."

When we are stuck in the "must have"/"can't have" cycle, the subject or concept (terminal) is treated as a scarcity and so the energetic solution is to imagine and create an excess of positive mental imagery that can easily be discarded, thrown away, wasted or dissolved without an emotional response engaging to "hold on" to it. After this is resolved, a Seeker is instructed to work in both directions of energetic flow, practicing fluid "acceptance" and "rejection" by alternately "throwing away" the images *and* "pushing them in" on the personal universe or "body." When we are treating the problem implants of "must avoid"/ "can't get rid of," the procedure is run in reverse, getting an individual to accept more of it by "pushing" an excess of the imagery into the personal universe until it can be "accepted" or "rejected" without fragmentation. This is not an instant process, but it may be accelerated with proper handling of mental imagery.

Δ Δ Δ Δ Δ Δ Δ

We are, throughout our Systemology, referring to various "fluid" conditions, freedom of willingness and various POV whereby *Self* can get "stuck" in. All of these surround the idea of "change"—and the ability or willingness and the inability or inhibition to "accept" and "reject" *changes* without emotional turbulence or other mental fragmentation. It may be that one of the closest points the **Western** world achieved in understanding this is referred to as the "Serenity Prayer," which is in more common use among a popular *Alcoholic &tc. Recovery Group* (we won't name directly) than anywhere else in society. It speaks strongly of the willingness to accept conditions and ability to change them; with the wisdom to *know* when to do each.

We have generally found that higher actualized *beta-Awareness* equals greater ability to *Self-direct* change. This also does not mean that things have to always be changing and that some things cannot remain as they are—but again we are concerned with the free-flow of energy in either direction. When it directly concerns patterns of imprinting and programming, we see a greater tendency to resist change, because energy holds the POV of *Self* in a suspension point—a "timelessness" that elusively provides an illusion of a similar near-stasis point: that of the actual Alpha Spirit ("I").

Information from painful and critically stressful events or other perceived threats to one's own environment or "person" is carefully "photographed" and stored as an imprint with all of the *facets* treated equally to the emotional encoding of the experience. The individual will "hold on" to this imprint very tightly believing that by carrying the full intensity of this experience they will "have" something to "know" in order to keep situations from getting any worse, or at the very least, being allowed to "repeat/duplicate" again. Well, this would all be fine and good if it were not encoded by reactive-responses and then thrown back up at us in the same way, filtering out the true knowledge and experience and *presence* of *Self* in the *present* by bringing "dead images" back to life as the *present...* and what strange *Necromancy* this is.

Ability to manage "change of energy"—which includes *all motion* of energy—is characterized by a willingness and certainty to channel energies, which is *not* here used in the same sense the mystics may have referred to channeling entities in the past. The "channel" here implies application to "communication" semantics, regarding personal energy and its interaction with "terminals." This means the *Self-directed* intention to "hold energy" and "move energy"; which we can apply demonstrations of as "objective processing" in material existence. Here, the *Pilot* may apply the *"Bell, Book & Bottle"* objective processing kit to a session; having the Seeker select an object and reach for it to hold it still several times; then selecting an object, the Seeker would repeatedly practice holding it to make it more solid (by intention); and finally, selecting an object, choosing to move it to another *Self-determined* location and then doing so. This would be a basic objective systematic processing example regarding "change." The same formula could be practiced on parts of the body, such as an arm or leg, *&tc.* (including trouble areas—since an individual is "out of communication" with those), and also in mental imagery exercises.

"Change"—and *alteration* in general—is a basic property of systematic control. Other than the initial start and stop of a flow or circulation of energy, about the only other thing energy actually does within and as any system is "change." Even the motion of energy itself is a "change" in state or location, which creates a flow-pattern that we measure in cyclic waves and generally define as "time." The two sides of change, as we have seen, regard holding something still (and keeping it from going away) and then the motion of **enacting** a change. We are, of course, looking for acceptance for both, free of reactive-responses and fragmentary energetic turbulence. The concept of change may also be introduced into processing as a "terminal" using any of the available "Routes" for *SOP-2C*. For example, a Seeker could use "Analytical Recall" (*Route-2*) or "Contacting Communication Channels" (*Route-3*).

BASIC CHANGE PROCESSING—ALTERNATING (GENERAL)

Circuit-1:   Get the sense of changing something.

                Get the sense of stopping something from changing.

SYSTEMATIC PROCESSING OF CHANGE (AR-ROUTE-2)

Circuit-1:   Recall a time you changed something.

                Recall a time you stopped something from changing.

SYSTEMATIC PROCESSING OF CHANGE (AR-ROUTE-2 EXTENDED)

Circuit-2:   Recall a time when (*terminal*) changed something.

                Recall a time when (*terminal*) stopped something
                form changing.

SYSTEMATIC PROCESSING OF WILLINGNESS TO CHANGE (ROUTE-3)

Circuit-1:   What would you be willing to have changed in
                "another"?[‡]

[‡]   This terminal is generally treated as "another person," though it could also be treated as any other "lifeform" or even the Spheres of Existence. If there is a problem terminal being processed, that can be used as well.

> Circuit-2:   What would you be willing to have another change in you?
>
> Circuit-3:   What would you be willing to have another change in others?
>
> A.T. (*Opt.*):   What would you be willing to change in you?

The Mind-System has a unique way of collecting and registering its data; in both instances, acting as a mirror and crystalline lens between the "observer" and the "observed." These mechanisms all act to create, store and display "mental images" which are essentially *facsimiles* or *copies* of what is registered as experience of existence. The motion of energies captured on these images is what gives a sequential record of "time."

The Alpha Spirit, from it stasis spiritual position, engages its attention by projecting toward "mental images" of motion (as a terminal), which then produces energetic activity. The **differential** between a static point and the image of activity is what creates the "charge." We are, in essence, imbuing a certain degree of "life" and "beingness" into these images, including all of our previous imprinted records of the Physical Universe. A fixed association of emotion or knowledge (both are source-points of *knowing* at their own levels) to any of these "charges" or "terminals" is what can get an individual stuck in patterns that they are either unwilling or unable (since the two are virtually the same) to "change."

An individual goes along thinking and acting as though such and such just *must be* the case so much, even against all odds, that they are unwilling to channel any other energy free-flow. They find themselves coming up hard against objective reality and other energies with repeated invalidation. Maybe the individual *is actually* correct in their knowledge, but what does that matter if the emotional and intellectual ties to this condition are destroying the individual from the inside due to their inability to release the hold on it. The mere unwillingness to *be* in any other POV is going to give them a difficult situation to manage and contribute to an existential demise; because we know that the willingness and ability to manage and adjust to all conditions freely is the key to our continued survival and upward progression.

∆ ∆ ∆ ∆ ∆ ∆ ∆

Elsewhere in our Systemology,[∞] the mental imagery that is captured dur-

---

∞ See *Grade-III* materials, particularly "*The Tablets of Destiny*" (*Liber-One*) and "*Crystal Clear*" (*Liber-2B*) also collected in the complete *Grade-III* Master Edition

ing times of pain, loss and other perceived threats to survival are referred to as *Imprints*. Unlike the associative knowledge and stored memory used in the analytical range of the Mind, these *Imprints* have very little rationale to their content. Any and every *facet* contained in one of these heavy *Imprints* can be given the label "must avoid" including locations, individuals, sights, smells, tastes, sounds, humidity, lighting... and just about any other possible *facet* of perception received at the moment of *Imprint,* which is an *Imprinting Incident.*

This fragmentation (automatic response mechanism) is later validated when stimulated by the environment, called an **Activating Event**, and then treated based on the content of the original *Imprint,* including any manner of sensation and emotion and pain that can be triggered by the RCC to alert the identity that they "must avoid." This develops into an automatic "flinching" or "recoil" any time *that* channel of communication is contacted. It should be understood that the internal mechanisms of the Mind-System are only stimulated into action by the environment; all of the actual energy contained, entwined and solidified in the emotional imprint as a "mass" is being supplied by *Self*—and since this is all happening automatically, the solution is to return the Seeker to a point where they can manage such products of the Mind-System clearly on their own determinism.

CHANGE/UNCHANGED SUBJECTIVE PROCESSING (ROUTE-3)

Circuit-1:	What *could* you change?
	What *would* you leave unchanged?*
Circuit-2:	What *could* change you?
	What *would* leave you unchanged?
Circuit-3:	What *could* change others?
	What *would* leave others unchanged?
A.T. (Opt.):	What *could* you change about you?
	What *would* you leave unchanged about you?

Objective processing may be applied using the same formula, simply having a Seeker look around the room, locating and identifying what they could change and what they would be willing to have remain unchanged. Essentially, the underlying *realization* behind all of this is, again, to demonstrate a fluid acceptance about the state of conditions

---

hardcover "*Systemology Handbook*" by Joshua Free.

* For some Seekers, "leave you *unchanged*" does not register as well as "allow you to *remain*" or "keep the *same.*" For the sake of processing, the wording should be brought to acceptance as "unchanged" as quickly as possible.

taking place in one's environment. Eventually a PCL can use the term "accept" and "reject" again, since these words qualify to mean the same, though they often carry heavier emotional encoding.

Circuit-1:	Get a sense of you changing X.
	Get a sense of not changing X.
Circuit-2:	Get a sense of X. changing you.
	Get a sense of X. not changing you.
Circuit-3:	Get a sense of others changing X.
	Get a sense of others not changing X.
Circuit-1:	What do you want changed about X?
	What do you want to remain about X?
Circuit-2:	What does X. want changed about you?
	What does X. want to remain about you?
Circuit-3:	What does X. want changed about *others*?‡
	What does X. want to remain about *others*?

By all means a person can decide to change something, but on their own determinism and not simply because they are compelled to or even forced to by other-determined factors. In fact, willingness to change is what empowers one to handle opposition, even if in the end we are still achieving the same result we originally intended.

Likewise, willingness for things to remain as they are also puts us in a position of acceptance and the ability to knowingly create, copy or duplicate something, again entirely on one's own determinism and without the obsessive need to repeat an action. These are some of the most critical skills of proper energy handling that seem to have escaped most mystical esoteric schools in the past. . . *They directly lead to metahuman destinations. . .*

---

‡ Alternatively, "What do others want changed about *X*?" or else "Others" can be treated as a "Sphere of Existence" terminal. The additional A.T. Circuit-0 would include Self as *X*.

:: 6 ::
MASTERS OF THE UNIVERSE
HELPING LIFE HELP ALL LIFE*

There is obviously a goal in mind with how systematic processing was first presented, then carried over from *Crystal Clear* into *Grade-IV Professional Piloting Procedure*, and now toward a finality of *Grade-IV*. I've been asked about minimum conditions, specific considerations for an individual to have *realized* in order to say, "yep, Wizard Level." Of course, we are calling *Grade-IV* a "Wizard Grade" to keep our former "Masters" from being discouraged [*laughs*], but seriously it is, in actuality, "Wizard Level-0." The end result of *Grade-IV* is the minimum that we want to be working with when confronting any further upper-level work.

The *Pathway* through the *Gateways* to higher *realizations* and points of acceptable *beingness* has been veiled—and we know this; but we have only just realized that it is *we,* each one of us, that has participated in the "covering" and "disguise" and "blocks" that bar the way out. The average standard-issue individual has not yet reached a point of *Awareness* to where they are able to confront such truths as reality; and thus they remain hidden as a Mystery—and we all know how much fear-imprinting there is on Mystery—and this is where the occupation of attention is directed: *down* into the state of unknowns that represent all that is dangerous to our survival. I suppose its actually a bit of *looking up*, if an individual as a spiritual being really were in that low of a **vantage** point, right? Down in the sub-ZU terrain on the standard model—that's the underworld. And why anyone would want to dwell in those depths is beyond me, but considerations and actual *Awareness* really do descend that low, almost into a hiding or a non-existence. *Stoop not down...*

This is all considered by a matter of choice, no matter how much responsibility has been given up for those choices and the power of choice is resumed only with the resumption of Awareness. So, what is it that really freed the magician on Earth and the priests and priestesses and the wizards from their ties to the material world? What was it that drove the shamans and mystics and healers—before they organized into medical institutions—along their *Pathway* in such a manner as to remain clear of the bombardment of fragmentation that undoubtedly surrounded them as much in their own times as we find among us today? Given that we had already had the properties of the *first, second* and *third* "Gates" to

---

* Based on transcripts to a lecture given by Joshua Free on the evening of June 21, 2020; first published in "*Now You Know!*" (*Liber-3C*).

examine, it seemed that the "push-button" nature on the *fourth* should be clear to see.

Although there were many clues provided throughout *Grade-III*, the real answer was only validated by asking ourselves a series of questions regarding what we *knew* for certain of the *Pathway* that brought us here. In point: *what* was an individual doing regardless of the point on the *Pathway* they were on that was propelling them forward. Of course, we knew the small answer to that for beta-existence was simply to exist. The being is, at its lowest point of certainty, a *being*, they have some quality of *beingness* whatever POV that might be granted toward. Great, so we know we are existing; that's something. As an existence we say that an individual must be *doing* something; there is some indication of a Will or Intention that is directing the *doing* when *Self-determined*. Of course the command of *doing* falls to lower and lower control centers as the consideration of *Beingness* and a decline of *Awareness* falls. And we know that is not promoting an continued existence.

Given all of the faculties and the abilities still accessible to the Alpha Spirit—who has merely given up the regard of these things in favor of hiding in a genetic vehicle POV—it is logical that the *being*, when defragmented, would be acting and *doing* in the direction of optimum existence and increase the quality of personal ability. We *know* that our POV is a projection of *Spiritual "Life" Awareness* or *Zu* entangled with the Physical Universe; but to call it a *Game* and be done with it, tells us just about as much about the purposes and rules as simply introducing to a person for the first time that "*mancala is a game*" and then giving them no further information on the subject. This only proves my point to those of you that don't already know what "*mancala*" is; but it's a game from Africa that is in some ways similar, though more primitive, to the game of "Twenty-Squares" played in Babylon.

Really, any hope of producing ideal conditions, or a certainty of continuance of existence, regards an individual actually believing in a future and their own determinism to *do*. Those who have succumbed to a nihilistic approach where "everything is pointless" and "there is no future"—these people have no "hope"; there is nothing to demonstrate to them—in their reality, meaning what they are able to confront as agreeable or acceptable—that there is any possibility of change and that nothing can help anyone. *There* is the underlying fragmentation that deteriorates the individual, the home and the society. A decline in the belief, acceptance, and therefore, ability to "help" anything, anyone, anywhere. *That* is what has entrapped us in *this* Physical Universe.

Therefore, the sum all of what we are reaching for at this stage of *Grade-IV,* is defragmentation on all energetic channels regarding the subject of "help." This is what is going to open up the *Gateways to Infinity* for the Wizard-levels of our Systemology. It is a critical and pivotal point for the Seeker; which has been slowly worked up to since its *realization* during the development of *"Crystal Clear."* You may be wondering how this standard relates to what is presented previously in Systemology. However, the word and concept surrounding it, seems to be the most underlying "keyword" to essentially open and close the Gates to higher realizations, because those realizations directly correspond with an increased *Awareness* regarding what one can—on each channel—be to others, accept from others, and apply to Self, *always* from a cause-point.

If one takes a close examination at the role of the magicians and priests, priestesses and mystics, shamans and all those of that type down the line, what is it that these individuals are doing in the Physical Universe? They are *helping* it to exist. Their goal is the aid, assistance and, otherwise, help of *Life.* Now, we aren't talking about misguided black magicians and evil sorcerers and such here, or the wicked witch that comes in to poison your crops for not buying a love potion; we aren't referring here to just anyone who carries the guise of *knowing,* but those that *do.* And we have found, as with the other invalidation that comes with using the Mind-System as a catalyst for *being,* that it is not the "help" and "change" and "problem-solving" in itself that causes the fragmentation through encoded imprinting or programming, it is the "failure" of such efforts that hangs us up.

If you think of the individuals in your life that you have been most angry with, I can almost guarantee it is those categorized as "failed to help"—and above all of these are those persons and situations where *you've* been the one that tried to help and registered the effort as a failure; you believed you could help someone as a cause-point and failed to manifest the effect. If we consider the aid, help and assistance of *Life* at one end of a spectrum, such as on our Standard Model, and then destroy down at zero, one can almost create a little flip-book scenario that demonstrates the lower and lower considerations for existence as one loses their *Actualized Awareness* as well; and some of this can be linked directly to the Spheres of Existence, which is how we modeled our version of Utilitarian Ethics for Mardukite Zuism.

As the whole matter of "help" and "ability" is betrayed at each Sphere of Existence, the individual finds less and less reach and acceptance in this area—which is, of course, tied to communication and the barriers and blocks set up to define the parameters of reality along the way. So let's take a minute just to track this little turn of the *Pathway* and how it relates to what all has led us here.

Now we have this subject of "assistance" and "help" to the greatest reach on the Standard Model, because it is the best channel of reach that pervades through each of the Gates and what we have modeled as Spheres of Existence to superimpose on our model. The Spheres, the Universes, the ZU-line; it all interrelates—as is mainly the subject of our Systemology at its core, especially if one reviews the *Grade-III* material. So let's backtrack from where we are: here is our whole world closing up on us on the failure to help and assist; which validates what we discussed regarding the fragmentation of "change" and then also the existence of "problems."

This whole cluster of stuff we call "problems" puts us out of communication and creates an automatic network of circuitry to handle the communication of reality for us, which failing to take responsibility for this, we lose the ability to clearly recall memory without fragmented imprinting and encoding; this last point being about where we left things with *Grade-III* as "Mardukite Systemology."

For *Grade-IV*, we are approaching a new vista for *Homo Novus* that we are calling "Metahuman Systemology," and by following these basic steps we have prescribed, I don't see any reason why a willing *Grade-IV* Seeker could not reach the plateau we have set up as the culmination of *Grade-IV*, assuming of course they have already worked successfully through *Grade-III* on their own, or have had a very "helpful" *Pilot* to "assist" them along the way. And now, maybe you see a hidden side to why we *Pilot*, too—or emphasize the applied spiritual technology accessible to a *Minister* that applies this Systemology to Mardukite Zuism.

Δ Δ Δ Δ Δ Δ

A Seeker can spend a great deal of time on their own "communication lagging" through all of the Self-Processing in "*Crystal Clear*," and some of the PCLs given in the *Grade-IV* "Pilot Course" and, of course all throughout the manuals we are preparing. That is certainly one option. Alternatively, a Seeker might decide to get together with a friend—presumably another *Seeker*—and proceed to work together to move through the PCLs. Now, if you don't know about how we are gauging the effectiveness of the process or what a communication lag is, this cooperative game with a friend might start to run into trouble around the point of systematic processing that we are reaching now. Of course, there is no actual reason you couldn't work through *Grade-IV* on your own, but we have found that it really helps to work with a *Pilot* that knows that they're doing.

In the past, particularly in *Grade-III*, the methodology was basic enough to where you could still get a lot of great results on your own, even if it took you a while to get through it. Even when we started to introduce basic communication training into our procedures in *Grade-IV*, the terminals and channels selected would still provide a lot of room for personal development and skill in delivering PCLs and practicing the fundamentals of what was presented a few months ago as *SOP-2C*. We want Seekers to get this right because there is no point in my going on to develop a presentation of *Grade-V* until we can do this. As we have narrowed down our semantics of energy flow as a "communication line," there is very little, if anything, that can substitute this foundation for operating our spiritual technology. When you are getting right down into the core of systematic processing, there is no substitute for skilled communication.

Our emphasis in this conference has been on the problems of the Human Condition and what we can do to help the situation. That's all. [*laughs*] But these are two elements that are critical to making progress using systematic processing. Both require that the *Seeker* provide true "presence" of Awareness to the systematic processing. The ability to focus and participate in a session is characterized by these two things: ability to handle the attention that is fixed on a problem and the certainty that help is possible. We don't even have to *do* anything about it right now, we just want the Seeker *willing* to be *helped* and able to *help others*. It may seem trite to some of you, but this runs parallel with the state of *Actualized Awareness*.

The interesting experience that one receives by achieving higher *realizations* about protest, problems, change and help—the greater we defragment these channels and increase *Awareness*, the less "driven" an individual feels in *needing* to *do* something about something. Now, what I mean is not a passive laziness; I'm speaking about the emotional urgency and mental fixations that get attached to these "trouble areas" in the game of Life. Those imprinted compelling, compulsive, turbulent hurricanes of confusions—those are states of fragmentation; they are not necessary POV.

Let's say you are *Piloting* a *Seeker* and getting a systematic session started and so you ask them if they are having any troubles or worries that are occupying their mind. Sometimes they are not very forthcoming about where their mental attentions are, which is why working at communication is so important. Or, let's say they are disconnected from everything and just *passe* with it all, because nothing bothers them, because nothing matters or something. Yeah, watch out for that guy—because he's totally out of communication with existence. But we are talking about the stuff going on in the Seeker's life that is occupying them.

For example, the Seeker you are about to process, they got a traffic ticket—a DUI or something—the weekend before. So, they are talking about the fines they have to pay, points on their license, the court appearance they have to show up for in two months, the affect that losing their license may have on their job...all of that. Well, *is* that problem there in the room with you? Are they coming in to arrest him? Is this session making him late for the court appointment in 60 days? Well, I can tell you that for this Seeker it is. They aren't there systematically running processing from *Self*; they are still stuck back on the weekend getting the ticket and then running through all the possible imagery that could eventually happen down the road. They are everywhere else *but* sitting right there in the chair in front of you being processed. We emphasize this *"Presence in Space-Time"* in our *Grade-IV* material, and it is listed as a preliminary of *SOP-2C* for a reason.

Most typical human problems we are approaching in a systematic session are not meant to be literally solved in session by a Pilot. This is a big misconception that follows along with the programming we have regarding the magicians and priestesses and healers and such in our memory. We aren't *solving* what the problem is in session; we are *solving* getting a Seeker out from the clutches of the problem. Funny thing is, when we do that, we realize that the consideration of a "problem" was just that. We want to take the hold it has off of us or get out from under it, however you want to see that. It is a POV that is held in suspension and nothing more. Okay, maybe there *are* certain actions that could be done for it, but the individual is so busy running around in their Mind feeling that they *must do* something that the door is left wide open for all that emotional imprinting to come rushing in. This is what actually keeps the Seeker suspended in the problem.

Other traditions; they have these "psycholo-spiritual advisers" or what-have-you, and you are supposed to go to them for all your answers because they are the only authority within the paradigm to tell you how it is. Well, that's just nuts. Anyone that has been working with *us* over the past year knows darn well that we haven't been training *Pilots* to provide answers; we've been training them to ask questions. This is something we know took place in ancient Mesopotamia, but seemed to be popularized, or at least carried down in visible history, from the ancient Greeks —presumably attributed to Socrates, but as we know, the Classical-period civilizations had imported their philosophies, "kabbalahs," "world-trees" and Hermetic pursuits from even more ancient, nearly prehistoric, civilizations in the regions scholars once referred to as the *Ancient Near East*, which is to say Egypt and Babylon.

I tell you though: one very actualized guy that seemed to have figured this out a couple thousand years ago would go around doing wonderful things by asking a Seeker, "Do you believe I can heal you?"—"Do you *believe help is* possible?" Never said, "Okay, now I will heal you whether you like it or not." Nope. He said, "By *your own faith*, you are healed."—"You did this to your self, *buddy*; I'm just reminding you." And its funny, the authorities of the societal systems at the time didn't seem to much care for this and then somehow they got humanity to fight one another in his name for so long that any usefulness of the messages became so lost on people so long ago that now the whole system is just used to trap and control parishioners into supporting a material organization on the hope that they can buy their way into some lofty afterlife.

There is a progressive pattern that unfolds in all systems and this understanding contributes greatly to why we call our work "Systemology." It is reduced, in the past, as "**general systematology**" in the realm of academics, but rather than using that information to work out a method of producing a *metahuman* state via spiritual technology, the material emphasis of the new millennium and its 20th century predecessor was all aimed at the external technologies and a *transhuman* evolution that would undeniably eliminate *Human Life*, or rather seal it into an even lower condensation of *reality* in a digital universe—which, I might add, is *beneath* this one, not some grandiose astral realm above it.

The main subject of our newest processing is "universes"—specifically *this* one, and how you got your POV stuck here. This seems wildly metaphysical, but it is a fundamental ledge for our *Metahuman Systemology*. Now we have a better understanding of the restrictions of consideration that led to the condensation of universes. We've figured upon a few of the hot-button issues; and dedicated the past six months of research and discovery toward this *Grade* of the *Pathway*. And it has been critical for demonstrating that these levels or *Grades* or *Gates* actually do mean something in regards to the Human Condition, the Alpha Spirit and the layers of miscommunication and fragmentation that have sealed in each of the higher universes and veiled them from sight. As we increase our responsibility and command for these conditions, so too will the veils be lifted.

We've come right down to it now: the final *realizations* of this step. It is the uncovering of the secret of universes; no secret really—more of a distant foggy memory that seems to come into clearer view as we clean those lenses of perception. When we use the Standard Model to represent the Spheres of Existence—and essentially "spheres of reach and influence"—we are demonstrating the solidification and condensation of all *Awareness* and considerations of *beingness* at each stage. What we are left with is an individuated Alpha Spirit, which after a progression through various stages of betrayal in higher universes, succumbs to a very isolated existence as the standard-issue POV of humanity. You can literally gauge an individual's true chronic state of *beta-Awareness* on our scales, simply by examining the degree to which they can exchange fluid communication; and the apex of this is specifically "assistance and help."

There are some in the past that have put a lot of stock in this word "*faith.*" Well, "faith" is funny, because on a practical level it is the actualized energy generated by the being themselves. Some religious leaders seem to talk about "faith" as if its something you can *have*, in fact you had better *have* it or their whole paradigm crumbles to pieces. Where others have indicated some special rising level of "faith" as **paramount**, we have instead found the more effective semantic as "help." This is because the degree of universal fragmentation that an individual would otherwise be told to categorize as "faith" (regarding various aspects of existence) is really a matter of where they still maintain trust, open lines of communication and a fluidity of help and assistance. When this clarity is betrayed or broken in any way, the individual goes out of communication on that line and a veil or barrier is put in its place. In many instances, the veil is a thin screen or filter that simply processes that channel of information on an automated-response mechanism. And it would be just fine to screen our calls, as the Alpha Spirit first started to do in the beginning, but now we aren't even getting our messages! So, it's a slippery slope when we start to create patterns.

Self has always considered itself to occupy some level of existential codependency with an environment, even within the highest Alpha spiritual universes—when *Self* was first individuated away from Infinite Beingness, or Nothingness, however you are still chewing on that one. *It's a Nothingness, by the way.* But that is the Infinite Nothingness—and the Alpha Spirit dwells as a near-static point at the edge of Infinity. But in the Alpha spiritual universes, the Alpha Spirit *is* an individuated being; they are a true individual—the "identity" part gets taken on later and is later replaced with a personality that is believed to somehow substitute individuality within material existence. It makes it easier to anchor the Alpha Spirit to a locatable body maybe.

"Betrayal" is probably the most severe emotional encoding that exists on a spiritual timeline. It is linked directly to this concept of "failure to help." It is the betrayal at each level of existence—or at least the perception of the same—that sealed up the Gates behind us on or descent through the universes. It is for this reason we are repairing these fractured lines of communication and lifting the veil of the *fourth Gate* with a defragmentation on the subject of Help, and for the moment, we will settle for beta-defragmentation up to the Fifth Sphere of Existence, which is essentially *All Life* on Earth, all the way to include the Green World or Kingdom of Animals and Nature. Some of the Druids, during the apex of their Mystery School, would have presumably made it at least that far—and thereafter one Christian saint, named Francis, seems to have as well.

What we are getting down to is a return of control of a Seeker's considerations, which have otherwise become fixed and limiting by all that supposedly useful "experience" that they are carrying around with them; all those energetic masses of emotional imprinting and reactive-response filter-screens that can basically do all the *looking* and *reaching* on a patterned deterioration of what is considered safe and acceptable. Obviously, when a person dies they must have decided there is no where else that is safe and acceptable from that POV and that the energetic lines have all been cemented to a point of weight and mass that the person just isn't going to get up and move anymore. They come to a point where they say, you know what, I'm done.

Don't get me a wrong. *Self* should be free to leave the POV of a physical body on its own determinism, particularly if it has somewhere to go, and might just as easily come back to command that organism again. This is entirely different than the desperation and confusion that results in an individual getting "spun" or feeling quasi-suicidal. You've got most of the population that doesn't know where they came from or where they're going, but they know damn sure that they can't confront any of that or even where they are right now. I mean: you're telling me you don't know what comes next but you're in a hurry to get there? Wow!

Those individuals that didn't break the chains of *beta-existence* will wind up right back here again, or worse, since they're going to have one more layer of validated fragmentation to carry around from the start. And this is part of the decline of spiritual ability, the descent and limitation of the Alpha Spirit's POV to the human condition and naturally the condensation of the Physical Universe. Here, everything has been reduced to a near zero-point of inert matter and energy—which is still in motion, by the way, but not nearly to the same degree as what we see in the creations of the higher Spiritual or "Alpha" universes. And there are many universes; each with its own qualifications of the Gates and veils—and this is why we suggest very strongly that those esoteric practitioners previously accessing their perception of "Seven Gates" while occupying the POV from the Earth Gate (and the fragmented identity installed) have only accessed a sequence of awakening that still resides within the *First Gate*. Those that have worked so diligently with that rigid ceremonial conception of the lore may have come to a new point of *realization* at the end, but still have only pierced the first level using those methods. We've been able to reach much higher now, that is for sure.

△ △ △ △ △ △

I think "Help" was once recently a hot topic in some circles—back in the 1960's and 1970's was it?—something like, "Helping You Help Me Help Others Buy More Self-Help Books" or some such, wasn't it? I guess that seemed more ethical than the "How to Influence Friends and Win People" angle. But we're hitting the subject of "help and assistance" in our Systemology and I know we are in the right direction, because just the other day I heard someone go on one of the most fragmentary rants on the topic, about how no one can help anyone and how all help has strings attached and well, they don't think they can be of help to people anymore—and I think I literally heard the word "help" a dozen times in a minute or two... yes, this is a "magic button" and should not be under-valued for your ascent on the *Pathway*.

If you consider what actions we are actually taking in Mardukite Zuism & Systemology—what we are *doing*; what you are *doing*; what everyone is here today to do—we are helping others, they are helping us, they are helping help each other and ultimately, we are helping ourselves. How we do this best? Of course, we are clearing debris out of our communication channels, extending our reach and increasing our *Awareness*—and when we consider any gradient scale or chart for this, the most objective conceptual understanding we can apply on a practical level is our ability to help and assist one another, all life and ourselves.

So let's break this down; I've given you a lot of theory and examples, but let's see how this all plays out in systematic processing. We have our Standard Model and its various external spheres of existence that we correlate *Awareness* to while operating in beta. So, yeah on the one hand we have "1" as the low points of a physical body and "2" as the react-ive-response mechanisms and so forth. That's the Zu-line or personal identity continuum. Superimposed on this information, we discover that the Spheres of Existence line up quite well; so we have Self as "1" and our domestic situation or home equilibrium as "2" and then our societies at "3" and on up. Those are the Spheres of Existence and it seems as though the ability and willingness to reach along these spheres can be easily defragmented using the concept of "help."

To engage or receive help from any sphere is to be in communication with it and to be willing to freely give and receive help—which is a high level of communication—on those channels. We could just as plainly state that the resolution of beta-fragmentation regards the handling of communication, problems, protest, change and willingness—and the common point that employs all of these is snow-capped with this concept of "help and assistance." Following this logical succession in *Grade-IV*, we are essentially leading to the highest point we can really un-derstand the channels of communication in a practical way for this beta-existence and that is the assistance and help of all life to help all life to the highest regard of life as a sphere of existence. This not only applic-able to the *Gateways* of our Systemology, but has become the basic standard behind the Utilitarian Ethics of our religio-spiritual presenta-tion of Mardukite Zuism. You see, it's not just some standard of morals of dogma like you find elsewhere; our ethics in regard to a Utilitarian viewpoint of the Standard Model actually makes sense.

We have spoken of "betrayal," and previously of failed efforts, failed communications, failed change and other control mechanisms put in place in society whereby we have become entirely fragmented on the channels of communication regarding help and assistance. And again, it is not as if someone *must* run around the world saving everyone and everything, because that would be driven some underlying implanted compulsive need. All we can determine with certainty at this juncture is that as the highest form of communication expression in *beta-existence* that we *can* act, do, know and observe upon, this button called "help" is the key to reaching beta-defragmentation, even undoing all these other short-circuited facets of life, because once we have resolved the ability and willingness to help along any channel, we know we have remedied the other forms of potential communication on that line too.

When we talk about "failed help," we do not just mean a failure *to* help, or apply the intention to *help* because that is what happens after the fact once we start to put up the communication barriers and other filter-screen mechanisms to handle all that for us. What prompts this pattern of activity is when we did make those intended attempts in the past and the efforts failed; or when others had genuinely intended to help us but it seemed that it didn't work out. These "experiences" start to get added up and associated with the concept of help, just as much as any other imprinting or programming—but this one seems more critical to selectively defragment due to the sheer amount of weight that it is given in the Mind, concerning personal ability, willingness and reach. Since the Mind has already associated our ability to help with our ability to reach, it makes sense to work with this as part of systematic processing.

It is logical that we should approach the subject of "help" as a hot-button for achieving spiritual evolution as *Homo Novus*, and at the very least extend the reach of our metahuman Systemology. In theory, this is already dangerous territory, because this is the power to end wars; and certainly there are more than a few authorities in this realm that benefit from keeping the masses suspended in confusion. But just imagine if both sides of conflict were to focus on how they could help an enemy and how their enemy could help them; well, help them other than being dead of course. I'm meaning that we apply the same methods of achieving defragmented fluidity as you've seen (with previous lessons). But you'll sometimes get that kind of response early on or in low-level states with systematic help processing. The *Pilot* asks, well, "How could so-and-so help you?" And the guy's all like, "well, the sonofabitch could be dead, not exist, that'd be a big help to me..." You know? And a well-trained *Pilot*, maintaining their composure all professional-like, not phased, will just acknowledge an acceptance of the communication—I mean, the guy gave an answer, right?—and we ask again.

∆ ∆ ∆ ∆ ∆ ∆ ∆

When we expand our processing to include the general "terminals" of the Mind-System as opposed to specific events and incidents, we approach a wider range of potential *recall* in our processing. This is what immediately led to our interest in exploring "past lives" in future Wizard Grades, because it seems to be about the only way we can be certain of approaching anything close to a standard operating procedure for *Alpha defragmentation*, but I'm not trying to get you focused on that direction yet; simply the consideration that, for example, the treatment of "parents" or "bosses" as a terminal for systematic processing accesses more of the operating system than only treating a specific target from *this* life, such as your biological or adoptive parent from *this* life, or an employer from *this* life, &tc.

By tapping into the greater content of a "terminal" with a broad approach, there are reactive-response tendencies and programming that may **resurface** that just don't seem to fit with events and memories of this lifetime—and this is when we realize we are encroaching on new territory for Systemology that I intend, as I said, to take up in *Grade-V.* But, let's just get a handle on things that we have here before us in taking responsibility for, not necessarily everything that happened *to* us in this lifetime; but the mental imagery and storage and reactive-response encoding and associations that we are carrying around as a result of it. This state of responsibility alone would border on true *metahumanism.* But it should be understood that with each lifetime we have carried more and more of the same "game" with us and are undoubtedly it playing out over and over in the roles we take on and the personality-mechanisms attached to it.

The PCLs for *Grade-IV* systematic help processing use the same circuit patterns and methodology as what you learned for "*Route-3*" and "*Route-2.*"[‡] We are still using the same procedures to defragment the channels; I'm not sure if you were expecting some radical new curve-ball here at the end, but no this is really basic if you've been following along to this point. Naturally, I want each and every one of you to be successful at this, which is why I've dedicated my life to breaking it down this way for you and doing the grunt work and long hours in the library and the thousands upon thousands of dollars in research expenses to bring this forward. Most of you that have been following along over the years know that I've spent a lot of time in the underground figuring on these *Gates,* and ways of accessing them for real—and while Systemology might seem like a lot of fancy word-play and creative psychology, I can say that after a quarter-of-a-century journey of being a messenger on these matters, I have found no better access point to achieve the genuine goals behind all former traditions of spirituality, mysticism, religion and philosophy. This is a delivery of the "Great Work" in its purest simplicity —because anything more esoteric and you could miss it. And we've already been coming back here to Earth over and over for however many thousands of years; always missing it. So let's not miss it this time.

---

‡ "*Crystal Clear*" (*Liber-2B*).

Unless a Seeker or Pilot is using a *Recall* approach to events and instances—which is what you would do to release emotional turbulence encountered—the "Route-3" approach often allows for more creative answers that are not restricted to a specific time something happened. You will notice this in the *Grade-III* and *Grade-IV* PCLs that use the word "*could*" or "*would*" rather than "recall a time when..."

When we use a PCL that says "*could*" or "*would*," we are in no way insisting action—only the considerations and whether or not they are reactive. An individual doesn't necessarily even have to help their enemies, but the free consideration that they *could* prevents the hatred from swelling up into an emotional mass that shuts down energetic communication along that channel and setting up a filter-screen of automatic response-reaction. If all you do is spend all day worrying about how to destroy your enemies, I can guarantee you that the one that will get messed up in the end is *you*. It isn't that you can't defend yourself in some situation either, that isn't what I'm talking about. But keep in mind that most of what we like to think we are in control of regarding our thoughts and what we think we are in command of concerning our actions is filtered through many filters and slams around many masses and barriers of failure and error, pain and loss, hatred and jealousy and so forth. If a person is having to duck-and-go around all of that, they are not in command of the Mind-Body connection, no matter how much they think they have got it all figured. It took me a long time to realize that "Turn the other cheek" simply meant "don't react."

It should be noticed—if you've been getting any actual progression on the *Pathway* from a genuine application of this work—that you've been coming up against layers of resistance as you've been playing at the game of systematic processing since *Grade-III*. Each time we apply these methods, or run a series of PCLs that are meant to increase our considerations, there is a series of barriers that one is breaking through with each level of responses. If you aren't hitting these barriers, you may not be running the processing long enough. Usually the first time you are running low on answers, you are not running out of answers, you've just cleared a level of rubble that you've been working with and if you get past the next veil or layer of resistance, you will find a whole new level of stuff to work with, no matter how ridiculous it seems for this *beta-existence*, those answers are a new level of consideration. This is generally only worked until a *Seeker* no longer carries a heavy mass or emotional charge on that line, but in theory, you could extend the basic methodology of systematic processing all the way up the chain of existence to the highest sphere fathomable.

If you want to apply "*Route-2 AR*" in order to get a session moving in the direction of contacting the help channels, then by all means. That application should, however, be run on the circuits of "*Route-3*" and preferably with full two-way communication about the subject matter, making certain that the Seeker is willing to communicate on these lines with the *Pilot*. All you would do here is run them through the circuits on recall with: Self helping another; another helping them; another helping others or another; and of course Self helping Self, if you are running all the way to *A.T.* with it. If we are being more general with the terminals, however, we can simply apply a PCL directly to the concept of willingness to help on any terminal.

Circuit-1:   Who (or what) would you be willing to help?

Who (or what) would be acceptable for you to help? (*Alternative version*)

Circuit-2:   Who (or what) would you be willing to have help you?

Who (or what) would you be willing to accept help from? (*Alternative version*)

Circuit-3:   Who (or what) would you be willing to have others help?

Who (or what) would be acceptable for others to help? (*Alternative version*)

The most basic systematic processing we have on these lines has run in "New Thought" circles for nearly one-hundred years. The most important part of defragmentation is clearing predisposed inclinations and associations that close off our communicative energies along the channels we are connected to. Only once these are all opened up can we hope to be free of the fixed considerations that hold the abilities of the Mind-System to *this* Physical Universe. So, we have the *Pilot* direct a five-way series of PCLs that should get a Seeker over the basic humps of help.

Circuit-1:   How could you help "someone else" (*terminal*)?

Circuit-2:   How could "someone else" (*terminal*) help you?

Circuit-3(a): How could "someone else" (*terminal*) help others?

Circuit-3(b): How could "someone else" (*terminal*) help themselves?

Circuit-AT: How could you help yourself?

This is similar to what we described earlier regarding lines of communication with terminals. Instead of staying on that same general idea of "communicating with" such and such a terminal or sphere or object or concept, we are speaking of "helping" as an active expression of high-level communication that promotes the Prime Directive of existence toward its ideal state or condition of beingness. If each and every one of us was promoting each others Prime Directive, none of us would have needed to be down here in this dungeon universe. You can work up this chain on the practice of "get the sense of" type PCLs to start loosening the fragments of a *Grade-III* Seeker too.

Circuit-1:   Get the sense of you helping "someone else" (*terminal*)?

Circuit-2:   Get the sense of "someone else" (*terminal*) helping you?

Circuit-3(a):   Get the sense of "someone else" (*terminal*) helping others?

Circuit-3(b):   Get the sense of "someone else" (*terminal*) helping themselves?

Circuit-AT: Get the sense of you helping yourself?

It is obvious that the RCC has registered and imprinted many "failures" and "losses" onto our stores of experience and memory—but it has not always been found to be the best route of systematic defragmentation to exclusively process out turbulence with commands that focus on "failure." It is true that "failure" is a hot-button and we *should* be able to confront it without emotional reactivity, but this is not what we are demanding of our Seekers at this time; only that they work toward it with each pass through the material. But yeah, if you start running at the Seeker with PCLs on all the times everything has failed, you're just going to get them spun and shut down to where they don't want to communicate at all. This is a dangerous point to reach since all of our systematic processing is rooted in communication.

There are lower levels of processing one could scrape at here if necessary. All we need to do is go back into our arsenal of PCLs and start plugging in "help." Most of them will work. For example, you could theoretically run something as basic as "What help could you accept?" and "What help can you reject?" up to a point where the Seeker understands that they should not automatically reject any consideration of true help.

If you want to link this work with problems, you might use something like "What problem *could* your help be to another?" or even "What problem *has* your help been to another?" if you are approaching it from the *Analytical Recall* angle. If you do this, make certain to then apply the other circuits from "*Route-3*" for a full *beta-defragmentation* regimen, such as "What problem another's help has been to them" and so forth. Once you understand the patterns inherent in the PCLs of our systematic processing, it becomes easier to apply the right type or level of processing to the individual, knowing that you have an entire gradient scale to work with.

When dealing with "past recall" or experiential defragmentation of imprinting and programming, it's not as if we can completely get around the energy attached to "failed help," but that isn't the wording that we plug into our PCLs. You combine *Recall* with "*Route-3*" and alternate "help" and "no help" on each circuit. That's all. Very basic. In the actual processing of it, you may need to state it in terms of "given help" and "not given help." And we say "not given help" or "not giving help" in the place of "failed help," because even when someone had said they are helping, but it turned out they were not or it did not seem to produce the proper result, that is still registered as a failed communication on the line of help, you see? The same is for those situations of betrayal by certain social roles that are supposed to help but don't and then we cut off lines of communication and put up blocks because we don't see how we can help them any longer either.

Circuit-1:	What help have you given to (another)?
	What help have you not given to (another)?
Circuit-2:	What help has (another) given to you?
	What help has (another) not given to you?
Circuit-3:	What help has (another) given others?
	What help has (another) not given to others?
Circuit-AT:	What help have you given yourself?
	What help have you not given yourself?

This general formula works pretty well with all terminals and Spheres of Existence. You can then apply an extension of the five-way formula I mentioned previously, but adding the alternations of "no help" on each circuit. And this should be done with as many "terminals" as possible, with particular attention to those representing an "trouble targets" in a Seeker's life. This should be run on any terminal that symbolizes the various Spheres of Existence and influence, primarily—let me read off a list here—mother, father, or parent, guardian; child, stranger; spouse or lover; teacher; healer or doctor; priestess, priest or even holy man; policeman, states official; and yes, I want to see *Grade-IV* Seekers working toward defragmentation on their connection with the Green World of the animal kingdom and nature as well. There's been a communication break between the Human Condition and the planet Earth as a living organism and all of its creatures for far far too long.

Honestly, the easiest answer that I've come up with over the past several years, on the subject of helping and assisting humanity is "*processing*"—systematic processing via the methodology presented in Mardukite Zuism and its advanced *metahuman systemology*. Processing. Help? How to help? You processing others. Teaching others to process others. You getting processed.

But above all else—HELP ONE ANOTHER!

Thank you!

—UNIT FOUR—

THE IMAGINOMICON

—LIBER-3D—

:: 1 ::
THE GATES OF HIGHER UNDERSTANDING
UNIFYING MARDUKITE ZUISM & SYSTEMOLGY
INTRODUCTORY COURSE FUNDAMENTALS
VOCABULARY AND SEMANTICS
GRADE-IV WIZARD-0 IMAGINOMICON EDIT

Many **esoteric** models of universal **cosmology** and spiritual ascension appear on the **timeline** of acutely recorded history over the past 6,000 years, and the most ancient of these records—the *Arcane Tablets*—reveal a simple account of *Cosmic History*, that which later inspired an entire planet of cultural mythologies and religious interpretations. Yet none of these further fragments and facets of the original *Crystal* ever brought a clearer experience or more perfect **understanding** than what had come before. As a result, the truth inherent in the simplicity once shared became forgotten and lost to a sea of "symbols" and "representations" that reflected the poorest shadows of a former age—and the **Ancient Mystery School** was born.

Patterns demonstrated by this marked descent of civilization are cyclic in nature and apply to all "systems"—including the **condensation** of "universes." Some have classified tendencies of this "downward spiral" using terms for energy, such as **"entropy"**—whereas others think in terms of material "degradation." Regarding a relative direction between states or **conditions**, there are also those that refer to these motions as "condensation" and "evaporation." In our Systemology, we use a "Standard Model" (also **treated** as the **"ZU-line"** when it applies to the individual "*Self*") with a systematic **continuum** between "zero" and "Infinity." We use this to easily demonstrate understanding of varying **gradients**: conditions of **existence** and **"degrees"** by which they are experienced.

As we move our consideration of viewpoint—the ***"Point-of-View"* (*POV*)**—closer to "zero" on the Model, experience of **manifested** space-time energy-matter is more greatly **fragmented** and condensed. By the time we reach "0" on this model, we are at a basic singularity or **continuity** of **beta-existence**, or with the *stuff* of this "Physical Universe."

With each descent of a Universe, the same **considerations** of existence that composed the first **postulated** Universe are fragmented and then reformed and compressed into another "lower" more "solid" continuity. When we apply this model to the "beta"-*Awareness* level of an **individual**, we say that they are "withdrawing" **attention** and *Awareness* and thus becoming more the "effect" of the Physical Universe as their consi=

deration of *Beingness* approaches "zero."

Our **methodology** greatly differs from former manic-type spiritual philosophies seeking spiritual oneness with continuity of *this* Physical Universe. Rather, we seek a return to former oneness as *Self* in a Spiritual Universe. Our systems logic demonstrates that occupying a POV at the zero-point of this Universe is the equivalent to occupying a "dead body" or a "rock"—because at the continuity point of a Universe, all matter is equally identified with all other matter. And "down here" the solidity of matter is uncomfortably dense.

Similarly, as we consider points further *away* from "zero," the same energetic patterns appear more "vapor-like" and "fluid" and increase in their "**potentiality**" as an existence or potential beingness and as a POV. Likewise, an individual's *Awareness* increases along with their "reach" in an upward direction as "cause," which is to say true **Actualization** and **Self-determinism** to the extent they may Self-Honestly project or extend their POV.

Although considerable discrepancy in **semantics**, vocabulary and human understanding exists in regards to our **Cosmic History** and the original *map* and *key* left to us on the *Arcane Tablets*, most of this "mythology" and "**symbolism**" has previously only been used as a basis for lesser purposes—including further solidification and fragmentation of an individual's considerations the longer they occupy this Beta-Existence outside of **Self-Honesty**. This is one of the primary concerns with basing our Systemology on the Standard Model or any fixed **paradigm**: that its classification and demonstration of "divisions," "levels" and "layers" of existence will be over-identified as "symbols" that poorly substitute true understanding as a *knowing*.

Foundations for our higher graded work—including *Systemology Grade-IV* —is grounded firmly on the basis of research and discoveries presented in *Grade-III*; particularly as introduced in *"The Tablets of Destiny"* (*Liber-One*) and its companion manual *"Crystal Clear"* (*Liber-2B*). [These materials also appear in the complete Grade-III Master Edition text, *"The Systemology Handbook."*] The entire **premise** of our "Standard Model" and "ZU-line" is established within those texts, supplemented by suggestions for practical systematic "**processing**" that correlates with each installment of instruction. The subject of "processing" itself, and the complete course on "Communication, Control and Command" is what opens our present *Systemology Grade-IV*, with the publication, *"Metahuman Destinations"* (*Liber-Two*).

The most ancient recorded chronicle of our Cosmic History on Earth—that which includes cosmological information predating even the existence of *Life* on Earth—is best found on **cuneiform** tablets; and among these, the *"Babylonian Epic of Creation"* known to scholars as the *Enuma Eliš*, so named for its opening lines. Unfortunately, even in ancient **Babylon**, these and other *Arcane Tablets* functionally assisted those that sought further fragmentation and **successive** programming of the **Human Condition** rather than liberating it. This is another pattern that we have seen many times since whenever similarly derived paradigms sought to provide any aid to the spiritual "Rescue Mission" (via "**defragmentation** of the Human Condition") presently taking place in the Physical Universe and on Earth.

> In fact, these efforts have been going on for quite some time—so long, in fact, that it seems as if all the interested parties have already now arrived *here.*

In previous *Grade-III* instruction for *"The Tablets of Destiny,"* a basic systemological interpretation of themes and events for the *Enuma Eliš* are provided in order to demonstrate, describe and illustrate the Standard Model. This is of significant benefit to a Mardukite **"Seeker"** continuing from the *Grade-II* "Mardukite Core."

At the completion of *Grade-III Mardukite Systemology*—or *"The Complete Mardukite Master Course"* at the Academy—a Seeker is expected to have mostly **"flattened the waves"** that **collapsed** around even those considerations fixed regarding ancient **Mesopotamian** semantics, even though our Systemology is originally drawn from it. We accurately state that our applied Systemology is a progressive futurist development of what was discovered in our revival of "Mardukite Zuism." It directly prompted the discovery of an applied spiritual technology for the 21st Century AD that is clearly present, but somehow lost, during the 21st Century BC—from the time of the "Age of Aries" (c. 2160 B.C.). Behind the scenes, an actual *Mardukite Babylonian systematization* has carried through to today, and it rests in our hands now—and for all those who wish to journey along up the *Pathway* with us.

Does this mean we are, in any way, rejecting the historical premise on which we first drew our **knowledge**? ...certainly not. But, let us just say that it took thousands of years to uncover (or recover, depending on your perspective) and translate the cuneiform source of global cosmologies, mythologies and creation myths from ancient Babylon—the *Enuma Eliš*—and in more than a century since its widespread academic circulation in the late 1800's, it has still taken until *now* to develop any workable cohesion of its information for any effective spiritual ideal or application other than exploration of its cultural mythology as a series of esoteric symbols and traditions. This is very much akin to the understanding and knowledge that hovers around that *first* level or "Gate" of realizations; which we have markedly explored within *Grade-I Route of Magic & Mysticism* [see *"The Great Magickal Arcanum"* by Joshua Free] with the intention that a Seeker will "flatten" programming that keeps them suspended as the "effect" of that level of understanding.

During personal investigations into evolutions of Western mysticism, which led to the formal 2008 launch of Mardukite Ministries (Mardukite Zuism), one key avenue from *Grade-I* served as a greater platform then any other for an early precursor to our NexGen Systemology, notably referred to as "Druidism." This information is explored directly in our material for the *Grade-I Route of Druidism & The Dragon Legacy*. [Refer to *"Merlyn's Complete Book of Druidism"* by Joshua Free.] It is actually on *this* very foundation, and explorations into the origins of ancient Druidism, that led the author to develop Mesopotamia (and specifically Babylon) as a "public" emphasis for further work continued underground, by the Mardukite Chamberlains (Mardukite Research Organization), primarily from 2009 until 2012, when the *Grade-II* "Mardukite Core" reached its apex; and the *second* "*Gate*" dislodged...

For the next eight years, "Mardukite Systemology" developed quietly in the underground as a futurist or "NexGen" movement dedicated to achieving the "next step" on this *Pathway*—one that would inevitably lead up and out of the "systems" laid out to entrap occupation and ensnare the attentions, willpower and spiritual energy of "Self" to this *beta-existence.* How then might we use the best of what we had found effective and workable to return the individual Seeker toward the direction that they *truly* occupy as an **"Alpha"** condition in a higher spiritual plane? This was no simple task; requiring *eight* dedicated years to intensive underground research and experimentation.

A perceptive Seeker having followed the serpent trail through lower *Grades* will undoubtedly recognize many elements found in our Standard Model and "ZU-line" that are consistent in both the ancient Babylonian sources *and* those in Europe qualifying a "Druid's Cabala" (from Welsh sources) and the Druid Triads. The gradient distinction plotted as a "seven-plus-one" methodology is mirrored in throughout the globe and across the timeline of human tradition—from the Eastern **chakras** to the *StarGates of Babylon.* An entire volume could be prepared exclusively on esoteric associations and correspondences—such as found in our Grade-I

Master Library—information that an individual could otherwise spend their entire lifetime correlating and associating various symbols to things, but still not reach any greater level of ***realization*** or higher point of *Actualized Awareness* that carries them on upward toward a more ideal state of *knowing* and *being*.

With the exception of a few semantics from Mesopotamia, we carry very little of the "*stuff*" along with us as we progress through higher gradients of understanding and personal *Awareness*. This has long been one of the shortcomings of previous attempts toward *Ascension*, whereby an initiate is not given tools to properly "let go" of the material programming and personal **imprinting** along the way, and is instead applying excessive effort to make a journey toward accumulation of "things" rather than a reduction. Former methods have not proved effective in producing much more than an incredible collection of cliché axioms and fancy spiritual doctrines that yet continue to keep the Human Condition in a fragmented state.

Within our Systemology, at each gradient of *Awareness,* a Seeker is systematically processed to "lighten their load" of *stuff*, because quite frankly, it will not all fit through as one moves further and further. And it was not meant to. Even the astral "levels" and energetic "layers" envisioned around the **Alpha-Spirit's** consideration of a "finite body" should be *lessening*, not *increasing*, as one reaches towards *Infinity* on the *Pathway*. For this reason, many who have attempted "astral work" and "Gatewalking" (&tc.) in the past, and based on the esoteric instruction and other paradigms predating Mardukite Zuism and Systemology, have not found true successes toward the ultimate goal that could have otherwise been reached.

Many underground esoteric and mystic practitioners, that have known no better, *have* actually traversed the sevenfold system—but they have only done so from within the *first* sphere or "Gate," not realizing that the system repeats itself as a **fractal**-like **macrocosm** and microcosm in **relative** "directions" of magnification; seven times in each of seven Gates. Most practitioners have either become lost in **entanglement** of the "Gates" at a *first level* of understanding or end up abandoning their reach on the *Pathway* altogether.

Even many of the brightest and most aptly trained and skilled individuals in such practices have found themselves permanently encircling the first level of continuity with a genuine feeling that they have "arrived" and therefore tend to look no further, only fragmenting the continuity of what they have found into a greater amount of potential correspondences. This is because there *is* a continuity at each level of understanding whereby everything can be made to seem to fit within *that* potential level of knowledge accessible from *that* Point-of-View; just as much as we could restrict a total knowledge of purely physical phenomenon using a purely physical understanding of chemicals and forces and still be made to seem "correct" for *that* level of understanding and knowledge base.

> More important than determining or demonstrating if any of our knowledge is representative of some "Absolute Truth," the emphasis of Systemology is toward specific ancient lore which is found to be **objectively** effective in predicting and workable in producing targeted results.

Our concern in presenting the "Standard Model"—and likewise why it is not introduced directly until *Grade-III*—pertains to previous associations an individual tends to attempt to apply to this material as just more "esoteric lore" to incorporate into an existing databank. Our model is specific but representative; fluid as opposed to rigidly fixed; interconnected systematically rather than a compilation of parts treated in exclusion. All of the parts and facets and elements it represents, maintain a complete energetic circulation of communication with one another as a dynamic system; a system that is always changing, shifting and altering its **apparent** face; and hence why these systems continue to persist with solidity.

Therefore, we have found, as a basic barrier to increasing an individual's *Awareness*—and as a basis of the "problems" facing the Human Condition—inability to adjust significances and reassign "importances" for new evaluations, while simultaneously under the hold and command of reactive-response programming and other heavily imprinted (or energetically **charged**) past experiences. As this personal inability continues to be **validated**, presumably across multiple lifetimes, the Self finds itself becoming more and more the "effect" of fixed mental implants and finite considerations of reality—and thus we find ourselves now stuck here, as the ultimate result of trillions of Alpha Spirits all **succumbing** to the same downward spiral of considerations and manifestation, imprisoned in a very solid Physical Universe. An individual's apparent personal stability is often based on conditional **"agreements"** they have made concerning Reality—which is to say a determination of considerations about what is *real.*

At its core, this is actually so important, that any useful meaning it might have carried was lost to the cliché sentiment that "everyone creates their own reality." But such statements have done nothing to effectively and successfully liberate considerations of the *Self* from its material entrapment. We tend to speak of "well-adjusted" individuals quite simply as those that seem to face new data and experiences *anew*, without overly fixating, comparing or automatically **associating** all past data in judgment. This, in itself, is milestones ahead of the **standard-issue** Human Condition—and a quite accessible first step in reaching toward our ultimate *metahuman destinations.*

:: II ::

UNIVERSAL COMMUNICATION, CONTROL AND COMMAND
SYSTEMOLOGY GRADE-IV CRASH COURSE

Systemology of "Communication, Control & Command" is an emphasis of material for *Grade-IV* Metahuman Systemology. At this Grade, we apply the same training and processing "routes" to individual "Seekers" working alone with books and resources *and* those practicing systematic processing as "Professional **Pilots**" of Systemology and "Ministers" of Mardukite Zuism. A complete course on these subjects for *Grade-IV* is provided as the volume "*Metahuman Destinations.*" For present purposes—to both newcomers and returning Mardukite Systemologists—a **crash-course** of fundamentals will suffice in carrying the total spirit of Grade-IV into this present manual.

The Standard Model of Systemology demonstrates a vast network of communication between our proposed points of "zero" and "Infinity"—most of which, as it relates to the individual themselves, is experienced along a personal energetic continuum of potential "beingness" that we call the ZU-line. Combined, the two "concepts" represent all possible interactive points between an individual and a universe—*any* universe.

> The relay of energy, a message or signal—or even locating a personal POV (viewpoint) for the Self—along this continuum is referred to as *communication*.

> Communication relayed from an operative center or organizational cluster, which **incites** new activity elsewhere on the ZU-line, is considered *control*.

> Abilities of the Self (I-AM), from its ideal **exterior** POV as Alpha Spirit, to direct a communication for control that is perfectly duplicated along the ZU-line without fragmentation is true *command*.

From a systematic approach, *communication* is the primary **catalyst** by which all *Life* is learning and experiencing existence. We are directing and receiving communications from the **external** environment while interacting with the Physical Universe (*beta-existence*). These are all processed by communications **internal** and **interior** to the Mind–Body connection, upon which experience and command of the Human Condition seems primarily **anchored**.

Humanity has run through many phases of intellectual reach to properly resume this control, ever since perfected knowledge of the Mind–Body

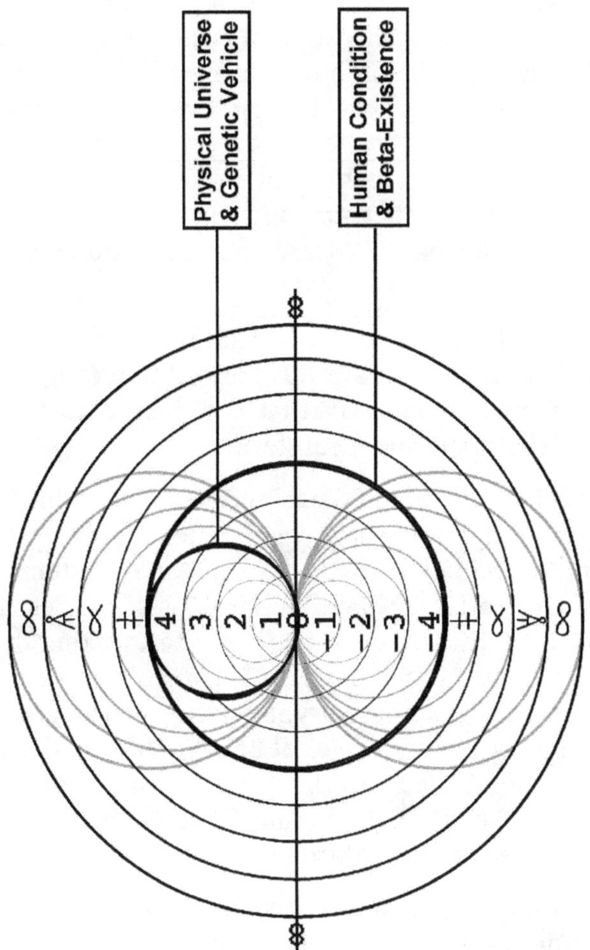

connection became fragmented thousands of years ago. Yet, there is an inherent *knowing* that behind, back of, and beneath the "surface" of what we are consciously facing as reality in this Physical Universe, there is an entire existence that is blocked, occluded, **occulted** or otherwise obscurely hidden from Human view, if following along to the beat of standard issue programming.

Physical sciences have offered little more than further "agreements" to confine our considerations of thought and spirit to this Physical Universe. Eventually an individual finds that all conceptions of potential beingness are either "reactive" or else tied strongly to "mental programming **implants**" that selectively direct and fix our attentions on the lowest denominator of beta-existence; that which we refer to as the

"RCC" or "Reactive Control Center," which generates bio-chemical and emotional experiences internally in a physical body ("**genetic vehicle**"). The purpose of any esoteric initiatory or mystical gradient system that mirrors facets of the "Gates" or "Levels" (which we demonstrate as a "zero-to-eight scale" on the Standard Model) were originally intended to systematically and progressively remove standard issue programming, **emotional encoding** and other implants that had been taken on, reinforced and validated during the course of an exceptionally long spiritual existence.

By reducing the weight of these lower level energy masses from the "banks" of the "spirit," an initiate was treated to a progressive journey toward a greater metahuman POV that put them back in contact with the ZU-line from their true and ideal state.

While a methodology of using "Gates" proved successful in the beginning (many thousands of years ago), these organized efforts to spiritually liberate individuals from the material system trappings of this Physical Universe (Earth-Gate or Zero-Gate) did not continue **undefiled** for very long. In no short time thereafter, we find the clear path obscured and confounded into "*Mystery Traditions*" with a now fragmented knowledge dispersed across varying cultures throughout the globe. This is the true nature of the "Tower of Babylon Incident" whereby complete, clear and present access to the "Gates of Understanding" was cut off from humanity. This is explored more directly in "*Tablets of Destiny*" and gleaned from the Grade-II "Mardukite Core."

In Systemology we do more than just suppose there is more than inert material continuity of this Physical Universe—we go forth to codify and systematize the understanding available to us on the Standard Model. As such, we have noted the existence of the "RCC" and "MCC" in previous texts, plotted at "2.0" and "4.0" respectively on the ZU-line. In fact, our primary introduction of the Standard Model and its systematic structure is a primary emphasis of education and systematic processing demonstrations provided in *Grade-III*.

What we have done with the Standard Model is provided a "systemology" for the Mind–Body connection that, when operated by a Self-Honest individual, is under the command of Self as the Alpha Spirit, free of entrapment to low-level considerations and automated reactivity to the environment. Between "0.1" and "4.0" is the "internal" nature of the Mind–Body connection, as within the range of *Awareness* and experience of the Human Condition, separate from "external" qualities attributed to continuity of the Physical Universe at *zero*.

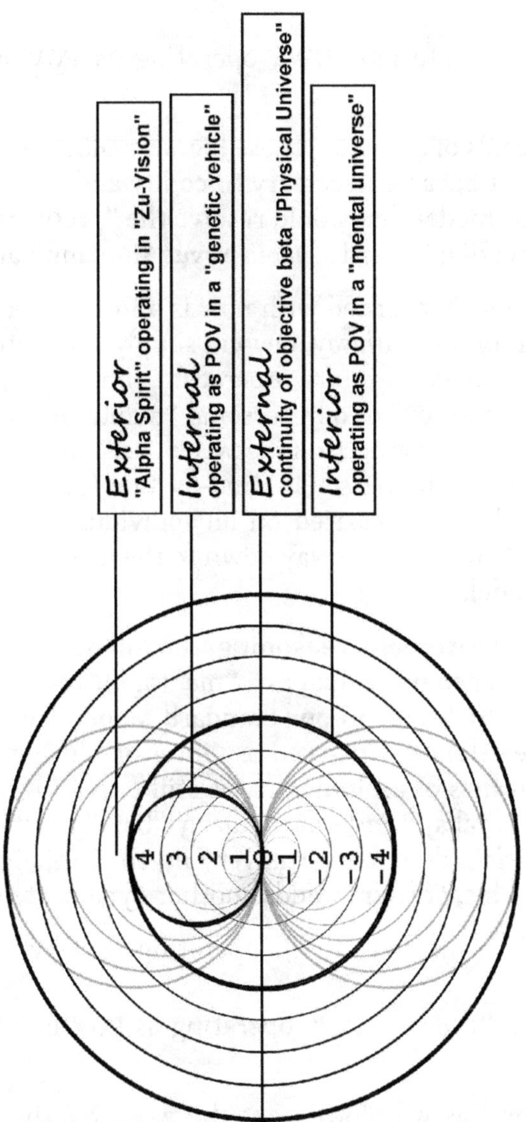

It is at the zero-point of our model that the most "solid" aspects of the "genetic vehicle" meet or match frequencies of "solid matter" in this Physical Universe. We tend to treat the entire range of "0.0" to "4.0" as *beta-existence*, because it reflects the total scope of physical, emotional and mental **parameters** as experienced "internally" from the POV of an Alpha Spirit operating its *beingness* "within" physical conditions of a "genetic vehicle"—and this is hardly an **optimum** position of command for a god-like Spiritual Beingness.

(0.0) : "External" (continuity of objective beta-existence; Physical Universe)

(0.1) to (4.0) : "Internal" (*Self*, operating as POV in a "genetic vehicle")

To accomplish goals of accessing these higher *realizations* to continue our graded *Pathway*, it became necessary to codify and systematize a wider-angle view of our model that would resolve the "problems" that we were left with in processing toward a **Homo Novus** "metahuman" state.

What we are simply concerned with now is a further reach that extends our progression on this *Pathway*, beyond simply the "internal" workings of the genetic vehicle we are operating, but the communications throughout the "interior" of our personal "mental universe"—which includes the Mind–Body connection (between "0.1" and "4.0") *in addition to* the full "interior" of the personal Mind-System (even independent of a specific "physical body") carried on an individual's persona energetic continuum (or ZU-line) all the way down to the (sub?) range of "–4.0" on our Standard Model.

By our systematic **rationale/reasoning**, the full operating system of the "Mind" exists for each individual as a "mental universe system" that extends from "4.0" to "–4.0" on our Standard Model demonstration. That entire zone of existence is marked as "interior" (using our semantics), because the *beingness* of an individual is still operating from a POV "interior" to the mental systems—particularly "beta" mental systems—thus it's stated that the individual is *still* very much "in their head" (figuratively speaking). This, of course, adds another dynamic to our model.

(4.0) to (0.1) : "Internal" (*Self*, operating as POV in a "genetic vehicle")

(4.0) to (–4.) : "Interior" (*Self*, operating as POV in a "mental universe")

It became evident, as we plotted out the work for the Wizard Grades, that we would have to make certain of our distinctions regarding these classifications on the Standard Model; particularly the differences between POV that are "internal," "interior" or "exterior"—because it becomes quite relevant when accessing the upper-routes.

This matter is not fancy word play and semantic tricks. Previous "traditional" attempts at our goals for Wizard Level-0 were ambiguous lower-Grade instructions regarding "astral vision" and "spirit bodies"—which *did not* provide actual effective tools for getting an individual *exterior* to even a "mental universe" fixed to an **intermediate** "Mind-System." Greater clarity was needed to complete "*Imaginomicon*" (*Liber-3D*) and realize our most basic goals for the Wizard Grades, as we move upward through the *Gateways to Infinity*.

Δ Δ Δ Δ Δ Δ Δ

The abilities of an Alpha Spirit throughout its own creative journey are linked precisely to the communication systems that are demonstrated on the *Zu-line* of the Standard Model. We see that when an individual is operating from their "MCC"—represented with the symbol of the upward pointing triangle—they are "facing up" or "confronting" the reality of their universe, reaching and extending across spheres of influence in the existential or objective universe, and is learning from the association and incorporation of its own experiential knowledge.

In our previous manuals for Systemology, a *Seeker* or *Pilot* is primarily dealing with "*products of*" the Mind-System when treating conditions found within the "internal" systems. It was not until we began to systematize knowledge of *how* emotional encoding, imprinting and other programming, actually takes place and the way in which it is even stored between lifetimes as part of a spiritual **identity**, that we realized that there was a more deeply ingrained chain of potential "**terminals**" or "nodes" by which all of these later programs, tendencies, fixations, **compulsions**, avoidances (*&tc.*) could even attach to an individual in any way. Since a few of us began to call these types of interior **facets** "implants" early on in our research, the name stuck.

On an energetic level—whether physical **kinetics**, emotional charges and mental circuits—we find varying "lines" and "connections" formed with various "terminals" of existence that we may have a communication with. Many Seekers discover that they have a great many "ties" with various objects and people; but specifically as a representative symbol that is interacted with in *beta existence*. These same "terminals" may be contacted or envisioned internally using mental **faculties** just as they are sprung up on automatic as "screens" to our view, whenever they are triggered or stimulated by the environment.

It has been realized that the average individual carries a great deal of energetic "charge" on their personal "**mental images**" which are treated as a reality substitution for the objective universe. In brief, the individual is interacting and reacting based on the mental and emotional stores connected to a "terminal" rather than the objective nature of the "thing." An individual goes as far as to "create" their copy of the objective universe based on automatic mechanisms and even begins to take for granted the concept that walls and other solids are *more real* than anything that could be created by the Self. When the individual has ceased to consciously create, they have succumbed to considerations that they are simply an effect. Naturally, the more numerous the strong "ties" to terminals in the Physical Universe, the stronger the "pull" to remain at such a level in order to receive whatever the individual is now wired to experience as an effect.

"Systematic Operating Procedure 2-C" is a Professional Piloting methodology introduced in the text "*Metahuman Destinations*" (*Liber-Two*). There are other "Routes" explored in *Grade-IV* specifically for *Wizard Level-0* contained in "*Imaginomicon*" (*Liber-3D*) that pertain to handling "*mental images*" directly. Prior to approaching this final **threshold** of the fourth *Gate* and *Grade*, "*Metahuman Destinations*" focused on clear communication relay between the most accessible considerations and terminals using these methods. Such techniques tend to be "generalized" in their approach so that a Seeker may insert their own applicable examples and yet still arrive at the ultimate conclusion or end-state *realization* that each systematic process is intended to achieve.

"Processing" or "systematic processing" that we "run" in our Systemology is composed of "Processing Command Lines" (PCLs) that function on the Mind-System very similarly to how you might operate a computer. These are essentially "command postulates" delivered by a *Pilot* that knows the way to where a *Seeker* wants to go, until the *Seeker* is certain in their ability to get there on their own. This, of course, actually requires properly directed attention and the Seeker's **willingness** to provide their actual ***presence*** to a "processing session."

The key is to always process with what *is* within the reach, accessibility and willingness of the Seeker as they are at present and then cumulatively extend that willingness to reach or *do*, building on the validation of what *is* within the known control of the individual. What we are then doing is reversing the programming and imprinting that has been stored, which has been found to limit the power of thought and consideration to smaller and more fixed parameters.

This degradation took place systematically throughout the course of the *Self's* own journey, projecting its POV through more and more rigid and condensed universes until finding all of the remaining "willingness" for consideration right now here in this beta-existence, tightly wound up as a box that we prize, guard and protect: the artificial **personality**. It is *this* that entraps the Human Condition to beta-existence.

The basic premise that we began with is very simple to consider, perhaps just as simple to manifest in today's world. Systemologists learn to think systematically and **holistically**, applying the fractal-like gradient scale of the Standard Model to daily life—and those training to be "Pilots" and "Ministers" within our tradition go on to expertly apply these same elements to processing procedures systematically designed to elevate *Actualized Awareness* from POV controlled by lower-level energy-driven mechanisms. Here we provide a *Seeker* with the tools to finally return effective command of their experience of *beta-existence* and the Human Condition to *Self* knowingly as Alpha-Spirit.

:: III ::

.: GRADE-IV AND THE STANDARD MODEL :.

CONDENSATION OF UNIVERSES AND FRAGMENTATION
OF THE HUMAN CONDITION

Most sources alluding to the true Cosmic History—one that predates this version of planet Earth and even *this* version of the Physical Universe—are based on the most ancient writings we have access to; carefully scribed at the **inception** of writing systems during this current version of human civilization. These narratives relay mythographic symbolism and as a result we find development of specific portrayals of a literal "mythology" that now, thousands of years later, have all been blown down for the "straw men" that they are. But!—they were all inspired by something, some memory, and the oldest of these recollections may be found on the *Arcane Tablets* and records from ancient Mesopotamia.

Previous relays of "Cosmic History"—including the systemological interpretation of the *Enuma Eliš* that is provided in "*The Tablets of Destiny*" (*Liber-One*), which directly contributed to the formation of our Standard Model—describe a linear pattern that reflects the "condensation of universes" and degradation of the Alpha Spirit as it became imprisoned within the POV and considerations of *beta-existence* and entrapped to the low-level hard-wiring of the standard-issue Human Condition.

We know very succinctly *how* it happened; progressing from an Infinite Nothingness; to individuation of Alpha Spirits; and onward through more condensed Universes and increasingly fragmented reality associations with their existence. This is reflected strongest in the "Gate-System" paradigm of ancient Babylon; then afterward, remnants appear in various lore regarding systems like various forms of *kabbalah* and *chakras*, which attempted to achieve the same reach of actualization.

But methods proposed over the past four millennium have done little for the Human Condition other than **enforce** more stringent considerations toward more restrictive reality agreements; such that, by our measuring —using a greater understanding of the Standard Model than before—is going to send the entire Physical Universe "out the bottom" quite soon, relative to our **Spiritual Timeline**. Direction of movement has been "downward" for too long, sending our Awareness to follow along, leading considerations to further "spiral inward"—validating and reinforcing the track direction we are unknowingly on, following standard issue programming. Without correction, this actually is quite a dangerous direction for an *eternal spirit* to be headed in for its existence. It undoubtedly echoes a truth that is otherwise buried in unnecessary religious dogmas and moral conventions.

As an individual unit of Awareness or *Spiritual Beingness*, *Self* establishes a personal identity continuum or track on the "Spiritual Timeline" known as "I." The Alpha Spirit practices selectively gives up **responsibility** for creating what is "not-I" near the uppermost level of our Standard Model (*ZU-line*). Esoterically, it has been referred to as the "*I-not-I monad*," but really it is *Self-"Aware"* of its *Self* as *Self* at the highest point of *beingness* that is possible from this **static** point (at "7.0" on the Standard Model).

In order to **differentiate** "I" from the "not-I," the Alpha Spirit adopts a selective practice of imposing various barriers, communication lags and distances to perceive across, so as not to simply be the mirror of other "I's" (Alpha Spirits) also differentiating themselves as wave peaks, crests or uppermost tips of icebergs emerging from out of the Infinity of Nothingness ("8"). At the highest level of *knowingness* and *beingness*—prior to the fragmentation of "**Alpha Thought**" in order to experience Shared-Games Universes ("6")—an Alpha Spirit maintained a perfect undefiled command of its own Personal-Home Universe.

An individual still very much occupies its own Personal Universe and is able to shift its considerations and creations freely by command postulates, generating the space and energy at will and without requiring any automated machinery. The whole of an individual's experience of existence is consciously created by *Self*, and in the beginning, the Alpha Spirit *knew* it was *creating* the conditions of its own *beingness* without **inhibition** or restriction. We speak in relative linear terms here, because the static position of *Self* as Alpha Spirit continues to remain unchanged in the present—only its considerations of *Point-of-View* (*POV*) and Self-**identification** given an experience of "time" as a successive degradation of personal willingness, reach and creative ability.

The only effective corrective measure inherent in the system is to simply run this programming and its circuits *backwards*. The way through and out is actually a *backtrack*; not some newly fragmented direction of action. Behind the considerations assumed and energetically imprinted on a personal "Spiritual Timeline," the *Self*—Alpha Spirit—is still there, bright, beautiful and powerful; the "I" that *is* the *Actual Awareness* of the individual... if you can just remember what you chose to forget...

In a shared "Creative Universe," other Alpha Spirits can also create. The Alpha Spirit is aware of their own creations and how they are separate as barriers and energetic masses at a distance, freely shifted and arranged at will; but they *are still* barriers of a sort, even only to maintain ones own individuality. This is not a crime; it is completely natural. But, it also sets up the Self for a practice in being the effect of another being's creations—and a desire to create automated energetic machinery to resolve this for them. Since an Alpha Spirit can put up its own screens and images and walls, it can also shield or filter or create walls.

Of course, what this did at a higher level of Self-determinism and creation is *knowingly* put a condition in place by which a once "all-knowing" Spirit *could* now be surprised by unexpected creations found on the other side. Enter: the inception of "*Mystery*" and a clear way ahead by which additional fragmented conditions and agreements resulted in further condensation of "*Space*" and "*Energy*" to the point where such "things" were now considered of value; and the way ahead was clear for establishment of "Games Universes."

> To be a "**player**" in a "Games Universe," the Alpha Spirit identifies *Self* with lower states and conditions of *beingness* to share a common reality agreement with other players. An Alpha-Spirit, which cannot be affected except by the consideration that it can, agrees to be the consideration of effect just to be part of the *Game.*

Δ Δ Δ Δ Δ Δ

Willingness of reach and extent of withdrawal is learned and "tracked" along the *Spiritual Timeline* of an individual, carried from "lifetime" to "lifetime"—or "**incarnation**" to "incarnation" since it is actually one continuous lifetime for the Alpha Spirit—for personal consideration. Unless otherwise directed, it apparently is only added to, never discharged, thus subjecting the Alpha Spirit to accumulate more and more solid energetic masses and more stringent considerations for existence as they descend into more and more solid, rigid and fixed POV from which to grant *beingness* even to themselves.

When the Alpha Spirit first occupied only POV in what is now an "exterior" existence or Alpha Universe, acceptance and rejection of energy communications was originally based on personal inclination and determination; but slowly these tendencies formed into patterns that we assigned as "aesthetics"—a *sense* of "beauty" or "ugliness" that transcends standard-issue beta-concepts of analytical thought or even emotional imprinting. "Aesthetic Consideration" is not really a quality that inherent to beta-existence. It is applied from a higher position than can be measured as *beta-Awareness*—meaning, markedly higher than

"4.0" on our Standard Model.

Personal tendencies toward "aesthetics" laid further groundwork for potential miscommunication and automation even above the level of "thought" connected to the Mind-System. Of course, a highly actualized being would be able to fully change their considerations and willingness to reach by a matter of personal choice. That which inhibits executing this directive fully is not a fault with the *Self* or Alpha Spirit maintain its true existence at "7.0," but from accumulation of energetic fragmentation along the "lines" between the "I" and command of its own POV *beingness.*

What we find to be the case early in our spiritual existence is not much different than what we discover to be true about the systems we find our POV now occupying: the entire matter is related to a communication of energy along specific **channels** and **circuits**. The only thing that has changed is the rigid automation of these channels and the fixed solidity found in physical mediums of communication exercised in *beta-existence.* This is why an understanding of the systemology of communication, control and command is functionally useful and effective "across the boards" and not simply in one or a few specific instances.

Even in the earliest "Creative Universes" we can see seeds of fragmentation stirring. Just as we might withdraw our reach, close off communication and reject creations of others, so too can others demonstrate a rejection of admiration toward our own creations. All various channels of **energetic-exchange** are created and then treated with some consideration that could be very well reduced to whether or not we "*like*" such-and-such. As *Self* moves its POV to more strict and narrow parameters of reality agreements, the automatic nature of these inclinations and tendencies is not only a personal hindrance to Self-determinism, but it could also be manipulated and programmed, then passed off and accepted as a "personality" that is quite artificial in nature when compared to the truest ideal state of the Self as Alpha Spirit.

Once a *Seeker* is able to understand the base structure of their own programming here in *this beta-existence* that the POV is presently confined to with *Systemology Wizard Level-0*, then we can press further onward into treating *Higher Universes* that we have "fallen" through to eventually arrive here. Such work continues throughout the "Wizard Grades." We are now charting our *backtrack* through minefields and trappings that we have picked up along the way. No steps are to be skipped along this course if we are to progress **surefooted** on the *Pathway* ascending toward a true metahuman evolution for the Human Condition.

Δ Δ Δ Δ Δ Δ

Simultaneous with the condensation of universes and the agreement to confine the POV of *Self* to such universes, the *Self* became fragmented as a result of its own consideration that it could be. This started with the basic acceptance and rejection of energy very early on the timeline and later developed into various automatic mechanisms that we might consider "solids" from a purely physical perspective and semantic. As most of us know, "solid matter"—any solid form—in some way obscures the view of what is behind or in back of it. This is no less the case when we consider the creative forms and vices that were composed even in higher reaching Spiritual Universes.

Once we find *Self* in a position of operating a Mind-Body connection from a Mind-System ("4.0"), the implanted programming for a standard-issue Human Condition is simply a matter of logic—and entirely and systematically demonstrable with the Standard Model. The sequence of diminished ability and rigidity of fixed agreements and considerations becomes quite apparent when we take a step back and look at mechanisms inherent in beta-Awareness; but let us examine them one by one, from the inside out—keeping in mind that *Self* is somehow convinced to agree to each one of these conditions along the way as part and parcel for the course down the spiral. But hope is not lost. We are able to clearly see these systems for what they are now, and the way out is very much in reach.

Let us consider that at the root behind all systems in existence, the most fundamental "Prime Directive" is simply *to exist*, which is the consideration *"to be."* But, this is obviously not the only driving factor; it is simply the most basic applicable common denominator, by definition, to *all* "existences." What we are interested in now are the *implanted* directives that may be introduced as programming for the Mind-System; essentially everything between "0.1" and "4.0" on our Standard Model. We have quite adequately divided the Mind-System into two "control centers" that relay communications commanding the Human Condition; one which is primarily "reactive" and the other is primarily "analytical"—referred to as the "Reactive Control Center" (RCC) at "2.0" and "Master Control Center" (MCC) at "4.0" on our Standard Model.

Naturally, in that truest, highest, most ideal state, the Alpha Spirit cannot be affected; but *what if* the *Self* made a sequence of agreements that led to unknowing automated assumption that the "spirit" *is* the "body"? By forming this connection of pre-programmed considerations for a

POV, we discover the "Mind-System" as it pertains to a "Mind-Body" connection. The POV of this Mind-System is not the actual *Self* either, but it *is* what many philosophers and mystics have treated as a "higher self" (from their perspective), although it is still very much tied to whatever implants and programs it is operating on, even in the upper-levels of *beta-thought* near "4.0" on our model.

Using the expanded version of the Standard Model (that includes sub-zero classifications), it is easy to demonstrate basic "fragmentation" inherent to the assumption of a "physical body" by simply threatening the *survival* or *existence* of that "body." It's literally that simple. Just get an eternal *Spiritual Being* to believe and postulate its own existence *as* a mortal body and suddenly it can be conditioned with "pain" (from the body) and also additional programming through various states of "**biological unconsciousness**" or reduced beta-Awareness.

Sub-levels of the Mind-System, beginning with identification and registry of "pain" and "unconsciousness" for a genetic vehicle, are deeply embedded and encoded *implants*—or rather, specific *imprints* encoded on specific *implants.* In the past, the primary issue with referring to any of this as "un–" or "sub–" anything, is a presumption that these inner workings are fundamentally inactive, except during perhaps sleep or physical unconsciousness (such as coma states); but this is not the truth at all. If anything, it is the clear view and upper command from the Alpha Spirit ("7.0") and control of the Mind-System ("4.0") that periodically drops out. But so long as POV is restricted to standard fragmentation of the Human Condition, these other sub-systems are *always on* and can be incited later to trigger direct reactive-response mechanisms outside the command and control of Self-determinism.

> Now, it might seem that we have gone as far as we can possibly go down the "Ladder" upon reaching the Earth Plane. Assuming the cosmic pattern continues, for those who have not achieved Ascension toward Higher Universes, when this Physical Universe collapses, the only POV left lower will leave *Self* "hanging on" as a mere perpetually enduring existence, functionally as static as a rock at a "zero-point" continuity in juxtaposition to the true stasis of the Alpha Spirit.

Before Self is "aware" of controlling a "body" it must *know* that it can *have* "things." And whatever it must *know* at this level of programming must be equal across all living systems that maintain even a cellular-**organic** "reactive-response" nature. But again—the problem and solution were the same and it was not hard to realize that emotional encoding is linked to *having* and thereby could be affected by the opposite qualities of "loss."

As a POV connected to sensory functions of an organic "genetic vehicle," the *Self* takes on the hard-wired programming that enables sensory reception of data, using a "physical body" to perceive material qualities of the physical environment. Programming and encoding at "2.0" on the Standard Model would thus be connected to a POV that is "aware" of the physical nature of creation (*beta-existence*) and that its composition of condensed solidified energy points creates matter, mass... "things."

Creative Ability of the Alpha Spirit while operating within a Home Universe, or even a shared Creative Universe, allows anything to be created and dispersed an infinite number of times without even a consideration of requiring energy. On the other hand, considerations for creations and position of energy-matter in *this* Physical Universe is concentrated and identified in such a way where a "thing" is uniquely rare from any other "thing" and cannot be truly duplicated even if resembling the same form.

By treating "things" with finite consideration in exclusion to all other "things," we generate an agreement with the concept of "possession"— or else a concept of *owning* or *having* "things" that are unique in finite creation to any other "thing" that is, was or could be. Fluid instantaneous and unlimited creation of "things" becomes something of a scarcity as one progresses down the condensation of Universes. As a result, at each level, there is a heavier tendency or desire to "hold on" to things more strongly or tightly. This only occurs when the Alpha Spirit becomes convinced it cannot easily create them again.

Therefore, as soon as Self enters the POV of any Games Universe where material things are scarce and therefore should be *had*, *protected* and treated with high regard, emotional imprinting enters the picture—because now the Self can "lose" things; and this sense of "loss" (at "2.0") is treated as the same nature of threat to survival and existence as we might treat the care, protection and stewardship of a "physical body" (at "1.0"). Therefore, the most basic implant at this level is the command: "*knowing* and *being* is precise identification with the *having* of things and the avoidance of *pain*."

Δ Δ Δ Δ Δ Δ

When treating the interior of the Mind-System, the "RCC" (at "2.0") constitutes only one part of the range that maintains the Mind-Body connection To the upper part of mental command (of beta-thought), we give the name "Master Control Center" (or MCC), plotted at "4.0" on the Standard Model. Within this upper **band** of "beta-thought"—between "2.1" and "4.0"—Self may occupy all manner of POV within the Mind-System.

At the level of "1.0" we can say that the observable programming of the Human Condition from the POV of the genetic organism is "fight-versus-flight"—and this is compounded by the other half of the RCC system at "2.0" with a primary "stimulus-response" automation system installed. That about wraps it up for the "genetic vehicle" as a bio-chemical emotional entity. Just above this level, we discover the larger framework of the Mind-System; and its manner of computation is wholly different from the "identity-based" imprints of the RCC, which tends to generalize "knowledge" as emotional encoding and includes all *facets* found within an experience indiscriminately.

Within the band of beta-thought (or else the Mind-System/MCC) operating between "2.1" and "4.0" on our Standard Model, we find "grouping" and "categorization" of associated knowledge. Although analytical (not reactionary), the MCC can still be fragmented by individual experiences of "failure" and "error." It uses its stores of information to calculate certain efforts and make **evaluations** about the Universe, then it looks to observable cues in the environment to see if this is correct. Misleading or **erroneous** knowledge leads to miscalculation and a deteriorated mental state if personal data is repeatedly **invalidated**.

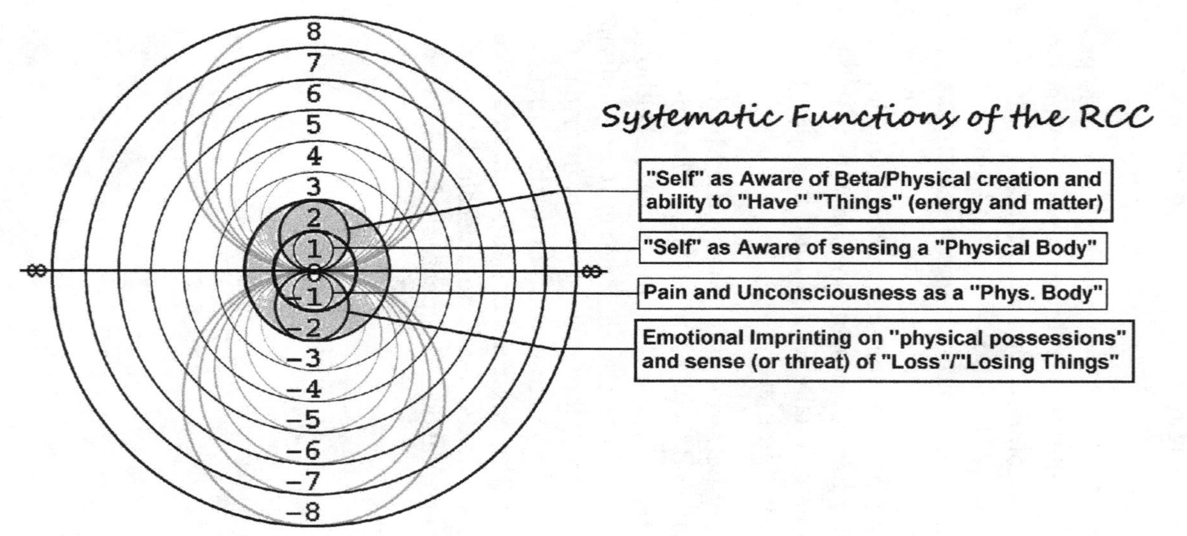

Systematic Functions of the RCC
8
7
6
5
4
3
2
1
0
1
0
1
2
3
4
5
6
7
8
"Self" as Aware of Beta/Physical creation and ability to "Have" "Things" (energy and matter)
"Self" as Aware of sensing a "Physical Body"
Pain and Unconsciousness as a "Phys. Body"
Emotional Imprinting on "physical possessions" and sense (or threat) of "Loss"/"Losing Things"

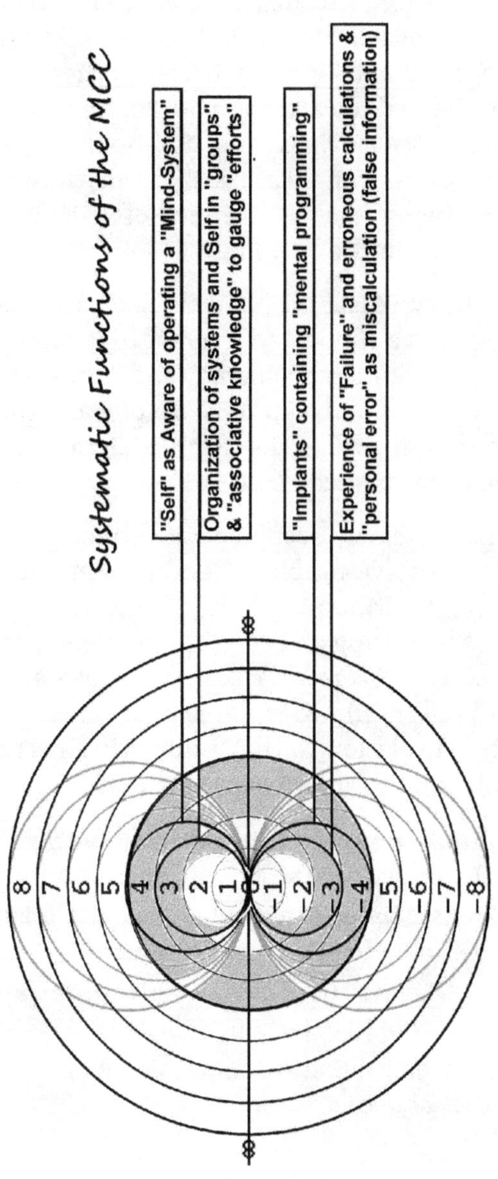
Systematic Functions of the MCC
"Self" as Aware of operating a "Mind-System"
Organization of systems and Self in "groups" & "associative knowledge" to gauge "efforts"
"Implants" containing "mental programming"
Experience of "Failure" and erroneous calculations & "personal error" as miscalculation (false information)
8
7
6
5
4
3
2
1
0
-1
-2
-3
-4
-5
-6
-7
-8

It is a Self-Honest "clearing" of the channels that restores full command of the Mind-System to the Alpha Spirit. Too many of the functions and systems have been set on "automatic." The lower one descends in consideration on the Standard Model, the more solidly mechanistic and automatic the programs and circuitry become. These lower mechanisms tend to push an individual toward having a "pattern" or "tendency" outside of full *Actualized Awareness* and *Self-Determinism.* Eventually an individual is no longer knowingly at *Cause* for anything; and when one finally succumbs to being the total effect of a Universe, there is no direction left to go but out the bottom.

The latest 21st century researches and discoveries of Mardukite Zuism and its Systemology have supported the fact that *there are solutions* to all of what is considered "human problems" and it has been further recognized that these problems and solutions are one and the same and given any consideration only because the Mind-System is running in such a way as to perceive them as such.

The Mind-System is primarily occupied with computations of knowledge and effort in order to solve problems; and its computations are perfect to the degree of the programming that it is given and the state of fragmentation that it is operating at. [To gauge this in any relative workable form, we developed the "*Beta-Awareness Scale*"—as described fully in the text "*Crystal Clear*" (*Liber-2B*).] In summary: personal fragmentation and Universe implants, in relation to the systematic structure of our Standard Model, logically follows an orderly sequence.

> 4.0 Mind-System (Human Condition)
> –4.0 ... able to experience "programming"
>
> 3.0 Associated Knowledge (Calculations)
> –3.0 ... able to experience "failure"
>
> 2.0 "Having" (Emotional Association)
> –2.0 ... able to experience "loss"
>
> 1.0 Physical Body (Genetic Vehicle)
> –1.0 ... able to experience "pain"

:: 0 ::
THE "CREATIVE ABILITY TEST" {"CAT"}
WIZARD LEVEL—TRAINING REGIMEN

<u>PURPOSE</u>:

The "*Creative Ability Test*" (*CAT*) was developed to assist *Mardukite System-ology* Seekers gauge personal progress during their Pre-A.T. "Wizard Level" grades of work, but also to directly accelerate "*Creative Ability Training*" using methods described throughout materials of "Metahuman Systemology"—specifically:

> *Creative Ability* maintained by an individual *Alpha-Spirit*, in its management of a *genetic vehicle* (to experience *beta-existence*), and also while operating independently *exterior* to reality agreements with the *Human Condition* and *Physical Universe*.

Unlike the "*Beta-Awareness Test*" (*BAT*)—first introduced in "*Crystal Clear*," then reprinted in the "*Systemology Handbook*" and "*Way Into The Future*"—the "*Creative Ability Test*" (*CAT*) is relatively subjective and virtually "unlimited" in its application. It requires no numeric assessment values.

<u>BACKGROUND</u>:

The author accumulated a large collection of esoteric exercises and New Thought techniques over a 25-year period. These were then tested by members of the Systemology Society and evaluated for their relevance to *Grade-IV* "end-goals" "Metahuman Systemology" leading to "Wizard Level" work. A precise study of "background theory" for the exercises is *not* necessary for them to be effective. However, supportive technical knowledge is found throughout related publications: "*The Complete Mardukite Master Course*," materials from "*The Systemology Handbook*" (primarily "*Tablets of Destiny*" and "*Crystal Clear*") and "*Metahuman Destinations*"—in addition to information in this present volume and its appendix.

After two years of intensive experimentation with innumerable "basic techniques" by many *Seekers* around the world reporting their results to the Systemology Society, surprisingly few exercises survived our rigorous testing and scrutiny for inclusion as both a Wizard-Grade "primer" and "*Creative Ability Test*" (*CAT*). Some versions of these exercises have appeared in previous Mardukite and Systemology publications; others may bare striking resemblance to "mystical" and/or "occult" techniques found elsewhere in esoteric lore—as recorded during the past 6,000 years, since the inception of cuneiform writing.

<u>APPLICATION</u>:

A Seeker will notice that as they develop greater degrees of *Creative Ability*, these "exercises" may be repeated with cumulatively better results. The "*CAT*" is not a traditional gradable "test." These "exercises" are approached on a gradient scale of "success" that relatively extends to *Infinity*. An individual will get a "sense" of their own present *ability*, which admittedly, can always be expressed "stronger," "longer" or "clearer" with additional practice.

"*Time*" is a common measure used by Seekers to chart their personal development; the *duration* period an individual can maintain duplication of an exercise with perfect clarity. Another measure is the actual degree of "*clarity*"—which is to say, a subjective certainty of completion or perfection successfully realized—that is maintained while carrying out exercises. This will all undoubtedly *increase* with each effective pass through "creativeness training sessions."

Data that *may* be recorded (for training purposes) is virtually identical to traditional "systematic processing sessions," including: the session environment (*location, weather, day of the week, &tc.*); your apparent condition (*a personal Beta-Awareness or Emotimeter evaluation*) at the start and end; the specific exercises or techniques applied; the duration of time spent on each exercise and the entire testing session; energy handling (*clarity of the operation, certainty of success, new realizations*); the material objects encountered and other "body phenomenon" (*solid forms, imagery, physical/emotional reactions, discomfort or pings sensed from the genetic vehicle*).

<u>INSTRUCTIONS</u>:

Even if an exercise seems "familiar," pay particular attention to specific wording of directions for each application, treating each step in its own unit of time (separate from previous exercises). The "*CAT*" may be *Self-Administered* or *Piloted*. In either case, to provide lasting "gains," it is necessary to focus validation on what an individual *is able* to do, rather than "exercising" in the direction of failure and shortcomings. We have found it more effective for beginners to cycle through as many of the basic steps of each exercise as possible during a single "creative training session"—because, when starting out, Seekers are likely to "try" too intensely on the extended particulars of a particular exercise, in exclusion to others, straining for a specific result or effect to occur. No effort should be applied; a *Seeker* should emphasize validating what they *can* do with each pass.

> :: NOTICE :: Exercise cycles applicable for this "test" and "training regimen" follow an intensive systematic methodology resulting from twenty-five years of esoteric research and experimentation with numerous applied philosophies of spiritual technology. Although we are quite casual in their relay here (emphasizing light practice to encourage accumulating greater certainty), actual realizations and stable gains develop only by pushing through whatever fragmentation appears during practice—discomfort, **somatic "pings,"** intrusive thoughts, reactive images, various emotional responses. Only by working through these to the height of personal certainty and clarity are they useful tools for defragmenting such automatic phenomenon.

At first, a Seeker may only be able to focus for a few minutes on the more basic steps of each exercise cycle, *realizing* it to the extent that present *Actualized Awareness* and attention allows—even if the extent of "success" is a vague *sense* of certainty. As the individual continues their studies and practice—increasing their understanding, willingness and ability—the "test" results become more vivid, certainty is stronger, greater realizations provide for higher "ledges" of Actualization, and personal development relevant to approaching *Gateways to Infinity* is demonstrably more apparent.

As an individual works toward *Spiritual* (or "*Alpha*") *Actualization*—emphasized for the "Wizard" (or "*A.T.*") work of our Systemology—any one of these exercises produces increasingly better results the longer its clarity is able to be held. It is not unreasonable, as an individual advances, to eventually apply 30, 60 or even 120 continuous minutes—and entire *two-hour creative session*—toward a single exercise with increasing results.

Each section represents a specialized cycle, building upon previous cycles. Even after greater certainty is established on a particular cycle: for each new creativeness session, an individual should start at the beginning ("#1") and move through each, however briefly, before going to the next. There are no other "short cuts" to getting *through* and *out* from the trappings of this *Beta-Existence*—our Systemology *is* the most direct path we can access and best chance humanity has had toward its own Ascension, for at least 6,000 years.

Due to debut appearance of the "CAT" in a rather introductory position for *Liber-3D*, an individual is likely to overlook true significance behind the following cycles of exercises in lieu of researching "deeper meaning" or "studies" behind this methodology. But, those who have walked this part of the *Pathway* ahead of you can attest that, indeed, *the whole meal is tasted within the first bite.* In the beginning, a *Seeker's* sense of reality on many of these experiences will be mostly "imaginary" in nature—but as real practice continues, actual perception will increase, permitting certainty and ability to *create* a higher ledge of *Beingness* to reach from, as we continue our journey upward the *Pathway* approaching the *Gateways to Infinity.*

:: NOTICE :: Before proceeding take factual note that the directives for this training regimen *do not* include personal intention or commands for a creation or image to persist. Any "masses" *Imagined* or *Copied* and any *Mental Images* "manufactured" in our Systemology exercises and systematic processing should be handled by (**Alpha Thought**) consideration or command postulate, either: discarded, reduced down to a ball to toss away, dissolved to nothing, treated as being given away—or even pushed into the body from time to time to satisfy the illusion of replenishing energy (though all energy is actually manufactured by the Unlimited Self when necessary). The Alpha-Spirit is a god-like artist with unlimited *Creative Ability*, access to limitless ink and pad of unending paper at their disposal. But over time, it became increasingly fixed on its one track of compulsive creation. Once we can rehabilitate *Self* with certainty of its own *Creative Ability* again—only then might an individual be convinced enough to finally tear off that top of sheet of paper and regain the freedom of its true *Spiritual Beingness.*

Δ Δ Δ Δ Δ Δ Δ

"CREATIVE ABILITY TRAINING" ("CAT")

—#1— "PRESENCE: ENVIRONMENTAL SECURITY"
• *Look around your environment and spot objects that are acceptable—that you don't mind being present.*
• *Look around your environment and find objects that you wouldn't mind having.*
• *Look around your environment and spot locations where you are not.*
• *Look around your environment and notice persons that are not present; objects that are not present; animals that are not present; locations that are not present; times and incidents that are not happening.*

—#2— "MENTAL IMAGERY: TURNING ON PICTURES"
• *Recall an actual event that has happened. When was it? Where was it? Who was there? What is its duration? Imagine the scenery. Notice as many facets of perception as you can—time of day, sensations, touch, weather, humidity, objects, brightness, smells, tastes, sounds, communications, dialogue, emotions of others, personal emotions, gestures, body positions, external motion, personal movement, &tc.*
• *Repeat the above step several times (with eyes closed if it is easier); recalling, imagining and looking at times/events which are acceptable to view, noticing all the details and facets—for example: when you saw something beautiful; when you heard something you enjoyed; when you smelled something pleasant, &tc.*
• *Continue until a clearer perception of Mental Imagery is realized.*
 :: *Persistent Blackness/No Images—Imagine a duplicate of the blackness in the same space as the one you're looking at. Make a copy of it beside it. Make another copy. And another. Several more. Push the copies together and compress into nothing. Make eight more copies; then push them together and throw it away. Make eight more copies; push them together and then push them into the body. Continue this step until the compulsively generated blackness is under your control and you can perceive imagined or recalled images.*

—#3A— "PRESENCE: BETA-EXISTENCE SPACE-TIME"
• *Select two walls in a room with a clear path to walk between them. Start in the center facing one wall and get the sense that you are making the body perform these actions: Look at that wall; Walk over to that wall; Touch that wall; Turn around. Repeat the actions numerous times between both walls, each time giving the same attention to each action as if it's the first time.*
• *To advance this further, perform the previous step as directed, then from the center of the room with eyes closed, perform it again using only directed attention to alternate your Awareness between the walls and touch them. Then,*

repeat the actions, focusing on getting an actual sense of the perception of touching the wall. If this doesn't happen right away, just imagine the feel of the wall.

—#3B— "PRESENCE: SPATIAL CORNER-POINTS"
• *Eyes closed, sitting near the center of a room—Reach up with Awareness and locate an upper corner-point in back of the room. Then find the second upper-corner. Focus all Awareness on these back two corner-points without thinking anything else. Keep all attention on these corner-points.*
• *To take a step further as an advanced practice, during a separate creative session, perform the same procedure treating all four back corner-points.*
• *This exercise can be extended to include all eight corner-points defining a room. This demonstrates basic principles behind the "imagined" or "spiritual" version of this exercise called "Creation-of-Space."*

—#4A— "FACSIMILE-COPIES: WHAT ARE YOU LOOKING AT?"
• *Eyes closed. What are you looking at? Imagine another copy just like it. Make another copy next to it. And several more. Then compress them all together into a ball and discard or toss away.*
• *Eyes open. Spot an object in the environment. Imagine a duplicate or copy of it right beside it. Spot another object and repeat. Continue to do this with various objects.*
• *With eyes closed, get a sense of looking at the objects in the environment. Imagine a duplicate or copy beside each, one by one.*
• *With eyes closed, while indoors, get a sense of looking at objects outside the environment/room/building; and imagine a duplicate or copy beside each.*
• *Practice each of the above—but imagining a perfect duplicate of the object, making it in the same space, using the same energy-mass; then consider that the object is there again; then make a perfect duplicate; then consider the object is there again. Alternate repeatedly.*
:: *Persistent Images/Imprints—Imagine a duplicate of the image in the same space as the one you're looking at. Make a copy of it beside it. Make another copy. And another. Several more. Jam the copies together into a ball and compress into nothing. Make eight more copies; then jam them together into a ball and toss it away. Make eight more copies; jam them together into a ball and push them into the body. Continue this step until the compulsively generated image is under your control.*

—#4B— "FACSIMILE-COPIES: IDENTIFICATION & BODIES"
• *Eyes closed. Imagine a duplicate (identical copy) of your presently owned human body out in front of you. Make a copy next to it. And another. And several more. When you have eight or so, push them together into a ball and*

collapse it into nothing. Imagine another duplicate. Make a copy next to it. And many more copies; then push them together into a ball and toss it away. Continue this step until you feel comfortable in creating bodies.

   –Imagine a duplicate of your present body as ideal and healthy; then unmake it. Make it again; then unmake it. Alternate repeatedly.

   –Looking into a mirror. Get the sense that there is "something there"; then get the sense there is "nothing there." Alternate these considerations repeatedly.

• Eyes closed. Imagine a busy or crowded place, mall, depot or street corner. Place your point-of-view in a fixed location; then look around and spot objects, motions and people in this scenery. Practice this for multiple locations (preferably until an increase in actual perception).

   –Choose the location you like best from the previous stop to use for the remaining cycle of exercises; Imagine making a facsimile-copy of your present human body to use as a point-of-view; then unmake the body and remain looking as an Awareness. Alternate repeatedly.

• Perform the previous step, but this time: Imagine an identical copy of the body out in front of you, using a point-of-view outside the body to look around the location; then use a point-of-view from inside the body to look around the location. Alternate viewpoints repeatedly.

   –Perform the previous step, but this time adding: Get the sense of other persons acknowledging your presence when they are near or walking by (even if they don't look at the body).

• Select a basic solid object (pyramid, cone, cube, sphere, &tc.); Imagine using the "object" as your body to practice each previous step of this locational-cycle of exercises; making and unmaking, alternating viewpoints, spotting other objects, noticing motions and persons, and receiving acknowledgment ("hellos") for your presence. Now add to this cycle: unmaking the body and point-of-view in one spot, then making it again at other spots in the location. Get a sense of moving that body like a "playing piece."

   –As before; Imagine using a duplicate copy of your present body.

   –As before; Imagine use of an elderly body.

   –As before; Imagine use of a child body.

   –As before; Imagine using a body of a different gender.

   –As before; Imagine using a body that appears strong.

   –As before; Imagine using a body that appears wise.

   –As before; Imagine using a sparkly cloud of silvery-white energy for a body with small golden balls for eyes.

   –As before; using only the point-of-view as an Awareness with nothing added as a body.

—#4C— "FACSIMILE-COPIES: MACHINERY AND BODIES"
• Select an object that has a basic mechanical function "to produce a flow."

(This may be best practiced with a "sink" or "water-spigot" until there is an independent reality on electricity and basic motions.)

–With eyes open. Look at the mechanical-object in its "off" condition and imagine an identical duplicate beside it. Look between the two and spot any differences, adjusting your created duplicate to match the original. Continue until satisfied with the certainty of duplication.

–Turn the mechanical-object "on" and look at it in this condition, noting the motion and getting a sense of the energy-flow driving it. Adjust your imagined duplicate to match this in every way, noting the motion and getting a sense of the energy-flow involved.

• For advancing these steps, with eyes closed; use an object not present.

• Select a mechanical-object that has a basic "motor" function. (This may be best practiced with an "electric fan" until there is an independent reality on generators and engines.)

–Apply the previous basic steps for imagining duplicate machinery; this time giving particular attention to its internal mechanics: at basic, a circuit or energy flow that drives or propels spinning motion of the blades and is started and stopped by a switch. As it runs (is "on") get a sense of the internal mechanics and match this energy and motion in your duplicate.

• For additional practice: use more complex machines; use machinery not present; use electronic devices. A basic study in physical mechanics on "how things work" is of benefit.

• Eyes closed. Imagine being a "motor-vehicle"; create the machine, the internal mechanics, and get the sense of identifying with it as a body. Establish a point-of-view from the car, while maintaining a sense of the energy and motion mechanically operating inside of it.

• For advancing this step further, move your point-of-view through each mechanical system of the vehicle as you imagine it running: steering, brakes, the engine, transmission, &tc. (to the best of your reality on these systems). Get a sense for how it operates from the inside.

• Apply basic directions for using a solid object in locational-cycle exercises (#4B), this time using a vehicle (such as a car) for a body. Run the whole cycle using the vehicle: everything from "making and unmaking" to considerations as a "playing piece."

• Imagine the creation and unmaking of various machinery, devices, motors, vehicles, engines, generators, and power plants. Imagine as much detail in your creations as you can.

–Additionally; Imagine being various machinery. Alternate your point-of-view between inside and outside various vehicles and machines.

• Imagine the creation and unmaking of various personal "mental machinery": devices that inform you of things, so you don't have to know; devices that react for you, so you don't have to remember; devices that show impressions of what

things are, so you don't have to look; devices that make your creations invisible as soon as you imagine them; devices that turn mental images into dark screens and black clouds when you try to remember them; devices that make mental images for you, so you don't have to create. Consider other mental mechanism that could be created.

–Additionally; Imagine being various mental machinery. Alternate your point-of-view between inside and outside various mental machinery.

• Eyes open, outdoors, public area. Spot a person that is standing or sitting for a while (like at a bus-stop). Imagine the creation of an identical duplicate copy beside them. As in previous steps; look between the two and spot any differences, adjusting your duplicate to match.

–Additionally; if the person leaves your view during practice, simply select another. If they change positions or spots in the area, adjust your duplicate copy to match the motion. Practice this step with several persons.

• Once certainty is established with the previous step: use the step to duplicate a person; this time giving particular attention to copying the internal parts of that body (bones, organs, muscle, &tc.) and get a sense of the organic systems functioning inside (as with the previous exercise on machines).

–Additionally; apply this step to duplicate a moving person, copying the motion in your duplicate. Get a sense of how the internal organic machinery drive various motors and systems during the motion. Practice this step with several persons. Practice this step repeatedly.

—#5A— "<u>CONTROL: WHAT IS THAT BODY DOING?</u>*"*
• Get the sense of you making the body do "what it's doing." Get the sense of making the body sit in a chair. Get the sense that you're making that body hold a book, &tc.
• Get the sense that you are behind the body, controlling its movement by strings or beams. Decide when to lift a finger of the body and then do so, imagining its control by a string. Decide when to lower it and then do so. Practice this on other movable parts of the body.
• Decide to conduct some activity (walk outdoors, &tc.) and focus Awareness behind the body's head. Expand your POV to encompass the entire space around the body. Move the body around, still using its eyes, but imagine controlling the body from behind it.
• Perform the previous step, emphasizing attention on the presser (push) and tractor (pull) energy beams directed to control movement of the body.
:: Compulsions/Ticks and Twitches—Consider a behavior that the body does compulsively on its own. Now decide to do this on your own determinism and you do so. Decide to stop and you do so. Start it again and decide to increase/exaggerate the action; then you do so. Decide to decrease the action and you do it. Decide to stop again an do it. Repeated this cycle until the

behavior is under better control.

—#5B— "PRESENCE: DISTANCE & CONNECTEDNESS"
• *Eyes open. Spot two objects and notice the differences between them; then note the distance between them. Then get a sense of the space between them.*
• *With eyes closed, repeat the above step.*
• *Eyes open. Look around and spot an object that you wouldn't mind connected to you. Get the sense of making that object connect to you. Then get the sense that it is separate from you. Alternate. Determine how you could make it connect. Then consider in what ways it is different from you.*
• *With eyes closed, repeat the above step.*
• *Eyes open. Spot an object. Decide that you will walk over to the object and do so. Decide that you will reach out and touch the object and do so. Decide that you will let go of the object and do so.*
• *With eyes closed, repeat the above step by extending your Awareness.*
• *Walking outdoors; get the sense of being stationary and moving space around you, then get the sense of moving through space.*
• *Eyes open, then eyes closed. Indoors and outdoors; spot two objects and notice the distances between the objects and you. Then get a sense of the space between them and you.*
• *Perform the above step using three objects.*
• *Look around and spot something that is still; then spot something that is in motion. Alternate repeatedly.*
• *Eyes closed, repeat the above step, using a point-of-view from spaces or locations where you are not.*

—#6— "ALTERNATION: BELL, BOOK & CANDLE"
• *Select a small simple object (such as a "bell, book or candle") that is easily moved. Locate two spots. Move the object uniformly back and forth between these exact two spots at a consistent speed. Reach and let go for every spot change, leaving the object in precisely the same position at each spot for a moment.*
• *Select two small dissimilar objects (such as a "bell, book or candle") that are easily moved. Locate two spots (on a table). Place an object in each spot. Pick up "Object-1" and look at it. Notice its weight, its feel and its appearance. Get the sense of you making it more solid. Put it back in the same exact spot and position. Pick up "Object-2" and look at it. Notice its weight, its feel and its appearance. Get the sense of you making it more solid. Put it back in the same exact spot and position. Alternate this step between the two objects, each time treated as the first time.*
• *Continue the previous step until there is no compulsion toward automatic actions or responses, no fluctuation in attention and no desire to "leave" the*

exercise.

• *For advanced practice, perform the physical version of the previous step, then close your eyes and imagine six walls forming a room that is not located in the Physical Universe. Imagine two tables or pedestals in the room. Imagine "Object-1" is on one table; hold it still and make it more solid. Imagine "Object-2" is on the other table; hold it still and make it more solid. Imagine "Object-1" floating up in the air; get a sense of its weight, its feel and its appearance; then have it float back down. Imagine "Object-2" floating up in the air; get a sense of its weight, its feel and its appearance; then have it float back down. Alternate as described above.*

• *Continue the previous step until there is increased perception of actual solidity and weight (in addition to imagined).*

—#7— <u>"ALTERNATION (POV): AWARENESS OF SPOTS"</u>

• *Eyes open. Locate a spot on the body, decide to reach out and touch it, then do so. Decide when to let go and do so. Find another spot on the body, and repeat the step. And again.*

• *With eyes closed, repeat the above step.*

• *Locate a spot in space, decide to move the body and touch it, then do so. Decide when to let go and do so. Find another spot in space, and repeat the step. And again.*

• *With eyes closed, repeat the above step.*

• *Locate a spot on the floor, decide to move the body over it, then do so. Find another spot on the floor, and repeat the step. And again.*

• *With eyes closed, repeat the above step.*

• *Locate two spots on the floor, decide to move the body over one, then walk toward it. Before reaching the spot, decide to change your mind and move the body over the other one instead. Find another two spots on the floor, and repeat the step. And again.*

• *With eyes closed, repeat the above step.*

• *Locate three points in the body; direct all attention on these three points in the body. Locate three points in space; direct all attention on these three points in space. Alternate these repeatedly—three points in the body; three points in space.*

• *With eyes closed, perform the above step; rapidly and repeatedly.*

• *Continue until there is perception separate from a body.*

—#8— <u>"PROCEDURE 1-8-0, ROUTE-8: NOTHINGNESS"</u>

• *Eyes closed. Imagine you are extending your Awareness, reaching through the entire Physical Universe, as far as you can imagine. Now reach a little further beyond and outside of all dimensional space and find the Nothingness. Hold your point-of-view on the Nothingness, without thinking or imagining anything else.*

 –*Extend your reach out on the right side, getting a certainty of the Nothingness.*
 –*Extend your reach out on the left side, getting a certainty of the Nothingness.*
 –*Repeat the previous step for each other direction; reaching in front, reaching behind, reaching above, reaching below.*
 –*Extend your reach out to the right and left simultaneously, holding the perception of Nothingness in both directions.*
 –*Repeat the previous step for each direction-pair: in front of and behind you; then above and below you.*
 –*Extend your reach out on all six sides of you at once, maintaining a certainty of Nothingness in all directions.*
 • *To take practice a step further, alternate between this point-of-view with eyes closed and the point-of-view of the Physical Universe with eyes open. Look around each time and orient Self to the environment.*
 • *Alternate getting full perception of Nothingness and full perception of the Physical Universe.*

:: 1 ::
IMAGINATION—HANDLING MENTAL IMAGES AND CREATIVE ABILITY

IMAGINATION is the vehicle or catalyst for an individual's *Creative Ability*. Such abilities originate at the level of the "Spirit" or "*Alpha Spirit*." They are "*Alpha*" qualities originating within one's own "Personal Universe" apart from any programmed or encoded "reality agreements" concerning *Beta-Existence*, which is to say, the "Physical Universe." The two "Universes" are separate—and it is only when an individual confuses the Reality of *one* with the *other* that they tend to find their experience of Life and Existence especially difficult... and *fragmented.*

Being an Alpha quality, Imagination is above or *senior* to "Associative Thought" of the Mind-System as it applies to experience of *Beta-Existence.* Where the common denominator of personal thought and effort in *Beta-Existence* is toward the Existential Prime Directive: "*To Survive*"—the "name of the game" in all upper-level Universes and truer Alpha **echelons** of spiritual existence is: "*To Create.*"

The Spirit is able to create, essentially, from *Nothingness*—and does not require fragmentation or condensation of *other* "energy-matter" *parts* in which *to be* creative. In this wise, an Alpha Spirit exists and operates in an unlimited Home Universe that defies some of the hardest-held beliefs about the Physical Universe. For example, fixed "conservation of energy." is an untruth given the fact that *Life*—or the Spirit—is able to employ *Imagination* and literally imbue *Beta-Existence* with energies from a point *exterior* to it. Perhaps this is what accounts for an "expanding" Universe: something we wouldn't expect to see *if* all energy-matter really *was* rigidly "conserved" as a fixed constant.

Present-day "adult" society pays a lip-service in support of "imaginative ability"—and what is laughingly called "creative thinking." All typical demonstrations of social education and "enforced reality" suggest that the value of Imagination has been ranked quite low, put somewhere on a back-shelf beside "childish" things and "play." For the average individual, ability and willingness to "play" or "pretend"—just as "To Create"—diminishes over time as more and more fixed **thought-forms** or "beliefs" (and other "imprinting" and "programming") are accumulated.

Most individuals are taught to put personal value in "experience." In order to get a sense of worth—to feel as if they can show something for it; or *have* something as the ultimate goal—the information is stored for "future" use. It's only valid function is evaluation of "effort" necessary to "act" in the Physical Universe (*Beta-Existence*) using a "body" that exists to communicate with a similar material **continuity** level. But unfortunately, as an individual puts more and more energy into storing data and other "*Mental Images*" that mirror *Beta-Existence*, their considerations and willingness become increasingly rigid and fixed—essentially forming "energy ridges" and "mental machinery" to manage and control experience with a physical body-form (*Genetic Vehicle*). This is also one aspect of how an *exterior* Alpha-Spirit became entrapped *interior* to the Human Condition of the Physical Universe.

Some schools of philosophy and spirituality have sought a resolution to this entrapment by treating the entire subject of the Physical Universe—and its facets of *space-time energy-matter*—as "unreal" or a "delusion." Such modes of operation contradict earlier agreements and postulates the Alpha-Spirit is already "carrying" concerning the Human Condition, so the individual gets "hung up" or "stuck" in a "Mystery" concerning their certainty on Reality. These other methods have already been attempted by our organization and were found unworkable and unproductive to reaching the ultimate goal of returning to the Spirit its own (true and original) Actualized Awareness and ability of operating as Self, independent and *exterior* to *Beta-Existence.*

In spite of the numerous times an Alpha-Spirit has connected with a *Life-form* in a *Beta-Existence*, the fact remains that we continue to consistently apply spiritual energy to create our "Personal Universe" in *Alpha-Existence*. Of course, the Self-Determined knowledge of this gradually fades to black as an individual enshrouds considerations of Self and Reality with further "agreements" concerning the nature of the Physical Universe in exclusion. For this reason, most other traditional "sciences" and "applied philosophies" have failed to do anything other than keep consideration and attention entrapped *interior* to *Beta-Existence*—providing no regard for the Spirit, its true nature or abilities.

> On a practical level—and in regards to "systematic processing"—before a *Seeker*, or *Pre-A.T. Wizard-In-Training*, focuses attentions too heavily on Higher Universes—their creation and management—the individual must arrive at full realization and *Awareness* that the Alpha Spirit *is* at *Cause* in *creating* them; that Self *is* at *Cause* in *determining* its own true spiritual existence and that the mechanics of *Beta-Existence* are wholly separate, but mirrored in an individuals consideration of a Personal Universe.

The nature and existence of this Physical Universe, however, is simply the result of common denominator agreements made by countless Alpha Spirits **participating** in this *reality* as a Point-of-View (POV) remote from, and simultaneous with, their own true continuing position as a *Spiritual Being* inhabiting a Personal Universe within Alpha-Existence (with is marked at "7.0" on our Standard Model). It is at this "point" that the Alpha-Spirit may turn "180 degrees" to **confront** the *Infinity of Nothingness*, but the fact that we are here now suggests that we became far more interested in the survival of potential *Somethingness.*

It is apparent from our Standard Model, our Systemology—and allegories from "Arcane Tablets"—that as an Alpha-Spirit became increasingly unwilling to confront communications of a "game" within a particular Universe, their considerations for existence as Self "fell down" or "degraded" to "lower" condensations and goals than former Universes. Descriptions of the Pathway back "up" and *out* are relayed to "esoteric initiates" using symbolism of ascending "Gates." This application is frequently misunderstood if treated exclusively within paradigms of former mystical religions and occult practices. In any case, an individual goes "out of" *Communication* with "higher" spiritual levels on their descent *interior* to the present Human Condition. The "Wizard Grades" of our Systemology *systematically* pursue a repair of this.

"Imagination" is the most appropriate semantics we can apply to the Alpha-Spirit's *Creative Abilities* as experienced in the Human Condition. It is a crude word to use, at best, given that most individuals associate it with "unreal," "artificial" or "mental fluff." Although an Alpha-Spirit may direct imagery (energetically down the ZU-line) to the "Mind-System" for *Beta-Existence:*

> Imagination is a *creation* originating directly from
> the "Spirit"—not a *product* of the "Mind."

However, as a *Being* descends in their considerations, *Point-of-View* (POV) and lower "seats" of *Beingness*—particularly below "4.0" on the Standard Model—cumulative programming and implanting of the "surrounding" Mind-System *caves in* on the individual. This promotes automated reactive tendencies, preset patterns of thought and stimulus-response behavior (such as treated in our *previous* Systemology materials concerning systematic **"Beta-Defragmentation"**).

Once a Seeker has effectively *cleared the **slate*** using *Grade-III* "Tech" from "*Crystal Clear*" combined with our initial *Grade-IV* advancements in "*Metahuman Destinations,*" then they are better prepared to realize for themselves—as an *Actualized Awareness*—the upper-level goals of "Wizard

Grades" such as relayed throughout this *present* book.

Δ Δ Δ Δ Δ Δ Δ

Each and every one of us has the ability to *incite* or *dissolve* "creation" with our *Attention*—our focused application of *Self-Directed Awareness.* We tend to do this several times a day: forming an **intention** in the "Mind," *creating* an entire "*Mental Image*" within our "Personal Universe" of Reality and then often *erasing* it in fear and/or doubt. Within higher realizations of an Alpha Spirit's "Home Universe" and other shared "Creative Universes" within Alpha-Existence, the same faculty described as "imagination" in *Beta* is actually pure "*Creation*"—perhaps the highest ability and directive purpose *of* the Alpha-Spirit.

Of course, an individual is no *more* "free" to *Self-Determine* the nature of their own "*Creations*" or "*Creative Ability*" than they are in confronting and handling other elements of the "*Reactive Control Center*" and Mind-System, *if* their considerations are still fixed locally and exclusively to the Point-of-View (POV) of the *Human Condition*—particularly the specific *Genetic Vehicle* to which it is operating. Such considerations inherent to the *Human Condition*, such as "I" or "Self" being "held in," "snapped in" or "keyed-in" *to* the "body" are implanted "pass-not" barriers to achieving higher states suggested by "Wizard Levels" of Metahuman Systemology.

The Alpha-Spirit is the "I"—the *Self* or individual as they actually are. At its highest realized point of *Being* or *Beingness* ("7.0" on the Standard Model), the Alpha-Spirit is a *unit* or *point* of Awareness, which is *Aware* of its *Awareness.* At its most basic state, *this* is all that an Alpha-Spirit really is, free of all other considerations, creations and even postulates of knowingness. All the rest is *secondary* and first *realized* into being in order for it to be actual; and all is a *product of* the Spirit. Unlike former philosophies—and even early schools of **epistemology**—we have discovered that the *Self* or "I" or Alpha-Spirit *is* the "I-AM"; not the Mind. "Self" is not *a* "Thought."

Descartes broadcast his error widely, when he famously wrote "I think; therefore, I am" (in his logical proof called the "*cogito*"). But he wrongly identified the "thinkingness" with the "beingness" of *Self.* Although it received far less attention, eventually this error philosophically earned a correction in Jean-Paul Satre's insight: "The consciousness that says 'I-Am' is not the same consciousness which 'thinks'."

> The *Being* is *Aware* that *it is* "thinking"
> —that *Awareness* is not a *part of* the "thinking."
> The *Being* is independent of the "thought."

What we have here, is a consideration of various potential POV or "viewpoints"—that we might otherwise consider "seats" of *Beingness*—whereby an individual is operating their *Awareness* from. It is bad enough to be "stuck" in a Mind-System POV, but when operating solely on considerations that *Self* is *a* "physical body," an individual has dropped extraordinarily low in *Beta-Awareness* (as demonstrable on the Standard Model).

Systemology Wizard Levels emphasize techniques that go *beyond* the scale of *Beta-Awareness* (the range of "0" and "4" on our Model). Previous materials introduce "personal defragmentation" for *Beta* levels, such as within the texts "*Tablets of Destiny*," "*Crystal Clear*," "*Power of Zu*"[‡] and "*Metahuman Destinations*." This earlier work is quite necessary for Seekers to establish successful (stable) certainty and effective reach and reality on higher goals in place for *Grade-IV* (*Wizard Level-0*), which includes not only full Awareness and **responsibility** for creation and personal experience of "Mental Imagery," but also operation of imagination and "Creative Ability" *independent* and *exterior* to the "Human" Mind-System. These are the keys to unlock *Gateways to Higher Universes* and stabilize "beta-defragmentation."

To adequately complete *Grade-IV Wizard Level-0*, an individual should *know* to the fullest extent of their *Beingness* that they are *not* the "physical body" (*genetic vehicle*)—to the same extent that they had once fixed or trapped their *knowing* in a consideration that they *were* identified as some other "body" or such. This is not an intellectual **semantic** trick or something learned from books; an individual *must* knowingly maintain *Actualized Awareness* "outside of" the *Beta* range and limitations of the *Human Condition* in order to move forward and "upward." Establishment of *Self* as Alpha Spirit is not some arbitrary "rule" that our organization on Earth is imposing for social purposes. The gradient structure of the "Gateways" we **illuminate** in our Systemology is already established as it is: the same "route" by which an individual once "descended" to reach present conditions.

Previous attempts at reaching the same goals as our Systemology often resulted in failure because of overemphasis on handling "energy" directly. It is now concluded that an individual's inability to directly handle

---

[‡] Materials from "*Tablets of Destiny*," "*Crystal Clear*" and "*Power of Zu*" may also be found in the Grade-III Master Edition anthology "*The Systemology Handbook*."

"energy" is supported by the amount of "relays" and "screens" and "filters" and "catalysts" fixed in place to prevent them from doing so—barriers to direct communication and knowingness. If an individual *were* practiced in handling energy directly, there would be no dependency on using sensory-organs and perceptions of a *genetic vehicle*. One could still do so by choice; but there would be no compulsive necessity behind it.

Systemology Wizard Level-0 redirects emphasis on precise control, and responsibility for, "Mental Images" and "Masses"—*forms, objects, manifestations* and *"terminals"*—that an individual maintains an energetic circuit-**flow** with. It was discovered during the "2019 Crystal Clear Convocation" that when an individual properly *Self-Directed* handling of their *realizations* of consideration connected to *imagery* and *symbols* representing the "terminals" themselves, the energy-flows simply followed in suit; the circuitry connected to them "defragmented" as if the operator handled the energy. Elements of this are described in "*Metahuman Destinations.*"

Imprinted encoded information and memory develops the basis of an artificial personality, one which the individual *identifies* with and operates a POV from. Of course, the Alpha-Spirit also possesses its own "personality" of sorts—a basic *Individual Identity* or *Beingness*. In regards to the *Human Condition*, additional considerations are then attached to this *Beingness* as one makes increasingly more agreements entrapping the individual within an artificial personality POV. For most individuals, there is no POV *outside of*—or *exterior* to—*Beta-Existence* and what it "means" to be "Human."

Encoded information imprinted on the Mind-System shares characteristics of a library or databank (of specific details). Details are stored based on classifications: assigned significances for consideration in association (or comparison) with other previously established details. This forms a "set" or "data set"—contributing to the common phraseology: "Mind-Set." Of course, total capability (or creative range) for the Alpha-Spirit (or *Self*) is not restricted to any particular Mind-Set, unless it considers or "postulates" that it does, as an Alpha-Thought—in which case:

> In its misguided *Self-Direction*, the Spirit *is* powerful enough
> to *forget* or hide its own nature, if it *commands* it to be so,
> even if pressured or coaxed into agreeing to the same.

△ △ △ △ △ △ △

Using previous material provided in Grade-III, Grade-IV and this present volume, a Seeker, Master—or *Pre-A.T.* Wizard-in-Training—increases Self-Determinism and understanding, and thereby certainty to "face up to" or *confront* "Reality," which is to say: personal agreements and significances regarding not only *Beta-Existence*, but *all* "Universes." In *this* book, we emphasize control and responsibility for "Mental Imagery"—control of our "associative knowledge response" to experiencing the "world-at-large." To be fully *Actualized*, an Alpha-Spirit must be free, once again, to fluidly consider potentiality of the "ALL"—called "*AN.KI*" in Mesopotamia—or else the total potential sum and differentiation of considerations for all existences, *Alpha* and *Beta*.

Highest potential creativity of the Spirit and its upper-level *Point-of-View* (POV) is brought down to lower points of *Beta-Awareness* and fixed within parameters of *that* existence, becoming obsessively attached to a *genetic vehicle* (or "physical body") POV for its sense of *Beingness*. Through a long sequence of programmed imprinting on implants reinforced with excessive emotional encoding:

> an individual comes to believe certain factors
> are true of *Self* and their Personal Home Universe,
> when they actually only pertain to considerations
> of the *genetic vehicle* and the *Physical Universe*.

Fragmentation of Beta-thought reduces an Alpha-Spirit's true spiritual individuality as it begins to "identify" itself with other "things." When it too solidly identifies with agreements of low-level *Awareness*, it becomes a locatable "effect" of *Beta-Existence*, succumbing to "mundane forces" of the "Physical Universe." Having forgotten its own creative ability, it is convinced on dependency of a *Beta-Existence* to provide all force, energy, space, matter and so forth—providing the individual with an entirely *other-determined* "reality" in which to exist. This fact is the real delusion of the Physical Universe; not the solidity of its material substance. It continues to persist in existence, as a sort of "prison for Alpha-Spirits," because no one takes responsibility for its original creation and every Observer consistently alters what it *is* and makes it more solid.

Inability to control or manage *Self-Determined* flows of energy (communication, reactivity, mental images, *&tc.*) is remedied by practice of consciously, intentionally and knowingly *Self-Directing* these flows in the same way that their handling has come to be "automated" as "push-button responses" managed *by* the *Beta*-environment or Physical Universe. The key component to this type of practice or "creativeness processing" is *Imagination*—literally, personal control of "Mental Imagery" and recording of experience.

Mechanisms of the Mind-System store data for "Mental Imagery" which entangles it with the same energy and *Awareness* that is *imprinted* during an experience or **Imprinting Incident**. Not only does this reduce an individual's *Actualized Awareness*, but also leads to reliquishing responsibility for creating and handling *Mental Images* over to the automated mental machinery. This same *imprinted* data creates energetic **turbulence** later when reactively incited as an individual's "Reality." This happens if the external environment is similar to an **Activating Event** that stimulates circuitry for a programmed response with a certain *facet*.

As explained in former Systemology texts, *Imprints* are essentially "stamped" holographic-type imagery—a snap-shot of energetic *facets* associated with an experience. When an individual is not maintaining high levels of *Actualized Awareness*, energetic-flows activate emotional encoding or programming (stored on and as implants). When insufficient *"Presence"* and *Self-Determinism* is applied to its handling, automated response-mechanisms are "unconsciously" generated in place of it; they generate a "Mental Image"—and an Alpha-Spirit *"looks"* at *that* in place of the actual energy.

When *Self* is not knowingly at *Cause* in the experience of *Life*, no responsibility is taken for creation of that experience—or one's own Personal Universe. The individual, as an *effect*, tends to put up more "resistance" to the Physical Universe being as *Cause*—therefore making considerations and agreements to *Beta-existence* more solid and apparently less controllable (one thinks) by *Self*.

In *Metahuman Destinations*, "energy-flows" are treated as "circuits" on "channels of communication"; **"terminal** nodes" are also defined. By understanding Systemology, we can see that the flows on these circuits are fixed by our "resistance" *against* some rejection, barrier or communication break with Universes and Spheres of Existence all the way down to present time *Beta*-experience. Over the course of our very long spiritual existence, this has created more solid barriers and added greater solidity to our fixed considerations of what something *is*. This happens "on automatic," using automated response-mechanisms we have created to handle the "circuitry" for us.

When we analyze the nature of
emotionally encoded *Imprinting*,
we often find "snap-shots" of
what we are resisting against.

For example, in a resonating "Image" remaining from a physical accident, it is a "snap-shot" of what we are attempting to *stop*, and thereby *control*. Failing this, the "Image" remains—it becomes a barrier-wall or backdrop on our Reality (for that "channel"). It contains only stopped motion or no motion and becomes timeless. Of course, because we don't want to *see* or *communicate* with it, we tend to "flip" the "Image" around, now seeing the "backside," which is a kind of "blackness" representing "Mystery."

But *facets* of the *Imprint* (and its mechanisms) all still exist "running in the background," yet now even less under control of *Self*, which no longer *sees* it for what it *is*. This energetic solidity and fragmentation hinders a *Self-Honest* state of true Spiritual Freedom and *Creative Ability*. A remedy for this is found with one of the primary theories behind the application of "systematic processing":—

> to get an individual to consciously, willingly and
> knowingly practice actions that are otherwise
> taking place unknowingly on automatic
> or using response-mechanisms and other filters.

Such mechanisms and filters were once our own creations, but *control* of them became more automatic the longer they were used and the greater they were relied upon as "sensors" for information and experience. Keep in mind, that this same quality of energetic communication is taking place all up and down the Standard Model (ZU-line), including throughout the Mind-System.

We are now treating what *Self* experiences as obstructing "screens" or "fields" *and* the automatic-response "*Imagery*" (along with its associations of identity). Without this component, "Route-1" methods described in "*Tablets of Destiny*" concerning the "Reactive Control Center" (the "RCC" at "2.0" on the Standard Model) have a "*limited*" application. They benefit a Seeker up to the point of overemphasizing validation of preexisting "RCC" patterns—as do "behavioral modification" exercises, or "cognitive therapies."

Thus, we systematically practice knowingly "duplicating" or "copying" *Mental Images* that are otherwise considered an imposition or barrier. When an individual recognizes that they "own" it, then the responsibility and command-power of creating all *Mental Imagery* experienced, increases.

:: 2 ::

ROUTE-ZERO—USING "CRYSTAL CLEAR" AND OTHER PROCEDURES FOR GRADE-IV "PRE-A.T." WIZARD TRAINING

An individual fragments—and may defragment—*their own "Mental Image"* stores, considerations (programming; postulates), thoughts (reasoning; association) and emotional encoding (as a personal imprint) *all* regarding "some thing" (a form or mass; "terminal"). Such "things" *remain* "things"—there is no delusion in this respect; but the *significances* "imagined" *about* "things" are what compose our own "image" of Reality (or "worldview). For this reason, in "systematic processing" we practice fluidity of energy-communication (as an alternation) along each channel (to a "terminal") to free up the unlimited considerations an Alpha-Spirit naturally would maintain at its highest basic state.

Often, too close a "reality association" exists between our imprinted responses (and implanted circuitry) to automated *Mental Imagery* senses and experienced as *Beta-Existence* from a *Human Condition* POV. An individual loses control of their own "Personal Universe"—which they ironically continue to create and experience—as more attention is fixed on mirroring "identity associations" and "reality agreements" with the (shared) "Physical Universe."

Grade-IV (*Wizard Level-0*) material emphasizes applications that promote responsibility and certainty to control *Mental Imagery*—the ability to *know YOU* are creating the *Imagery*; that you can *choose* to make it more 'solid' and 'real' or simply 'dissolve' it; and realizations that no thing is permanent or can affect the Spirit permanently, except as a consideration that it can.

"Routes" of systematic processing given in previous materials have one thing in common: they are treating the *past* in *this* lifetime—"scanning" this lifetime or "resurfacing" a specific event, or an event that is linked to communications from an earlier event by its *facets*. Such methodology is not only effective for *this* lifetime, but to have any greater applications, the Seeker would require an increased Reality on *former* lifetimes— and quite often, the "screens" and "filters" maintained during experience of *this* lifetime act as "blinders" to higher spiritual realizations.

"Route-1"—as demonstrated in theory for "*Tablets of Destiny*"—assists an individual in reclaiming some former energies "entwined" or "entangled" with emotional intensity held from former experiences. It was intended to *assist* an individual in reaching enough *Actualized Awareness* to apply other forms of systematic processing. The method by itself is somewhat limited due to its exclusive treatment of instances where the Seeker is at "effect" of something other-determined—"what others have done to you"—and therefore can potentially reinforce "victimization" if used intensely for all purposes, in addition to over-validating functions of reactive mechanism. [It required revision in 2022.]

"*Crystal Clear*" introduced "Route-2"—or else, "Analytical Recall"—which has a far wider range of application in addressing personal significances, reasoning and *facets* of "associated knowledge" tied to an event (*any* event) or consideration. "Route-3" from "*Metahuman Destinations*" follows a similar philosophy; though it went beyond only events, treating communication lines with "terminals" as energetic channels, and *three* specific circuits of *facet imprinting*:

> Circuit-1: what *Self* has done (outflows);
> Circuit-2: what *Self* has received (inflows); and
> Circuit-3: what *Self* has observed of others (crossflows).

All former "Routes" primarily treat actual incidents from *this* lifetime—and their "Recall." There is no question that they are effective methods for goals in place at each step of the way; and it is highly recommend that a reader of this book actually work through previous materials. But —you are *here* now—and if these other "Routes" should have demonstrated anything to you as a *Systemologist*, it is that you are *here* in the present where "past events" are *not.*

Too much attention is spent trapped in "old" viewpoints (POV) where an Alpha-Spirit was so overloaded with energy that they have, in essence, "stuck" themselves—or rather, part of their Awareness—there on a "*Spiritual Timeline*" to *figure it out* for eternity. But there is really nothing to figure upon when the truth of the matter is: those events and conditions are *not* here and now—regardless of what "similar" *facets* of existence we may be confronted with that seem to "snap us" *unwillingly* "back" to relive a "timeless" experience or *filter* and *process* present experiences from a POV held suspended.

Wherever an "energy-flow" has been fixed in place, or control of a "channel" has been abandoned, or considerations concerning a given "terminal" have been **calcified** or fragmented into debris: an individual can be said to be "out of communication" with that aspect or part of existence. And since all parts work *systematically*, there is an ensuing *systematic* break-down of the remaining systems—at least as it concerns

Self-Determinism, control and command, of and by *Self*—as Alpha-Spirit. To be effective at all:

> the "Routes" of "systematic processing" rely on
> a Spirit's ability to *control* and *dissolve* its own *creations*,
> even if not directed instructed as such in the directions.

When we consider the Grade-III anthology, "*The Systemology Handbook*"—containing "*Tablets of Destiny,*" "*Crystal Clear,*" "*Power of Zu*" and "*Systemology: The Original Thesis*"—in addition to "*The Complete Mardukite Master Course*" Academy Lectures *and* the first half of *Grade-IV* material published as "*Metahuman Destinations,*" the present author has already dedicated *over half-a-million words* to establishing a complete basic theory and applied philosophy for developing this "New Thought" spiritual science of "Mardukite Systemology"—of which we will not rehash in this present volume, when our goal remains to reach *higher* still.

Precise methodology for an additional *Grade-IV* "Route" has not been previously provided. It is, however, unofficially listed as "Route-0" in "Unit Three" of "*Metahuman Destinations*"—and its steps are oversimplified for the outline (in that book) of "Systemology Operating Procedure 2-C." No other information is given for it, other than that it would be covered in "*Liber-3D, a forthcoming Grade-IV textbook*"—this present volume you now hold in your hands.

Δ Δ Δ Δ Δ Δ Δ

The two-step process given for "Route-0" in Pilot Procedure **SOP-2C** is: *Imagine* and *Create It*—which sufficed to give an idea of the direction that "*Pre-A.T.*" work was headed. This might even be better stated as: *Imagine/Create* and *Make it More Solid*; or even *Realize It* and *Make it More Actual.* Additionally, SOP-2C "Route-3" lists a further "A.T." application as "Circuit-0," which is what *Self* has created (or is creating) for *Self*—"What *Self* has done to *Self*." This method emphasizes personal responsibility for creating all *Mental Images* and "identity associations" of what things *are.* "Circuit-0" is only used in processing once reaching *Wizard Level-0* (*Seekers* using this present book).

Any point where the Alpha-Spirit is using a Mind-System to experience *Beta-Existence* from a POV *interior* to the *Human Condition*, a significant amount of its own spiritual energy is taken up in the "unknown" validation and solidification of various "*wall-like screens*" and "*filter-mechanisms*" inhibiting free circulation of energetic-flow between an Alpha-Spirit's true Beingness and any of its potential creations or POVs.

Fragmentation of any kind "blocks" clear communication maintained between *Self* and anything which it is still creating or in "possession" of. We may carry strong energetic "ties" with terminals in our past that hold a significant amount of our attention fixed—and even other times when attention was too dispersed to be properly focused at all. Our former "Routes" (1, 2 and 3) allow a Seeker to resume communication with what they *"screened"* or *"filtered"* in the past, thereby reclaiming control and command of those channels.

The basic goals of defragmentation using our applied spiritual philosophy has not changed in *Grade-IV*. Working through the appropriate gradients of understanding—and "Gateways" they correlate to—an individual's *Actualized Awareness* increased up the **tiers** of the *Pathway*; a wider-encompassing "arsenal" of tools is suddenly accessible and effectively workable. Such must first be within the realm (or Reality) of the operator, who then may actually understand and employ them properly.

In essence, all of our "Routes" have approached the same goal on a gradient scale: the *conversion* of old fixed *Mental Images* and significant channels of energy-flow that *Self* maintains with these creations. In "Route-1" we called it *Resurfacing* (or **Cathartic Processing**); "Route-2" is obviously *Analytical* or *Recall Processing*; and "Route-3" is commonly referred to as **Communication Processing**. This leaves us with with an obvious classification for this present "Route-0" methodology as *Creativeness Processing*—as applied to *Grade-IV Pre-A.T. Wizard Level-0*. We now have a very concise schedule of basic procedure.

> "Route-1" Resurfacing/Cathartic Proc. (*Tablets of Destiny*)
> "Route-2" Analytical/Recall Processing (*Crystal Clear*)
> "Route-3" Communication Proc. (*Metahuman Destinations*)
> "Route-0" Creativeness Processing (*Imaginomicon*)

The most basic "keyword" used as a *"Processing Command Lines"* (PCL) of "Route-0" is: "IMAGINE." Although originally introduced as a spiritual technology during the "2019 Crystal Clear Convocation," we held back "imagination" for "higher-level" application after realizing many *Seekers* required working (solo) through *"Crystal Clear"* material several times in order to have a strong Reality on it. We developed *"Metahuman Destinations"* and "Route-3" not only to introduce "Professional Piloting Procedures" to Systemology, but also to make certain a *Seeker* had cleared *enough* channels—had enough "reactivity" under their control—before making their *Mental Imagery* and other creations any "stronger" or "more solid."

"Route-0" methods may be applied directly to the same types of "terminals" and "events" targeted by other "Routes," but only if applying "IMAGINE" properly to the *Processing Command Line* (PCL) and properly processed. [For example, one can easily replace "RECALL" with "IMAGINE" for PCLs suggested in previous texts.] "*Imagining*" and/or "*Creating*" also provides a wider range of application as *Systematic Processing*. This includes those that increase ability to "*confront*" (what they were unable to adequately "*recall*" or have "*screened*"/"*filtered*") and points of *Recall* that prove too turbulent for a *Seeker* to approach by other "Routes."

Most any "terminal" or "incident" one might treat by another method of systematic processing could be treated with *Creativeness Processing* (Route-0) *if* the "terminal" or "subject" is within the reach (Reality) of the Seeker. If not, then the same methodology is employed on a gradient scale—getting an individual to simply *Imagine* some small part of the whole, each time gradually increasing the amount of scope (or magnitude) that they *are* willing and able to "*confront*." This is especially applicable to *any* "terminal" associated with reactive *Mental Images*; or to "mass" or a "situation" in one's environment, associated as a particular *facet*, that automatically stimulates generation of a particular imprinted *Image*. When reactive-response phenomenon occurs, it is "out of communication"—and thereby "control"—of the operator.

Δ Δ Δ Δ Δ Δ Δ

Effectiveness of "Route-0" is dependent on an individual *creating* and *imagining* independent of memory, Beta-thought or "associative reason." When using "*creativeness processing*," in no way should an *Imaginary Scene* or *Mental Image* be a duplicate or "*facsimile*" of something that has actually happened unless the technique specifically calls for it. The basic purpose is to resume control of the very mechanisms and functions already causing "associations of identity" to be automatically fixed in "*facsimile imprints*" and ("reaction-response") experiences.

Use of the term "*Mental Image*" is not restricted to only "visual pictures" or "scenery" viewed from the Mind—or within one's Personal Universe. As a Seeker learns in former Mardukite Systemology studies, the *facets* of an *Imprint* include all sensory perceptions along with other associative information. In addition to scenes depicting places and things, "*Crystal Clear*" suggests several other significant *facets* including: brightness/dimness, time of day, time of year, sounds, noises, vocal tones, spoken language, hardness/softness to touch, weights, physical efforts, tastes, smells, temperature, humidity, motion/movement, body actions, body position... the potential list is nearly endless.

True *Imagination* originates from a "higher" point on the Standard Model than Beta-Thought. The source is outside of, or *exterior to, Beta-Existence* and the *Human Condition* POV, similar to "*Alpha-Thought.*" Alpha-Thought is referred to as "postulates" in past literature: a decision for something *to be* or *not to be*—a much higher level faculty of the Alpha-Spirit than "considerations" or associations taking place as "thinking." In fact, these higher faculties were once used to *create circuitry* of the Mind-System relied on for "thinking" as the willingness and ability of the Spirit began to slump into states of *Beta-Awareness*. Therefore, rehabilitation of *Creative Ability* allows an Alpha-Spirit the understanding and certainty to regain freedoms it holds in its truest basic state.

Perhaps one of the benefits to having a *Professional Pilot* administer "Route-0" early on is: an individual new to this systematic approach may repeatedly succumb to drowning in *real* scenes from their past—which is not the purpose of this technique. Benefit gained from *Creativeness Processing* is not as a result of a *Seeker* "facing up to" the Reality of *this* Physical Universe. Ability to *confront* this *Beta-Existence* is increased by practicing with their own Personal Universe—which is a truer spiritual existence they closed off responsibly communicating with, by unknowingly superimposing experience and POV of *Beta-Existence* using the *Human Condition.*

We are dealing with higher-level processing skills when dealing with *Creativeness Processing*. The range of "Creative Alpha-Thought" occurs in the domain of approximately "6.0" on the Standard Model—exceeding even the level of "Will-Intention" at "5." We are, of course, treating the POV of *Self* from a higher echelon than "Beta-Thought" or "surface thought" between "2.1" and "4.0" in the Mind-System; and naturally well beyond the "below-surface thought" of "reactive-response" mechanisms from "2.0" on downward. *Creativeness Processing* follows a logical systematic progression of work along the *Pathway*.

"Route-0" is intended to steer away from *real* "scenes" from *this* lifetime. *This* Physical Universe is not the only *Beta-Existence* an individual has occupied—nor is *this* lifetime the only incarnation-cycle that has been experienced in *this* Physical Universe. Unfortunately, the more an individual's POV is entrapped in *Beta-Existence*, the more their considerations fall "in line" or "in step" *with* the Physical Universe; and both become more solid.

When occupying low-levels of *Beta-Awareness* for too long, an individual often "mechanizes" their considerations—rather than willingly controlling "postulates" and knowingly directing "actions" to *create* effects.

An individual may also come to believe that Physical Universe is all there is—that it is the source of all the materials and energies within it; that they must use efforts of *Beta-Existence* in order to *Be* or *Have* anything in a Spiritual Universe. Yet, we discover that Alpha-Existence—and one's own Personal Universe—does not actually require any physical effort in order to *Create.* It only requires "postulates" or "considerations" that things *are,* in order *to be.*

Defragmenting (and controlling) "stores" of *Mental Imagery* seems particularly important for our *Spiritual Actualization.* An Alpha-Spirit "records" personal experience as *Mental Imagery* on a "*Spiritual Timeline*" and this is carried between lifetimes.

Some "**genetic memory**" is taken on from the continuing legacy of a *genetic vehicle* itself, but for the most part, it is our own *created* and *carried* "storage" of "things" that seems to affect our "mode of operation" the greatest—particularly when one identifies *Self* and the *genetic vehicle* as the same POV; at which point it is very hard to distinguish whether the Spirit *or* the "Body" is in command of the experience (or even differentiate identification).

An individual is often occupying a POV surrounded by "*screens*" and "*Imprints*" based on fixed locations in "space-time"; which they refer to as "experience." But these experiences tend to "change" the perception of what and who the Alpha-Spirit *thinks* they are; which is a big step down from *knowing.*

Communication of energy is retained as a continuous flow (or "wave") on a particular "channel" up to *now* in present time. In truth, an individual isn't really *stuck* anywhere themselves, so much as they have *stuck* "pictures." But the individual is no longer carrying *Actualized Awareness* on that "channel" in the *now*, which is why it is not "actual" *Awareness*, but instead, a "Reality" agreement that has kept a "presence" of *Awareness* fixed on some point in the "past."

The subject of "*Point-of-Views*" (POV) and "*Identity **Phases**" is treated in previous imaterials, but much like what is formerly described as "*Imprints*," "*facsimiles*" and "*snap-shots*," an application of these semantics seems more "correct" or understandable to a *Seeker* when approaching our Systemology on the basis of "*Mental Images.*"

> A *Point-of-View* (POV) *is* a "point" in which to view out from.
> These "*screens*" and "*filters*"—and circuits of *Mental Images*—
> are "*Identity-Phases*" an individual takes possession of;
> a pattern of "thinkingness" to substitute true "Knowingness."

In other words, an individual gets to "play a game" by assuming a "role"—and there is, of course, nothing wrong with the ability of the Alpha-Spirit *to Be* anything it chooses, so long as it *is* knowingly and willingly *choosing* to do so on its own Determinism; and is freely able to "get up" from the *Game*.

It is also important to realize *when* we *are* "playing a game"; and that the experience of moving little pieces around a board is not the same as the Identity of the *Self*—as Alpha-Spirit—that *is* the one playing the *Game* from a truer POV that is outside of—or *exterior* to —the Reality of the "game-board" dimension.

:: 3 ::
ESTABLISHING THE ALPHA-SPIRIT

The applied spiritual philosophy of Mardukite Systemology is rooted on one primary axiom: that the *Self* is a point or unit of *Spiritual Awareness* that we refer to as the *Alpha-Spirit*—the first-form or primary principle of "I-AM" that exists as a center of our true Alpha-Existence. The *Alpha-Spirit* has *one* true lifetime or continuous eternal Alpha *Beingness*, which is only separated by consideration of individual life-cycles (*incarnations*) that it has located its POV and identified as a *Beingness* to some level or plane of communication: in order to *do* something, in order to *have* something.

Self-Actualization, as it applies to our *Metahuman* and *Spiritual* "Systemology," is a higher state of *Beingness*, *exterior* to the *Human Condition*, that includes a true *Self-Honest* perception and realization of the "I-AM." Although the concept has appeared in the semantics of many spiritual philosophies and mystical religions in the past, the *map* is not the *territory*—and in the past 6,000 years we have found few demonstrations of these higher ideals experienced by individuals still entrapped within the POV of the *Human Condition*. In short: former attempts have not delivered satisfactory results.

It is true that many who remain suspended within "parameters" of the *Human Condition* cannot *actually* conceive of *Self* as a "Spirit" operating *exterior* to states of "feeling" (sensation) and "thinking" (associative reason), which have far too long substituted actual states of "*Knowingness*." Even magicians, mystics and priests—with their "astral bodies" and "mental bodies" and "etheric bodies"—are still yet unable to *realize* a *Self* that is not tied to forms and bodies. We have experienced phenomenon of *Seekers* in processing: some of which are stuck in a body POV; some of which are stuck in a head POV; some of which are stuck apart from wanting anything to do with control of "bodies," leaving the one they identify with to run completely on its own stimulus-response impulses.

As techniques within this book demonstrate, *Self-Actualization* of *Self-Awareness*—which we refer to as gradients of *Actualized Awareness*—is not being *Aware* of the "outside world" in *Beta-Existence*, or even of one's own *genetic vehicle* as separate from other "bodies" and forms—such as impressed by the mystic's "I–Not-I monad." Upper-level states of *Spiritual Awareness* (and "**Zu-Vision**") that often accompany the completed experience of "Beta-Defragmentation" (*Self-Honesty*) surpass even an *Aware-*

ness of operating one's own Mind-System, as we have realized that Descartes was only part of the way "there" when he stopped with "thinkingness."

"Individuality"—as the true nature of *Self*—is plotted high, one-to-one with the Alpha-Spirit, at "7.0" on the (*Zu-line*) Standard Model; higher than the range of even Alpha-Thought, which is the product of the Alpha-Spirit—and well beyond the level of "association" and, of course, "identity." The I-AM—*Self* as Alpha-Spirit—*is* an Individual. It is above any of the personality-persona-packages and *genetic vehicles* and *forms* that it may later attach to its own consideration of *Beingness*.

The basic methodology and "esoteric exercises" suggested are meant to assist a Seeker in more fully *realizing* the *Awareness* of "Spiritual Individuality" as opposed to the "*beta-personality*." The total *realization* of "I" as *Self* as Alpha-Spirit *is* a prerequisite to the attainment or *Actualization* of that high-level Awareness. This is not "word-play"; the fundamentals of this principle are outlined more clearly in the text "*Crystal Clear*" and many other collected works within the "*Systemology Handbook*" anthology. An actualization of these same fundamentals is also necessary for a *Seeker* or "*Master*" to achieve the highest goals for "*Wizard Level-0.*"

Practice of *Self-Awareness* falls within a subset of the domain of "*Imagination*," which we might refer to as "*POV Processing*" when administered systematically. Mystics and adepts would practice such exercises until they became as habitual to consider as the former considerations once were of being fixed within the *Human Condition*. Once the stable gains for Grade-IV have been achieved—as an individual reaches closer to total *Beta-Defragmentation*—the basic methodology of the present volume provides for more certain and lasting results.

The most critical component to operating "out" and *exterior* to this *Beta-Existence* is to attain a "crystal clear" certainty and realization—complete reality agreement—that the I-AM, *Self*, is: not the Mind, not the Body (or any *genetic vehicle*), but is commander and operator of these instruments in *Beta-Existence* from a point of true *Spiritual Awareness* that is not directly identifiable within the boundaries or parameters of the Physical Universe; it simply operates the machinery there. As an individual Alpha-Spirit becomes fragmented by "associative thought," the circuitry of the Mind-System offers POV that make it seem as though the individual *is* confined to within those Systems as a point of *Beingness*. But these "implants" are not truth—the total remedy for which falls within an even higher pursuit that we might refer to as "*Alpha-Defragmentation*."

In order to get a *realization* that *Self* is apart from—and the superior master to—the *genetic vehicle* as a "body," the Seeker should take time to focus *Awareness* through each part of the body: beginning with the feet and moving up into the head (and including the brain). In the past, mystics referred to these techniques as "*Activating the Light-Body*"—but, what we have found in our Systemology is that the *Awareness* itself act as "Light," not any "body." The Alpha-Spirit operates as an *Awareness* independent of *any* "body"—even a "spiritual" one. Of course, it has had many layers or levels or dimensions of "energetic body" assumed during its experiences through various "Universes"; and the more rigid, solid and condensed the energy-matter of a Universe, the more rigid and solid the *genetic vehicles* are for Life to communicate at that level of *Beta-Existence.*

When *Self* is operating as an *Awareness* "outside" sensory perceptions and energetic rigidity of a "material body," it may, in effect, *look into* the *genetic organism* and view its workings—practice in which will demonstrate that the "I" or *Self* is not identical or identified *as* the "body." For some it is easier to consider that they are operating *exterior* to this Physical Universe, but are "projecting" their *Awareness* to a POV that *is within* another form or "body" to experience a *Beingness.*

"*Creativeness Processing*" tends to operate best on a gradient scale of reality. A Seeker achieves best results by systematically confronting the "whole" in "parts" until they are prepared to maintain a full realization on the whole. For example, in basic treatment of a "body" using these methods:

Begin with full directed attention—as *Awareness*—on just the feet (even prior to treating the entire limb), or if that proves challenging at first, just one toe of one foot. Then concentrate that *Awareness* in that location; and using *Creative Ability*, imagine that: if the feet were nonexistent, then *Self* would still continue to exist unchanged as the Alpha-Spirit. Next, consider that they are useful tools for communicating activity when operating a *genetic vehicle* in the Physical Universe, but they are not the "feet" *of* the Spirit; and *Self* is not dependent on the feet of a "body" to act.

It is not the intention of the exercise to lessen or reject the *genetic vehicle.* An individual not getting along well in this lifetime—or experiencing a great deal of pain—is already excessively and compulsively "out of communication" with the "body." The *genetic vehicle* is exactly *that*—a vehicle or instrument or tool that should be cared for like we might any other "possession," but it should not be obsessed over or confused with an "identity" for *Self*.

The same exercise may be continued with the remainder of the body—the pelvic region (sexual organs), digestive tract, chest, arms, neck, head, *&tc.*—treating each with the same considerations, and moving off from each with the same realizations, as with the feet. When this is accomplished throughout the whole body, then the *Seeker* may look to consider the "body" as the whole of the *genetic vehicle*, an instrument useful for communication in the Physical Universe, biologically adapted to this *Beta-Existence*; but that *Self*—I-AM; Alpha-Spirit—*is* above and superior, independent and apart, from the *genetic vehicle*, and actually exists *exterior* to it in a "Spiritual Universe."

△ △ △ △ △ △ △

Practice of *exterior* "Zu-Vision"—the *Awareness POV* from *Self* independent of a "body" in *Beta-Existence*—ensues until a *Seeker* has an increased *realization* (reality) on the matter; and such practice requires "Imagination" and *Creative Ability* for that *realization* to become *actual.* Here, an individual should not invalidate their own experience—or a *Pilot* to invalidate a *Seeker*—concerning exactly what is happening within the realm of one's "Imagination" and Personal Universe. An individual "*imagines*" the potentiality of something until it is *realized*, from which it may then be *actual.*

It is interesting to discover a few workable premises for our Systemology scattered throughout human history—pieces waiting to be picked up and assembled into foundations for a new level of "*Metahuman*" understanding. For example: although more precise and systematic applications of our philosophy and spiritual techniques have since developed, we read similar suggestions for practical exercises voiced by *William Walker Atkinson (1862-1932)*—a founding pioneer of American "New Thought" over a century ago. We find written in his esoteric library of arcane teachings:

"Let the **Neophyte**, in imagination, leave the physical body and gaze upon the latter. A little mental practice will enable one to do this in imagination, thus bringing fully to mind the realization that it is possible for the *Self* to leave the body and dwell apart from it. When the mind has once grasped this possibility, the body will ever after be recognized as merely a physical machine, sheath or covering, of the *Self*—and one will never again commit the folly of identifying the 'I' with the physical body.

> "Then let the Neophyte imagine themselves leaving behind their physical body, until, as Holmes says: '...thou at length are free, leaving thine outgrown shell by life's unresting sea.' Let them then consider themselves as occupying other and different bodies, one at a time, in different phases of life and condition, in different ages, &tc. This will bring about the realization that *Self* is something higher and independent of the particular physical shell or machine that it is now using, and which it may have at one time considered identical with itself. Then will the particular body occupied seem, in reality, to be *'my body'* instead of *'I'* or *Me*."

Of course, where one does find persistent difficulties in managing the *genetic vehicle*—or some reoccurring psycho-somatic condition—it is found that the Mind-System "short-circuits" energetic communication flows to locations of the "body" that are injured. Being a composite system, that "part" of the *genetic vehicle* is treated unaffectionately by the "automated" network—and this causes the *pings* and *pains* of life to continue being *created* as they are, until *Self* resumes control and responsibility for total command of the "body."

As an experimental example, when a particular part of the *genetic vehicle* has been injured or pains us, we "prefer" to *not* "think" about it—or put any *Awareness* onto that region of the "body" because it "hurts." An individual can go as far as to start "damning" and "cursing" that part of their "body" and even succumb to lower levels of physical mutilation—all simply to avoid actually *confronting* that part of a "body" any longer. A better approach is to "imagine" *Mental Image* copies or create Self-Determined *facsimiles* of that "part" within the vicinity of the "part." This reestablishes that the "part" exists and that there is no "mental shortage" of energy passed to the "terminal." As a "Route-0" application of *Communication Processing*: an individual might even *imagine* literal spoken communications between *Self* and that "part," complete with "*Hello's*" (greetings) and **acknowledgments**.

By working with *Imagination* and *Creative Ability* in one's Personal Universe, a *Seeker* is able to focus more of its attentions on incidents and experiences *exterior* to this *Beta-Existence* as recorded on one's "*Spiritual Timeline.*" Recovery of "Past-Life" memory is set for a higher gradient in our Systemology—such as *Grade-V* (*Wizard Level-1*)—we are already building up greater certainty of *realization* toward our Alpha-Existence, which of course, must be attained and actualized as Reality for us to reach any further.

For now, the *Seeker* may contemplate—or *Imagine*—the etheric and incorporeal nature of the Alpha-Spirit that exists independent to *this* Universe. They may experience *Mental Imagery* conjured in old Mystic Initiations drawn from the *Chaldean Oracles*, wherein a "Neophyte"—while mentally separated from the "body"—is brought to confront *Mental Images* of the "rushing fires" or "swirling waters" and physical elements that would otherwise consume and waste the flesh, but to which has no hold or influence on the eternal qualities and individual existence of *Self* as a "unit" of *Spiritual Awareness.*

Alpha-Defragmentation theories *could* be derived from a variety of mystical teachings and esoteric exercises—however the longevity and certainty of their stable results has always been in question, even among most "New Age" practitioners, which still seem to operate more on the basis of "thought" and "Mind" than the "Spirit." Consequently, many are on a "route" that does little more than validate the traditions they participate in. There is no sense of *Knowingness* attained; only that there *must* be some *thing* to *know.* Therefore, these organizations and groups continue to swell in numbers composed of members that simply have not *realized* anything "greater than" whatever their new presentation of old beaten ideas has to offer.

Many ongoing "Alpha-Defragmentation" experiments at the Systemology Society are born from archaic "New Thought" formulas found in old forgotten corners of dusty esoteric libraries—many of which bare similarity to various methods of "Eastern Tradition," but we emphasize *Self-Actualization* as an Alpha-Spirit (a point of pure *Spiritual Awareness*) that is not the same as an "Astral Body" or even a "thought"—although it is capable of *creating* both "thoughts" and "bodies." The very fact that *Self* is able to *observe* all these faculties should suffice to *realize* that the actual I-AM is above, superior to, and fully able to control and command its own *creations.* Even when we are presented with something *externally*—creations of others—the actual *facsimile* "copy" we store in our databanks and all associations we identify with it are completely our own *creations* to manage.

∆ ∆ ∆ ∆ ∆ ∆ ∆

At the end of Grade-III work, during the "2019 Crystal Clear Convocation" a special process was given to attendees—and later published in "*Crystal Clear*"—originally referred to as "SP-2B-8A." When combining full knowledge of our "Standard Model" with the "Spheres of Existence," it was designated "Systemology Procedure 1-8-0." It became apparent after "*Tablets of Destiny*" that, even for basic "Beta-Defragmentation," a

Seeker would have to *realize* well "beyond" the point they sought to effectively *actualize* as a stable gain.

"Systemology Procedure 1-8-0" remains the primary experimental *route out,* if completely actualized, even should we later discover more direct or effective means of achieving similar *realizations.* Although the concept seems basic, the present author can attest to the fact that over two decades of experimental practice with variations of the same, used by different operators, continues to yield great results. For us, it first began in the late-1990's, when reading from *Atkinson's* esoteric library of arcane teachings:—

> "Let the Neophyte meditate upon the great Ocean of Life in which the individual entities are but focal Centers of Consciousness and Force. Let them picture themselves, in imagination, as being an actual Center, with all the Universe revolving around them; see themselves as the pivot around which the Universe moves—the Central Sun around which the infinite world and planets circle in their cosmic flight. Let them feel themselves to be the focal Center of the Cosmos.

> "And this is indeed, in accordance with the centuries of old occult axiom, which informs us that 'the Cosmos is infinite—its circumference is nowhere—its center is everywhere.' Let the Neophyte lose all thought of the outside world in this meditation—let them regard it as totally unmanifest if they like—but see *Self* in Actual Existence and in Full Power. Let them realize 'I-AM' to the fullest extent of their power of imagination and conception."

Development of "Systemology Procedure 1-8-0" began with the various routes for which it was named for—though it is also named for the compass-direction of our *Pathway,* which is 180-degrees (*back the way we came*). Its "routes" were given as advanced *Grade-III* material, but allow progressive increased *realization* (personal reality) with practice.

The text for *"Crystal Clear"* only included directions for one of them: "Proc. 180, Route-1" (*SP-2B-8A*) exactly as given below. This was originally intended to move *Awareness* "out" from the *genetic vehicle* to personally experience one's impressions of *each* "Sphere of Existence"— along the "Zu-line"—on their approach to *Infinity;* but it was never written as such in the instructions and previously is only described that way at the Academy (*Professional Piloting Flight School*).

"Systemology Procedure 180, Route 8" is given in the *"Creative Ability Test"* (CAT), emphasizing its ultimate destination: the "Infinity of Nothingness"—directly experiencing the "Infinity of Nothingness" in all directions. The third and final tested demonstration is "Proc. 180, Route 0," whereby an individual directs their *Beingness* as an Alpha-Command to any point in space-time for any Universe—though it is generally practiced with the local planet and local solar system first. This would include *Processing Command Lines* (PCLs) such as "*Be* outside the body" or "*Be* above the Earth" and other similar practices that effectively prepare an individual to operate independent of the *genetic vehicle* (in "*Zu-Vision*").

To sum up very concisely—we have an advanced methodology called "Systemology Procedure 180" that includes practice of the following formula:

(1) Self-Awareness;

(8) Nothingness; and

(0) Beingness.

In essence, it is this basic applied philosophy that actually provides us with high-level defragmentation. However, other practices, procedures and methods of systematic processing are also employed in order to increase ability and certainty of reach that an individual actually has to attain higher-levels. This would be no great task *if* it were just a matter of subtly reminding everyone of their *true Spiritual nature*; but most individuals have been systematically plunged into *Beta-Existence* (and the *Human Condition*) pretty deeply—so, it requires a greater systematic approach to allow someone stable lasting results along the way *through and out* of the **dross**.

Δ Δ Δ Δ Δ Δ

For reference purposes, the procedural instructions for "*Systemology 1-8-0, Route-1*" are given below exactly as they first appear in the text "*Crystal Clear*." This same formula can be applied for each of the "*Spheres of Existence*."[*]

"SYSTEMOLOGY 1-8-0, ROUTE-1"

—IMAGINE your Awareness as outside and *exterior* to the body.
—FOCUS your *Awareness* on the *Eighth Sphere* of *Infinity*.
—IMAGINE the *Infinity* of *Nothingness* extending out "infinitely" on all sides as a great Ocean of Cosmic Consciousness.

---

[*]   1) Self; 2) Home; 3) Groups; 4) Humanity; 5) Life on Earth; 6) The Physical Universe; 7) The Spiritual Existence; and 8) Infinity.

—FOCUS your *Awareness* from *Self* as a singular focal point of individuated consciousness in the center of the *Infinite Ocean.*

—SENSE that the *Nothingness-Space* all around you is rising up as tides and wave-actions of invisible motion; its abyssal stillness broken by the singular point that is *You.*

—SENSE that as you press your *Awareness* against the *Nothingness*, there is no resistance, there is no sensation—no feeling of any kind.

—IMAGINE your totality of *Awareness* as the singular focal point of *Infinity*—then REALIZE that the waves you see crashing up against you and rippling into *Infinity* are an extension of your every thought, will and action.

—REALIZE that you are the *Alpha Spirit*; that "wave peak" in an otherwise *Infinity of Nothingness* stretching out within and back off all that was, is and ever will.

—REALIZE that your conscious *Awareness* as "I", your direction of WILL as *Alpha Spirit*, and the "central wave peak" born out of *Infinity* are all the same pure individuated ZU—are all *One; Infinity; None.*

—WILL yourself to project *Awareness* ahead of you and see an extension of this ZU as your projection of Identity extending infinitely in front of you—all the way to the *zero-point-continuity* of existence—and back to *Infinity.*

—REPEAT this several times, IMAGINING this ZU as a *Clear Light* radiant extension from *Self*, directed across *Infinity* to *Zero-point* and back to *Infinity*; then REALIZE that you are dissolving and wiping out all *fragmentation* from the channel as you direct the *Clear Light.*

—REPEAT this several times, until you feel confidant in your current results for this cycle of work.

—RECALL the instance you decided to start this present *session*—get a sense of the Intention you *Willed* to begin the session.

—REALIZE that your *beta-Awareness* and the true WILL of the Alpha Spirit are One continuous stream and that the *Self* is superior to, and master of, the *genetic vehicle*; End the session.

:: 4 ::
THE CONQUEST OF BETA-EXISTENCE, MENTAL IMAGERY AND IMPRINTING

"A faithful reproduction of the world around us collapses, and our world image, far from being identically duplicate with the 'real world', becomes but our specific interpretation of that world; our world is but *our* version of *the* world."

—*J.J. Van der Leeuw*

Imagination takes place "above" *Beta-Awareness* and is even superior to the WILL of an individual, for it effectively initiates the impulse for what a *Being* is "willing"—and how that will later correspond to reasoning, efforts and action that take place in *Beta-Existence. Imagination* most closely resembles the *Creative Ability* of the *Alpha-Spirit* in its basic natural state, existing in a personal Spiritual Universe that is receptive to *spontaneous creation.* Such instantaneous "manifestation" is not as apparent in *Beta-Existence,* where an individual uses a *genetic vehicle* to apply limited physical effort toward changing *energy-matter* of the Physical Universe and *create* effects in *Beta-Existence.*

Existence of "I-AM" *Self* as Alpha-Spirit is not dependent on any *survival* in *Beta-Existence,* except as the consideration of playing a "game" *here* and being able to continue the "role" and "personality" of a *genetic vehicle* that is equipped for communicating efforts of "change" in *Beta-Existence.* This is, of course, not the only Universe we could be operating in—but so long as we are fixed to the low-level considerations of the *Human Condition* as an "identity," it *appears* as if it is the "only game in town."

With *Imagination,* an individual is employing high-levels of *Creative Ability* as an Alpha-Spirit independent of considerations tied to the *Human Condition.* The highest function of the Alpha-Spirit is *Creation;* and this ability is reduced to functions of a Mind-System and associative reasoning when fixed to a *Human Condition* POV. *Life,* as operating in *Beta-Existence,* is simply playing a "game" of *survival*—trying to "get along" as best as possible, using associative reasoning of the Mind-System (rather than *Imagination*) to "solve problems" of *survival;* all the while waiting for something or someone *else* to open the prison-gates. Yet, it is only by our own consideration and realizations (or lack thereof) that keep us *creating* the "Gates" as intact and guarded.

Practice and certainty of *Creative Ability* is **paramount** to a *Seeker* being able to "release the hold" on *Beta-Existence* and its *Imprints,* knowing they are completely capable of *creating* any of these *Mental Images* again—and therefore not restricted only to those which have been *impressed* strongly upon them by other "forces" as *Cause*. The Alpha-Spirit has become more comfortable with *somethings*—where something is better than nothing—in preference to *confronting* the Infinity of Nothingness. This is resolved by providing an individual with certainty that they can *have* anything they can *create* at any moment; thus, they need not compulsively cling to what is keeping them "down."

An individual believes—or *feels*—as though they "*have*" something by retaining significances of past *Imprinted Imagery*, which they tend to maintain as a valid "present-time" POV. The logic behind this, of course, being that the experience must have some "value" or "*be something*" (solid) of which can be used at a later time—otherwise why would we keep it in storage. The individual starts wanting to keep it all—after having been implanted with the concept of "*loss*"—and starts energetically *pulling* these "solids" in on the "body" from the perspective of *Self* being *interior* to the *genetic vehicle*. This validates and strengthens entrapment of *Self* "inside" the *Human Condition*. Even the idea of "pushing" things *away* from *interior* to the *Human Condition* creates a "resistance" or "energetic turbulence" *against* some *thing*, adding further "solidity" to it as a *thing*. It is no wonder that the Alpha-Spirit found itself in quite a "spiritual trap" entering the Physical Universe.

While confined to the *Human Condition* or any *Beta-Existence*, a *Seeker* is using automated mechanisms to consistently "pull in" *Mental Images, Encoded Events, Thoughtform Beliefs*—all of which are the very *Imprinting* that is keeping them "trapped" *in* their present "mode" or Reality (level of realization). The mechanistic defense given to their compulsive creation, when *confronted* directly in systematic processing, is: "*but, they did happen...*"—and it is true: these are *Images* imprinted from *real* events that are located to some specific space and time; but that space and time is not *here* and *now*. Thereafter, these *Images* are simply maintained as "coiled energy" stores that fix (what would otherwise be unlimited) *Awareness* to "compulsive creation" outside total *Self-Determinism*.

Imprinted "snap-shots" often result from repeated "stops"—injury, punishment, going out of communication—all of which cause an individual to retreat (or retract or withdraw) from "control" on a particular communication line or "channel." Or, they might become "obsessive" about it. But neither extreme (tendency) provides for proper energy flow. The unwillingness to handle it proper forms energetic barriers—false *Mental Imagery* as a "screen," "filter" or "wall" in place of a *Self-determined* flow connected with some "terminal" or "stimulus."

Systematic processing has revealed that much of what we consider "personal fragmentation" results from an inherent nature to *create* and *collect*—in this case: "pictures" of experience—and to be able to carry evidence of this experience in the form of "energetically charged mementos"—and *Imprints* of the "moment"—that are kept in place as signals or flags intended to prevent an individual from having to experience such *again*. This also breaks down an individual's *Self-Determinism* and ability to "duplicate" intentions with full *Awareness.*

While it may seem fine to remember an incident as a warning to keep from "making the same mistakes," those conditions of the past are no longer present as "the same" ever again—and many other *facets* of experience are also tied to an *Imprint*, meaning that its inhibiting factors extend to domains aside from just that one exact scenario.

Experiences of "spiritual advisement" and "systematic processing" within our tradition also revealed that: individuals are likely to reflect their "mode" of handling *Imprints* and *Mental Imagery* in the same manner they treat physical "objects"; since both are "masses." Many individuals have a tendency to be irresponsible about "masses"—whether compulsively "collective" or "destructive" in that regard. A "psychotic" may be hell-bent only on destruction of things in absence of any realized ability to *create*. But in most cases, it will be found that a *Seeker* is as well off as they are able to freely "rid themselves" of "masses" and have more "space"; and as bad off as they are surrounded by physical objects and "mental masses" with no "space" for *Beingness*. A *Being* that truly *Knows* they can *Create* at any instant will find little value (or need for) storing and carrying *mass*.

When we consider what the Standard Model (*Zu-line*) of Systemology represents—in terms of *Space-Time Energy-Matter*—the point of *Beingness* for an individuated Alpha-Spirit ("7.0") is all *Space* with nothing really happening within it. The spiritual unit of *Awareness* that is "I-AM"-*Self* certainly is not a "mass" in itself, which is why it is relatively "Eternal." As we move (down the "Model") into the Personal Universe and Alpha-Thought (toward "6.0") generated by an Alpha-Spirit, we begin to observe "action" or else "space with motion" in it—or else "energy."

As best we can understand, the energy potential at this level of operation by the Spirit is essentially unlimited. However, as more and more energy is created finitely, we get a condensation of space. Thus, by a directed concentration of the spiritual (Alpha) equivalent of "effort"—which is Will ("5.0")—we arrive at an "object" or "*mental mass.*" In theory: *space* condenses as *energy*, which condenses into *matter*; and the closer and more "solid" the *matter*, the more finite the appearance of *time* as "action across/over distance." This would explain the changing conditions as we move into "lower" Universes and "shorter" cycles of action (sometimes depicted in "wave-form" as "frequency").

It is difficult to introduce the Systemology of *Imagination* and its *Mental Image Pictures* (thought-images) without also differentiating these "knowingly" *Self-created Images* from other **thought-waves**; which is to say "thought-forms" or "*thoughtforms*"—the energetic patterns surrounding an individual—that they are creating, usually on automatic or else "unknowingly." Some past philosophies have treated these thought-forms as everything from "auras" to "light shields" to "entities"—because there *is* a resulting phenomenon that mystics and spiritualists have long sought to classify; but never as the thing actually *is*, and always in combination with some other semantics or paradigm of understanding.

Δ Δ Δ Δ Δ Δ Δ

When we treat the Systemology of *Creative Ability*, a *Seeker* increases their ability to knowingly manage "*mental pictures,*" but it is not only the "thought-image" being handled, so much as the energetic "thought-forms" attached to it. Frequencies of various energies impress against the fields of *Beta-Existence* and *Self* must then process this information into what it considers "recognizable."

This means external energy is received by a sensor,
relayed on a communication line,
hits against a "screen" of sorts
and then the Alpha-Spirit *looks* at *that* "image"
rather than *confronting* the actual energy-flow itself.

From this, the concept of the "*Mental Image*" is created—and we say "mental" because it is using the "field" of the Mind as a backdrop to do this; and we are not restricting this idea to only a "Human Mind," but the actual "field" of mental energy does enshroud the *Human Condition* when operating such a *genetic vehicle.* It is also why someone operating *interior* to a fragmented Mind-System has difficulty *realizing* the goals of Systemology Wizard Grades—and why we first begin a Seeker with former "Routes" and materials.

The value of our applied spiritual philosophy—as an effective technology—is proved to an individual only by application: to the **acid-test** of everyday life. A "*Systemologist*" has entire Universes for a laboratory. As we are concerned with *Creative Ability*, this "spiritual technology" is a living truth only when applied. It provides a *Seeker* with little more than mental occupation as "knowledge" when treated solely as an intellectual pursuit. *Creativity* comes not from having and accumulating a collection of dry postulates, but in the act of *creating energy*.

Goals for our work are meant to be treated in the "objective" world that a *Seeker* experiences everyday. Although we may establish objective truths, the "knowledge" earned from book-learning alone becomes a very "subjective" ordeal. A Systemologist is not deluded into thinking that there is not "objective" Physical Universe "out there" as a shared meeting ground of communications at this level of *Beta-Existence* agreements (reality).

> Issues only emerge when this Physical Universe—and its reality agreements—are confused with the true nature of *Self* and its own truer "Alpha" existence, operating from within a Spiritual Universe. The *Human Condition* is often implanted to *forget* this key point; and it seems that it cannot be simply and subtly reminded—thus, we have our systematic methods for a *Seeker* to gradually work this out for themselves, called "processing."

Systematic processing employed at the former "Master Level" (*Grade-III*) of Systemology—and "Route-3" from (*Grade-IV*) "*Metahuman Destinations*"—should have at least increased a *Seeker's* reality on the basic facts that:

> a) the "Alpha-Spirit" operates as an individual "I-AM"-*Self*,
> b) in command of a *genetic vehicle*
> c) by using a "Mind-System."

This much should at least be demonstrable before moving forward. At "Wizard Levels," we are concerned with establishing the Alpha-Spirit as a *creative* force capable of generating space-time energy-matter; at the very least, from within their own Personal Universe. Furthermore, the "Wizard Levels" must establish a Reality for the *Seeker* that:

> *a*) there *is* a "Personal Universe" or "Home-World Universe" that the Alpha-Spirit is native to in its original basic state of existence;
> *b*) that the I-AM-*Self* (as this Spirit or point of *Awareness*) exists independent of a *genetic vehicle*—just as much as we are not our

"cars"; and

c) that an individual can operate from a truer POV remote from a body—*exterior* to the body and *beta-fragmented* "Mind-System."

Although *death* is also a direct transition point of *Awareness* "exterior" to the command of a specific *genetic vehicle*, thousands of years of practices by various monks and shamans demonstrate that "alternative states" have been hit upon many times by the *living*. But in the case of death, the *genetic vehicle* and considerations of its operator have become the over-whelming effect of *external* forces—and the Alpha Spirit abandons control of the organism. Of course, if not freed from an implanted Mind-System (encoded by *beta-existence*), the individual typically remains fixed to this Physical Universe in their next "incarnation" experiences.

Contrary to "thought-formed beliefs" established by various religions in the past 6,000 years, it is far more logical and demonstrable—not to men-tion more certain in regards to one's own *Self-knowledge*—that we have experienced "past-lives" and continue our "spiritual existence" beyond this one. The idea of an "eternal stopping point" seems to defy the truth. Each one of us already has some reality on a spiritual past. Of course, "Mind-System" implants do not allow proper memory of past-lives on an individual's "*Spiritual Timeline*" very easily. The matter is not particularly dealt with in our "basic" Systemology work due to its likelihood of dis-tracting from responsibilities of *this* life, while they are still increasing basic horsepower of *Actualized Awareness* enough to properly *confront* the reality of higher "levels."

There is a vague concept relayed in the semantics available in *beta-exist-ence* regarding what is most primitively understood as a contrast between an "external world" environment (or "objective" Physical Uni-verse) and the "internal" (subjective) "consciousness" of the "I" or "Eye of the Observer." Our Systemology breaks down these concepts *systemat-ically*—as External, Internal, Interior and Exterior.

The basic issue of being *fixed* or *stuck* "*interior*" to the *Human Condition* is just *that*: it *is* a condition—a conditional parameter or limitation of standard-issue "*internal*" sensory perception of an "*external*" environ-ment. Yet, different *Awareness* levels, which incidentally have nothing to do with a "body," can allow a wider (or narrower) "reality" or "scope" of consideration—and potential *realization*—by which to evaluate en-ergy-flows and/or directly establish a *Knowingness*.

Although there are many levels of condensation—each essentially a Uni-verse unto itself—the basic systemology behind space, time, energy and matter, seem to be mostly in common across all levels as we understand them. In the Physical Universe, we are dealing with a *beta-existence* that still operates on similar principles as "higher ones," but the manifestations present—and our standard-issue faculties to perceive them—fall in a very low-level range of existence for experience.

> An individual while maintaining considerations for a POV rigidly fixed *interior* to the standard-issue *Human Condition* is unable to *confront* the "actuality" of energy-matter directly and must therefore rely on "organs" and "sensory screens" of a *genetic vehicle* to give them "cues" of an *external* world.

That alone should trigger some signals that a true existence of *Self* could not actually be confined to this *beta-existence* when all indicators seem to illuminate the now apparent fact that it remote-operates the experience "from outside."

> This was one of the frustrating issues the present author has found with semantics of "remote viewing"—because the true position of *Self* is always "remote" from a *body*, it just seems to be particularly attached to one as an exclusive POV. That *Self* can also direct its viewpoints *elsewhere*—or into other objects—is no more or less "remote" than its fixing or localizing a POV to a *genetic vehicle.*

△ △ △ △ △ △

Apart from the *Infinity of Nothingness*, the *Self* exists as a point or unit of *Spiritual Awareness* as the "I-AM" amidst that *Sea of Infinity*. All else is Universes—or what some have called "dimensions"—and we typically *know* them by their "space" and "forms" existing against a background matrix, which is itself backed by *Nothingness.* So, the Alpha-Spirit *creates* and *experiences* a "World of Lights" no matter what level of condensation those *spots* and *points* may manifest as.

Even in the Physical Universe, the green trees and blue skies and yellow suns and white clouds are all simple demonstrations of color and form, which is information transferred onto a screen and then given some sense of conceptual "reality" meaning. Otherwise, all we really have is *forms* and *colors*—the same as what we are likely to perceive as the *thoughtformed* "ridges" enshrouding the *Beingness* of *Self* and what mystics and esoteric practitioners have termed "auric bodies" or "astral shields" and the like. Condensation of universal energy-matter can obviously get as solid as a *genetic vehicle*—or even a "rock."

Mental Imagery is always *generated* with energy created by *Self*, even when it is a "response" to some external stimulus and/or created using automatic-mechanisms and "filter-screens"—such as information received through "eyes" of a *genetic vehicle* and then broadcast as an "image" in the *"Mind's Eye"* (as it used to be called; and as people generally are likely to understand it at first), which is then viewed by *Self*. But all that is actually taking place is an encounter with the *forms* and *colors* of an "impression."

These "impressions" give our directed *Awareness* "cues" of an objective Physical Universe (*beta-existence*)—qualities of light, color and form, which make up the visual *facets* of the images we register as our "view" of an "external" environment. These varying "qualities" are treated as *facets* of the experience in "systematic processing"—each *facet* representing some type of recognizable energy or potential perception that can be recorded. All of the significance and meaning—all of the data for reasoning and future evaluation—is entirely *Self*-generated and maintained as an experience. But the truth is that the considerations of the *imagery* are completely up to an individual to determine; as theosophical philosopher, *J.J. Van der Leeuw*, even suggests:—

> "We, as it were, clothe the nakedness of the unknown reality with the image produced in our consciousness. The same facts, which are true for the sense of vision, hold good for our perception through any of the senses; thus there is no question of 'should' but in our consciousness, no question of 'taste' or 'smell' but in our consciousness, no question of 'hardness' or 'softness', of 'heaviness' or 'lightness' but in our consciousness; our entire world-image is an image arising on our consciousness because of the action on that consciousness by some 'unknown reality'."

We address this directly in with the systematic procedure **'Bell, Book and Candle'** treated at great length in the text *"Metahuman Destinations"*—a procedure included in the "Creative Ability Test" (CAT) for *Liber-3D*. The "objective" Physical Universe is the external other-determined force impressing actions that *Van der Leeuw* refers to as the "mysterious unknown reality"—because to an individual operating at low-levels of *Beta-Awareness* or even fixed within the *Human Condition* at all, an "outside world" is continuously hungry for our *attentions*. It prompts compulsive *looking* and *validation* by maintaining itself as a Mystery. It literally gets participants to do all the work in continuing the perception of its existence—even though an individual is really only interacting with a "world-image" that they themselves have created and then later refer to as an experience happening *to* them.

The form and **fodder** of the Physical Body (*genetic vehicle*) is also a part of *Beta-Existence*—a part of the projected "world image" of a personal reality experience in a projected "world image" of a Physical Universe. Due to Mind-System circuitry with the *Human Condition* and the amount of time the POV is validated or "snapped-in" tighter through pains and pleasures and other contact with the Physical Universe (its energetic frequency vibrations and particles), the **physiology** and sensory perception of the *genetic vehicle* incites "internal" stimulation of a type that registers "familiar" enough to seem as though *it* is actually happening *to* the Alpha-Spirit, when it is only happening in *beta-existence*. *Van der Leeuw* goes on from earlier:—

> "It is the peculiar relation in which we stand to our own body, the intimate link we have with it and which we do not have with regard to any other object in the outer world, which makes us feel that we know all about its reality. We have an *inside* feeling of our body which we do not have in regard to a stone or a tree, our body appears to us as part of ourselves and we forget that it is as much part of that *outer* world as the tree or the stone, and that our perception of it as a visible and tangible object takes place in just the same way as our perception of the tree or of the stone. Even the *inner* feeling we have of our body is but a variety of sense-perception which exists for our body alone..."

We come to the conclusion that: all perceptions of an objective reality are *Self-created* or generated based on impressions or suggestions from participation (reality agreement) with a Universe—regardless of what considerations or assignments of value are given to those perceptions. It is quite clear that the standard-issue Human operator is not aware of any higher *Creative Ability* to change the nature of objective reality at will —or we would expect that they would not manifest the experience and "world image" (Reality) that they ("knowingly") perceive.

Some individuals find it incredibly difficult to have any "reality" on what is *Imagined* and *Created* as *Mental Imagery* within one's own "Personal Universe"—or the "illusive" energetic qualities described of these "higher metaphysical" dimensions. But!—even when dealing with the more condensed "concrete solidity" of the Physical Universe, *Self* as the Alpha-Spirit is still interacting with *fields* and *screens* and treating the "reality" communicated as *Mental Imagery.* In either case, whether experiencing a "Personal Universe" (or a "Physical Universe"), the individual, as a *Spiritual Awareness*, is interacting from a point *exterior* to the projected images of a holographic-reality that appear viewable on the *"screen"* of perception and are treated as "experience."

> This would all just be simple intellectual curiosities to ponder in our "free time" were it not for how detrimental these truths are to the *Human Experience* and the liberation of the *Human Spirit* to higher states.

This information would be lost in large pools of untested philosophy if it were not the case that the Mind-System is implanted to accumulate programming and collect encoding to validate fixed "associations of identity" and rigid considerations for what things *are. Van der Leeuw* reminds us with a clear message:—

> "When an event takes place in this world of reality, there is produced, in the consciousness of each creature concerned, an *Awareness*, or *mental image*, which is the event as we see it. Unreality or illusion never resides in the event, or the thing in itself, nor even in my interpretation of it, which is true enough *for me*, but in the fact that I take my interpretation to be the thing in itself—**exacting** to it the stature of an absolute and independent reality.

> "The illusion or unreality is neither in the thing itself, nor in the image produced in my consciousness by that thing—but in my conception of the image in my consciousness as the thing in itself; as an object existing independent of my consciousness. We can see the way we have to go: we must withdraw ourselves from the enticing images of our own production and turn towards that center through which the production of our world image takes place—*Self* as a unit of *Awareness*."

We are quite close to completing a final leg on the current cycle of the spiral-like *Spiritual Timeline*; and generally by the end of such cycles of action, everything equals everything else and a Universe collapses into yet one more level of condensation. If we allow identification of *Beingness* to get much lower, there is less likelihood for an individual to get themselves *through and out* again.

Effective systematic processing should include an increased *Awareness* along with the ability to clearly differentiate—rather than associate and categorize—the qualities of *energies* and *forms* and Universes encountered.

First we *clear* the *slate*; then we can truly *create.*

:: 5 ::
PERSONALITY PACKAGES, IDENTITY PHASES
AND VIEWPOINTS OF REALITY

"As this processing continues, the Neophyte will find, much to their surprise, that while their most cherished and firmly rooted characteristics are sheared away from them, *Self* remains. They will find that when all their mental feelings, as well as the objects thereof, are removed from their mental vision, they, themselves, as *Self*, remain. They will find a *Something* remaining, that is back of, underneath and at the basic center of all these feelings and characteristics, and which persists in full vigor when the rest has been stripped away."
—*William Walker Atkinson*

"Personality-Persona-Programs" or "identity-phases" are taken up in previous Systemology publications—though, even at Grade-IV, one is not yet likely to be totally free of such considerations. Until then, we continue to treat this cycle of systematic components at each gradient step—simply at a higher level of *realization*. Note that:

of everything that is *identifiable* and *apparent*
in the course of one's *Ascension* up the *Pathway*,
it is perhaps the sense of *Self*, *Awareness* or
knowledge of *Self* and image of *Self*
that is most noticeably refined as a *Seeker* progresses
with their work from our Systemology.

Just as Universes condense as we perceive lower and lower levels of existence, working our way back up through the *Gates* requires increasingly greater degrees of personal refinement. Metaphorically speaking, an individual is essentially purging additional layers of low-level artificiality with each *Grade* and *Gate*. Only energy-matter of a specific type or frequency is manifest at each tier of the *Pathway*—and behind each *Gateway to Infinity*.

An individual is allowed to carry less and less "mass"—even "mental mass"—along with them at each level of ascent. It is the "mass"—the rigidly fixed "resistance" on the *Zu-line*—that keeps an individual's POV or sense of *Beingness* suspended by the low-level "gravity" and tethered to a locatable mass that "forces" can act upon.

When we've applied **"game theory"** to our Systemology—regarding Universes of *action* and "game-play"—we often refer to the individual as a "player." This immediately denotes that we are assuming a "role" in which to "play" a "game" toward a specific *goal*, which is what lets *Self* "have" something to "do" with any 'randomity' (or other-determinism). One often forgets that this is what is happening in *beta-existence.*

In a previous lesson, we discussed placing an *Awareness* "on" and then "dismissing" the characteristic components of the *genetic vehicle* as a "body"—the same methodology can be applied to scanning and locating the characteristics inherent in the "personality package" or "identity phase" that a *Seeker* is "wearing" as a "player" in this "game."

Of course, it requires a bit of systematic processing and *Self-analysis* to properly identify the "phase" an individual is operating from. This is something that is given attention right from the beginning with the texts "*Tablets of Destiny*" and "*Crystal Clear.*" An individual must also first understand what an "identity-phase" is, along with its components. Most often they come under the heading of "tendencies" and "inclina-tions" that are over-identified with *Self* or "I-AM"—when really they belong to the "personality package" one is wearing as the "Me" or "My" in order to "play a game."

An individual is already a *Being*, maintaining a *Beingness* that is the I-AM-*Self* or Alpha-Spirit (at "7.0" on our Standard Model) and which, in its own "Personal Universe" can *Create* anything and *Know* anything by *Be-ing* it (and then not) without a concern of fragmentation. And that *is* our most basic state—but that isn't a *game.*

> As the Alpha-Spirit seeks to *do* something apart from *Beingness* as *Self* in this basic state, we enter a realm of "Universes" and "Games" (at "6.0") just subordinate to former superior "Creative Universes." Below or after the "Game Universes" an Alpha-Spirit began emphasizing use of "Will" (at "5.0") during "past-lives" in a "Magical Universe" (sometimes referred to as the "Magic King-dom" in our *Systemology Wizard Levels*), which immediately pre-ceded the type of effort-based "mechanistic" "electrons-on-a-wire" *beta-existence* that we identify as this "Physical Universe."

Thus:

<u>BASIC PROCESSION OF UNIVERSE CONDENSATION</u>

```
||HOME BASE||
    —> Creative Universes
        —> Games Dimensions
            —> Magic Kingdom
                —> Physical Universe
```

The key to understanding "phases"—particularly the unknowing ("unconscious") assumption of various roles, personalities and attributes—as with other elements of our Systemology, is through personal practice. If an individual is able to knowingly ("consciously") *create*, greater control may be attained over the "automatic-mechanism" that *Self* has continuously and obsessively *creating* on its own behalf. In this instance, *Imagination* plays a key role in the resolution.

"Systemology Procedure 1-8-0, Route-1" is written out with a series of progressive steps that essentially just shoot the individual off toward *"Infinity"* as a preparation for *"Proc. 180, Route-8,"* which is the instantaneous experience of the *"Infinity of Nothingness" on command.* But, the full intention behind this procedure as an exercise is not so clearly given in the original relay of the steps and so it is worth us reiterating the correction: an individual is meant to practice ("Imagine") *Beingness* of as many different "types" as possible within *each* "Sphere of Existence" *progressively* up *to* the *"Infinity of Nothingness."* This full version described here is what effectively prepares a *Seeker* for applying "Proc. 180, Route-0," which is the practice of instantaneous experience of *any "Beingness"* or *"POV" on command.*

At first, *facets* of a "personality package" (a "role") or "Identity-Phase" (representative of a "specific person") may be more difficult to identify and analyze. It is often easier to first locate facets of a "role" because they are more widely understood **archetypes** with socially educated definitions. For example: a mother, a father, a teacher, a priest, a lawyer, a politician—these are all "roles" that have certain attributes, characteristics or *facets* "associated" with them as a consideration. When we speak of "Identity-Phases," we mean more specifically the attributes, characteristics or *facets* "associated" with a *specific* individual: their beliefs, the way they talk, certain phrases they say, the mannerisms and behaviors—even physical ailments can be assimilated from persons we know and have assumed the "phase" of.

After working through a list of all roles and persons, the *Seeker* is likely to identify certain ones that correlate with significant "terminals" and "implants" in their own lifetime—or lifetimes. Some of this processing can be assisted greatly by mechanical **bio-feedback** aids (such as discussed in *The Way of the Wizard* or *Liber-Three*) to pinpoint "terminals" and "points" on the *Spiritual Timeline* where a *Seeker* is carrying "emotional encoding." It is found that heavy charges of energetic "programming" can actually raise detectable levels of "mass/resistance" in the fields surrounding the *genetic vehicle*. In the past, such observations were treated with exclusively mystical or esoteric semantics, which simply are not as workable with out present understanding of the *Pathway.*

Regardless of using any processing aids to the technique, the basic systematic methodology for uncovering this information follows rules of *Analytical Processing, Route-2* (given in *"Crystal Clear"* or *"The Systemology Handbook"*)—particularly when applying "alternating" PCLs. This continues until a *Seeker* comes to the *realization* that the role is simply a reality agreement; the specific identity/person (from their past) is not actually present; and none of these have anything to do with the true individual *Self*, which lies at the center, which has been *looking* out through a lens or POV that is artificial to the Alpha-Spirit.

PHASES: IDENTIFIER-SEPARATION (ALTERNATING BASIC 3D)
  —How are you similar to ___ ?
  —How are you different from ___ ?

△ △ △ △ △ △

Self-Directing POV is simply a matter of *attention* as *Awareness.* Systematic processing is designed to uncover "where" (or on "what") *attention* is compulsively fixed; and in the case of confusions and energetic dispersals, "where" (or on "what") it is unable to be concentrated or fixed upon by command of *Self.* Rather than treating "energies" directly, a *Seeker* is introduced to mechanics of directing attention with "command of the Mind–Body connection"—as explored in *"Metahuman Destinations."*

Furthermore, the ability to manage responsibility for thought activity, communications, ability to change or remain the same, attitudes of **protest**, abilities to assist and help *Life* achieve higher states of *Being*, and the circuitry carrying betrayal on all "Spheres of Existence," is also described (primarily in Unit-Three, *Liber-3C*) of *"Metahuman Destinations."* Such is an immediate precursor to systematic processing of our present work for *"Wizard Level-0."*

Collected work from our previous materials should not be overlooked if a *Seeker* expects to achieve the highest level of *Self-Actualization* using this present volume. Previous work moved forward along an effective gradient scale. Comprehension and use of former material allows us to introduce POV or *"location-based processing"* in Grade-IV, which directly moves us outside the confines of emphasizing only *Beta-Awareness* and the Mind-System, and concentrating more of our attention on *Creative Abilities* and progressive mastery of *"Zu-Vision."*

In its original state—and occupying a "Home Universe"
—the Alpha-Spirit, quite god-like is able to *Create* and *Be*
any thing, uninhibited and devoid of external forces,
other-determined creations, and enforced considerations.

Some mystics and spiritualists in the past have referred to this state as *Spiritual Innocence.* We have referred to various parts of it as *Self-Honesty.* But in whatever way a "clearing of the slate" is to be understood, this critical step is missing from past attempts to accomplish *Metahuman* or *Spiritual Ascension* "out of" this "Physical Universe." Yet, there are a few teachers that discovered basic elements of the *Pathway* we travel, such as reflected in the words of mystic philosopher, *Deepak Chopra*, in his own training of Wizards:—

"The wizard sees themselves everywhere they look, because their sight is innocent; unclouded by judgments, labels and definitions. A wizard still knows they have a self-image, but is not distracted by such either. All these things are seen against the backdrop of the totality, the whole context of life—where our worldview is also a looking glass.

"The 'I' is your singular point-of-view. In innocence, this point-of-view is pure, like a clear lens; but without innocence, the focus is extremely distorting. If you think you know something—including yourself—you are actually seeing your own judgments and labels. The simplest words we use to describe each other—such as *friend*, *family*, *stranger*—are loaded with judgments. The enormous gulf between *friend* and *stranger*, for example, is filled with interpretations. A friend is treated one way; an enemy, another. Even if we do not bring these judgments to the surface, they cloud our vision like dust obscuring a lens."

When we are dealing with POV, we are treating the same fundamentals as *Creation*, which is *Being—Beingness*, "to be." This contrasts greatly with conditions of *beta-existence*, wherein individuals are forced to engage in "motion" or "effort" to accomplish similar results in the Physical Universe. When a *Seeker* is operating "*Proc. 180, Route-8*" and "*Proc. 180, Route-0*" there is no sense of movement; and no effort is necessary. The Alpha-Spirit says "*Be*" and it *is so.* Of course, at *Systemology Wizard Level-0*, this may still seem somewhat out of *reach* to *actualize*—but it can be practiced and *realized* and then gradually *actualized* further until there is a better handling of what is behind all of this. A *Seeker* should also not underestimate the value of using the *Creative Ability Test* (CAT) exercises consistently while pursuing the other parts of the material.

An individual has spent most of their spiritual existence *operating* or *occupying* various POV, none of which are the actual perspective of the "undefiled Self" as Alpha-Spirit. Now, it is true that any POV can be assumed by *Self* as directed attention—but the standard-issue *Human Condition* is quite "fixed" (or entrapped) in POV exclusively *interior* to "beta-existence" (and confined to a *genetic vehicle*), already consistently reinforced, validated and agreed to, by experience of "internal sensation" prompted by an "external" Physical Universe.

At its truest basic state, the I-AM-*Self* (Alpha-Spirit) is not actually located in space—*any* space; but, down the course on the *Spiritual Timeline*, by the point of occupying the *Human Condition*, an individual considers (thinks) themselves quite locatable in *beta-existence* "space-time." They accept implanted reality agreements that fix or restrict *Awareness* to beliefs that they must operate exclusively from the POV they consider themselves located: as a fixed POV in "space-time." This leads to erroneous beliefs of: "Okay, I'm a spirit, but only after I die."

When assuming a POV in a *beta-existence*, the Alpha-Spirit fixes its attention on a *living system* anchored in that space-time—the "physical body" itself is a composite organic mass of energetic concentration made solid. The Alpha-Spirit establishes a locational POV, then starts to "identify" with a *form* that *can be* contacted or reached. Dependency on energetic *mass* cause a *Spiritual Being* to carry platforms, palettes or fields of implants and recordings along from one *incarnation* to the next.

If a POV is too badly fractured or damaged, the individual generally abandons control and responsibility of it. As more POV are considered "unsafe," the Self-determination of *reach* gradually diminishes; hence the condensation and collapse of Universes that the Alpha-Spirit formerly maintained communication with.

> Personal experience of a Higher Universe "collapses"
> when all "points" in "space" are treated as "unsafe."

Even in *beta-existence*, an individual increasingly *withdraws* from more "space-time energy-matter" as they *associate* more "terminals" and "things" with pain and loss—including ability to manage *Mental Imagery* representing the same *facets*. An individual eventually succumbs and "quits" as a result of over-associating *Self* with the "external world" and internal mechanisms of a "body"—both of which are objectively temporary in comparison to Alpha-Existence.

Δ Δ Δ Δ Δ Δ Δ

Our standardized methodology of "Route-0" is traditionally classified as "*creativeness processing*," but we have found that this also includes processing "acceptance of viewpoints" or increasing the "ability to confront POV"—which all seem to go hand-in-hand. This is applicable to "Wizard Levels" because rather than *reducing* every energetically turbulent "charge" on the "line"—such as emphasized with "Route-1" in "*Tablets of Destiny*"—a "Wizard" must effectively demonstrate abilities to manage and handle "POV" at face value. This is a bit of an extreme gradient for some, but its benefits are necessary for securing stable gains, increasing *Actualized Awareness* and progressing further upon the *Pathway*.

Abilities to directly *confront*, manage, handle, ...*create* "energy" is increased as one cumulatively works with methods of each higher "route" within our applied philosophy—*Route-1*, *Route-2*, *Route-3* and our anomaly in numeric sequence, *Route-0*. Each has developed out of the former; each has its own specialized uses—and all are effective in what they are.

> Some have said that each "Route" can be used for getting "quicker" results than a former—but that is also dependent on the state of the individual applying it and/or receiving it; it must be within their *reach* as a *Reality*.

An individual that is not *Actualized* to a point of *confronting* the responsibility of *creating* their own *Mental Images* is not just going to "get there" because you or this book says it's a "truth." Systematic processing is meant to "steer" an individual's handling of considerations in the direction of *realizing* the basic material for themselves, which may then be expanded with training from these books and lectures.

We have emphasized, in this book and previous material, "response-mechanisms" and "reactive imagery" tied to circuitry in the Mind-System that we *are* prepared to *confront*; but what about that which seems "hidden" from view? The subject of "memory" has long fascinated "social" and "neurological" scientists—but how well does it pair up with our Systemology?

We consider that individual's tend to *abandon* their past POV, particularly when it has been overrun by effects; they no longer wish to *confront* it, because they believe they literally cannot "tolerate" it—meanwhile the *Imprinting* still exists, albeit "hidden" from view. Considering the amount of emotionally-charged incidents that an individual doesn't want to face up to along the *Spiritual Timeline*, it is no wonder that a clear memory of it all becomes difficult.

Furthermore there is a diminishing scale an individual succumbs to with lower considerations. A complete "falling out" with each Universe—by some means or another—brought Alpha-Spirits to only consider occupying the *Human Condition* as a POV. Even still, tolerance for *beta-existence* usually continues to decline, more or less, with each *incarnation* within it. In short:

> An individual's *willingness* to *Be* or use potential POVs diminishes with *Actualized Awareness.* The less an individual is *willing* to *Be* and the less they are willing to *look at* or *communicate* with, the less they "survive" their experience of existence—and the less they are able to *see clearly* on the "backtrack" or *Spiritual Timeline.*

"*Imprints*" are, in fact, "*Mental Images.*" "Emotional encoding" builds up an energetic response to such "*Mental Images*" with repeated experiences. This provide us with a certain sense of "time." The more an individual doesn't want to be responsible for, the less "time" it seems they *have.* This is demonstrated by even their outer behaviors. Another example is the "occluded childhood" that is "*forgotten*" due to deep levels of "*Imprinting.*" The amount of "encoding" taking place thereafter during the course of a lifetime can also greatly affect what is generally referred to as "memory."

Our systematic processing often seems to lead to some highly esoteric and mystical *realizations* concerning the Alpha-Spirit and what *Self* is "doing" with the *Human Condition.* For example, the very fact that an individual refuses to *confront* or take responsibility for *Mental Images* is what actually constitutes their compulsive creation. In essence, an individual wants nothing to do with it, so they are stuck with it. On the surface, such things seem to defy basic reason—but we should not be surprised when the truth of things is not *one-to-one* with the information that we have had impressed upon us from those individuals (and POVs) that are heavily conditioned by the Physical Universe and its reality agreements.

We systematically practice "reach and withdraw" in processing. As basic as it seems, an individual is not accustomed to *willing* the "letting go" part of life—sudden abandonment, unconsciousness, the sense of loss, the heat of a hot surface, and so forth, all arranges this for us, outside *Self-Determination.* The standard-issue *Human* has very little practice in "letting go," when the implanted game objective has always been accumulation, and more accumulation—and when an individual is still not satisfied with that, they decide what will "do the trick": just a little bit more accumulation.

Applying "Route-2" methods to "Identity-Phase POV Processing" is introduced in *"Crystal Clear"*—and its reissue in *"Systemology Handbook"*—but additional breakthroughs in that technique resulted later at the Systemology Society, with experiments developed by Grade-III participants researching for Grade-IV.

For example: applying *"Analytical/Recall"* to directly apply principles from our philosophy that are not already provided in a "scripted procedure." Some PCLs are provided to suggest the best of what we've found to work, but is certainly not the limit to what a *Seeker* or *Pilot* can apply based on the books—and possibly not even yet the *best* possible methods or techniques; but they work. We've simply gone with the best of what everyone at a particular level can generally understand and apply well.

PHASES: IDENTIFICATION AND SEPARATION (RTE-2 POV 3D)
—Recall a time when you were ___ .
—Identify someone who is ___ . (*use answer below*)
—Find a time when someone said you were like ___ .

Alternatively, a *Seeker* might "spot a time" (they) "decided to be like *so-and-so*." Sometimes the first step of increasing a *Seeker's* handling of POV is to get them to recognize—or *realize*—the one(s) they are compulsively occupying or *"looking through."* The amount of fragmentation an individual is looking through contributes to the "communication lag" monitored in systematic processing (typically by a trained professional *Pilot*). The next step is, of course, getting an individual to *realize* that other POVs are "safe"—or to use language of PCLs: "would be acceptable" or "wouldn't mind."

Although the Standard Model typically demonstrates *"Beingness"* at the top of the scale—relative to the *Spiritual Beingness* of an Alpha-Spirit—the fact remains that an individual seems to take their sense of *Beingness* with them as they descend into the *Human Condition* to experience *Beta-Existence*. In fact, as one descends the scale into and through *beta-existence*, we find a fragmented individual will apply a great deal of *effort* in order to *"Be"* something—having forgotten the true nature of *Self* and its own ultimate *Spiritual Beingness.*

> The pattern of personal *creation* in most Universes
> operates as we would expect for an Alpha-Spirit:
> a *Beingness* that can *do* things in order to *have* things
> —consciousness, action, substance.

But, when we hit the point of *Beta-Existence* and the "MCC" (*Master Cont-*

rol Center) on the Standard Model—and all the implants on which the *Human Condition* is programmed and encoded—we find an individual working in the opposite direction: now they *have* something—at the very least, a "body," which requires protecting to survive—and they *must* "*do*" something, applying the efforts of the Physical Universe, in order to get a sense of *"Being"* something again. And that is among the clearest examples of "fragmentation" that we can easily demonstrate with our Systemology.

:: 6 ::
IMAGINATION—HANDLING SPACE AND CREATION

Our description of the "Alpha Spirit" *is* not a figurative construct or philosophical abstraction: it *is* the individual or spiritual being as they *actually* are: a "point" or "unit" of *Awareness* (as "I-AM") existing outside "Beta" in an *Alpha-existence* or "Spiritual Universe." All of Mardukite Zuism and Systemology is developed from this basic *a-priori* statement or maxim.

> The Alpha-Spirit is the point of purest "Beingness" surpassing all other considerations. In fact, all other considerations and postulates (of Alpha-Thought) are generated by this point of *Awareness.*

When operating from a point of beta-fragmentation, carried through successive beta-incarnations, programming and encoding, the *Human Condition* is "wired" to sense, feel, associate and react according to the "Imagery" and "Imprints" displaying what is *imagined* to be "true" about the condition of *Self* and stability (safety and security) of the environment surrounding the POV.

Things *are* because *Self* considers they *are*—what we "existentially" treat as the "is" of something; it's "*is-ness*" factor. The basic characteristic of an Alpha-Spirit is *to be* an Alpha-Spirit—to "be its own beingness"—but the imposition of "other-determined" *space-time* in *beta-existence* causes an individual to "feel" or "believe" and validate with "postulates" and "considerations" that *Self* is a "physical being"; which, of course, puts the individual (their POV and perceived state of Beingness) out of "phase-alignment" with the true POV of *Self* as Alpha-Spirit.

> The Alpha-Spirit does not require any "Mind-System"
> as a catalyst to operate its own highest faculties
> —creation, command postulates and consideration.

"Mind-Systems" apparently developed during condensation of Universes, while an Alpha-Spirit's consideration of its own sense of *Beingness*—its willingness and ability to command and be responsible for creation—also condensed and solidified into implanted patterns and fixed energetic circuits. Failing to remain in full *Awareness* of these energetic flows and creations, "ridges" formed patterned circuitry, automated response-mechanisms and other "energetic machinery," which take on more "mass" and "fragmentation" as the individual continues along their "*Spiritual Timeline.*"

"Beta-Defragmentation" is a basic systematic processing goal that is accomplished by "clearing out" energetic debris and "mental masses" accumulated as fragmentation in circuits of communication channels between the Alpha-Spirit, the "Mind-System" and the "Mind–Body" connection when commanding a *genetic vehicle* in *beta-existence*. Most of our previously released material on Systemology pertains to this subject.

—During *Beta-Defragmentation*, *Seekers* increase enough *Actualized Awareness* to "break gravity" of the heavy emotional encoding fixing them to low-level POVs and *Imprinting* from the *"Reactive Control Center"* (RCC).

—*Alpha-Defragmentation* methodology (for future *Wizard Levels*) depends on an individual effectively regaining responsibility and control over their compulsively created *beta*-POVs pertaining to a "Body" and "Mind."

When considering a *beta-existence* restricted to dense masses, symbolic objects, physical "efforts" and a necessity to destroy, fragment or transmute Physical Universe energy-matter in order to "create," it should come as little surprise that a *beta*-fragmented individual carries many of these same considerations about *Self* being identified *one-to-one* with conditions of *beta-existence*. An individual finds great difficulty in exercising "freedom of the spirit" when they are tied to a mortal POV. Actual conditions for an Alpha-Spirit are independent of the Physical Universe —and any effective regimen for rehabilitating *Actualized Awareness* to a point beyond the "Mind" (or "Master Control Center") must include full *realization* of *Self* independent of lower-level considerations.

An Alpha-Spirit essentially has infinite potential and ability to *Create*, and it continues to exercise this quality of its nature all the way down the line—whether it knowingly commands such, or unknowingly and compulsively doing so "on automatic."

In one's personal universe, there are no concerns of "where" energy comes from in order to *Create*, because the Alpha-Spirit needs only "consider" or "postulate" for something *to be*. Similar to "internal" experience of a Human Mind, subjective *reality* of an individual's personal universe is as *real* to the individual as they *realize* it; and that is all the consideration necessary for *Self* to cause something to *be* what it *is* for *Self*.

Although we often compare the "Will" of an individual, in actuality, there is no "Alpha-state" equivalent to the type of "material effort" employed by "material means" in order to *act* in this "Physical Universe."

Consensual beliefs concerning "fixed conservation" in *beta-existence*, or scarcity of available *energy* and *material*, increases perceived value of solid and substantial "things" of this Universe (in preference to what an individual can produce in *Imagination*). Somehow *others* convinced Alpha-Spirits that to be of *value*, the "force" and "consequence" of their *creations* must be more solid, more objective, and it had to be *experienced* to be *known*. Then, as reality agreements to experience *effects* of their *Creations* increased, the willingness and ability to be responsible for them diminished.

Spontaneous generation of infinite potentiality and direct flows of raw energy apparently became too overwhelming to manage properly in a (now) fragmented state. Where *Self* once actualized a level of "god-like" *Beingness*; now it was creating something to *know* about—which meant it *chose* to "forget" aspects of its own *Beingness* in order to *have* something to know about. In the balance, the Alpha-Spirit withdrew conscious participation from "higher" existences, figuratively sealing up and locking out high-level *knowing*—creative ability and handling direct energy-flows—closing off communication-lines with, and responsibility for, abandoned POVs that an individual still maintains energetic ties to.

An individual's true *Spiritual Beingness* still very much remains on the other side of the "Gates."

Any energy required to perceive a reality experience—any reality—comes from *Self* directing *Awareness* as attention like a "beam," on agreed upon patterns and archetypal matrix codes that are "seen" as *forms*. Both, "internal" thought-waves and "external" material energy patterns are only approximated as the *forms* we are implanted to recognize while using a Mind-System as an intermediary interface or catalyst between *Self* and environment. This limits or shields *Self* from handling (or even experiencing) energies directly as they *actually* are, and instead, only to the extent that they are *realized* by "looking" at "second hand" information or a potentially **aberrated** "mirrored" reflection. This concept of a "telescopic spiritual lens" led to our phrase, and previous title, "*Crystal Clear.*"

Rather than eternally confront an *Infinity of Nothingness*, the Alpha-Spirit turned around the "other way" and became very interested in the business of "pictures."—which our materials tend to generalize as "*Mental Images*"—even if they are higher-level "facsimile copies" an individual began to collect and experience in *Alpha-Existence*. This even begins prior to formal solidification of a *Human* "Mind-System" implanted like a circuit-board to key-in various types of *Imprints* and additional *coding*.

Traditional social sciences carry very little interest and (or true data) regarding "*Mental Images.*" Whether attributed to "memory" or some other phenomenon, modern "psychology" texts still treat the subject of "*Mental Images*" as abnormal "hallucinations." No regard is given for every individual essentially creating their own facsimile "mockups" of *beta*-experience and treating it as reality. This is not some "rare" or abnormal phenomenon. On the contrary, a relatively small percentage of the population does not experience "pictures" in the mind—or demonstrate ability to visually "imagine."

There are many ways we could classify, code and systematize qualities and types of "*Mental Images.*" We are beginning to treat not only the Mind-System in beta-existence, but also experience of *Self* in *Alpha-Existence* and "higher spiritual universes." Herein we discover the highest qualities of the Alpha Spirit directly, including unlimited *Imagination* and *Creative Ability*:

• Will and Intention	• Aesthetics and Art
• Ethics and Organization	• Games and Novelty
• Logic and Reason	• Alpha Postulates

> There are two main types of "*Mental Image*":
> those an individual *knows* they are creating; and
> those which they *don't know*, but are still creating.

Even when they *don't know*, an individual still participates in "facsimile-copying" and continuous creation thereafter. This directly correlates to the amount of "attention units" and/or *Actualized Awareness* and individual maintains in the "present." A primary difference between the two types going back to our original emphasis in Grade-III: *Self-Determinism.*

"*Mental Images*" themselves simply *are.* Fragmentation ensues when "labels" are assigned. Even this might not be an issue, if it weren't for the "associations" and "identifications" attached to not only the primary subject or form, but all of its *facets.* This is where the "power" of Alpha Thought (consideration) comes into play—and also why some previous spiritual philosophies warn against "forming judgments." In this light, the state of *Self-Honesty* might be most simply defined as: the ability to experience existence without judgment.

The Alpha-Spirit is an individual *Spiritual Beingness* (I-AM)—an epicentric unit of *Awareness*—described in Hermetic/Mesopotamian interpretations ("*Tablets of Destiny*") as:

a *consciousness* that exists independently

from *action/motion* and *form/substance.*

Where we have an *Awareness* observing *forms* in *action*, we have perception of "manifestation." An individual copies and stores an *impression* of all information perceived about the environment. This develops the more permanent *"Spiritual Timeline"* (of registry) carried by an individual from one lifetime incarnation to another. After cumulatively collected "memory" is crystallized, an individual can begin falsely *identifying* it one-to-one with *Self.*

Mental Imagery treated in our previous material is of the type referred to as an *"Imprint."* In some ways, an *Imprint* could be any experience which makes an "impression" on recordings kept by *Self.* We are most concerned with those that significantly "impinge upon," "hang up" or "stick" an individual—and units of attention somewhere on their *"Spiritual Timeline."*

Heavily charged *Imprints* containing PAIN and/or LOSS
add *emotional encoding* to existing frameworks of *Implants.*
There are FAILURE/ERROR and INVALIDATION *Implants.*

Future "Wizard Grades" of the Systemology Society will better approach and systematically explore the subject of a *"Spiritual Timeline"*—or "past-lives." But a continuing *Seeker* begins to "clear the way" for such realizations *now*, in *"Wizard Level-0."* Access to clearer memory of one's own *"Spiritual Timeline"* is occulted/ filtered/screened/blocked/&tc. by implants carried between lifetimes, composed of *Mental Image* stores and other strongly encoded emotional *Imprints.*

From the **vantage** point of the Alpha-Spirit, *all* of *beta-existence* is an "environment"—and this includes the physical makeup of a *genetic vehicle.* For this reason, we established appropriate semantics to describe the position of all potential *Points-of-View*—whether:

"interior" to *beta-existence;*
"internal" to a *body;*
"external" in the *Physical Universe;* or
"exterior" in *Alpha-existence.*

For example, the entire Mind-System is maintained *interior* to beta-existence, but not *internal* to the body and not *externally* out in the Physical Universe. These classifications allow for a more systematic approach that simply "internal/external" as treated in other paradigms.

The RCC is an "energetic mechanism" that is not found within physiologic anatomy of the "brain"—nor is the "Mind-System" in general. But, an Alpha-Spirit's stores of *Mental Images* and *Imprints* can affect the body—producing various observable effects and *internal* sensations. Standard material sciences draw conclusions based exclusively on observable effects taking place in the Physical Universe: no consideration is made regarding anything that **perturbs** actions from "outside" of it.

Devices measure certain electrical impulses in the "brain" when a person moves their hand—and various manner of biochemical systems of motion "inside" the *genetic vehicle*; but what of the originating Will and Intention that directs this as a *Self-determined* choice? An Observer would have to be simultaneously *under* the "microscope" and *looking through* it.

> When an Alpha-Spirit—"7.0" on the Standard Model—could no longer tolerate or confront its basic state for whatever reason, it shifted its POV away from the *Infinity of Nothingness* into an Alpha-existence of seemingly unlimited potential.

As first described in *Grade-III*, we refer to this next lower level continuity (at "6.0") as the domain of "Spiritual Universes" and "Games." This point on our Spheres of Existence Model correlates with personal *"Zu-line"* levels of "Alpha Thought" (postulates, consideration and logic).

Having established the Models and a basic description of their parts, we can use our Systemology to gauge a specific logical sequence of "spiritual events" that led to considerations for *beta-existence*—though presently, much of this **Backtrack** is still left to a *Seeker* to work out and **discern** from our existing materials until our *"Wizard Grades"* are more solid and published in the future from the Systemology Society.

Very early on the *Spiritual Timeline*—possibly as *Awareness was* "awakening" a POV in the "Home Universe" of *Alpha-Existence*—the Alpha-Spirit first "discovered" (the likely was given a primitive demonstration of) its own inherent *Creative Ability*. And this discovery or demonstration would have been among the first "recordings" made, revealing self-evidently, that an Alpha-Spirit can create (at the very least for itself) its own duplicate "facsimile-copy," "mirrored reflection" or "snap-shot" of anything in its *Awareness*; including creations originated by others and even entire Universes of existence.

Systematic use of *Imagination* and *"Creativeness Processing"* is introduced within "Wizard Level-0" because it takes us one step beyond basic goals of *Beta-Defragmentation* described in previous literature. We are beginning to treat the nature of Alpha-*Existence*, emphasizing rehabilitation of "knowingness" (*Actualized Awareness*) responsibility and control of Self-

Creations. Even if (or when) the Alpha-Spirit no longer wants to "look" or "acknowledge" their existence—since it is powerful enough in its command of *Beingness* and Alpha-Thought to deliberately "not-know"— more often than not, those *Imprints* and automated energetic-mechanisms (which are themselves only compacted sets of "pictures") are *still* being created and stored—*still* active to produce effects—just beneath the surface of whatever level an individual is willing to knowingly handle directly.

> An individual *Creates* in order to *experience.* Recording every action and form is also how an Alpha-Spirit generates its own "sense" of passage along a "Spiritual Timeline." This is also marked by significant changes of consideration and conditions of *Beingness* as *Self* fixes its POV and "personal identification" to lower states of existence and experience. This "timeline," by definition, is built up as a **chronological** sequence. Each additional *experience* is cumulatively recorded/imprinted and stored as "new" information. An individual assigns personal meaning or significance to these encounters (energy-flows) using their own collection of *Mental Images* and previously established considerations (Alpha Thought postulates) about existence for a comparison.

Simple observance of "creation and destruction" cycles—the rise and fall of a **sine-wave**—is all that is necessary to *experience* considerations of communication, movement, action/ motion—the "ebb and flow" of manifest existence—across perceived distances of space-time. But eventually, an Alpha-Spirit is no longer willing *to be* responsible for its own creations and stores of *Mental Images* or the handling of "unlimited potentiality." So the attention-energies that went into conscious *creation* of the *Mental Images* and *Imprints* are sorted by "*facet-association*" and systematized as "patterned circuits" or "tendencies."

> These rigid energy circuits are compacted or condensed to form energetic-mechanisms continuously and compulsively *created* by *Self* and run in the background on automatic, foregoing knowingly applying personal attentions to manage energetic receipt, interpretation and communications on that line.

"Route-0" is a systematic method of processing toward *realizations* about the native (and often forgotten) condition and true faculties of the Alpha-Spirit early on in the *Spiritual Timeline.* Unlimited abilities to *Imagine* anything into *Being,* create a facsimile copy of any form, and duplicate any POV in existence, requires maintaining exceptionally high-level *Self-Honest* responsibility and control. Failure to do so—as apparently is the case—results in Alpha-Fragmentation: formation of a basic "platform" or "circuit-board" for potential *Implants*. Here we find the underlying systematic network array of energetic receptors. Each records a specific type or quality of *emotionally encoded imprints* and other "heavily charged" *Mental Images* impressed by future encounters.

Alpha-Fragmentation carries over during a command of a "Mind-System" and naturally affects *beta-experience.* The basic native true "ability" of *Self* is *fragmented* to support apparent automated circuits of "compulsive action" and "unwillingness." An Alpha-Spirit has recorded an exceptionally long *Spiritual Timeline*, compulsively *creating* and collecting *Mental Images* and other *Imprints* in the name of "experiential knowledge." This began before even reaching *this* Physical Universe.

There are many *imprints* an individual doesn't want to confront or handle; but rather than "uncreate," "destroy" or postulate them out of existence, their creation is misappropriated to another "source" and hidden away from view, yet still active and compulsively created.

> An Alpha-Spirit becomes "effect of their own cause"
> as they lose control and **relinquish** responsibility of
> *created* and *copied* (mirrored, facsimile) *Mental Images.*

Certain "control centers" or "relays" on the *Zu-line* communicate sensory experience and existential data between *Self* and an environment. These become automatic response filters that hide, occlude or occult the *actual* nature of existence in fragmentation. As an individual adds more "experience" to the "pile," more content is associatively cross-identified with other associative data and then assigned meaning or value. Each time, less freedom (space) remains and more rigid finite parameters are installed for future considerations and willingness to reach along that channel.

The Alpha-Spirit's original state of *Beingness* is a pure *Spiritual Awareness* of "I-AM." As a *Spiritual Awareness* unit maintaining an optimum POV of Beingness, an Alpha-Spirit requires no *imprinted images* or *energetic masses* in order to "Know" anything. In fact, it can simply *create* whatever it is it wants to "Know" or "look at" instantaneously. But an individual's *Beta-Awareness* (or *Actualized Awareness*) decreases as more personal energy is continuously routed to keep surrounding *Imprints* "alive."

Even when their own *Imprints* and *Images* are tearing them to shreds, an individual still feels as though they "*have something*" by retaining it; and of course, this "something is better than nothing" philosophy is what got an Alpha-Spirit fragmented in the first place.

In short: *Awareness* descends to lower levels of *beta-existence* as an individual *considers* themselves increasingly the *effect* of its environment; and more dependent on it for their sense of solid reality. Personal tolerance to handle energy, existence and even directly "look" at things also decreases. From this point, an Alpha-Spirit descends to a POV *below* conditions for any "Direct Knowingness." Communication with, and experiential knowledge of, a world-at-large is fragmented—heavily "filter-screened" by surrounding *Imprints* and circuitry that **feedback** information from "sensors" and "automated response-mechanisms" that actually do the "looking."

This patterned progression extends all the way down to a complete relative absence of *Actualized Awareness* at the continuity level of the Physical Universe (or a *beta-existence*) marked "0" on the Standard Model. This **"singularity"** point on our Model/Zu-line indicates a condition where the actualized POV identifies with a "dead body"—and at this continuity level of manifestation: inert matter *is equal to* inert matter *is equal to* inert matter.

> By our logic, this is the *only* position in known existence where a POV could *actually be* at "One with the Physical Universe" in perfect agreement—and it is *not* the "place to be," leaving us with little need to further question why past spiritual methods and mystic systems sound "good on paper" but provide no stable workable "route out" to effectively liberate a practitioner from heavy gravity and spiritual (energetic) trappings of the *Human Condition* in *Beta-Existence*.

△ △ △ △ △ △ △

When we consider systematic handling of *Imagination*, *Creative Ability*, *Space* and *POV*, there is the pragmatic matter of *where* an individual *is* present.

> Standard-issue "identification with a body"
> has fooled many into validating beliefs that
> *Self*—an individual *Being*—must be somehow
> "residing in" a physical body with the fullness
> of their presence, *Awareness* and *Beingness.*

A Professional Pilot of our applied spiritual technology learns quickly how to gauge an individual's actual "presence" by their "communication lag" in systematic processing. Greater skills and training are still needed in this area for differentiating between: "no-lag" and automated responses generated off a "circuit" or some other mechanism.

Before semantics for "fragmentation" and "Self-Honesty" widely caught on for our Systemology, the most commonly used term to describe the aberrated state of the *Human Condition* was: STUCK. The term is a crude generalization, but carried a close enough sentiment to be effective during the "pre-Graded" era of our early underground development. As we approach the "Wizard Grades," it is relevant, if not necessary, for us to go back to this concept.

It is over-critical to reinforce semantics evaluating that someone is "stuck" somewhere. It is not "good practice" for *Pilots*, so the concept was mostly left alone. In an apparent sense, it does seem most individuals *are* figuratively "stuck" somewhere other than the present. When someone refers to someone else as "stuck," they generally mean that they are "rigidly fixed" or "set in" some aspect.

Systematic treatment of POV is typically an extension of *creativeness processing*. It is also a prerequisite for additional upper-route experiments and procedures, such as "*Zu-Vision*" and "*Backtrack*." Increased realizations intended for "*POV Processing*" include:

—willingness to manage the present POV and phases;
—ability to transfer between any POV freely;
—tolerance and certainty handling any other viewpoint;
—full realization that no POV is the existence of Self.

Consider what a person is actually doing in a typical state of fragmentation: the individual has suspended some portion of their *Awareness* to a particular moment in "time," *copied* its information and now compulsively creates a *picture* of it to *look* at; and they are still expecting to "change" that *image* or somehow *stop* the motion that it represents. Alternatively, they may also be fixed on a confusion or a "compulsive maybe" that is being held in place to "be figured" out perpetually.

Rather than take responsibility for continuing creation and ownership (*create*), properly managing it (*control*) and letting it go (*destroy*), a person will often "blame" (attribute responsibility to) someone or something *else* for its creation. They hold onto it permanently as a "rare" or "unique" thing to "have"—something of value they can use to later evaluate their present environment or use on a circuit. This not only makes it more solid, but more difficult to manage. As a compulsive creation, an individual is lending to it their own energies for sustenance. This is handled better by an individual who carries no *masses* with them, allowing for unlimited *Self-directed* energy to simply *Create* whatever they want to "see" or "know" without holding a POV in suspension indefinitely.

Each different "personality phase" has its own circuitry and basic collection of "things" used to associate knowledge of other "things"—which is why the standard issue *Human Condition* doesn't really "know" anything, it just compulsively "figures" and "thinks" about things in relation to other things.

Herein, one also realizes that *creations* are actually a "cycle of actions," and to manage full responsibility for *Creative Ability*, an individual should be able to handle all three parts of that cycle: *Create-Control-Destroy* (CCD)—and technically, these are the *only* three types of directive action actually employed.

By its own semantic application, "*defragmentation*" represents collecting dispersed parts to reform a whole. The Alpha-Spirit is already a singular unit of pure *Beingness*, but once realization of this is fragmented, an individual lessens their *Awareness* and *Knowingness* and assumes various roles and *phases* to get a sense of "*Being*" something again. This is a consequence of *identifying* "I-AM"-*Self* with anything other than *Awareness* as an Alpha-Spirit. At first this must have provided *Self* with a "sense" of something to "*do*"—being in communication with a shared existence or reality separate from the individual's own personal "Home Universe."

Evidently, as additional considerations were compacted together, an individual simply forgot they were playing a *game*—or chose to forget, in order to have "more" *game*.

:: 7 ::

RESPONSIBILITY FOR IMAGINATION
AND THE MIND-BODY CONNECTION

Mystical and spiritual use of the term "remote" is too ambiguous to apply to our upper-level considerations of Systemology Tech.

> When regarding a *Point-of-View* (POV) as "remote,"
> it is important to specify "remote from *what.*"

In most instances, we found intended implications concerned "remote from the POV of a body." This serves to increase considerations that the individual *Awareness* as "I-AM"-*Self* could be separated from a *genetic vehicle*—although they were usually still fixated on the "Mind" or a "mortal body." Today, this all seems like obvious truth to us; but, the only reason there is a truth here in any regard, is because:

> the POV maintained from within a "body" (or "head")
> is *already* "remote" from the actual existence of
> the Alpha-Spirit that is doing the "*viewing.*"

A POV is a "point" *from which* "to view." There is little doubt that an individual has directed *Self-Awareness* to billions of "remote" POV along the course of their full "*Spiritual Timeline.*" If a *Seeker* had to go back and recollect every single one in order to advance through the *Gateways*, we would not get very far along on the *Pathway*.

At each major tier or gradient (or *Gate*), there is a significant quality or a certain type of "*Barrier*" that *Self* is imposing on *itself* by its own considerations and the relative "space" occupied by the recordings and energetic *masses* still compulsively carried forth.

Once "heavier locks" are removed—that bar the "Gate"—the "lighter" stuff seems to either dissipate automatically or comes off more freely when applying the higher *Actualized Awareness* attained at that "level" and greater command of Alpha Thought. It all only seems overwhelming or unattainable when still holding a *vantage* that requires looking "upward" toward higher conditions and *realizations* that an individual has yet reached. This is when *Self-defeatism* plays in—and why relying on fragmented "associative reasoning of a Mind-System"—particularly at our "Wizard Levels"—has a tendency to just ger a Seeker more "spun" in to where they already are.

Managing "points" is similar to "presence" as treated in "*Standard Procedure 2-C*" when a *Pilot* directs the *Seeker* to make contact (communicate) with the immediate environment. One reason is to get directed *Aware-ness* "present" and the other, which is related, is:

> to establish that the "points" in one's environment
> are actually "safe" to both "look at" *and* "view from."

An Alpha-Spirit does not like to *knowingly* leave its attentions on a space that is considered unsafe (or containing "cues" from *facets* that are considered unsafe by fragmented associative reasoning)—but, if there is a strong enough impression, it does so *unknowingly* anyway, leaving part of its *Awareness* there to hold that *image* in suspension so as not to completely "turn its back" on something that *might* "get" them. They don't destroy the creation, as they should. They keep a facsimile-copy of it in existence with a big warning sign that says: "Must Never Duplicate"—but there it is, maintained continuously created with entangled energy all the while.

In order to succumb to identifying with the standard-issue *Human Condi-tion*, an Alpha-Spirit has already dispersed a great amount of their *Actualized Awareness* with attentions simultaneously on many POV across the entire "*Spiritual Timeline.*" Contrary to the apparent "sense" of it one might carry in *beta-existence*, the Alpha-Spirit is not "imbued with" or "imbuing" any less of their own *Beingness* or ability to create energy as it progresses along, but the degree of entangled *mass* compulsively created between the position of the Alpha-Spirit and its POV-experience of a *beta-existence*, causes a lot of its attentions and energetic channels to be "tied up" or otherwise "occupied" and seemingly unavailable in the present.

> Willingness—and therefore, ability—to locate and access
> a particular Universe collapses for an individual when
> all possible extant POV are intolerable or deemed unsafe.

In most instances, the key consideration is "betrayal." The certainty of what is safe to *view*, and acceptable points to *view from* reduces. The indi-vidual is willing to be responsible for fewer and fewer POV. We generally equate "ability" with "willingness" in our Systemology, because: the in-dividual is less able when they are less willing; and less willing when they are uncertain in ability.

It may be said that an individual declines in their optimum condition the less they are willing to *look at* and be responsible for. This can also be so-cially manipulated if "how bad it is everywhere" is consistently rein-forced or validated by others. This is also one of the means of entrapment because the implanted reaction to something labeled "Not Safe" is not to *look*. This has even taken place during our own development of the **Master Grades**, where most of what we discovered of value or as outside inspiration, came from examining sources that contemporary spiritual authorities would "highly *not* recommend" or even tell others "not to look at" (either blatantly or by degrading it).

△ △ △ △ △ △

Systematic processing—as a supplement to educational training—is a means for an individual to practice *Self-Determinism* and alternating "viewpoints" which effectively free up tendencies and considerations operating on "automatic." For example, we use objective methods involving "corners" or "points" that anchor the space of a room, because they are considered "determined" and "owned" by something separate from *Self*.

> An individual operating in *beta-existence* starts to believe they cannot be responsible for (or create) *Space*, because it all seems to be already "determined" for them. We are erroneously told that even the "ideas" have all been thought of before and thus *belong* to someone else.

An interesting situation takes place for the standard-issue *Human Condition*, when an individual considers that they would be "nothing" or "not" if they weren't *identified* with some "thing"—and, of course, at the Physical Universe level of *beta-existence*, the identification is with "objects" (solid masses). Therefore, one of the objectives of Grade-IV (*Wizard Level-0*) is to detach an individual from a compulsive POV from the *genetic vehicle* they "think" they are. This is systematically accomplished by introducing viewpoint "shifts" into a secondary alternate POV and then practicing alternation between them on one's own *Self-Determination*.

> Metaphysical/mystical practitioners usually are quite familiar with concepts of an "astral body," which previously even received the most attention in former methods of freeing up and shifting POV out of the *genetic vehicle*. Our upper-level emphasis is on "*Zu-vision*" as a point of Awareness; not another intermediate "body."

An individual *can* assume a POV from within a *genetic vehicle*, but when one *knows* they are willingly doing so, they also know they have freedom and ability to shift to other POV independent of any body. Since occupation of the *Human Condition* POV is generally "enforced" and "implanted," the Alpha-Spirit forgets considerations that its own true nature is located *exterior* to this beta-existence of a Physical Universe.

Its own actual point of true pure spiritual *Beingness*—its existence—the Alpha Spirit is not located in any mutual Universe. Its own original state is and as a Personal Universe. The whole matter of being fixed to a location is subject to reality agreements and considerations, whether we remember "making" them or not.

In practicing our techniques, it is preferable to shift to a POV that is not dependent on any type of form or body, astral or otherwise, in which to maintain existence as a "point." Tolerance for this can be increased by applying "*creativeness processing*" methods that treat "points" and "spots" in space. The reason many practitioners have worked with "astral bodies" in the past, is because it still provides a "sense" that they *have* something.

The goal of operating as a point of pure *Awareness* can be a steep gradient to take on all at once. In "*creativeness processing*" an exception to this might be the practice of *Self-directing* an alternation of POV between shifting "into" and "out of" an *imagined body.* The primary difference is that processing treats a *form* that the individual *knows* they are *creating,* can take a responsibility for, and then stop creating (and dissolve) it when the exercise is completed.

As an entity or *Awareness,* the Alpha-Spirit has long been out of practice with operation of its own faculties and relying on its own *Creative Ability* and perception. Considerations at the degree of the Physical Universe result in a standard-issue *Human Condition* that believes itself dependent on a "physical body" to communicate with an "external environment."

The goals of our "Wizard Grades" takes this a step further in developing tolerance and willingness for POV that are "*exterior*" to not only considerations of a *genetic vehicle,* but the fragmented circuitry of the "Mind-System" as well. If desired, such a vantage would be optimum for treating conditions of a "Mind" and "Body" when one does not feel as though they are "stuck" within them. This concept is also found at the heart of many archaic forms of *shamanism.*

The generally accepted belief that an individual *must* be occupying a POV exclusively *interior* to a Mind-Body in order to operate that *genetic vehicle* is quite false. *All* of the potential POV are actually "remote" from existence of *Self,* therefore an Alpha-Spirit could maintain a POV "just outside" the Mind-Body system and still very adequately operate it independent from an *Identity with Self,* just as one might operate a marionette puppet. This is preferable for many reasons; most importantly, it more closely matches the truer state of things *just prior* to compulsive standard-issue POV creation fixed exclusively *inside* the Mind-Body system.

Reality agreements that an individual maintains, and fixed to, a POV *"interior"* to *beta-existence* are reinforced and validated the longer a consideration or computation is held outside full *Self-Determinism*—and the amount of "impact" an individual experiences from "external" (or "environmental") sources while doing so. This is one of the only reasons that "pain" and "loss" are considerable points of solid *beta-fragmentation*: an individual considers they are *Identified* as the *genetic vehicle* and thus it associates all of its experiences as happening *to Self* as the Alpha-Spirit. Because we consider this heavily—that things in this Physical Universe are *happening to us*—significant amounts of energy are "wound up" or "entangled" with keeping "hold on" these *Imprints* across a *"Spiritual Timeline"* of many "existences."

The idea of *"Zu-Vision"* (under one label or another) is not a *new* concept, but a very very ancient one. A proper understanding of it failed to be duplicated across history, but with the rise of the "New Thought" movement in the early 1900's, the esoteric ideal of "operating as Self" or accessing "Spirit Vision" became more prominent in many spiritual circles up to the mid-20th Century. But, attentions in the world started shifting again as World Wars ensued, the atomic bomb was created and migration to "space" within the Physical Universe began to take priority. Human civilization has been operating in the shadows of this mechanical-technological paradigm shift ever since.

Although much of the methodology is fairly simple, the premise of *"Zu-Vision"* is not introduced prior to "Wizard" work, because earlier materials focused on *Seekers* reducing energetic intensity of the "field" created and automated by circuitry of the Mind-Body system as *"Beta-Defragmentation."* Such circuitry is often created and/or reinforced while an individual is "keyed-in" or "fixed to" those *interior* considerations—and this "electric field" seems to also have a "magnetic" quality to it. An individual *does* have a natural ability to "get out" on command. There is, however, also a tendency to "snap in" again with the sensation or some force of impact. This sense of "pull" or "gravity" can accumulate and decrease willingness and ability to knowingly *Self-direct* "getting out" *again*. To correct this properly for accessing higher gradients of realization, we have *"Wizard Level-0."*

Δ Δ Δ Δ Δ Δ Δ

Several years ago, a member of the Systemology Society suggested a basic technique inspired by an old obscure volume of German mysticism. Therein, "transference of consciousness" is described—where:

> an initiate practices imagining their POV "going inside"
> solid masses separate from the *genetic vehicle.*

However, the original methods all seemed to emphasize one direction of flow, and we can improve this for our practices:

> using alternation—"going in" *and* "going out"
> —with repetition and fluidity.

Our experiments demonstrated that better results could be earned initially by selecting large masses, which one is familiar with but that are not in the immediate vicinity—which returned us to the original suggestion of "a mountain" (one which the individual is not already sitting on). This differs from other "magical" suggestions where beginners use a candle in the room or the tree they are in front of. For this practice, we still want to start with an "imagined facsimile-copy" of an actual mass in the Physical Universe. And "a mountain" works well for this.

Practice of "Locational POV" may be *Self-processed* or *Piloted.* When *Piloted,* the *Pilot* is not to evaluate significances or invalidate results for the experience. Whatever is happening in a *Seeker's* perception of reality *is* what is happening *for them.* To ensure proper continuation of processing (and to keep the *Seeker's* attention "on the mark" so to speak), a *Pilot* may follow up a "Route-0" or "*creativeness processing*" PCL series with: "Did you?" But this is only to be certain a *Pilot* remains in communication with a *Seeker* during their subjective use of imagination. It should never be asked with skepticism. So long as the *Seeker* says "Yes," a *Pilot* should only respond with acknowledgments that the message was received, such as "Okay."

LOCATIONAL POV—ALTERNATING (ROUTE-0, BASIC 3D)

—Imagine being above (*a mountain*) looking down on it.

—Imagine your POV moving in *to* it.

> \ Imagine your POV moving out *from* it.

LOCATIONAL POV—ALTERNATING (ROUTE-0, A.T.-SP 3D)

—Be near (*or above*) ___ .

—Be inside of ___ (*it*).

> \ Be outside of ___ (*it*).

> —Be at the center ___ (*it*).
> \ Be outside ___ (*it*).
> —Be on the surface ___ (*it*).
> \ Be above ___ (*it*).

> This may be practiced with eyes closed and by imagining a "secondary POV" independent of the *genetic vehicle*. By establishing a new viewpoint, a *Seeker* is not demanding themselves to reach much higher-level goals: completely separating from a compulsive POV within the "body." Certainty and skill for that will follow greater actualized success.

When an individual *is* practiced in commanding their POV (for *ZU-Vision,* &tc.), an extended "Actualization Tech" (A.T.) version (included above for reference) is applied to upper-route Wizard Grades to direct *Actualized Awareness* to various POV in the Universe—and beyond it—on command. It is based on a popular meditation technique appearing in Eastern Mysticism concerning "journeys to other planets."

By effectively working with an "imagined point" and focusing attention of *Awareness* on that "secondary POV," an individual may notice that noise and interference from the Mind-Body "field" is "quieted down" during this practice. This is because the energy that keeps the "field" *created* is supplied by the individual themselves on automatic. An Alpha-Spirit is certainly able to maintain circuits with multiple POV simultaneously and shift its *Awareness* fluidly among them.

> Once an individual has certainty on the basic technique, it may be expanded to include practice maintaining multiple POV. With the above example, a *Seeker* "anchors" the POV they are using above "the mountain" and holds it there. They can begin alternating attention:

> between an "imagined POV" with eyes closed and
> the POV maintained by the *genetic vehicle* with eyes open

> —making sure that the "secondary POV" is held stable in the imagination, so when one closes their eyes they are immediately assuming this other viewpoint.

As an additional gradient of practice, a *Seeker* can develop enough perception with this experience to simultaneously "*look*" through both POV. It will be noticed, of course, that perceptions of the *genetic vehicle* POV are considerably "louder" than a "secondary" one. All an individual needs to do, even with eyes open, is increase the attention that is direc-ted to the "secondary POV" to keep it from completely fading out. "Alternating Locational POV" may be incorporated into an individual's regular "*Creativity Session*" regimen, since certainty on this ability can al-ways be increased—and it quite critical for upper-level development.

With personal development of this type of work, an individual increases their own willingness on what is acceptable or "safe" to *view*—and toler-able "points" to *view* from. When one considers that this free *Awareness* is able to do so without consequence to the body, an individual's "spir-itual" reach or *realization* increases. They can begin to *look* and *know* without consideration of a *genetic vehicle* or sensory limitations and com-putations of the standard-issue *Human Condition.* Although these exer-cises may be, themselves, imaginative practice—the gains in *Creative Ability* and higher "spiritual" realization are *actual.*

:: 8 ::

RESPONSIBILITY FOR IMAGINATION
AND THE CREATION OF SPACE

Applying Systemology to POV management is important for rehabilitating abilities of the Alpha-Spirit in many ways—one of which being the creation and handling of *Space.* This first and foremost:

> begins with a *point* in which to consider that Space *is.*

When the mystic says that "space extends infinitely in all directions," it assumes an **epicentral** *point* in which to "view" *out* into "Space" *from.* We can also consider that there are specialized points—such as we treat in geometry—that define "boundaries" of a dimensional plane of space.

> The concept of distance and time enters in when
> there is more than one existing *point* to consider.

To truly *create* energy, matter and various forms, there must be space for them to exist in.

The Alpha-Spirit has forgotten its own ability to create and handle space —relying on an existence of *genetic vehicles* and the Physical Universe in which to *have* any sense of space. Many treat the concept of Space (and Universes) as a *spherical* nature—such as a mystic or magician that "casts circles" or *imagines* a "shield-like sphere" surrounding their ritual area. However, our experiments show:

> —easier and more effective, in basic practice, to represent
> six directions of a three-dimensional space with a "cube."

As a demonstration, this basic idea can be put into practice as an extension of the exercises given in the previous lesson-chapter. However, rather than use "a mountain" as it exists within the "actual" Physical Universe (*beta*), this time we want to actually *imagine* "a mountain" within one's own "Personal Universe." This is "practiced with imagination" by:

a) first *creating* and defining dimensions of "space";

   and then

b) *creating* the masses and objects within.

Humans tend to consider forms and experiences on Earth or in the cosmos—those representing a shared common reality communicated with others—as more *real* than those created and existing just for *Self.* The primary difference in "reality" between a "Personal Universe" and the "Physical Universe" is the level of common agreements. This is explored in prior material regarding the semantics of "reality" and "agreements."

In "*creativeness processing*," an individual *could* just close their eyes and "*Imagine*" certain forms that they perceive, which satisfy written directions for techniques (or from a *Pilot*)—but, if greater attention is given to the *creation* of *space* the *form* exists in, than greater certainty on actual *Creative Ability* can be earned.

> "*Imaginative*" work increases *realizations* so that an
> individual's *Awareness* can even receive *actual perception.*

Rather than closing your eyes and "recalling" an actual mountain from memory in order to duplicate a scene, this time we want to *create* fixed dimensions of finite *space* in our "Personal Universe" for which to *imagine* "a mountain" of our own unique design.

"*Creation of space*" may be practiced progressively—because it is dependent on an individual's ability to perceive a "*point*"; something developed increasingly as personal "*Creativity Sessions*" continue. The following process applies basic steps to create a "cube of space." Once an individual has a sense of this, a more direct method is simply to *Imagine* the eight points to form a cube and *Create* it as a single-step. However, This isn't a "race"; it is more important that an individual has absolute certainty on their *creation* of each point as fully as possible. It has taken some *Seekers* a significant amount of time to simply achieve total realization of holding even a single "point" still enough to perceive it solidly. This is far more important for accelerating progress on the *Pathway* than simply "flash creating" a random series of thin imagery.

CREATION OF SPACE (ROUTE-0. PRE-A.T., BASIC 3D)
—Imagine a *point* that is independent of *beta-existence.*
—Imagine a *line* stretches to a second *point.*
—Imagine those two *points* extend *lines* upward to another two *points.*
—Imagine these four *points* connected by *lines* form a *square.*
—Imagine another set of four *points* connected as a second *square.*
—Imagine lines connecting the *squares* to form a *cube.*
—Imagine that this *cube* is pure *space.*

Once there is certainty on effective "*Creation of Space*," an individual can then go on to *Imagine* creation of "a mountain" *inside* the "cube." This is why it is important to *create* a large enough space to work in.

> Effective "*creativeness processing*," requires an individual make certain the imagery *created* is not a *reactionary imprint,* or *mental image* that spontaneously surfaces into view. For example: at the mention of the word "*mountain.*" This is ensured by "throwing away" any "pictures" that "come to Mind"—and then further, *creating* changes in whatever is *imagined.* For example: reforming and adjusting the shape and color (and other *facets)* until it is absolutely certain that *Self* is fully responsible for the *creation* of every detail.

As an individual considers applying exercises from the previous lesson-chapter to their uniquely imagined mountain, a realization may occur that equally applies to the structure of POV in every Universe. There is a fixed or "anchored" POV in place that maintains *creation* of space and form. Meanwhile the "secondary POV" may still be directed "in to" and "out of" the object. The same exercises may be applied. As an additional step, the POV is alternated between the "copied beta-mountain" (from the previous chapter-lesson) and the "uniquely created mountain" (from this one). For best results, rather than simply flashing between the two scenes each time, use the POV to *actually look* at some detail or *facet* that is interesting, acceptable and/or safe to look at.

This type of work is mimics events that took place early on the "*Spiritual Timeline.*" It is "refresher practice" for an Alpha-Spirit that otherwise has forgotten how it once *created* and *viewed* in this manner (with full *Awareness*) prior to any existence of a "common agreement" Games-Universe shared with other Alpha-Spirits. The exercise relates the idea that:—

> The POV of a *Spiritual Being* as a unit of *Awareness,* can:
> *create* dimensional boundary points to define a space;
> *create* forms to view by condensing points in that space;
> shift its POV to be any point in a form or point in space,
> while maintaining POV on *creation* of forms and space.

We could fill many volumes of text with various concepts, theories and research underlying all of this work—but with consistent practice and development, intended *realizations* for this gradient of our Systemology should become increasingly self-evident.

Δ Δ Δ Δ Δ Δ Δ

As a practice, "*Creation-of-Space*" has a long-standing esoteric and mystic history. But previous systems never truly explored its full potential. And there are, of course, numerous variations and extensions of our basic procedures. Most importantly, we are treating *Self-determined* creation and management of *space*, so the Alpha-Spirit can *knowingly* practice and rehabilitate *Creative Ability* and responsibility for its existence.

A beginner would find it invalidating to attempt this in a *beta-existence* where strong reality agreements restrict one to only "borrowing external" space-time and energy-matter to *do* or even *have* anything in the Physical Universe. The base materials and fodder, the objects and *space* they occupy—we perceive it has already been put in place prior to the Alpha-Spirit's entry; elsewise it is "other-determined." In fact, the conservatism imposed on the **physics** of continuity in this *beta-existence* is a reality agreement in place specifically to prevent an individual from manifesting "spontaneous generations"—which would, of course, "spoil the game."

At this juncture of development, we are most concerned with what can be managed within an individual's own *"created space"*; and even the very *"creation-of-space"* for a "Personal Universe." It is far better to train and practice our brand of "Wizardcraft" in a dimension of "personal space" independent of Physical Universe reality agreements. The previous exercises are intended to direct attention toward realizations that: the Alpha-Spirit, as a "point" of *Awareness*, can *create* space and forms within it using one POV and then experience it with another. This defies many commonly held beliefs about *beta-existence* and yet is a simple truth in Alpha-Existence.

Using traditional styling of former mystical texts, basic instruction of our procedures offers guidance for what may otherwise be overlooked (often due to the very "simplicity" of the directions). The entire idea that "one step is preliminary to some other step that yet might produce an effect" causes a student (or initiate) to overlook significance of the more "basic" step—not realizing that a more actualized certainty on a particular level, or foundation, will actually increase the potential "reach" for what follows thereafter. This commonly occurs in contemporary "magical traditions," where high-level mastery of basic rudiments (that actually determine any results) are carelessly put aside in favor of more "interesting" rituals and "elaborate" ceremonial dramatics (which carry no living power exclusively in themselves, regardless of what gestures or words are uttered).

Many key suggestions for practice are given as the *Creative Ability Test (CAT)* and various other techniques throughout this present volume (and former literature). As an Academy Grade and tier on the *Pathway*—what we are most concerned with (for *Wizard Level-0*) is just how certain an individual can be in their *creating* and just how strong of a perception they can eventually have on it (relative to the solidity perceived of the Physical Universe).

> It is important that *Awareness* is strengthened in a safe session environment and practiced within one's own Universe. No other considerations about *beta-existence* are applied. While establishing greater reality on *Self* and developing personal *Creative Ability*, we are certainly not treating apparent "manifestation"—"spontaneous generation" "teleportation" "levitation"—of these *creations* for common-agreement *beta-existence*. Apparent reality for an individual in their Personal Universe is subject to their own level of actualization on those perceptions; as a personal experience, there is nothing to invalidate an individual and their progress.

In actual practice, an hour or more spent developing total certainty on *creation* of a single "point" is more significant for ongoing development (progress) than considering a whole "cube" vaguely with only a slight perception on its reality.

> The *"point"* is an interesting fundamental encountered by
> a Seeker during the *Creation-of Space*; because the *"point"*
> represents *no-dimension* and *no-mass* and thus closely resembles the
> nature of the Alpha Spirit's own existence.

It takes *two* "points" to create a line (segment) and a single *"spatial dimension."* This makes the "point" an effective tool (in systematically processing) to "reach" higher states. Holding the concept of a "point" by itself runs an individual very close on having to confront "non-motion" and "non-existence." This is comparable to experiences on the *"Spiritual Timeline"* that an Alpha-Spirit had difficulty prior. Hence, our Systemological compass points toward a *180*-degree turnabout regarding condensation and restriction of our considerations of *Beingness.*

When we practice *"creation-of-space,"* no attention is given to other considerations or *mental imagery.* This also means—after reaching a stable condition of Beta-Defragmentation—we expect no interference of "automated" *imprints* or impinging *pings* sensed from the *genetic vehicle* while an individual is holding the *creation* of a single "point" in place within their own Personal Universe. If understood properly—in connection to training given in previous Systemology volumes—"Route-0" methods can actually be used to carry out high-power Beta-Defragmentation processing.

As an individual maintains total focus on basic existence of the "point," these other automatic response circuits *will* "turn on" if not already defragmented. This is one more reason we held back this material until after an individual potentially works through the previous Systemology books.

However, if determined enough, the personal phenomenon (fragmentation) that occurs while maintaining attention on a single "point" can simply be treated right then and there. This is effective for clearing out debris from channels that may not have fully defragmented during earlier Routes.

> Total *Actualized Awareness* and full *Creative Ability* is hindered only by "automated circuitry" and "mental machinery" that an Alpha-Spirit formerly *created* (or *copied*, then *compulsively creates unknowingly*) to manage control of all these functions.

Our ongoing solution is to knowingly take responsibility and control over whatever is compulsively unknowingly or reactively happening automatically. Such is the basic theory behind the exercise regimen provided as the *Creative Ability Test (CAT)*, which can more appropriately be considered our standard *Creative Ability Training*. This should make greater sense as an individual practices with a "point."

> For example, the natural tendency is to put in "*effort*" to "stop" (destroy) what is taking place outside personal control and determination; but a more effective method of regaining control is to "change" what is happening or make it happen more strongly. An individual might create their "point" with structural intent of no mass or dimension, yet it takes on characteristics on its own; perhaps of a "spot" by expanding its size, or flashing as a light rather than remaining a static point.

A static point, whether as a point "anchoring" corners of *created space* or a point within space, should be able to be fixed in a location and suspended from motion. In either case we have "other-determined" actions affecting the basic command postulate directed to hold a single "point" still. If it's faintly flicking in and out of *Awareness* or flashing, the individual can intend for it do so strongly and more boldly. If it won't remain still, the course or direction it travels can be changed. If it keeps moving in on the body, give it a little "knock" the other way back toward its intended location, rather than giving in to withdrawing your POV backward.

Anything that impinges on a specific/fixed "postulate-of-creation" can be systematically put under control of *Self* using gradients of *change* to increase or decrease what is already happening, even if it seems contrary to the original intent. A fast moving *image* or *point* can be more easily *changed* to go faster before there is enough certainty to slow it and hold it still.

The same degree of attention and certainty should be applied to each basic "step" to "*Creation-of-Space*." An alternative "Universes" method treats the flat two-dimensional *plane* ("square") as the base (or bottom for corner-points) of the "*cubed-space*," rather than as a "wall"-surface that one is facing (as suggested in the basic version).

Once there is certainty on creating and viewing "out in front" (of their POV), the next applicable gradient is *creating* eight points around the individual's own POV—so as *to be* the only existential-point and *Awareness* within the "cube" of *created space* that is otherwise intended as "empty" of *creations* and *imagery*.

Responsibility is connected to *ability, knowingness, willingness* and *control*—all of which are treated at length in former volumes. *Responsibility* for "*Creation-of-Space*" increases with certainty of command and control of it; hence remaining at "*Cause*" throughout the cycle-of-creation—including discard, dissolve or destruction—when an individual intends to no longer create it and has not intended on it to persist compulsively on some automatic-circuit of creation (because we now know that *Self* contributes to that as well).

Placing attention on "corners" of space, as suggested in the *Creative Ability Test (CAT)*, this can be done while remaining stationary within the *created-space*. An individual can also rotate their view to inspect the boundaries as well. To further increase certainty on the *creation* and its contents (or lack thereof), the individual can go *look* from other POV to see that it is empty and simultaneously determine the level of control, responsibility and ability. For example, unlike points that define the dimensions of this space, the individual's POV *can* be relocated, such as from one corner to the next and *look* inward at the space. A *realization* should become increasingly actualized that: *Self* completely owns and is totally responsible for this independently created personal space.

Δ Δ Δ Δ Δ Δ Δ

Many of our goals for Systemology "Wizard Grades" follow an arcane pattern or sequence that we often refer to as the "*Gates*"—and there are traces of this lore throughout 6,000 years of recorded esoterica, regarding "veils" and "kabbalistic spheres" and "dimensions" and "aethyrs" of existence. In such instances, the "initiate" primarily relies on familiarity of an "astral body" while "pathworking" (or "imagining") a "predetermined mental image set." This is meant to induce or incite some new impression of *"Beingness."* This is the approximate extent to which the practical applications of *Grade-I* and most *Grade-II* material actually reach.

Even then, such techniques can only be realized as *actual* to the degree an individual is able to *actually* handle the *space* they are operating in. And if their presence is not masterfully **immersed** in a vivid experience (due to unpracticed handling of *Imagination*), then those former methods —which arcane schools and lodges have long relied on quite heavily—do not provide an individual with much more *reality* than when simply reading them.

Standard-issue operation of the *Human Condition* is restricted by a heavily implanted Mind-System that orients the POV toward "protecting" the survival of a *genetic vehicle*. All of the mental machinery presently operating with this intention interrupts our experience of a *Self-Honest* existence with an entire *imprinting* factory and *personality package* that cumulatively associates more of an individual's Universe, and more of an individual's potential action in that Universe, to low-level misemotional response-mechanisms. Eventually, the entire slate is filled up with scenes and signals that provide a sense that the individual has no space and no action remaining in the "game."

When an individual is convinced that this is the only game around, it is quite difficult to *imagine* something else that is independently created from familiar parameters of the Physical Universe. One of the reasons mystical practitioners rely on "mental bodies" and other "mental scenery" in alleged "astral work" is because they are still operating, to some great extent, *within* or *interior to* the Mind-System; thus they still are very heavily affected by its fragmentation and implants. Traditional practices of this sort do not necessarily free *Awareness-as-Self* (*Actualized Awareness*) beyond or *exterior* to mental circuitry, since without full control and responsibility for *Space* and *Creation*, an individual still relies on self-generated mental machinery to manage all *creating, looking* and *evaluating* on automatic.

Practicing, imagining and eventually establishing a POV in a *created-space* of one's own Personal Universe is an objective goal for *Wizard Level-0* completion; not only for its function, but also to increase subjective certainty or personal reality that:

> *Space* can exist independent of the *Physical Universe* and
> experiencing existence of exterior Universes depends on
> an *Exterior POV* and not a *genetic vehicle* in *beta-existence*.
> I-AM is an *Alpha Spirit* existing independent of any body
> and any universe other than its original *Alpha-Existence*
> as a unit of *Awareness* with unlimited Creative Ability.

Actualization *follows* Realization. Only when the I-AM-*Self* (Alpha-Spirit) is certain enough that there is *somewhere to be* existing outside of this *beta-existence*, can enough willingness and determinism break ties that have long fixed one's attention exclusively on existence in this Physical Universe. The range of *Actualized Awareness* under full control of the Alpha-Spirit is fairly unlimited in ability to direct its POV and locate itself in existence, but logically: an individual must first realize that a destination exists for them to actually be there.

Our methodology of "spiritual rehabilitation" still follows the same effective formulas of handling *Self-Determination* and automatic-mechanisms that brought us up to this point on the *Pathway.* These are simply applied to conditions of each gradient or "Gateway." Here, we have illuminated true boundaries of this Physical Universe and operation of POV-implants; we are reintroducing *Self* to handling imaginative faculties and ability to command Creative Ability, taking back control of and responsibility for mental machinery that reinforced fixed attention circuits validating solidity of this *beta-existence* further.

As we complete the selection of standard discourses intended for this volume, treating the end of a cycle or a departure of communication, there is one additional matter to call attention to—one which must be consistently treated at each level of *Personal Defragmentation,* because it is a basic implant installed and then impressed more strongly the more an Alpha-Spirit began to participate in Game-Universes: "*Loss.*" And this implant, like the others, is an ongoing chain or branching tree of associations built upon intensity and charge of a preexisting incident: "*Loss of Space.*" This is certainly a deeply *imprinted* experience on the "*Spiritual Timeline.*" An individual has a certain sense that a Universe can cease to have any occupied existence—in fact, we have all known the loss of at least one Universe due to violent collapse or some other type of explosive phenomenon.

There is a considerable amount of imprinting tied to a sense that we might "lose something we have" by not compulsively existing in this Physical Universe—or that it might cease to be if we weren't here to somehow reinforce and support its existence "for ourselves and our fellow citizen" because in such fragmentation, there is no other *beingness* possible.

> The majority of those presently operating the *Human Condition* are here by similar circumstances—the most basic being: entrapment of an Alpha-Spirit's consideration of *Beingness* from a "higher" Universe, interior to enforced spatial dimensions of *beta-existence*, where *Awareness* is fixed as a "point" locatable for that other-determined *space*, subject to being the effects of reality agreements concerning external energies and forces of the Physical Universe. As anyone can see, this is clearly just a very technical description for *a prison.*

Certainty on the *Beingness* of *Self* correlates to the level of *Actualized Awareness* available. An individual heavily fixed in their singular *Identification* with the *Human Condition* as their only existence carries no considerations for any existence *exterior* to those conditions.

> And that is the only reason a *Spiritual Being* would
> remain trapped in a *material prison* where the
> only one guarding the gate, *is themselves.*

With use of *Imagination* and practice of *Creative Ability*, we continue to systematically process a *Seeker* in the direction of taking control of whatever *Self* is participating in unknowingly or else by some other determinism. It does require a bit of intuition for individual application; the scope of any single book is tied to specific goals and objectives, while variations for its potential use are virtually unlimited.

> All our experience, thought and action
> is a created product of imagination.
> We can never express any thing
> that we do not first imagine.
> Imagine freely and often.
> Live as a Free Spirit.
> Create. Create.
> Create.

:: A ::
IMAGINATION AND SYSTEMATIC PROCESSING
TECH REPORT FOR SYSTEMOLOGY PILOTS
GRADE-IV WIZARD-0 ROUTE-0

IMAGINATION is the primary subject of *Systemology Grade-IV Wizard Level-0*, as explored in *Liber-3D*. Our methodology emphasizes increased *Self-directed* "control" (*willingness, knowingness* and *ability*) of communications and creation—the Alpha-condition of "responsibility" for cause and effect.

An Alpha-Spirit occupying POV in denser Universes along the "*Spiritual Timeline*" progressively considers their own *ability* to have less direct effect on their environment—possibly fearing some "punishment" for this control and responsibility. But, this leads them to eventually stop *knowingly* creating at all, putting these faculties on automatic—until finally forgetting their *Creative Ability* altogether.

Use of *Imagination* in systematic processing allows *Seekers* to *knowingly* practice command of *Creative Ability,* the control and responsibility of being at "*Cause*"—because they *know* they are *creating* this *illusion* in their own "Personal Universe" (where it is safe to do so). There is no kickback effect or consequence enforced by the "Physical Universe" as a result.

> The two Universes exist independent of each other. The more a *Seeker* is processed to realize this with certainty, the better their ability to handle existences of each Universe "*As-It-Is*"—not simply as they are "thought" *to be* using some filter or circuit to receive fragmentary information. Only after the *realization* is present can a *Seeker* can *actually* reassign their considerations.

Previous systematic process "Routes" mostly emphasized *recall* or *resurfacing* of events registered in "memory"—concerning what has actually happened. In addition to emotional qualities and other intellectual associations, these "memories" contain *facets* connected to specific types or pattern-forms of "energy-matter." *Mental Imagery* attached to *imprinted* experiences often carries an "*energetic charge*" of the original impression along with it. When stimulated as an automatic-response to some stimulus in the present environment, information from previous impressions containing similar *facets* is internally communicated as part of the reality experience.

> In the beginning, the Alpha-Spirit used its *Creative Ability*
> for "fun" - for "art" - and its own personal amusement.

> Getting "lost" and identified with POV of its own *Creations*
> not-knowing the true nature of *Self* as I-AM, came later.

Meanwhile, here in *beta-existence*, we can employ *Imagination* in systematic processing as a means of handling "assignment of consideration" along a circuit or channel without being restricting use only to *"activating events"* which have both actually occurred *and* are within the scope of reality for a *Seeker* to effectively confront or recall (reach) directly.

> Most *imprinting incidents* become heavy charged fragmentation only when an individual is not willing to directly *look*, and therefore take control and responsibility for either eliminating the creation or reassigning its value, instead of relying on mental machinery and other relays to handle perpetual creation and interpretation of the reality experience.

Concepts of "pain," "loss"—even witnessing violence or death—are compulsively created *imprints* which often seem *more real* to an individual than the true present environment. Of course, these events *did* happen, but a *Seeker* keeps the energy and attention entangled and suspended with *Awareness* around each. This is what holds *Self* back from breaking the gravity of *beta-existence.* Even when unknowingly and compulsively maintaining creation of mental machinery (and its products), the Alpha-Spirit is still *fragmenting* the wholeness of its *Awareness*—hence decline of *Actualized Awareness* "present" at a given moment.

An individual puts up so much resistance to the *mental image*, hoping to stop the motion it contains, meanwhile compulsively creating it. The force they apply against it makes it more solid and thus perceiving it as stronger and more difficult to handle. Then comes feelings of overwhelm as an effect and abandonment of control and responsibility for treating its contents. If handled directly with systematic processing, *imprinted* information can be *defragmented* from the circuits; but this requires ability and willingness of the *Seeker* to actually *"look"* at the *image* they carry around from it. Applying increased *Actualized Awareness* disintegrates the "charge" held on it—perhaps one reason that "stares" instinctively bother many beings.

Various training, exercises, techniques and processes given in *Tablets of Destiny, Crystal Clear* and *Metahuman Destinations* combine to establish a systematic regimen for "beta-defragmentation." We are now able to approach a new level of "beta-Actualization" by applying "*Imagination*" and "*Creativeness Processing*" to our methodology. Material for this is covered in *Liber-3D* (released as "*Imaginomicon*") including these updated tech reports. "Route-0" is a result of new *realizations* achieved using our former work as a *ledge.* This has been the pattern of our development all along. Suggestions contained herein may be *added* to previous material; applicable to both *Self-Processing* and *Professional Piloting.*

Δ Δ Δ Δ Δ Δ Δ

Systematic processing goals are achieved only when a *Seeker* directs actual attention to the exercises. This is referred to as "presence" in the outline for Standard Operating Procedure (#2C) for *Grade-IV.* The first steps begin with increasing *Awareness* given to the present environment, especially the session. Processing is directed toward *Self*, not one of the phases or circuits or *imprints* created by *Self.* Instructions are referred to as "commands" because they introduce Alpha-Thought considerations for a *Seeker* to "run" on their own "operating system"—

> "command lines" are received from the text or *Pilot* until an individual *Self-determines* control of the command. And a Seeker must actually *be* "present" *doing* the exercises.

Most individuals operate on so much automatic circuitry—looking through so many filters—that very little *Actualized Awareness* is present. At the start, before "upper-level" considerations are treated, we apply a standardized systematic processing method. The assumption is that some part of an individual's *Awareness* is fixed somewhere (or else too dispersed) apart from their present environment.

> When an individual stops *looking*—for whatever reason— they use mental machinery to do the "*looking*" for them.

Therefore, most "objective universe" methods of increasing attention-on-the-present have to do *literally* with "*looking*" "*contacting*" and "*communicating*" with the present environment. This demonstrates enough certainty in the "safety" of the environment for *Self* to actually apply its *Awareness.* Proper handling of various "Points-of-Views" (POV) is an integral part of "Route-0" because:—

> while this "crystal lens" remains fragmented, so too is the view taken regarding *Imagination* and *Creative Ability.*

At the beginning of a session, a *Seeker* is directed to "look around" at their environment and notice things, one to the next. The environment may even appear to get "brighter" as this happens.

> So much of what an individual really believes they are

> perceiving is actually fragmented by circuits and filters
> before the information is even communicated to *Self.*

This is better demonstrated, for example, when an individual enters a new environment: more attention is placed on what is around them. It does not take long for "familiarity" to set in. Then "scenery perception" is mostly created on automatic—not even really "looked at" anymore. The average individual is not educated to remain at "cause" over their own selective directed attention. There are exercises that direct a *Seeker* to look at precise points, one to the next, as opposed to simply glancing around lightly. Several examples are actually included in the *"Creative Ability Test"* (CAT).

Techniques and training for "Wizard Level-0" are intended to increase an individual's certainty toward operating as the Alpha-Spirit. This includes using *"Zu-Vision"* independent of a *genetic vehicle* or *beta-existence.* The most direct technique (or PCL)—*"Be outside that body"*—is not necessarily the most effective if other strongly held reality agreements and fragmented considerations still impinge on an individual.

> *Systemologist Seekers* practices exercises to increase
> the reach on *knowing* their own spiritual existence,
> rather than agreeing to carry a vague idea about it.

Additionally, "Route-0" may be applied to all previous "objective processing" methods. These are just a few ways that suggestions from former texts may be retained and returned to again for upper-levels of practice:

> Practice while seated, with eyes closed, using "Imagination" (or assumption of a secondary POV) to treat the environment. An individual places full attention on the room (or object), closes their eyes and uses *Imagination* to create a facsimile-copy of it. If an exercise requires contacting or moving an object in some way, then the *Seeker* is to remains in place and focus on a "sense" of it happening as fully as possible.

Other "objective processes" practice *Self-directing* communication with objects, masses and walls in the environment. A *Seeker* may be directed to pick a spot on an object and touch it; and then they are directed to let go. When this is carried through without lag, the *Seeker* is to get a sense of making a decision of when to touch and when to let go. For "Wizard Level-0," an additional step is added: to direct (or project) a *"beam"* (or *Awareness*) that is used to touch and let go. A *Seeker* may upgrade methods of *"Presence in Space-Time"* (SOP-2C), contacting walls while remaining still, directing a POV (or *Imagination*) to move back and forth across the room.

Δ Δ Δ Δ Δ Δ Δ

> Fragmentation inhibits clear communication between Alpha-Command of *Self* and the resulting activity.

Systemology focuses on the Alpha-Spirit, the *Self* that controls a Mind-System and a *genetic vehicle.* But what is *actual* for the Alpha-Spirit exists in a domain of Alpha-existence, not beta. When an individual is fragmented, their experience of "thought" is restricted to associative information kept in circuits of the Mind-System. Creative expression in *Beta-existence* results from material/physical *efforts* first circulated through the Mind (from *Self*) and only then manifest in *Beta* by efforts of a physical organism. An original *action* (from *Self*) precedes and originates this communication. The impulse directing this comes from *Self*, even when fragmented channels communicate (on the Zu-line) improperly toward "*efforts*" and "actions."

CREATIVE ABILITY (ROUTE-3, CIRCUIT-0, BASIC 3D)
—What have you done using imagination or creativity?
—What have you kept yourself from doing using imagination or creativity?

There are many reasons why an individual becomes less willing to be *Cause* of things. This basic PCL can be expanded to include other "circuits" (described in *Metahuman Destinations*) for recovering entangled energies set by: what you would allow others to do and keep from doing; what others have done and kept themselves from doing, &tc. As with most systematic processing, this cycle is run until an individual has freed their considerations and willingness; in this case regarding use of imagination and creativity—with no reactive or automatic tendencies regarding the concept.

> In our natural state, the I-AM-*Self* (Alpha-Spirit) can only have its own abilities reduced as a result of its own Alpha-Thought—a high-level consideration or command-level postulate on existence. We have the ability to place *Awareness* at any POV, even where our consideration for *Beingness* is less than we actually are.

We have accepted suggestions lending toward our own Self-invalidation as reality." It allowed implantation of considerations rigidly fixed to a

POV, such as the standard-issue *Human Condition.* Fear of invalidation can prompt an individual to decrease their willingness and certainty on ability. Regardless of where an invalidating cue or suggestion originates from, it is only by our own acceptance and incorporation of it as a reality agreement that allows us to become its effect. The circuits introduced for "Route-3" (in *SOP-2C*) may be applied to handle "Invalidation" with systematic processing.

Δ Δ Δ Δ Δ Δ

On our Standard Model, the *Zu-line* represents a continuum of "Identity" that an individual Alpha-Spirit associates with itself. But this something of a misnomer because the actual existential position of an Alpha-Spirit (7.0) is as an Individuated Beingness—not an identity as might "identify" it with a "thing." It is not actually located in any *space.* It is a single unit or point of pure *Spiritual Awareness*—often imagined as a single island-peak emerging from out a drop of the *Sea of Infinite Nothingness* ("8") or else *Infinity.* However, the Alpha-Spirit may directed its POV toward *creation, space* and *Universes.* As *Awareness* "descends" on the *Zu-line* toward *beta-existence,* an individual more strongly associates its own *Beingness* as *Self* with lower POV that it is operating from.

In the past, mystics and magicians emphasized control of the body by operating from the Mind; and their POV is very much entangled within the Mind-System and the "mental plane." This is particularly evident in themes and semantics of their paradigms. It is from the "mental plane" that an individual is very *Aware* of "mental fields" surrounding "mental bodies" and a whole vast network of circuits and relays composing "mental machinery."

> In most cases, "New Age" practitioners remain *interior* to the Mind-System. Of course, this is a step above fixation *interior* to the *genetic vehicle* itself. However, it is not enough to access Higher Gates of Realization, which permit a potential for direct experience of Higher Universes. Assuming an individual has successfully defragmented emotional stores (*Reactive Control Center*), this still leaves them somewhere around the *third* (or *fourth*) "Gate" (or "Veil")—still yet to break free of the Mind.

There are many instances when the POV of an Alpha-Spirit can be pulled-in or snapped-in on the fields and mechanisms inherently part of a "body." This may take place during intense emotional stress or **trauma** when the perspective of *Self* is fixedly tied in with (and distracted by) sensations and *pings* of a "body." This strengthens circuitry for *Identity*, propagating that *Self* is located in a "body." This happens much more often when an individual is already suspended *interior* to a Mind-System, already surrounded by the associative thought and emotional encoding circuits of the *vehicle*.

> The Alpha-Spirit is capable of commanding a *genetic vehicle* and its functions (mechanisms and energetic fields) while retaining its original POV *exterior* and independent of the *vehicle* they are operating and Universe they operate in.

Δ Δ Δ Δ Δ Δ Δ

Entrapment in a Mind-Body Identity is possible and later cemented by "*Implants.*" There are many implant platforms and on which specific circuits operate. At this present level of work, our concern is with a general realization that they exist and that their installation has a tremendous impact on the POV and considerations remaining with an individual to knowingly handle. Rather than prompting by a PCL directly, the *implants* on which *programming* and *encoding* occurs, are increasingly more accessible (and less sensitive) after a complete and thorough application of all materials comprising *Grade-III* and *Grade-IV* Metahuman Systemology. *Implants* are treated in upper-level work when they "surface" and/or when a *Seeker* is in a position of *Awareness* to confront them directly.

> Many who already have a sense of their entry into this Universe and *Human Condition* will often liken it to *falling into* or being *sucked into, &tc.* But in all cases where we have considered the action taking place to "*Implant*" an individual with the *Human Condition* in *this* Universe, the common theme suggests that one is *outside* and then one is suddenly *inside*—and during the disorientation between, *something* happens.

Depending on whether an individual is working with *this lifetime* or has begun *Backtrack* work on the *Spiritual Timeline*, the same methodology is employed to start opening up these channels for exploration. Processing includes considerations (and sensations) attached to "going in" or "getting in" something or somewhere.

Significant "energetic charge" is entangled with "Entry into Universes" or "Implanting." Much of this work is still under research and review at the Systemology Society for inclusion in higher Wizard Grades. You might wonder why we mention its background before closing out Grade-

IV. We discovered—some might say "by accident"—that *Tech* applied for "Wizard Level-0" *can* potentially trigger actual realizations of how a *Seeker* arrived "here." It is often reacted to without understanding and without realizing the nature of this phenomenon ahead of time. Fragmented automatic-response circuits connected to these events add some difficulty in maintaining high enough Awareness to fully achieve goals set forth for *Grade-IV.*[*]

> By processing the concepts of moving *inside* and *outside*, a
> *Seeker* is less likely to handle it with automatic circuitry.

Systematic processing using *Route-3* (and/or *Route-0*) is applied to defragment considerations for accessing "Zu-Vision," operating "*exterior*" to the physical body, or even the handling of space and creation of a "Personal Universe." So long as a POV can be "snapped in" on the Mind-Body system outside of *Self-Determination*, the individual's *Identity* is still very much entangled and associated with those mechanisms.

- Incidents when you wanted to get inside but can't
- Incidents when you were kicked out from where you
  wanted to be
- Being forced inside
- Incidents of being trapped inside
- Pulled in
- Pushed in
- The feeling or sense that you must get in
- The feeling or sense that you can't get in...

Such types of incidents potentially carry a heavily imprinted charge. This greatly reduces *Self-Awareness* and *Self-Determination* and therefore, *presence*, when left uncontrolled. You can use the above concepts for PCLs to treat circuits with *Recall* or you can *Imagine* incidents and see what *Mental Imagery* seems most correct. In either case, experiencing some release assists handling basics of upper-level work.

> An Alpha-Spirit exists apart from thought and creation,
> but once it *believes* it is located among them,
> it is subject to its reality agreement with
> external conditions & environmental factors.

Another heavily-charged spiritual incident may also be "restimulated" and "detrimental" to effective progress at *Wizard Level-0* is Collapse-of-

---

[*] Additional work to resolve this may be found in "The Way of the Wizard: Utilitarian Systemology" (*Liber-3E*) by Joshua Free.

Space and Collapse-of-Universes. This is something that all individuals have experienced intensely at some point on the *Spiritual Timeline* at least once (with their Home Universe).

> Our exercises depict the basic structure of a *space* or *Universe* as a "cube"—defined by eight "corners" or "points" that *anchor* the boundaries of the dimension. Just as there are experiences of one's own POV "snapping in" or "caving in" on a new plane of *space* or *mass*, so too are there times when the *space* and *energy-matter*—and the very corners of a Universe itself—"collapse in" on the individual. Heavy fragmentation charges on this experience can affect a *Seeker's* willingness to be responsible for "*Creation-of-Space*" as found in Grade-IV exercises.

The "***hot buttons***" treated in systematic processing for "Collapse-of-Universes" are quite similar to the "going in" and "interior/exterior" buttons used previously. In this instance, rather than a POV being "snapped in" to some *space* or *energy-matter*, the reverse is treated:

- Incidents of *space* collapsing in on the POV
- The world closing in; the world folding up
- Energy imploding; energy collapsing in on the POV
- Corner-points collapsing; corner-points snapping in on the POV
- Sudden "uncreation" or folding up of all form
- The environment caving in on the POV
- Pulled backward from
- Falling away from
- Sense of everything suddenly becoming unreal...

As with the case of "POV snap-ins," these "creation cave-ins" may be encouraged or prompted by external sources and other-determined events —however, much like "invalidation" and other *facets* of personal (degradation that we *choose* to "accept" or *agree* to as "reality"), experience of any POV is still *Self-Determined* on some level; including "Entry into–" and "Collapse of–" Universes.

Δ Δ Δ Δ Δ Δ Δ

After the point of pure *Awareness* (I-AM), the next point on the Standard Model (or *Zu-line*) treats the Personal Universe or Home Universe of an Alpha-Spirit. This is created by (and subject to) the *first* Alpha-Thought: direct considerations and command postulates for any existence *to be* or *not be*. It is composed of that which an Alpha Spirit has created for and as their own consideration, when the:

> "Home Universe" is the *highest* of "Creative Universes";
> not "shared" in agreement; the true form of individuality.

In actuality—though outside realizations of the average human—an individual as Alpha-Spirit (true I-AM; highest POV) is still existentially occupying the existence of their original Personal "Home Universe" foremost to any other Universe or POV. However, considerations and postulates for this Home Universe began to blur. Other reality agreements fix a POV in remaining "shared universes," in which *Self* could engage in "creative display" and eventually "games" with other "*Selves.*" A reduction in *Awareness* and ability occurred when eventually:

> Alpha-Spirits substituted considerations
> for the creation of their Home Universe
> by rigidly fixing reality agreements and
> POV in place with other Universes.

The command postulates and considerations of creation and space around "6.0" on the Standard Model required no energy or force in which *to be.* Later agreements to use force—energy (in Alpha-Existence) and effort (in Beta-Existence)—is a "game condition" only. At first, things could be brought into being for a Creative Universe by "Alpha Thought" alone—and in many respects, the actual considerations and commands still originate at this level. However, with condensation of Games Universes and individuals *considering* creation as more solid *energy-matter* at each one, the action requires applying a similar degree of *energy.* This further validates the *substance* and *reality* of a particular Universe.

> When POV is anchored to *beta-existence* and
> controlling the functions of a *genetic vehicle,*
> the Alpha-Spirit is still using energy beams.

These are commanded at the level of Alpha-Thought, but they are conducted by Will-Intention even when attention is focused on *beta-existence,* such as a "body" or the "Physical Universe" in general. Both are treated as environment (or setting). There is also the matter of the Mind-System (4.0), meaning mental machinery and fragmented communication/energy circuits.

All operations of a *beta* Mind-System are below *exterior* Alpha qualities of "Direct Will and Intention" (5.0) on the Standard Model. In Alpha-Existence, we chart a point of Alpha-Command (7.0):

—followed by Alpha-Thought (6.0),

—followed by Will-Intention (5.0) treating energetic action at the con
tinuity-level of a "typical" Spiritual Universe (4.0).

The *depths* of Alpha-Existence (4.0) are fragmented to compose the
height of (and control point for) *beta-existence.* This follows a similar
pattern of energy as before, with the same style of harmonics—but
taking place at lower-frequencies as the manifest Physical Universe. The same pattern repeats itself through condensation of *all*
Universes; only the *parameters* shift for *what* is treated as *above* and
below the "line" for consideration as "physical" or "apparent."

For example, if establishing a POV in the "Magic Universe" (immediately
preceding the present Physical Universe), one would still consider its
continuity a *beta-existence* with its own relative degree of solidity (which
is actually not much different than the present Physical Universe). All
else beyond and "above" that—the *"Other"*—is still treated as Alpha-Existence. For this reason, the Standard Model can be used to represent all
possible states of all viewpoints for any Universe. It is far more workable
than any former description of "planes," energetic bodies, or mystical
cosmology found in esoteric occultism.

An Alpha-Spirit uses energy beams for command of a Mind-Body system.
These are treated lightly in other types of "energy work" regarding certain "circuits" and "flows" of the body—such as *kundalini, yoga, chakras,
&tc.*—but like other forms of mysticism, the practitioner has a tendency
to remain quite fixed to the mental circuitry itself (rather than a perspective *outside* of it). One can use these other methods and sometimes
get lucky in managing some kind of repair of an existing state, but seldom does it permanently treat *encoded* and *programmed* conditions
causing an individual to continuously require such corrective actions.
While the methods may produce an effect, they also validate operating
reactively only, which puts the individual at effect.

Handling of energy beams and flows requires operating with clear channels from a point of direct consideration and command postulates in
order to *Will* or *Intend* an energetic effect. It requires no actual effort, because we are not using a physical means to affect physical mass. A *Seeker*
may find working directly with energy is a bit out of their "reality" to
grasp at first. It is quite different from how they have agreed to consider
standard operation and action in the Physical Universe.

For example, when controlling a *genetic vehicle*, the Alpha-Spirit will connect up circuitry and energy beams—running to the inside of a head, the
back of the neck, all along the central nervous system or spine, the area

called the Solar Plexus, and so forth. In the past these specific areas have been treated as "energy centers" or "light centers" that circulate specific types of energy. Yet most traditions just *assume* them to *be*, not realizing that *Self* is not only operating them, but also responsible for agreeing to and maintaining their *creation* each step of the way.

> There are essentially *seven* of these "centers" and *seven* "shells" "bodies" or "veils" that enshroud considerations of an individual that occupies this Physical Universe. In Systemology, we have been navigating our ascent up the "*Ladder of Light*" using calculable systematic correlations between these personal "*layers*" that were added and the cosmic "Gates" we descended.

Before heavy fragmentation occurs, an Alpha-Spirit is *Aware* that they are not actually located *interior to* a Creative Universe, but are instead "reaching inside" one to both operate and experience that operation. As when practicing exercises for "*Creation-of-Universes,*" the individual (as an *Awareness*) is completely *outside* the boundaries of the space, looking *in*. [This applies to everyone, not only individuals named Timothy Leary.] The Alpha-Spirit is already *exterior* to the entire Universe as an actuality, so the best "Secondary POV" (they think) is not located behind the "body" it wants to operate and experience, but from a POV that is *inside* it. Which is, of course, how an individual gets over-identifies with (and can fixedly snap into) a "body" more permanently.

The more an individual associates their personal *Identity* (or Beingness) with the *genetic vehicle*, the greater energy will be applied to *protect it* and maintain its survival *above all* other considerations. It is the "*above all else*" to the detriment of *Self-Awareness* that allows more personal fragmentation.

When an Alpha-Spirit *identifies* with "pain" or other sensations of a physical body, additional circuitry is crystallized (or calcified) in place, which we call *imprints*. The "shock" snaps the POV into the body with force.

The Alpha-Spirit now wants to protect itself and considers itself to share the same fate as the body. It develops all manner of shields, filters, relays and other automatic mechanisms to assist protecting the *genetic vehicle*. This mode of action repeated numerous times through many incarnations. The inherent sense of "betrayal" inevitable down the line is sure to put an individual out of communication with bodies and spaces throughout this *beta-existence* altogether. The conclusion is another Universe collapse. Then, we'll find considerations for the next shared-agreement Universe to sink one notch lower as a common denominator.

The Alpha-Spirit maintains an *interior* POV for the *genetic vehicle*, but realizing it is not always a "safe" place to be, sets up additional "points" to view from just outside of it. This is the area that *Awareness* will suddenly move to, using *Self-generated* response-mechanisms, during severe accidents. These points of "unconsciousness" are actually times when the POV has been spontaneously expelled from the *genetic vehicle*. It is also from this point that *Awareness* will suddenly "snap-in" on the body again. The very fact that these incidents result in sudden shifts of *interior* and *exterior* and *interior* (again) POV, outside of one's direct *Self-determinism*, contributes to the ongoing difficulty one has in "getting out" as a stable condition and resuming control of a body knowingly and willingly as opposed to being "stuck" inside one.

Proper handling of the fundamentals lends greater understanding on primary areas of "energetic charge" and ability to target channels and terminals associated with turbulent incidents. This package is what led a *Seeker* to the point they are now. A *Professional Pilot* gains the training, skills and certainty necessary to effectively assist others to redirect their course and increase their reach to fly out and beyond the boundaries of *beta-existence*.

:: B ::

APPLICATION OF CREATIVENESS PROCESSING
TECH REPORT FOR SYSTEMOLOGY PILOTS
GRADE-IV WIZARD-0 ROUTE-0

CREATIVENESS is perhaps the highest faculty and functional purpose of the I-AM-*Self* Alpha-Spirit in its basic state of Beingness as pure *Spiritual Awareness.* The more we increase a *Seeker's* level of *Creative Ability,* the more certain they will be in ability to control the creation of various *impressions* and *imprints*—the *Mental Imagery* and its *facets*—that they copy and continue to compulsively *create* in order to "*have*" something. Until an individual has systematically reduced encoded effects from former "*loss*"—including loss of creations and universes—and practice *Self-determining* their own "withdrawal" of attention or reach, difficulties may arise, quite common to the *Human Condition*:

ability to let go of and disconnect from what we *have.*

"*Creativeness Processing*"—Route-0 and "Wizard Grades"—provides *Seekers* sufficient practice of their own *Creative Ability* in order to demonstrate that:

Self can create whatever, whenever, and everything that is experienced and recorded is copied by *Self* as a personal creation. We are, in essence, creating a facsimile-copy of the Physical Universe around us and treating the *Mental Imagery* of that copy within our Personal Universe. All perceptions are communicated indirectly through circuitry and relays and screens.

The Universe that many individuals occupy when they close their eyes and *Imagine*, is very often still a duplicated facsimile of *beta-existence.* This means all their considerations for creation and ability and reality agreements for a Personal Universe are tied exclusively to *beta-existence* as well. Systematic application of "*Creativeness Processing*" and *Imagination* assist in defragmenting these considerations and returning additional certainty to *Self* about its own true nature as a *Free Spirit.*

Seekers should begin with previous Routes and methods of *Beta-Defragmentation* (procedures in *Crystal Clear* and *Metahuman Destinations*). This reduces heaviest charges of *imprinting* or reactive "*pictures*" prior to increasing perception of *Mental Imagery.* Otherwise reactive *imprints* are perceived more vividly and have more "bite."

It may be the case that spiritual rehabilitation of *Creative Ability* is the master key to stable *Beta-Defragmentation.* All other systematic processing essentially makes *this* more possible. For processing, early steps regarding "Presence" in environment and "Control" of the body are necessary for increasing *Awareness* enough to actually make *"creativeness processing"* effective for our purposes.

If a *Seeker* (as an *Awareness* point) is not truly "present," than all exercises, procedures and fancy PCLs will only be performed using some automatic response circuit. The individual, as *Self*, may still not be executing the commands at all. Most procedures for "Route-0" focus the *Seeker* on a subjective universe to work from, giving a *Pilot* only certainty on action that is actually observable. If an individual is still having difficulties with exercises and processes that *can* be observed and communicated easily, a *Pilot* should be careful **investing** too much time toward applying "upper-routes."

Δ Δ Δ Δ Δ Δ Δ

Increasing a *Seeker's* tolerance of POV and *Creative Ability* involves confronting *space* and "points" in *space.* Traditionally, an individual is more comfortable with *mass,* calcified *energy-matter.* Many *"Wizard Level-0"* exercises and techniques deal with "points" and "spots," which have, in themselves, no *mass* or color or shape or feel. Of course, these "points" can be collapsed within a Universe and condensed into greater solidity— but that is not the level of solidity we are dealing with in higher existences.

> "Route-0" emphasizes what *Self* is doing in regards to its own Personal Universe. Our past work has treated other circuits of energy-flow and stored imprints regarding what has happened to *Self,* what *Self* has done to others, and what *Self* has observed others doing to others. All of this is stored within the Mind-System. Even when it does not have strong emotional encoding, if *Self* assigns significance and association to it, this information contributes to what an individual carries for their considerations as Alpha-Thought. But this is entirely subject to an individual's own participation, command postulates and creation—even when information and cues are strongly suggested by external forces.

Another application of "Route-0" is found embedded in the most esoteric part of Systemology since the beginning, and that is *"Procedure 180."* Here, *Self* is in command of its own *Beingness* from the POV of the Alpha-Spirit and not fixed to a specific dimensional anchor. We treat this upper work as *Imagination*, or "knowingly creating an illusion," when *Seekers* are first introduced to the "Wizard Grades." This safeguards against any invalidation of results. The *"Creative Ability Test"* (CAT) and other suggestions in the *"Imaginomicon"* (*Liber-3D*):—

> may simply be *gotten a "sense of"* until they can be *Imagined*;
> and they can be *Imagined* until *Actualized Awareness* is at
> such a level that *Self* starts to experience *actual* perceptions.
> *Imagination* increases *realization* and *potential* for the actual.

To knowingly *Be* an *Awareness* at various "spots" and "points" in existence (and be able to scan the *"Spiritual Timeline"*), a *Seeker* must increase their tolerance to *look.* This means actually applying attention to a "locational point" in *space-time.* The Alpha-Spirit has the ability to direct its POV to any location that it is willing to "see." We now practice this differently than previous arcane mystic schools have taught.

Rather than considering a "spirit in flight," a *Seeker* should strengthen realizations that the true static I-AM-*Self* POV is actually a non-local point "moving the scenery"—or rather *creates it*—around them.

A *Seeker* that works through material from earlier volumes relatively easily, but only sees "blackness" or "darkness" when applying *Imagination*, may have heavy Alpha-Fragmentation impinging on their ability to handle *space* and other concepts beyond *beta-existence.* They may require more practice with "Wizard Level-0" exercises before moving forward. Such *Seekers* may also have to practice observing "points" or "spots" in their physical environment before treating an "imaginary" or otherwise "spiritual" one.

A *Pilot* should practice with them in locating and touching "spots" in the room that are not in relation to an object or *mass.*

"*Wizard Level-0*" goals should be approached gradually rather than invalidating what a *Seeker* is unable to reach at their present state. Certainty on the "abstract" can be strengthened by practicing with "objective."

Similar to techniques for "Presence" and "Control of the Body," a *Pilot* can place marks on objects and have a *Seeker* direct themselves between those, even resuming the function of "choice" by deciding when to "touch" and "let go." The *Seeker* can practice moving the body over various spots in alternation.

When this has been satisfied, only then should a *Pilot* have a *Seeker* "imagine" spots in their physical environment and perform the same steps. It is important that they can repeatedly indicate exactly where it is with certainty and that it is a "point" in "space" and not in relation to another object or *mass*.

A *Seeker* that is able to practice these things objectively can then apply the same methodology to their *Imagination* and use of *Creative Ability*. For whatever the reasons, the POV for Alpha-Existence is confined to "blackness" for some individuals. This is not the same as an Infinity of Nothingness, but the *Imprinting Incident* has left something so similar that it produces a fear of approaching the Gates of Infinity and standing for-and-as *Self*, the point of pure *Spiritual Awareness*.

A *Seeker* can practice putting out "black points" and getting a sense of them, even if they are not objectively visible. Once the *Seeker* is certain enough of their existence and control of their creation, they can turn them white. As with the traditional application, any impinging or automatic phenomenon can be accelerated, changed, exaggerated or alternated until the individual has its creation under their control as intended.

∆ ∆ ∆ ∆ ∆ ∆ ∆

Another element of "*creativeness processing*" became more critical the longer our experiments were treating "points" and "spots" with no *mass*. An individual is likely to not feel very well during the session when constantly confronting or standing before *space* (which prompts toward *Nothingness*). An individual finds *energy-matter* more interesting and enticing as their *Awareness* decreases because it gives them something to "know about." When sole consideration is a "Personal Universe" and everything is known, because everything is *Self-directed*, there is no such "game" conditions involved.

Although "games" and "energy" are what got an Alpha-Spirit into trouble early on the "*Spiritual Timeline*":

it is difficult to increase *Actualized Awareness*
back to its original state without also consistently
giving the Alpha-Spirit something
to *do* with a *purpose*—or something to *play with*.

When one is raising a young person—or even, for example, training a dog—they are likely to get into things that they shouldn't or start playing with something that is dangerous.

> If you want to take something away and
> not leave them unhappy,
> you give them something in its place.

This is no different than an individual that has come to depend on their stores of *Mental Images*, each assigned meaning from former events that still carry *facets* of significance into the present. This alters how an individual experiences existence. An individual would feel quite lost, disoriented and unhappy if we were to simply take away all *imprints* at once. It became clear to us that for a *Seeker* to "let go" willingly, they would have to be able to knowingly *create* something in its place.

> An individual has grown accustomed to being an
> "energy unit" rather than an "Awareness Unit."

Systematic processing *reduces* emotional intensity, analyzes imprints to the point of *dissolution*, and *defragments* circuits of "pictures" and "programs." A *Seeker* can feel as though they are *losing*, not just the things themselves, but their sense of "game." They are no longer in a state of non-knowing, dependent on their stores of "thinking" debris in which to "know."

> If this is not handled systematically, a *Pilot* may find that as one "automatic circuit" is reduced, another one "turns on" with full intensity. This can happen if *implanted compulsions* remain where an individual "has to have" something.

Our method is to neither "strip down bare" or "feed stuffed full." Covert goals of *Imagination* and *Creativeness* processes are to assist *Seekers* in being free of implanted compulsions to "*have*" things. Work with "mass" is one basic step to this. We've mentioned having a *Seeker* really "*look*" at things around them in the "session room" to orient their presence. This is just as effective in one's usual environment, when already dealing with POV in this Physical Universe that are simply no longer "game enough" to be occupied. Thus an individual is willing to duplicate, or repeat, less and less in each Universe.

Scenery has a tendency to fade into the background when its registry is set on automatic; it has no life or beingness given to it by *Self* until its restimulated in some way. Suddenly, being asked to *really* look at a tree or a hillside and notice its substance, even one they have "seen" a thousand times before, the perceptions are suddenly much more vivid.

> An individual "sees" a tree and registers a facsimile-copy of it in their "Personal Universe"; they no longer will look at the tree, even

when its present; they have the picture they generated and they will treat the recorded picture as the thing for "thought" and "consideration."

Even when live impressions are recorded from the present external environment, an individual is still looking at impressions of waves and particles hitting sensors and relays within a circuit; not the actual thing that *is*.

In theory, an Alpha-Spirit seeing something truly "*As-It-Is*" would have the ability to dissolve its creation instantaneously. This may be more difficult to demonstrate in the *Physical Universe* of shared consensual reality agreements, yet this is exactly why any defragmentation processing is effective in our Systemology. An individual is handling their own version of *it* within a Personal Universe.

∆ ∆ ∆ ∆ ∆ ∆

Refinement of "*Creativeness Processing*" refinement occurred at the Systemology Society as an upper-route alternative to "Route-2" (*Analytical Recall*). (Much as "Route-3" is an upper-route alternative to "Route-1.") Each former Route would apply to a particular set of subjects or imprint-types, but proved more tedious when applied to later goals.

Applications of "Route-0" emphasize what *Self* is *doing*, but specifically what it can *create*—or *is* creating. The more a *Seeker* practices handling their *Creative Ability*, the greater the realizations concerning just how significantly *Self* plays a role in compulsively and unknowingly creating with various types of energetic-machinery all along. This is incredibly difficult for some individuals to accept properly; but it is among the minimum requirements for proceeding beyond *Grade-IV* and *Wizard Level-0.*

Working with energy directly is quite obscure to communicate for *Grade-IV* Systemology. Therefore, we treat *Mental Images* for the energy that they contain; partially like a magician uses a *symbol* in substitution for the *actual*. But it is not the same. Rather than symbols, our *encoded imprints* actually do contain a reserve of entangled energy of personal *Awareness* on a particular channel. Handling circuitry on that channel affects the *imprint.*

Our *Mental Images* are very personal to us and they carry a lot of personal energy within them. Each time they are restimulated from various *facets* and generated with automatic-mechanisms, the entire fragmented *Hu man Condition* is given more solidity. This is because an individual is also responsible for continuous creation of the machinery at work. In short: "*Creativeness Processing*" may allow a *Seeker* to regain control over their creation of *Mental Imagery* along a certain channel or representing a specific terminal that is not otherwise resolved easily using other "Routes."

There is a consideration of something specific in "Games Universes" and below that does not exist in an individual's own "Home Universe." This is:

> "Scarcity-and-Abundance"—This exists as a consideration
> only if there is a dependency on "energy" to communicate
> actions and intention, rather than direct "Alpha-Thought."

This reality agreement is installed as part of an *implant platform*. It solidifies certain limitations and conditions placed on lower "Shared Universes"—providing a certain order-and-sequence to "forms" moved by "energy" (and the creation of both). Everything gets knocked down a notch with each Universe condensation. Everything that was, becomes a "way to" something else. And this continues on.

> The perception of "scarcity" is what causes an individual to cling
> that much tighter to what they perceive they "have." The more
> "pictures" they copy, the less an individual begins to *create* on
> their own. Failing to knowingly create, they hold onto compulsively created *imprint* as something rare.

Most encoded information tends to be a hindrance to experiencing and *Self-directing* that experience. It's easy to see how a very long existence across the "*Spiritual Timeline*" could have a tendency to cumulatively degrade abilities and fragment *Awareness* of an otherwise Unlimited *Spiritual Being*.

> Collecting experience hinders *Awareness* for new experience.
> The only reason we keep it to "learn from" is because we put
> ourselves into a position of "not-knowing" in the first place
> —it was something to do; we've done it; now its one more
> consideration restricting what we will do next.

A *Seeker* carrying automated-images and other reactive-responses connected to "pain" is doing so because they perceive a "shortage" of such *Mental Imagery* in their "files" or ability to "create." So, it continues to be created on automatic and held in close to the POV. The information, sensory triggers, pings and other uncomfortable sensations will all continue to be generated by this reactive *Image* and encounters with its *facets* until control can be maintained over its *creation.*

As explained in Grade-III, particularly in *"Tablets of Destiny,"* a tendency to develop and depend on these primitive "survival" mechanisms is part of the evolutionary make-up of the *genetic vehicle.* As an *implant* it came to define parameters of the *Human Condition.*

> these are *just* response tendencies and impulse patterns;
> an individual doesn't *have to* "listen to" and "obey" them.

It is quite difficult for someone still working through heavy beta-defragmentation steps to come to a solid actual realization that: *they are creating this experience.* That is a lot for someone to take responsibility for all at once, especially if pushed before they are ready to handle it. The idea will certainly be rejected if it comes from another source. There-fore, the bulk of "beta-defragmentation" hangs on the amount of time it takes for an individual to come to this realization, for themselves, with complete certainty.

> Each "Route" is intended to "free up" enough
> *Actualized Awareness* to apply additional routes
> and higher gradients of systematic processing.

"Route-1" is mainly effective for lower-level cases that are heavily sus-pended in emotionally encoded *imprinting* in the present; those things which are so intrusive that no next-level "analytical" work can be effect-ively processed. It is used by *Pilots* when necessary and as a basic coun-seling methodology for *Ministers* of the Church of Mardukite Zuism. If operated beyond its intended purposes, "Route-1"—erasure or reduction in *dissolving fragmentation*—not only validates reactive-mechanisms too often, but due to a perceived "energy loss," other *imprinting* may become stronger and "snap in" tighter. An individual starts to "hold on" with a sense that something is taken away. "Route-0" and "Circuit-0" applica-tions of *Creativeness* and *Imagination* can resolve this when alternated in between other Routes. Prior to, and including, *"Wizard Level-0,"* a *Pilot* should be very observant of the *Seeker's* condition regarding "energy loss"—alternating use of "objective" and "subjective" exercises.

△ △ △ △ △ △ △

"*Creativeness Processing*" negates automation and associated im-printing along a certain channel by replacing it with a new creation of the same type, degree and frequency. The one essen-tially cancels the other out.

An individual could spend several lifetimes retracing each of their steps, each *imprint* and each facsimile-copy *Mental Image* they took on. But, this would not have given us the results we were after here, of which we may summarize quite completely and concisely for the first time:

BETA–DEFRAGMENTATION VERSION 2.0*
SYSTEMOLOGY OPERATING PROCEDURE

Once a *Seeker* has completely worked through Grade-III (see *"Tablets of Destiny"* and *"Crystal Clear"*; or *"The Systemology Handbook"*) and the "hot-buttons" of Grade-IV using "Route-3" and SOP-2C (see *"Metahuman Destinations"*), all remaining beta-defragmentation is primarily accomplished with *"creativeness processing"* (see *"Imaginomicon"*).

This also requires imagining the creation and handling various terminals—possibly hundreds of different objects, masses and incidents —that have emotional encoding (or associative imprinting) restricting "free" consideration and fix *Awareness* outside Self-determination.

Each *Mental Image* representing a terminal is systematically handled in one's Personal Universe until the *creation, protection (preservation)* and inevitable *destruction* of it is freely treated and comfortably acceptable on all of its channel circuits.

Finally, a *Seeker* reviews *all former* work, but applying *"Imagination"* to all PCL, adjusting all processing so as to not invoke any physical actions or recall pertaining to *beta-existence.*

When an individual is clear of compulsive and unknowing tendencies to *create,* has fully rehabilitated *creative faculties* of a Personal Universe, and regained a commanding viewpoint as the Alpha Spirit exterior to any considerations for the Physical Universe, we consider that individual defragmented -or- *Actualized* up to a *beta-state* of *Self-Honesty,* a basic stable point, just outside the Mind-System, from which to knowingly continue to experience the Human Condition— and if so inclined, pursue a higher spirituality with the Mardukite Wizard Grades of Metahuman Systemology.

* * * * * * *

[*As addition beta-defragmentation booster, the *"Way of the Wizard"* (*Liber-3E*) established Ethics and Integrity Processing in Spring 2022.]

---

* Version 1.1: 30. April 2021; revised: 22, June 2021; Version 2.0. revised 30. April 2022

Humans typically have difficulty handling *imprints* with heavy energetic charges. The purpose of the *imprint* and other mechanisms is as a "buffer." They will each have different reactions to being responsible for their "*Mental Images.*" It may be that when they *Imagine* something very clearly, and then make it more solid, that it is difficult to do anything with it other than admire—least of all, throw it away or destroy it.

Destruction is really counter-creation or no-creation. Making something more solid or persistent is a continuous creation of many copies tightly compressed together. It may be that some *Seekers* would have to be prompted to create several copies of an *imagined mass* before they are willing to discard or dispense with any. The ultimate goal here is for a *Seeker* to be able to freely create, confront and discard anything it can *imagine*, without an automatic tendency, associated response or consideration aside from: practice of Alpha-Thought to make something *Be* what it *is*.

Ideally, "*Creativeness Processing*" (for defragmentation processing) requires some type of *assessment* on a *Seeker* concerning the terminals and forms that carry an energetic charge. There are ways of even using various "galvanic skin response" biofeedback devices in conjunction with "word-association." This is even suggested by Carl Jung.[‡] An individual could list out all various items, as best they could, paying close attention to those that they are unwilling to create or be responsible for; also those that they have an emotional response-reaction to.

> Some *Pilots* introduced a PCL that query a *Seeker* alternately: "What are you willing to create?"/"What are you not willing to create?" Others have used the keyword "confront" in place of "create." This primarily works best for more advanced *Seekers* experienced with *Piloted Procedure.* A less direct PCL would replace "are you" with "would you be."

Concerning applications to earlier materials: "Route-1" treats the heaviest incidents that act as the thickest blinders to maintaining present *Awareness*; "Route-2" employs "*recall*" PCLs, which can be converted to "*imagine*"; all of the "hot-button" terminals and circuits treated with "Route-3" in "*Metahuman Destinations*" can also be converted. Make certain that imagined incidents and events are uniquely and knowingly created, not something that the *Seeker* has a sense is a facsimile-copy from actual experience. Reactive images are those that "come to mind" as soon as a terminal, subject or object is named (or contacted).

---

‡ See "*The Way of the Wizard*" (*Liber-3E*) by Joshua Free.

The original "two-step maneuver" given for "Route-0" (Grade-IV, SOP-2C) appears as: a) *Imagine*; b) *Create It*—with no other commentary. In order to take what is *Imagined* and use it for "*Creativeness Processing*," the *Seeker* must have a sense that they are actually creating it and that it is not a reactive-response. It must not be generated for them by some other mechanism that they, long ago, set up to deliver "pictures" on a "screen."

> A *Pilot* can suggest any particular terminal (object, mass, &tc.) for the *Seeker* to "*Imagine*." This is followed up with a PCL to "make it more solid." Essentially take what one has imagined to *be* and, by consideration, grant it *more beingness.* Until this is effectively done by postulate command, a *Seeker* can start with making many copies and pushing them together to make a solid or turning up a "dial" to make it "brighter." At first, in lack of certainty on direct postulates or Alpha-Thought, a *Seeker* may be likely to rely on *imagining* a means of accomplishing the action in a way that is "in agreement" with experience of the Physical Universe.

Because an individual is constantly creating *energy-masses* that snap-in or pull-in on their POV, whether that is the *genetic vehicle* "body" or some other consideration of "*Self*," it is necessary to facilitate this on one's own determinism. However, a PCL directing this:

> should *never* be a "pull" action (from inside),
> but rather a "push" or "shove" (from outside).

The individual has enough "caving-in" on them when they are fixed to a *genetic vehicle* POV. Therefore, we employ methods to establish a "secondary POV" that allows them to "push" or "shove" their *Creations* into the *genetic vehicle* from a point *exterior* to it. This is also excellent *pre-A.T.* practice for "*Zu-Vision*." The *Pilot* should direct an end-cycle to each *Creation*, alternating: "push into that body" and then "throw away." If necessary, the *Seeker* can "squish it into a ball" before the end-cycle action.

In addition to exercises selected for the *Creative Ability Test* (CAT), other processes described throughout *Grade-IV* materials, and attainment of necessary realizations, there is another primary "test-out" for "*Wizard Level-0.*" This is inspired by arcane ritual texts extending back into nearly-**prehistoric** Mesopotamia, almost 6,000 years ago. The same methodology can be found in modern rites of "ceremonial magic"—although little regard is made to it otherwise.

These archaic scripts refer to the individual standing within created-space while keeping a solid image on all six sides from going away.

In some cases, a practitioner envisioned a "deity"; in others a "star" or "symbol"—but most importantly, the entire effectiveness depended on the *Creative Ability* and *Actualized Awareness* to maintain this for the duration of a ceremony.

While we are not as concerned with "magical" semantics for our application of Systemology, the fact remains that the minimum to effectively aspire beyond Wizard Level-0 is:

ability to handle *Creation-of-Space* on all sides of an individual; then on each side, to imagine an object, keep it still in place, make it more solid, make copies of it, and suspend it before proceeding to the next side.

This can be practiced alone as part of regular *Creativity Sessions*. Select an object with no energetic charge or personal significance for best results. When *Piloted*, make certain that PCLs refer to "that body" or "the body" and not "your body." For example: "In front of that body, imagine..." and then applying to each direction of "that body."

Realization goals for *Grade-IV Wizard Level-0* include: handling automatic and compulsive creation of *Mental Images*; freeing associative restrictions on *Creative Ability* and *Imagination*; detaching *fixed POV* from the *genetic vehicle*; assuming responsibility for *Creation-of-Space* and handling *points in space*; and ability to maintain a stable Alpha-Spirit POV to freely experience a *Personal Universe* that is independent from, outside of and exterior to the *Physical Universe*.

—UNIT FIVE—

THE WAY OF THE WIZARD

—LIBER-3E—

:: ETHICS, CODES, MORALS & DOGMA[‡] ::
—General Information for All Systemologists—

Semantically named from the Greek word *"ethos"*—meant to infer an **individual**'s "moral character" (and the corresponding "customs" or "principles" thereof)—formal intellectual pursuit of *"ethike philosophia"* became a fundamental subject among famous "high minds" of the *Classical World*—including Aristotle, Plato and Socrates. Of course, the **concept** itself is actually much older; extending far back to the *Ancient Near East*—"**Mesopotamia**"—and **inception** of *cuneiform* writing and other civic **systems**. Even the Ancient Druids of Western Europe had already perfected their own independent philosophy of *Ethics* by the time of their first direct encounters with the Greeks—and the *Classical World*—nearly 2,500 years ago. Unfortunately, many contemporary scholars of the past century continued to falsely favor the *Classical Period* (for example, Greece and Rome, *c. 500 BC*) as the singular source or **epicenter** of all substantial **knowledge** carried forth from the ancient world.

We tend to **treat** a much wider array of source material at the Mardukite Academy and Systemology Society than practically any other "**esoteric fellowship**" in history. But, our efforts are not entirely unlike those of the Greek and Hermetic traditions from the *Classical Period*—enigmatic and "cultish" Pythagorean Schools and secretive "underground" Socratic Societies.[*] With much of the cuneiform records already lost to the shifting sands of Sumer by this time, the *Classical Age* witnessed its own revival of "**epistemological**" philosophies regarding the "truth" of "things" and strong efforts toward preserving an "absolute" **knowledge** —such as was once retained in **Babylonia**, and which once served as the true "heartbeat" of ancient **systematization**. As time bore on, similar intellectual pursuits became diluted and reduced to a wider subjective **treatment** as "moral philosophy," eventually influencing human "**consciousness**" strongest through common practices of **religious "dogma"** and upheld (or **enforced**) by whatever element of civilization stood socially responsible for maintaining civic "justice."

[‡] Portions of this chapter-lesson are based on the July 2021 *"Grade-IV, Freedom From"* lectures given by *Joshua Free* to the *Mardukite Academy of Systemology* at *Mardukite Babylonia SLV Borsippa HQ*; additional *"Notes On Philosophy"* sections are specially adapted from the *Grade-I (Route-A)* Master Edition textbook: *"The Great Magical Arcanum."* These were issued as supplemental lecture handouts.

[*] Referencing John Toland's *Pantheisticon* available from Mardukite Esoteric Research Library; reprinted in *Grade-I (Rte-D)* Master Ed. textbook: *"Merlyn's Complete Book of Druidism"* by Joshua Free.

With small regard for linguistic analysis and the true meaning of words, common-use English is seldom a perfect language for us to communicate Systemology to the "average" individual. It can take a considerable amount of time and training to indoctrinate one of these "**standard-issue**" lifeforms to even the most basic wide-angle **understanding** of our Systemology... Unless, of course, all specialized vocabulary and terms are uniquely and concisely defined to our complete satisfaction in relation to basic purposes of our organization. This is the only way we can share certainty that a *Seeker* (or reader) is receiving (and perfectly duplicating in their Personal Universe) the exact meaning communicated (in this book) as intended. As a systematic approach to philosophy and spirituality concerning *"Life, Universes and Everything,"* our Systemology naturally recognizes separate semantics for each significant component—*ethics, morals, dogma, justice* and so on—since they are not actually **identifiable** synonymously equal to one another.

> *ethics* : an intellectual philosophy concerning *rightness* and *wrongness* based on "**logic**" and "**reason**" combined with observable consequences and tendencies of action or conduct; formal name for a "moral philosophy" (study of moral choices); in ancient times, originally treated *one-to-one* with "**Cosmic Law**" regarding *causation, order* and *sequence*; an **objective** (Universal) philosophy of *rightness* and *wrongness*, treated separate from culture-specific (subjective/ "**relative**") **considerations**, such as *morals* and *dogma*; in *NexGen Systemology* (*Grade-IV* **Metahuman** *Systemology*), a **dynamic** philosophy (applying "**logic**-and-**reason**") to understand the nature of "reality **agreements**" concerning *rightness* and *wrongness*, then treating the most "**optimum**" **conditions** of continued **existence** ("SURVIVAL" in *Beta-existence*; "CREATION" in *Alpha*) for the highest affected "Sphere of Existence" (on the *Standard Model*).

> *morals* : widely held culturally conditioned (socially **learned**) ethical standards of conduct used to "judge" *rightness* from *wrongness* of an individual's character, **personality** or actions (which may or may not be intellectually and emotionally influenced by "local" religious customs, taboos and *dogma*; basic social reality agreements determining "proper conduct" and "right actions" (behavior) based on civic *laws*, social *codes* and religious *doctrines* of a particular society or group (and its own cultural experiences of *Reality*.

> *dogma* : religious doctrines or opinion-based beliefs (**data-set**) treated socially as fact, especially regarding "divinity" or "God" (the common "Human" interpretation of the "Realm" or "boundar-

y" of Infinity) represented by the "Eighth Sphere" on our original Standard Model of Systemology; religiously defined values, taboos and ethical standards emphasized by cultural/religious socialization and mythographic beliefs (held superior to observable causal effects, logical sequences or verifiable proofs).

code : an outline of *ethical* standards regarding social **participation** and acceptable behavior; not generally enforced as *law* itself, but a standard that reasonable individuals are **actualized** (or civil) enough to *Self-Determine* (by choice) their own following (or adherence) if it is *right* and *good*; shared reality agreements that promote optimum conditions of continued existence ("SURVIVAL" in *Beta-existence*; "CREATION" in *Alpha*) for the highest affected "Sphere of Existence" (on the *Standard Model*).

law : a formal **codified** outline (or list) of *ethical* standards regarding social participation and acceptable behavior, like a "*code*," except that it *is* enforced by civic consequences (or even "*Cosmic Law*") when not adhered to, usually with punishment coming either by the group (exclusively) or by involvement with an "outside party" or societal (legal) **authority**; a predictable sequence of naturally occurring events that will consistently repeat under the right conditions (such as "*Cosmic Law*" or "*Natural Law*").

justice : observable social actions (or consequential reaction) and predetermined civic (legal) processes employed in a society or group to uphold or enforce their reality agreements concerning "*law*"; a civic authority and administrative body responsible for carrying out practical/physical responses and penalties; the words, "*just*," "*justice*" and "*justification*," all stem from the Latin "*jus*" (meaning "*morally right*," "*law, in accordance with*" or "*lawful*") and "*iustus*" (expressing what is "true," "proper," "up-right" and "justified").

Fortunately, in view of the fact that this course is for the Mardukite Academy of Systemology—and strongly connected to "**Mardukite Zuism**" ministries and related spiritual advisement techniques—we do not exclusively restrict our understanding to contemporary academia or even 0the *Classical World*. We have a tangible 6,000-year archive to draw from. It is familiar territory for us "Mardukite Systemologists" to reference our ancient stores of "*Arcane Tablets*" and esoteric "*Mystic Scrolls*" when necessary; or when supplementing Clear Understanding for an individual's personal vision maintained of antiquity and progressive development of building upon the same **archetypal** Systems of Civilization. Yes, we treat you with a history lesson; even now as we transition from Grade-IV, when our own "total recall" of the past is still uncertain, obscured by many thin veils solidly compacted together; meaning the Self-created barriers and "unknowns"—or more correctly, what we specifically chose (at some point on the *Backtrack*) to "Not-Know" and/or not be "responsible" for.

Imposition of critical *Ethics*—in the form of *Justice* and *Law*—only increased as civic populations (and the complexity of their systems) grew. This is easily demonstrable with a simple *Back-Scan* of the past 6,000 years on Earth. Drawing from **'common knowledge'**, Babylon carries a pretty bad reputation for the severity of its *Laws*, but ironically, you don't find a lot of significant criminality during that *Age*, like you might expect. Yes, of course, nations were always pitted against each other for one territorial reason or another—which is ironic when you consider just how much energy had to go into keeping that land sustainable and viable for life; you'd think at some point they would have all just banded together and overtaken more plush regions elsewhere. But, they didn't; so, obviously there is a greater significance to the hold on Mesopotamia —one which escapes more obvious observations available to the average individual. Post-Alexandrian invaders that overtook Mesopotamia did not even maintain the aqueduct system and then newer populations just let the whole place go to pieces.

In both **Sumerian** and **Babylonian** tradition, the Sun—"*Shammash*"— represents "truth," "justice" and the "wisdom of ethics." Such is the domain of *Shammash*, both: literally, as an Anunnaki representative; then celestially, as the actual embodiment of the Sun. This is also the classification for the *Fourth* "rung" along the *Pathway* on the "Ladder of **Ascension**" or "Ladder of Lights" (or "step" on the "Stairway to Heaven") and, likewise, representative of the *Fourth Gate*. This is what immediately precedes the *Fifth* gradient—or *Grade-V*—in the original "Star-Gate" **methodology**; and it seems particularly fitting and prophetic that we should be taking up the concise Systemology of *Self-Honesty* and systematic **processing** of *Ethics* at this **level**. For those that reached the basic point of *Beta-Defragmentation* attainable at this level of our applied spiritual technology (since the release of **Liber-3D**, "*Imaginomicon*"), my intent is that [**Liber-Three**, *Ethics*] will successfully "boost" and "stabilize" all personal gain achieved from completely working through *Grade-IV*. This newly released material on *Ethics*, *Self-Honesty* and "**Responsibility**" provides an effective and necessary "bridge" between *Grade-IV* and *Grade-V* for our "Pathway" in Systemology.

Looking back at records from ancient Mesopotamia—we do not find significant emphasis on violent criminality or imprisonment. While the severity of Babylonian "**Codes**" and "Laws" are particularly famous **rhetoric**, the actual Mardukite legal system is practiced with emphasis on "equality" and "balance"—with "making things whole." During initial installation of civic systems, the Anunnaki most likely held-back restimulating "Prison **Imprints**" too deeply in order to keep the masses from prematurely "waking up" to realizing that this Earth is itself something of a "Prison-Planet." Early progression of formal "*Ethics*" in Mesopotamia is concisely taken up by E.A. Wallis Budge in his century-old treatise titled "Babylonian Life and History":—

> "In primitive times in Babylonia each community or each tribe formulated its own laws and administered them according to custom, which was probably already age-old. The laws at that time were few and simple, and were drawn up chiefly to protect the property of the god and the community. Of these we know nothing. When the Sumerians conquered Babylonia and settled down in it, they observed their own laws, and it is possible they adopted some of those of their predecessors in the country..."

> "When Khammurabi* conquered the whole of Babylonia, he formulated a Code of Laws, by which he intended all his subjects to regulate their lives and affairs. The Laws were not invented by him, but were drawn up from earlier codes which had been in existence for many centuries. He had this Code cut upon a large stone *stele*, which was set up in the Temple of **Marduk** (*E-Sag-Ila*), so that any and every [person] could consult it... The **condition** of peace existing throughout the country under the firm, just and vigorous rule of Khammurabi made application of the Laws of the Code comparatively easy. The property of the rich and the rights and privileges of the poor were alike safeguarded, and during the time that the Code was observed, a woman could travel unmolested from Babylon to the Mediterranean Sea. The text of the Code was also edited for use in schools and studied as a text-book for many centuries after Khammurabi's death..."

Therefore, in c. 1800 B.C., "The Code of Hammurabi" greatly expounded on precepts of former Kings and the cultures they governed;‡ though he had admittedly received the "Code" from *outside* sources, Divine (as attr-

---

* Budge employs the archaic spelling "*Khammurabi.*"

‡ The oldest surviving written legal code predates Hammurabi by three centuries and is attributed to the Sumerian King Ur-Nammu.

ibuted) or otherwise. While his "Code" might seem rather "excessive" at first glance, to members of present-day **Western Civilization** now studying Babylon, its original presence in society was intended as a cultural deterrent (to crime) and standard of protection (for the people), which did not require excessive **enforcement**. [Although less famously known, their Assyrian neighbors to the north held far stricter and more militant laws.]

Early in the development of civilization, the "Law-Giving Kings" were highly celebrated for their wisdom. Legal "codes" in Mardukite Babylon were stylized in a very particular style of "ought not or else consequences"–type statements, which were readily accepted by the community as a standard of safety and protection. These were not written out as a list of demands, such as you find with the Judeo-Christian "Law of Moses" or "Ten Commandments"—instead, they describe scenarios like: "if this man harms this other fella, he must pay him such and such or be his servant for three years."

Aside from critical matters of state or crimes against the Temple, the highest "order" or "governmental system" was seldom employed. Citizens were encouraged to handle their own affairs at a local **level**; public display copies of the "Code of Hammurabi" were simply reminders that the "World Order of Marduk, son of Enki, son of Anu" was present among the population—and that the "Sun-god of Justice" was ever watchful. Stephen Bertman notes, in his "*Handbook to Life in Ancient Mesopotamia*":—

> "If the law codes of Mesopotamia signify an ideal of justice that should govern society, how was the ideal made an everyday **reality**? To begin with, there were no lawyers. Nor was there a regular court system, as we understand it. Nor were there prisons, or even a police force. How then was justice achieved, or even approximated? The key was an innate compliance to a higher authority, a behavioral characteristic that permeated Mesopotamian culture. Society's prime personal virtue was humble and unquestioning obedience—to the gods and their earthly surrogates."

> "Most controversies were resolved on the local level—the village or neighborhood—by a Council of Elders whose members were impaneled as judges when circumstances warranted. There were no juries selected from the population at large to hear cases. Instead, litigants presented their arguments to the judges, witnesses were called, and evidence (a written contract, for example) was examined. Trials were often held on the grounds of temples and

those who testified were required to swear an oath on a sacred **symbol** of the local god. Perjury was punished not by law but by divine retribution..."

Another cuneiform series—the *surpu-tablets*—is treated in our original Mardukite "Liber-9"[†] concerning cultural "taboos" referred to as *mamit* in the Akkadian language (Old Babylonian). Lengthy lists of "taboos" or "sins" appear in the series, all of which are actions potentially "causing" an illness or affliction (which might otherwise be religiously treated as "demons"). The tablets also reassure that *"The MAMIT of any kind that afflicts man, MARDUK, Priest of the Gods, can attend."* The list is fairly extensive, detailing numerous "causes of headache, disease and possession" that we might otherwise treat as common-sense in the Western World (concerning health and cleanliness), whereas the remainder appear to illustrate a *Code of Ethics* that is suggestive or implied, rather than imposition strict rules.

An individual is warned (on the *Surpu tablets*) about causing themselves trouble, for example, if they have:

> "...sinned against their god or goddess; ...slighted what is due to the gods; ...caused obstruction between family or friends; ...held hatred toward an elder; ...propositioned their neighbor's spouse; ...used a false balance in business affairs; ...stolen or caused another to steal; ...unjustly entered their neighbor's house; ...spoken of what is unholy; ...promised pleasure and joy but not giving it; ...offended the righteous; ...pointed at the holy fire; ...struck the young of an animal; ...torn up plants and trees; ...eaten from an unclean cup, plate or dish."

Mesopotamian-oriented Anunnaki Traditions—ancient or modern—place particular emphasis on themes of "Cosmic Ordering" or "The World Order of... this god or that one"; essentially anything along the lines of order, structure, sequence and systematization in place of "chaos." Even the notorious "Eye for an Eye" rhetoric is really relaying a cuneiform version of "*karma*" (or "Causal Law") more than anything else—especially when we discover that most "Free Citizens" were, in actuality, charged significant monetary fines or required to "repay in kind." The "Code" required a "victim" be "made whole"—in some cases, the offender would have to work for them.

[†] The text of *Liber-9* is incorporated into *"The Complete Anunnaki Bible"* (or *"Necronomicon: The Anunnaki Bible*), in addition to the Grade-II Master Edition textbook *"Necronomicon: The Complete Anunnaki Legacy"* and a 10th Anniversary reissue of *Liber-R+9* titled: *"Novem Portis: Necronomicon Revelations and Nine Gates of the Kingdom of Shadows."*

Nowhere among Hammurabi's "282 Laws" do we find mention of imprisonment. In fact, such methods of "correction" are not effective for anything other than getting an individual further "spun in" to the **Human Condition.** The experience restimulates existing unresolved "**fragmentation**" and makes it more "solid"—further separating an individual from their potential to experience a basic state of "***Self-Honesty***" (*Beta-Defragmentation*); And we expect *Seekers* to have achieved a basic state of *Self-Honesty* after using *Grade-III* and *Grade-IV*—in combination with *Liber-Three (3E)*, this present volume—before approaching "*A.T.*" ("*Actualization Tech*") in *Grade-V* as *Wizard Level-1*.

* * * * * * *

<u>NOTES ON EPISTEMOLOGY</u>

"Epistemology" is a school of philosophy containing theories about the basic structure of **knowledge** and reason. An understated, misrepresented and much misunderstood field, epistemology is actually the heart of every other philosophy and science because it pertains to how we might know anything about anything with any certainty. "Logic" offers a means by which we can analyze **semantic** reasoning—later divided into subjects: physio-logic, meteor-logic, even sciento-logic... But, epistemology is where our study of knowledge, reasoning, knowing, and truth interacts directly with "metaphysics" and what we hold true about the appearance of "reality."

Essentially every bit of knowledge—every belief, every idea or concept—is a *bit* of data an individual carries and supports as their view of "reality." Regardless of its **actual** or *factual* truth, logic or reasoning, this personal **agreement** (as data) affects how an individual "sees" and interacts with the "world." The materialist interpretation by Rene Descartes led academia to the standard "scientific method," which became something of a stumbling block for post-modern sciences, such as quantum and string theory. Materialist science would have us believe that everything is separate and that reality is something that **exists** "out there" completely independent of the observer. Yet, we find in our Systemology that reality is quite dependent on personal cognition, "observation," sensory **perception** and realizations for it to actually "exist" and persist "*As-It-Is.*"

When we consider all of the partitions of knowledge—the "-ologies" and "-logics"—by their own classification, each "school of thought" is entirely dependent on its own closed-**circuit "paradigm"** of semantic vocabulary in order to functionally operate. Although an individual might examine observable "causality" within a particular "field" of science, only consequential end-results are **apparent** from standard-issue **levels** of observation. Any supposed "absolute knowledge" objectively yielded from such observation does not reveal the true nature and/or source-cause of what is observed. This is one reason why Descartes originally put "God" into his epistemology. With "God" in the equation, all models work—so long as they are *dualistic* models. [Of course, an emphasis on God also protected Descartes from persecution as a "heretic" during the era of Galileo.]

Personal interpretation of any system's language or vocabulary (**semantic-set**) can be objectified and then later "agreed" upon (or accepted) as "reality" by mainstream society. In essence, we generally and socially call "truth" really results from "**authoritarianism**." The authoritarian scientist and/or reality **engineer** wants you to accept knowledge that you cannot personally verify outside the boundaries of the paradigm (and its use of language) specifically created to **identify** and prove the very knowledge in question. Most specific paradigms are self-serving and self-supporting in exclusive isolation.

French philosopher Rene Descartes (*1596-1650*) is credited with originating some significant modern contributions to epistemology, which he demonstrated to be the basic general philosophy back of all other "modern" scientific thought. From within his entire literary work, only a few simple key principles distinctly stand out, although thousands of words and multiple essays were composed to offer additional explanations and clarification to the era and audience he wrote for. During his time, as humanity emerged from its "Dark Ages," this was revolutionary thinking. Descartes caused the very foundations of modern science to tremble with his new "epistemology." But, he is accused (by some critics) of overly generalizing to a point of incompleteness. A closer examination reveals that rather than attempt to persuade the reader to "buy" a particular **patter** "sold" as "Absolute Truth," Descartes is more interested in uncovering a route by which an individual can discover this for themselves.

In "*Discourse on the Method of Rightly Conducting Reason and Seeking Truth in the Sciences*" (1637), Descartes describes—

> an intensive process by which the operator must attempt to clear their **slate** of all knowledge that can be doubted; which proves to be essentially everything determined through sensory perception and "human" experience in the Physical Universe.

Descartes suggests that these things can be added back into a personal paradigm later on, after vigorous scrutiny and in a logical order of certainty. First and foremost, *Self-knowledge* is given priority, proved by the *Self-Aware* **consciousness** of an individual; then *God*, the perfect **encompassing** generative force and source in the Universe; and finally *mathematics* and *geometry*, the means in which one might measure and quantify existence in the Universe. However, pursuit of mathematics necessarily loops a seeker back toward contemplation (or interpretive use) of symbols and language. Descartes even illustrates that as a model of observable (empirical) materialist science—even if we are certain of what our senses tell us about a causal "how"—no absolute knowledge of "why" can be determined by the same methods.

"Meditations on the First Philosophy in which the Existence of God, Reality and the Real Distinction of the Mind and Body of Man are Demonstrated" (1641) is Rene Descartes most famous work, though many readers have found *"Discourse on Method"* more practical. *"Meditations on First Philosophy"* does, however, reveal the thought progression distinguishes his epistemology. It also presents his most famous **axiom** of *"a-priori"* knowledge [the *"Cogito"*]: "I think, therefore I am." This is famous, though flawed; and logicians point out that it is not a true propositional proof—simply a statement. We can apply the most basic rule of "inferential logic" [*"modus ponens"*] to create a simple "if A then B; A, therefore B" conditional proposition: "If I think, then I exist. I think, therefore I exist." But, this does not solve the entire issue, which is a point directly addressed in the text for *Liber-3D*, *"Imaginomicon"*:—

> "Descartes... wrongly **identified** the 'thinkingness' with the 'beingness' of *Self*. Although it received far less **attention** [than the original 'cogito'], eventually this error philosophically earned a correction in Jean-Paul Satre's insight: The consciousness that says 'I-AM' is not the same consciousness which *thinks*."

> The *Being* is *Aware* that *it* is "thinking"
> —that ***Awareness*** is not a *part of* the "thinking."
> The *Being* exists independent of the "thought."

Perhaps the least cited, but most concise discourse by Descartes is *"Principles of Philosophy"* (1644). The work composes over one hundred propositions, each with an explanation, as well as significant **axioms** and other clarifications of his unique paradigm. Its demonstration style of Axioms and Logics has influenced and inspired many more recent "New Thought" presentations in the past century. Though the title might suggest some all-encompassing resolution or textbook for a broad study of general philosophy, this slim volume reduces philosophy to only two main aspects:

—the nature of human knowledge (*epistemology*) and

—the nature of material existence and reality (*metaphysics*).

Descartes puts forth the idea that "the senses deceive; and all that we can determine of material existence is accessed by material senses, then processed cognitively." What's more: when rigidly fixed to the *Human Condition* as a **Point-of-View** (**POV**) for **Awareness**, anything "beyond the physical" (or "meta-physical")—such as cognitive **faculties** and the "Mind-Body" connection—cannot be determined with material senses; therefore it lies beyond the domain of "empirical" science. Development of future "meta-sciences" (such as our *Systemology*) must also take into account the "spiritual" factor of *Self* (the actual 'I-AM') and the other Universes and alternate levels of existence not directly experienced from the POV of a "Human Body."

Standard models that radiate **apparent** truth may be overturned by new developments of understanding in spite of public/mass acceptance of the prior knowledge. The *Human Condition* is **implanted** to resist accepting large changes in paradigms or methodologies. As creatures wired by experience and habit, most common knowledge is taken for granted, but based on former knowledge foundations previously adopted. Many philosophers suggest a comparison of one's personal belief (paradigm) against the objective or social world-at-large. On the other hand, *Wizards* are more concerned about the effects of beliefs on reality. In the end, the knowledge we receive from the **external** world must still be processed through various sensors and relays and then weighted against some existing form of established knowledge.

Descartes also inspired German philosopher Immanuel Kant (*1724-1804*). He set forth to revise his own revision of a similar epistemology, which he describes in *"Critique of Pure Reason"* (1781). With rising interest in "empirical objectivism," Kant's *Ethics* requires the existence of an "abstract moral agent," what he called the "Good Will"—and which we might identify as the *"conscience."* An equally abstract **"maxim"** exists as a driving force or core **imperative** that Kant tries to impress as a Universal. It, of course, fails to be Universal if personally subjective, like a "conscience." While it may be actually true that "you" and "I" exist, proving the existence of one does not necessarily prove existence of the other.

> True **premises** carried to a false conclusion and
> true conclusions drawn from false premises
> are both **invalid** usages of logic and reasoning.

Kant's emphasis on "reasoning" and "logic" circled around *Ethics* as "the purest **evaluation** or practical application of epistemology." Reason—or rather, "Pure Reason"—is the pot-of-gold at the end of Kant's rainbow. Using the propositions of Descartes as a base, Kant determined that "reasoning" is the "highest cognitive ability **capable** to man." It is from this faculty that humans possess ability to obtain "self-knowledge"—by which all other understanding and judgment about reality is formed. "Reason" can be used to describe what is observable, communicable within the **Beta**-range of action and causation; but it may not adequately explain its underlying nature or true source. And that's all there really is to say about famous high-ranking founders of contemporary epistemology.

The standard-issue *Human* uses experience as the essential **catalyst** for interpreting knowledge. Experience is described in terms of *"sensation"* and *"perception,"* which are often confused with each other:—

> —*Sensation* involves receipt of *external* stimulus
> and **"internal" communication** from sensory organs.
> —*Perceptions* regard internal **processing** of data
> received and communicated from the senses.

For example, your senses pick up and receive the light off of this page, revealing *form*. Perceptually, however, you have abilities to distinguish symbols as coherent letters—and their meaning as *words*. Humans are predominantly programmed (encoded) with audio-visual cues. This makes it quite easy to implant impulses to *label* all *forms*. This means that in addition to a communicable language (to objectively describe a **concept**), sensory experience is dependent on light and/or other detectable *Electromagnetic* (*EM*) **vibrations** in order to distinguish or **differentiate** its "reality." The primary limitation in this method is the "ladder of abstraction," where our words do not share a *one-to-one* (or *A-for-A*) relationship with the forms that they describe.

* * * * * * *

<u>NOTES ON ETHICS</u>

Ethics is the social science or study of moral philosophy, which is to say the extent to which one's actions are objectively "right" or "wrong." Most arcane mystical and esoteric systems operate on the **premise** that an individual is primarily responsible for everything that happens to them in life—everything they experience and the manner in which that experience is treated. Wizards study *Ethics* to better understand how to actively handle personal **responsibility** for their lives. Though a fragmented individual is not necessarily knowingly *Aware* of all processes taking place, their consciousness is constantly (and often compulsively) building and rebuilding their position in reality to have an experience.

Total responsibility for *Ethics* as **metahumans** also includes *ethically* handling matters pertaining to the organization, function and representation of **Mardukite Zuism** and the Systemology Society.

> A "true" *Ethic* requires "*true knowledge*" for "*knowing*"
> what is "right" and what is "wrong"
> —moral philosophers are often also epistemologists.

Semantic debates regarding this perceived knowledge are called "moral arguments." If we were forced to label it, a Wizard's *ethic* blends "objective rationalism" with "Utilitarianism" using set premises regarding *Creeds* and *Codes* of Mardukite Zuism. Some consider this effort "***Utopian***" idealism; yet quite simply, personal systematic **defragmentation** increases an individual's "clear vision" (and reality or understanding) on the highest ideals and levels of *knowingness* regarding ethics.

An "individual" (or for purposes of general philosophy, an "ego-con-science") has the ability to go beyond considering what is *only immediately* "good" for Self; they can see the entire "**holistic**" **dynamic** system of existence. An individual is certainly capable of interpreting "objective laws of the Universal Imperative" governing the ***Prime Directive*** of this *Beta-Existence*, which is implanted *sixty times* over with the **command**: "TO SURVIVE." The **Alpha-Spirit**, as an eternal being, has no need to be concerned with its own "survival"—because that is one thing it is innately doing already (by the nature of its *Beingness*) in **Alpha**-*Existence*. The "I-AM"-Self is carrying out an entirely different (upper-level) "directive" or "imperative" for the Spiritual Universe, which is "TO BE" and "TO CREATE." [A more detailed relay of these concepts is communicated in "*Imaginomicon*" (*Liber-3D*).]

In his discourse, "*Grounding for the Metaphysics of Morals*" (1785), Kant introduces semantics for two different types of "imperative": the "**hypothetical** imperative" and the "categorical imperative." He argues that the Universal Imperative (of Universal Law) must be a "categorical imperative." To clarify, a "hypothetical imperative" appears conditional and relative, or perhaps not universal toward survival of all people.

These are the "*if*" statements that are subject to an individual's own personal inclinations—however much **Self-determined** these may be. The effects are consequential or hypothetical: "If you do 'A', then 'B' could happen to you." In contrast, Universal or "categorical imperatives" are typically "*you ought*" sentiments, emphasizing that they are not solely motivated by inclinations or personal **considerations** of subjective consequences and conditionals.

Wide-angle (systematically holistic) consideration of objective effects and subjective consequences—getting the "whole picture"—is an integral part of effective *Utilitarianism* as a moral philosophy; and this is as good of a time as any to begin introducing the subject of *Utilitarianism* directly. [Although the subject will be treated further in the next section "*On Utilitarianism.*"] Many individuals claim to have already discounted "Classical Utilitarianism" as a flawed system of ethics—so our organization apparently has very little modern competition for its application.

For the first act of "**Ethics Processing,**" a *Professional* **Pilot** (of Mardukite Systemology) would inquire *what* the Seeker's idea of "Classical Utilitarianism"*actually* "*is.*" Whatever answer is given with, the *Pilot* responds with a "Thank You," **acknowledging** the *Seeker* for **participation** in the "**communication** cycle" (and "**processing** session"). The *Pilot* directs a similar acknowledgment after each "**Processing Command Line**" (PCL) or question, once answered. A *Pilot* doesn't **evaluate** content of the response directly. A note is made, especially if the answers are "way off base" or "coming out of left field." (This example illustrates the basic fact no system of "Classical Utilitarianism" exists...) [Systemology of Communication (as it relates to basic practices of systematic processing), is described fully in material for "**Metahuman Destinations**" (**Liber-Two**). These "basics" served (for nearly two years) as a placeholder in *Grade-IV*, substituting a much greater disciplined and complete "Course" for standardizing *Professional Piloting Procedure.*]

In most cases, a *Seeker* is processed toward "defragmentation"; and this means, by *definition*, that some of their own *definitions* are actually "fragmented"—regardless of how reasonable they may *seem* to the individual. As with other fields, areas and subjects of *knowingness*, philosophical debates often erupt from lack of semantic clarity regarding that subject, its vocabulary, and/or varying interpretations of the same... All because a word, concept or idea was not understood properly as intended—which is why the statement (phrase) "A-for-A" or "One-to-One" is used to describe perfect duplication of communication.

The two individuals most famous for its propagation (Jeremy Bentham and John Stuart Mill) each had their own slant on the philosophy called "Utilitarianism." Understand that we are treating applications of "philosophy"—a **facet** of learning that most individuals are likely to be either disinterested in completely, or else carry very specific emotionally **charged** opinions (which are actually *their* "beliefs") on the matter. There could be many factors present to **incite** this, but more often than not it stems from the fact that philosophy, mathematics, history and physical or natural sciences have all been mishandled in modern contemporary education systems. This strongly affects an individual's ability to study and learn beyond their formal education—and this affects Systemology, because we have never pretended that the pursuit and relay of this work did not appear somewhat on the "nerdy" side of the **spectrum**.

> Utilitarianism is actually a consequential ("*teleological*") moral philosophy rooted in a belief that ethical actions in nature (physical phenomena, *Beta-Existence*) are dependent on consequences of these actions as a determinant or explanation, as opposed to a "rule" or "law."

An emphasis on end-goals and consequences is what provides the concept (and namesake) of "utility" for Utilitarianism. Some philosophers in the past have had difficulty "reading between the lines" or even taking a position other than one extreme side of a **dichotomy** or another. In most instances of philosophy, our "excluded middle" becomes the "path less traveled by." It provides workable concepts that probably better represent the "Truth" of things far more than those positions taken in the past by the "better-known" extremist philosophers. The present author finds no contradiction to incorporating "objective reasoning" into *our* "Mardukite" version of *Ethics* as Utilitarian Systemology. "Thought" and "Reasoning" actually do apply to Utilitarianism. When combined, our meta-paradigm allows an individual freedom to rise above mundane/material (man-made) laws, if those laws are deemed unjust or destructive toward the "greatest number" or more specifically: the highest inclusive (or affected) "Sphere of Existence."

* * * * * * *

NOTES ON UTILITARIANISM

John Stuart Mill (1806–1873) launched his philosophical literary career from London (England) when he completed writing his two-volume set, titled: "*A System of Logic, Ratiocinative and Inductive*," published in 1843.

However, the work he is best known for is "*Utilitarianism*"—a title based on the concept derived from Jeremy Benthem, a close friend of Mill's father, James. His treatment of ethics is clearer and more readable than Immanuel Kant. Mill was even once the editor for the "*Westminster Review*," which had provided the very first English translations of Kant's "*Metaphysics of Morals*," but Mill was extremely critical of "German Metaphysics," claiming it had a tendency to "deprave one's intellect."

Mill illustrates faults of "*a priori*" moralists; for example, Kant's "first moral premise" (or "golden axiom"), which suggests a person should act as if such actions should be "the rule" for all men. Mill remarks that there is no logical contradiction found in that philosophy (as there should be) that would prevent a person from simply seeing or accepting that all other "**rational** beings" adopt a similarly "outrageous" immoral rule of conduct. This means that conventional "golden rule" ethics is flawed, because a person can act "unethically" using the excuse that others could also just act similar. Such a view is held by contemporary society in many ways. This has actually led to environmental destruction, wildlife abuse and capitalist fascism.

> Jeremy Benthem states that "the greatest happiness of the greatest number is the foundation of morals and legislation." Benthem's philosophy focuses on "quantitative" amounts of happiness—known as "Quantitative Utilitarianism"—not "quality." But according to John Stuart Mill, right and wrong should be connected to "pleasure" and "pain," employing faculties an individual innately possess.

"Pleasure" and "Pain" are frequently treated by humans as valid determinants of "Good" and "Bad." In our Mardukite Systemology we recognize (and treat) a "***Reactive Control Center***" (*RCC*), a primitive survival mechanism installed in the "Mind–Body Connection" for a ***genetic vehicle***. The "*RCC*" emotionally encodes experiences of "pain" and "loss" as "***Imprints***." This mechanism is responsible for all "fight–flight" and "stimulus–response" reactions. Such "*Imprints*" are more easily restimulated into action, when an individual maintains a low-level of **Awareness**.

While these terms—*pleasure, pain, good* and *bad*—all seem highly subjective and encourage ideas of "value hedonism." On the surface most will agree that *pleasure* and *pain* do play an important role in what an individual deems "good" or "bad" as based on personal "experience." This form of experience is sometimes called "conditioning" or "reinforcement" in traditional social sciences. Those outside of our Systemology paradigm will understand (using their own semantics) that through an action's consequential reinforcement, emotional states (response-reactions) are developed concerning a cycle-of-actions or **Imprinting Incident**.

> These emotionally **charged** imprinted recordings
> develop into what some refer to as a "tendency"
> *toward* or *away* from particular actions in the future.

We cannot demean our statement by calling it a "preference," as such implies only a weak subjective moral premise. "Preferences" can also be *implanted*; so, much like reaction-response "tendencies," these "**personality**" traits do not necessarily remain under full (*Self-*)*determinism* of an individual This does not make an argument based on preference completely untrue; simply weak. A rational being prefers to endure "pleasure" and avoid "pain" whenever possible. If a "*facet*" from an *Imprinting Incident* (when "pain" or "loss" had occurred) is present in the environment while an individual is maintaining low-Awareness, then automated mechanisms ("**Reactive Control Center**"/ *RCC*) may take over considerations ("**control**") of the Physical Body ("*genetic vehicle*"), removing the "**Master Control Center**" (*MCC*) from the **circuit**—and likewise removing a clear "Self-Honest" "line of communication" between *Self* (Alpha Spirit/"I-AM") and *beta-Existence.*

> A *tendency* automates **willingness** to "*reach* or *withdraw.*"
> Additional validation makes the tendency more demanding
> until the response is operating automatically (reactively)
> to yield positive results and avoid those that effect poorly.

On the surface, Utilitarianism might not appear very "spiritual" since most individuals only recognize its hedonistic views—where "pleasure" and "pain" become the only "ends" in material life. However, Mill disuades propagating this inaccurate generalization by explaining that "*spiritual inclinations*" of an individual are what ultimately contribute to their supreme happiness and highest optimum experience of existence. Material "things" and worldly "goals" are not generally desired as the "ends" in their own right—but instead as a means to promote greater pleasure and happiness in the Physical Universe. All persons must be held accountable for consequences of their actions. This does not require libraries worth of laws and precepts to understand. In *Utopian Philosophy* (explained in the next section), Thomas More considers it morally unjust to subject people to so many laws and of such obscure language that no one—except their authors and lawyers continuing to propagate their reality—actively knows or understands them all.

Given a choice between two options, a Utilitarian is encouraged to choose the path that "employs the highest faculty" and this is where we see a strong connection between Mill's philosophy and the *Pathway*—the "Right Way to **Ascension**." Intellectual pleasures are obviously of a higher quality (value) than physical ones alone.

> Mill warns, however, that those who learn to operate on these higher faculties will require a higher quality of life to remain happy and can potentially have greater suffering than a person driven only by physical mundane inclinations. In other words, the higher you fly, the greater the distance of a potential fall.

According to Utilitarian philosophy there are two main causes of unhappiness that can be more detrimental to life than just the physical pain and emotional loss alone:—

Firstly, there is "selfishness"—acting as though the individual is the "*only one*"; that the *only* Sphere of Existence is the *first.* This completely goes against the basic tenets of Utilitarianism.

Secondly, and perhaps more importantly, there is the "want of mental cultivation." Serious emotional depression often results for an individual not making use of their "higher faculties."

Mill frequently used "intelligent appreciation of music and art" as a primary example of high-value intelligence in "*aesthetics.*" In fact, *music* and *art* were the two specific facets of life that his father had forbidden him to take interest in as a child.

A Wizard-Level Systemologist [*Grade-V* and above] is earning critical data regarding the Spiritual Systemology of Alpha Existence—all previously experienced **condensations** (versions) of shared common-agreement Universes. This is particularly relevant in this instance, because it is during the "Wizard Grades" that we turn our **attentions** toward understanding the Standard Model from a "higher-level" *point-of-view*—turning around 180-degrees to **confront** *Gateways of Infinity* as opposed to the "Veils" of a "low-level" (*Beta*) existence.

Upper-level *Gateways of Infinity* represent even higher "**Spheres of Existence**" (though they are better defined as curves or arcs of the "infinity-loop") that are not critically aimed at "survival in *beta-existence*" so much as they are balancing the *Infinity of Nothingness* equation with potential *Infinite Creation.* The "dynamic systems" demonstrated as "Eight Spheres of Existence" in our Standard

Model repeat at a higher resonance with **Alpha** qualities. The ninth and tenth, harmonizing with the first and second, are: *Ethics* and *Aesthetics.*

Mardukite Systemology, is an applied spiritual philosophy and "high-level" spirito-intellectual pursuit. It qualifies as a "higher pursuit" for Utilitarian purposes, operating toward the highest Sphere of Existence a *Seeker* holds a reality on. Our Systemology not only provides increased happiness and certainty in *this* lifetime (**incarnation**) and *this* version of *Beta-Existence*, but it also provides "lasting gains" that significantly assist the *Seeker*, *Master* and/or *Wizard* while "between" "lifetimes" and into the "next."

This hybrid neo-Utilitarian *Ethic* was first developed for "Wizards" during the early-2000's, while the present author still operated under the name "Merlyn Sone." Its earliest version appeared in the 2008 publication: "*The Great Magical Arcanum*" by Joshua Free. Refinement of the "greatest number" concept applied to "Spheres of Existence" on our "Standard Model" is the newest application. Its appearance now in Systemology erupted from necessity; out of a need to resolve a way through a critical barrier **confronting** those that have reached far enough on the *Pathway to Self-Honesty* to seek clear passage up and across the *Fifth Gate.*

Considering the nature of the *Fourth Gate* ("*The Sun*") and the *Fifth* ("Mars"), we are now dealing with a lot of *FIRE*—purging emotional mass, dissolving fragmentary parts, immolating **iniquities**. In view of what is required for this part of the journey, it is clear to those of us—such as the present author—that have dedicated 100-hour work weeks to the "Gatework" for over a decade, there are few others that are likely to brave their way completely through this *wall of fire*, successfully passing through Sacred Flames that wash away all that is Human, leaving only Self to remain unscathed.

> A Wizard seeks "greatest happiness" for all affected Life,
> and by incorporating our Standard Model of Spheres,
> this includes Planet Earth as an necessary organism
> for continuation of existence on the lower spheres
> —for too long slighted out of moral considerations.

There is no reason to quantify, weigh out and/or balance moral values, which is where neo-Utilitarianism (Systemology) greatly differs from its predecessors (inspired by Bentham and Mill). For example: If A and B are competitors, some interpretations of former outdated Utilitarianism would allow A to put B out of commission using any means necessary, assuming that A's happiness and gain is quantitatively greater than B's unhappiness, pain and loss. For this reason, many critics shot holes in Utilitarian paradigms traditionally given. Essentially, A initiates actions that cause pain, which is "evil," and A also violates the rights and freedom of B. With a concise revision of Utilitarianism, we can prove this course of action to be unethical.

> Our society does not recognize that it can truly be stronger by having stronger, empowered actualized individuals. It instead creates and enforces a centralized epicenter and seat of power that pushes itself down onto the greater population of individuals and workers; conceptually represented in the past by a *"pyramid."*

Those uneducated regarding higher faculties of life are at an obvious disadvantage. Actually this is one reason that the New Age Movement grew so quickly. The mundane pleasures (and ideals) available to material-minded folk *will* actually pale in comparison to higher pursuits of life, once recognized. Some argue that people naturally possess these actualized abilities. Yet we can see everyday that folk repeatedly and blatantly compromise higher pleasures for lower ones. Some believe that our "standards" of **Self-Actualization** (or in Utilitarianism) are simply too high of a "standard" for present-day standard-issue humanity. Hence our Systemology **heralds** the arrival of metahumans—*Homo Novis*, the "New Human."

John Stuart Mill saw a possible Utopian world available to humanity if society could adhere to Utilitarianism. He stressed that law and order were important, but also ability to recognize when injustice is present in the mandates of supposed civic authorities. He often spoke out against corruption in government and personally contributed to the English Reform Bill of 1867. Some consider Mill "ahead of his time," but the message he carried is important for all times and in all places. It **validates** on paper, using written words of a noted philosopher, the beliefs that most folk already carry about how the world *ought* to be.

* * * * * * *

NOTES ON UTOPIAN PHILOSOPHY

Here we address a social philosophy and ethic for (primarily) independent rural (country-dwelling or pagan) living communities adopting a neo-Utilitarian moral philosophy (as suggested by Systemology) to enhance "greater happiness" and **"Ascension"** of all participants.

"*Utopia*" is a little-treated concept in our vocabulary and contemporary academics. It is not easily definable, since each individual is certain to hold their own unique version of an "ideal" worldview. Some believe *Utopia* is a type of "Nirvana-on-Earth" free of any labor and suffering or tangible quality to experience. This is not a realistic view as the agreed upon Physical Universe presently stands. *Utopians* actually labor quite intensely when they are working, but such a society emphasizes only necessities of material happiness, and thus work is performed by necessity. No one labors needlessly. A typical workday consists of six hours divided by a meal and two hours to pursue individual inclinations at the peak in the day (when outdoor labor conditions are not always efficient).

A utopia requires all citizens earn proficiency in agriculture in addition to whatever other craft or trade they intend to contribute to the community. This means all folk take turns working the fields (or at least one complete cycle under direct supervision of a more experienced farmer). Some citizens also maintain agriculture as their sole trade, seldom trading off to work in other parts of the community (by choice).

Everything is manufactured from natural materials with an emphasis on longevity and value. Building structures and produced goods are not expendable; anything repairable or reusable is kept, mended or re-purposed. In most instances, "money" is non-existent within the community —though a store of "fiat currency" is kept for emergency dealings with the "outside world." In many respects, no one person has more "wealth" than anyone else. All necessary clothing and supplies are made, stored and dispersed as needed. It is each citizen's responsibility to maintain their own supplies in good order as well as the condition of any essential tools required for their craft.

There is never a short supply of what is needed. Tendencies to "hoard" are dissolved. No one has a need for more than what they can functionally use. As things eventually wear out or are destroyed, they are fixed or replaced. In most cases, an "expected duration" is set for replacing each type (a farmer will obviously require more durable clothing than a boot-maker) and as suggested, Utopians seek to reuse as much as possible. If a particular supply of something is deemed "surplus," then efforts are redirected toward other foreseen shortages or deficiencies. "Surplus" goods may also be exchanged in fair trade with other similar communities.

Traditional (academic) "*Utopian Philosophy*" emerged with Sir Thomas More's novel, "*Utopia*" in 1516; a treatise describing the "best form of commonwealth." [More was also beheaded for treason, refusing to swear to the "Act of Succession."] "*Utopia*" chronicles social philosophy of a fictional island—"Utopia"—named after its original settler, "Utopus." The island was previously called "Abraxas." He describes the living spaces on the island, divided by equally spaced cafeteria halls, storage houses and "buildings of industry." Retail outlet are not necessary, nor taverns and superlative office-space. Advertising, marketing and excessive packaging are non-existent in non-competitive industries. Essentially, even "leaders" in the community do not live more lavishly or possess more "wealth" than others. In fact, More suggests that the living quarters of each household could be rotated every ten years. However, an individual might accumulate more aesthetic craft-items or surround themselves with more of their own artistic works and inventions as they progress in years. Such would seem only natural.

Wizard-Level Systemologists are interested in *Utopian* models, like More's, as fundamental examples for esoteric study and practiced application. There is no continuing interest in failed New Age communal efforts of "quasi-hippies"—such as gained prominence several decades ago. More's vision of *Utopia* does not condone polygamous relationships, which actually "compromise the central family unit" that make a *Utopian* community so strong. Much as in ancient Mesopotamian law, sexual infidelity is essentially intolerable; even divorce is generally frowned upon (with obvious exceptions).

Specialization is a common factor of *utopian* visions. Inescapably, a person should contribute what they best can. *Utopian* ideals keep labor efficient, minimizing the actual time spent performing it. An individual is then left more personal time to pursue their own inclinations toward happiness, usually intellectual or craft-related—not to mention the ability to pursue spiritual freedom from this existence. This makes for a more productive "working man," one that doesn't feel like they have slaved for all their waking hours to primarily benefit another—or only toward care for and feed of a material body.

Idleness and sloth is, however, not tolerated and the primary function of a "chief" is to provide certainty and security by maintaining productivity in the community. The "head" of each household is responsible for making requests and obtaining the supplies for the house. Rotating "*guildmasters*" of each trade will report their own inventories and supply needs for (craft) production. Medical treatment and sick houses are offered to those who both need and want them. Services are not denied to those who request them, nor are they forced on those who do not want them. The same applies to euthanasia as a means of ending suffering during critical venerable periods.

All of this reflects the best of what *Philosophy* represents through the ages. It is, however, in no way a fixed criteria or standard for modern *Mardukite Zuism* and/or *Systemology*. The idea of *Utopia* has ever after remained a theoretical construct of philosophy. In the broad sense, most communes/ communities are not nearly as efficient, or self-sufficient, as they would like to believe. At their operative size-level and with no other similar communities to network with, most cannot actually functionally employ the minimalist lifestyle described here. The question remains as to whether such a community would even be possible today based on the standard-issue Humans Condition—or, is the rise of a tyrant, operating outside the state of *Self-Honesty* always inevitable?

:: UTILITARIAN SYSTEMOLOGY FOR SEEKERS[‡] ::
– Systematizing Ethics for a Pathway to Self-Honesty –

When *Ethics* is applied to our Standard Model of Systemology—its *Spheres of Existence*—it should seem easy to classify the strongest Moral Philosophy based on observation of survival in *Beta-Existence*. What promotes the greatest conditions of survival would therefore be the highest good. Most ancient 'moral codes' and 'taboos' regard observable consequences —actions that had either promoted or **thwarted** survival; and naturally this is reduced to the most fundamental sensory experience of the Human Condition (pertaining to the *First Sphere*): "pleasure" and "pain."

The purpose of *Ethics* is to determine what is right action and wrong conduct universally across the boards, in all **times** and **spaces**, regardless of an authoritarian regime or what cultural paradigm-set is in place. This is what makes *Ethics* a high standard of thinking—"high thought"—for philosophy. It has perhaps only recently been perfected to any applicable extent. Given that our primary emphasis has been on *"Self-Honesty"* ever since the inception of the Pathway, it should come as no surprise that proper handling of *Ethics* is the Key to reaching true Metahuman destinations.

* * * * * * *

UTILITY AND THE SPHERES OF EXISTENCE

One of the challenges with using the Standard Model in relaying Metahuman Utilitarianism: it tends to emphasize the individual as identified in space-time of *Beta-Existence.* This is the orientation point at "1.0" and why we are able to effectively use the Standard Model to navigate experiences of *Beta-Existence* and "rise above" it. The Standard Model is essentially the blueprint for lower Universes. Hence, the motivator of *Life* in "Beta-Existence" relates to perpetuating its own existence, or else "survival." Of course, this can *only* be the case while identified with *Beta-Existence.* By its own nature, an Eternal Spirit can only (or must) "survive" in "Alpha Existence" as an *Alpha Spirit.* An immortal spirit is implanted with the motivation to survive only when fixed to a particular identifiable "genetic vehicle" as a particular **Identity** (or *Self-Identifica*

[‡] Portions of this chapter-lesson are based on the *"Grade-IV, Freedom From"* lectures given by *Joshua Free* to the *Mardukite Academy of Systemology* (in July 2021) at *Mardukite Babylonia SLV Borsippa HQ*; remaining sections were issued as supplemental lecture handouts.

tion). The individual is seeking to *Be* its own basic nature—as something to "*Do*"—applying efforts toward *Infinite Survival* (*Sphere Eight*) or else to achieve Immortality, but which is already its natural state in Alpha Existence.

After **succumbing** to present positions and considerations of the Human Condition, awakening as the Alpha Spirit, eternal in nature, is now something to *Do*. A Seeker then discovers *seven veiled layers* set between the two states. Infinite Survival *within* Beta-Existence still speaks nothing of conditions of the Alpha Spirit. There is no physical/material boundary of the Physical Universe that would deliver *Self* (using a *genetic vehicle*) at the doorstep of the next Universe beyond. To approach another Universe requires breaking the gravity of this plane as an Alpha Spirit, then knowingly having Awareness and ability to either create an appropriate form for the newer plane or simply take **command** of one that is bioengineered or birthed for communication at that range of existence. This is, of course, assuming the individual has not already mastered the art of *Beingness* without dependency on a "locatable body"—but, again, such vehicles can be useful for communicating within a particular "shared" Universe.

As relayed in *Unit-2* of "*Metahuman Destinations*" (*Liber-Two*)—then illustrated more clearly in *Unit-3*—the more recent the **implant**, the lower the Spheres (harmonic) it manifests on. This means that at "1.0" where Self is *Aware* of *Life* existing as a *genetic vehicle* or "material body," it now can be "hurt" and experience "pain"—whereas in higher existences, this is not possible. The fixed *Point-of-View* (*POV*) for Self had to fall pretty far down to reach such a state; but that also tells us that we have been imprinted on the idea of "pleasure/pain" for far less time on the **Backtrack** then the older a more deeply ingrained implant incidents. Yet, one can also see that they get more and more solid in their effect as you get down to "1" on our scale.

> There are four implant **patterns** for each Sphere. The (most recent) implanted platforms (or circuitry) appear on the *First Sphere* (1.0) and are, from lowest "frequency" (most recent) to highest "frequency" (earliest, happening further back): *To Endure, To Survive, To Eat* and *To Feel.*[*]

Implants are patterned platforms on which other encoding and imprinting of a certain type (or experience) may be recorded. They are particularly significant in systematic processing and other advanced studies at higher-level Wizard Grades; but implants are mentioned in *Grade-IV*

---

[*] This effectively updates the chart list from *Liber-Two, Unit-3*.

(*Wizard Level-0*) to prepare *Seekers* with a general idea of how all this imprinting and programming is actually involved (and/or entangled) with the Human Condition—and solidly fixed energetic "mass" that accumulates through countless lifetimes on the **Spiritual Timeline.** Such "mass" ultimately resulted in weighing down considerations of the individual to exclusively place themselves *here.* This is what we are to correct, if there is any hope in liberating the *Human Spirit* from the *Human Condition.*

The *Second Sphere* is traditionally labeled "Home (and Family)" because it extends directly from stable security maintained by *Self* in *Beta-Existence* (when identifying with a "genetic organism"). The *Second Sphere* also **correlates** with "2.0" on our Standard Model for *Beta-Existence*, which is to say the "Reactive Control Center" (RCC), which is emotionally encoded with imprints of "Havingness" and "Loss" (in addition to the lower scale of "Pain" and **"Biological Unconsciousness"** from "1.0"). These first two Spheres are treated for "survival" in Beta-Existence, but they share a harmonic quality resonating with the first two higher Alpha-Spheres (or arcs of Infinity, when treated as an extension of our Standard Model) of *Ethics* and *Aesthetics.* This is easy to understand if we consider the relationship between *Ethics* ("9") to a "Body" at "1.0" and the idea of *Aesthetics* ("10") as a higher-level equivalent of "human emotion" at "2."

beta "*SURVIVAL*"	alpha "*CREATION*"
8	16
↑	↑
7	15
6	14
5	13
4	12
3	11
2	10
1	9

The four implant patterns for the *Second Sphere* are, from lowest (most recent) to highest (earliest, happening further back): *To Protect (Care For), To Satisfy (Cope), To Reproduce* and *To Join.*[*]

---

[*] This effectively updates the chart list from *Liber-Two, Unit-3.*

Although we speak of "Home" and "Family," the encoding for the *Second Sphere* pertains to anything an individual can "*Have*" and therefore potentially "*Lose.*" Hence, an organism expands efforts to "survive" (or *enhance* "survival") by *having* certain things; and even continuing existence through a legacy, mainly children. This is also where we find heavy **emotional encoding** and other imprinting regarding the "reproductive act" ("sex") itself.

> From our examination of basic fragmentation,
> it is logical to state: any action encouraging or
> causing *Pain* or *Loss* to any Sphere is unethical.

At the *Third Sphere*, the basic dynamic systems expand to concern "*Organizations*" and "Grouping." This applies to "organizational grouping of data" (**internal** to a Mind-System) as well as "organized groups of individuals" (externally) manifest in the world-at-large. It is from this "Sphere" that we derive our three circuits of imprinting/programming involving "others" (as treated in **SOP-2C** and **Route-3** circuit-processing): *Self* to *Others*; *Others* to *Self*; and *Others* to *Others*. Information received and encoded on these three circuits contributes to an individual's association (or grouping) of data (as knowledge) and calculation of effort (in *Beta-Existence*) to be "right" in their communication (including actions) in producing the appropriate (intended) effect.

Where systematic functions of the Human Condition pertain to the Mind-System, or "Master Control Center" (MCC), we treat the range between the RCC (at 2.0) and "4.0" on our Standard Model. This is the limited range of "Beta-Thought" relating specifically to the Human Condition. All remaining upper-level thinking (outside of **associative** and **experiential knowledge**) is for "Metahuman" consideration. In "Unit-3" (of *Liber-Two*, "*Metahuman Destinations*"), the *Third Sphere* of existence (and implanting) is precisely defined as: "Organization of systems and alignment of Self in groups; associative knowledge used to gauge efforts" all at "3" with "groups"—and "experience of failure and **erroneous** calculations; personal error as miscalculation from false knowledge" at "*minus*-3."

As the *Third Sphere* applies to "society," an individual is extending their reach into dynamic systems which are not restricted only to a "family unit" and "home-life." This means participating as a member of a group ("3") composed of representatives from many different families ("2") and, of course, the various individuals ("1") themselves. Whether we refer to various social circles, clubs, religious associations and even the community we reside in, an individual participates in the **existential** survival of the group. This correlates to a perceived value (or esteem) that contributes to their own survival on the *First* and *Second* spheres in Beta-Existence.

> The implant patterns for the *Third Sphere* are, from lowest (most recent) to highest (earliest, happening further back): *To Expand, To Participate, To Cooperate* and *To Organize.*[*]

An individual also tends to withdraw participation ("**presence**") in a *Second* or *Third* sphere, if they feel they have wronged the group (or partnership)—or feel wronged themselves—and this includes "*failed* **help**." On the downward journey and trapping of the Human Condition, an individual does not "go out of communication" with all of existence at once. Such takes place gradually—knowingly at first—with a few lines selectively closed off or set on automatic. But eventually the avoidance is quite sweeping as the individual completely withdraws their reach and thereby becomes the total effect of environment.

As much as we would expect a *Seeker* to carry fragmentation concerning a *genetic vehicle* or "body" ("1") and even family life ("2"), we discover older experiences imprinted on a deeper laid platform of incidents involving "groups" ("3") and an individual's *participation* therein.

The *Fourth Sphere* **encompasses** all human individuals, human families and human groups—and thus is the representation of the entire "Human Condition" in its standard-issue Beta-state. In previous volumes of our material, the *Fourth Sphere* is given as: All Human Life. Each group, subgroup, family and individual is a component of "Humanity" as a whole. The Human Condition is a dynamic system. It would make sense that any motivation or ethical action should serve the betterment of all Humanity and a healthy continuation of its material Beta-survival. When handled outside of *Self-Honesty*, this is where the "chain" breaks down. Upper-**echelon** "metahuman" understanding includes *utility* of the *Fifth Sphere* and above.

> Implant patterns for the *Fourth Sphere* are, from lowest (most recent) to highest (earliest, happening further back): *To Unite, To Control, To Share* and *To Establish.*[*]

Our "new ethics" is for Humanity (including present and future "metahumanity" or the "New Human"). It does not stop (or end) with a short-sighted consideration of only what pertains exclusively to one species of little beasties we often identify as "*humans.*" Such "*Fourth Sphere*"

---

[*] This effectively updates the chart list from *Liber-Two, Unit-3.*
[*] This effectively updates the chart list from *Liber-Two, Unit-3.*

limitations of the standard-issue Human Condition and low-Awareness handling of the Mind-System has led planet Earth (*Fifth Sphere*) to its ecological imbalance and brink of annihilation; the classic case of a species that never learned "not to shit in its own nest."

The *Fifth Sphere* is not only the Earth as a living organism, but also a composite of All Life on Earth—meaning not only plant-life and animals, but the very same **organic** *genetic vehicle* used for the Human form ("4"). As such, it encircles the boundaries of the Human Condition on our Standard Model. Since continued survival of a human-like species on Earth *is dependent on* an Earth to inhabit (both existentially and by semantic logic). An even higher ethic is necessary than standards formerly treated in modern civilization—and this necessarily must include the Earth (Planet) and its eco-systematic balance as the "greatest number" above (and *as*) all lower spheres.

> Even an ego-centric worldview, if executed *in Self-Honesty*, should have reached this same logical conclusion from the very beginning. Hence, the alleged "best of **intentions**," when acted upon *outside of Self-Honesty*, tends toward disaster. In a state of *fragmentation*, especially regarding *Ethics*, an individual cannot possibly *Know* what is *Best* when operating on mortal programming of "eat today; die tomorrow."

Not surprisingly, an examination of early-period esoteric paradigms (such as *Grade-I, Route-D*[‡]) toward their own "metahuman" ideals (by some other semantic) are exceptionally Nature-oriented. This focus on the natural environment seems to increase the likelihood that an individual will "rise up" out of their confounding Human Condition and gravity of the systematic social structure impinged on that condition in civilization. Otherwise, too often we find the needs of the *group* ("3") or even the *individual* ("1") given more weight than the optimum survival of all humanity ("4"), all *Lifeforms* on Earth ("5") and all existences in the Physical Universe ("6").

> Implant patterns for the *Fifth Sphere* (pertaining to *Lifeforms*) are, from lowest (most recent) to highest (earliest, happening further back): *To Adapt, To Heal, To Live*[†] and *To Grow*.

While *ecological responsibility* is certainly not a "new" concept for philosophy or "ecopsychology" (whatever that is and for whatever it's done),

---

[‡]   See the Master Edition anthology "*Merlyn's Complete Book of Druidism*" by Joshua Free; additionally refer to "*The Complete Mardukite Master Course*" transcripts.

[†]   Possibly a better translation is "*To Experience.*"

it has not been properly introduced to *Ethics*, and certainly not in former "algebraic utility" or "utilitarian calculus" inspired by Bentham and Mill. Our Standard Model of Beta-Existence also considers planet Earth ("5") as yet one component of an even larger dynamic system—or *Sixth Sphere*—which is essentially all *Beta-Existence* itself, or else, any Universe. As much as we might like to gripe about entrapment within our own agreements *here*, there is a "cosmic imperative" where we seek to sustain continued existence of the Universe—for what would happen if it were to collapse short of our individualized achievement of *Self-determined Ascension* of *Actualized Awareness* back to "Alpha"?

When we consider "6.0" on the Standard Model (of Beta-Existence), we are at the theoretical point of Alpha-Thought and the ability to construct, create and participate in shared/common Universes in general. In most cases, however, we treat the *Sixth Sphere* as other-determined *Beta-Existence*, or else that which an individual *superimposes* onto their personal "Home Universe" ("7") by agreement/**postulate** (Alpha-Thought).* From the perspective of the basic Standard Model of *this Beta-Existence*, other "**Games** Universes," "Penalty Universes"—and even the recently previous "Magic Universe"—would all fall under the *Sixth Sphere.*

> Implant patterns for the *Sixth Sphere* (pertaining to *Universes*) are, from lowest (most recent) to highest (earliest, happening further back): *To Own, To Gather, To Locate* and *To Discover.*

Naturally, we not only label our philosophical approach due to its intended audience, but—

> "Metahuman Utilitarianism" (in our Systemology) is perhaps the only formal model of moral philosophy published (on Earth, anyways) that calculates entire universes and other non-Human *Lifeforms* into its ethical equations.

We are, in all seriousness, equally factoring in POVs for species *apart* from those which are "Human"—or even those exclusively "terrestrial" to Earth. We must consider the unspoken truth that our Standard Model of Spheres is *relative* to any *individual*, the *planet* they occupy and corresponding *universe*. The common conceptual perspective of "Humans on Earth" (in *this* version of Beta-Existence) is simply the most accessible example.

Realizing and calculating any higher Spheres of Existence requires, at

---

* See also "*Imaginomicon*" (*Liber-3D*).

the very least, a basic state of *Beta-Defragmentation.* Individuals carrying extreme fragmentation about *who they are* (at "1.0") are seldom in the best position to demonstrate certainty about the *Spiritual World* ("7.0") or the truth of *Divinity* or *Infinity* ("8.0"). And yet, we discover the majority of low-Awareness individuals professing a lot of knowledge about "God." What's more, such erroneous paradigms are often used as basis and justification for erroneous ethics. So, we end up with half-wits conducting harm with hostile actions (which they don't understand) in the name of a higher authority (which they also don't understand), under the premise that it will all "just work itself out" in the afterlife.

> Implant patterns for the *Seventh Sphere* (pertaining to *spiritual life-forms*) are, from lowest (most recent) to highest (earliest, happening further back): *To Embody, To Collect, To Influence* and *To Predict.*

An individual's perception of a "Spiritual Universe"—or *Seventh Sphere*—*does* play a role in the "Ladder of Awareness" they are using to climb up out from the mire of *Beta-Existence*; it directly represents the "Other" or "greater than" *this.* However, in previous traditions, the *Self* as (Alpha) Spirit is not really emphasized until *after* an individual has "died"—for only *then* are they considered a "Spirit" in some worldviews. But the fact remains that:

> an individual *is* a Spirit first and foremost. Spiritual Beingness is the natural state of Self. The very idea of having "TO SURVIVE" as any other **Identity** is clearly an implant.

Our present survey of the basic Standard Model naturally concludes with "Infinity" as the *Eighth Sphere*—which is how it is classified throughout Grade-III and Grade-IV (and even in prior Grade-II presentations of *Mardukite Zuism*). From a *Beta-Existence* POV, "Infinity" and "Divinity" are essentially synonymous. Using a standard-issue Human Condition POV, the concept of "Infinity" is "conceived of" individually based on a Seeker's state of Awareness. For some in a low-Awareness high-fragmentation state, the concept of "Infinity" is simply whatever the individual considers the "utmost" "topmost" or "ideal" aspect of all existence, simply extended to all points and spaces and times (for their Reality).

Very often, the specific identification made with Infinity/Divinity contributes to fragmentation. For others, it involves symbols representing "goals" that an individual is implanted to "work toward achieving" during their lifetime/incarnation. After a *Seeker* (or Pilot-in-Training or Mardukite Minister or Grade-III+ Mardukite Master, *&tc.*) has worked through the *Pathway to Self-Honesty* as outlined in the basic "Beta-Defragmentation Systemology Operating Procedure"‡ (which requires all of *Grade-III* and *Grade-IV*), these other matters of the *Backtrack* are treated in the "Wizard Grades" (otherwise referred to as the *Gateways of Infinity*).

> Implants for the *Eighth Sphere* (pertaining to *Infinity-Divinity*) are, from lowest (most recent) to highest (earliest, happening further back): *To Worship, To Commune, To Convert* and *To Enlighten.*

The implant patterns for Religious Conviction and Divine Worship are among the oldest and most basic in any *Beta-Existence*, constituting the primary "Pass-Not" boundary between the basic Standard Model (*Beta*) Spheres of Existence and their Alpha-Octave or upper-level harmonic qualities as "Arcs of Infinity." This upper-**band** of All-Existence (*Creation, Creativity*) is what balances out the "*Infinity of Nothingness*" equation—and likewise encompasses, enshrouds and encircles *All* "Beta-Existences" as a higher echelon of dynamic systems. These "Arcs" are treated further in our forthcoming advanced (*A.T.*) Systemology "*Wizard Levels*" (Mardukite *Grade-V* through *Grade-VII*).

* * * * * * *

<u>UTILITY AND HUMAN BEHAVIOR</u>

Humans primarily behave as a result of:
(1) personal Awareness levels; combined with
(2) implanted goals; and
(3) imprinted experience.

Apart form this, we can consider that all creation—anything that exists for *Beta-Existence*—relatively may be categorized with one (or more) dynamic systems represented by our Standard Model of Spheres. By understanding these factors, a Systemologist is able to glean the "utility" of our methodology and its real-world applications; both for increasing one's progress along the Pathway and for predicting behavior of others. By considering the existential dependency of all *Life* amidst our Model of Spheres, the *moral philosophy* of "right" and "wrong" is clearly illustrated and establishes a structure for our *Ethics.*

Calculating someone's reach and even predicting their actions is simple when based on data of how they associate or align personal understanding and prioritization of the Spheres. Whether pictorially demonstrated

---

‡ "Beta-Defragmentation S.O.P. v.1.1" (*Grade-IV, Wizard Level-0 Metahumanism*) from *30, April 2021* is given in "*Imaginomicon*" (*Liber-3D*) premiere edition; "v.1.2" revised on *22, June 2021* with minor formatting changes.

with nice tidy concentric rings or not, each person carries their own individual Awareness of "values" concerning all existence. For example, some will devote most of their energy and **attention** to "Family" (*Second Sphere*), whereas another may follow a lifestyle (or give preference) to "Environment, Animal Life and Pets" (*Fifth Sphere*) as their primary motivation. There are no spheres directly "against" any others—but it will be demonstrable that an individual favors certain Spheres of Existence while opposing emphasis on others. It is possible that a person can misalign or misappropriate "**terminals**" and significances associated with these dynamic systems—and such is also a indicator of fragmentation.

Using *Utility*, an action is more ethical the more/higher
Spheres of Existence it promotes (assists survival of)
and the fewer (lower) systems it harms or hinders.

An individual's relative condition of success and survival is primarily dependent on the relationship held with each Sphere of Existence. A *Seeker* that is systematically defragmented on each of the Spheres of Existence —thereby maintaining clear communication **channels** with each—is going to get along better and reach farther in *Beta-Existence*. This "reach" is part of the "ticket" *out*. The way *out* is *through*; not withdrawal and individuation into lonely caves and mountainsides—not fortification of the *First Sphere*. "Seclusion" is not wisdom; it's just "hiding." It's no different than an alcoholic that "solves" the issue by avoiding environments containing alcohol. Well, they haven't actually *solved* the issue of alcoholism that way; there is no increase in developmental faculties—there is no increased ability to *Hold-Back* with Self-determinism as such.

In *Grade-III* ("*Crystal Clear*"; **Liber-2B**) we applied the "*Beta Awareness Scale*" to the first four "spheres" and "zones" of the Standard Model (of Beta-Existence) to illustrate dynamic systems composing the Human Condition. This is also valid data for determining how actualized an individual's reach is (in the Physical Universe), their *Ethics* (conduct and behavior), their ability to clearly communicate (or relay communication) and chronic conditions or level of optimum survival (success) in daily life. These are all elements for consideration that compose the total system of our Systemology Ethics.

In most instances, increased Awareness means an increased ability to "foresee" future results and act toward them. This includes maintaining a wide-angle view of the entire Standard Model at all times. Individuals that can only "think" or "operate" regarding the first few spheres have a tendency to be shortsighted. This is worse when an individual is not even Actualized (defragmented) regarding the *First Sphere* as Self. Such individuals are "Potential Dangers" to optimum survival of both the Systemologist and the community at large. The only resolution we have discovered is our systematic processing; making it the most important activity you can *do* for someone.[†]

A standard-issue (fragmented) Human being does not know to "process out" their perceived "problems" and thereby applies shortsighted actions to resolve them. Such efforts are referred to as **"Harmful Acts"** in Systemology, or more accurately **"counter-survival"** actions.

> *harmful-act* : a counter-survival mode of behavior or action (esp. that causes harm to one or more *Spheres of Existence*)—or—an overtly aggressive (hostile and/or destructive) action against an individual or any other *Sphere of Existence*; in *Utilitarian Systemology* —a shortsighted (serves fewest *Spheres of Existence*) **intentional** overtly harmful action to resolve a perceived problem; a revision of the rule for standard *Utilitarianism* for Systemology to distinguish actions which provide the least benefit to the least number of *Spheres of Existence*, or else the greatest harm to the greatest number of *Spheres of Existence*; in *moral philosophy*—an action which can be experienced by few and/or which one would not be willing to experience for themselves (*theft, slander, rape, &tc*); an iniquity or iniquitous act.

Fragmentation and energetically **charged** masses (sometimes called "ridges") are connected to *Harmful and Hostile Acts*. This includes what we have done to others, others have done to us, and what we witness others having done to each other. These are all "systematic processing" points (and **Hot Buttons**). These are critical for achieving "Wizard Level-1" and working through *Mardukite Grade-V*, where *iniquities* must be "incinerated" in order to rise above. Therefore, the *Ethics* (or *Liber-Three/3E*) portion of the *Pathway* is not an afterthought, filler or some arbitrary supplement—it is a detrimental factor for Ascension through the upper "Wizard Grades."

> There is a considerable difference between:
>
> —the individual that struggles to adhere to a *moral code* or *law*, doing so only for fear of civic/social punishment or for religious purposes (a belief in metaphysical punishment, karma *&tc.*); and
>
> —an *Ethical* individual that performs "right actions" and the "highest good" for its own sake.

[†] Get trained to do processing, or refer to a "Professional Pilot."

Therefore, we note differences between a *moral* standard, as socially defined (by a particular group or society) and the "metahuman" observation of actual *Ethics*, which treats absoluteness of "rightness" and "wrongness" as it pertains to the Standard Model of Spheres.

> The individual, as "I-AM"/*Self* or Alpha Spirit,
> beneath fragmentation, is basically "*good.*"

This truth about the "Spirit" (of *Lifeforms*) is what allows Systemology techniques (systematic processing technology) to yield positive effects in *defragmenting* veils of erroneous consideration clouding or distorting clear vision of what is "right" and/or (for) the "highest good." All individuals act in Beta-Existence to "SURVIVE" and thus, in their own fragmented POV (which they refer to as their "own right" or "opinion"), believe themselves acting "justly" for what is "best." None truly believe that they are acting upon "evil" or "false" fixated purposes for the sake of "evil" alone; not even the "villains."

An individual's "*Spiritual Timeline*" is explored in greater detail as they progress through the Wizard Grades. At this juncture, we can determine that the *Alpha Spirit* begins its existence with a very high *Ethics*, superior to even what is demonstrable within the Standard Model of Beta-Existence. Proper *Ethics* is actually an upper-level dynamic system, equivalent to a "*Ninth Sphere*"—or more accurately, *First Arc of Infinity*, carrying a "harmonic" with Alpha-Existence relative to the *First Sphere* in Beta-Existence.

The Alpha-Spirit seeks to operate and act in the most optimum manner, which is most evident with their original "Home Universe." Eventually, cohabitation considerations within "Shared Universes" and "Games Universes" (which are, themselves, superimposed over one's own personal "Home Universe")* results in more and more behavior that is less and less optimum—and from which a being may lose its ability to *Hold-Back* the *Harmful Acts.*

> **hold-back** : withheld communications (esp. actions) such as "*Hold-Outs*"; an intentional (or automatic) withdrawal (as opposed to reach); Self-restraint (which may eventually be enforced or automated) to not practice *Harmful-Acts*; not reaching, acting or expressing, when one should be; an ability that is now restrained (on automatic) due to inability to withhold it on Self-determinism alone.

---

* Refer to "*Imaginomicon*" (*Liber-3D*).

Loss of high-level *Ethics* forms a perceived need for *moral codes* and *penalties* as a guide. This also leads to *Hold-Outs*.

> **hold-outs** : withheld communications; energetic withdrawal and communication breaks with a *"terminal"* and its *Sphere of Existence* as a result of a *"Harmful-Act"*; unspoken or undiscovered (hidden, covert) actions that an individual withholds communications of, fearing punishment or endangerment of *Self-preservation* (*First Sphere*); the act of hiding (or keeping hidden) the truth of a *"Harmful-Act."*

We selected the term *"Hold-Outs"* for our Utilitarian Systemology semantics, based on its application in professional photography—where numerous snapshots/pictures are *withheld* from final selections openly communicated to present an event, *&tc.* Oftentimes, an individual carries around many *Hold-Outs*—hidden, but occupying their attention. They are fed energy as compulsive creations. The individual participates in Reality with a constant anxious worry (problem) that someone else will "find out." Therefore, they are forced to *Hold-Back* their reach and communications (**energetic-exchange**) *outside* of *Self-Honesty*. And, as it turns out:—

> these *Harmful-Act–Hold-Out* sequences are what keeps
> a Spiritual Being entrapped within a Prison Universe.

Therefore, the Wizard's *Way Out* of Beta-Existence requires *clearing* the *slate* of what is emotionally and energetically carried as "mass"/"matter" by the Spirit: to be certain that the "heart" is "light enough" to be weighed against a feather.[‡] Many religions have established their own methodologies for confessional procedures. Yet, none seem to be effective for *systematically rehabilitating* the Power and Beingness of the Spirit. Former attempts simply enforced "guilt" and other enforced programming, fixing attentions on a *moral code* rather than a higher *Ethic*.

Ethics is the lowest *Arc of Infinity* for Alpha-Existence. Imposition of a *moral code* (and *penalties* when an individual *fails*) resulted in construction of "Penalty Universes" or "Prison Universes." The *Beta-Existence* (Physical Universe) we consider present, is actually a "Penalty Universe" created by those (once) occupying a previous manifested universe, referred to (in our Systemology) as the "Magic Kingdom." Even the "Magic Universe"—similar to *this* one, except that the "electron is free" (and able to be utilized without "wires")—was itself first constructed as a

---

‡   Alluding to "afterlife judgment" in ancient Egyptian mysticism. See also *"The Vampyre's Handbook"* by Joshua Free for additional details.

"confined existence" *beneath* an even wider encompassing shared "Games Universe." Hence, *Ethics* is no small matter once we consider how large a part it plays in why an individual consistently finds themselves "located" in (and "fixed" to) a *Beta-Existence* "space-time" as they do.

The I-AM-*Self* once experienced an essentially unrestrained existence as a *Free Spirit*, due to the naturally high *Ethic* "in" place. During accumulation of experience across a *Spiritual Timeline*, this deteriorated into rigid *moral codes* that promote imposing (or enforcing) restraints (*Hold-Backs*) on Self and others. **Validation** of "guilt" leads to further "*Hold-Outs*" due to regret—*Hold-Backs* and *Hold-Outs* being "no-action" *imprints*, or else of "regret" when one did not *Hold-Back* an action and now *Holds-Out* admission and responsibility for it. Just as *facets* of other types of *Imprinting* and *Programming* can affect the freedom of an individual Alpha-Spirit, so too will these energetically charged masses tied to *Harmful-Act/Hold-Outs/Hold-Backs*. These specifically affect ability to reach optimum states of *Self-Honesty* with our "Wizard Level" work.

Once a *moral code* is in place (or *Ethics* are implanted), a series of "hidden" restraints are agreed to and become Reality—even when an individual operates in opposition to this programming. In fact, when a *Seeker* negates *morality*, they are at once in **conflict** with their own true values (and nature) as Alpha-Spirit. In addition to *Hold-Outs* and struggles over *Hold-Backs* (personal restraint), an individual will also employ a sequence-"**pattern**" or programmed-circuit of "justification" to explain motivation for their *Harmful-Acts*. In many instances, this **displaces** personal responsibility onto some "other" *terminal*—which further **inhibits** one's own *Self-Determined* restraint. This creates mechanisms that automatically *Hold-Back* ability.

The present author has spoken ambiguously at length (amidst several **gradients** and volumes of "Gatework")—concerning a perfected state of *Self-Honesty* sought as "Beta-Defragmentation." The standard experiential boundary of *Beta-Existence* is fixed at "4.0" on the Standard Model; also relative to the "Beta-Awareness Scale."[†] But it is a true solid "4.0," elevated solely by an individual's freedom of *considerations* and handling of *Self-Determinism* that is apart from, or outside of (**exterior** *to*), any POV held rigidly as the "Human Condition."

The ultimate state of *Self-Honest Beta-Defragmentation* requires going above and beyond the Human-Mind or "MCC" (4.0) on the Standard Model. Hence, *Grade-III* and *Grade-IV* include emphasizing actualization

---

[†]   Introduced in "*Crystal Clear*" (*Liber-2B*).

of "Will-**Intention**" (5.0), "Creative **Imagination**" (6.0), and "**Alpha Thought**"/"**Postulates**" (7.0), to the extent that a *Seeker* is able at a given level of **realization.** These additional factors are correct concerning handling of the Mind-Body connection. They are still drawn from our Standard Model—one developed using a POV (perspective) of Beta-Existence *looking outward* toward Infinity. However, once the **threshold**-cover was lifted on Wizard-Level "Alpha/Ascension-Tech" (*Actualization Techniques*/"*A.T.*"), it became quite clear that *Ethics* is the fundamental "keystone" for accessing (and surviving) the "Fifth Gate" and its *immolation of iniquity.*

> A "charge" on *Harmful-Act/Hold-Outs* may be "confronted"
> and "flattened" by a *Seeker* using (*pre-A.T.*) Self-processing
> before they are certain to surface for *Piloted A.T. Processing.*

** * * * * * **

UNDERSTANDING THE SYSTEMOLOGY OF ETHICS

Many individuals are likely to consider "Ethics" and "moral philosophy" as serious intellectual studies that only apply to the most serious criminal cases or social offenses. An individual is not always *Aware* enough to *realize* the *actual* consequences of their actions. Much of the time, the accumulated actions that breakdown clarity of (or "fragment") a communication line (whether for "SURVIVAL" or "CREATION") are not blatantly considered "*Harmful-Acts*" or outright overt attacks on a "terminal"—or against some "Sphere of Existence." In most cases, the responsibility and acceptance, coupled with realization and ability to confront, all increase as a *Seeker* peels away more layers of "*Hold-Outs.*" Our methodology of *Ethics* (toward "spiritual rehabilitation") is based on such observable progressive gains. For example:—

> Let us consider a well-to-do productive office-worker; and one day they accidentally damage a piece of company equipment. At the time of this particular incident, no one else is around to know what happened. But the office-worker knows that what happened is "bad" and fears consequential repercussions, so they "*Hold-Out*" admittance of cause and responsibility—of any knowledge at all regarding the incident or the equipment. Because it is now a **Mental Image** of a "stopped-**flow**" (which the individual has to keep secret) an "energetic mass" forms and is suspended on the *Spiritual Timeline.*

In this situation, "*Ethics Fragmentation*" is compounded further by developing an automatic *"Hold-Back"* response-reaction mechanism. This is because, while a *"Hold-Out"* remains in suspension: free reach (expression, communication) within the "organization"/ "company" (*Third Sphere*) is now restricted; and the individual may later experience *"pings"* when encountering *facets* of the experience (such as in the location of the incident or in the presence of similar office equipment). This is just one illustrated example of how easy it is to fall away from "high-power" *Self-Honesty* when operating as standard-issue "Human"—even when one has no blatantly malicious or "hostile" intentions at the start.

The same systematic principles for *Imprinting Incidents* (described in *Grade-III*)* apply to processing *Harmful-Acts*, *Hold-Outs* and *Hold-Backs*. In fact, "R1R" (**Route-1 Revised**)° is a preferred processing method for incidents on the *Backtrack*—particularly during *Pre-A.T.* work in Grades *IV* and *V*. But any systematic processing serves an individual better than allowing the standard-issue (pre-programmed) tendencies to take over. Humans often attempt "intellectual negation" or "Self-determined forgetfulness" of an *Imprinting Incident*. Rather than confront the *Mental Imagery* with full *Awareness*—and dissolve any charge on its *facets*—the reflex is to make nothing of it; to more easily stop its existence (communication) from reaching others. Of course, we know from Systemology that imprinting is made more solid if treating it—responsibility for its cause, its nature, its mass, &tc.—as anything other than what it *Is*.

> Although *"Harmful-Acts"* have their own ethical considerations to analyze (in addition to treating the *Imprinting Incident*), it is the resulting *"Hold-Backs"* and *"Hold-Outs"* that accumulate and really reduce *Actualized Awareness*—prompting an individual to withdraw their reach from "higher" *Spheres*.

This very sequence of actions results in an individual breaking off more and more relationships and closing communication channels with increasingly greater *Spheres* of a "Beta-Existence." Experience of a fragmented *Life* continues. The being succumbs to the effect end of the scale via their un**willingness** to *Be* or *Do* anything, then alone be in communication or social fellowship with anything. If uncorrected, this spiritual and physical atrophy often marks the (relatively) nearing collapse of any tolerable POV maintained by the Alpha-Spirit with an **extant** Universe. An individual does not suddenly "go out of communication" with an entire Universe all at once; nor is "intending to" a necessary condition for

---

*   *"Tablets of Destiny"* (*Liber-One*); *"Crystal Clear"* (*Liber-2B*).

∞   Formerly RR-SP-1; *"Tablets of Destiny"* now revised in 2022.

it to gradually happen. For example:—

Let us consider a well-to-do productive postal-carrier delivering mail daily to residences; then one day they find themselves encountering a painful experience with a stray tomcat. Without warning, the cat leaps out from the bushes and begins savagely attacking the mail-carrier's face. A blur of feline tooth and nail flail about wildly frantic—as if the cat were deliberately designing an art-doodle in blood-drawing scar lines. The mail-carrier freezes in place stunned, hurt and embarrassed: a *Mental Image* of the cat preparing to pounce is suspended in time, emotionally encoded with *facets* of the environment, and of course, the searing pain.

From a *Grade-III (Master-Level)* perspective, record of the event seems typical of an *Imprinting Incident*—and, of course, there are several systematic "Routes" at one's disposal to remedy the light **degree** of *fragmentation* that ensued. But who is to say in this case (other than the postman) how "light" the experience may have actually been. Emotional and analytical "charge" on the incident itself may be rather "light"—but without *Self-Honest* exploration of the *Backtrack*, we cannot be completely certain of how this actually "stacks up" with an individual's existing *Implants, Programming* and *Encoding.*

A *Grade-IV/V (Pre-A.T. Wizard-Level)* Systemologist has a much wider view and understanding of *Life* and *Existence* than even a "Master." In this example, our mail-carrier is the recipient (or "effect") of a *"Harmful-Act."* We know that the incident is stored with a *Mental Image* and associated with environmental *facets.* This is recorded (along with the registry of pain) as a survival-mechanism by the "Reactive Center" (*RCC*) so that it may issue "warnings" when restimulated in the future.

Embarrassed by "losing a fight" to a cat, our main character establishes a *"Hold-Out"*—or unwillingness to communicate the incident to others. The longer this is maintained in suspension, the more solid the *"Hold-Back"* becomes until the individual no longer feels comfortable extending their reach at work (*Third Sphere*) or in the presence of cats (*Fifth Sphere*). **Affinity** for (or "liking") cats and similar animals is likely to fall away, blocking and/or fragmenting communication channels with the *Fifth Sphere.* This is likely to continue so long as the individual remains fragmented with the subject/terminal "*Cats.*" Additionally, the *"Harmful-Act"* is registered as "motivation" to justify future considerations of action. When left unchecked from this point onward, the matter becomes a *slippery-slope.*

Ethical fragmentation occurs via *Imprinting* and *Facets*, meaning we are again in the domain of the "RCC"—or "Reactive Control Center" (a **Zu-line** relay point at "2.0" on the Standard Model). It wasn't until the Systemology Society had worked beyond this point once already in *Grade-III*, and into higher faculties through most of *Grade-IV*, when the "RCC" reared up on us again and threatened to undermine an individual's preexisting gains on the *Pathway.* In brief: *Ethics Processing* experiments began July 2020 synchronous with our *Grade-IV Professional Piloting Course* given for "*Liber-Two.*" [*Ethics Processing* is also a remedy for *Seekers* that made slower gains in Grade-IV and/or had difficulty previously achieving basic Beta-Defragmentation (after using the combined texts: **Liber-One**, *Liber-2B*, *Liber-Two* and *Liber-3D*).]

A considerable amount of attention is given in our Systemology toward resolution (or proper handling) of the "Reactive Control Center." Whether the mechanism first evolved genetically or spiritually, the RCC is a "mental construct" inherently attached to the "Mind-System" of all *Life-forms* on planet Earth (at the very least). Its original purpose is to automatically (and non-analytically) "record wrongness," then display the data (when restimulated) to "increase survival by minimizing pain and exposure to dangerous facets." Of course, the RCC seems to produce the opposite experience at this present evolutionary stage of civilization and the Human Condition. Any supposed benefits once obtained from this "safety system" became obsolete a long time ago—and yet the (standard-issue) "mechanism" remains "operationally" in place.

Although *Ethics* is an "analytical" endeavor, any
Imprint Charges, Hold-Outs and/or *Hold-Backs*
keep the RCC actively involved (if restimulated).

Both examples (*office-worker* and *postal-carrier*) involve a "*Hold-Out*" concerning a previous "*Harmful-Act.*" This begins with a small amount of withheld communication, but then results in a growing series of personal "*Hold-Backs*" on *ability* and *reach.* The employee (in both examples) starts appropriating their "workplace" (*facets*) as a dangerous environment. This causes a decline in performance (productivity) and increased separation (or fragmentary individuation) from the organization (job), social groups—the *Third Sphere* in general.

Not only is personal energy (*Awareness* "units") spent compulsively keeping a "*Harmful*" or "*Hostile*" incident (*Mental Image*) suspended, but the individual also perpetually maintains (creates) a highly-charged "worry" (fragmented energetic "ridge") about "others *finding out*." This is referred to as "*Missed Hold-Outs*" in our Systemology Ethics.

> **missed hold-out** : an individual's *Hold-Out* that someone else nearly found out about, or which leaves the individual wondering if they did actually find out or not; undisclosed event when someone else's behavior (or speech) restimulates emotional-response-reactions ("worry" &tc.) about potential discovery of withheld data, a *Harmful-Act* or *Hold-Out*; also less often referring to, in *systematic processing*, a Seeker's "held-out" (hidden) data that they expect (or "worry" &tc.) to be discovered during a *session*, but which is *missed* by the Pilot.

Where a "*Hold-Out*" involves the Seeker's own undisclosed actions (which should still be addressed in *Ethics Processing*), a "*Missed Hold-Out*" involves someone else's actions. It is possible that the "*Hold-Out*" was not even treated as such by the Seeker—may not even be thought about ever—until the energetic charge on the incident is nearly found out and then missed. This directly restimulates any charge on the energetic-mass. Since the Seeker is erroneously left with an *uncertainty* to "wonder" about (thereby reducing Awareness and presence), the whole sequence-chain is a source of present-time fragmentation.

For this specific application, the nature (or contents) of the "*Hold-Out*" itself is quite secondary in significance (by comparison) to the primary fact that: "*something* was almost found out"—contributing to the fragmented state of a *Seeker's* present condition. Unlike systematic methods for processing-out *Imprinting Incidents*, the exact moment of uncertainty (or Mystery) should be "spotted" on the *Backtrack* (and realized/discharged "*As-It-Is*"). Otherwise, a *Seeker* risks accumulating additional "*Hold-Backs*" due to a perceived confusion and/or **degree** of (un)willingness to act or reach.

Mardukite Systemology, insofar as it relates to the "Power of Choice," frequently references the logic of **Games Theory**, supplementary to standard/academic "*systematology*," which is crossed with knowledge from the *Arcane Tablets* and 20th Century American New Thought. The "*Harmful-Act-Hold-Out*" sequence is comparable to the "Offensive/Defensive" *dichotomy* of "play" in standard *Games*. An individual can certainly be bogged down with "things" in *Beta-Existence*. There is a general sense (implanted) that a "**player**" is meant to gather and accumulate energy-masses, while simultaneously minimizing losses. This is why a Seeker practices physical (objective) processes of "reaching" and "letting go" on Self-determinism. Otherwise, the challenge is how to override tendencies that "hold a person back" from adequately "releasing" their grip on "things."

> An individual needs only to "*consider*" a *reality* that
> they are "weighed down" or "stuck" in order to feel
> "entrapped" and *actually* restrict their own actions.

The Mind-System buffers direct experience (projection and reception) of energy between the Alpha-Spirit and its perceived Universe. Where it concerns *Beta-Existence*, direct **manifestation** of *Alpha-Thought* (*Will-Intention, &tc.*) is reduced to physical *Effort*. Therefore, the original intention of a Mind-System is estimation of *Effort* (to be applied toward a particular result). Fragmentation affects this estimation, and considerable emotional **turbulence** is connected with the "misses" and "close calls" of life experience. An "accident" might be an *imprinting incident*, but this goes on to include further situations with potentially deeper emotional encoding. It doesn't only concern times when we were impacted from a car, but the nearness of an accident—a missed accident—that seems to incite the greatest reactive-response. Or, for example: a *test* that is only missed by a "point" or two. In this application of *Ethics Processing*, we are also interested in what others have "nearly found out."

All "circuits" are applied to *Ethics Processing*. Failure to do so proved to be a shortcoming in the original version of Route-1.[*] "Processing-out" each circuit or POV on an incident (or event type), even if one or more has to be *imagined*, provides opportunities for optimum energetic release on that channel. This means for any *Harmful-Act* you have committed and then *Held-Back* ("**circuit-1**"), you would also *run* the concept of having someone else commit it against you ("**circuit-2**"), and of course, another/others to another/others ("**circuit-3**"). This will remove enough residual energy from a channel to prevent incidents from restimulating "*automated motivation*" or considerations for future actions and responses.

> **hostile-motivation** : an *imprint* of a counter-survival action ("*Harmful-Act*" or "*Hostile-Act*") committed by another against Self, stored as data to justify future actions (retaliation, *&tc.*); any *Sphere of Existence* (though usually an individual) receiving the effect of a "*Harmful-Act*"; an *imprint* used to rationalize "motivation" or "justification" for committing a "*Harmful-Act*"; in systematic *games theory*—the *modus operandi* concerning "payback," "revenge" and "tit-for-tat."

---

[*] "RR-SP" given in the First Edition of "*Tablets of Destiny.*"

The "Mind-System" records and stores all parts (*facets* and *POVs*) of similar incidents on an associated-knowledge chain. As a result, there are some instances when fragmentation remaining from incidents of "being the effect" (something happening *to you*) will not "process out" (or reduce in charge) until similar incidents of "being the cause" (doing something *to others*) are fully confronted. If not resolved systematically, these "action-motivation sequence-chains" can actually remain suspended (actively awaiting restimulation) across many lifetimes/incarnations.

Along the course of an Alpha-Spirit's long existence on a *Spiritual Timeline*, many patterns of harmful behavior are recorded and stored. Therefore, it is also necessary to **flatten** "Circuit-3" turbulence in *Ethics Processing*, which is frequently overlooked. Witnessing the actions of other "beings" (even when imaginary or fictional) has a tendency to restimulate energetic charge and/or solidify fragmentation of the first two *circuits*.

> Metahuman Wizards maintain a higher actualized Power
> and higher degrees of Awareness
> through Acceptance and upper echelon Responsibility,
> demonstrated by a superior Ethic
> rooted in Spiritual Utility, Self-Honesty and Forgiveness.

["**Route-0**"/"**Circuit-0**" emphasizes *Responsibility* ("*Power*") and *Self-at-Cause*. This is applied during an additional advanced *pass* through all basic processing from *Grade-III* and *Grade-IV* as a "check-out" for completing *Beta-Defragmentation Standard Procedure (Version-1)*[‡] and prerequisite for employing *Wizard Level-1 (Grade-V)* as "A.T." (*Actualization Technology*). If there is no energetic-charge on a particular "line" or area, then there is no need to process it again. Listing and checking for charge does not restimulate *Imprints*, *Incidents* or *Implants*; but, "over-processing"—for example, something that has already been *reduced*, **flattened** or *resolved*—can cause a Seeker to **inadvertently** apply Alpha Thought (postulate) "compulsively create" the same energy-mass again.]

* * * * * * *

[‡] Instructions appear in "*Imaginomicon*" (*Liber-3D*).

<u>BASIC ETHICS PROCESSING: "SPHERES-ASSESSMENT"</u>
(PRE-A.T./GRADE-IV, WIZARD LEVEL-0, ROUTE-3E)[†]

This present volume (*Liber-Three/"Ethics"*) extends a continuation of processing given in *"Metahuman Destinations"* (*Liber-Two*). That volume concludes (in Unit-3) with systematic processing of **"HELP"** on "circuits" to channel-*terminals*. An individual's concept or definition of *"Help"* shifts with *Awareness* levels and degrees of *Self-Honesty*. So, for present purposes: "HELP" is defined as assisting (continuation) of optimum survival. ["Help" and "Failed Help" are processing *"hot-buttons."* Personal realizations that "Help is Needed" and "Help is Possible" are fundamental conditions for effective application of Systemology techniques.]

The "Spheres-Assessment" may be Self-processed[∞] using the PCL: —"...ASSIST SURVIVAL OF..." (rather than *"Help"*). **Assessments** may be expanded with prepared standard lists of terminals. It is sometimes much more effective—assuming a *Seeker* has heightened Awareness at this gradient of the *Pathway*—to apply basics at the extent of understanding that an individual actually realizes with each "pass" through the material. We do not expect a *Seeker* to become a winged saintly angel overnight—or perhaps ever. We recognize that personal reach—and ability to confront—is increased gradually with continued study, meditation (**thought experiments**) and systematic processing in a specific "area" of focus.

A complete assessment treats all *Eight Spheres of Existence.* It may require a *Seeker* multiple session periods (or sittings) to work through all eight sufficiently. Although this is classified as an assessment, it is systematically processed, which means new realizations and actual defragmentation can occur. The simplest application is a **Route-2** PCL format using the most basic "terminal" for each Sphere. In fact, many processes (from previous publications) concerning "terminals" may substitute treating entire *Spheres of Existence*—assuming the *Seeker* appropriates correct understanding of what each Sphere represents.

When first starting out, a *Seeker* scans through each ascending *Sphere of Existence*—starting with "1. SELF"—spotting and listing whatever "terminals" ("things" or "masses") **resurface,** or are recalled, which appropriately represent that particular *Sphere.* For this example, we would at

---

†   For additional systematic processing instructions, a *Seeker* should refer to both *"Crystal Clear"* (*Liber-2B*) and *"Metahuman Destinations"* (*Liber-Two*).

∞   As a *Piloted Procedure*, professional assessments are a prerequisite for admittance to *Wizard Grades* when following the official structure of our Systemology organization (or Mardukite Academy).

the very least assume an individual would correspond the "body" or "*genetic vehicle*" as a *terminal* for *Self* (*First Sphere*) in *Beta-Existence*. [An individual may prepare worksheets or record data in a "processing journal." In any case, the PCLs (used) and responses should be written down.]

> *Self-processing* a standard "Spheres-Assessment" requires alternating PCLs (until a new realization or absence of further answers is achieved). Apply "Route-0" or "**Route-3**, Circuit-0" *Pre-A.T.* commands to *Self* as "YOU" for *Solo-Piloting*—such as (for the *First Sphere*):
>
> A.) How could (your physical body) assist your survival?
>
> B.) How could you assist survival of (your physical body)?

This continues through each successive Sphere:[*] "2. HOME-LIFE" (Family, Children, Partner, Sex...); "3. SOCIAL GROUPS" (Organizations, Job/Workplace, Religious Groups, Church of Mardukite Zuism, Clubs, Systemology Society...); "4. HUMAN SPECIES" (Nations/Society, Civilization, Mankind/Human Condition...); "5. ORGANIC LIFE" (Lifeforms, Plants, Trees, Animals, Planet Earth...); "6. PHYSICAL UNIVERSE" (Beta-Existence, Matter, Galaxies, Extraterrestrial...); "7. SPRITUAL UNIVERSE" (Alpha-Existence, Alpha-Spirits, Creative Beingness, Decayed Entities...); and "8. INFINITY" (Infinite Creation, Supreme Beingness, Divinity/God).

> When *Professionally Piloted*, the correct PCL for a basic assessment is: "What are some things that would represent (*sphere* or *terminal*)?" or "Tell me some things that could represent (*X*)." [Be consistent with PCL wording once a set patter is found most effective or deemed best understood.]

When a *Seeker* is familiar enough to refer to (and understand) the *Spheres* by number, then do so. Otherwise, this data (above) may be used to prepare a "word-association" list suitable for newcomers. As usual, a *Pilot* is especially interested in any particular *Spheres* or *terminals* that incite "reaction-responses."[‡] If a *Seeker* misappropriates associations ("items") to Spheres/terminals (that do not analytically/rationally make sense), this is also noted. "Items" that *stand out* as "fragmentary" are given additional processing attention, once the assessment part is completed.

Ethics Processing is introduced in systematic sessions with basic PCLs given above. At *Wizard Level-0*, the *Seeker* can begin to recognize and person-

---

[*] A script for all eight will not be given here, but may be included in "procedure manuals" released/published in the near future.

[‡] Skilled use of "*GSR*"/"*Biofeedback Technology*" is particularly useful here—and becomes necessarily essential for processing upper-level *Wizard-Grades*.

ally "process out" or "discharge" energetic stores (*Hold-Outs/Hold-Backs*) connected to fragmented *Spheres* or terminals (which typically also have *Harmful-Acts* and *Hostile-Motivators* associated). Even at *Grade-IV—Wizard Level-0*—the key to opening a channel is still "Willingness to Confront" (or "face up to"); and to "increase horsepower" on the upward journey, the emphasis is still on "*Responsibility as Self-at-Cause.*"

Standard "**Route-3E**" Procedure is introduced by running a basic "confront" PCL on all three "*circuits*" of a channel using Route-3 methodology. [During an additional Route-0 (*A.T.*) pass though all basic procedures for a *Beta-Defragmentation Check-Out*, Circuit-0 is also included: "What part of yourself..." *&tc.*]

> A.) What part of (*X*.) could you confront?
> B.) What part of (*X*.) would you prefer to not-confront?

Systematic processing is applied to any noted "items" with:

> A.) What have you done to (*X*.)?
> B.) What have you held-back from (*X*.)?

The other *circuits*—"What has (*X*.) done..." (*&tc.*)—also apply. This PCL wording is overtly direct. It is most effective for advanced *Grade-IV/V* applications (when a Seeker already maintains higher-than-average *Awareness*). However, if applied *earlier* on the *Pathway*, a "stepped-gradient" approach is necessary to reach a better (more certain) reality on the process, all "*circuits*" may be run through using a more accessible (alternative) PCL, such as "Think of something you have..." or even "Recall something..."

* * * * * *

ETHICS PROCESSING: "SELF-HONESTY: SOLO PURGE"
(GRADE-IV ETHICS, PRE-A.T. SOLO, 3E)[†]

Unknowingly or naively "following" the "**command**" or programmed *Implant* patterns has a tendency to cumulatively lower one's *Awareness* (and state of *Beingness*) further away from *Self-Honesty* like a dwindling spiral. Not only will increased *Harmful-Acts* and *Hold-Outs* fragment continuous communication shared among participants in a Reality/Universe, but heavily charged weights and energetic-masses accumulate and keep an individual's spiritual aspirations ("Ascension" *&tc.*) out of reach.

[†]   For additional systematic processing instructions, a *Seeker* should refer to both "*Crystal Clear*" (*Liber-2B*) and "*Metahuman Destinations*" (*Liber-Two*).

As with other types of fragmentation, the co-creation and fragmented participation with dynamic systems of *Life, Universes* and *Everything* binds an individual to their own rules and contracts—subsequently and unknowingly making them the *Effect* of their own *Cause.* The most recent (lower) Universes are increasingly solid-state as "thicker" agreements add to previous structures. In this present *Beta-Existence*, agreements of "restriction" were made to balance the equation of any "force" applied to act (action) in the Physical Universe. Here we see an inevitable condition of *Hold-Backs* placing limits on ability.

The more an individual demonstrates inability to *Hold-Back* on their own judgment and Self-determinism, the greater the restrictions (enforcement and denial) are imposed by the agreed-upon systems. For example, **"Cosmic Law"** or "Causal Law" governs a system that is commonly understood as "*karma*." However, the idea of *karma* as a individualized punishment via Divine intervention is not altogether true.

> By **insistence** and agreement that "all actions must be balanced," the individuals themselves—those occupying Beingness/ POV within these systems and Universes—impose their own criteria for "backlashes" and "kickbacks" when acting in a common environment. In short: an individual "does it" to themselves based on:
>
> > (A) what they have done; and
> > (B) what they will not confront.

These Universes are shared by other participants, each *implanted* to uphold a similar enough "reality agreement" to combine and make the apparent structure experienced as *Beta-Existence* even more solid for all concerned. Logic behind the "*hostile-motivation*" factor is rooted in "balance"—although it never actually leads closer to a balanced equilibrium. An individual is harmed; data is recorded; then data is used as motivation to "do unto others." Of course, one can also find themselves at cause for many "unmotivated" *Harmful Acts*, each carrying their own charge—an equation that must be balanced. After which:—

> energetic charge from a *Hold-Out/Hold-Back* accumulates
> enough mass to "pull in" necessary conditions for
> a "*hostile-motivator*" to manifest in the individual's future.
> A *Hold-Back* is essentially a "pull back" from a terminal,
> strong enough to "pull in" undesired phenomenon
> as a *motivation* for previous *Harmful-Acts.*

To be completely and systematically clear on this point:

> *Hold-Outs* are a "social" variety of *Hold-Backs*.
> Thus, all *Hold-Outs* are *Hold-Backs*;
> but not all *Hold-Backs* are (known) *Hold-Outs*.

It is possible an individual may not even be *Aware* (as in "consciously" "knowingly") of the many *Hold-Backs* subtly restricting and defining **parameters** of their own tendencies and personal inclinations. A *Beta-Defragmented* state of total *Self-Honesty* lifts the "bars" or shackles, allowing further *reach* on the *Pathway*—upward to *Gateways of Infinity*. In combination with *Grade-III* and *Grade-IV*, our present systematic *Pre-A.T.* resolution of "Systemology Ethics" (or "Metahuman Utilitarianism") is the "hidden key" to reaching a stable basic state as **Homo Novus**—the "New Human." This is the ideal direction and destination for humanity's present (and future) "spiritual evolution" (or *revolution*, if you prefer).

On our *Route to Ascension*, this refined culminated library of published "*Mardukite Systemology*" material (spanning several volumes since the "*Original Thesis*" by Joshua Free, published in 2011) now represents the first necessary (prime) milestone achievement—of which there is no substitute for; not even at "higher levels." Such "upper" *Wizard Grades* are dependent on a Seeker having already reached a basic state of *Self-Honesty* (*Homo Novus*) to be most effective.

> The purpose of our Systematic Ethics Processing is to
> rehabilitate an individual's willingness to be at Cause.

As an introductory application, the first basic step of a "Self-Honesty Solo-Purge" is for a *Seeker* is to actually *spot* the things they've done on the *Backtrack* (in the past). Prior to any additional treatment or consideration of these things, an individual must first take responsibility for action—being at Cause for the doing of things. A retraction from this point results in *Hold-Backs*. As an additional step, we would want to *spot* points of *Hold-Back*—actual instances of inhibited (*Held-Back*) action. The more "charge" can be taken off the *Backtrack* with preliminary "Solo" work, the easier and more effective a *Piloted Check-Out* for the "Wizard Grades" will be.

Ability to spot and confront these actions increases on a gradient scale; as more is lifted, more becomes available within reach. It is suggested to begin with an area of life (partner, family, work, &tc.) that they are commonly having difficulty with—and which is most accessible for recall, &tc.

[One would also note which *Sphere of Existence* it pertains to.] A *Seeker* is then prompted to *write down exactly what action(s) they did.* Such confessional-style "therapies" are common to many traditions and religions, but we are concerned with a specific systematic approach here. For example, we are not interested in attaching any reflections, rationalizations, thoughts of shame or regret and so forth. At this stage, we want to emphasize *actual physical actions done by Self*, regardless of any considerations, justifications or additions.

> An individual raises *Awareness* to free themselves from
> a *"Harmful-Act—Hostile-Motivation"* sequence cycle by
> taking responsibility/confronting what Self has done
> without feeling regret, guilt, shame or a need to blame.

This first part (of listing) treats the nature of the actions systematically. Then afterward, if necessary, the process may be cleaned up (specific charges "flattened") further by a second part: writing confessions; letters of "admittance" (admitting *doing* actions). These are directed to persons and groups that the *Seeker* maintains *"Hold-Outs"* (and *"Hold-Backs"*) from—often times even related to *actions* formerly listed. The letter should include *all details on display with nothing hidden or withheld*. This is continued until there is a noticeable sense of "release." These letters are generally *burned* afterward; not retained or sent anywhere; although they may increase ability or prompt interests in opening a closed-off channel of communication. As a personal choice, this does not actually have to happen afterward—but a *Seeker* should not continue to experience any automatic "flinch" or "withdrawal" from (communicating/connectivity with) that terminal (and its Sphere).

The standard (*Piloted*) layout of Systematic Ethics Processing (Route-3E) of a specific *"Harmful-Act—Hold-Out"* sequence may be applied to the form or method of Solo/written processing. Some *Pilots* have practiced this in training sessions by recording the *four points of data* on note (index) cards. It is more common to use a "steno-book" or appropriate journal/log to record full *systematic processing sessions.* However, the *Wizard Level-0* application of Route-3E often involves what many individuals consider "sensitive information." To be fully effective, a *Seeker* must both understand the value (personal gain/benefits) of *Ethics Processing* and feel safe exploring it without fear of punishment (guilt, evaluation or judgment of any kind) from others. The more critical or sensitive "3E" (*Ethics*) records are generally only kept long enough to qualify a *Seeker's* transition to *Wizard Level-1* proper.

Much like *systematically processing* an *Imprinting Incident*, the act/action must be specifically located in the "Space-Time" of the *BackTrack* and confronted *"As-It-Is."* At a *Pilot's* discretion, the *Seeker* may be prompted to follow up basic data listing with a more formal and complete "confessional letter" written and read out loud in session (to resolve heavily charged fragmentation) and then is destroyed. The *four pieces of data* collected for each action are:—

HEADING : Short description of *"What"* as a title.

A.) WHEN (TIME) : The *"Exact Time"* the event occurred; time, date and duration (how long was spent carrying the action out). This distinguishes/separates entanglement of a specific time from the reality experience of all other times (including how the "present time" is treated).

B.) WHERE (SPACE) : The *"Exact Place"* where the event occurred; including not only location, but also unique facets of the environment. This distinguishes/separates entanglement of a specific location (and environmental condition) from the reality experience of all other locations (including how an individual's "immediate surroundings" are treated.

C.) CONSIDERATION : The *"Exact Considerations"* in which the event occurred; including what kind of law, code, rule or social convention was violated, and whether it was an error/mishap or civic crime. Essentially, answer the question of "What were you *thinking* 'at the time' (or 'immediately prior')?" Another standard PCL is "What problem 'was it' (or 'might it be') a solution to?"

D.) WHAT IS (DETAILS) : The *"Exact Event"* actions that occurred; an account or script of activity detailing exactly what the individual has physically done, step-by-step, as if viewed by a third-party observer. Only actions the individual has done and not what others have done or anything that would fall under *'Considerations'* (above). This also distinguishes/separates entanglement of the physical event actions recalled from personal considerations.

If a *Seeker* is unable to achieve any sense of "release" using *systematic 3E-processing*—or significant turbulent fragmentation is still restricting free-**flow** on a channel—there is likely to be a *"Missed Hold-Out"* connected to that area, or else all critical information has not yet been recalled and addressed (confronted *"As-It-Is"*). As an additional safeguard, it is standard practice for *Pilots* to end any 3E-session by applying PCLs that remedy these conditions.

* * * * * * *

ETHICS PROCESSING: "SELF-HONESTY: FORGIVENESS"[*]
(PRE-A.T. WIZARD LEVEL-0, ROUTE-0, SOLO 3E)[†]

"Forgiveness" is a much misunderstood subject, influenced by religious connotation and other social applications among standard-issue Humans. When treated conventionally, the concept accepts and validates the *Harmful-Acts* of another. At a low-level of application it says, "I see you've caused me harm and it's okay." But, of course, *the hell it is okay.* So, here we find a kink in trying to be "right" while occupying the Human Condition. Someone with low-Awareness bumps into you and presses "play" on an automatic circuit to apologize and you're supposed to say "it's fine." Society has actually run this circuit into the ground to where we all have come to accept that "it's fine" actually means "it isn't fine," you know?

In our *Systemology Ethics*, "Forgiveness" is treated at a higher order of meaning, next to "Understanding." It suggests a *Seeker* "Understands" something "*As-it-Is.*" In systematic processing, "Forgiveness" is a *concept,* not a *terminal,* because it is not a "mass" (object) or "energetic-mass." It is, however, descriptive of the quality of a channel (to a terminal) or personal significance given to an "energetic-mass" by consideration. Therefore, when applied in processing:—

| The *concept* of "Forgiveness" *may be run on* a terminal. |

So, in the end, what we are really dealing with is another semantic for "release" of "emotional encoding" and "freedom from" fragmentation. It is, essentially, letting go of the hold on, or a rigid fixed attachment to, the space-time-event that has already passed and survived. Meanwhile, the unprocessed fragmented state tends to stick one's POV in treating experience of a present time environment as if the previous conditions are still present in it.

"Failed Help" and *"Betrayal"* are the two aspects contributing greatest to the collapse of communication channels with any relevant terminal— and further to entire *Spheres of Existence*. They are detrimental to Ascension. They individuate a person away from higher Spheres and put them in a position to think and act as if they are the only one in Existence— hence the *First Sphere* of *Self.*

Technically, the person will still feel as though they are operating toward the "greatest good" (for "SURVIVAL") even if the extent of that

---

realization is reaction-responses born from hatred or revenge. Such a mode of operating will generally "stick" the person right in the middle of the fragmentation they would rather avoid. But, they base willingness to act solely on an accumulation of *Hostile-Motivators.*

Grade-IV methodology is used for training not only *Professional Pilots* of the Systemology Society, but also the *Mardukite Ministers* of the Church of Mardukite Zuism. In addition to materials already released, *Liber-3E* is an integral part of "pastoral" or "spiritual" advisement available to *Seekers* —either to get along with a happier life, or to continue further and achieve *Self-Honesty* as a "Meta-Human Condition" and access *Gates of Infinity.* Our applied methodology is an advancement and improvement on how the concept is used by religions in the past. So, whether applying solo-exercises or receiving formal *Piloting,* an individual should get a sense of "relief" by confronting their actions—and should understand that they are *forgiven.* If this acknowledgment is not positively received, or a *Seeker* is still feeling heavy emotion, it is likely that only part of a *Hold-Out* or *Harmful-Act* has been confronted or processed. Acceptance of "Forgiveness" is then an excellent monitoring tool regarding the completeness of Route-3E applications.

> In order to pursue upper-level Wizard-Grades with full effectiveness, a *Seeker* simply cannot have attentions still rigidly fixated on *guilt, Hold-Outs* or low-level *justification cycles* of any kind. Thus, we are impressing achievement of *Self-Honesty* in *Liber-3E* more strongly than ever before.

The most Basic "Route-0" *forgiveness* PCL (*Routine-3E* circuitry) include:

> A.) IMAGINE you are treating others with *forgiveness.*
> B.) IMAGINE others are treating you with *forgiveness.*
> C.) IMAGINE others treating others with *forgiveness.*

> An advanced (*A.T.*) "Circuit-0" application would include the concept of *Self-Forgiveness,* or else "treating *Self* with *forgiveness.*" Ultimately this is really what it all leads up to: each individual having to fully let themselves *off the hook* from stored/charged energies of what has happened in the past.

When we consider how long the Alpha Spirit has existed—how many Universes it has occupied, how many roles it has identified with—it is not surprising that each of us has *done* virtually all you can possibly think of *doing*—both good or bad. It is also not very surprising that many of us would rather choose to forget a lot of the misdeeds. Apparently, there even are *Hold-Outs* we *Hold-Back* from ourselves. But, of course, these accumulate—building up energetic-mass over time—and often conceal or close off channels with various Spheres of Existence and even entire Universes. Somehow or another, this is the case for each and every one of us involved with this whole mess of operating (or entrapment to) the Human Condition in the Physical Universe.

> An individual decides "I don't want to know"
> and winds up on the effect end of a Mystery.

Unlike *Analytical Recall* (*Route-2*), application of *Imagination* and **Creativeness Processing** (*Route-0*) to *Ethics Processing* allows a *Seeker* the freedom to consider a wider range of possibilities that are not restricted to *known* (consciously recalled) events from this lifetime. Often times there are some nearly-automatic practically-reactive "ideas" that one has regarding personal events on the *BackTrack*. Without need of validation or concern about whether one's speculations are accurate, *Route-0* may be used to treat real matters that remain just below the surface of *Awareness*. If the imagined event is fictitious, *Creativeness Processing* will only add greater fluidity to considerations a *Seeker* maintains on the line. However, if the imagined event does, in fact, include facets of an actual event (even if "out of sight") than the processing can actually assist in resurfacing more of what is hidden—or at the very least, provide a very real sense of relief and release. So, either way, there are gains; but this process can also be applied to known events.

FORGIVENESS (PRE-A.T. ROUTE-0 ETHICS/0E, BASIC 3E)[‡]

Circuit-1 — What *Harmful-Act* "might" you have done?
         \ IMAGINE[*] yourself being *forgiven* for it.

Circuit-2 — What *Harmful-Act* "might" others have done to you?
         \ IMAGINE them being *forgiven* for it.

Circuit-3 — What *Harmful-Act* "might" another have done to others?
         \ IMAGINE them being *forgiven* for it.

Circ-0/A.T. — What *Harmful-Act* "might" you have doe to yourself?
         \ IMAGINE you *forgiving* your Self for it.

[‡] Refer to a later section ("*Metahuman Ethics: Entering the Wizard's Way*") for additional processing enhancements.

[*] *Conceptual-Certainty* (*Route-0E*) may be substituted for *Route-0*, if a *Seeker* has not yet worked on *Creative Ability.*

:: UTILITARIAN SYSTEMOLOGY FOR PILOTS ::
—Professional Processing to Bridge Grades IV. & V.—

Historically, social and civic use of Ethics for justice, religion, medicine and penal systems, all impresses the Human Condition with concepts regarding "apparent dangers" of *Truth* and *Honesty.* In fact, we find no shortage of examples describing coerced confessions, enforced communication (under duress) and interrogative interviews for thousands of years—and that's just including our "most recent" version of *Earth Civilization.* Essentially, all relevant *Mental Images* and considerations are "imprints" encoded to "fear"—*facets* of punishment and pain, guilt and shame, potential loss of property, personal freedom or even one's own *Life.*

> There is also a more deeply implanted *Fear of Discovery* or
> *Fear of Being Discovered* present among all Life-on-Earth—
> and once we find out why, we release ourselves from it.

Using our established semantics and systematic logic to understand: this low-Awareness "fear" point of Beingness is synchronous with the "Reactive Control Center" (of the Mind-System) and what some would call the "Fight-or-Flight" survival-response-mechanism of the standard-issue Human Condition. Therefore, the *BackTrack* is likely to have entire chains of encoding from assuming various Identity **"Phases"** as both "interrogator" and "interrogated"—"executioner" and "executed" *&tc.* Naturally then, the concept of *Truth* is easily fragmented by association as-equal-to "pain" and **"unconsciousness"** or even "death."

Piloting systematic processing for "Route-3E" requires a higher level of skill and training than former Routes. To be certain there are no "hidden communication channels" in the Systemology Society, details from our *Professional Piloting Course* for *Ethics Processing* are given here alongside other chapter-lessons better directed to all *Seekers.* There is every reason to believe an individual that worked through all four former "Routes" (and primary texts) can understand and benefit from *Pilot* information—or even enhance *Self-Processing* efforts. The official *"Pre-A.T."* Wizard-Levels (particularly *Grade-V*) are *Piloted*; after which, much of the upper-band of higher-grade prep-work for *A.T.* ("*Actualization Tech*" or "*Ascension Tech*") may be resumed *Solo.*

> The primary methodology of *Ethics Processing* (*Route-3E*)
> is to *Confront* something *As-it-Is.*

> The "RCC" (if active) prevents someone from *"confronting"*
> by doing all looking, **computing** and evaluation for them.

When processing *Seekers*, a *Class-3E Pilot* must operate at high-Awareness with ability to *confront*—face-to-face handling and proper management—of "discreditable" and "hostile" *Hold-Outs* by certain individuals using the *"phase"* of a malevolent personality-package. An Alpha-Spirit does not directly set out to occupy a POV from an "evil" *phase-personality.*

A being will often times start out on this part of the pattern as a high-Ethics enforcer of some kind, essentially minimizing the "Evil"; and so, it gets to where you start having to classify what is evil and hating it and it's that thing *over there*, so to speak. Naturally, we participate in creating solidity of this part of our Reality. The Enforcer is trying to do everything right—everything by the book—and suddenly there are enough *Harmful-Acts, Hold-Outs* and *Hostile-Motivators* on their path, that they suddenly "drop down" a notch on the scale, or in *Awareness*, so to speak. So now, they are an Avenger, using force to balance the "evil acts" they are faced with; and all the while they have been creating this "Mental Image" of the "evildoer" and making ir more solid and more solid until ultimately in the end, the Avenger crosses over and into the "phase" of his nemesis, the **Malefactor**. Therefore:—

> we do not need to judge and chastise our fellow Seeker;
> we defragment the view of the path which led them there.

* * * * * * *

BASIC APPLICATION OF ROUTE-3E ETHICS PROCESSING

Many systematic *Grade-IV* PCLs introduced for "Route-3" and "Route-3C" within SOP-2C[‡] also apply to "Route-3E" for *Ethics Processing*. [If the language used in the former sentence is confusing in any way, especially to a newcomer to this paradigm, be certain to spend additional time reviewing the vocabulary given in the glossary and/or supplemental materials preceding this publication.] If a Seeker has already received and successfully flattened a complete run through that processing, it may be left alone until the *"Pre-A.T. Personal Integrity Check-Out"* required for Grade-V.[*]

[‡] Refer to *"Metahuman Destinations"* (*Liber-Two*).

[*] Until the org be certain that training, skill, ability, technology and equipment is properly duplicated by independent practitioners, the full "Check-Out" to access upper Wizard-Grades (as of January 2022) is administered exclusively at the "Borsippa HQ" (*Colorado*) for Mardukite Academy & Systemology Society.

However, during *Piloted systematic processing*, if a *Seeker* is painfully struggling to achieve *Grade-IV* realizations, has not effectively achieved any, or is not progressing forward on the *Pathway*, it is only due to one or more of the following, with a slight push to considering the latter:—

— the *Seeker* is feeling hungry, thirsty, tired or restimulated by the environment;[†]

— the *Seeker* is maintaining a misunderstood word/ concept;

— the *Seeker* is not applying presence to the session, due to attention fixed on an outside problem;

— the *Seeker* is not trusting of Systemology methods, or has been mishandled by a Pilot;[∞] or

— the *Seeker* is suspended in place, maintaining *Hold-Outs* and *Hold-Backs*, or with attentions directed at *Harmful-Acts* and even *Hostile-Motivators.*

It is detrimental to successful application of our methods that these conditions be determined or resolved. This list should be briefly checked-out before starting *any* systematic processing session, *Piloted* or not.

> Whether or not a *Pilot* (or *Seeker*) utilizes mechanical **biofeedback** tools (described later) to assist, the ability to provide high-power processing in Systemology requires high-level intuition and proper application of this applied philosophy. The keyword here is *"applied"*—that means you're supposed to *do* something with it. When it comes to *Wizard-Grades*—when it comes to *Actualized Alpha Ascension*—you won't be able to just *think* your way up and out. Handling the *"Way Out"* requires a high-tone ability to *Confront*; as does the gradient of *Gatework* we are presently treating.

In some situations, an early emphasis on *Ethics Processing* is necessary just to get an individual *moving* at all on the *Pathway*. It is not for us to judge a *Seeker's* misdeeds. Our only interests concern improvement of their own ability and spiritual freedom. Progress on the *Pathway* is the importance here—and some *Seekers* find the weights they have burdened themselves with in this material existence, prior to pursing this *Pathway*,

---

†   In substance abuse/chemical dependency ("twelve-step") programs, the acronym H.A.L.T. is used to remind an individual to stop and evaluate if they are experiencing any of the main conditions that hinder rehabilitation: Hungry, Angry, Lonely, or Tired. If these are left unattended, personal progress tends to *halt.*

∞   This includes actual or imagined events. Mardukite Systemology—as a concept and group entity—also has a tendency to restimulate fragmentation, especially connected to "education" and "religion."

are already too much for them to *Confront* and resolve at their present *Awareness*-level.

For this reason, Route-3E (and *Liber-3E*) is introduced for Grade-IV rather than Grade-V. It may be introduced immediately as an integral of Route-3 (described in *Metahuman Destinations*). Therein, we process *Three Circuits* regarding channels of *Communication, Interest* and *Agreement* (in that sequence). The emphasis of those series regarded *Recall* and *Analysis* of "demands" (enforced, coerced, &tc.) and "rejection" (withdrawal, inhibition, &tc.) on those lines. This is quite similar to our present focus on what someone "*has done*" and what they have "*held back*." When an individual *rejects* some thing, they are *Holding-Back* on those lines, and essentially withdrawing responsibility.

To our existing array of PCLs, we have but to add "*Hold-Outs*" to each of the series. For example: where we have *Communication Demanded* of others, of us, and cross-flow; then *Communication Rejected* by others, by us, and cross-flow; we then add *Communication Held-Out* on others, on us, and cross-flow. A Grade-III or early Grade-IV *Seeker* may need to have explained that a "*Hold-Out*" is an intentional inhibition, withdrawal or refusal to reach, communicate or connect. PCLs are not effective if a *Seeker* is uncertain of a word's meaning, or if the meaning they associate is misapplied.

> Initially, we are not as concerned with targeting justifications (or excuses) in basic "Route-3/3E" as much as we are interested in distinguishing imprinted considerations (and *facets*) of a particular space-time event as separate from present-time and present-environments. Personal computations and justifications are often revealed when properly processing (more accessible) considerations.

HELD-OUT SUBJECTIVE COMMUNICATION
(EXPANDED RECALL, BASIC 3E)

Circuit-1 — RECALL a time you *held-out* communication on someone.

Circuit-2 — RECALL a time someone *held-out* communication on you.

Circuit-3 — RECALL a time someone *held-out* communication on another.

Notice that some existing *Grade-IV* PCLs already cover similar ground. "*Inhibited Objective Interest in Communication,*" where an individual is demanding that someone *not* communicate with someone or some thing, is the same as "*Enforced Hold-Outs*"—though at the time of initial development, these were not considered as a matter of *Ethics.*

HELD-OUT SUBJECTIVE EMOTIONAL INTEREST
(EXPANDED RECALL, BASIC 3E)

Circuit-1 — RECALL a time you *held-out* on liking someone.[‡]

Circuit-2 — RECALL a time someone *held-out* on liking you.

Circuit-3 — RECALL a time someone *held-out* on liking another.

HELD-OUT SUBJECTIVE REALITY AGREEMENT
(EXPANDED RECALL, BASIC 3E)

Circuit-1 — RECALL a time you *held-out* on agreeing with someone.

Circuit-2 — RECALL a time someone *held-out* on agreeing with you.

Circuit-3 — RECALL a time someone *held-out* on agreeing with another.

These are just a few examples of appropriate PCL. While a *Pilot* (or *Seeker*) should not vary wildly from those PCL given in previous material, it requires the "intuition" and a great deal of "listening" to apply the right sequence or series that actually creates a change in *Awareness.* There are actually more processing examples given throughout *Grade-III* and *Grade-IV* than would be critically necessary to resolve *Self-Honesty* for a typical *Seeker.* The remainder are given so that a *Professional Pilot* can apply a complete intensive **Systemology-180** rundown for any *Seeker* at their existing level of understanding (or *Awareness*) and produce results—which is to say a positive change in a Seeker's *Awareness.*

But *Grade-IV* is separated from *Grade-III* for a reason—and we should expect that a solitary *Seeker* has minimally completed a *Grade-III* understanding prior to applying *Grade-IV* to Self-Processing. Furthermore, a *Pilot* should be trained on all relevant professional materials (ideally up to *Grade-V*) prior to applying *any* of the methodology to others. The *Systemology Society Professional Piloting Course* for Metahuman Systemology minimally includes the texts **"Tablets of Destiny"** and *"Crystal Clear"* for *Grade-III*; then *"Metahuman Destinations"* and *"Imaginomicon"* for *Grade-IV.*

There are also *Grade-III* supplements, including *"Systemology: The Original Thesis of Mardukite New Thought"* and *"The Power of Zu"* which are available as stand-alone titles or in the *Grade-III* anthology, *"The Systemology Handbook."* The first distinguishable *Grade-IV* supplement is the present volume, *"Liber-3E."* An expanded version of the *"Basic Course"*[*] that appe-

---

‡ Or "something"; or a specific charged terminal, if applicable.
* "Principles of Systemology" (*Published in 2022*).

ared in the premiere edition of "*Imaginomicon*" (but which was removed from the Mardukite Academy Revised Edition) is also in development as a stand-alone title, in addition to the complete Pre-A.T. *Beta-Defragment-ation* procedures manual, "*Systemology-180.*"[†]

"Route-3C" (in *Metahuman Destinations, Unit-3*) closed with considering various persons, places and terminals (even *Spheres of Existence*) with the aspect: "HELP." We considered "willingness to help," "help given" and "help not given," but focused on mostly "positive" expressions. We did not touch upon more serious detrimental imprinting regarding "*Failed Help.*" This *facet* (or aspect) and "*Betrayal*" are the two key *hot-buttons* from *Grade-IV Processing* that **correlate** most to *Harmful-Acts* and *Hostile-Motivation* in *Ethics*. In turn, these are the avenues leading to close-off reality channels (total "*Hold-Back*") in an existing Universe. There are a few more aspects of this subject that require defragmentation for *Self-Honesty*. These may be used during the earlier series of "Help" if the individual is not gaining new realizations with that aspect; otherwise they are standard practice for a *Route-3E* Ethics-cleanup prior to Grade-V.

HELP—PROBLEMS AND HELP (EXPANDED 3C, BASIC 3E)

Circuit-1 — How has your *help* been a *problem* to another?
             \ Tell me about it. (*Two-Way Communication*)

Circuit-2 — How has another's *help* been a *problem* to you?
             \ Tell me about it. (*Two-Way Communication*)

Circuit-3 — How has another's *help* been a *problem* to others?
             \ Tell me about it. (*Two-Way Communication*)

C-0/A.T. — How as *helping* yourself been a *problem* to you?
             \ Tell me about it. (*Two-Way Communication*)

It is important for a *Seeker* to realize that there are *no real problems* with actual *Help*. A basic systemology of problems itself is treated in "*Metahuman Destinations*" (*Liber-Two*), to which we can state that it is two *flows*, postulates, goals, modes, considerations (*&tc.*) directly in conflict with one another. We are mostly concerned now with flattening any turbulence on the lines of *Help*, correcting and defragmenting a *Seeker's* willingness to reach at terminals that they have had difficulties with. This includes general *facets*, those similar terminals that are tangled up a cross-association with a "past failure." This happens all the time, for example, where an individual has difficulties with their "mother" and then displaces considerations on all reflections of "Mother," *&tc.*; issues with a

---

† Forthcoming publication by Joshua Free in 2022.

specific "boss" or "employer" is processed as a general terminal encompassing *all* "bosses" or "employers" after it has been run on the specific.

> By processing general terminals rather than only specific names, the range of consideration for application is increased to include other earlier similar aspects that could be contacted. Early on, this is also one of the keys to tapping into memory of "past-lives"—or even other "hidden data" that has not yet resurfaced about *this* lifetime.

The following are processed by running alternate PCLs of each circuit repeatedly to a satisfaction or realization before treating the next circuit.

FAILED HELP—REJECTED HELP (EXPANDED 3C, BASIC 3E)

Circuit-1 — How might you reject another's *help*?
    \ How might you fail to *help* another?

Circuit-2 — How might another reject your *help*?
    \ How might another fail to *help* you?

Circuit-3 — How might another reject *help* from others?
    \ How might you fail to *help* others?

C-0/A.T.   — How might you reject *helping* yourself?
    \ How might you fail to *help* yourself?

> Experiencing *"Failed Help"* and/or perceived *"Betrayal"*
> promotes (or prompts) *Hold-Outs* and *Hold-Backs*—
> fragmentation, *"justifications"* (*illogical computations*),
> *"Self-created disabilities"* and *"motivations"* (*hostility*).

In the systematic process below, make note of all names and terminals that surface. If any carry an energetic charge, incite reactivity or represent difficulties and problems, they may be run appropriately on *"Help-Defragmentation"* following second below, which is an expanded version of a standard process given in *"Metahuman Destinations."*

INTENTION TO HELP (EXPANDED 3C, BASIC 3E)

Circuit-1 — Who have you intended to *help*?
    \ Who have you intended not to *help*?[*]

---

[*] A direct approach considers doingness and actuality, such as: "..have helped" and "have not helped" rather than intention, but in *"Route-3E"* we must gradually "draw the *Seeker* out" from their darkness and concealment to the extent that they feel safe and secure in reaching. Another advanced application for "Route-3E" is "have given" and "have not given." These are called "direct" because they allow a *Seeker* to directly treat what has actually happened "As-it-*Is.*"

Circuit-2   — Who has *helped* you?
          \ Who has intended not to *help* you?

Circuit-3   — Who has *helped* others?
          \ Who has intended not to *help* others?

C-0/A.T.   — How have you *helped* yourself?
          \ How have you intended not to *help* yourself?

HELP–DEFRAGMENTATION (EXPANDED 3C, GENERAL 3E)

Circuit-1   — How could you *help* a ___ ?
          \ How could you fail to *help* a ___?

Circuit-2   — How could a ___ *help* you?
          \ How could a ___ fail to *help* you?

Circuit-3   — How could a ___ *help* others?
          \ How could a ___ fail to *help* others?

C-0/A.T.   — How could you help yourself concerning a ___ ?
          \ How could you fail to help yourself concerning a ___ ?

The previous should be run on all "trouble terminals" and all *Spheres of Existence*. It may even be run on a list of various terminals for each *Sphere* to determine remaining charge or fragmentation. Based on information provided in "*Imaginomicon*" (*Liber-3D*), we discovered a "final touch" *should* be added to a series or cycle (and this is not exclusive only to the "*Help*" series): the **conceptual processing** command line ("get the concept of")[‡] or even "*Imagining*" (Route-0).[†]

> By prompting the *Seeker* to assume responsibility and control of intentionally created *Mental Images* without emotional reactivity or cross-association, the level of defragmentation (*Self-Honesty*) and effectiveness of a series-run can be determined. The following is an example for "*Help*."

HELP–DEFRAGMENTATION (CONCEPTUAL ROUTE-0E/3E)

Circuit-1   — IMAGINE[Δ] *helping* a ___ .
          \ IMAGINE not *helping* a ___ .

Circuit-2   — IMAGINE a ___ *helping* you.

[‡] *Conceptual-Certainty Processing* (*Route-0E*) is treated further in a forthcoming section of this chapter-lesson.

[†] *Route-0, Imagination* and *Creativeness/Imaginative Processing* are described in more detail within "*Imaginomicon*" (*Liber-3D*).

[Δ] "Get the idea" or "Get the concept" can replace "IMAGINE" for *Seekers* not yet officially processed on "*Route-0.*"

```
              \ IMAGINE a ___ not helping you.
Circuit-3  — IMAGINE a ___ helping others.
              \ IMAGINE a ___ not helping others.
C-0/A.T.   — IMAGINE yourself being a ___ and helping you.
              \ IMAGINE yourself being a ___ and not helping you.
```

* * * * * * *

ETHICS PROCESSING: STANDARD SPHERES-ASSESSMENT
(PRE-A.T. WIZARD LEVEL-0 STANDARD R-3E CHECK-OUT)

The following PCL-skeleton (SP-R-3E) is a systematic formula for applying *Ethics Processing* to all key areas and any applicable terminals representing *Spheres of Existence*. It may be used as a general assessment, as a check-out, or specifically targeting charged "turbulent terminals." We are concerned most here with *Confronting* all actions, *Hold-Outs* and *Hold-Backs* that are accessible.

> The systematic logic we have applied here is:
> "Defragmentation via Direct Confront As-It-*Is*."

It may be that lighter more reachable answers must be pulled off the channels before deeper heavier incidents (and imprinting) can be contacted and released (knowingly and willingly).

> The method applied here introduces "R-3E"—literally the Standard Procedure for (back of and beneath) all *Ethics Processing* as "Route-3E." It differs from traditional *"Expanded Route-3"* because this is intended to resurface key points of specific data, rather than analyzing and distinguishing intertwined or entangled *Communication Circuits*, which is the systems logic behind "Route-3." This is a Wizard-Level Procedure, systematically intended to not exclusively restrict answers to this lifetime or incarnate-body when run extensively at high-Awareness levels.

ETHICS PROCESSING FOR STANDARD PROCEDURE R-3E
(PRE-A.T./GRADE-IV, WIZARD-LEVEL, ROUTE-3E, SP-R3E)

Basic Terminals (as Sphere-Representations) for Ethics Processing—(1) "YOUR BODY"; (2) "SEX" "CHILDREN" "FAMILY" "HOME"; (3) "WORK" "COMMUNITY" "A 'TYPE' OF PERSON"; (4) "SOCIETY" "HUMAN SPECIES"; (5) "ANIMALS" "NATURE"/"ENVIRONMENT" "PLANET EARTH"; (6) "A 'TYPE' OF OBJECT OR MACHINE" "SOLAR PLANETARY SYSTEMS" "GALA-

XIES" "PHYSICAL UNIVERSE." Treating higher *Spheres* such as (7) "SPIR-ITS" *&tc.*; (8) "RELIGION" *&tc.* are also important, especially given the 'religio-mystical' backgrounds many *Seekers* have before finding the *Pathway* with our Systemology.

Advanced Wizard-Level Applications—this same formula may be applied to upper-level work to handle terminals representative of the *"Arcs of Infinity"* (the upper-Alpha *Spheres* beyond "8" on the Standard Model of Beta-Existence for the Human Condition) which concern a truer Alpha-Directive, primarily with "SURVIVAL" of *Creations* and *Universes*, rather than an already "ETERNAL" *Alpha-Spirit* that is only convinced of its need to survive through a body after heavy implanting and entrapment in *Beta-Existence* systems.

** When using a **Biofeedback** *Device*, it is important to check each individual word of a PCL for an existing charge prior to use in session processing. Every series or process should begin with communication between *Pilot* and *Seeker* regarding what process is about to be run and the words used for it. It is possible that a particular button or concept carries a *charge* on its own; it is also possible to get charge-reads on a misunderstood word. **

[*Ethics Processing* is a *Seeker's* best chance to get everything out in the open—to confront, handle and discharge everything accessible *As-it-Is* prior to upper-level *Wizard Grade* check-outs and further ("A.T.") *Actualization-Ascension Tech.*]

— What *Actions* have you done involving ___ ?
\ What have you *Held-Back* from doing involving ___ ?

— What *Actions* has another done involving ___ ?[‡]
\ What has another *Held-Back* from doing involving ___ ?

— What would you permit others to do involving ___ ?[∞]
\ What have you *Held-Back* others from doing involving ___ ?

— What could you allow others to find out about you involving ?[Δ]

---

‡ Or "*have others*"—based on an agreed upon PCL patter that the *Seeker* understands to mean "circuits other than 1."

∞ Alternative patter to "*permit*" (preferred) includes firstly "*allow*" and secondly (if needed) "*find acceptable for.*"

Δ "*Find out*" implies discovery or a revealing, as opposed to another version of this: "*What would be acceptable for others to know about you?*" A *Professional Pilot* may have to work, or rather "*word,*" a PCL around an individual's acceptance level (reach and understanding) as discussed prior to simply running a series of command lines out of the blue. There is an exchange of direct communication during the setup of each process or series. Lack of such

\ What have you *Held-Out*[*] on about yourself involving ___ ?

— What could others allow you to safely find out about themselves
  involving ___ ?

    \ What have others *Held-Out* on about themselves involving ___ ?

* * * * * * *

CONCEPTUAL PROCESSING FOR ETHICS ("ROUTE-0E")

Conceptual-Certainty Processing is applicably effective for any *Seeker* at any
gradient; however, its refinement at the Systemology Society was re-
served for experimental developments at Wizard-Levels. It is part of the
original "*Route-0*" research series, beginning years prior to the publication of "*Imaginomicon*" (*Liber-3D*). Starting with *Grade-III*—as an early precursor to *Imagination* and "*Creativeness Processing*"—it was discovered
that:

> a "*Concept*" of something can be systematically processed
> even if an actual *Recall* is difficult to obtain or
> a specific memory unavailable.

However, in late 2019 (and throughout developments of 2020), newly apparent shortcomings suggested it not be recommended as a direct or
primary route to *Beta-Defragmentation*. Where it came to treating terminals, the actual "energetic-mass" (fragmentation) did not always fully resolve because the "Source"/"Cause" was still *not-known* and often
remained *non-confronted*. Difficulties found in processing certain *computations* with *Conceptual-Certainty* led us directly to the existence and subject of *Implants*—yet this would require further investigation that
surpassed the scope of the "**Master Grade**" (*Grade-III*) and *Wizard Level-0*
(*Grade-IV*). [In fact, this upper-level experimental research and development cycle is still ongoing at the Systemology Society and Mardukite
Academy through 2021.]

"*Route-0*"—as specifically treated in "*Imaginomicon*"—became our *Grade-
IV* solution (or alternative) to *Conceptual-Certainty Processing*. "*Route-0*" is
applied to our first official completed version of *Beta-Defragmentation
Standard Procedure*.[Σ] However, for systematic practice-drilling personal

---

    communication will limit the success rate of our applied philosophy.

[*]   This assumes a seeker understands the intended systematic meaning of the phrase "*Hold-
Out*," otherwise alternative patter would be "*kept hidden.*"

[Σ]   Issued in the June 2021 premiere edition of "*Imaginomicon.*"

ability to freely or fluidly manage *Alpha-Thought* (*considerations* and *postulates*) fully on Self-Determination, the formerly given "*Route-0*" methods are either like using dynamite where shovels are needed, or else quite the opposite if a *Seeker* is still in preliminary stages of systematically developing "*Creative Ability.*" *Conceptual Processing* also makes some *Ethics* processes accessible/workable earlier on the *Pathway*, rather than only waiting until after a *Seeker* has officially worked with *Imagination* and *Creativeness* at the end of *Grade-IV.*

Wherever a PCL reads, "Get the sense of..." "Get the idea of..." "Think of..." and even the more blatant "Get the concept of..." we are treating considerations of a *concept* (as a thought or consideration, *&tc.*) and not a "feeling" or "sensation." Much like proper use of "IMAGINE" PCLs, processing *concepts* is useful for defragmenting *Imprints* and automation at a reactive (RCC) level; mainly because understanding and handling *concepts* is not restricted to associative-analytical thought levels. Many "computations" an individual makes about life are based on implanted *concepts* used as a foundation to encode relative *Imprinting* later on. And this is also where a *Seeker* comes around to face the nature of *Alpha-Thought* (*considerations* and *postulates*).

> *Concepts* may be run, but they do not represent "mass"
> —and therefore are not "terminals" themselves.
> But, "*Conceptual-Certainty*" may be run on "terminals."

Conceptual-Certainty was among the first methods used to handle "automaticities" during early days of the Systemology Society. The logic is rooted in very ancient spiritual practices pertaining to consciously "making" the body/mind *do* what it is doing on an automatic circuit, and thereby taking control. When a concept is run long enough (or high-power enough) for *certainty*, then total command is resumed by *Self* determining a change to the nature, motion or speed of the tendency, *&tc.* For example, if you are sitting down while reading this now:

> —*Get the concept of <u>you</u> making that body sit in a chair.*
> Or, alternatively:
> —*Think of <u>you</u> making that body sit in the chair.*
> Compare to an objective application:
> —*<u>You</u> make that body sit in the chair.*
> Or, a command postulate:
> —*Sit in the chair.*

"Route-OE" is not exclusively intended to handle physical behaviors. However, Mind-System response-patterns often promote obvious or observable reactions, **compulsions** and behaviors. The behavior exercised as physical effort in *beta-existence* begins as a thought—even if a programmed one; and if so, it most likely has emotional encoding or some other facet of sensation associated with it that might "***ping***" the *Seeker*. It is important to continue through the process completely, even if a given concept, subject or consideration is causing physical discomfort. Safeguards and system-protections exist embedded into the basic foundation of fragmented Implant-programming patterns. These may then be encoded by some related event to have a "physical response" where a *Seeker* withdraws their reach on handling them due to an automatic "*ping*" or reoccurring chronic ailment that flares up each time.

Using these methods, a *Seeker* reclaims "energy-bits" of their past attentions that have been suspended on the *Backtrack* in connection to a particular area, subject or terminal. Typically, these units of our attention— or **AttEnergy**—were either *rigidly fixed* or *widely dispersed* by some "other-determined prompting" (communication and social activity with others).

> Whatever impinging or obsessive thought an individual has, they would systematically process (or "run") the concept of having that thought (as *Self-Determined*). If the obsessive thought is, for example, a worry over buying a house; the *Seeker* runs the concept of worrying over buying a new house. Eventually, the "worry" can be turned off or changed into a "healthy interest" or even "enthusiasm" (on the *Beta-Awareness Scale*). Preferably, a *Seeker* runs the process until not only is there no automatic obsession to worry about buying houses, but no intrusive compulsion to think about buying houses at all. Afterward, the individual is free to more clearly think about, or not think about, buying houses as they choose—and without attached misemotional facets of anxious worry.

There is also the other side to consider. We have mentioned the obsessive circuit, but—what about a desired or intended thought or idea that is not surfacing? Rather than being compulsively fixed, there are matters that an individual finds difficulty "thinking on" by choice. If a *Seeker* finds that they are unable to "think" on a certain line or channel, run a process on the concept of being *denied* access to that line or *Held-Back* from reaching a certain *Sphere* (of existence or actions)—since that is what is automatically taking place.

> *Hold-Outs* and *Hold-Backs*, by semantic definition,
> "hold" *Attenergy* to an incident on the *BackTrack*.

Even if the exact mechanism qualifying this condition has not yet been "spotted" in space-time on an individual's *Spiritual Timeline*, just work with what is readily apparent at this stage of the *Pathway*—and do your best. As standardization of our *Beta-Defragmentation* procedure is reaching completion, we still seek to handle management of any accessible response-tendencies inhibiting a *Seeker's* total freedom and ability to knowingly "reach" and "withdraw" their attention, energy and personal power on their own determinism.

ETHICS PROCESSING FOR CONCEPTUAL R-3E PROCEDURE
(PRE-A.T./GRADE-IV, WIZARD-LEVEL 0/1, EX. RT. 0E/CR-3E)

Key Concepts (Hot-Buttons) for Route-OE Ethics Processing—"**INVALIDATING**" "**BEING CRITICAL**" "**WORRYING**" "**ATTACKING**" "**HOLDING BACK**" "**FAILING TO HELP**" "**LOSING CONTROL**" *and* "**MISCOMMUNICATING**."

** When using a *Biofeedback Device*, it is important to check each individual word of a PCL for existing charge prior to use in session processing. Every series or process should begin with a communication between *Pilot* and *Seeker* regarding what process is about to be run and the words used for it. It is possible that one of these buttons or concepts carries a *charge* on its own; it is also possible to get charge-reads on a misunderstood word. **

** *A point-of-fact for training* :: This PCL makes an excellent example of demonstrating the systematic relationship between the *Circuits* (in most of our "Route-3" processing methods) and the *Spheres*. **

[Run the entire process inserting the same "*Key-Concept*" in the blanks. Flatten any significant turbulence on a *circuit* before leaving off of it for another. Record notes regarding any contacted or surfacing thoughts, memories, realizations or additional *Harmful-Acts*, *Hold-Backs*, *Hold-Outs* and other charges discovered on channels to terminals, communication-circuits, **phases**/identities, *Spheres*, and so on. *Ethics Processing* is a *Seeker's* best chance to get everything out in the open—to confront, handle and discharge everything accessible *As-it-Is*, prior to upper-level *Wizard Grade* check-outs and further ("*A.T.*") *Actualization-Ascension Tech.*]

> Circuit-1 — Get the concept* of ___ something.‡
> \ Get the concept of not ___ something.

---

*   If needed, the alternative standard patter is "Get the idea of..."

‡   The PCL can be left general ("*something*") unless there is a particular terminal (person, animal, place, thing) that is assessed as heavily "charged"—preferably "reading"/"indicating" as such on a mechanical *'Biofeedback'* device.

> \ Get the concept of *something* being ___ .

Circuit-2 — Get the concept of another ___ *something.*
\ Get the concept of another not ___ *something.*
\ Get the concept of *something* being ___ to another.

Circuit-3 — Get the concept of others ___ *something.*
\ Get the concept of others not ___ *something.*
\ Get the concept of *something* being ___ to others.

C-0/A.T. — Get the concept of ___ yourself about *something.*
\ Get the concept of not ___ yourself about *something.*
\ Get the concept of *something* being ___ to yourself.

After running *Expanded Route-0E Conceptual Processing* (above) to a completion, the next step is to run the same "*Key Concepts*" with *Basic-Conceptual Route-0E* (below). Emphasis here returns specifically back to *Self*—what has *out-flowed* "from" and *in-flowed* "to" the *First Sphere of Existence*, representing the perceived position and POV of *Self* experiencing *Beta-Existence.*

Circuit-1 — Get the concept of ___ .
\ Get the concept of not ___ .

Circuit-2 — Get the concept of another ___ *you.*
\ Get the concept of another not ___ *you.*

Circuit-3 — Get the concept of others ___ *something.*
\ Get the concept of others not ___ *something.*

C-0/A.T. — Get the concept of *you* ___ *yourself.*
\ Get the concept of *you* not ___ *yourself.*

* * * * * * *

METAHUMAN ETHICS: ENTERING THE "WIZARD'S WAY"

The WIZARD **archetype** represents an individual's highest echelon of *Beingness* attainable as a persona-phase or identity-role for 'Players' in the 'Game' of *Beta-Existence.* This computation is so deeply ingrained in consciousness that it doesn't even originate in *this* Universe, but the one preceding it—the *Magic Universe* or "*Magic Kingdom*" as it is often called in our Systemology. Of course, implanted or imprinted data, while logical in **syntax**, does not always result in the most rational computation of reality for present space-time. A logical evaluation of *this* present "*Mech Universe*" might suggest that an "advanced superpower alien race" might be the ultimate; and there is good reason for this, in view of the fact that some such superpowers in *this* Universe are *"High Wizards"* prior to crossing-over from the previous **condensed "continuity"**: the *"Magic Universe."*

In many ways, establishment of the '**Ancient Mystery School**' served as an *Implant-Reinforcement Station* for those brought into this current incarnation of *Human Civilization* on Earth prior to formal systematization of the present *Human Condition*, which began during the first era of Mardukite Babylon over 4,000 years ago. A minimal amount of the original "magical" and "mystical" regalia, symbolism and philosophy crossed-over into this present cycle-phase of *Beta-Existence* via the *'Ancient School'*. Essentially only enough to restimulate *facets* of "hidden memory" and personal implant programming that most individuals continued to carry with them on their descent from the *"Magic Kingdom"*—the minimum critically necessary to "seem innately and intuitively familiar."

> ** Flattening the concept of being the effect of *"magick"* and *"mysticism"* (using *Grade-I* material and the volume titled *"The Complete Mardukite Master Course"*) is highly suggested for all Master-Level (or higher) *Seekers.* **

> Inciting a sense of the "unknown" or "not-known" equally incites computations that "there is something to be known about"—hence the obsessive "pursuit of the *Great Mystery.*"

A Wizard-Level Systemologist is processed toward a realization on the *Great Mystery* of the Universe, which reveals itself to be that: *there is no Great Mystery of the Universe.* All of *'that'* has been imposed by the individuals themselves and is dependent on others to be in agreement with it enough to a point to where it becomes a 'thing' duplicated in all realities within its reach. The higher the Awareness-level, the greater the scope on exactly what is going on.

At one level of *Existence*, we "knew" (and still "know") what *'Is'*—and on a level of Truth that expounds far and beyond a sense of *'words'* and *'definitions'*. But then we agreed that it would be more interesting—more of a *"Game"*—if we could "not know" all these things, so we might have something 'new' to *Do* in trying to *'find out'* again. Hence, the Human Condition sets out to *create things* to *know* about. But in *Beta-Existence*, this hardly reflects the state of *Knowingness* that was once maintained. And the individual has sunk fairly low in the not-know to be meandering about blindly in the Human Condition, enough to where it has to remember to *'find their own way out'* again.

The "Way of the Wizard" represents access to the upper-routes leading to *Gateways-of-Infinity*, which is to say "Ascension," far and beyond the scope of what it means to be "*Human.*" Fields of technological science and mechanical development usurped concepts of "**transhumanism,**" so our Systemology Society settled on the terms "METAHUMAN" and "HOMO NOVUS" to denote our "spiritual" applications of techniques that elevate the *Knowingness* and *Beingness* of an individual toward their optimum states. It is difficult to even consider this a new "evolution," since we are peeling back layer after layer of artificial programming that ultimately returns an individual to their true, basic and original position prior to entering the Physical Universe and its implanting. And this is what the "higher" *Wizard-Grades* represent. The way out... The way back... *The Way...*

> Even at *Wizard Level-0*—as introduced with "*Imaginomicon*"—a *Seeker* discovers that the *Reality* being experienced may be an illusion, but it is one that is projected by *Self* as part of a shared or common agreement. We are still, in essence, creating our own personal universe as we always have been—but as we take on more layers of agreement with others about what *Reality 'Is'*, such become part of the postulates and consideration for how we design our Personal Universe. These layers each become cumulatively more convoluted, restrictive and solid until we either *clear the slate* or become the total *Effect* of our own *Cause.*

In the simplest systematic terms, we remain an individual fragment of the ALL within our own Universe that we are projecting in order to have an experience, but we superimpose a *'duplication'* in that Universe of whatever we are in communication with. For this reason, we emphasize defragmenting the channels of communication with systematic processing as a primary step toward *Self-Honesty.* The underlying blueprint of *Reality* is formed by communication-circuits and the continuous flow maintained between *Self* and all others acting as "*terminals*" in this Universe.

We maintain some level of reality agreement with whatever we identify or are in communication with. In any situation where there is actual contact or flow, both sides must 'duplicate' the full cycle of communication as *Reality*. A person acknowledges, recognizes or identifies a certain individual as the *Source* of the communication just as much as they must 'duplicate' the content communicated by willingly being a receipt point. The entire *'Cycle-of-Action'* must be projected as *Reality* and 'duplicated' by each each party "*A-for-A*" in order to have actual communication. And all of these *Mental Images* (and subsequent encoding from the content) are stored along each appropriate channel and contribute what we "take away from it" or register as "experience."

> Our "experience" is not a source of "fragmentation"
> until we find ourselves not-confronting it "As-It-*Is*."
> That means not only the "acceptance" of what is done
> but also the "willingness" to be at either *Point-of-View*.

Ethics Processing is introduced on the *Pathway-to-Self-Honesty* to systematically resolve this issue. It is gravely overlooked or directly left out of what former basic systematic methods targeted. There are some individuals that do not seem to earn any stable gains from the *Pathway* until this area is resolved. It is not so much a matter of the actions themselves, but the significances assigned to them and other considerations attached. Most encounters are not permanently fragmentary, but that which is not-confronted directly will hang up on the *Spiritual Timeline* as a confusion—a fragmentation of the certainty, muddying the clear vision and experience of *Reality*.

> During a "*Harmful-Act*" there is a 'duplication' of all **viewpoints**
> by all persons, easily allowing a "*Phase-shift*" with the others.

There is a tendency for an individual to **dramatize** what has happened to them—or solicit assistance and support from others—with the old "look what they've done to me" while occupying a *Victim-phase.* This is derived from a basic survival tactic that projects "I am already wounded; please do not attack." The tendency is validated and strengthened by memories and imprints of when others might have "taken care of the individual"—such as with a childhood illness or injury. This tends to apply mostly to encounters with other friends and loved ones, where one might earn "**sympathy**" as the sole means of remaining in communication.

There are other environments throughout the greater *World-at-Large* where this computation of victimization is highly counter-survival mistake to employ. In such instances, the individual is likely to take on the (more aggressive) *Malefactor-phase*, based on a completely separate computation that "*that one* is the winning position to be in," or the mode one must operate with in order to achieve a surviving position. So we have the issue of a fragmented personality-package that has "turned Evil" solely because of being on the receipt (*enforced effect*) end of too many non-confronted "Evil" acts.

We already began treating *Victim*-fragmentation at the very beginning—

starting with *"Route-1."* Unfortunately long-term use of our original[*] *"Route-1"* methods—in exclusion to all others—tends to reinforce being the *Effect* or what we later consider *Circuit-2* (*"in-flow"*). *"Route-1"* is still a valid stepping-stone and place to begin for many *Seekers* that haven't yet regained control of enough *"AttEnergy"* or *"attention units"* (*Awareness*) to progress forward on the *Pathway* with higher studies and other *Routes* of processing. However, it does overlook other important aspects of fragmentation, such as what the individual, themselves, has done as an *"out-flow."* The total sum of these aspects contributes to later *"acceptance levels"* or *Hold-Outs* on free-flow communication and the *Hold-Backs* that Self-impose a restriction or unwillingness to act, or else *reach* thereafter.

Whatever is non-confronted becomes a "hidden influence."

The *malefactor* committing a *"Harmful-Act"* carries just as much, if not more, fragmentation at *Cause* as their *"victim"* does at *Effect.* Keep in mind that the experience of both POV is recorded by both. This means that when an individual is unwilling to confront their own created effects or completely unwilling to experience the *"other side"* of the situation, the event and all of its facets will be registered and carried as a fragmentary energetic-mass suspending *Awareness* and attention on the *Spiritual Timeline.* It is simply waiting to be *"pulled in"* and manifested against themselves as a *"Hostile-motivator."* Subscribing to the balance of all action in this Physical Universe, the *malefactor* has an incident happen to them *"after the fact"* that would seem to justify or motivate the former action—but it is happening afterward. This phenomenon is misunderstood as *karma.*

We have briefly mentioned "sympathy" as a means of maintaining low-level connectivity or communication. There is also the matter of "empathy"—or else the ability to experience another POV apart from one's own: to literally see what it's like "in someone else's shoes." This should be practiced as a *Pre-A.T.* exercise—and since it is related to use of *Imagination,* it may even be incorporated or cycled into the *Pre-A.T. Wizard-Level "Creative Ability Training"* (*CAT*) regimen.[‡]

Before treating more significant Ethical concerns, "empathy" may be repetitively practiced (or "drilled") with a partner free of the inhibition that may be applied to casual contact in public or with strangers.

—Entire instruction behind the exercise is simply: to attempt a 'du-

---

[*] Given in the premiere first edition of *"Tablets of Destiny"* (*2019*) and inclusion of that text in *"The Systemology Handbook."*

[‡] Refer to *"Imaginomicon"* (*Liber-3D*).

plication' of sensations from another POV.

—If you are even just speaking with someone, *Imagine* the impression you are projecting (how you appear and sound) from their POV.

—If there is physical contact, *Imagine* the feeling or sensation of touch received by the other POV.

When we refer to "*Harmful-Acts,*" we are not exclusively treating physical violence. All manners of projected unkindness apply to *Ethics Processing*, particularly where the effect is a reduction (any perceived "*Loss*") in an individual's *Beingness* and/or *Awareness*-level. "*Pain*" and "*Unconsciousness*" are simply two common examples of more violent acts. We are reaching for genuine ability to face-up to the *BackTrack* as we increase progress on the *Pathway*. To ensure "wins" for a *Seeker*, the "lighter" incidents should be treated masterfully prior to tackling "bigger" *Ethical* hang-ups in one's past.

> Empathy may be applied to "supercharge" effectiveness
> of '*Forgiveness*'—as given in the previous chapter-lesson.

In fact, an ability to actually confront environmental facets and personal experiences from all POV of an incident "As-It-*Is*," is a high-power key to discharging accumulated turbulent energetic-masses that restrain (or *Hold-Back*) true freedom of the Alpha-Spirit.[†]

* * * * * * *

ETHICS: "SEARCH AND DISCOVER (ON THE CIRCUITS)"
(GRADE-IV, PRE-A.T. WIZARD LEVEL-0, EXPANDED 3E)

Standard and Conceptual methods of *Ethics Processing* usually reveal quite a bit of material for resolve. It may be, however, that at a certain stage of release (or even at the very start) some significant attention must be given directly to a "search and discovery" effort. Although no specific instructions are given to restrict its application to *this* lifetime, there are also no specific instructions given as *Wizard Level-0* (*Grade-IV*) for targeting a *Seeker's* "*past lives*" directly.[∞] [This is an experimental for-

---

[†] When processing an incident (or running "*Forgiveness*"), also *Imagine* the experience from the opposing POV. The Mind-System tends to classify and group imprinting incidents on a "chain." If a your sense of an incident is becoming stronger (more solid) in its restimulated charge (rather than releasing), spot a similar non-confronted incident "parked" earlier on the *BackTrack*.

[∞] An exception being the note regarding incidents that do not readily discharge because they are linked to a larger, stronger, *older* "chain" requiring a *Seeker* to "scan for" and "spot" a

mula directly distinguishing communication-circuit energy-flows as treated throughout *Ethics Processing*.]

> NOTE: Energetic discharge and sense of release only takes place if what is discovered is fully confronted "As-It-*Is*" using methods and instruction given throughout our present *Liber-3E* text. "Discovery" and "Discharge" processes may be more effective when conducted by a *Professional Pilot* and/or using a mechanical biofeedback device to assist (as explained in the chapter-lesson: "Utilitarian Systemology for Wizards").

"Search and Discovery on Circuits" is worded very directly for use by experienced Systemologists. It is originally intended as a *Pilot's* "tool" for accessing layers of significance surrounding *Ethical* fragmentation. Each circuit is treated separately. The four PCL are run alternately in sequence repeatedly (1-2-3-4; 1-2-3-4) for a single circuit until a *Seeker* has no more readily available answers, they are interested in the discovery process and optimistic or relieved by the results. [If a *Seeker* reaches this point on one PCL of a circuit before the rest, that one part may be omitted from repeated runs.] This process may be run *Solo* as a personal data-inquiry toward *Self*, but its function is primarily to "root out" information—a list of which should be recorded for later use.

Circ-1 — What have you made another *Out-Flow*?
What have you made another *Hold-Out*?
What have you made another *In-Flow*?
What have you made another *Hold-Back*?

Circ-2 — What has another made you *Out-Flow*?
What has another made you *Hold-Out*?
What has another made you *In-Flow*?
What has another made you *Hold-Back*?

Circ-3 — What has another made others *Out-Flow*?
What has another made others *Hold-Out*?
What has another made others *In-Flow*?
What has another made others *Hold-Back*?

Circ-0 — What have you made yourself *Out-Flow*?
What have you made yourself *Hold-Out*?
What have you made yourself *In-Flow*?
What have you made yourself *Hold-Back*?

---

similar type of incident earlier in "time." This sometimes inspires *Seekers* with a "*sense*" of something that is only logically connected via a former incarnation.

:: UTILITARIAN SYSTEMOLOGY FOR WIZARDS ::

— Advanced Tech Toward "Wizard Level" Processing[‡] —

> "AHA, A LOOKING GLASS INTO THE UNCONSCIOUS!"
> —*Carl G. Jung* about GSR-Meters

Research supporting application of a **GSR-Meter** for *systematic processing* includes: Volney Mathison's "*Manual of Electropsychometry*" (1951) and "*Super-Visualization: The Duplicative Techniques of Applied Creative Energy*" (1956); Mark L. Gallert's "*Electropsychometry: A New, More Effective and Faster Psychotherapy*" (1955); Peter Shepherd's "*GSR-Meter Course: Biofeedback Monitoring Skills in the Context of Transformational Psychotherapy*" (1994, 2001); Inna Khazan's "*Biofeedback and Mindfulness in Everyday Life: Practical Solutions for Improving Your Health & Performance*"; Dr. Michael Apter's "*Reversal Theory*" and "*Personality Dynamics*" among others; Frank A. Gerbode's "*Beyond Psychology: Traumatic Incident Reduction*"; and, of course, Carl G. Jung's "*Studies in Word Analysis*" (1908). Additional controversial sources were also explored—as cited in this chapter-lesson. Various different applicable "Meter" models now exist with several "patents" filed and on record for the same.

"Wizard Grade Systemology" optionally incorporates *GSR-Meters* to assist many upper-level *Systematic Processing* applications. If used, success depends on a *Pilot/Seeker* carrying a working knowledge of, access to, and certainty in ability to use, such a device.

"*Psycho-Galvinometers*" (or *GSR-Meters*; *Galvanic Skin Response*) measure electrical resistance of the skin surface. Experimental use of *GSR* for "transpersonal psychology" is as old as "psychology" and "psychoanalysis" itself. It has been little more than 150 years—since the field of Psychology separated itself from general Philosophy. [All sciences are originally "breakaways" with Philosophy—including such as **physics** and **physiology**. That the surface of skin is electrically active—and that detectable resistance changes occur based on emotional stimulation—dates back to the mid-to-late 1800's. Early "word association" investigations by Carl Jung compared measurable "critical arousal" ("**electro-dermal**

[‡] This chapter-lesson is based on "*Wizard Level-1 Experimental Research and Demonstrations for Ethics Processing and Beyond*" as overseen by *Joshua Free* in August 2021–January 2022 for the *Mardukite Academy of Systemology* at *Mardukite Babylonia SLV Borsippa HQ*. It is compiled from the notes prepared by the author in addition to those Staff members already participating at these levels/Grades of the organization.

**activity"/*EDA*) to the "emotional charge" held by an individual regarding key words and concepts.

By the 1930's, the field of criminology applied *GSR*-equipment as a key component of the "polygraph," which also measures heart-rate, temperature, blood pressure and breathing. For both legal and practical reasons, a *full* "polygraph" is not employed within our Systemology—the additional measurements being quite unnecessary. However, it is no surprise that *biofeedback* devices and instruments used to gauge our *Ethics Processing* for *Personal Integrity* are also associated with what is commonly referred to as a "lie detector." We are, again, dealing with something called "*Self-Honesty*"—so...

For our purposes, a *GSR-Meter* (or *EDA-Meter*) detects *emotional fluctuation*, measures *energetic fragmentation* and monitors changes in *Awareness* whenever a *Seeker* contacts "charged" terminals, *imprints* or *implants* on a particular channel. Although design improvements (transistors, amplifiers, adjustable range/magnification, &tc.) expanded potential applications after the 1930's, the basic technology remains stable and relatively unchanged since intensive experimental research of "New Thought" movements emerging the 1950's and 1960's.

A *Systemologist* (*Pilot* or *Seeker*) does not require an extensive background-education in electricity/electronics in order to understand and operate a *GSR-Meter*. As with taking up an exploration, study and practice of any other new pursuit—much like when the *Seeker* started up on the *Pathway* with our Systemology—we will accomplish all that is necessary for transition into *Grade-V* (*Wizard Level-1*) by relaying a basic introduction to *Electronic Biofeedback Technology*, combined with concise communication of fundamental vocabulary and appropriate examples.

<u>GSR-METER DEVELOPMENT FOR DEFRAGMENTATION</u>

Research suggests that infamous Swiss psychologist Carl Jung was first to employ *GSR-Meters* in psychotherapy and psychoanalysis. He conducted "word association" experiments and "interviews" (asking questions, much like our *PCLs*) while measuring "galvanetic skin responses"—meaning observing, detecting and measuring change in electrical resistance across the surface of the skin (or Electrodermal Activity/EDA). It is important to note that such meters do not literally "read the mind."

One or two "electrodes" are held by, or attached to, a *genetic vehicle* and only *reflects* conditions of the Mind-System to the extent that it is affecting the body. Early meters were little more than the "*Ohm-Meter*" you

An example GSR-Meter

might find inexpensively on the market today; they lacked amplifiers and range control, making them difficult to use. [A traditional "*Ohm-Meter*" is not suggested for modern practice.]

Various book publications (and patent records) from the mid-20th Century "New Thought" era suggest that two men in particular were primarily responsible for standardizing modern *Electro-Psychometers* ("*E-Meters*")—and even systematically applying them toward *defragmenting* the Human Condition:—

• Volney G. Mathison (1950, *Patent #2684670;* "*Mathison Electrometer*"—using a single electrode held in one hand)

   –and–

• Lafayette Ronald Hubbard* (first version filed 1961, revised in 1966, *Patent #3290580;* "*Hubbard® Electrometer*"—"a device for measuring and indicating changes in the resistance of a human body"—using two electrodes, one held in each hand).

Dissatisfied with existing "*polygraph*" experiments Volney conducted in the 1940's, he invented his own type of *GSR-Meter* that included transistors (an electronic switch with no moving parts) for the first time in 1950.

---

*   In an effort to maintain a monopoly on his work, legal complications allegedly prohibit reference to "*Lafayette Ronald Hubbard*" by his more commonly recognizable name, which is apparently trademarked by "The Church" he established in 1953/1954. Elsewhere in the paragraph, the device name is printed ("*Hubbard® Electrometer*") in the style given on copyright pages of "Church" literature written by him. Usage of the name appears in the present text for educational purposes only, to describe historical development of GSR technology and is not intended to infringe on any legal trademarks or organizations that hold them.

At least by 1951 (possibly even 1950), he began regularly attending (and was significantly impressed by) Lafayette's "New Thought" lectures. He worked on perfecting his device, which detected and measured the type of "personal energy" (*Zu*) "*reads*" and "*fluctuations*" that Lafayette described. This allowed their brand of "*Pilot*" (called "*auditors*") a greater certainty toward "*Clearing*" an individual of their emotional and mental fragmentation. For several years after—until circuitry of the "*Mathison Electrometer*" became too convoluted for Lafayette's practical use—the two men sporadically collaborated on improving the equipment; all the while following very specific premises:—

• "Matter" is the physical appearance of "Energy" (*Zu*) as visible or detectable within the normative range of the *Human Condition*.

• "Energy" (*Zu*) is a "super-frequency" visible or detectable to Humans as "matter" or else manifest as the "stuff" of "*Mental Image Pictures.*"

• "Energy" (*Zu*) may be directed by the (*Alpha*)-*Spirit* or *Self*; "raised," "lowered," "released" &tc.

• Improperly directed (misdirected) "Energy" (*Zu*), "reduced flows" and "stuck flows," influences personal illness and disease.

• An individual can modify "Energy" (*Zu*) flows, selectively redirecting and applying attention, by intentionally duplicating "*Mental Image Patterns*" at the level of conscious *Awareness*.

• "Psycho-Physical" Energy (*Zu*) flows of the *Human Condition* register on, and may be relatively measured with, an "*Electro-Psychometer*" ("*E-Meter*").

"*E-meters*" received most public attention as "religious artifacts" of Lafayette's "Church"; but the "*Hubbard® Electrometer*" was not the first one developed and used for *defragmentation*—nor is it technically the only option now available today for a *Seeker* or *Pilot* of our Systemology. In the past few decades, several versions of this device have been constructed and marketed to "*Clearing* practitioners" independent of "The Church." They currently own a commercial (proprietory) trademark for the word "*E-Meters.*"

Alternatively manufactured biofeedback devices (applicable for *our* Systemologists) are not presented or referred to as "*E-meters*" either, as per —carrying names like: "Ability Meter" (*UK*); "Clarity Meter" (*US*); "Clearing Meter" (*generic term*); "C-Meter" (*Austria*); "Delta-1 Meter" (*Germany*); "Freedom-2 Meter" (*Russia*); "Mindwalker" (*UK*); "OM-Meter" (*Russia*);

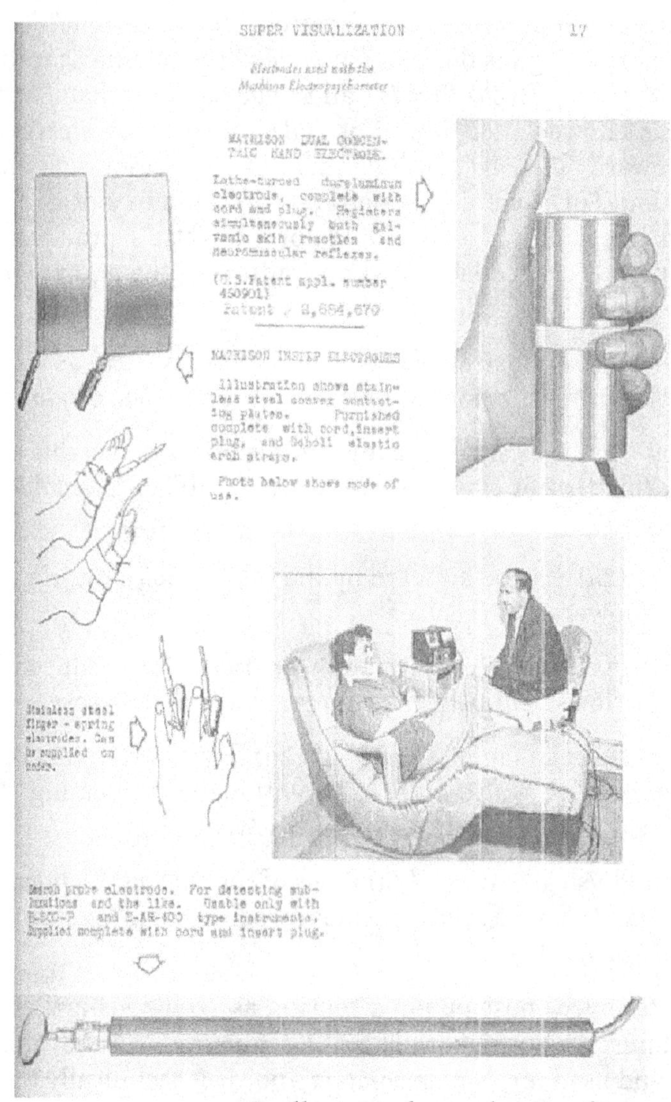

An illustrated sample page from
Volney Mathison's "*Super Visualization*"

"Phoenix Meter" (*US*); and "Theta-Meter"—to name a few commonly used ones.

A more recent design trend involves computer software, requiring minimal expense for hardware—typically two hand-held electrodes connected to a "black-box" that is then read and displayed on a personal computer rather than the device purchased. A brand new computer-based setup is a few hundred dollars, which is comparable in price to a quality second-hand refurbished/reconditioned *"Hubbard® Electrometer"* (perferably from a source in the *FreeZone*‡ that can check out the equipment before you get it; as opposed to the cheaper garage sale finds that have questionable pasts. This is not the area you'll want to 'skimp' on.

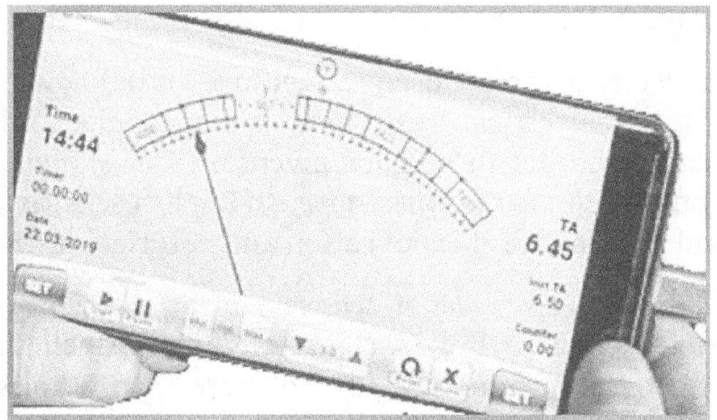

An example GSR-Meter
using cell phone technology

ELECTROPSYCHOMETRIC BIOFEEDBACK: HOW IT WORKS

> "Volney Mathison† was a pioneer in the discovery that all fears, feelings and resentments—all thought and emotion—were electrical in their nature. He found through experiments with lie-detectors during the 1940's that when a person was reminded of certain past events, or when a change of mood was induced in him, the needle in the meter would jump erratically; the degree of jump was in **proportion** to the strength of unconscious reaction. In skilled hands, the meter could be used to locate particular mental content, the nature of that content, the location of that content in space and time, 6and the amount of force contained within it."
>
> —Peter Shepherd, <u>GSR Meter Course</u>
> *Tools for Transformation, 2001*

Electrical "current" is electrical energy "flow"—meaning a *flow* (motion or action) of *electrons*, usually through a conductive wire; much like a flow of water moves through pipe or a hose. A "closed-loop" where electrons circulate is called a "circuit." We quite often treat personal energy

---

‡   The *Free Zone* or *FreeZone* is an international network of individuals and groups that continue the work described within Lafayette's material independent of "The Church."

†   Volney Mathison (*1897-1965*) psychoanalyst, chiropractor, writer, inventor.

"flows" and "circuits" in our Systemology. However, when referring to "electrical resistance" of a circuit, we quite literally mean: an "energetic-mass" (material) with an ability to "restrict" (slow down) electron flow. Larger or greater resistance in a circuit indicates greater or denser "mass" *resisting* free-flow of electrons in that circuit. And unless an individual intends on constructing their own Meter, this is really the extent of traditional electrical knowledge that a *Seeker* or *Pilot* needs

> The basic electrical circuit used to measure an unknown (or variable) value of electrical resistance is called the *"Wheatstone bridge"*—named not for its original inventor (*Samuel Hunter Christie* in 1833), but for *Sir Charles Wheatstone*, an English scientist that improved and popularized its application and notoriety in 1843.

When a *Seeker* holds *electrodes*[Σ] ("*sensors*") of an *Electro-Psychometer* in their hands, they are part of a closed-circuit. A small unnoticeable amount of electrical current (usually no more than 2 volts) is passed through the body, which now acts as one "leg" of "resistance" in the circuit. To determine the unknown value of resistance from the body, a *"potentiometer"* ("*variable resistor*" and "*range adjuster*") is attached to the other "leg" and controlled externally by a rotating "knob" or "arm." This "balancing arm" (or "baseline control") is manually rotated to a position where the "display-dial needle" is visibly at the "set" point, indicating a "balance point" is reached for the circuit. While the "needle" is at the "set" point, the circuit is balanced: the "balancing arm" (or "baseline control") position on one "leg" or "side" of the "circuit bridge" is indicative of the electrical resistance value present across the surface of the skin on the other "leg" or "side" of the circuit.

> This fundamental action compares to applying weights (with known values) on one side of a "balancing scale" in order to determine an unknown, but equivalent, weight (value) of mass on the other side.

Bringing attention out from the inner workings and mechanisms, it is more critical that all operators (*Pilots, Co-Pilots* and *Solo-Seekers*) are fami-

---

Σ Although semantically and scientifically accurate, a few experimental participants at the Systemology Society found terms like "electrode" and "probe" to personally carry reactive association with something *invasive*. If not applying physics vocabulary, as above, to introduce a proper electrical-education ("*how they work*"), a preferred day-to-day name (and for sessions) is "*sensors.*" Another acceptable term is "*cans*"—which is part of the original terminology found in this practice. It simply references the fact that metal soup-cans were actually the first standard "*electrodes*" applied—attaching to the meter wire-leads with alligator-clips. Even after specially manufactured "electrodes" were designed, the term "*cans*" has remained in use among practitioners all the way up to the present.

liar with the external controls and dials of whatever model/type is chosen for use. Basic functions and controls of an *Electro-Psychometer* have remained standard for at least half-a-century. Whether using older styles, where every detail is represented by an analog knob, or newer models that employ digital technology—and even computers, the operation is the same. External appearance of some newer models is different than what will be described here, depending on how many analog functions (on older/standard models) are now "automated" (internally), such as "*balancing action.*"

[Our *Systemology Society* 'covert' 2020-2021 planned project was originally: "to design and produce (in-house) a 'SELF-HONESTY METER' or 'DEFRAGMENTATION METER' or 'ZU-METER' (preferred names for our *Systemology* application) and/or develop an instructional course pertaining to inexpensive manufacture of the same for practical personal use" Well, we fell short on that, on *every part of it!*—*Time, Results*, and so forth. By Autumn 2021 it became clear that attentions should be redirected back toward *Grade-IV* completion: finalization and release of "*Liber-3E.*" If so desired, education materials exist 'out there'—primarily from or linked-through the *FreeZone*—to assist constructing your own Meter.]

There is one particular anomaly worthy of mention here—because all meters directly inspired by designs and operative uses from the Volney and Lafayette models continue to carry a misnomer forth. In the early 1950's the two men were giving a lot of attention to their *New Thought* concept of "emotional tone" or "tone scale"—similar in purpose to our "*Beta-Awareness Scale*" introduced in "*Crystal Clear*" (*Liber-2B*). The "range adjustment arm" that controls the "balancing action" (meaning the needle "balance point" or "set" position) was thought to indicate an individual's emotional tone level on the scale. Well, *it didn't*—but once labeled as a "tone arm," the name stuck.

Rather than indicate a display of the actual "electrical resistance"— measured in "*Ohms*"—by the Meter, Volney and Lafayette used basic numbers "1" through "6" (sometimes even up to "7"). The balance-set position is indicative of some things, but it is really the needle motion and pattern characteristics that become the critical reads during a process. While they do not necessarily indicate an individual's "emotional tone," the simple single digits aren't arbitrary and may have perhaps made the Meters easier to apply and interpret from memory, rather than actual "*Ohms*" values.

For example: up until release of Lafayette's *Professional Mark-VI* (in 1978), the "2" also had an "F" next to it and the "3" had an "M" next to it. This originally denoted target "clear readings" for each bio-physical sex. According to the story given by Lafayette in late-1950's lectures, skin resistance measurements were tested on dead bodies. Therefore, at *basic*—meaning emotionally and reactively defragmented; unaffected by any turbulence from the Spiritual Self—the meter-reads on the bodies were consistently 5,000 *Ohms* (*5000 Ω* or *5kΩ*) for females and *12,500 Ω* (*12.5kΩ*) for males. These figures are actually simplified on the standard Balance-Arm as "2" and "3" respectively. These set values are also useful to know for calibration before each use.

In many respects, it may actually be easier and more efficient for these application to use simple representative numbers. Otherwise, again, we are left with the hard figures—for example, the way the information just given is relayed in a **Traumatic** *Incident Reduction* (*TIR*) manual (Frank A. Gerbode's "*Beyond Psychology*"):—"...in most people, under ordinary circumstances, the resistance will be found in the range of 5,000–15,000 *Ohms*." Some *GSR-Meter* models do display actual electrical resistance in *Ohms*. To be consistent across the boards, we want to have the 'big picture' as a reference—if our *Systemology* is to have 'Universal' application as intended.

Balancing Arm	Electrical Resistance
1	400 Ω
2	5000 Ω
3	12,500 Ω
4	25,800 Ω
5	56,500 Ω
6	190,400 Ω

An *Ohm*-meter, such as you would find in a hardware store, does not work well for detecting *fragmentation*. Usually the display-dial will cover such a large range that you are not going to see precise movements, if at all. On the other hand, *GSR-Meters* allow an individual to display a smaller portion or range—and generally have controls that increase or decrease amplification (sensitivity). Although we can cover basic theory and technical information in this text, there is really no substitute to actually working with an operative model to gain personal experience, familiarity and certainty with these devices. This doesn't mean experience in memorizing a lot of data—we mean practicing with various individuals to see patterns and differences and feeling certain about the device before utilizing it as a *systematic processing* tool. If you're not certain in your general handling of *GSR-Meters* for *processing*, then better to skip it.

UNDERSTANDING GSR-METERS FOR DEFRAGMENTATION

> "It is a remarkable fact that the real sources of one's anxiety may be so deeply hidden in one's subconscious that one will go about believing all sorts of other things are causing all the trouble, and erroneously blaming these other things which are *secondary effects*, not *causes*. Meanwhile, the true cause remains hidden, growing ever more powerful in its effects."
>
> —Volney Mathison, <u>*Super-Visualization*</u>
> *Manual of Electropsychometry, 1956*

Prior to Carl Jung's incorporation of *GSR-Meters* for 'Word Association', the standard gauge of psychoanalytics primarily consisted of "*Comm-Lag*"[‡] (*communication lag*), which is the amount of time it takes to get a question answered. When used for *Systematic Processing*, a *GSR-Meter* may be used to detect *fragmentation*, specifically information that is suppressed, but accessible—meaning, able to be *confronted As-It-Is*—by a *Seeker*. This is not only useful for achieving true *Beta Defragmentation* in *Self-Honesty*, but is almost necessary to achieve any certainty of *Alpha (Spiritual) Defragmentation* at higher-level Wizard Grades.

The intended purpose of *Systematic Processing*—as described in *Grade-III*—is to bring undesirable, implanted and artificial *programs*, *imprints* and *postulates* into clear view for a *Seeker* to analytically inspect. Suppressed *fragmentation*, *imprints* and *programming* are uncovered in layers—as some is taken off, more becomes accessible that previously might not even register on a Meter. This is elevation of *Actualized Awareness* in action and objectively on display.

> "When restimulated mental content is confronted, repression dissolves into Awareness. When not confronted, detachment may suffice, but if further involvement is enforced, then anxiety results."
>
> —Peter Shepherd, <u>*GSR Meter Course*</u>
> *Tools for Transformation, 1994-2001*

An individual that avoids "handling their stuff" runs the risk of having the *charge* restimulated by their environment in everyday life. Energy-flows encounter resistance from *mass*, just like damming up a stream of water. Hence, in most cases, the higher the resistance, the greater the *mass* encountered. Here we mean quite specifically and literally "*mental mass*" (or "*fields*") surrounding certain 'ideas' and 'concepts'—or as Carl Jung was researching, associated with certain 'words'

---

‡   See also *Unit-1* of "*Metahuman Destinations.*"

and 'memories'.

> As *energetically-entangled mental masses* are brought up to the surface for a *Seeker* to confront, the resistance increases—or "*rises.*" When the *mass* <u>is</u> actually confronted *As-It-Is* and disintegrated with the *Seeker's attention* ("*attenergy*")—Actualized Awareness—then the Meter reads a resistance reduction, or "*fall.*"

GSR-Meter use is only introduced at our "Wizard Grades" to supplement higher levels of *systematic processing*, because the device is not a substitute for understanding. A *Seeker* would already have to be familiar with vocabulary and concepts applied to a *process* or *PCL.* For example, a misunderstood word given in a *process* can cause false readings. Therefore, it is also important to check each of the actual words used in a *PCL* prior to applying them in order to be certain they do not already have a "charge" on them. This goes back to the original Jungian application of *GSR* for "word association."

A Meter is particularly useful when *Piloting* a *Seeker.* Although they do not indicate exactly *what* the *Seeker* is thinking about or confronting, they will indicate shifts in attention and *how* the *Seeker* is handling it. They do not necessarily "read" the *Mind*—but they do register how the *Mind-System* is affecting the body as it operates. For example, by observing the *Seeker* and Meter, a *Pilot* can determine when a "*hot-button*" is 'pressed' or *reached* during processing—or when the *Seeker* is *withdrawing* (backing off) from the same. There are indications for when the *Seeker* is experiencing restimulation of an *Imprint*—and when there is no longer a "charge" of entangled energy remaining on a particular circuit or channel. The Meters are intended only as *tools* to assist *systematic processing* and should not be the ultimate focus of observation. A *Pilot* is processing the *Seeker*; not the Meter device itself. It is not a substitute for observing the reactions and behaviors of a *Seeker.*

In spite of the fact that excessively sweaty, cold or dry hands can affect the baseline read from the electrodes (and should be remedied before a *systematic session* begins), use of a *GSR-Meter* as we describe and apply it does not have anything to do with perspiration—which is what many skeptics and critics suggest. The human body does not sweat and "unsweat" rapidly enough to provide the kind of instant reactive reads and changes we look for an observe during systematic use. By reactive read, we mean literally within an instant or second of a *Pilot* completing a statement, word or PCL. Anything more than three seconds and you are dealing with latent thought.

Fragmentation, by nature, is a state of *confusion*.

The purpose of all *systematic processing*, at some level or another, is to increase the *certainty* that an individual has about themselves, the management of *Self* and the environment. This also falls in line with what we know about *Self-Honesty* and the honesty exchanged with others. By desiring or wishing to know something, but not knowing it, the individual is unable to realize what something is—*As-It-Is*—and therefore unable to confront it. One cannot face what is not known. And this is why forthright honesty is critical for *actualization*.

> This is contradictory to the social **fallacy** that
> "what they don't know won't hurt them."
> In fact, it is what "they don't know"
> that causes the greatest energetic turbulence.

This factor is particularly strong between individuals sharing "interpersonal" or intimate relationships. This is why infidelity—or "cheating"—in relationships carries such significant *charge*. It is a *betrayal* of the highest order.

E-METERS, LIE-DETECTORS & SELF-HONESTY, OH MY!
(& SOME COMMENTARY ON THE POLITICS OF TRUTH)

> "Detection and recording of galvanic skin response is often combined with detection and recording of other autonomic-[*ANS (Autonomic Nervous System)*]-dependent psychophysiological variables such as heart rate, respiratory rate and blood pressure. The device that detects and records these (additional) variables is called a *polygraph*—meaning *'many measures'*. Changes in emotion associated with intentional falsification of answers to carefully selected and worded questions involuntarily and subconsciously alters autonomic output in such a way as to cause recognizable changes in recorded physiological variables. Keep in mind that although the procedures and measures used are similar to a polygraph recording, this is not a 'lie detector test'. All you will do here is record the [*Seeker's*] physiologic responses to certain questions. Some types of physiological responses are typically associated with 'lying'—although under the best conditions, one-third of innocent people 'fail' lie detector tests."
> —Pflanzer & McMullen, *Galvanic Skin Response & The Polygraph*
> *Lesson 9, Biopac Systems Inc., 2000*

The quotation above appears in a manual of "*Physiology Lessons for use with the Biopac Student Lab (BSL)"* produced by a California-based educational-technology company, *BIOPAC Systems, Inc.* Their aim is replacing former analog methods of collecting "psychophysiological" (how the mind affects the body) research data with more economical digital tools that rely on a personal computer rather than stand-alone hardware. This effectually enables academic-students an ability to experiment with areas of medical science that previously required costly *chart-recorders* (used for traditional "polygraph") and *oscilloscopes* (for example, the ECG/EKG).

"Old-school" analog *GSR-Meters* (as described throughout this chapter) maintain solid popularity and practicality. However, in the past few decades, *"spiritual clearing"* *Biofeedback* practitioners have developed newer more modern versions that frequently integrate computers and "smartphones." This is likely to be the trend into the future. It is not surprising that we now have many alternatives to the original devices developed by Mathison in the 1950's, and of course, Lafayette's professional models. Cost and availability is another factor. For example, the particular model used exclusively by the author at Mardukite Systemology Offices for the past several years—a Blue-Diamond-Dust *"Mark-VII Super Quantum"* refurbished from the *FreeZone*—would have required the original owner make a $4,000 donation to "The Church" to possess it. This is usually not a widespread issue, since an individual (that is not training to be a professional) really only works with a Meter alone by themselves when processing the upper-most levels.[‡]

For several years during the mid-1950's, Lafayette's courses and lectures did not include use of Meters. And nearly a decade later, the FDA militantly raided "The Church" and, among other things, confiscated all the unsold *"E-Meters."* These were eventually returned with the requirement that a disclaimer[*] be placed on them—but, American-Medical-Gestapo

---

[‡]   "The Church" completed mass manufacture of a *'Mark-VIII Ultra'* behind-the-scenes by 2004. These were not made available to general members for another ten years. However, some of the higher-level Staff *'swapped out'* electronics in their *Mark-VII* with the new technology.

[*]   *U.S. v. An Article of Device*; September 29, 1971—No. D.C. 1-63. "In a seizure action by the Government against the Hubbard E-Meter, the court ordered, *inter alia* [Latin—*"among other things"*], condemnation of the seized articles, and release of condemned E-Meters and literature to claimant for the purpose of bringing the devices and literature into compliance with the law (*Federal Food, Drug and Cosmetic Act*). The court further ordered that E-Meters be restricted for use only in bona fide religious counseling. Each E-Meter shall bear a warning, printed in 11-point type, permanently affixed to the front of the E-Meter, so that it is clearly visible when used: *The E-Meter is not medically or scientifically useful for diagnosis, treatment or prevention of any disease...*" The strangely worded message actually found on devices—and on a plate found at the front of every book issued since 1971—reads: *"The E-Meter, by itself, does nothing."* You could almost make that statement toward any piece of

had continued monitoring Lafayette's practices since 1951, when he was charged with "unlicensed practice of medicine" during an "auditing" demonstration in New Jersey. Even today, many books released under the "New Age" genre—including our own—carry a disclaimer that they do not diagnose ailments, treat disease or replace professional medical advice. Although this is taken about as seriously as selling tarot cards and psychic services as "for entertainment purposes only," it is a critical factor in today's world.

Many *Biofeedback* and *GSR*-devices are on the market that do not possess the same features as Meters described in this chapter. Really though, many of them should not be considered "Meters"—acting more like "monitors," like a smoke detector. Those sold as "meditation trainers" or "stress-relaxation aids" likely resulted from a completely different type of experimental research and their applications seem contrary to our own. For example, clinical tests in some fields of psychology will show that relaxation elevates skin resistance—as does entering meditative states. Yet, in our work, increase in skin resistance essentially denotes greater tension and stress. So, why then do we work in the face of contradictory data in our Systemology? The short answer: contrary examples concern individuals that are not engaged in a *systematic processing session.*

Observation of this "paradox" demonstrates a basis for "*Reversal Theory,*" as pioneered in the 1970's by Dr. Michael Apter,[√] a university professor of psychology and author of several books on the subject. The full nature of this theory is well beyond the scope of the present discourse—but it is dependent on basic motivation as a dichotomy, treated differently between two different states. In one state, the individual is operating in the normal wakeful every-day physical reality of action; in the other, a state of contemplative or analytical thought. Another way it is presented is the "means/ends" dichotomy—or even "journey/destination." In several papers on the subject, it is even reduced to "playful" versus "serious"—but in terms of doing enjoyable things for the sake of doing them as opposed to engaging in an activity purely to reach or achieve a desired goal. While this sounds all fine and good, how does it relate to our Systemology?

As high-level *fragmentation* is already a state of energetic suspension and confusion (yielding lower states of *Beta-Awareness*), when we increase involvement, reach or arousal (by triggering heavier traumatic experienc-

---

matter.

√ In collaboration with psychiatrist/psychotherapist Dr. Ken Smith.

es), it produces stress, tension, anxiety and discomfort. In what might be considered "excitement" under other circumstances, we are pushing limits of tolerance while *systematic processing*. When an individual is in a relaxed state, the detachment or withdrawal from worldly matters is invited and generally pleasant. But when the same reaction is applied in *systematic processing*, the *Seeker* is "dodging" or moving away from what should be confronted, which produces tension and stress. This is why, in session, we are most interested in points when a *GSR-Meter* indicates a sudden reduction of resistance—or "fall"—because it denotes something that the *Seeker* is able to handle, reach for and is ready to confront; it denotes an increase in *Awareness* applied and a willingness to take responsibility. An increase or "rise" would indicate the opposite of this.

Of course, in order to have "falls" during a session there must be points when the Meter reads a rise, or that the Balance Point is a higher resistance. But, we are talking about *processing* each individual item or terminal, *imprinting incident* or event. A particular area or focus is indicated for *processing*, the needle (display) will indicate a reduction of resistance when the *Seeker* is no longer resisting the handling of it. A *Pilot* will keep an eye on the Meter to determine that a question or item is *"reading"* before it is *systematically processed.* This goes along with the answers a *Seeker* gives as well. *Processing* a "charged" terminal or incident continues so long as there is still a "read" (change) taking place. If there was no indicator or "read" to begin with, there would be no real way to gauge this; there would be no way to determine when a *Seeker* had flattened that *wave-action* (or energetic *"ridge"*).

A "ridge" is perhaps one of the most *solid-state* **waveform** patterns encountered when an individual is working with energies. It is essentially an energetic-mass formed from two energy-wave flows, typically in opposition to one another. In some ways, all of "matter" could be considered a highly condensed and compacted energetic "ridge"—and in all likelihood, that is how it came to be so in *beta-existence.* But rather than dissolving solid matter, we are concerned with *flattening* the "solidity" of the **collapsed wave-functions** that form and collect as "energetic-masses" around the individual.

The "stuck" *Mental Image Pictures* and "reactive" *imprinting* are formed on and as such "ridges." And they have a tendency to build up into greater and greater "masses" when left improperly handled, or in many cases, not managed at all. Essentially, this is what is being described in all of our previous *Systemology* material, in one way or another.

• In "*Tablets of Destiny (Secrets Revealed)*" we examined the *emotional* qualities of *imprinting* and its nature in general.

• In *"Crystal Clear (Handbook for Seekers)"* and *"Metahuman Destinations"* we *processed* the effects of *imprinting* on our *considerations* and *thoughts*.

• In *"Imaginomicon (Approaching Gateways to a Higher Universe)"* we treated *Mental Imagery* blatantly and directly.

But in every case, we are still dealing with the same *fragmentation* phenomenon. *Here* we see it for what it is as its observable electronic properties. And:—

> when a *Seeker* is truly able and willing to handle, manage
> and/or confront the nature of their "stuff" *As-It-Is*,
> that increased *Awareness* is enough to "blow" it apart.

There are many types of experiments and training drills that can be conducted to understand more about the function of a *Meter*—and also to understand more about your 'subject' or *Seeker.* For example, in the BIOPAC manual quoted at the beginning of this section, a student instructs their subject to concentrate on each of a square sheet of colored paper, which is held two feet in front of their face; and *Biofeedback* is recorded for each. Sequential order of the colors presented are: *white, black, red, blue, green, yellow, orange, brown* and *purple.* A pause between each is necessary to get the baseline read again. This could be incorporated with additional questions to have some therapeutic value, but mostly it is for learning (and gaining experience) of the Meter itself.

Another common experiment is to learn the "yes"/"no" *Meter*-reads and reactions by working with a list of questions (or generating them at the time) for which there is no mystery about the answers. For example: Are you sitting down? Are we presently inside/outside? Do you drive a car/have a license to drive a car? But nothing that digs to deep under the surface. To get an even further handle on what is taking place when using a *Meter* in session and for Ethics (or Integrity Checkups), you can instruct the *Seeker* to intentionally "lie" about an answer to a question that is otherwise obvious. If they are sitting down—if they are indoors—have them answer that they aren't to each and see what and how things *read.*

SOME VERY BRIEF THOUGHTS ON POLITICS OF TRUTH
(A PERSONAL NARRATIVE AND INTERLOGUE)[*]

> "If you can't tell the truth to
> the people you care about the most,
> eventually you stop being able
> to tell the truth to yourself."
>
> —*Cassandra Clarke*
> *Mortal Instruments: City of Ashes*

"Truth was truth, whether I darkened my eyes to it or not."

"This earth appears to be a hell,
  or at best a planet condemned—
  A sort of purgatory..."

"Hide what you have to hide
  And tell what you have to tell.
  You'll see your problems multiplied
  If you continually decide
  To faithfully pursue
  The Policy of Truth."

(*Also used by Depeche Mode for their song "Policy of Truth"*)

> —William Batchelder Greene, *1819 – 1878*
> *Individualist anarchist, Unitarian minister, soldier, writer*
> *32° Scottish Rite Freemason, Massachusetts (1871)*
> *33° Sov. Gr. Inspector-General of Northern U.S. Jurisdiction (1872)*

"Our *Systemology*, first and foremost, began with a study of 'systems.' It was not a play on words or to relate to the work of an already existent organization with a similar name. It was not even entirely my own invention, because an academic pursuit called *systematology* had already been established nearly a decade ago—and apparently branched off to become *cybernetics* and work used to advance other material technologies. But, I was concerned with the spiritual technologies and philosophies that could actually be applied and not just debated and theorized by a handful of intellectuals for their own 'mental masturbation' as we used to refer to it as. I didn't believe that the material sciences and New Age spirituality was working well enough in solving the affairs on Earth or the

---

[*] Based on and quoting a "New Year's" lecture given by Joshua Free.

problem of the Human Condition—if anything, they were sealing folks into the mess even tighter, furthering the entrapment of Self into the Human Condition. But as a teenager at the time, living during an apex of New Age revival in the 1990's, I questioned my own potential efforts too. I mean: would the work I wanted to do bring an individual their spiritual freedom—or would it just be more empty hope for an 'enlightenment' that never comes?"

"At the time, a lot of the individuals I was surrounded with really didn't believe I was going to be doing anything innovative or significant during this lifetime. To them the whole question being, who was I, you know—and who were they that they would have happened to be on a first name basis with me. It was also quite difficult to advance anyone beyond what had already been established. It was easy to design, publish and distribute occult books that were cultural and/or ritual based—for example, traditions of Celtic Druidism. It was far more difficult to present a colorful enough 'creative psychology' or 'New Thought' that these type of ceremonial magicians and such would accept. I mean, I would expect that these Celtic Druids would have been *Systemologists*—not necessarily calling it that, but we are talking about the high-born intellectuals of Europe, credited with "systematizing the Celts." I would expect that the first established civic Human systems in Mesopotamia were also the product of an intensive intellectual knowledge of *Systemology* that, until recently, has primarily gone unnoticed."

"Nearly all of the elements that are effective in our *Systemology* relate back to the fundamentals that I developed, but kept to myself, as a teenager—thus over two decades in my past, now. But, there was not much I could think to *do* with it in the late 1990's, and it would take an entire decade for me to really try to synthesize any working knowledge of it for print-publications. Even in saying this, it has taken *three* different approaches to the subject before it caught on. The first attempt—'*Systemology 1.0*'—is still with us, but it is given as '*Systemology: The Original Thesis.*' While all of the theories and goals were adequately explained, it still left a *Seeker* wondering what to do with the knowledge. I'll admit that for a couple years even my own hat was thrown into that group. It wasn't until a few years later that I developed '*Systemology 2.0*' and released the title "*Reality Engineering*' (portions still appear in the appendix for '*The Systemology Handbook*'). Most of the critical previous elements were given more substance, but the presentation still lacked a certain demonstrable edge toward practical actualization. I did, however, start to notice a lot more of the Mardukite Alumni using the lingo in their everyday life. They knew there was *something* about all this, but I still had not fully driven in the nail yet. It took many more years of behind-the-scenes development before 'Tablets of Destiny' and 'Crystal Clear' could be presented—but it was obvious that now we had finally arrived at something that we could truly launch from. So much had gone into its unseen development that almost the entire Grade-III core took only a few months to refine and publish—and the rest, as they say, is history."

Seekers may well find humor in kick-starting new higher-level Wizard Grades with *optional* but-highly-suggested incorporation of *GSR-Metering*. This applies a more certain time-saving *Biofeedback Tech* toward accessing higher-level *Self-Honesty*. Of course, contrary to fantasy and enchantment themes denoted by its title, our "Wizard Grades" (*V*, *VI*, and *VII*) intend to provide *Seekers* a much needed "booster" for reaching Metahuman destinations—a much needed evolutionary *disillusion* and *dissolution* of what is otherwise an out-dated sub-standard model for the Human Condition.

Some individuals will undoubtedly be taken aback—or even unpleasantly surprised—by suggestion of *GSR* as given within Mardukite Systemology "*Liber-3E*" (*this present book*) based on how such controversial devices have gained public attention in the past and the types of non-medical organizations that employ them; to ensure the protection of ourselves and our fellows *Seekers*, we of course, won't name names—but one in particular even sounds like "systemology." Certainly, some reaction is considered normal whenever we introduce new material or new directions of work—and we get it; and we forgive that.

Many *Seekers* are getting seasoned to those mild shocks that accompany the work by now. Especially given the way a *Seeker's* attention is so masterfully routed, piloted and directed across the entire span of Systemology materials thus far; not even mentioning the Mardukite **Master Grades** which precede it. However, to prevent solidifying any Self-imposed barriers or road-blocks, any remaining reactivity (if present) should be *processed-out* (much like we did with the subject of "religion" in the "*Crystal Clear*" *Liber-2B* handbook) as erroneous considerations—those based on something which must have been heard or picked up along the way, but of which is nothing more than a baseless opinion assimilated from someone else (who was probably in no better condition to make a wide-sweeping judgment in the first place).

Needless to say that any subject, field, religion or group invoking the name of certain science-fiction author and spiritual pioneer is headed straight into a battle-zone for religious freedom. But, if one is *Self-Honest* —if one does not seek to retaliate against the Suppressors in kind; if one is willing to press onward naked to the world carrying only the *Sword of Truth* by their side—then that particular war-front is paper-thin at best, entirely dependent on certain interpretations of copyrights and a mis-guided infiltrated and usurped group with a bottomless pocket of means to pursue maintaining **fallacious** interests in holding onto a *Monopoly on Truth*. Of course, it all still requires managing things intelligently and with tact—two things that seem counter-intuitive to what it means to be a teenager, especially at the end of the 20th Century.

> "But, wouldn't you know it... I was listening to this song... and— okay, keep in mind I was 'Class of 2000' and so were most of my best friends. We were—or are—primed as the oldest year of the *'Millennial'* generation, yet we had been looking up to the Gen-X and they seemed so cool, but there was a separation. Even if only a few years difference, we had more in common with someone sev- eral years *younger* than us than we did with those graduating even a year or two sooner than us. We were born in the 1980's, but just young enough to not have been able to fully appreciate being '80s kids' or 'punk' or 'old-school Goths' and while in high-school, they released a volume of singles by *Depeche Mode* and I was listening to *Policy of Truth* and it got me thinking about how convoluted the whole matter of truth really is. Because there seems to be a ques- tion of whether or not to speak the truth with each other—to ad- mit the truth of things. And given how much this Universe is built upon lies, the truth generally cannot be hidden for long, even if we think we will get away with it. And the matter of who we are and what we've done is a big part of that. The manner of my own work, starting very intently and intensely as a teenager and continuing through to the present also falls under this category. Although, in my case, I have often found that hiding truth in plain sight can also work quite well. For some reason it is just not accepted factually. Now, you've got it to where you try and present some element and the other person goes, yeah yeah, I saw *'The Matrix'* too."

> "Concerning the sources of 'New Thought' inspiration, there are many *Seekers* mostly unaware of the 'other side of Reality'—what has been taken place for 70-years. Much of what I refer to in these statements is but a cute sentiment, albeit poetic. Putting that aside, there have been other *pioneers* in the past that have taken up

similar life-paths, but of a different flavor—for example, the route once forged in public view by Dr. Timothy Leary. While considerably influential to me in my youth, well, what I am about to say is an oversimplification that somewhat misrepresents true beliefs and ideals that Leary (and myself) maintained, but: I make no such promise to a *Seeker* that they—or any random person on the street—will find personal enlightenment at the end of a twelve-hour trip on five-dollars worth of LSD. You might as well be hunting for a pot-of-gold at the end of a rainbow. Yet in a former time—actually, a former millennium even—I made certain to test (and retest; and, of course, triple-check again, to verify) those waters for myself, too. But, that element was a part of *my own personal path*—a path which at some point or another had required me to look beneath every rock and down every alleyway to gain a handle of certainty as a *Messenger* of something greater—something that none of these other routes were reaching as a definite destination. If something like that really worked across the boards, its inclusion would be a part of this work; but there's no guarantees there. It may have been a part of my own journey, but it is found nowhere directly on *The Pathway* that Systemology represents. And this is just one example... But the point is: *Systemology* is not just a chronicle of *my* trip or some interactive diary to enforce following in *my* footsteps, which traced a tortuous journey; *Systemology* is the chronicle of us all—and for that reason *Seekers* have discovered that it speaks to them directly."

As you may have surmised at this juncture, development of this "Mardukite" brand and its related works up through the "lower ('Master') grades"—and now at the threshold of the Wizard—is a significant body of work that no one, other than the present author, truly saw coming. Although hints might have been dropped in one or another introduction or preface, the truth is that only the present author knew where it was headed when initial preparations were laid out in the late 1990's. At the same time, the most accessible literary presentations began to emerge at the apex of the "New Age Magickal Revival" by Joshua Free—then concealing himself behind the pseudonym *'Merlyn Stone'*.

Aside from using pseudonyms (which began while attending high school and leading some of the earliest "coven"-styled precursors to the Mardukite movement; and with a dozen individuals carrying copies of *"The Sorcerer's Handbook"* and such around school), the guise of the occult, New Age mysticism and emphasis on practical magic, ritualism, &tc., permitted a certain freedom from the *Policies of Truth*; particularly while the work demonstrated over the last two decades all remained in formative stages. There is not enough space allotted to this single discourse for a proper relay of what all takes place behind-the-scenes or beneath-the-surface of the *Material World* at large—at least not enough in exclusion to other materials to ready a *Seeker* to effectively fight in the true *Invisible War* of our times.

The *Politics of Truth* is deserving and worthy of an entirely separate book dedicated to it—because the general public, even many of the New Age practitioners, believes that "we are all in this together"; that everyone proposing enlightenment is on the same page and that we are working together toward the same ends. But, for the most part, it is just one more "industry" among many that keeps the Grand Game going. And if you have been paying attention, then you will know how to participate and play it out and still remain *Self-Honest*.

UNDERSTANDING GSR-METERS & HOW TO READ THEM

"When material [a mass or '*ridge*'] is restimulated by events or in session—if the material is too hard to experience or confront, it is repressed and there will not be an instantaneous response on the meter. The *ridge* will remain in restimulation but out of consciousness, until attention is directed to the item and it is confronted. This is a flight away from the material. If the client is able to view the material, some of the suppressed emotional charge is released, causing a *fall* in resistance. This happens instantly. However, mental defenses may kick-in and cause a backing off or resistance to the material, because its content may be hard to face. This stops the release of charge and the resistance may *rise*— still accessible but the client is fighting against it. A *rise*, then, relates to material that is being confronted, but is also fought against. If viewed directly, the contents may overwhelm the client, and the client moves away from it in fear, which causes high emotional arousal and *fall* in resistance, followed by a blocking-off of the material and subsequent *rise* in resistance and suppression of the experience."

—Peter Shepherd, <u>*GSR Meter Course*</u>
Tools for Transformation, 2001

In the late 1990's, the present author had the behavior of *Biofeedback Meters* demonstrated to them by an experienced individual. This introduction provided a great deal of certainty prior to reading, or being exposed to, oppositional literature and statements. Is there definitive proof that "heavy thoughts" are literally a "heavy mass" on an individual, complete with "electronic resistance"? Not necessarily. However, the activity seems to reflect that there is a relationship (a "positive coefficient" as you academicians would call it) concerning what *we* classify as *fragmentation*—and it may be that any opposition to this fact stems from a philosophic-semantic issue that does not concern us in the least so long as *we* can observe, record and communicate a reliable interconnected pattern of results (as we understand them) within *Systemology*.

> "The *Meter* was demonstrated to me while I was seated comfortably and holding the two *'cans'* (*electrodes*). So, he asks me to 'squeeze the cans'—and I did. A few seconds later, he repeated that—and I believe this happened three or four times; each time he made a small adjustment of the sensitivity. The final time he showed me that a deliberate squeeze caused the needle to move about two centimeters or about a third of the way on the *fall* or right-hand side of the dial-display. I thought, okay... He reaches over and gives my arm a little pinch and I watched the needle practically peg the pin on the *fall* side. A small adjustment of the Balancing-Arm and the needle was in the 'set' or 'balance' range again. Then he says, 'Now, go back to the moment I pinched you.' Sure enough, the needle swung over just as it had done before simply by directing attention to that moment. He said to go through the event, play it out so to speak, in my mind—and I did. He repeated for me to 'go back' and this time the needle swung, but not as severely. After resurfacing and confronting the event four or five times, the needle barely registered. I thought to myself: this is something I want to know more about..."

Even if our scientific semantics is not completely where it should be, this simple demonstration illustrates a lot of what is discussed in our preliminary Grades of Systemology. Does it always require this level of mathematical precision to determine success? Well, certainly not, or those previously using the *Tablets of Destiny*, *Crystal Clear* and *Metahuman Destinations* material would not have found any success. And we know for a fact that those who have utilized our work and properly participating with their presence to the procedures *have* found enough positive gain to keep them progressing and interested in pursuing this *Pathway*. What a *Biofeedback Meter* such as this allows for is a greater certainty, greater accuracy and a vast improvement in the amount of time it takes to "get something handled" and move forward with the work.

When working with a *GSR-Meter* for *systematic processing*, the most common term is "read"—such as when you hear someone say, "That *reads.*" More often than not it is indicating a decrease in resistance or "*fall.*" There are also rare instances where the *Meter*, or more accurately, the observed *needle*, doesn't read anything at all for anything no matter what you do. The term "stuck" is often applied and all this means is that the *Seeker* is not offering their presence to the session. There is a break in communication or reality for whatever reason. If such is truly the case, even the "pinch test" described above would not necessarily register anything. It is important to know whether or not a reaction is going to read, otherwise it gives an illusion that there is no "charge" on something that otherwise will be blown over—or *flown* over—when it should have been handled. Operating a session in this way, when the *Seeker* is not providing presence, will actually reduce a *Seeker's* participation even further because the session, methods and *Pilot* (ability) loses credibility—even at "subconscious" levels; even when the *Seeker* is the one causing, allowing or validating the break in reality or attention themselves.

So long as the sensitivity is kept constant—checked at the beginning with the "squeeze and release" tests described above—the *reads* on a *Meter* are able to be compared to other *reads.* For the "*falls*" you would be looking for the "largest" read or "*largest fall*" in relation to other reads. This is important when you are seeking to scout out a particular answer among variables. If you were to ask a *Seeker* which of their former jobs contributed the most fragmentation, there may be some "charge" on more than one answer; therefore you are looking for the biggest reaction or *read* when each is given.

We frequently use the term *resurfacing* to denote bringing something up from beneath-the-surface. The quicker the response from the *Meter*, the closer something is to the surface. If something doesn't read, a *Pilot* should avoid focusing further attention on it. Of course, this does not mean that the *channel* is clear or there is no energetic charge held on the terminal in question—but it is not accessible or presently within the *Seeker's* reach or tolerance level to confront at that given time. Not to mention, without a *read*, there is no guarantee a *Pilot* can determine full erasure of that *fragmentation* or an **End Point** on other types of processing. This is, of course, what we mean about continuing a particular process or area of work so long as it is producing change in Awareness, but not to overrun.

When using a *GSR-Meter* it is a little easier to determine when an End Point is reached. It is critical to fully eliminate "reactive charge" from anything that either does *resurface* or that can be made to *resurface* so long as it is *reading* on the Meter. If a *Pilot* doesn't treat a process through to finality, the "Universe" (society, &tc.) most certainly will keep running it and the *Seeker* will become increasingly withdrawn.

For the purpose of establishing a standard for recording a session, we have established a chart for our *Systemology* that applies to many models of *GSR-Meter* used for 'spiritual defragmentation'. On such models, the dial-display has a 90-degree range—a quarter of a circle—illustrated with a 9-centimeter arc of potential motion: *one centimeter* per *ten-degrees*. In most cases, the area given to read the *"falls"* constitutes half of the *Meter.* It is the differences between reactions in this zone that are of primary interest for the session and its records. Although not all practitioners will have the same interpretive classification for *reads*, using our chart offers the greatest stability or consistency in what we are looking for.

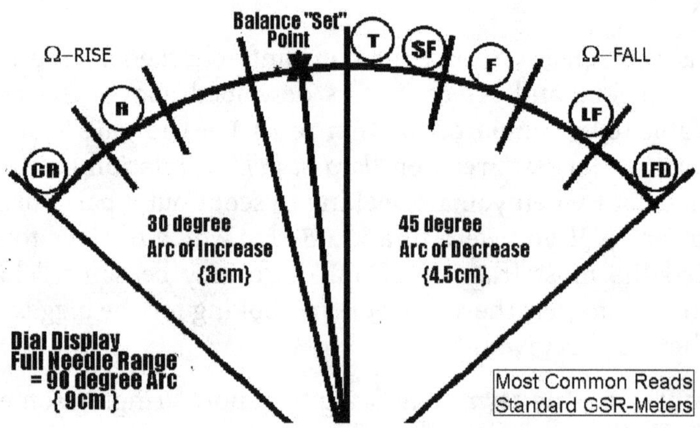

The Balance-Point or Set-Point provides a BASELINE reading and it reflects the basic state of the *Seeker* when at "rest" presently in the session, without being aroused or directly stimulated by inner thoughts or the environment, &tc. A *read* is then taken when the needle moves off of, or out of, the small 15-degree region given for this. Sometimes a TINY TICK is *read* within this region, but if all session activity remains that close to the Balance-Point, it may be that the sensitivity is too low. The answer to "Does it read?" can also be considered the answer to whatever yes/no question you pose as a PCL. Therefore a *read* typically means "yes."

The Physical Universe is solidified by compacted matter that philosophically are "lies." When an individual is confronting (facing up to) the truth about something, they are practically disintegrating it and hence you get a reduced mass and reduced resistance ("*fall*"). Therefore, it is possible to get an increase-decrease fluctuation during a single process. A PCL results in a FALL, meaning there is some level of energetic "charge" available for the *Seeker* to confront. But then they could find that while examining it, they suddenly feel "resistive" which literally adds "resistance" demonstrated by a RISE. However, if the *Seeker* overcomes this withdrawal and continues to confront it, you will continue to see a FALL (usually a "LARGE/LONG FALL"/"LF") until it finally and significantly "BALANCE DROPS" (requiring movement of the *Balancing-Arm* to keep it on the *Meter dial-display*). Since this is a LARGE/LONG FALL and a DROP it is often written "LFD" or LFBD. The basic *reads* as they appear marked on our chart are as follows:

(R) RISE (R)

Any movement of the needle on the left side of the "Set Point" (BA); no additional **differentiation** is made—unless it is a "Continuous Rise" (CR)—just the fact that the needle and resistance is *rising* (has *risen*). If it never did you would not get any "Balance-Arm action" at all in processing. An initial increase in resistance to a question means literally increased resistance *to* the question; it can *fall* once a *Seeker* permits themselves to confront it *As-It-Is*.

Since a *rise* generally indicates a *Seeker* does not want to confront what has been presented, it is best *not* to announce this *read* when it occurs. If pressed further in that direction the *Seeker* will break with reality and communication and potentially go "out of session."

(CR) CONTINUOUS RISE (CR)

A large enough *rise* to the left side of the meter that requires the Balance-Arm to be adjusted to keep the needle within range of the dial-display. A question that immediately "stops" a "rising needle" is a change in characteristics and should be considered the same as a *Fall*.

Sessions where the *reads* do not seem to be coming as expected may require monitoring such changes of characteristics rather than other *reads*. So, if the needle is continuously *rising* but a question stops its motion—or it has been doing nothing but then decides to dance a jig—this is the indicative pattern change.

(BA) or (BP)   BALANCE-ARM SET POINT   (BA) or (BP)

The reading taken when the armature fixes the needle on the set point (or at least in the balanced range). If *Low* BA/BP—is below "2.0" (5000 Ω)—exceptionally decreased resistance possibly hyper-vigilant or overwhelmed; If *High* BA/BP—above "4.5" (35,000 Ω)—increased resistance is possibly withdrawal, dissociation and/or detachment.

If the BA/BP is *High* at the start of the session, the *Seeker's* attention is already directed on some "mass" elsewhere. You can start to free up these attention units by two-way communication with the *Seeker* about "where" their attention is. "Do you have your attention on any-thing?" "Is there anything you would like to tell me?" "Since your last session, is there anything you would like to tell me about?"

Although "solo-metering" is not trained for this *Grade-IV pre-A.T.* level of work, when combining two electrodes with a coupler —making cer-tain they do touch—to hold in one hand, the BA/BP will be higher than standard (by a factor of as much as "0.5" higher) reads. There-fore what might be "2.1" when each electrode is held in its own hand, would then potentially be around "2.6" when soloing with one hand.+

(X)   NO/NULL READ   (X)

As the name suggests, there is no read and the needle remains at rest at the "Set Point" (BA). "No charge" or an answer of "no" should be distinguishable from a "stuck needle" based on characteristics of meter reads throughout the session up to this point or from a proper session setup that guarantees the *Seeker* is participating or has pres-ence in session.

(T)   TICK/TINY READ   (T)

A rapid *fall* of less than a few millimeters to the right of the "Set Point" (BA); as the name suggests, it barely counts as read. It may or may not even leave the "Balanced Range." If you get a small "trace read" from a question, trying varying the wording. If the same small "tick" or "tiny read" is all that occurs after three inquiries, move on.

(SF)   SMALL/SHORT FALL   (SF)

Up to one centimeter (or ½ an inch) *fall* to the right side of the "Set Point" (BA). Any amount of *fall* is still a *fall;* if you are still getting a *read* after several runs or exhausted question/answer, the *Seeker* still "hasn't told all" or else you are dealing with a "past life" or an area they do not "consciously know about."

If a decent *read* occurs when the *Seeker* hasn't said anything, inquire about it. "What was that there?" "What did you just think of there?" "Did you have a thought there?"

(F)   FALL   (F)

One to two centimeters (½ inch to one inch) *fall* to the right side of the "Set Point" (BA). Any length of *fall* is a standard *read* or "Yes" answer to your question; for some techniques the largest/longest read is the answer.

(LF)   LARGE/LONG FALL   (LF)

Two to six centimeters (1 to 3 inches) *fall* to the right side of the "Set Point" (BA). Among several possible *reads*, the largest/longest *read* or *fall* is the answer.

(LFD/LFBD)   LARGE/LONG FALL BALANCE DROP   (LFD/LFBD)

A large enough *fall* to the right side of the meter that requires the Balance-Arm to be adjusted to keep the needle within range of the dial-display. A massive discharge of this caliber accompanies the *Seeker* having confronted (faced-up-to) or seeing (knowingly duplicating creation of) something *As-It-Is*, thereby duplicating and eradicating what and where something is by consciously placing one's own there —seeing it for what *It Is* on one's own volition.

GSR-METERS APPLIED TO SYSTEMATIC PROCESSING[*]

> "If the [*Seeker*] knew about the subconscious reactive contents of the mind, they wouldn't be subconscious or reactive. But the *GSR-Meter* responds to the reactive emotional charge. Hence, you don't follow up something unless it gives a read. You don't let the [*Seeker's*] analytical (cognitive) mind control the session or give it free reign to talk about anything it likes. It is a [*Pilot's*] responsibility to control the session. The [*Pilot*] has more control over the [*Seeker's*] case, since the [*Seeker*] is influenced by the case."
> —Peter Shepherd, <u>GSR Meter Course</u>
> *Tools for Transformation, 2001*

This entire unit of our book has provided a tremendous amount of basic

---

[*]   Strongly based on Volney Mathison's "*Super-Visualization (formerly 'The Manual of Electropsychometry')*" revised 1956 edition.

fundamentals regarding history, purposes and usage of *GSR-Meters* for personal development when applied to *our systematic processing*. Mathison's own work "*Super-Visualization*" includes a sporadic "session script" that offers examples of what one might expect when applying *GSR-Meters* to standard methods similar to our own presentation in previous *Systemology* texts. Use of a *Meter* does not in itself solve the matter of getting the *Seeker* to participate *presence* in sessions, with attention fully on *processing*; there are no substitutes for skillfully *Piloting* a *Seeker*—it must be learned and practiced. This includes certainty of handling a *Meter* when applied to processing, which is best gained by experience.

Having the *Seeker* "squeeze the cans" (and then release) is a popular way of setting/adjusting the sensitivity before a session really begins. Once begun, it is best if it does not have to be readjusted. When you are rapidly comparing relative lengths of various *falls*, the sensitivity must remain constant. There are ways of testing this before a formal start of session. And then there are also instances (especially in *Ethics Processing* for *Personal Integrity*) when you really want to see if a question is getting a solid *read* or not. You can always raise the sensitivity for that particular PCL, but make sure to return it to where it was afterward.

If everything that you are asking or saying is getting large reads, you may need to turn the sensitivity down. A simple determinant of basic stress levels can be used at the beginning to check this. Simply as: "How are you going to feel about my asking you a lot of personal questions?" You aren't really concerned about the answer given so much as the read on the *Meter*. In fact, on an episode of the British comedy "*I.T. Crowd*," a "stress expert" is demonstrating just how little it takes to experience stress using a similar type of *GSR-Meter*. All he says is "Alright, I am now going to ask you a very personal question." And the needle surges very strongly. He doesn't actually ask anything else; the demonstration (as described) speaks for itself. If there is a strong *read* in response to this, it is likely that the *Seeker* has experienced uncomfortable interrogation in the past, either from a family member or some other source. It is helpful if communication can be used between the *Pilot* and *Seeker* to quiet these *reads* before proceeding.

If a *Seeker's* attention is not directed precisely on the session and PCLs, there is no way to determine what the *reads* on a *Meter* actually pertain to. Having the *Seeker* acknowledge the *Pilot*—a reality on the fact that the *Pilot* is the *Pilot*—is quite critical for the *Pilot* being able to get (and keep) the *Seeker* in session. There is at least one key reason why this is sometimes difficult—and this can be checked with the *Meter* prior to a true session start. *Pilot* asks: "Do I remind you in some way of a person you have known whom you feared or disliked?" If there is no *read* on that, or if there is only a *tiny tick*, consider rephrasing the PCL slightly: "Is there anything about me that is similar to some person that bothered or injured you in the past?" If any of these types of questions indicates a "yes," then *defragment* the line using basic communication to illustrate differences as with the previous question on being asked questions. Resolving things like this is, of course, critical for success; but it also directly facilitates getting the Seeker to participate with *presence* in the session.

As a chiropractor, Mathison's initial interests for using an *Elctropsychometer* pertained to the physiological body long before concepts of *spiritual defragmentation* became **paramount**. Therefore, in his manual—prior to the *Test Questionnaire* (given hereafter)—he describes a progressive *'Deep Meditation' technique* that is otherwise very similar to *'Energetic Body Scanning'*. The *Pilot* would give the PCL: "Toes, left foot, relax."[‡] The *Seeker* would then silently deliver the PCL/message to the *genetic vehicle* and report back with "Okay" after having done so. The *Pilot* closes that communication cycle with an acknowledgment ("Thank You") and begins the next: "Now, ankle, left foot, relax." And onward in this fashion they continue, treating each portion of the body. If at any point the *Pilot* sees a "sharp needle surge" on the *Meter* in relation to a certain part of the body, nothing is said, but a notation is made. Once the list of all body areas is completed, the *Pilot* returns to those which were indicated and if the unrest still persists, additional attention is given to them with the command "Be at ease."

<u>EXPLORATORY TECH. FOR SYSTEMATIC PROCESSING</u>[*]
OPENING ASSESSMENT QUESTIONNAIRE EXAMPLE

> "A sharp prolonged meter surge on *'How do you feel about your name?'* indicates one of two things: the (*Seeker*) is using a false, an assumed, or an altered name—or—more commonly, the (*Seeker*) dislikes their name for some specific reason which they can readily clarify. A disliked name has some unpleasant or silly connotation or association. Sometimes a name is changed to forget a hated parent, a past mate, or the like. Meter surges on such situations are all significant and should be discussed until tension on

---

‡   Alternatively, "Let go" or "Let go of the tension" could be used for this PCL in place of "relax."

*   Strongly based on Volney Mathison's *"Super-Visualization (formerly 'The Manual of Electropsychometry')"* revised 1956 edition.

> them subsides. Laughter, yawns and sighs will cause major needle surges, owing to flash metabolic effects, and may, in general, be disregarded. Do not permit the (*Seeker*) to tap on the electrode with finger or thumb. Minor needle surges may merely indicate mental activity. Major surges indicate areas of pain or tension."
>
> —Volney Mathison, *Super-Visualization Manual of Electropsychometry, 1956*

We conclude the present unit of our book with the original *Test Questionnaire* that appears in Mathison's *Electropsychometry Manual* from 1956. Strong *reads* or "surges" (as he calls them) should be reduced with *processing-style* communication (as learned throughout our professional *Systemology* texts). As an "assessment," this is really meant to "open a case" and not necessarily "solve" every aspect of a *Seeker's* life. It allows a *Pilot* to get a general idea of where significant trouble-spots are. An attempt should be made, however, to reduce the "charge" on anything found to give major *reads* before continuing on.

1. How do you feel about your name?

2. What is your occupation? How do you feel about it?

3. How do you feel about your mother? About your father?

4. What sort of person do you fear? Hate?

5. Mention, by way of example,° one of the worst things that has happened to you.

6. What do you think of a person that commits suicide?†

7. Have you ever been in a hospital?

8. Have you ever been injured in an accident?

9. Whom did you hate or fear most when you were a child?

10. Mention some things you are very anxious about or that you feel should not occur. Mention some things you would fight or struggle against to keep them from happening.

11. Who loves you?

∞   "*By way of example.*" We interpret this to mean a non-specific type.

†   Mathison indicates here that "sharp needle action" may mean the (*Seeker*) is or has been a "suicide hazard." In a later remark, he states that a "heavy surge" indicates the (*Seeker*) has lost someone close to them that way, or—"and more commonly"—that the (*Seeker*) has either attempted or considered it themselves. He recommends that the cause of this needle reaction be uncovered and explored (via communication) until "discharged or reduced" before continuing on with the questionnaire.

12. Who used to love you, but no longer does?

13. Can you think of a time when you wished someone would love you?

14. Do you feel remorse, regret or blame over the way you have treated some person? Mother? Father? Wife? Husband? &tc.

15. If you were writing a novel and you had to depict some injurious thing happening to a baby or a child, what would have this thing be?

16. Have you ever been struck or severely beaten?

17. What do you think of a homosexual person?[√]

18. How do you think women feel about you?

19. How do you think men feel about you?

20. How do you think children feel about you?

21. Have you ever been through an unhappy love experience?

22. Do you love your wife/husband?[‡]

23. How do you think your wife/husband feels about you?

24. Have you ever been attacked or severely shocked sexually?[*]

25. Are you satisfied with your present sexual relations?

26. Have you ever had a bitter quarrel with a man? Woman? Mention actual incidents.

27. What do you think about the use of contraceptives? Abortions?

28. What do you think about illegitimate children?

29. What do you think of a woman who is frigid? Or a man who is impotent?

30. What do you think of a sexual sadist? Masochist?

[√] This was written during a period of time when such was commonly and socially considered "deviant sexual behavior," just as "masturbation" was.

[‡] This is asked without the "mate" present. Mathison remarks that "surges on this may not indicate lack of love"—rather, they *do* but tension is attached, such as situations where the couple "fights too much" or they "fear losing" them.

[*] Mathison remarks later on that "if the (*Seeker*) registers tension on some of the sexual-area questions, it may not be advisable to explore causes or details unless the (*Pilot*) is certain they have the trust and confidence of the (*Seeker*)." Mathison is mainly concerned here about situations where the (*Pilot*) is male and the (*Seeker*) is female—or vice versa.

31. Have you ever been jeered at, made fun of, or painfully rejected?

32. What things do you keep doing that you wish you didn't do?

33. What changes do you wish to make in yourself?

34. Mention three goals or ambitions that you have wished to achieve —and which you have achieved.

35. Mention three goals or ambitions that you have wished to achieve —and which you have not achieved.

:: TOWARD A STRONG SYSTEMOLOGY SOCIETY ::
ORGANIZATIONAL ETHICS STANDARDS[‡]
WIZ-θ GENERAL INSTRUCTION

As stated in the original *Mardukite Zuism* introductory booklet:[*]

> "The greatest good contributes to the greatest continuation of optimum existence and survival for the greatest *Sphere* of inclusion."

This means by protecting and maintaining the integrity of a strong and healthy *organization*—"*Org,*" or "*Society*" as we often term it—we "best contribute to its continuation." And mostly all who have "*Self-Honestly*" participated in this *Pathway* will agree that our *Mardukite* and *Systemology* work is worthy of persistence.

It is each individual's responsibility to provide *Self-Honest* support to the *Organization* that has assisted them in realizing *Self-Honesty* (whether directly or by way of print-publications). This expectation appears within the very "*Creed*" of *Mardukite Zuism* (and *Systemology*):

> "We support the continuation of, and proper communication of, the true legacy of 'Human' history—and a fundamental ability of every 'Human' to realize that they are a 'Free Spirit' occupying a 'Free Zone' of Self-Determinism."

We can be certain that any 'group' (much like an 'individual') carries its own a calculable "*Beta-Awareness Score*" representative of its "general health"—and the *Mardukite Org* is no exception. Maintaining proper 'Utilitarian Ethics' in functional operations, the *Organization* ensures we maintain "Order" and (by demonstration of the *Spheres*) protect the integrity of 'individual' Seekers themselves—along with their 'homes' and families. In total, this supports a healthier 'Humanity'.

In some regards, the *Mardukite Org* represents 'dangerous' work—but only when misunderstood; either out of sheer ignorance, or blatant misrepresentation. Many individuals mistake our *Organization* as idealizing a "*Cure*" or "*Help*"—yet our methods quite literally epitomize the true spirit of "*Self-Help.*" We assist navigating a survey of the *Seeker's* own considerations. Breakthrough-insights and new realizations are still up to each

---

[‡] A revised facsimile based on original supplemental handouts written by Joshua Free for the *Mardukite Academy of Systemology* during the "*Intro to the Wizard's Way: Ethics and Beyond*" R&D cycle, which was active July 2021 through January 2022 at *Mardukite Babylonia SLV Borsippa HQ.*

[*] Material reissued in (*appendices* of) other Systemology/Zuism titles.

individual to wholly actualize themselves. We are not substituting "religion" for "Truth"; no "pills" or "magic spells" replace necessity of *actual* processing (work). Otherwise, an individual would simply be even more the "effect" of some outside, other-determined or enforced idea, rather than "originating" their own Reality Agreements.

When it comes to executing clear judgment and evaluation, our greatest asset is increased *Actualized Awareness*. This is important for development and security of an *Organization*, for a healthy and peaceful *Home*, and for a happy *Individual*. It is equally important that we have "true knowledge" in which to evaluate from—and that our process of evaluation is free of *fragmentation*. This is particularly important when involved with other individuals or their placement into positions and roles. **Beta-Awareness Test** *(BAT)* scores may be of particular significance here (where it concerns our own organization).

Human lives are composed of facts—pieces of data. All of the available data an individual knows about someone else is brought together to form the composite image or overall opinion that is carried in future considerations and interactions. In the future, when our underground *Organization* grows and requires greater centralization, it may be necessary to keep files on everyone and everything that we encounter—both personally and as an *Organization*. In the meantime, most of this data-storage and evaluation is handled with personal memory. Our heightened *Awareness*, more often than not, contributes to "right judgment." Those situations where it does not: we are often "too close" or carry too much "emotion" in those instances to always see clearly. This is another one of those little-spoken-of shortcomings of the Human Condition.

When necessary, the use of "Private Investigators" is preferred to personal involvement of our members and ranks. As many of the basic facts should be organized ahead of time—but where it concerns time and resources, the most serious instances generally require a P.I. to be most effective. This should only be used for specific applications and not for general circumstances. One key instance that always demands further investigation is any individual that openly communicates and/or acts against the *Organization*. In this wise, it is critical to know as many facts as possible about someone that is intentionally setting themselves up as opposition. In any instance where legal action is not to be taken, then open posting and wide distribution of collected data is preferred to stashing it away.

△ △ △ △ △ △

History demonstrates that one key revolutionary turning point is the most destructive on a wider scope, whether in an organization or for society (civilization) as a whole: *fragmented humans* in *large masses* with *crude weapons.* This is what has forced out the "gods" represented in all ancient mythologies. Certainly the "gods" had their own issues with each other, but what changed things the most from the *'way they were'* to the *'way they are'* now is exactly as just described. Usually this does not happen all at once or "come from nowhere" as it were—there are obviously small demonstrations, revolts and coups that all lead up to it.

At an "organization" level, it is the responsibility of *Organization Members* to safeguard themselves and the property (physical and intellectual) of the *Org* in order to ensure its continuation.

In the United States, the right to **protest** is protected under the First Amendment—and this applies to all sides. As carefully explained to the present author by those involved in such demonstrations, these rights apply the strongest in "traditional public forums" that include streets, sidewalks and parks. When it concerns private property, such as that of an organization, uphold of this right is discretionary to the owners of the property. For example, in a public park you may photograph anything "in plain view." However, if held on private property, it again is at the discretion of the property owners.

The idea that an individual organizing a protest requires a permit is a misconception. However, that being said, a "peaceful protest" is not allowed to block or inhibit the flow of traffic. If a march or demonstration is to do so, then a permit *is* required. When not "permitted" a law-enforcement officer does have the authority to have you move out of the way of automobile traffic. Another instance requiring a permit would be an assembly or rally that intends to use "sound amplification" of any kind—such as a P.A. System (and potentially a megaphone). This information is provided because we cannot definitively predict the future of our *Org*, nor how it will be viewed once its infrastructure and purpose publicly extends beyond the written word.

> Remember that as a *Systemologist*, you represent the full body
> of the *organization* and its *membership* in your everyday life.
> *Conduct yourself accordingly.*

Concerning law enforcement representatives: *respect them*—or in the case of heavily fragmented one's, *respect the position they represent.* Al though they do become conditioned over time to "suspect everyone" and generally get to handle the "worst" of how humanity behaves, even this must first begin with fragmented individuals unable to control themselves properly. *Fragmentation* is spread like a disease. If all individuals were able to conduct their actions in line with the *Ethics* illustrated in this book, we would still employ peace officers, but their jobs would be much easier. Any individual put under intense stress and strain is at risk for trigger *reactive-responses*; so don't give them a hard time.

To ensure the highest caliber of behavior, safety and legality when conducting protests, one of the leading activist organizations on the planet, known as *Anonymous*, expresses five key points when training their members for demonstrations:

    1) *Respect Police*;

    2) *Never <u>use</u> violence*;

    3) *Never <u>threaten</u> violence*;

    4) *Do not throw anything*; and

    5) *Do not be insulting.*

If our Organization—and its membership—can execute the same tact in their behavior (and when encountering opposition) it will always be the *other side* that comes out looking criminal. We are not a criminal organization—and there are no laws governing against replacement of a standard-issue Human population with *Metahumans*. If given the means we could "upgrade" the entire planet to *Metahuman* status within a single generation—but, just do your *Self-Honest* best. That's all anyone can ask of you.

:: SYSTEMOLOGY OF PERSONAL INTEGRITY ::
TECH REPORT FOR SYSTEMOLOGY PILOTS[‡]
GRADE IV/V WIZARD-0/1 ROUTE-3E/0
RESPONSIBILITY & JUSTIFICATION

A *Self-Honest* and "Awakened" *Seeker* needs only to look out in the world around us to see just how far down a dwindling spiral the Human Condition has progressed. Yet, in looking out, it seems just as critical that we are looking "in"—as the world that is manifested "out there" is an agreement of participation by what is going on "in here" and there really is no distinction between the two when we get right down to it. We all strongly benefit from the fact that at its basic state, the *Alpha Spirit* is actually righteous and good—if not otherwise *amoral* down here when serving a higher Ethic—simply working to get along in the continuation of its own existence. Were this not the case, we would have no chance at rehabilitating presence and *Awareness* of the actual *Self* that is behind the helm and restoring to it the full control of how we experience the *beta-existence* that we each participate in maintaining as reality.

Although programmed purposes and implanted goals are treated more directly at higher level Wizard Grades (because they pertain to lives prior to this one), it is easy to see that this subject reoccurs sporadically within our *Systemology* texts (and Grades) all along the way. Even in "*Crystal Clear (Handbook for Seekers)*" we began to ask a *Seeker* if the goal and motivation for their behavior is actually their own—*Self-determined*—or does it come from another—*Other-determined*—source. Accumulated involvement in dangerous situations, states of confusion, unjust destruction and being at the effect end of faulty—or blatantly false—information, all lend to fragmented purposes that may very well be painted to appear "for our own good." Instead they are actually non-survival (or counter-survival) oriented, leading us away from routes to achieve "greater heights"—higher more ideal states of *Beingness*—including the "Universe" preceding this one.

As ancient Babylonian Star-Gate lore suggests—and even the better known Judaic Kabbalah based on it—our *Awareness as Self* has descended a great many "Spheres of Existence," each one a little more condensed and a little more solid, and *fragmentation* carried with us certainly reflec-

---

[‡] A revised facsimile based on original Tech Reports compiled by Joshua Free for the *Mardukite Academy of Systemology* during the completion of the "*Intro to The Wizard's Way: Metahuman Ethics and Beyond*" cycle of developmental work at *Mardukite Babylonia SLV Borsippa HQ* in January 2022; officially issued in February 2022.

ts that—becoming more rigid and fixed each time. Again, some of this has been done *to* us, implanted by a class of beings seeking to seal away our access to their realm. But, once this is the case, we are quite effective in doing it to ourselves and each other. This very pattern is what constitutes our occupation of *Awareness* and POV to a "prison" or "penalty" Universe such as the one treated around us as *beta-existence.* But, of course, we have descended to a lower grade *beta-existence here* than what was once considered former, which is only slightly referenced within pre-Wizard Grades of Systemology as the "Magic Universe" or "Magic Kingdom."

> Just as we certainly did not all-at-once "fall from grace" of our perfected *Alpha* state, so must we *ascend* on a gradient scale—each carefully mapped step guaranteeing certainty for occupying our *Beingness* or *Awareness* in higher universes. It is obvious then that it is into the "Magic Kingdom" that we next seek to open a "Gateway." We have moved in that direction since the beginning, carefully releasing our hold on—and the hold on us—as we progress through the gradients of Systemology. Material given in *"Imaginomicon"* (*Liber-3D*) builds up from premises first established in *"Crystal Clear (Handbook for Seekers)"* (*Liber-2B*), just as the present volume (*Liber-3E*) advances upon where we have successfully reached with *"Metahuman Destinations"* (*Liber-Two*). All of which are, in turn, treating a fundamental development of ledges to reach upward from.

For a *Seeker* that is 'approaching' the Wizard Grades, there is no doubt that there are amazing and fantastical vistas yet to be explored within our work. This present *"Way of the Wizard"* volume is one of several checkpoints along the *Pathway.* But it is entirely critical for any lasting success in the higher ranks and levels of if of our *Systemology.* By reclaiming a true Ethic—by resolving the matters of *Hostile-Acts* and *Hold-Backs* that are determinable from *this* lifetime—the way forward is cleared much faster.

The *Pilot* must address any and all *"Problems"* that a *Seeker* has their 'present attention' (*Pressence*) on—focus on the *"elephant in the room"* (*factual/actual* or *imagined/realized*) before addressing other considerations. The subject of "Problems" is taken up in *"Metahuman Destinations,"* but the truth is that the lower on the *Beta-Awareness Scale* an individual is, the more of their attention and sense of *Beingness* is wrapped up or entangled with problems—the more problems they perceive they have which are not solved. In fact, the lower a person is in *Awareness,* the more insistent they are that the problems have to be solved "right now." [If the GSR's *Balance Point* is high at the start of session, *do not* conduct '*standard processing*'; find out what the *Seeker's* attention is on and/or what "*Loss*" they are 'sad'/'upset' about. No other '*systematic*' gains will occur while a *Seeker* is in this position.] In order to dissolve significance of emotional entanglement, the *Seeker* should be prompted to identify as many aspects of the event, time and place *As-It-Is.*

In the instance of Goals and Purposes, the problems are often hidden or buried from view—they are not "confronted" and when using GSR in processing, they cause the needles to "*rise*" significantly. Basically, the individual is increasing their resistance against whatever it is they don't want to face. We might say it indicates being overwhelmed. This is where we find the "breaks" in communication and/or reality. This is why our *Acension* is handled on a gradient scale—an individual must have reality on it—realization—before they can find themselves confronting the *actuality.*

Major *Self-determined* life-changes (not necessarily enforced)—or actions/movements—are generally preceded by a major confusion. These are moments when *Awareness* is reduced and therefore susceptible to programming, encoding and implanting. The same thing could be said for physical trauma, shock or unconsciousness. The effects on a *Seeker* can be reduced if the "imprinting incident" (*&tc.*) is resurfaced—but it must be at the point of origination, the very first moment or instance of the event. Otherwise the results will not be permanent. It is not unlike a chain, which is found in *systematic processing* to only reduce if the earlier incident or earlier beginning is found. Otherwise the imprinting and/or associative Mental Imagery can potentially become stronger. This is why after being processed a couple of times, the *Pilot* asks the *Seeker* if the intensity or imagery is getting stronger or thinner. If it does intensify, then you're not working with the "whole thing." Just as if the *fall* on the GSR continues, there *Seeker* still has more *Hold-Backs* -or- the incident is rooted in a "past life" and the *Seeker* has no reality on it.

A *Fragmented Purpose* is rigidly fixed in place in such a way that the *Seeker* didn't likely agree to it or may not even be 'aware' of it—thus it is not *Self-determined* and is certainly not resolved (or dissolved) *"As-It-Is"* in basic processing or managed in regular every-day life. Such a purpose may or may not be overtly displayed with *Hostile* or *destructive* intentions, but they are certainly present—even if, again, beneath the surface and outside the normal reach of a *Seeker.* When '*processing-out*' a *Fragmented Purpose*, the *Seeker* must confront the nature of the actual intention they have and not simply a statement of action or what someone else intended. When it comes to *Ethics Processing* and personal integrity strengthening, we are concerned primarily with the "intention" that the *Seeker* had—and without attempts to justify it. When asked what they've done, too often a *Seeker* will set up their *Awareness* on the "defensive side" and immediately begin to give obvious facts, excuses and justification. These are not the type of answers we want to see accepted in Route-3E (*&tc*).

Fragmented Purposes reduce the appearance of an individual's integrity. They are not necessarily always "on" or dramatizing the programming—it may be triggered or stimulated into action by any number of things. However, when they are in this "*mode*," they often are perceived by others to be at least a little bit "crazy" if not fully insane depending on the intensity of the programmed purpose. It is a patterned tendency and not random, which means that there are indicators that can be watched for and this information leads to better 'processing-out' the whole thing. The *Pilot* is looking to find the underlying *Fragmented Purpose* that systematically leads to a behavioral-chain or pattern of *Hostile-Acts.* Whether or not the *Fragmented Purpose* is installed as part of between-lives implanting, at Grade-IV (and *pre-A.T. Wizard-0*) the focus remains on the present life. However, higher treatments of the same applied-philosophy would undoubtedly reveal more information from the *BackTrack*—and of course the *Pilot* is not permitted to invalidate whatever a *Seeker* says.

One of the main reasons why this type of *processing* is so significant is because of how much attention and energy is placed on personal restraint —the *Hold-Backs.* An individual is actually straining themselves to not do "the usual." A skilled *Pilot* [*Class-3E* or higher] that has worked into Grade-V is permitted to process a *Seeker* into the Abyss or chasm that separates this life from others—which we refer to as the *BackTrack* because it is the course already laid down behind us. When we say "purpose" we of course mean the *Alpha* qualities beyond only this existence, pertaining likely to "*Will-Intention*" (5.0) and/or "*Alpha Thought*" (6.0). As such, *Purpose Defrag* methods are not a replacement for standard *Ethics Processing.* Application of *Justification Processing* may also be required for the full defragmentation effect.

Underlying the *Fragmented Purpose* is a *Hostile-Act* of "commission"— something they have *done*, as opposed to one of "omission" (something they didn't do or neglected) that the *Seeker* is likely to 'give up' much easier under questioning than something they've done. Like other forms of *Processing*, a "*Purpose Defrag*" is incredibly basic, requires specific expert handling and will not result in a *Seeker* sprouting wings and rising up to be an instantaneous deity. This is just one of many aspects to breaking through and past this juncture of the *Pathway* and into the *Actualizing-Ascension Tech* ("*A.T.*") of upper-level Systemology. As such, it can be overrun beyond its *End Point*, at which you risk losing the gains it provides.

Unlike use of *Grade-III* materials, such as "*Crystal Clear*"—or even application of "*Metahuman Destinations*" and "*Imaginomicon*"—a *Pilot* must be specially skilled with practice and certified as "<u>*Class-3E*</u>" (or above) to operate this material in a session. Also: while this will not come without difficulty to some that have been following along the *Pathway*, the odds of complete success *without* using an appropriate type of *GSR-Meter* (which requires its own area of expertise as described in *Liber-3E*) are about 1000-to-1.

THE SYSTEMOLOGY OF JUSTIFICATION, MANIPULATION & RESPONSIBILITY[†]

As long as the *Pilot* handles *processing* fully and systematically, which may include necessary application of *"The Systemology of Justification and Responsibility,"* it is possible to free up the *Seeker* enough to pursue the higher-level Wizard Grades. However, if the *Pilot* does not maintain proper control and steering of the session, allowing the *Seeker* to run all around the actual procedure, then they've both *had it* and are wasting processing time. This is not meant to sound overly harsh or rigid—but we are dealing with a key area here that is going to essentially make or break progress on the *Pathway*. It wasn't until intensive work on *Grade-V* began at the *Systemology Society* in 2021, that we realized *"The Way of the Wizard"* (*Liber-3E*) was critical—necessary as an intermediary transition.[*]

Another critical step to handling and elevating *Personal Integrity* is *"justification defragmentation."* If the matter is not obvious—assuming the *Seeker* has not focused on their own *justifications*, they can be obtained by asking for them. Whenever a *Hostile-Act* or *Hold-Out* is discovered, the *Pilot* simply asks if the *Seeker* has justified that behavior in any way. If using GSR, the matter should be asked about until there is no charge regarding the act. Although standard *Pilot* training in "3E" distinguishes a "read" on a *GSR-Meter* to mean "yes," it can also mean that there is still a charge on a line. So if after there are no immediate reads on a interrogative question, and you ask "Do you agree that this PCL is clear/defragmented?" and you get a read, then there is still a charge on the line.[‡]

You do a *Seeker* a great disservice by allowing vague answers and generalities to "fly" during *Personal Integrity Defragmentation.* A *Pilot* is also encouraged to have gotten their own *Hold-Outs* defraged (as part of their *"Class-3E"* certification) so that they are not likely to sidestep the same areas in others. Although we are concerned with actions, the 'things' that a *Seeker* has "heard" (from others) or "thought" (but not acted on) can also create "mental mass" and thus should be flattened with two-way communication, but not emphasized or targeted directly. Spending an entire session on such will not advance the *Seeker*; yet, parts of these

---

†   Supplemental to the former document; officially issued March 2022.

*   All fundamentals should be run as a repetitive PCL until the *Seeker* appears to run out of answers. Any further answers hidden may be detected by GSR—asking the *Seeker* what '*that*' is that came to mind each time there is a read (however slight or tiny).

‡   According to an anonymous professional therapeutic processor that this article is written in collaboration with, the *Pilot* should never say "that *still* reads" and should say instead that "there *is another* read here" or "I'm getting *another* read here." Otherwise you risk invalidating the *Seeker.*

actually relate to a *Seeker's* "justifications" and so they are (to that degree) important. However, *Hold-Outs* on actual *Hostile-Actions* are immensely more important. It is also critical to pinpoint the time-place of events to be certain a *Seeker* desensitizes the charge *As-It-Is.* If *GSR-Meter* reads aren't quieting down, ask for a similar occurrence that took place earlier in the past. You want to target the *first* time the *Seeker* acted in such a way—which is the *imprinting incident* on which all other mass/ fragmentation is built upon.

At the inception of the Games Universes, *Alpha-Spirits* went to great lengths to trick and deceive each other with "*Illusion*" for the sake of fun and entertainment—similar in nature to the purpose of "special effects" in movies and formerly "stage magic." Eventually this became a means for entrapment and slavery. This is not always easy to detect because of illusive shields and veils that—at **WILL**—can conceal thoughts and intentions. In the old days of Systemology—circa 2008 through 2012—the key word was "distraction"; and by this we meant the misdirection of attention and *Awareness* that kept a *Seeker* from facing up to (confronting) the truth of Reality of *As-It-Is.* "Route-2" (*Analytical Recall*) and "Route-3C" (*Circuits*) methodology may be used to increase *Awareness* on these occurrences.

Those who are familiar with "*Systemology: The Original Thesis*" (the "Patterns and Cycles" section) understand that civilization on this planet socially operates to the tune of an 84-year cycle (congruent with the orbit of Uranus). It is not unrealistic to assume that we are entering into a period that is consistent with conditions similar to what led us into *World War II.* To prevent: How is this type of travesty safeguarded against (?), you may wonder. Well it requires "proofing up" or "strengthening" against succumbing to the type of confusion that will allow the patterned sequence to take place in the world... In the case of WWII, we find (at its inception) a major economic depression—which is, of course, a large-scale social "confusion" for society as a whole. This is not unlike conditions the world is streaming toward today, where we start seeing a division of the population forming two main classes: the truly needy and the truly greedy.

FALSEHOOD—FIGHTING (EXPANDED 3C, BASIC 3E)

Circuit-1 — Recall a time when you tricked another into fighting.

Circuit-2 — Recall a time when you were tricked into fighting.

Circuit-3 — Recall a time when another tricked others into fighting.

FALSEHOOD—DISTRACTION/ATTENTION (3C, BASIC 3E)

Circuit-1 — Recall a time when you intentionally distracted another.
Circuit-2 — Recall a time when another distracted you.
Circuit-3 — Recall a time when another distracted another.

FALSEHOOD—CONFUSION (EXPANDED 3C, BASIC 3E)

Circuit-1 — Recall a time when you confused another or others.
Circuit-2 — Recall a time when another/others confused you.
Circuit-3 — Recall a time when another confused another/others.
Cr.0/A.T. — Recall a confusion.
            \ What concept was used to handle or reduce it?

The term "instigator" seldom appears in common conversation—but we know that there are those out there that encourage confusion, or at the very least have learned to take advantage of it. There are especially those that profit or benefit, even if only for personal entertainment, from *instigating* conflict between others—sometimes even to have an opponent eliminated for them. Well, this is what happens in the midst of a confusion that leads to something like *WWII*. In the state of confusion, an individual is left to grasp onto something *real*, some "stable data" that may or may not be analyzed for its truth before it is accepted. In the case of *WWII*, the Jewish population was targeted as the enemy or cause for the depression. Of course, this wasn't true—in spite of what some *Protocols of the Learned Elders of Zion* document might suggest.

There are several ways in which information may be mishandled, thereby becoming false information or false data. When operating in a confusion or points of low-*Awareness*, this data is often accepted without scrutiny. Many of the tactics further reduce *Awareness* and affect clarity of memory.

• "Passing the Buck" — Shifting the blame onto an individual, family, group or society (race, nation, &tc.), which is misdirecting *Awareness* from the true Source to a false one; this includes false accusations.

• "Remember When" — Shifting the dating/timing of an event from actual data to invented data, thereby obscuring the facts and sometimes diminishing significance by presenting events as longer ago then they actually are.

• "Shifting Significance" — Exaggerating or downplaying the significance or importance of some data; this includes intentions to belittle, shame or embarrass an individual.

FALSEHOOD—BLAME (EXPANDED 3C, BASIC 3E)

Circuit-1 — Recall a time when you shifted blame onto another.
Circuit-2 — Recall a time when another shifted blame onto you.
Circuit-3 — Recall a time when another shifted blame onto others.

FALSEHOOD—SHIFTING TIME (EXPANDED 3C, BASIC 3E)

Circuit-1 — Recall a time when you were misleading about the time some event occurred.
Circuit-2 — Recall a time when another misled you about the time some event occurred.
Circuit-3 — Recall a time when another misled another about the time some event occurred.

FALSEHOOD—SIGNIFICANCE (EXP. ROUTE-2, BASIC 3E)

Circuit-1 — Recall a time when you exaggerated the importance of something.
             \ Recall a time when you downplayed the importance of something.
Circuit-2 — Recall a time when another exaggerated the importance of something to you.
             \ Recall a time when another downplayed the importance of something to you.

FALSEHOOD—EMBARRASSMENT (EXP. 3C, BASIC 3E)[‡]

Circuit-1 — Recall a time when you acted to make another feel embarrassed.
Circuit-2 — Recall a time when another acted to make you feel embarrassed.
Circuit-3 — Recall a time when another acted to make another feel embarrassed.
Cr.0/A.T. — Recall a time when you made yourself feel embarrassed.

FALSEHOOD—MANIPULATION 1 (RTE 3C/3E, PRE-A.T.)

::A::   — Spot a time when you were told someone or something was

---

[‡] *"Falsehood—Stupidity Exp. Route-3C (Basic 3E)"* is run identically, but replacing "embarrassed" with "stupid."

"bad."

::B::   — Identify the person that told you.

::C::   — Did that person have "personal interests **invested**? How did they?

FALSEHOOD—MANIPULATION 2 (PRE-A.T.)

::A::   — Spot a time when you were told something that you found out to be true.

::B::   — Spot a time when you were told something that you found out to be false.

FALSEHOOD—MANIPULATION 3 (ADV. 3C, Route-3E)[*]

Circuit-1   — How have you manipulated another?

Circuit-2   — How has another manipulated you?

Circuit-3   — How has another manipulated others?

When using the *GSR-Meter*, a *Pilot* learns to recognize the significance of an immediate reaction of the needle or 'instant read'. Even when the *Seeker* does not have an immediate answer, because they are now searching their databases for it, the immediate response of a needle should be used as the indicator. Assuming the *Seeker* does take a moment to 'think' about it, it is likely that when they hit upon it, the *Pilot* will see the same quality of needle reaction on the *Meter*. With these kinds of processes, it is *then* that a *Pilot* should indicate a 'read' to the *Seeker*, by saying "*there*" or "*that*" or "*what is* that(?)" (of which a *Seeker* would know from previous experience or education that they are being asked *What-Is-It* they are looking at; and the *Pilot* is to acknowledge the *As-It-Is* answer received).[√]

As expressed throughout Grade-III and Grade-IV work, "*Willingness to be Responsible*" has nothing to do with blame and guilt; it has everything to do with *True Power*—the ability to be *at cause* over things. "Justification" is a common occurrence when handling "Route-3E" because when an individual acts in a manner that is later considered "wrong," there is a natural encoded tendency to "lessen the importance/significance" or else "justify" the actions. This not only strengthens the imprinting of the "*Harmful-Act*" but also requires that the individual maintain certain false

---

[*]   "*Falsehood—Manipulation 4, Advanced Route-3C (Route-3E)*" is run identically, but replacing "manipulated" with "misled."

[√]   An addition review (read through) of "*Metahuman Destinations*" (*Liber-Two*) may be necessary after completing *Liber-3E* in order to achieve effective *Pilot*-training to the extent that we can.

beliefs in order to support these "justifications." Maintaining any false-hoods is a conflict with *Self-Honesty* and perpetuates distortions in 'thinking' and the way in which one views and interacts with the 'world'. It is high-time that you are able to confront (*face up to*) actions without feelings of regret, blame or the urge to justify them; without which it is impossible to shed skin of the Human Condition and rise above the gravity of this *beta-Existence.*

JUSTIFICATION—HOSTILE-ACTS DEFRAG. (EXP. 3E, A.T.)

Circuit-1 — What have you done to another?
          \ How did you justify that?
Circuit-2 — What has another done to you?
          \ How did they justify that?
Circuit-3 — What has another done to others?
          \ How did they justify that?
Cr.0/A.T. — What have you done to yourself?
          \ How did you justify that?

JUSTIFICATION—EXCUSES (EXPANDED ROUTE-2, 3E)

Circuit-1 — What do you use as an excuse?
          \ How could you survive without excuses?
Circuit-2 — What do others use an excuse?
          \ How could they survive without excuses?

The final key for accessing *The Wizard's Way*—and the transition from Grade-IV to Grade-V and the upper-level Wizard Grades—is to **process-out** what facets we carry regarding "Domination" of others for our material survival; the material survival of these "bodies" anyways. We have been in the habit of attacking and competing with one another for far too long, under an illusion that there can only be one "winner" or that "more for you equals less for me." The systems are designed for this, but it is not truth. Not really. PCLs for this may begin with spotting and analyzing what you have done to "dominate" "stop actions" and "inhibit" others. All of these contribute to our sense of personal "superiority."

Superiority and Domination games are implanted to "keep the masses from uprising" against those that are actually in a position of superiority in calling the shots of the *Game* and the implants themselves. Keep them fighting amongst each other and they will never "remember who the enemy is." But these are *Games* of the lowest order; they are not for our greater good or for the greater survival of the whole. They keep us trapped on a dwindling spiral that will ultimately doom us all if we allow it. If you examine your *kabbalistic* models you will see just how far things have progressed—or rather digressed and regressed—from the Source. Where do you think things will go from here?

Although future "Wizard Grade" materials will expand upon the next steps on the Pathway toward our Ascension—treating the *BackTrack* of our spiritual existence—the present author closes this volume with a quote from the late defragmentation-philosopher *Ken Ogger:*—

> "Each of us has something by which we prove that we are superior to others. It will be some basic characteristic that we have worked on to the exclusion of other things, and so you will be good at it. It will be something like being *holy* or *good* or *strong* or *intelligent* or some similar thing by which you make yourself better than others. Even the enlightened beings who have managed to pull out of this game of domination will have this item. The difference is that they choose not to use it against others. And please note that this is a self-destructive game. You're best characteristic, which you use against others if you choose to play this game, will eventually deteriorate because of the harm that you are doing with it. And so eventually you must abandon it and shift over to something which is not so badly deteriorated. As a result, this item will only stretch back for a limited number of lifetimes. If you go back early enough, you will find some other thing which you once used and have since abandoned."

In the Magic Universe, the name of the *Game* was "*To Enjoy*"—and down here it is "*To Survive.*" Once we descend to an even lower level of "*To Exist,*" the gravity of the next Universe down will be inescapable. Imagine your consciousness being trapped within a rock or granule of sand for all eternity. Sure you'll remain an eternal being, but what chance of movement upward will remain then?

This is the reality that is facing us today.

And we are approaching the end of this cycle quite quickly.

:: BOOK OF THE LAW OF THE NEW WORLD ::
SYSTEMOLOGY PILOT TECH REPORT[‡]
GRADE-V WIZARD-1 CLASS-3E
A METAHUMAN ETHIC
2022 VERSION 1.1

The "Mardukite" Organization—and its movement—was launched in 2008, exactly *14 years* ahead of the coming dawn of a *brave* "New World" for Metahumans in 2022. This development over a decade ago was intentionally and purposely directed by certain Anunnaki factions, particularly those in support of "Marduk" and the vision and call of ancient Babylon; and in our case, a "*New Babylon.*" The *Armageddon Clock* begins ticking strongly in 2022, after *14 years* of being warned and coddled. And while this latest volume—*Liber-3E*—is set to be released in the middle of that year, those few who are the *Chosen Ones*, from the *many called*, will have already heard the trumpet-cries for *Self-Honesty* and personally beheld the *vision and the voice* for several years leading up to 2022. If you have been waiting for a cataclysm, for a 'second coming', for an obvious momentous occasion in which to begin changing your life, you're too late. For the rest of us, there is *The Pathway*.

"*Book of the Law of the New World*" was a codename for "*Projekt Ethics*"—or else "Liber-3E" during its original development from mid-2021 through early-2022. Basic principles of "The Law" (as a written code illustrated here) are based on a combination of *A New Metahuman Ethic*, the guidelines set down for *Utilitarian Systemology*, and information gathered by other spiritual and metaphysical leaders that have had some type of contact with the Anunnaki, during the past several decades, in regards to the "*New World.*"

*** <u>MINOR INFRACTIONS</u> ***

Those individuals conducting "*minor*" acts of 'counter-survival' are subject to critical review of *Ethics* and implanted *False Purposes*. They are likely salvageable if they are able and willing to defragment themselves *and* change their order of conduct in the immediate future.

• Those who produce and propagate (via distribution, marketing,

---

[‡]   A revised facsimile based on original an Tech Report compiled by Joshua Free for the *Mardukite Academy of Systemology* during the completion of the "*Intro to The Wizard's Way: Metahuman Ethics and Beyond*" cycle of developmental work at *Mardukite Babylonia SLV Borsippa HQ* in January 2022; officially issued as a supplement to former documents in March 2022.

&tc.) material goods and/or ideas that are harmful to individuals and/or the ecological environment of planet Earth.

• Those who are oppositional to positive social reformation of civic policies that better equalize the survival and betterment to the highest *Sphere of Existence*, meaning both individuals *and* the ecological environment on planet Earth—and elsewhere in the **cosmos** (since the *False Purposes* of humanity appear to seek a reach onto other planets, *&tc*).

• Those who are not *Beta-Defragmented* and perhaps even suppress others from achieving such—including those operating under implanted *False Purposes.*

*** <u>INTERMEDIATE VIOLATIONS</u> ***

Those individuals who are following implanted *False Purposes* that lead to an '*Intermediate*' degree of *Fragmentation* are on the cusp of being salvageable; though it entirely depends on the individual themselves and how tightly they seek to cling to their materialistic programming. They will require a greater degree of *processing* in order to let go of their superiority and greed—which has given the gravity of this existence a greater hold on them, due to material *and* mental masses that they cling to. Quite simply, a *Pilot's* work is '*cut out for*' them; resources *may* be better applied to those operating under '*minor infractions*' such as those who are simply ignorant of how to attain *Beta-Defragmentation*, and that "*help*" is available.

• Those "*Irresponsible Parents*" that have enforced physical punishment on their children or promoted that their children have values that would otherwise be deemed infractions of the *New World*.

• Those who kill, particularly animals—and including hunters believing their justification that it's "for food."

• Those who own and operate "*factory farms*" where animals live out "*miserable lives*"—even if they are not blatantly "*tortured.*"

• Those who eat meat.

*** <u>MAJOR CRIMES</u> ***

Those individuals guilty of "*major*" crimes are generally not worth the time and attention of a *Pilot*, whose efforts could be better served for treating those that are more likely to achieve *Beta-Defragmentation* and are thus more salvageable. Certainly an individual could have a 'change-of-heart' during their lifetime, but if they are still committing "*major*" crimes at the inception of the "New World," they are more than likely expendable members of the population—suppressive persons that are treated as "Fair Game" by up-and-coming Metahumans (provided their treatment does not incite a "*good*" person to commit violations). NOTE: Leave their handling to the Anunnaki Elite and pursue your own *Pathway to Self-Honesty*. Fight them peacefully using social reform until the point in which they are deemed unnecessary by those powers that are here (or coming here) to 'clean up the mess'.

• Those who are violent and physically abusive to any lifeform.

• Those who use their careers, "*religious fanaticism,*" elected offices —or any form of justification—to support torture, murder, rape, enslavement and "forced prostitution" of any lifeform, including animals, or the destruction of the ecological environment on planet Earth.

• Those who participate in any form of animal abuse, including abandon, neglect, indefinite chaining, physical punishment, blatant "dog-fight" type activities, "*legal mutilation*" (*removal of claws, vocal cords, &tc.*), or operation of "puppy mill" type activities.

• Those who have "*sold out for power or greed*"—and/or participate in any agenda set forth by the *Zeta Reticuli* (*Grays*), which are technically enemies of this Anunnaki "New World" Agenda.

:: THE CREED OF MARDUKITE ZUISM ::
PRINCIPLES OF BELIEF

1.) We believe in an Absolute Being, which is Infinite—(the ABZU)—the All-as-One encompassing Source of all Being, Knowing and Awareness to all Alpha/Spiritual (AN) and Beta/Physical (KI) states of existence.

2.) We believe in a spiritual energy of all Life and Awareness (ZU) in the physical universe that is an effect of a spiritual cause; a Spirit that is cause. This Spirit—in its Alpha state—is the True Self "I-AM" Individual Identity that many have called the "soul."

3.) We believe that the Human Condition is a genetic vehicle used by a spiritual source (AN) to experience the Finite as physical existence (KI)—that we are Awareness (ZU) projected onto a genetic vehicle—and that while the vehicle/body may perish to physical **entropy**, the "Alpha Spirit" remains immortal and Self-directed to the extent of its own Actualized Awareness.

4.) We believe that the highest form of worship and spirituality is the actualization and advancement of our "Self" as Spirit in Self-Honesty—and that Self-Honesty is the I-AM Alpha state of Being and Knowing, which is realizable in this lifetime.

5.) We believe that the purpose of all existence is: to exist—and that the **Prime Directive** of all spiritual Life is: continued existence of spiritual Life and co-creation of habitable Reality. "Good" and "Moral" actions are evaluated to the extent of this end.

6A.) We believe that no Life exists in exclusion to all other Life—and that the conditions of a habitable Reality extending from Self include: Home; Community; All Humanity; All Life on Earth; All Life in the Universe; All Spiritual Life; and the Infinite.

6B.) We believe in a continued evolution of Alpha Spirit awareness developed beyond one physical life, and that a Spirit experiences many.

7A.) We believe Mardukite Zuism is: a 21st Century AD synthesis of the 21st Century BC wisdom collected on cuneiform tablets and experienced in ancient Mesopotamia, esp. Babylon.

7B.) This cuneiform library includes details concerning: beings called the Anunnaki; ordering of the Cosmos; creation of Humanity; and an entire legacy of systematized traditions.

8.) We believe in the continuation of, and proper communication of, the legacy of true Human history—and the ability of every Human to realize that they are a Free Spirit in a Free Zone of Self-Determinism: No "evils" can affect intentions if an individual is holistically Self-Actualized in Self-Honesty.

—APPENDIX—

NEXGEN SYSTEMOLOGY GLOSSARY v4.4

—A—

A-for-A (one-to-one) : an expression meaning that what we say, write, represent, think or symbolize is a direct and perfect reflection or duplication of the actual aspect or thing—that "A" is for, means and is equivalent to "A" and not "a" or "q" or "!"; in the relay of communication, the message or particle is sent and perfectly duplicate in form and meaning when received.

aberration : a departure from what is right; in chromatic light science, the failure of a mirror, lens or refracting surface to produce an exact *"one-to-one"* or *"A-for-A"* duplication between an object and its image; a deviation from, or distortion in, what is true or right or straight; in *NexGen Systemology*, a term to describe *fragmentation* as it applies to an individual, which causes them to "stray" form the *Pathway*.

abreaction : the "burn off" or "purging" or "discharge" of "unconscious" (re-active response) as applied to early 20th century German psychology, from *abreagieren*, meaning "coming down from a release or expression of a repressed or forgotten emotion; in *NexGen Systemology*, fully "resurfacing" traumatic past experiences consciously (on one's own determinism) in order to purge them of their emotional excess (or "charge"); also *"Route-1"* and *"catharsis."*

acid-test : a metaphor refers to a chemical process of applying harsh nitric acid to a golden substance (sample) to determine its genuineness; in *NexGen Systemology*, an extreme conclusive process to determine the reality, genuineness or truth of a substance, material, particle or piece of information.

acknowledgment : a response-communication establishing that an immediately former communication was properly received, duplicated and understood; the formal acceptance and/or recognition of a communication or presence.

activating event : an incident or occurrence that automatically stimulates a conscious or unrecognized reminder or 'ping' from an earlier *imprinting incident* recorded on one's own personal timeline as an emotionally charged and encoded memory; an incident or instance when thought systems are activated to determine the consequence or significance of an activity, motion or event— often demonstrated as *Activating Event → Belief Systems → Consideration.*

actualization : to make actual, not just potential; to bring into full solid Reality; to realize fully in *Awareness* as a "thing."

affinity : the apparent and energetic *relationship* between substances or bodies; the degree of *attraction* or repulsion between things based on natural forces; the *similitude* of frequencies or waveforms; the degree of *interconnection* between systems.

agreement (reality) : unanimity of opinion of what is "thought" to be known; an accepted arrangement of how things are; things we consider as "real" or as an "is" of "reality"; a consensus of what is real as made by standard-issue (common) participants; what an individual contributes to or accepts as "real"; in *NexGen Systemology*, a synonym for *"reality."*

allegorical : a representation of the abstract, metaphysical or "spiritual" using physical or concrete forms.

alpha : the first, primary, basic, superior or beginning of some form; in *Nex-Gen Systemology*, referring to the state of existence operating on spiritual archetypes and postulates, will and intention "exterior" to the low-level condensation and solidarity of energy and matter as the 'physical universe'.

alpha control center (ACC) : the highest relay point of *Beingness* for an individuated *Alpha-Spirit, Self* or "I-AM"; in *NexGen Systemology*—a point of spiritual separation of ZU at (7.0) from the *Infinity of Nothingness* (8.0); the truest actualization of *Identity*; the highest *Self-directed* relay of *Alpha-Self* as an *Identity-Continuum*, operating in an *alpha-existence* (or "Spiritual Universe"–AN) to *determine* "Alpha Thought" (6.0) and WILL-*Intention* (5.0) *exterior* to the "Physical Universe"–(KI); the "wave-peak" of "I" emerging as individuated consciousness from *Infinity*.

alpha-spirit : a "spiritual" *Life*-form; the "true" *Self* or I-AM; the *individual*; the spiritual (*alpha*) *Self* that is animating the (*beta*) physical body or *"genetic vehicle"* using a continuous *Lifeline* of spiritual (*"ZU"*) energy; an individual spiritual (*alpha*) entity possessing no physical mass or measurable waveform (motion) in the Physical Universe as itself, so it animates the (*beta*) physical body or *"genetic vehicle"* as a catalyst to experience *Self*-determined causality in effect within the *Physical Universe*; a singular unit or point of *Spiritual Awareness* that is *Aware* that it is *Aware*.

alpha thought : the highest spiritual *Self-determination* over creation and existence exercised by an Alpha-Spirit; the Alpha range of pure *Creative Ability* based on direct postulates and considerations of *Beingness*; spiritual qualities comparable to "thought" but originating in Alpha-existence (at "6.0") independently superior to a *beta-anchored* Mind-System, although an Alpha-Spirit may use Will ("5.0") to carry the intentions of a postulate or consideration ("6.0") to the Master Control Center ("4.0").

amplitude : the quality of being *ample*; the size or amount of energy that is demonstrated in a *wave*. In the case of audio waves, we associate amplitude with "volume." It is not a statement about the frequencies of waves, only how "loud" they are—to what extent they are or may be projected (or audible).

AN : an ancient "Sumerian" cuneiform sign for Heaven or "God"; in *Mardukite Zuism and Systemology* designating the *'spiritual zone'* (or *'Alpha Existence'*); the *Spiritual Universe*—comprised of spiritual matter and spiritual energy; a direction of motion toward spiritual *Infinity*, away from or superior to the physical (*'KI'*); the spiritual condition of existence providing for our primary *Alpha* state as an individual *Identity* or *I-AM-Self* which interacts and experiences *Awareness* of a *beta* state in the *Physical Universe* (*'KI'*) as *Life*.

anathema : a thing or person to be detested, loathed or avoided; a thing or person accursed or despised such as to wish damnation or "divine punishment" upon.

anchor (conceptual) : a stable point in space; a fixed point used to hold or stabilize a spatial existence of other points; a spatial point that fixes the parameters of dimensional orientation, such as the corner-points of a solid object in relation to other points in space; in *NexGen Systemology*, "beta-anchored" is an expression used to describe the fixed orientation of a viewpoint from Self in relation to all possible spatial points in *beta-existence* ("physical universe"), or else the existential points that fix the operation of the "body" within the space-time of *beta-existence*.

Ancient Mystery School : the original arcane source of all esoteric knowledge on Earth, concentrated between the Middle East and modern-day Turkey and Transylvania c. 6000 B.C. and then dispersing south (Mesopotamia), west (Europe) and east (Asia) from that location.

antinomian : a term applied to *Gnostics* (popularized by Martin Luther during the Christian reformation) denoting a rejection of formal religious morals and dogma—decreed, written and interpreted by humanity—as a true pathway to Ascension (some elements appear in all forms of religious protest and reformation but as an extreme, would be considered spirto-religious rebellious punkdom by some modern standards, but it should be understood that it does follow a higher ethic, such as Mardukite Utilitarianism.

apotheosis : from the *Greek* word, meaning *"to deify"*; the highest point or apex (for example, of "true knowledge" and "true experience"); an ultimate development of; a glorified or "deified" *ideal*, such as is a quality of *godhood*.

apparent : visibly exposed to sight; evident rather than actual, as presumed by Observation; readily perceived, especially by the senses.

a-priori : from "cause" to "effect"; from a general application to a particular instance; existing in the mind prior to, and independent of experience or observation; validity based on consideration and deduction rather than experience.

archetype : a "first form" or ideal conceptual model of some aspect; the ultimate prototype of a form on which all other conceptions are based.

ascension : actualized *Awareness* elevated to the point of true "spiritual existence" exterior to *beta existence*. An "Ascended Master" is one who has returned to an incarnation on Earth as an inherently *Enlightened One*, demonstrable in their actions—they have the ability to *Self-direct* the "Spirit" as *Self*, just as we are treating the "Mind" and "Body" at this current grade of instruction; previously treated in *Moroii ad Vitam* as a state of Beingness after *First Death*, experienced by an *etheric body*, which is able to maintain consciousness as a personal identity continuum with the same *Self-directed* control and communication of Will-Intention that is exercised, actualized and developed deliberately during one's present incarnation.

assessment scale : an official assignment of graded/gradient numeric values.

associative knowledge : significance or meaning of a facet or aspect assigned to (or considered to have) a direct relationship with another facet; to connect or relate ideas or facets of existence with one another; a reactive-response image, emotion or conception that is suggested by (or directly accompanies) something other than itself; in traditional systems logic, an equivalency of significance or meaning between facets or sets that are grouped together, such as in *(a + b) + c = a + (b + c)*; in NexGen Systemology, erroneous associative knowledge is assignment of the same value to all facets or parts considered as related (even when they are not actually so), such as in *a = a, b = a, c = a* and so forth without distinction.

assumption : the act of taking or gathering to one's Self; taking possession of, receive or behold.

attenergy : *NexGen Systemological NewSpeak* for "attention energies"; the flow of consciousness "energy" that is directed as "attention"; semantic recognition of an axiom from the *Arcane Tablets* that states: "energy flows where attention goes."

attention : active use of *Awareness* toward a specific aspect or thing; the act of "attending" with the presence of *Self*; a direction of focus or concentration of *Awareness* along a particular channel or conduit or toward a particular terminal node or communication termination point; the Self-directed concentration of personal energy as a combination of observation, thought-waves and consideration; focused application of *Self-Directed Awareness*.

authoritarian : knowledge as truth, boundaries and freedoms dictated to an individual by a perceived, regulated or enforced "authority."

auto-suggestion (self-hypnosis) : auto-conditioning; self-programming; delivering directed affirmations or statements repeatedly to *Self* in order to condition a change in behavior or beliefs; any *Self-directed* technique intended to generate a specific "*post-hypnotic suggestion.*"

awareness : the highest sense of-and-as Self in knowing and being as I-AM (the *Alpha-Spirit*); the extent of beingness directed as a POV experienced by Self as knowingness.

axiom : a fundamental truism of a knowledge system, esp. *logic*; all *maxims* are also *axioms*; knowledge statements that require no proof because their truth is self-evident; an established law or systematic principle used as a *premise* on which to base greater conclusions of truth.

—B—

Babylonian : the ancient Mesopotamian civilization that evolved from *Sumer*; inception point for systematization of civic society and religion.

Back-Scan : to apply Awareness, *Zu-Vision* or "Alpha-Sight" (*exterior* to the

Human Condition) and *resurface* impressions for recreating *Mental Imagery* of the *Backtrack* within one's own Personal Universe and treat with Wizard-Level (*Grade-V+*) methodology.

Backtrack : to retrace one's steps or go back to an early point in a sequence; an applied spiritual philosophy within *Metahuman Systemology "Wizard Grades"* regarding continuous existence of an individual's "*Spiritual Timeline*" through all lifetime-incarnations; the course that is already laid behind us; a methodology of systematic processing methods developed to assist in revealing "hidden" *Mental Images* and *Imprints* from one's past and reclaim attention-energies "left behind" with them by increasing ability to manage and control personal energy mechanisms fixed to their continuous automated creation.

band : a division or group; in *NexGen Systemology*, a division or set of frequencies on the ZU-line that are tuned closely together and referred to as a group.

BAT (Beta-Awareness Test) : a method of *psychometric evaluation* developed for *Mardukite Systemology* to determine a "basic" or "average" state of personal *beta-Awareness*; first developed for the text "*Crystal Clear.*"

"bell, book & candle" : three dissimilar objects that are kept accessible during a processing session (the book is often a copy of *The Systemology Handbook* or a hardcover copy of *The Tablets of Destiny* with the dust-jacket removed if it is less distracting that way); a term meant to indicate a Pilot's "objective processing kit" of objects generally present in the session room (accessible on a shelf, table or pedestal stands); in *NexGen Systemology,* the name of an objective processing philosophy pertaining to command of personal reality; historically, a formal ritual used by the Roman Catholic church to ceremonially declare an individual "guilty of the most heinous sins" as "excommunicated (to hold no further communications with) by anathema"—whereby a *bell* is rung, a *holy book* is closed and all *candles* are snuffed out—thus we therapeutically use the same symbolism historically representing religious fragmentation for modern systematic defragmentation purposes.

beta (awareness) : all consciousness activity ("*Awareness*") in the "Physical Universe" (KI) or else *beta-existence*; *Awareness* within the range of the *genetic-body*, including material thoughts, emotional responses and physical motors; personal *Awareness* of physical energy and physical matter moving through physical space and experienced as "time"; the *Awareness* held by *Self* that is restricted to a physical organic *Lifeform* or "*genetic vehicle*" in which it experiences causality in the *Physical Universe*.

beta (existence) : all manifestation in the "Physical Universe" (KI); the "Physical" state of existence consisting of vibrations of physical energy and physical matter moving through physical space and experienced as "time"; the conditions of *Awareness* for the *Alpha-spirit* (*Self*) as a physical organic *Lifeform* or "*genetic vehicle*" in which it experiences causality in the *Physical Universe*.

beta-defragmentation : toward a state of *Self-Honesty* in regards to handling experience of the "Physical Universe" (*beta-existence*); an applied spiritual philosophy (or technology) of Self-Actualization originally described in the text "*Crystal Clear*" (*Liber-2B*), building upon theories from "*Systemology: The Original Thesis.*"

biological unconsciousness : the organism independent of the sentient *Awareness* of the *Self* to direct it; states induced by severe injury and anesthesia.

biomagnetic/biofeedback : a measurable effect, such as a change in electrical resistance, that is produced by thoughts, emotions and physical behaviors which generate specific 'neurotransmitters' and biochemical reactions in the brain, body and across the skin surface.

—C—

cacophony : dissonant, turbulent, harsh and/or discordant sound or noise.

calcified : in nature, to calcify is to harden like stone from calcium and lime deposits; in philosophic applications, refers to a state of hardened fixed bone-like inflexibility; a condition change to rigidly solid.

capable : the actual capacity for potential ability.

CAT / "Creative Ability Test" : a method of increasing personal freedom and unlimited creative potential of the Alpha-Spirit (Self) independent and exterior to conditions and reality agreements with beta-existence; a Wizard-Level training regimen first developed for the Grade-IV text "*Imaginomicon*" (*Liber-3D*).

catalog / catalogue : a systematic list of knowledge or record of data.

catalyst : something that causes action between two systems or aspects, but which itself is unaffected as a variable of this energy communication; a medium or intermediary channel.

catharsis / cathartic processing : from the Greek root meaning "pure" or "perfect"; Gnostic practices of "consolamentum" where an individual removes distorting/fragmented emotional charges and encoding from a personal energy flow/circuit connected or associated with some terminal, mass, thing, *&tc.*; in *NexGen Systemology*, the emptying out or discharge of emotional stores; also "*abreaction*" or "*Route-1.*"

causative : as being the cause; to be at cause.

chakra : an archaic Sanskrit term for "wheel" or "spinning circle" used in *Eastern* wisdom traditions, spiritual systems and mysticism; a concept retained in NexGen Systemology to indicate etheric concentrations of energy into wheel-mechanisms that process *ZU* energy at specific frequencies along the *ZU-line*, of which the *Human Condition* is reportedly attached *seven* at various degrees as connected to the Gate symbolism.

channel : a specific stream, course, current, direction or route; to form or cut a groove or ridge or otherwise guide along a specific course; a direct path; an artificial aqueduct created to connect two water bodies or water or make travel possible.

charge : to fill or furnish with a quality; to supply with energy; to lay a command upon; in *NexGen Systemology*—to imbue with intention; to overspread with emotion; application of *Self-directed (WILL)* "intention" toward an emotional manifestation in beta-existence; personal energy stores and significances entwined as fragmentation in mental images, reactive-response encoding and intellectual (and/or) programmed beliefs; in traditional mysticism, to intentionally fix an energetic resonance to meet some degree, or to bring a specific concentration of energy that is transferred to a focal point, such as an object or space.

circuit : a circular path or loop; a closed-path within a system that allows a flow; a pattern or action or wave movement that follows a specific route or potential path only; in *NexGen Systemology*, *"communication processing"* pertaining to a specific flow of energy or information along a channel; *see* also *"feedback loop."*

Circuit-1 : in *Grade-IV* "communication processing" (introduced in *Metahuman Destinations* as *Route-3*), the flow of energy and information connected to outflow, what *Self* has expressed, projected outwardly or done.

Circuit-2 : in *Grade-IV* "communication processing" (introduced in *Metahuman Destinations* as *Route-3*), the flow of energy and information connected to inflow, what "others" have done to *Self,* what it has received inwardly or had *happen to*.

Circuit-3 : in *Grade-IV* "communication processing" (introduced in *Metahuman Destinations* as *Route-3*), the flow of energy and information connected to cross-flows, what *Self* has witnessed of others (or another) projecting or doing toward others (or another).

Circuit-0 : a more advanced concept introduced to *Grade-IV* "communication processing" (as listed on SOP-2C in *Metahuman Destinations* for *"Pre-A.T"* or *"Route-0"* applications), which targets *'postulates'* and *'considerations'* generated and stored by *Self* for *Self* and the direction, energy or flows representing what *Self* "does" for and/or to *Self*. This circuit is treated further in *Wizard Level* work,

chronologically : concerning or pertaining to "time"; to treat as "units" of "time" ; to sequence a series of events or information with regard to the order it happened or originated (in time).

clockwork : rigidly fixed gear-like systems that operate mechanically and directly upon one another to function; a "clockwork universe theory" is a "closed-system design" popular in Newtonian Physics attributes all actions of energy-matter in space-time as reactions in accordance with a "Divine Decree" or fixed design that functions like a "clock-mechanism" and does not account for the "Observer."

code (ethics) : an outline of *ethical* standards regarding social participation and acceptable behavior; not generally enforced as *law* itself, but a standard that reasonable individuals are actualized (or civil) enough to *Self-Determine* (by choice) their own following (or adherence) if it is *right* and *good*; shared reality agreements that promote optimum conditions of continued existence ("SURVIVAL" in *Beta-existence*; "CREATION" in *Alpha*) for the highest affected "Sphere of Existence" (on the *Standard Model*).

codification : process of collecting, analyzing and then arranging knowledge in a standardized and more accessible systematic form, often by subject, theme or some other designation.

collapsing a wave : also, "*wave-function collapse*"; in *Quantum Physics*, the concept that an Observer is "collapsing" the wave-function to something "definite" by measuring it; defining or calculating a wave-function or interaction of potential interactions by an Observation; in *NexGen Systemology*, when a wave of potentiality or possibility because a finite fixed form; Consciousness or *Awareness* "collapses" a wave-function of energy-matter as a necessary "third" Principle of Apparent Manifestation (first described in "*Tablets of Destiny*"); potentiality as a wave is collapsed into an apparent "*is*", the energy of which is freed up in systematic processing by "*flattening*" a "collapsed" wave back into its state of potentiality.

command : in *Metahuman Systemology*, responsibility and ability of Self (I-AM) as operating from its ideal "exterior" *Point-of-View* as Alpha Spirit; to direct communication for control of the *genetic vehicle* and Mind-Body connection that is perfectly duplicated from a source-point to a receipt-point along the ZU-line.

command line : see "*processing command line*" (PCL).

common knowledge (game theory) : facts that all "players" know, and they know that all other "players" also know—such as the very structure of the "game" being played.

communication : successful transmission of information, data, energy (&tc.) along a message line, with a reception of feedback; an energetic flow of intention to cause an effect (or duplication) at a distance; the personal energy moved or acted upon by will or else 'selective directed attention'; the 'messenger action' used to transmit and receive energy across a medium; also relay of energy, a message or signal—or even locating a personal POV (viewpoint) for the Self—along the *ZU-line*.

communication (circuit) processing : a methodology of Grade-IV Metahuman Systemology that emphasizes analysis of all Mind-System energy flows (information) transmitted and stored along circuits of a channel toward some terminal, thing or concept, particularly: what Self has out-flowed, what Self has in-flowed, and the cross-flows that Self has observed; also "*Route-3*"

compulsion : a failure to be responsible for the dynamics of control—starting, stopping or altering—on a particular channel of communication and/or regarding a particular terminal in existence; an energetic flow with the appearance of being 'stuck' on the action it is already doing or by the control of some automatic mechanism.

computing device : a calculator or modern computer; a mechanism that performs specific functions, particularly input, output and storage of data/information.

concept : a high-frequency thought-wave representing an "idea" which persists because it is not restricted to a unique space-time; an abstract or tangible "idea" formed in the "Mind" or *imagined* as a means of understanding, usually including associated "Mental Images"; a seemingly timeless collective thought-theme (or subject) that entangles together facets of many events or incidents, not just a single significant one.

conceptual processing : a Wizard-Level methodology introduced intermittently throughout materials of Metahuman Systemology that emphasizes fully "getting the sense of" (or "contacting the idea of") a particular condition as prompted by a PCL and on one's own determination; a systematic practice-drill regarding considerations and postulates (Alpha Thought) regarding various reality agreements; a *Route-0* variant employing *Creativeness* and *Imagination* for systematic processing; also *Route-0E* when used for *Ethics Processing.*

condense (condensation) : the transition of vapor to liquid; denoting a change in state to a more substantial or solid condition; leading to a more compact or solid form.

condition : an apparent or existing state; circumstances, situations and variable dynamics affecting the order and function of a system; a series of interconnected requirements, barriers and allowances that must be met; in "contemporary language," bringing a thing toward a specific, desired or intentional new state (such as in "conditioning"), though to minimize confusion about the word "condition" in our literature, *NexGen Systemology* treats "contemporary conditioning" concepts as imprinting, encoding and programming.

conflict : the opposition of two forces of similar magnitude along the same channel or competing for the same terminal; the inability to duplicate another POV; a thought, intention or communication that is met with an opposing counter-thought or counter-intention that generates an energetic cluster.

confront : to come around in front of; to be in the presence of; to stand in front of, or in the face of; to meet "face-to-face" or "face-up-to"; additionally, in *NexGen Systemology*, to fully tolerate or acceptably withstand an encounter with a particular manifestation or encounter.

consciousness : the energetic flow of *Awareness*; the Principle System of *Awareness* that is spiritual in nature, which demonstrates potential interaction with all degrees of the Physical Universe; the *Beingness* component of our existence in *Spirit*; the Principle System of *Awareness* as *Spirit* that directs action in the Mind-System.

consensual (consensus) : formed or existing simply by consent—by general or mutual agreement; permitted, approved or agreed upon by majority of opinion; knowingly agreed upon unanimously by all concerned; to be in agreement on the objective universe and/or a course of action therein.

consideration : careful analytical reflection of all aspects; deliberation; determining the significance of a "thing" in relation to similarity or dissimilarity to other "things"; evaluation of facts and importance of certain facts; thorough examination of all aspects related to, or important for, making a decision; the analysis of consequences and estimation of significance when making decisions; in *NexGen Systemology*, the postulate or Alpha-Thought that defines the state of beingness for what something "*is.*"

continuity : being a continuous whole; a complete whole or "total round of"; the balance of the equation ["–120" + "120" = "0" *&tc.*]; an apparent unbroken interconnected coherent whole; also, as applied to Universes in *NexGen Systemology*, the lowest base consideration of space-time or commonly shared level of energy-matter apparent in an existence, or else the lowest degree of solidity or condensation whereby all mass that exists is identifiable or communicable with all other mass that exists; represented as "0" on the *Standard Model* for the Physical Universe (*beta-existence*), a level of existence that is below Human emotion, comparable to the solidity of "rocks" and "walls" and "inert bodies."

continuum : a continuous enduring uninterrupted sequence or condition; observing all gradients on a *spectrum*; measuring quantitative variation with gradual transition on a spectrum without demonstrating discontinuity or separate parts.

control (systems) : Communication relayed from an operative center or organizational cluster, which incites new activity elsewhere in a system (or along the *ZU-line*).

correlate : a relationship between two or more aspects, parts or systems.

correspondence : a direct relationship or correlation; see also "*associative knowledge.*"

Cosmic History : the entire continuous *Spiritual Timeline* of all existence, starting with the *Infinity of Nothingness* and individuation of Self and its Home Universe, running through various Games Universes and ultimately leading to condensation and solidification of this Physical Universe experienced in present-time.

Cosmic Law : the "Law" of Nature (or the Physical Universe); the "Law" governing cosmic ordering; often called "Natural Law" in sciences and philosophies that attempt to codify or systematize it.

cosmology : a systematic philosophy defining origins and structure of an apparent Universe.

Cosmos : archaic term for the "Physical Universe"; semantically implies chaos brought into order; in *NexGen Systemology*, can also include considerations of "Universes" experienced previously as a *beta-existence*.

counter-productive : contrary to the greater or original purpose or intention; in *NexGen Systemology*, anything which brings *Life* away from its sustainable goal or position of *Infinite Existence*.

crash-coursed : a very intense or steep delivery of education over a very brief time period, usually applied to bring a student "up-to-speed" or "up-to-date" for receiving and understanding newer or cumulatively more advanced material.

creative ability test : see "*CAT.*"

creativeness processing : a *systematic processing* methodology introduced in *Grade-IV Metahuman Systemology* (*Wizard Level-0*) that emphasizes personal use of "*Imagination,*" or else "creative ability" of Self and freeing considerations of the Alpha-Spirit to *Be* or *Create* anything within its Personal Universe, independent of reality agreements with beta-existence; also "*Route-0.*"

Crossing the Abyss : to enter the spiritual or metaphysical unknown in "Self-annihilation" to purify the Self and "return to the Source."

Crystal Clear : the second professional publication of Mardukite Systemology, released publicly in December 2019; the second professional text in Grade-III Mardukite Systemology, released as "*Liber-2B*" and reissued in the Grade-III Master Edition "*Systemology Handbook*"; contains fundamental theory of "*Beta-Defragmentation*" and "*Route-2*" systematic processing methodology.

cuneiform : the oldest extant writing system at the inception of modern civilization in Mesopotamia; a system of wedge-shaped script inscribed on clay tablets with a reed pen, allowing advancements in record keeping and communication no longer restricted to more literal graphic representations or pictures.

cuneiform signs : the cuneiform script, as used in ancient Mesopotamia, is not represented in a linear alphabet of "letters," but by a systematic use of basic word "signs" that are combined to form more complex word "signs"—each sign represented a "sound" more than it did a letter, such as "ab," "ad", "ba", "da" &tc.

—**D**—

data-set : the total accumulation of knowledge used to base Reality.

dead-memories : outdated, inadequate or erroneous data.

defragmentation : the *reparation* of wholeness; collecting all dispersed parts to reform an original whole; a process of removing "*fragmentation*" in data or knowledge to provide a clear understanding; applying techniques and processes that promote a *holistic* interconnected *alpha* state, favoring observational *Awareness* of continuity in all spiritual and physical systems; in *NexGen Systemology*, a "*Seeker*" achieving an actualized state of basic "*Self-Honest Awareness*" is said to be *beta-defragmented*, whereas *Alpha-defragmentation* is the rehabilitation of the *creative ability*, managing the *Spiritual Timeline* and the POV of *Self* as Alpha-Spirit (I-AM); see also "*Beta-defragmentation.*"

degree : a physical or conceptual *unit* (or point) defining the variation present relative to a *scale* above and below it; any stage or extent to which something *is* in relation to other possible positions within a *set* of "*parameters*"; a point within a specific range or spectrum; in *NexGen Systemology*, a *Seeker's* potential energy variations or fluctuations in thought, emotional reaction and physical perception are all treated as "*degrees.*"

demographics : segments of the population uniquely identified, whether real or representative; targeting a specific portion of the population, such as for marketing or statistics.

destiny : what is set down, made firm, standard, or stands fixed as a constant end; the absolute *destination* regardless of whatever course is traveled; in *NexGen Systemology*, the "*destiny*" of the "*Human Spirit*" (or "*Alpha Spirit*") is infinite existence—"*Immortality.*"

dichotomy : a division into two parts, types or kinds.

differential : the quantitative value difference between two forces, motions, pressures or degrees.

differentiation : an apparent difference between aspects or concepts.

discernment : to perceive, distinguish and/or differentiate experience into true knowledge.

displace : to compel to leave; to move or replace something with something else in its place or space.

dissonance : discordance; out of step; out of phase; disharmonious; the "differential" between the way things are and the way things are experienced; cognitive dissonance could be demonstrated as A = abc, or C = A, the duplication of truth/communication is not A-for-A.

dogma : religious doctrines or opinion-based beliefs (data-set) treated socially as fact, especially regarding "divinity" or "God" (the common "Human" interpretation of the "domain" of Infinity) represented by the "Eighth Sphere" on our original Standard Model of Systemology; religiously defined values, taboos and ethical standards emphasized by cultural/religious socialization and mythographic beliefs (even above any observable causal effects, logical sequences or verifiable proofs).

dramatization / dramatize : a vivid display or performance as if rehearsed for a "play" (on stage); a *'circuit'* recording *'imprinted'* in the past and, once restimulated by a facet of the environment, the individual "replays" it as through reacting to it in the present (and identifying that reality as present reality); acts, actions and observable behaviors that demonstrate identification with a particular character type, "phase" or personality program; a motivated sequence-chain, implant series or imprinted cycle of actions—usually irrational or counter-survival—repeated by an individual as it had previously happened to them; a reoccurring or reactively triggered out-flow, communication or action that indicates an individual "occupying" a particular *'Point-of-View'* (*POV*)—typically fixed to a specific (past) identification (identity) that is space-time locatable (meaning a point where significant *Attenergy*—enough to compulsively create and maintain a POV—is "stuck" or "hung up" on the *BackTrack*).

dross : prime material; specifically waste-matter or refuse; the discarded remains collected together.

dynamic (systems) : a principle or fixed system which demonstrates its *'variations'* in activity (or output) only in constant relation to variables or fluctuation of interrelated systems; a standard principle, function, process or system that exhibits *'variations'* and change simultaneously with all connected systems; each *'Sphere of Existence'* is a dynamic system, systematically affecting (supporting) and affected (supported) by other *'Spheres'* (which are also dynamic systems).

—E—

Eastern traditions : the evolution of the *Ancient Mystery School* east of its origins, primarily the Asian continent, or what is archaically referred to as "oriental."

echelon : a level or rung on a ladder; a rank or level of command.

eclipse : to cast a shadow or darken; to block out or obscure a comparison.

EDA : "electro-dermal activity"; see also *GSR-Meter.*

electro-psychometer ("E-meter") : see *GSR-Meter.*

elocution : the skillful use of clearly directed and expressive speech; the expert demonstration of articulation, pronunciation and dictation to express a message.

emotional encoding : the readable substance/material (data) of *'imprints'*; associations of sensory experience with an *imprint*; perceptions of our environment that receive an *emotional charge*, which form or reinforce facets of an *imprint*; perceptions recorded and stored as an *imprint* within the "emotional range" of energetic manifestation; the formation of an energetic store or charge on a channel that fixes emotional responses as a mechanistic automation, which is carried on in an individual's *Spiritual Timeline* (or personal continuum of existence).

enact : to make happen; to bring into action; to make part of an act.

encompassing : to form a circle around, surround or envelop around.

end point : the moment when the goal of a process has been achieved and to continue on with it will be detrimental to the gains; the finality of a process when the *Seeker* has achieved their optimum state from the current cycle (whether or not they run through it again at a later date with a different level of *Awareness* or knowledge base doesn't change the fact that it has flattened the standing wave

energetic exchange : communicated transmission of energetically encoded "information" between fields, forces or source-points that share some degree of interconnectivity; the event of "waves" acting upon each other like a force, flowing in regard to their proximity, range, frequency and amplitude.

energy signatures : a distinctive pattern of energetic action.

enforcement : the act of compelling or putting (effort) into force; to compel or impose obedience by force; to impress strongly with applications of stress to demand agreement or validation; the lowest-level of direct control by physical effort or threat of punishment; a low-level method of control in the absence of true communication.

engineering : the *Self-directed* actions and efforts to utilize knowledge (observed causality/science), maths (calculations/quantification) and logic (axioms/formulas) to understand, design or manifest a solid structure, machine, mechanism, engine or system; as "*Reality Engineering*" in *NexGen Systemology*—intentional *Self-directed* adjustment of existing Reality conditions; the application of total *Self-determinism* in *Self-Honesty* to change apparent Reality using fundamentals of *Systemology* and *Cosmic Law*.

entanglement : tangled together; intertwined and enmeshed systems; in *NexGen Systemology*, a reference to the interrelation of all particles as waves at a higher point of connectivity than is apparent, since wave-functions only "collapse" when someone is *Observing*, or doing the measuring, evaluating, &tc.

entropy : the reduction of organized physical systems back into chaos-continuity when their integrity is measured against space over time; reduction toward a zero-point.

epicenter : the point from which shock-waves travel.

epistemology : a school of philosophy focused on the truth of knowledge and knowledge of truth; theories regarding validity and truth inherent in any structure of knowledge and reason; the original "school of philosophy" from which all other "disciplines" were derived; the study of knowing how to know knowledge, reason and truth.

erroneous : inaccurate; incorrect; containing error.

esoteric : hidden; secret; knowledge understood by a select few.

etching : to cut, bite or corrode with acid to produce a pattern.

ethics : an intellectual philosophy concerning *rightness* and *wrongness* based on "logic" and "reason" (rationale) combined with observable consequences and tendencies of action or conduct; formal name for a "moral philosophy" (study of moral choices); in ancient times, originally treated *one-to-one* with "Cosmic Law" regarding *causation, order* and *sequence*; an objective (Universal) philosophy of *rightness* and *wrongness*, treated separate from culture-specific (subjective/relative) considerations, such as *morals* and *dogma*; in *NexGen Systemology* (*Grade-IV Metahuman Systemology*), a dynamic philosophy (applying "logic-and-reason") to understand the nature of "reality agreements" concerning *rightness* and *wrongness*, then treating the most optimum conditions of continued existence ("SURVIVAL" in *Beta-existence*; "CREATION" in *Alpha*) for the highest affected "Sphere of Existence" (on the *Standard Model*).

ethics processing : a *systematic processing* methodology introduced for bridging *Grade-IV Metahuman Systemology* (*Wizard Level-0*) with *Grade-V Spiritual Systemology* (*Wizard Level-1*) that emphasizes personal realization of "*Ethics*" and increased ability and responsibility to confront the "rightness" and "wrongness" of past actions (on the Backtrack), including defragmentation of "*Harmful Acts*" (as *Imprinting Incidents*) and any corresponding "*Hold-Backs*" and "*Hold-Outs*" (which reduce *Actualized Awareness* and prompt an individual to *withdraw* their *reach*); also "*Route-3E.*"

etymology : the origins of "words" and their development.

evaluate : to determine, assign or fix a set value, amount or meaning.

exacting : a demanding rigid effort to draw forth from.

executable : the supreme authoritative ability to carry out according to design.

existence : the *state* or fact of *apparent manifestation*; the resulting combination of the Principles of Manifestation: consciousness, motion and substance; continued *survival*; that which independently exists; the *'Prime Directive'* and sole purpose of all manifestation or Reality; the highest common intended motivation driving any "*Thing*" or *Life*.

existential : pertaining to existence, or some aspect or condition of existence.

exoteric : public knowledge or common understanding; the level of understanding and *Knowing* maintained by the "masses"; the opposite of *esoteric*.

experiential data : accumulated reference points we store as memory concerning our "experience" with Reality.

extant : in existence; existing.

exterior : outside of; on the outside; in *NexGen Systemology*, we mean specifically the POV of *Self* that is *'outside of'* the *Human Condition,* free of the physical and mental trappings of the Physical Universe; a metahuman range of consideration; see also *'Zu-Vision'*.

external : a force coming from outside; information received from outside sources; in *NexGen Systemology*, the objective *'Physical Universe'* existence, or *beta-existence*, that the Physical Body or *genetic vehicle* is essentially *anchored* to for its considerations of locational space-time as a dimension or POV.

extrapolate : to make an estimate of the "value" outside of the perceivable range.

extropy : *NexGen Systemology NewSpeak*—the reduction of organized spiritual systems back into a singularity of Infinity when their integrity is measured against space over time; reduction toward an infinitude; the opposite of *entropy*.

—F—

facets : an aspect, an apparent phase; one of many faces of something; a cut surface on a gem or crystal; in *NexGen Systemology*—a single perception or aspect of a memory or "*Imprint*"; any one of many ways in which a memory is recorded; perceptions associated with a painful emotional (sensation) experience and "*imprinted*" onto a metaphoric lens through which to view future similar experiences; other secondary terminals that are associated with a particular terminal, painful event or experience of loss, and which may exhibit the same encoded significance as the activating event.

faculties : abilities of the mind (individual) inherent or developed.

fallacy : a deceptive, misleading, erroneous and/or false beliefs; unsound logic; persuasions, invalidation or enforcement of Reality agreements based on authority, sympathy, bandwagon/mob mentality, vanity, ambiguity, suppression of information, and/or presentation of false dichotomies.

fate : what is brought to light or actualized as experience; the actual *course* taken to reach an end, charted end, or final *destination*; in *NexGen Systemology*, the *'fate'* of a *'Human Spirit'* (or *'Alpha Spirit'*) is determined by the choice of course taken to experience *Life*.

feedback loop : a complete and continuous circuit flow of energy or information directed as an output from a source to a target which is altered and return back to the source as an input; in *General Systemology*—the continuous process where outputs of a system are routed back as inputs to complete a circuit or loop, which may be closed or connected to other systems/circuits; in *NexGen Systemology*—the continuous process where directed *Life* energy and *Awareness* is sent back to *Self* as experience, understanding and memory to complete an energetic circuit as a loop.

flattening a wave : see "*process-out*" for definition; also see "*collapsing a wave.*"

flow : movement across (or through) a channel (or conduit); a direction of active energetic motion typically distinguished as either an *in-flow, out-flow* or *cross-flow.*

fodder : food, esp. for cattle; the raw material used to create.

forgive(ness) : to let go of resentment (against an offender, source of *Harm-ful-Act*) or give up emotional (energetic) turbulence connected to inclinations to punish; a legal pardon; to intentionally "overlook" (as opposed to "forget") the repayment of a debt or sense of something owed.

fractal : a wave-curve, geometric figure, form or pattern, with each part representative of the same characteristics as the whole; any baseline, sequence or pattern where the 'whole' is found in the 'parts' and the 'parts' contain the 'whole'; a pattern that reoccurs similarly at various scales/levels on a continuous whole; a subset of a Euclidean space explored in higher-level academic mathematics, in which fractal dimensions are found to exceed topological ones; in NexGen Systemology, a "fractal-like" description is used specifically for a pattern or form that has a reoccurring nature without regard to what level or scale it is manifest upon. Examples include the formation of crystals, tree-like patterns, the comparison of atoms to solar systems to galaxies, &tc.

fragmentation : breaking into parts and scattering the pieces; the *fractioning* of wholeness or the *fracture* of a holistic interconnected *alpha* state, favoring observational *Awareness* of perceived connectivity between parts; *discontinuity*; separation of a totality into parts; in *NexGen Systemology*, a person outside a state of *Self-Honesty* is said to be *fragmented*.

—G—

game : a strategic situation where a "player's" power of choice is employed or affected; a parameter or condition defined by purposes, freedoms and barriers (rules).

game theory : a mathematical theory of logic pertaining to strategies of maximizing gains and minimizing loses within prescribed boundaries and freedoms; a field of knowledge widely applied to human problem solving and decision-making; the application of true knowledge and logic to deduce the correct course of action given all variables and interplay of dynamic systems; logical study of decision making where "players" make choices that affect (the interests) of other "players"; an intellectual study of conflict and cooperation.

general systemology ("systematology") : a methodology of analysis and evaluation regarding the systems—their design and function; organizing systems of interrelated information-processing in order to perform a given function or pattern of functions.

genetic memory : the evolutionary, cellular and genetic (DNA) "memory" encoded into a *genetic vehicle* or *living organism* during its progression and duplication (reproduction) over millions (or billions) of years on Earth; in *NexGen Systemology*—the past-life Earth-memory carried in the genetic makeup of an organism (*genetic vehicle*) that is *independent of any* actual "spiritual memory" maintained by the *Alpha Spirit* themselves, from its own previous lifetimes on Earth and elsewhere using other *genetic vehicles* with no direct evolutionary connection to the current physical form in use.

genetic-vehicle : a physical *Life*-form; the physical (*beta*) body that is animated/controlled by the (*Alpha*) *Spirit* using a continuous *Lifeline* (ZU); a physical (*beta*) organic receptacle and catalyst for the (*Alpha*) *Self* to operate "causes" and experience "effects" within the *Physical Universe*.

gifted : attributing a special quality or ability; having exceptionally high intelligence or mental faculties.

gnosis : a *Greek* word meaning knowledge, but specifically "true knowledge"; the highest echelon of "true knowledge" accessible (or attained) only by mystical or spiritual faculties whereby actualized realizations are achieved independent of specialized education.

Gnostics : a name meaning "having knowledge" in Greek language (see also *gnosis*); an early sect of Judeo-Christian mysticism from the 1st Century AD emphasizing true knowledge by *Self-Honest* experience of metahuman and spiritual states of beingness, emphasizing defragmentation of "illusion" and overcoming of material "deception"; an esoteric proto-Systemology organization disbanded by the Roman Church as heretical.

godhood : a divine character or condition; "divinity."

gradient : a degree of partitioned ascent or descent along some scale, elevation or incline; "higher" and "lower" values in relation to one another.

GSR-Meters ("galvanic skin response"–"electropsychometer") : a *biofeedback* device used for measuring electrical resistance (in "Ohms") of the skin surface; one of many parts used in a polygraph system; a highly sensitive "Ohm-meter" with variable range, set points and amplification used to monitor electrical fluctuations of the skin surface.

—**H**—

harmful-act : a counter-survival mode of behavior or action (esp. that causes harm to one of more *Spheres of Existence*)—or—an overtly aggressive (hostile and/or destructive) action against an individual or any other *Sphere of Existence*; in *Utilitarian Systemology*—a shortsighted (serves fewest/lowest *Spheres of Existence*) intentional overtly harmful action to resolve a perceived problem; a revision of the rule for standard *Utilitarianism* for Systemology to distinguish actions which provide the least benefit to the least number of *Spheres of Existence*, or else the greatest harm to the greatest number of *Spheres of Existence*; in *moral philosophy*—an action which can be experienced by few and/or which one would not be willing to experience for themselves (*theft, slander, rape, &tc*); an iniquity or iniquitous act.

help : to assist survival of; aid continuing optimum success.

heralded : proclaimed ahead of or prior to; officially announced.

hold-back : withheld communications (esp. actions) such as "*Hold-Outs*"; intentional (or automatic) withdrawal (as opposed to reach); Self-restraint (which may eventually be enforced or automated); not reaching, acting or expressing, when one should be; an ability that is now restrained (on automatic) due to inability to withhold it on Self-determinism alone.

hold-outs : in photography, the numerous snapshots/pictures withheld from the final display or professional presentation of the event; withheld communications; in Utilitarian Systemology—energetic withdrawal and communication breaks with a *"terminal"* and its *Sphere of Existence* as a result of a *"Harmful-Act"*; unspoken or undiscovered (hidden, covert) actions that an individual withholds communications of, fearing punishment or endangerment of *Self-preservation* (*First Sphere*); the act of hiding (or keeping hidden) the truth of a *"Harmful-Act"*; a refusal to communicate with a *Pilot*; also *"Hold-Back."*

holistic : the examination of interconnected systems as encompassing something greater than the *sum* of their "parts."

Homo Novus : literally, the "new man"; the "newly elevated man" or "known man" in ancient Rome; the man who "knows (only) through himself"; in NexGen Systemology—the next spiritual and intellectual evolution of *homo sapiens* (the "modern Human Condition"), which is signified by a demonstration of higher faculties of *Self-Actualization* and clear *Awareness*.

Homo Sapiens Sapiens : the present standard-issue Human Condition; the *hominid* species and genetic-line on Earth that received modification, programming and conditioning by the *Anunnaki* race of *Alpha-Spirits*, of which early alterations contributed to various upgrades (changes) to the genetic-line, beginning approximately 450,000 years ago (*ya*) when the *Anunnaki* first appear on Earth; a species for the Human Condition on Earth that resulted from many specific *Anunnaki* "genetic" and "cultural" *interventions* at certain points of significant advancement—specifically (but not limited to) *circa* 300,000 *ya*, 200,000 *ya*, 40,000 *ya,* and 8,000 *ya*; a species of the Human Condition set for replacement by *Homo Novus*.

hostile-motivation : an *imprint* of a counter-survival action (or *"Harmful-Act"*) committed by another against Self, stored as data to justify future actions (retaliation, *&tc.*); any *Sphere of Existence* (though usually an individual) receiving the effect of a *"Harmful-Act"*; an *imprint* used to rationalize "motivation" or "justification" for committing a *"Harmful-Act"*; in systematic *games theory*—the *modus operandi* concerning "payback," "revenge" and "tit-for-tat."

hot button : something that triggers or incites an intense emotional reaction instantaneously; in *NexGen Systemology*—a slang term denoting a highly reactive *channel*, heavily *charged* with a long chain of cumulative *emotional imprinting*, typically (but not necessarily) connected to a significant or "primary" *implant*; a non-technical label, first applied during *Grade-IV Professional Piloting "Flight School"* research sessions of Spring-Summer 2020, to indicate specific circuits, channels or terminals that cause a *Seeker* to immediately react with intense emotional responses, whether in general, directed to the *Pilot*, or even at effectiveness of processing.

Human Condition : a standard default state of Human experience that is generally accepted to be the extent of its potential identity (*beingness*)—currently treated as *Homo Sapiens Sapiens,* but which is scheduled for replacement by *Homo Novus*.

humanistic psychology : a field of academic psychology approaching a holistic emphasis on *Self-Actualization* as an individual's most basic motivation; early key figures from the 20th century include: Carl Rogers, Abraham Maslow, L. Ron Hubbard, William Walker Atkinson, Deepak Chopra and Timothy Leary (to name a few).

hypothetical : operating under the assumption a certain aspect actual "is."

—I—

identification : the association of *identity* to a thing; a label or fixed data-set associated to what a thing is; association "equals" a thing, the "equals" being key; an equality of all things in a group, for example, an "apple" identified with all other "apples"; the reduction of "I-AM"-*Self* from a *Spiritual Beingness* to an "identity" of some form.

identity : the collection of energy and matter—including memory—across a "*Spiritual Timeline*" that we consider as "I" of *Self,* but the "I" is an individual and not an identification with anything other than *Self* as *Alpha-Spirit.*

identity-system : the application of the *ZU-line* as "I"—the continuous expression of *Self* as *Awareness* across a "*Spiritual Timeline*"; see "*identity.*"

illuminated : to supply with light so as to make visible or comprehensible.

imagination : the ability to create *mental imagery* in one's Personal Universe at will and change or alter it as desired; the ability to create, change and dissolve mental images on command or as an act of will; to create a mental image or have associated imagery displayed (or "conjured") in the mind that may or may not be treated as real (or memory recall) and may or may not accurately duplicate objective reality; to employ *Creative Abilities* of the Spirit that are independent of reality agreements with beta-existence.

Imaginomicon : the fourth professional publication of Mardukite Systemology, released publicly in mid- 2021; the second professional text in Grade-IV Metahuman Systemology, released as "*Liber-3D*"; contains fundamental theory of "*Spiritual Ability*" and "*Route-0*" systematic processing methodology.

immersion : plunged or sunk into; wholly surrounded by.

imperative : a high-level authoritarian command; a command triggering urgency and necessity of a certain goal or directive; see also "*Spheres of Existence*" and "*Prime Directive.*"

implant : to graft or surgically insert; to establish firmly by setting into; to instill or install a direct command or consideration in consciousness (Mind-System, &tc.); a mechanical device inserted beneath the surface/skin; in *Metahuman Systemology*, an "energetic mechanism" (linked to an Alpha-Spirit) composing a circuit-network and systematic array of energetic receptors underlying and filter-screening communication channels between the Mind-System and *Self*; an energetic construct installed upon entry of a Universe; similar to a platen or matrix or circuit-board, where each part records a specific type or quality of *emotionally encoded imprints* and other "heavily charged" *Mental Images* that are "impressed" by future encounters; a basic platform on which certain *imprints* and *Mental Images* are encoded (keyed-in) and stored (often beneath the surface of "knowing" or *Awareness* for that individual, although an implanted "command" toward certain inclinations or behavioral tendencies may be visibly observable.

imprint : to strongly impress, stamp, mark (or outline) onto a softer 'impressible' substance; to mark with pressure onto a surface; in *NexGen Systemology*, the term is used to indicate permanent Reality impressions marked by frequencies, energies or interactions experienced during periods of emotional distress, pain, unconsciousness, loss, enforcement, or something antagonistic to physical (personal) survival, all of which are are stored with other reactive response-mechanisms at lower-levels of *Awareness* as opposed to the active memory database and proactive processing center of the Mind; an experiential "memory-set" that may later resurface—be triggered or stimulated artificially —as Reality, of which similar responses will be engaged automatically; holographic-like imagery "stamped" onto consciousness as composed of energetic *facets* tied to the "snap-shot" of an experience.

imprinting incident : the first or original event instance communicated and *emotionally encoded* onto an individual's *"Spiritual Timeline"* (recorded memory from all lifetimes), which formed a permanent impression that is later used to mechanistically treat future contact on that channel; the first or original occurrence of some particular *facet* or mental image related to a certain type of *encoded response*, such as pain and discomfort, losses and victimization, and even the acts that we have taken against others along the Spiritual Timeline of our existence that caused them to also be *Imprinted*.

inadvertent : an unintended (knowingly) result caused by low-Awareness actions; applying effort (enacting change) outside Self-Honesty, leading to negligent oversights with harmful outcomes.

incarnation : a present, living or concrete form of some thing, idea or beingness; an individual lifetime or life-cycle from birth/creation to death/destruction independent of other lifetimes or cycles.

inception : the beginning, start, origin or outset.

incite : to urge on or cause; instigate; prove or stimulate into action.

indefinable : without a clear definition being currently presented.

individual : a person, lifeform, human entity or creature; a *Seeker* or potential *Seeker* is often referred to as an "individual" within Mardukite Zuism and Systemology materials.

infinite existence : "immortality."

infinitude : being infinite; quantity or quality of *Infinity*.

inhibited : withheld, held-back, discouraged or repressed from some state.

iniquities : wickedness or wicked acts ("sinful" in religious use); literal etymology, "that which is not equal"; synonymous with *Harmful-Acts*.

"in phase" : see *"phase alignment."*

insistence : repeated use of a communicated energy into a form that demands acknowledgment, is more difficult to avoid or ignore.

institution : a social standard or organizational group responsible for promoting some system or aspect in society.

intention : the directed application of Will; to intend (have "in Mind") or signify (give "significance" to) for or toward a particular purpose; in *NexGen Systemology* (from the *Standard Model*)—the spiritual activity at WILL (5.0) directed by an *Alpha Spirit* (7.0); the application of WILL as "Cause" from a higher order of Alpha Thought and consideration (6.0), which then may continue to relay communications as an "effect" in the universe.

inter-dimensional : systems that are interconnected or correlated between the Physical Universe and the Spiritual Universe—or between "dimension states" observably identified as "physical," "emotional," "psychological" and "spiritual." The only point of true interconnectivity that we can systematically determine is called *"Life"* or the POV of *Self.*

interior : inside of; on the inside; in *NexGen Systemology*, we mean specifically the POV of *Self* that is fixed to the *'internal' Human Condition,* including the *Reactive Control Center* (RCC) and Mind-System or *Master Control Center* (MCC); within *beta-existence*.

intermediate : a distinct point between two points; actions between two points.

internal : a force coming from inside; information received from inside sources; in *NexGen Systemology*, the objective *'Physical Universe'* experience of *beta-existence* that is associated with the Physical Body or *genetic vehicle* and its POV regarding sensation and perception; from inside the body; within the body.

invalidate : decrease the level or degree or *agreement* as Reality.

invest : spend on; give or devote something in exchange for a beneficial result; to endow with.

—J—

justice : observable social actions (or consequential reaction) and predetermined civic (legal) processes employed in a society or group to uphold or enforce their reality agreements concerning "*law*"; a civic authority and administrative body responsible for carrying out practical/physical responses and penalties; the words, "*just*," "*justice*" and "*justification*," all stem from the Latin "*jus*" (meaning "*morally right*," "*law, in accordance with*" and "*lawful*") or "*iustus*" (expressing what is "true," "proper," "up-right" and "justified").

—K—

"kNow" : a creative spelling and use of semantics for "*know*" and "*now*" to indicate the state of present-time actualized "Awareness" as Self (Alpha-Spirit), developed for fun dual-meaning messages made by early Mardukite Systemologists in 2008-9, such as "Live in the kNow" or "Be in the kNow"—and even "Drown in the kNow" (parodying a song featuring Matisyahu, by electronic music duo, *Crystal Method*).

knowledge : clear personal processing of informed understanding; information (data) that is actualized as effectively workable understanding; a demonstrable understanding on which we may 'set' our *Awareness*—or literally a "know-ledge."

KI : an ancient cuneiform sign designating the *'physical zone'*; the *Physical Universe*—comprised of physical matter and physical energy in action across space and observed as time; a direction of motion toward material *Continuity*, away from or subordinate to the Spiritual (*'AN'*); the physical condition of existence providing for our *beta* state of *Awareness* experienced (and interacted with) as an individual *Lifeform* from our primary Alpha state of Identity or *I-AM-Self* in the *Spiritual Universe* (*'AN'*).

kinetic : pertaining to the energy of physical motion and movement.

—L—

law : a formal codified outline (or list) of *ethical* standards regarding social participation and acceptable behavior, like a "*code*," except that it *is* enforced by civic consequences (or even "*Cosmic Law*") when not adhered to, usually with punishment coming either by the group (exclusively) or by involvement with an "outside party" or societal (legal) authority; a predictable sequence of naturally occurring events that will consistently repeat under the right conditions (such as "*Cosmic Law*" or "*Natural Law*").

learned : highly educated; possessing significant knowledge.

level : a physical or conceptual *tier* (or plane) relative to a *scale* above and below it; a significant *gradient* observable as a *foundation* (or surface) built upon and subsequent to other levels of a totality or whole; a *set* of *"parameters"* with respect to other such *sets* along a *continuum*; in *NexGen Systemology*, a *Seeker's* understanding, *Awareness* as *Self* and the formal grades of material/instruction are all treated as *"levels."*

Liber-One : First published in October 2019 as *"The Tablets of Destiny: Using Ancient Wisdom to Unlock Human Potential"* by Joshua Free; republished in the complete *Grade-III* anthology, *"The Systemology Handbook."*

Liber-Two : First published in October 2020 as *"Metahuman Destinations: Piloting the Course to Homo Novus"* by Joshua Free; an anthology of the *Grade-IV* "Professional Piloting Course," containing revised materials from *Liber-2C*, *Liber-2D* and (most of) *Liber-3C*.

Liber-Three : see *"Liber-3E."*

Liber-2B : First published in December 2019 as *"Crystal Clear: The Self-Actualization Manual & Guide to Total Awareness"* by Joshua Free; republished in the complete *Grade-III* anthology, *"The Systemology Handbook."*

Liber-2C : First published in April 2020 as *"Communication and Control of Energy & Power: The Magic of Will & Intention (Volume One)"* by Joshua Free; revision republished as an integral part of the *Grade-IV* "Professional Piloting Course," in October 2020 within *"Metahuman Destinations"* (*Liber-Two*).

Liber-2D : First published in June 2020 as *"Command of the Mind-Body Connection: The Magic of Will & Intention" (Volume Two)"* by Joshua Free; revision republished as an integral part of the *Grade-IV* "Professional Piloting Course," in October 2020 within *"Metahuman Destinations"* (*Liber-Two*).

Liber-3C : First published in July 2020 as *"Now You Know: The Truth About Universes & How You Got Stuck in One"* by Joshua Free; a discourse in the *Grade-IV* Metahuman Systemology series; a revision of one part republished in October 2020 within the *"Professional Piloting Course"* manual, *"Metahuman Destinations"* (*Liber-Two*), a revision of the remaining part republished in June 2021 within the *"Imaginomicon"* (*Liber-3D*).

Liber-3D : First published in June 2021 as *"Imaginomicon: The Gateway to Higher Universes (A Grimoire for the Human Spirit)"* by Joshua Free; a manual completing the *Grade-IV* (Metahuman Systemology) professional series with a treatment of "Wizard Level-0."

Liber-3E (Liber-Three) : First published in 00000 as *"The Way of the Wizard: Utilitarian Systemology (A New Metahuman Ethic)"* by Joshua Free; a professional manual bridging *Grade-IV* (Metahuman Systemology, *Wizard Level-0*) with *Grade-V* (Spiritual Systemology, *Wizard Level-1*).

localized : brought together and confined to a particular place.

logic : philosophical science of correct *reasoning*.

logic equations : using symbols and basic mathematical logic to establish the validity of statements or to see how a variable within a system will change the result; a basic demonstration of proportion or relationship between variables in a system.

logistics : pertaining to the movement or transportation between locations.

—M—

macrocosmic : taking examples and system demonstrations at one level and applying them as a larger demonstration of a relatively higher level or unseen dimension.

malefactor : a person that knowingly commits *Harmful-Acts*; a source of frequent turbulence and destruction on a system.

manifestation : something brought into existence.

Marduk : founder of Babylonia; patron Anunnaki "god" of Babylon.

Mardukite Zuism : a Mesopotamian-themed (Babylonian-oriented) religious philosophy and tradition applying the spiritual technology based on *Arcane Tablets* in combination with "Tech" from *NexGen Systemology*; first developed in the New Age underground by Joshua Free in 2008 and realized publicly in 2009 with the formal establishment of the *Mardukite Chamberlains*. The text *"Tablets of Destiny"* is a cross-over from Mardukite Zuism (and Mesopotamian Neopaganism) toward higher spiritual applications of Systemology.

Master-Control-Center (MCC) : a perfect computing device to the extent of the information received from "lower levels" of sensory experience/perception; the proactive communication system of the *"Mind"*; a relay point of active *Awareness* along the Identity's *ZU-line*, which is responsible for maintaining basic *Self-Honest Clarity* of *Knowingness* as a *seat of consciousness* between the *Alpha-Spirit* and the secondary *"Reactive Control Center"* of a *Lifeform* in *beta existence*; the Mind-center for an *Alpha-Spirit* to actualize cause in the *beta existence*; the analytical *Self-Determined* Mind-center of an *Alpha-Spirit used* to project *Will* toward the genetic body; the point of contact between *Spiritual Systems* and the *beta existence*; presumably the *"Third Eye"* of a being connected directly to the *I-AM-Self*, which is responsible for *determining* Reality at any time; in *NexGen Systemology*, this is plotted at (4.0) on the continuity model of the *ZU-line*.

"Master Grades" : literary materials by Joshua Free (written between 1995 and 2019) revised and compiled for the "Mardukite Academy of Systemology" instructional grades—"Route of Magick & Mysticism" (*Grade I, Part A*), "Route of Druidism & Dragon Legacy" (*Grade I, Part D*), "Route of Mesopotamian Mysteries" (Grade II) and "Route of Mardukite Systemology" or "Pathway to Self-Honesty" (*Grade III*).

maxim : the greatest or highest *premise* of a paradigm or particular literary *treatment*; a concise rule for conducting action or treating some subject; the most relevant "proverbial adage" applicable.

MCC : see "*Master-Control-Center.*"

mental image : a subjectively experienced "picture" created and imagined into being by the Alpha-Spirit (or at lower levels, one of its automated mechanisms) that includes all perceptible *facets* of totally immersive scene, which may be forms originated by an individual, or a "facsimile-copy" ("snap-shot") of something seen or encountered; a duplication of wave-forms in one's Personal Universe as a "picture" that mirror an "external" Universe experience, such as an *Imprint*.

Mesopotamia : land between Tigris and Euphrates River; modern-day Iraq; the primary setting for ancient *Sumerian* and *Babylonian* traditions thousands of years ago, including activities and records of the *Anunnaki.*

metahumanism : an applied philosophy of *transhumanism* with an emphasis on "spiritual technologies" as opposed to "external" ones; a new state or evolution of the *Human Condition* achievable on planet Earth, rooted in *Self-Honesty*, whereby individuals are operating *exterior* to considerations that are fixed exclusively to the *genetic vehicle* (Human Body) and independent of the *emotional encoding* and *associative programming* typical of the present standard-issue *Human Condition.*

Metahuman Destinations : the third professional publication of Mardukite Systemology, released publicly in October 2020; the first professional text in Grade-IV Metahuman Systemology, released as "*Liber-Two*" and containing materials from *Liber-2C, Liber-2D* and *Liber-3C*; contains fundamental theory of "*Professional Piloting*" and "*Route-3*" systematic processing methodology.

meter : a device used to measure; see *GSR-Meter.*

methodology : a complete system of applications, methods, principles and rules to compose a *'systematic'* paradigm as a "whole"—esp. a field of philosophy or science.

"mind's eye" : following semantics of archaic esoterica, the point where "mental pictures" (and senses) are generated that define what an individual believes they are experiencing in present time; activities or phenomenon described in archaic esoterica as the "Third-Eye" (or actualized MCC) where the *Alpha-Spirit* directly interacts with the organic *genetic vehicle* in *beta-existence*; in the semantics of basic Mardukite Zuism and Hermetic Philosophy, *Self-directed* activity on the plane of "mental consciousness" between "spiritual consciousness" of the *Alpha-Spirit* and "physical/emotional consciousness" of the *genetic vehicle*; *NexGen* 'slang' used to describe "consciousness activity" *Self-directed* by an actualized WILL.

misappropriated : put into use incorrectly; to apply ineffectively or as unintended by design or definition.

missed hold-out : an individual's *Hold-Out* that someone else nearly found out about, or which leaves the individual wondering if they did actually find out or not; undisclosed event when someone else's behavior or speech restimulates emotional-response-reactions ("worry" *&tc.*) about potential discovery of a withheld *Harmful-Act* or *Hold-Out*; in *systematic processing*, a Seeker's "held-out" (hidden) data that they expect to be discovered during a *session*, but which is *missed* by the Pilot.

morals : widely held culturally conditioned (socially learned) ethical standards of conduct used to "judge" *rightness* from *wrongness* of an individual's character, personality or actions (which may or may not be intellectually and emotionally influenced by "local" religious customs, taboos and *dogma*; basic social reality agreements determining "proper conduct" and "right actions" (behavior) based on civic *laws*, social *codes* and religious *doctrines* of a particular society or group and its own cultural experiences of *Reality.*

motor functions : internal mechanisms that allow a body to move.

—N—

Nabu : the *Anunnaki* "god of wisdom, writing and knowledge" for Babylonian (Mardukite) Tradition.

negligible : so small or trifle that it may be disregarded.

neophyte : a beginning initiate or novice to a particular sect or methodology; novitiate or entry-level grade of training, study and practice of an esoteric order or mystical lodge (fellowship).

neurotransmitter : a chemical substance released at a physiological level (of the genetic vehicle) that bridges communication of energetic transmission between the *Mind-Body* systems, using the "nervous system" of the physical body; biochemical amino acids and peptides (neuropeptides), hormones, &tc.

NexGen Systemology : a modern tradition of applied religious philosophy and spiritual technology based on *Arcane Tablets* in combination with "*general systemology*" and "*games theory*" developed in the New Age underground by Joshua Free in 2011 as an advanced futurist extension of the "*Mardukite Chamberlains*"; also referred to as "*Mardukite Systemology,*" "*Metahuman Systemology*" and "*Spiritual Systemology.*"

—O—

objective : concerning the "external world" and attempts to observe Reality independent of personal "subjective" factors.

occulted / to occult : hidden by or secreted away; to hide something from view; otherwise *occlude,* to shut out, shut in, or block; to *eclipse,* or leave out of view.

one-to-one : see *"A-for-A."*

optimum : the most favorable or ideal conditions for the best result; the greatest degree of result under specific conditions.

orchestration : to arrange or compose the performance of a system.

organic : as related to a physically living organism or carbon-based life form; energy-matter condensed into form as a focus or POV of Spiritual Life Energy (*ZU*) as it pertains to beta-existence of *this* Physical Universe (*KI*).

oscillation-alternation : a particular type of (or fluctuation) between two relative states, conditions or degrees; a wave-action between two degrees, such as is described in the action of the *pendulum effect*; a flux or wave-like energy in motion, across space, calculable as time; in systematic processing, alternation is the shift between two direction flows on a circuit channel, such as *inflow* and *outflow*, or between two types of processing, such as *objective* and *subjective*; alternation of a POV creates "space."

—P—

pantheism : religious philosophies that observe God as inherent within all aspects of the Physical Universe.

paradigm : an all-encompassing *standard* by which to view the world and *communicate* Reality; a standard model of reality-systems used by the Mind to filter, organize and interpret experience of Reality.

parameters : a defined range of possible variables within a model, spectrum or continuum; the extent of communicable reach capable within a system or across a distance; the defined or imposed limitations placed on a system or the functions within a system; the extent to which a Life or "thing" can *be, do* or *know* along any channel within the confines of a specific system or spectrum of existence.

paramount : the most important; of utmost importance; "above all else."

participation : being part of the action; affecting the result.

patter : fast-talk; a manner of quickly delivered speech/words, esp. used to persuade or sell something.

patterns (probability patterns) : observation of cycles and tendencies to predict a causal relationship or determine the actual condition or flow of dynamic energy using a holistic systemology to understand Life, Reality and Existence as opposed to isolating or excluding perceived parts as being mutually separate from other perceived parts.

patron god : the most sacred deity of a region or city, of which most temples and religious services are directed; the personal deity of an individual.

PCL : see *"processing command line."*

perception : internalized processing of data received by the *senses*; to become *Aware of* via the senses.

personality (program) : the total composite picture an individual "identifies" themselves with; the accumulated sum of material and mental mass by which an individual experiences as their timeline; a "beta-personality" is mainly attached to the identity of a particular physical body and the total sum of its own genetic memory in combination with the data stores and pictures maintained by the Alpha Spirit; a "true personality" is the Alpha Spirit as Self completely defragmented of all erroneous limitations and barriers to consideration, belief, manifestation and intention.

perturbation : the deviation from a natural state, fixed motion, or orbit system caused by another external system; disturbing or disquieting the serenity of an existent state; inciting observable apparent action using indirect or outside actions or 'forces'; the introduction of a new element or facet that disturbs equilibrium of a standard system; the "butterfly effect"; in *NexGen Systemology*, *'perturbation'* is a necessary condition for the *ZU-line* to function as a *Standard Model* of actual *'monistic continuity'*—which is a *Lifeforce* singularity expressed along a spectrum with potential interactions at each degree from any source; the influence of a degree in one state by activities of another state that seem independent, but which are actually connected directly at some higher degree, even if not apparently observed.

phase (identification) : in *NexGen Systemology,* a pattern of personality or identity that is assumed as the POV from *Self*; personal identification with artificial "personality packages"; an individual assuming or taking characteristics of another individual (often unknowingly as a response-mechanisms); also *"phase alignment."*

phase alignment or *"in phase"* : to be in synch or mutually synchronized, in step or aligned properly with something else in order to increase the total strength value; in *NexGen Systemology,* alignment or adjustment of *Awareness* with a particular identity, space or time; perfect *defragmentation* would mean being "in phase" as *Self* fully conscious and Aware as an Alpha-Spirit *in* present *space* and *time*, free of synthetic personalities.

philanthropy : charitable; the intention (or programmed desire) to generously provide personal wealth and service to the well-being and continued existence of others.

physics : regarding data obtained by a material science of observable motions, forces and bodies, including their apparent interaction, in the Physical Universe (specific to this *beta-existence*).

physiology : a material science of observable biological functions and mechanics of living organisms, including codification and study of identifiable parts and apparent systematic processes (specific to agreed upon makeup of the *genetic vehicle* for this *beta-existence*).

pilfering : to steal in small quantities; petty theft.

pilot : a professional steersman responsible for healthy functional operation of a ship toward a specific destination; in *NexGen Systemology*, an intensive trained individual qualified to specially apply *Systemology Processing* to assist other *Seekers* on the *Pathway*.

ping : a short, high pitched ring, chime or noise that alerts to the presence of something; in computer systems, a query sent on a network or line to another terminal in order to determine if there is a connection to it; in *NexGen System- ology*, the sudden somatic twinge or pain or discomfort that is felt as a sensation in the body when a particular terminal (lifeform, object, concept) is 'brought to mind' or contacted on a personal communication channel-circuit; the accompanying sensations and mental images that are experienced as an automatic-response to the presence of some channel or terminal.

player (game theory) : an individual that is making decisions in a game and/or is affected by decisions others are making in the game, especially if those other-determined decisions now affect the possible choices.

point-of-view (POV) : a point to view from; an opinion or attitude as ex- pressed from a specific identity-phase; a specific standpoint or vantage-point; a definitive manner of consideration specific to an individual phase or iden- tity; a place or position affording a specific view or vantage; circumstances and programming of an individual that is conducive to a particular response, consideration or belief-set (paradigm); a position (consideration) or place (loc- ation) that provides a specific view or perspective (subjective) on experience (of the objective).

postulate : to put forward as truth; to suggest or assume an existence *to be*; to provide a basis of reasoning and belief; a basic theory accepted as fact; in *NexGen Systemology*, "Alpha-Thought"—the top-most decisions or considera- tions made by the Alpha-Spirit regarding the "*is-ness*" (what things "are") about energy-matter and space-time.

potentiality : the total "sum" (collective amount) of "latent" (dormant— present but not apparent) capable or possible realizations; used to describe a state or condition of what has not yet manifested, but which can be influenced and predicted based on observed patterns and, if referring to beta-existence, Cosmic Law.

POV : see "*point-of-view*" and/or "*POV Processing.*"

POV processing : a methodology of *Grade-IV Metahuman Systemology* em- phasizing systematic processing toward realizations that improve a Seeker's willingness to manage a present POV and associated *phases*, their ability to transfer POVs freely, increased tolerance to experiences (or encounters) with any other viewpoint, and finally, an actualized realization that a POV is not one-to-one with *Beingness* of *Self*; an extension of *creativeness processing* and "Wizard Level" training that systematically handles *Awareness* of "points" and "spots" in space, from which an Alpha-Spirit may place its own viewpoint of a dimension or Universe—also a prerequisite to upper-route practices such as "*Zu-Vision*" and "*Backtrack.*"

precedent : a matter which precedes or goes before another in importance.

precipitate : to actively hasten or quicken into existence.

preconception : to assign values or evaluate a reaction or response to a past "imprint" of something and treat it as present knowledge or experience.

prehistoric : any time before human history is properly recorded in writing; prior to c. 4000 B.C.

premise : a basis or statement of fact from which conclusions are drawn.

presence : the quality of some thing (energy/matter) being "present" in space-time; personal orientation of *Self* as an *Awareness* (*POV*) located in present space-time (environment) and communicating with extant energy-matter.

prevalent : of wide extent; an extensive or largely accepted aspect or current state.

Prime Directive : a "spiritual" implant program that installs purposes and goals into the personal experience of a Universe, esp. any *Beta-Existence* (whether a 'Games Universe' or a 'Prison Universe'); intellectually treated as the "Universal Imperative" in some schools of moral philosophy; comparable to "Universal Law" or "Cosmic Ordering."

probability : the causal likelihood for something to result, "effect" or manifest in and as a certain way, manner or degree, based on "observed evaluation" of programming and tendencies that follow Cosmic Law.

"process-out" or **"flatten a wave"** : to reduce *emotional encoding* of an *imprint* to zero; to dissolve a *wave-form* or *thought-formed* "solid" such as a "*belief*"; to completely run a *process* to its end, thereby *flattening* any previously "*collapsed-waves*" or *fragmentation* that is obstructing the *clear channel* of *Self-Awareness*; also referred to as "processing-out"; to discharge all previously held emotionally encoded imprinting or erroneous programming and beliefs that otherwise fix the free flow (wave) to a particular pattern, solid or concrete "*is*" form.

processing, systematic : the inner-workings or "through-put" result of systems; in *NexGen Systemology*, a methodology of applied spiritual technology used toward personal Self-Actualization; methods of selective directed attention, communicated language and associative imagery that targets an increase in personal control of the human condition.

processing command line (PCL) or **command line** : a directed input; a specific command using highly selective language for *Systemology Processing*; a predetermined directive statement (cause) intended to focus concentrated attention (effect).

projecting awareness : sending out (motion) or radiating "*consciousness*" from *Self* ("I") to another POV.

proportional : having a direct relationship or mutual interaction with.

protest : a response-communication objecting an enforcement or a rejection of a prior communication; an effort to cancel, rewrite or destroy the existence or "is-ness" (what something "is") of a previous creation or communication; unwillingness to be the Point-of-View of effect or (receipt-point) for a communication.

Proto-Indo-European (PIE) : in Linguistic-Semantic Sciences, a hypothetical single-source Eurasian root language (c.4500 B.C.) demonstrating common origins of many "word-roots" found in European languages.

psychometric evaluation : the relative measurement of personal ability, mental (psychological/thought) faculties, and effective processing of information and external stimulus data; a scale used in "applied psychology" to evaluate and predict human behavior.

—R—

rationality / reasoning (game theory) : the extent to which a player seeks to play (make decisions, &tc.) in order to maximize the gains (or else survival) achievable within any given game conditions; the ability and willingness of an individual to reach toward conditions that promote the highest level of survival and existence and make the best choices and moves to see the desired goal manifest.

reactive control center (RCC) : the secondary (reactive) communication system of the "*Mind*"; a relay point of *Awareness* along the Identity's *ZU-line*, which is responsible for engaging basic motors, biochemical processes and any *programmed automated responses* of a living *beta* organism; the reactive Mind-Center of a living organism relaying communications of *Awareness* between causal experience of *Physical Systems* and the "*Master Control Center*"; it presumably stores all emotional encoded imprints as fragmentation of "chakra" frequencies of *ZU* (within the range of the "*psychological/emotive systems*" of a being), which it may *react* to as Reality at any time; in *NexGen Systemology*, this is plotted at (2.0) on the continuity model of the *ZU-line*.

reality : see "*agreement.*"

realization : the clear perception of an understanding; a consideration or understanding on what is "actual"; to make "real" or give "reality" to so as to grant a property of "beingness" or "being as it is"; the state or instance of coming to an *Awareness*; in *NexGen Systemology*, "gnosis" or true knowledge achieved during *systematic processing*; achievement of a new (or "higher") cognition, true knowledge or perception of Self; a consideration of reality or assignment of meaning.

receptacle : a device or mechanism designed to contain and store a specific type of aspect or thing; a container meant to receive something.

recursive : repeating by looping back onto itself to form continuity; *ex.* the "Infinity" symbol is recursive.

relative : an apparent point, state or condition treated as distinct from others.

religion : a concise spiritual *paradigm*, set of beliefs and practices regarding "Divinity," "Infinite Beingness"—or else, "God"—as representative symbol of the *Eighth Sphere of Existence* for *Beta-Existence* (or else "Infinity").

relinquish : to give up control, command or possession of.

repetitively : to repeat "over and over" again; or else "repetition."

responsibility : the *ability* to *respond*; the extent of mobilizing *power* and *understanding* an individual maintains as *Awareness* to enact *change*; the proactive ability to *Self-direct* and make decisions independent of an outside authority.

resurface : to return to (or bring up to) the "surface" of that which has previously been submerged; in *NexGen Systemology*—relating specifically to processes where a *Seeker* recalls blocked energy stored covertly as emotional "*imprints*" (by the RCC) so that it may be effectively defragmented from the "*ZU-line*" (by the MCC).

rhetoric : the art, study or skilled craft of using language eloquently (words, writing, speech preparation); expert communication using "words"; effectively using language for persuasive communication.

Route-0 : a specific methodology from *SOP-2C* denoting "*Creativeness Processing*," as described in the text "*Imaginomicon*" (*Liber-3D*).

Route-0E : a specific methodology (expanding on *Route-0* from *Liber-3D*) denoting "*Conceptual Processing*" applied to *Ethics Beta-Defragmentation*, as described in the text "*Way of the Wizard*" (*Liber-Three* or *Liber-3E*).

Route-1 : a specific methodology from *SOP-2C* denoting "*Resurfacing Processing*," as described in the text "*Tablets of Destiny*" (*Liber-One*) as "RR-SP" (and reissued in "*The Systemology Handbook*").

Route-2 : a specific methodology from *SOP-2C* denoting "*Analytical-Recall Processing*," as described in the text "*Crystal Clear*" (*Liber-2B*) as "AR-SP" (and reissued in "*The Systemology Handbook*").

Route-3 : a specific methodology from *SOP-2C* denoting "*Communication-Circuit Processing*," as described in the text "*Metahuman Destinations*" (*Liber-Two*); also the basis for *SOP-2C* routine.

Route-3E : a specific methodology (expanding on *Route-3* from *SOP-2C*) denoting "*Ethics Processing*," as described in the text "*The Way of the Wizard*" (*Liber-Three* or *Liber-3E*); also related to "Standard Procedure R-3E."

—S—

scions : a descendant or offspring; an offshoot or branch.

Seeker : an individual on the *Pathway to Self-Honesty*; a practitioner of Mar dukite *Systemology* or *NexGen Systemology Processing* that is working toward *Spiritual Ascension.*

Self-actualization : bringing the full potential of the Human spirit into Reality; expressing full capabilities and creativeness of the *Alpha-Spirit.*

Self-determinism : the freedom to act, clear of external control or influence; the personal control of Will to direct intention.

Self-evaluation : see *"psychometric evaluation."*

Self-honesty : the basic or original *alpha* state of *being* and *knowing*; clear and present total *Awareness* of-and-as *Self,* in its most basic and true proactive expression of itself as *Spirit* or *I-AM*—free of artificial attachments, perceptive filters and other emotionally-reactive or mentally-conditioned programming imposed on the human condition by the systematized physical world; the ability to experience existence without judgment.

self-sustained : self-supported; self-sufficient; independent.

semantics : the *meaning* carried in *language* as the *truth* of a "thing" represented, *A-for-A*; the *effect* of language on *thought* activity in the Mind and physical behavior; language as *symbols* used to represent a concept, "thing" or "solid."

semantic-set : the implied meaning behind any groupings of words or symbols used to define a specific paradigm.

sensation : an external stimulus received by internal sense organs (receptors/sensors); sense impressions.

sentient : a living organism with consciousness or intelligence; a "thinking" or "reasoning" being that perceives information from the "senses."

simulacrum : an tangible likeness, image, facsimile or superficial representation that is similar to or resembles someone or something else; in *NexGen Systemology,* any *genetic vehicle* or physical body is considered a reflective "simulacrum" of, and used as a "vessel-shell" by, the *Alpha-Spirit* or *Self* (I-AM), which otherwise maintains no true finite locatable form in *beta-existence.*

sine-wave : the *frequency* and amplitude of a quantified (calculable) *vibration* represented on a graph (graphically) as smooth repetitive *oscillation* of a *waveform*; a *waveform* graphed for demonstration—otherwise represented in *NexGen Systemology* logic equations as 'Wf,' or in mathematics as the *'function of x'* (*fx*); graphically representing arcs (*parameters*) of a circular *continuity* on a *continuum*; in the *Standard Model of NexGen Systemology,* the actual 'wave vibration' graphically displayed on an otherwise static *ZU-line* (of Infinity) is a *'sine-wave'.*

singularity : in general use, "to be singular," but our working definition suggests the opposite of individuality (contrary to most dictionaries); in upper-level sciences, a "zero-point" where a particular property or attribute is mathematically treated as "infinite" (such as the "black-hole" phenomenon), or else where apparently dissimilar qualities of all existing aspects (or individuals) share a "singular" expression, nature or quality; additionally, in *NexGen Systemology*, a hypothetical zero-point when apparent values of all parts in a Universe are equal to all other parts before it collapses; in *Transhumanism*, a hypothetical "runaway reaction" in technology, when it becomes self-aware, self-propagating, self-upgradable and self-sustainable, and replaces human effort of advancement or even makes continued human existence impossible; also, technological efforts to maintain an artificial immortality of the Human Condition on a digital mainframe.

slate : a hard thin flat surface material used for writing on; a chalk-board, which is a large version of the original wood-framed writing slate, named for the rock-type it was made from.

somatic : specifically pertaining to the physical body, its sensations and response actions or behaviors as separate from a "Mind-System"; also *"pings."*

SOP-2C : *Standard Operating Procedure #2C* or *Systemology Operating Procedure #2C*; a standardized procedural formula introduced in materials for *"Metahuman Destinations"* (*Liber-Two*); a regimen or outline for standard delivery of systematic processing used by *Systemology Pilots* and *Mardukite Ministers*; a procedure outline of systematic processing, which includes applications of *"Route-1," "Route-2," "Route-3"* and *"Route-0"* as taught for *Grade-IV Professional Piloting*.

space : a viewpoint or *Point-of-View* (POV) extended from any point out toward a dimension or dimensions; the consideration of a point or spot as an *anchor* or *corner* in addition to others, which collectively define parameters of a dimensional plane; the field of energy/matter mass created as a result of communication and control in action and measured as time (wave-length), such as "distance" between points (or peaks on a wave).

spectrum : a broad range or array as a continuous series or sequence; defined parts along a singular continuum; in physics, a gradient arrangement of visible colored bands diffracted in order of their respective wavelengths, such as when passing *White Light* through a *prism*.

Spheres of Existence (dynamic systems) : a series of *eight* concentric circles, rings or spheres (each larger than the former) that is overlaid onto the Standard Model of Beta-Existence to demonstrate the dynamic systems of existence extending out from the POV of Self (often as a "body") at the *First Sphere*; these are given in the basic eightfold systems as: *Self, Home/Family, Groups, Humanity, Life on Earth, Physical Universe, Spiritual Universe* and *Infinity-Divinity*.

spiritual timeline : a continuous stream of moment-to-moment *Mental Images* (or a record of experiences) that defines the "past" of a spiritual being (or *Alpha-Spirit*) and which includes impressions (*imprints, &tc.*) form all life-incarnations and significant spiritual events the being has encountered; in NexGen Systemology, also *"backtrack."*

standard issue : equally dispensed to all without consideration.

standard model : a fundamental *structure* or symbolic construct used to evaluate a complete *set* in *continuity* relative to itself and variable to all other *dynamic systems* as graphed or calculated by *logic*.

Standard Model, The (systemology) : in *NexGen Systemology*—our existential and cosmological *standard model* or cabbalistic model; a "*monistic continuity model*" demonstrating *total system* interconnectivity "above" and "below" observation of any apparent *parameters*; the original presentation of the *ZU-line*, represented as a singular vertical (y-axis) waveform in space across dimensional levels or Universes (*Spheres of Existence*) without charting any specific movement across a dimensional time-graph x-axis; The Standard Model of Systemology represents the basic workable synthesis of common denominators in models explored throughout Grade-I and Grade-II material.

static : characterized by a fixed or stationary condition; having no apparent change, movement or fluctuation.

stoicism : pertaining to the school of "stoic" philosophy, distinguished by calm mental attitudes, freedom from desire/passion and essentially any emotional fluctuation.

sub-zones : at ranges "below" which we are representing or which is readily observable for current purposes.

successively : what comes after; forward into the future.

succumb : to give way, or give in to, a relatively stronger superior force.

Sumerian : ancient civilization of *Sumer*, founded in Mesopotamia c. 5000 B.C.

superfluous : excessive; unnecessary; needless.

superstition : knowledge accepted without good reason.

surefooted : proceeding surely; not likely to stumble or fall.

symbiotic : pertaining to the closeness, proximity and affinity between two beings that are in mutual communication or maintaining mutually validating interactions.

symbol : a concentrated mass with associated meaning or significance.

sympathy : a sensation, feeling or emotion—of anger, fear, sorrow and/or pity—that is a *personal reaction* to the misfortune and failure of another being.

syntax : from the Greek, "to arrange together"; the semantic meaning that words convey when combined together; the manner in which words are arranged together to provide an understandable meaning, such as following the structure for a sentence.

system : from the Greek, "to set together"; to set or arrange things or data together so as to form an orderly understanding of a "whole"; also a *'method'* or *'methodology'* as an orderly standard of use or application of such data ar ranged together.

systematization : to arrange into systems; to systematize or make systematic.

Systemology : see *"NexGen Systemology."*

Systemology Procedure 1-8-0 : advanced spiritual technology within our Systemology, which applies a methodology of systematic practice for experiencing: (1) Self-Awareness, (8) Nothingness and (0) Beingness, introduced for "Crystal Clear" but expanded on for *"Imaginomicon"*; *'one-eight-zero'* is included in, but not the same as application *'one-eighty'*—or else the *Beta-Defrag-Intensive* called *"SOP-180"* or *"Systemology-180."*

Systemology-180 : an intensive systematic processing routine employing all *Grade-III*, *Grade-IV* and cross-over *Wizard-Level* work to date; the total sum of all effective philosophical and spiritual applications necessary to professionally *Pilot* a *Seeker* to reach a stable point of *Self-Honesty* and basic *Beta-Defragmentation*, as a prerequisite to treating *"Actualized-Ascension Technologies"* (*A.T.*) of upper-level *Wizard Grades*.

systems theory : see *"general systematology"*

—T—

Tablets of Destiny : the first professional publication of Mardukite Systemology, released publicly in October 2019; the first professional text in Grade-III Mardukite Systemology, released as *"Liber-One"* and reissued in the Grade-III Master Edition *"Systemology Handbook"*; contains fundamental theory of the *"Standard Model"* and *"Route-1"* systematic processing methodology.

teleological (teleology) : using the end-goal or purpose of something as an explanation of its function (rather than being a function of its cause); example—Aristotle wrote (in his discourse, *"Metaphysics"*) that the intrinsic (inherent or true nature) *telos* of an 'acorn' is to become a fully formed 'oak tree'; the ends are an underlying purpose, not the cause (also known as "final cause"), or else the famous phrase: "the ends justify the means."

terminal (node) : a point, end or mass on a line; a point or connection for closing an electric circuit, such as a post on a battery terminating at each end of its own systematic function; any end point or 'termination' on a line; a point of connectivity with other points; in systems, any point which may be treated as a contact point of interaction; anything that may be distinguished as an 'is' and is therefore a 'termination point' of a system or along a flow-line which may interact with other related systems it shares a line with; a point of interaction with other points.

thought-experiment : from the German, *Gedankenexperiment*; logical *considerations* or mental models used to concisely visualize consequences (cause-effect sequences) within the context of an imaginary or hypothetical scenario; using faculties of the Mind's Eye to *Imagine* things accurately with *considera-*

tions that *have not* already been consciously experienced in *beta-existence*.

thought-form : apparent *manifestation* or existential *realization* of *Thought-waves* as "solids" even when only apparent in Reality-agreements of the Observer; the treatment of *Thought-waves* as permanent *imprints* obscuring *Self-Honest Clarity* of *Awareness* when reinforced by emotional experience as actualized "thought-formed solids" ("*beliefs*") in the Mind; energetic patterns that "surround" the individual.

thought-habit : reoccurring modes of thought or repeated "self-talk"; essentially "self-hypnosis" resulting in a certain state.

thought-wave or **wave-form** : a proactive *Self-directed action* or reactive-response *action* of *consciousness*; the *process* of *thinking* as demonstrated in *wave-form*; the *activity* of *Awareness* within the range of *thought* *vibrations/frequencies* on the existential *Life-continuum* or *ZU-line*.

threshold : a doorway, gate or entrance point; the degree to which something is to produce an effect within a certain state or condition; the point in which a condition changes from one to the next.

thwarted : to successfully oppose or prevent a purpose from actualizing.

tier : a series of rows or levels, one stacked immediately before or atop another.

time : observation of cycles in action; motion of a particle, energy or wave across space; intervals of action related to other intervals of action as observed in Awareness; a measurable wave-length or frequency in comparison to a static state; the consideration of variations in space.

timeline : plotting out history in a linear (line) model to indicate instances (experiences) or demonstrate changes in state (space) as measured over time; a singular conception of continuation of observed time as marked by event-intervals and changes in energy and matter across space.

tipping point : a definitive "point" when a series of small changes (to a system) are significant enough to be *realized* or *cause* a larger, more significant change; the critical "point" (in a system) beyond which a significant change takes place or is observed; the "point" at which changes that cross a specific "threshold" reach a noticeably new state or development.

transhumanism : a social science and applied philosophy concerning the next evolved state of the "*Human Condition*,"; progress in two potential directions, either "spiritual" technologies advancing *Self* as an "Alpha-Spirit," or the direction of "external"-"physical" technologies that modify or eliminate characteristics of the *Body*; a theme describing contemporary application of material sciences emphasizing only "physical" and "genetic" parts of the *Human* experience, such as brain activity, cell-life extension and space travel; *NexGen Systemology* recently began distinguishing its emphasis on "spiritual technology" as "*metahumanism*."

transmit : to send forth data along some line of communication; to move a point across a distance.

traumatic encoding : information received when the sensory faculties of an organism are "shocked" into learning it as an "emotionally" encoded *Imprint*; a duplicated facsimile-copy or *Mental Image* of severe misfortune, violent threats, pain and coercion, which is then categorized, stored and reactively retrieved based exclusively on its emotional *facets*.

treat / treatment : an act, manner or method of handling or dealing with someone, something or some type of situation; to apply a specific process, procedure or mode of action toward some person, thing or subject; use of a specific substance, regimen or procedure to make an existing condition less severe; also, a written presentation that handles a subject in a specific manner.

turbulence : a quality or state of distortion or disturbance that creates irregularity of a flow or pattern; the quality or state of aberration on a line (such as ragged edges) or the emotional "turbulent feelings" attached to a particular flow or terminal node; a violent, haphazard or disharmonious commotion (such as in the ebb of gusts and lulls of wind action).

—U—

unconscious : a state when *Awareness* as *Self* is removed totally from the equation of *Life* experience, though it continues to be recorded in lower-level response mechanisms (fixed to a simulacrum or genetic vehicle) for later retrieval.

undefiled : to remain intact, untouched or unchanged; to be left in an original "virgin" state.

understanding : a clear 'A-for-A' duplication of a communication as 'knowledge', which may be comprehended and retained with its significance assigned in relation to other 'knowledge' treated as a 'significant understanding'; the "grade" or "level" that a knowledge base is collected and the manner in which the data is organized and evaluated.

Utopian Philosophy : a social philosophy and ethic for (primarily) independent rural (country-dwelling or pagan) living communities that adopt a neo-Utilitarian moral philosophy (as suggested by Systemology) to enhance the "greater happiness" and "Ascension" of all participants.

—V—

validation : reinforcement of agreements or considerations as "real."

vantage : a point, place or position that offers an ideal viewpoint (POV).

Venn diagram : a diagram for symbolic logic using circles to represent sets and their systematic relationship; popularized by logician *John Venn*.

verbatim : precisely reproduced or duplicated communication *one-to-one* or "word"-for-"word" (*'A-for-A'*).

via : literally, "by way of"; from the Latin, meaning "way."

vibration : effects of motion or wave-frequency as applied to any system.

viewpoint : see *"point-of-view" (POV)*.

vizier : a high ranking official; a minister-of-state.

—W—

wave-form : see *"sine-wave."*

wave-function collapse : see *"collapsing a wave."*

Western Civilization : modern contemporary culture, ideals, values and technology, particularly of Europe and North America as distinguished by growing urbanization, industrialization, and inspired by a history of rebellion to strong religious and political indoctrination.

will *or* **WILL** (5.0) : in *NexGen Systemology* (from the *Standard Model*), the Alpha-ability at "5.0" of a Spiritual Being (*Alpha Spirit*) at "7.0" to apply *intention* as "Cause" from consideration or Alpha-Thought at "6.0" that is superior to "beta-thoughts" that only manifest as reactive "effects" below "4.0" and *interior* to the *Human Condition*.

willingness : the state of conscious Self-determined ability and interest (directed attention) to *Be, Do* or *Have*; a Self-determined consideration to reach, face up to (*confront*) or manage some "mass" or energy; the extent to which an individual considers themselves able to participate, act or communicate along some line, to put attention or intention on the line, or to produce (create) an effect.

—Z—

ziggurat : religious temples of ancient Mesopotamia; stepped-pyramids and towers used for spiritual and religious purposes by Sumerians and Babylonians, many of which are presented as seven tiers, levels or terraces representing "Seven Gates" (or "7 Veils") of existence, separating material continuity of the Earth Plane from "Infinity" ("8").

ZU : the ancient Sumerian cuneiform sign for the archaic verb—*"to know," "knowingness"* or *"awareness"*; in *Mardukite Zuism and Systemology*, the active energy/matter of the "Spiritual Universe" (AN) experienced as a *Lifeforce* or *consciousness* that imbues living forms extant in the "Physical Universe" (KI); *"Spiritual Life Energy"*; energy demonstrated by the WILL of an actualized *Alpha-Spirit* in the "Spiritual Universe" (AN), which impinges its

Awareness into the Physical Universe (KI), animating/controlling *Life* for its experience of *beta-existence* along an individual Alpha-Spirit's personal *Identity-continuum*, called a *ZU-line*.

Zu-Line : a theoretical construct in *Mardukite Zuism and Systemology* demonstrating *Spiritual Life Energy (ZU)* as a personal individual "continuum" of Awareness interacting with all Spheres of Existence on the Standard Model of Systemology; a spectrum of potential variations and interactions of a monistic continuum or singular *Spiritual Life Energy (ZU)* demonstrated on the Standard Model; an energetic channel of potential POV and "locations" of Beingness, demonstrated in early Systemology materials as an individual Alpha-Spirit's personal *Identity-continuum*, potentially connecting *Awareness (ZU)* of *Self* with "*Infinity*" simultaneous with all points considered in existence; a symbolic demonstration of the "*Life-line*" on which *Awareness (ZU)* extends from the direction of the "Spiritual Universe" (AN) in its true original *alpha state* through an entire possible range of activity resulting in its *beta state* and control of a *genetic-entity* occupying the *Physical Universe (KI)*.

Zu-Vision : the true and basic (*Alpha*) Point-of-View (perspective, POV) maintained by *Self* as *Alpha-Spirit* outside boundaries or considerations of the *Human Condition* "Mind-Systems" and *exterior* to beta-existence reality agreements with the Physical Universe; a POV of Self *as* "a unit of Spiritual Awareness" that exists independent of a "body" and entrapment in a *Human Condition*; "spirit vision" in its truest sense.

THE GREAT MAGICKAL ARCANUM:
A MASTER COURSE IN MAGICK
FOR MODERN WIZARDS
Deluxe—Master Edition Hardcover
Collected Works by Joshua Free

The ultimate book of Magick and Mysticism for all Wizards of the 21st century! Collected writings and founding materials on which Mardukite Zuism and Mardukite Academy were founded; the most complete guide, reference and course curriculum on occultism—ancient and modern—a spiritual, mystical and magical legacy of legendary renown first released underground in 2008. This classic is revised and updated, including all material from the Merlyn Stone "Sorcerer's Handbook" in one amazing volume; nearly 1000 pages.

Complete Your Master Edition Esoteric Library!
The most Amazing Grimoire on the subject of Magick!

MERLYN'S COMPLETE BOOK OF DRUIDISM:
A MASTER COURSE IN DRUIDRY
FOR MODERN DRUIDS
Silver Anniversary—Master Edition Hardcover
Collected Works by Joshua Free

The ultimate book of Druidism for all Druids of the 21st century! Collected writings and research spanning a quarter of a century are culminated together to present the most complete guide, reference and course curriculum of druidry—ancient and modern—a spiritual, mystical and magical legacy of legendary renown that speaks relevantly to present times and will carry human evolution into the future. Classic materials originally composing over 7 books in total are expertly arranged for Truth Seekers in one amazing volume!

Complete Your Master Edition Esoteric Library!
Over 25 Years of Research and Discoveries!

NECRONOMICON:
THE COMPLETE ANUNNAKI LEGACY
10th Anniversary—Master Edition Hardcover
Collected Works by Joshua Free

The ultimate "Necronomicon" of the 21st century. A decade of research and discovery unified together to present the most complete source book of Mesopotamian, Sumerian, Babylonian and Anunnaki knowledge unearthed by humanity. Discover the oldest and most complete spiritual, mystical and magical tradition ever known to exist. Classic underground materials from over 15 books by Mardukite director Joshua Free are expertly arranged for Truth Seekers in one volume!

Complete Your Master Edition Esoteric Library!
The most ancient writings on the planet revealed!

THE SYSTEMOLOGY HANDBOOK:
UNLOCKING TRUE POWER OF THE HUMAN SPIRIT
& THE HIGHEST STATE OF KNOWING AND BEING
Deluxe—Master Edition Hardcover
Collected Works by Joshua Free

A decade of writing forms a complete record of research and discovery, revealing revolutionary advancements of a 21st Century "New Thought" movement known as Mardukite Systemology. Here is the technology to guide our evolution toward a spiritually idealist "transhuman" future. This textbook includes all materials from "The Tablets of Destiny," "Crystal Clear," "Systemology: The Original Thesis" and "Power of Zu"—combined in a single volume that also prepares Seekers for the "Mardukite Master Course."

Complete Your Master Edition Esoteric Library!
The most important pursuit an individual can explore!

THE COMPLETE MARDUKITE MASTER COURSE: KEYS TO THE GATES OF HIGHER UNDERSTANDING
Deluxe—Master Edition Hardcover
Based on Academy Lectures by Joshua Free

The most complete definitive single-source delivery of ultimate "New Age" understanding through Applied Philosophies and Spiritual Tech available to the public for the first time! Now you can experience precision instruction of the "Mardukite Master Course" for all three Master Grades from anywhere in the Universe exactly as Joshua Free gave in person to the Mardukite Academy in September 2020. Over 800 pages of material are collected in this Master Edition, providing Seekers with transcripts to all 48 Academy Lectures, including all course outlines, supplemental reports and critical handouts from the original "Instructor's Manual."

Complete Your Master Edition Esoteric Library!
Experience Mardukite Academy Master Training Anywhere!

A mystic philosopher, world renowned underground occult expert and prolific writer of over 50 books on systemology, ancient history, magic and "esoteric archaeology" since 1995. He founded Mardukite Ministries (Mardukite Zuism) in 2008, is director of Mardukite Research Organization (Mardukite Academy) and its New Thought division "The Systemology Society."

PUBLISHED BY THE **JOSHUA FREE** IMPRINT REPRESENTING

**The Founding Church of Mardukite Zuism
& Mardukite Academy of Systemology**

mardukite.com

THE JOSHUA FREE IMPRINT
JFI PUBLICATIONS

CPSIA information can be obtained
at www.ICGtesting.com
Printed in the USA
BVHW011802270522
638315BV00003B/50